# ROUTLEDGE LIBRARY EDITIONS: ARTHURIAN LITERATURE

Volume 7

# MEDIEVAL ARTHURIAN LITERATURE

I0591522

# MEDIEVAL ARTHURIAN LITERATURE
## A Guide to Recent Research

Edited by
NORRIS J. LACY

LONDON AND NEW YORK

First published in 1996

This edition first published in 2015
by Routledge
2 Park Square, Milton Park, Abingdon, Oxfordshire OX14 4RN

and by Routledge
711 Third Avenue, New York, NY 10017, USA

First issued in paperback 2015

*Routledge is an imprint of the Taylor & Francis Group, an informa business*

*British Library Cataloguing in Publication Data*
A catalogue record for this book is available from the British Library

ISBN: 978-1-138-02487-8 (Set)
ISBN 13: 978-1-138-98078-5 (pbk)
ISBN 13: 978-1-138-78808-4 (hbk) (Volume 7)

**Publisher's Note**
The publisher has gone to great lengths to ensure the quality of this book but points out that some imperfections from the original may be apparent.

**Disclaimer**
The publisher has made every effort to trace copyright holders and would welcome correspondence from those they have been unable to trace.

# Medieval Arthurian Literature
## A Guide to Recent Research

Edited by
Norris J. Lacy

Garland Publishing, Inc.
New York and London
1996

**Library of Congress Cataloging-in-Publication Data**

Medieval Arthurian literature : a guide to recent research / edited by Norris J.
　　Lacy.
　　　　　p.　　cm. — (Garland reference library of the humanities ; vol.
　　1955)
　　　　Includes bibliographical references.
　　　　ISBN 0-8153-2160-0 (alk. paper)
　　　　1. Arthurian romances—History and criticism.　2. Literature, Medieval—
　　History and criticism.　I. Lacy, Norris. J.　II. Series.
　　PN685.M43　1996
　　809'.93351—dc20　　　　　　　　　　　　　　　　　　　　　　95-4761
　　　　　　　　　　　　　　　　　　　　　　　　　　　　　　　　　　CIP

Cover illustration: "Arthur" from Malory, *The Storie of the Most Noble and
Worthy Kinge Arthure* (1578?). From the Berg Collection, New York Public Li-
brary. By permission of the New York Public Library. Photo courtesy of The
Newberry Library, Chicago.

Printed on acid-free, 250-year-life paper
Manufactured in the United States of America

# CONTENTS

# PREFACE

The study of Arthurian literature has increased at an extraordinary rate over the past decades. The *Bibliographical Bulletin of the International Arthurian Society* (BBIAS), which provides an annual census of Arthurian scholarship, listed 226 items in its first number, the bibliography for 1948 (published in 1949). Forty years later, the most recent volumes contain some seven hundred entries each, and they are by no means exhaustive.[1]

The scholarship devoted to the Arthurian legend has grown not only in quantity but in scope. When J.D. Bruce published his important *The Evolution of Arthurian Romance From the Beginnings Down to the Year 1300* (1923; 2nd ed. 1928), he offered some discussion of Celtic texts, especially as source material, and gave a reasonable nod to some Latin material. (By ending his study at the year 1300, Bruce necessarily excluded most Middle English material.) His emphasis remains solidly on French romance, and the scant attention—scarcely more than a listing of titles—given to other literatures dramatically illustrates where interests lay in the early part of the century. Hispanic, Italian, and Dutch get decidedly short shrift, and German romances are only slightly better represented. Bruce devotes less than a page to Scandinavian texts.

Roger Sherman Loomis's *Arthurian Literature in the Middle Ages: A Collaborative History* (1959) partially redresses this imbalance both

---

[1] The bibliography is compiled by committees in each of the national branches. Some are far less thorough and efficient than others, and one of the branch bibliographies has been missing for several years. In addition, the bibliography concentrates on research on medieval Arthurian literature, excluding most of the work in art history and other disciplines and excluding as well most scholarship on modern texts. Once these problems and omissions are taken into account, it becomes apparent that the amount of research on Arthurian subjects has doubtless increased fivefold since the *Bibliographical Bulletin* was first published.

by the strong emphasis on Celtic Arthuriana and by the inclusion of
chapters treating "Arthurian Literature in Spain and Portugal," "The
Dutch Romances," and "Scandinavian Literature." Yet a number of
these are brief presentations, not always prepared, even allowing for
the state of our knowledge of texts in the late 1950s, with the care
given to other chapters. The chapter on Italian literature is entitled not
"Italian Arthurian Literature" but "Arthurian *Influences* on Italian
Literature from 1200 to 1500" (my emphasis). On the other hand, the
volume devotes separate chapters to Wace, to the *Livre d'Artus*, and to
other French texts.

By pointing out these features of two monuments of Arthurian
scholarship, I intend no criticism of their authors and editors but wish
only to define the interests and the state of our knowledge at an earlier
period. Since Bruce and Loomis, we have discovered or rediscovered
additional texts, and scholars have provided editions of romances
formerly available only in manuscript or in inadequately edited form.
No less important, many Arthurian scholars have broadened their focus
and ceased to think of medieval Arthurian literature as consisting, to
stretch a point only slightly, of a few great masterpieces: Geoffrey of
Monmouth, Chrétien de Troyes, the German triumvirate (Hartmann,
Wolfram, and—if we even consider his work Arthurian—Gottfried), the
French Vulgate, *Sir Gawain and the Green Knight*, Malory, and few
if any others.

Thus, an important trend discernible in Arthurian scholarship is the
recent interest in texts that we would formerly have considered
secondary or even minor. In part, this interest is a natural reaction to
the enormous body of scholarship devoted to Chrétien, Wolfram,
Malory, and a handful of others. Yet it is not a purely negative
phenomenon: it surely represents also a tendency, shared by recent
critics in all fields, to expand the canon to include texts once largely or
entirely ignored. This trend represents a welcome recognition that some
texts have been rarely taught and almost as rarely read for reasons—
prejudice,[2] custom, historical accident, availability of editions—that
may have very little to do with their quality. No less important is the
realization that, even if study demonstrates that a work is minor or

---

[2] By this, I mean in particular the traditional preference for texts that pass muster when
measured by criteria (e.g., unity) more appropriate to modern literature.

flawed, our understanding of the genre, the literary tradition, or even the masterpieces themselves is enhanced by the expansion of the canon.

A gratifying development is the increasing attention given to what we might call the "second-tier" Arthurian literatures (Hispanic, Italian, Dutch, Scandinavian) and the acknowledgment that they are secondary only in a quantitative sense. Scholars have begun to recognize that these literatures include texts, whether adaptations, translations, or indigenous compositions, that are important not only as historical witnesses but as literary creations fully deserving of our attention.

Undeniably, the traditional view of Arthuriana, emphasizing the centrality of French texts, has considerable justification in the sheer number of Arthurian works composed in French and in their influence on authors writing in other languages, and it would be foolish to underestimate the importance of Chrétien de Troyes's romances, the Vulgate Cycle, Thomas's *Tristan*, and a good many other compositions. Yet this scholarly "gallocentrism," however justified, is surely an attitude that has too long inhibited the proper study and appreciation of other literatures. A single but revealing example is the controversy over the origins of the Middle Dutch *Walewein*: some scholars have found it inconceivable that this important romance could be indigenous and have consequently posited for it, despite a paucity if not an absence of evidence, a lost French source. Without intending to settle such problems, we hope to provide a study that, while acknowledging the prominence of French, Celtic, German, and English Arthuriana and documenting their numerical dominance, will demonstrate unambiguously the importance and value of second-tier literatures.

The focus of this book is medieval vernacular literature in western Europe. That focus thus excludes discussion of the scattered texts from the East (e.g., the Byelorussian *Tristan*) and particularly of Latin material. That is not in any way intended to deny the importance of Latin texts, whether of the voluminous chronicle materials or of the few examples of romance. Geoffrey of Monmouth, the author of the most prominent Latin Arthurian text, is in fact included here; although he wrote in Latin, he can be seen as functioning to an extent within the English tradition, and James Carley discusses his work briefly in his chapter on England. (John Koch deals in passing with the Welsh-language manuscripts of Geoffrey's work.)

The chapters presented here have been prepared by acknowledged authorities in their fields. Those authors have been accorded considerable latitude, both in the presentation of the subject and in the choice of material and titles to include. Their commission was simply the following: present to scholars and students the current state of scholarship in your field, both through a narrative presentation and through bibliographical listings of significant recent studies.

Although authors have generally taken a common approach, some modifications have been made to accommodate the specific scholarly situations that pertain in Celtic and French Arthuriana. Celtic scholarship in particular differs in certain ways from that of the other literatures represented here, and those differences account both for the larger chronological spread and for the greater length of John T. Koch's essay. First, as Koch notes, research in Celtic studies, for a variety of reasons, has progressed more slowly and sometimes more fitfully than in French, German, and the others. Consequently, whereas the adjective "recent" has generally been taken in this book to designate roughly the past twenty or twenty-five years, Koch has prudently chosen to expand that definition. As a result, although most of the chapters include a few older monuments, going back in a few cases to Loomis's 1959 *Arthurian Literature in the Middle Ages* or beyond, the chapter on Celtic Arthuriana offers a good number of references to studies of that age or older—works that for better or for worse still represent the current state of scholarship.

Moreover, it is undoubtedly true that most users of this volume will find Celtic scholarship less accessible and more difficult than scholarship devoted to other literatures. For that reason as well, we considered a fuller and more detailed treatment advisable.

French, too, offers particular problems. The sheer volume of scholarship devoted to French Arthurian literature in recent decades makes it impossible to deal as exhaustively with its subject as other authors do with theirs. To control the length of that chapter, we have devoted less space to the essay on French than to some others, and we have concentrated on scholarship published since 1980, with a small number of titles included from the 1970s. Moreover, our selectivity has led us to exclude from the bibliography a number of important books devoted to broader subjects, such as the romance form or courtly love, even when they study Arthurian texts alongside others. The titles of such books are generally included in the annual *Bibliographical Bulletin of the International Arthurian Society,* to which readers are referred for additional information concerning all the national literatures considered in the present volume.

In addition to discussing and listing scholarly and critical studies, the chapters of this book include recent editions, and all of them except French (owing to its length and to the volume of material presented therein) refer as well to translations into English. An appendix also deals, though by no means exhaustively, with trends in Arthurian translation through all the literatures treated in this volume. It will, we hope, offer useful information about what has been accomplished in the interest of anglophone readers and also, no less important, about the gaps, sometimes dramatic, in translated material.

The bibliographies included in each chapter represent the authors' judgments (with suggestions but few interventions by the editor) concerning essential materials. Some, as noted, are far more selective than others, but in every case they have responded to a single imposed criterion: is this article, book, edition, or translation an important contribution that ought to be known by anyone dealing with the literature in question? The listings are generally divided into sections devoted to 1) bibliographies (and sometimes general studies), 2) editions and translations, and 3) scholarly and critical studies. Editions and translations, which are sometimes given in separate categories, are listed under the scholar's name, rather than by title or author; because the bibliographies were designed for use in conjunction with the essays, it will most likely be the editor's or translator's name that will lead the reader to that section of the bibliography. The contrary approach, listing by works or authors, would in some cases (e.g., Chrétien de Troyes) require the reader to peruse a good number of entries before locating the one being sought.

Within the essays, contributors identify scholars simply by name, if they are represented by a single entry in the bibliography, or by name and date if the bibliography lists several titles by the scholar in question. Consequently, we have adopted a chronological arrangement within bibliographies. However, we separate a scholar's own books and articles from books edited by that person and, further, from titles that represent collaborative efforts. The titles within each of these three groups are listed chronologically.

Finally, since these chapters are fundamentally independent of one another, the order in which they stand is largely arbitrary and, given the difficulties frequently involved in dating compositions and tracing influences, is the result of a conscious decision not to imply the priority of some literatures and the merely derivative nature of others.

Inevitably, any study of the present state of scholarship, by the time it is published, has already become a study of the recent past state, and important studies in most or all of these literatures will surely have appeared after the contributors to this volume have completed their work. Insofar as possible, we have responded to this implicit problem by indicating work in progress, but it is certain that the flood of Arthurian scholarship will not soon abate, and that means that this kind of study is never quite finished. Nevertheless, we hope to have provided readers with a thorough and reliable guide to recent trends, problems, accomplishments, and desiderata in research on medieval vernacular Arthurian literature.

I have naturally incurred a number of debts while preparing this volume, and I have privately thanked a number of persons for their advice or suggestions. Here I wish to express my gratitude to three in particular. First, I thank Douglas Kelly for his counsel and his generosity; although his name is not attached to a chapter of this volume, his assistance was substantial and much appreciated. Second, my thanks to Donna Nix for her editorial and computer expertise. Finally, I am as always grateful to Gary Kuris, my friend and my editor, who supported and encouraged this project from the beginning.

# ENGLAND[1]

## James P. Carley

I n a 1988 study of progress and trends, Keith Busby argued that "French Arthurian literature stands at the beginning of the Arthurian literary tradition in whatever language and whatever period." In his view, Chrétien de Troyes is the initiating point of the tradition, and Chrétien also dominates the later developments to such a degree that his *oeuvre* assumes a central place in the Arthurian corpus as a whole. Subsequent Arthurian texts can, in other words, be seen primarily as a reaction in one form or another to Chrétien. From the perspective of the English tradition, Busby's thesis has much to recommend it—and many scholars have remarked on the irony that the *matière de Bretagne* is a French creation codified within the French language—but the thesis also depends on the way in which "literature" is defined. Certainly, if this term is restricted to its modern meaning and is placed in binary opposition to history, then English Arthurian literature falls markedly under the shadow of the French romances and much can be considered translation, in the most general, or at least medieval, sense of the term. To a large extent, nevertheless, the firm separation of fiction and history represents an anachronistic reading of the past. Rosalind Field (1991), considers that the quality of the Matter of Britain romances derives precisely from their conscious historicity, their blurring of the distinction between fiction and history. Suzanne

---

[1] Various individuals have read this essay or sections of it in draft, and I should like to acknowledge their assistance here: Richard Barber, Jennifer Goodman, Ann Hutchison, Lesley Johnson, James Noble, Helen Phillips. Gillian Rogers, in particular, applied her sharp bibliographer's eye to it and made many helpful suggestions. I have made constant reference to the *Bibliographical Bulletin of the International Arthurian Society* but have been unable to make use of Caroline Palmer's Arthurian Bibliography for the years 1978-92, which was not available when my research was being undertaken.

1

Fleischman (1983) has observed more generally that once the demands of narrativity are imposed on the representation of reality, distinguishing between fiction and history becomes theoretically problematic no matter what the period.[2]

In the English context, in any case, it is almost impossible to ignore the so-called historical side of things, since Geoffrey of Monmouth's *Historia Regum Britanniae* (ca. 1138) is such a firm reference point and would have strongly influenced the view of the past held by almost any medieval writer or audience; indeed, it is a work that dominated historiography in England to such an extent that "Brut" ultimately became a synonym for any history. Even though the *Historia Regum Britanniae* does not fall within the actual boundaries set for this essay, especially since it was composed in Latin, it is worth noting that in recent years there has been a revival of interest in the textual tradition, and Wright (1985, 1988) has issued the first two volumes of his series of critical editions of all variant versions of the text. Crick (1989, 1991) has undertaken careful studies of the transmission of the *Historia Regum Britanniae*, examining and categorizing the more than two hundred and fifteen surviving manuscripts; her work is complemented by Reeve's shorter study (1991). Martin B. Shichtman and Laurie A. Finke (1993) have completed a long contextualizing essay on "history as symbolic capital in the *Historia Regum Britanniae*," which forms part of a book-length project on the social significance of the Arthurian legend in Geoffrey and in other Arthurian chronicles of the Norman period. Kennedy (1989) has provided a commentary and bibliography of "historical" writings in English between 1050 and 1500, almost all of which ultimately derive in part from Geoffrey and many of which contain Arthurian materials: Laȝamon's *Brut*, Robert of Gloucester's *Chronicle*, the *Short Metrical Chronicle*, Robert Mannyng's *Story of*

---

[2] In a useful study of the Arthurian materials in Robert Mannyng's *Chronicle of England* (1991), Lesley Johnson has raised similar historiographical questions and has argued that the verse chronicles in particular defy the departmental organization of modern medieval studies' programs.

*England*, the Prose *Brut*, John Hardyng's *Chronicle*,[3] translations of Ranulf Higden's *Polychronicon*, John Capgrave's *Abbreuiacion of Cronicles*, and others. Matheson (1990) has prepared a study of the chronicles working from Antonia Gransden's definition of a romance tradition of historiography; in his view, many of the romances were accepted as historical and some of them seem more like chronicles or biography. In general, however, Matheson would suggest that the romances tended to deal with individual characters and their exploits, whereas the chronicles provided a historical framework and cultural context.

Although there are some problems in defining romance within the French tradition—Busby (1988) refers to "the hornet's nest of genre-definitions"—the issue seems even more complex in the English context. The classic survey is that of Dorothy Everett (1955), who argued that one could articulate a "grammar" of romance. She also rejected the distinction between *roman courtois* and chanson de geste, considering it more useful to distinguish between romance and epic poetry in general. Building on Everett's work, Pearsall (1965) gave a fine summary of the texts involved, not including in his discussion prose versions and alliterative texts, however, since these have "a strong enough formal and social identity to warrant exclusion."

The excluded alliterative material has in itself been the focus of general studies: Levy and Szarmach (1981), Lawton (1982, 1989), Cable (1991). These have dealt with questions of classification, formal characteristics, authors, audience, and manuscript reception. Lawton (1982) pointed out that although the evidence is enigmatic—we know little about the origins of the so-called fourteenth-century revival, its practitioners, or the reasons for its demise—it is important to make a basic distinction between composition and reception. In his more theoretical essay (1989), which summarizes earlier work in the field, he came to the conclusion that in spite of all the scholarship to date, the subject remains confusing—"plural traditions, in multiple texts passing through multiple centres and revealing diverse and variant patterns of composition and circulation"—and may well need some kind of

---

[3] Felicity Riddy is preparing an edition of the Arthurian sections of this text. Both she (1991) and Kennedy (1989) have written on Arthurian aspects of the chronicle.

reformulation. Nor do the texts provide evidence for a closely delineated textual community; for this period, "English" literature must define itself as literature in three languages: Latin, French, and English.

Pearsall (1965) distinguished between "epic romance," almost always in four-stress couplets, and "lyric romance," in tail-rhyme. The former are more prosaic, more "historical," and more martial, whereas the latter are more emotive and are concerned with love and the marvelous. The epic romances, moreover, start to decline in popularity after 1320. Barron (1980) argued that one can detect traces of a specifically English romance tradition for which certain common features can be identified: an interest in dynastic significance, a moral earnestness in the treatment of themes, a "realistic" viewpoint, and a preference for alliterative verse. In his fuller study (1987), he insisted that we should in any case move away from the concept of genre and look at the fundamentals of the romance *mode*, where experience is approached as part fantasy, part reality, and where there is a balance between idealism and realism. In some ways, this is not unlike the conclusion drawn independently by Finlayson (1980–81). Finlayson suggested that difficulties arise because scholars conceive of romance as a genre and at the same time as a particular treatment of that genre. He believed that romance, whose core is *aventure*, must be viewed as a mode, in which a particular kind of activity becomes the vehicle for the presentation of an attitude to experience. Nevertheless, Finlayson was more narrow in his definition than Barron and did not consider, for example, that "chronicle romance" is a useful category. Nor did he think that classification by *matières* is at all helpful, whereas Barron used this traditional division as an organizing principle for his book-length study.

Recent years have seen other attempts to formulate a definition of Middle English romance in terms of genre categories—in particular, Strohm (1977, 1980) and Fichte (1981)—but none has been entirely successful, and Busby (1987) argued that many of the problems in classifying the English material are a direct result of the fact that it does not conform to the genre pattern of Old French.

What all these studies indicate, however, is that, as Brewer (1988) has observed, "an explosion of interest in medieval English Romances has taken place in the 1980s." This is all the more remarkable in a way (or perhaps more typically academic), given the fact that most scholars dismiss the texts in themselves as inferior creations: Finlayson (1980) stated that "*[r]omances* of the quality of *Sir Gawain and the Green Knight* are extremely rare in English—in fact, one might easily assert that apart from the *Knight's Tale*, *Sir Gawain*, and a few others, the English achievement in the *romance* form is not of a very high order." Boardman (1988) was even more scathing: "Some of the writers were so unskilled that the current critical fashion for preferring texts to writers becomes attractive, although one is tempted to say that many of these works have more 'inter-' than 'textuality' about them." Barron (1987), it appears, is one of the few to defend the romances as literature, maintaining that we foist expectations conditioned by the French *romans courtois* on the English materials, which should rather be judged by their own aims and characteristics.

The discussion of "aesthetic" value leads back to audience expectation and relationship to French materials. Finlayson (1980) assumed that more sophisticated, more aristocratic readers would have turned to French romances and would not have read the inferior English imitations. J.D. Burnley (1989), who is one of a number of scholars dealing with translation theory, has examined the cultural context of the translations and has concluded that "the transition from French to English involved a cultural descent, or at the very least a considerable broadening of appeal. Anglicization often meant popularization, adaptation to a new audience of less sophisticated tastes." In a more general context, Susan Wittig (1978) has used linguistic means, Pike's tagmemic linguistics and Lévi-Strauss's mode of analysis, to determine how the romance form originated and what cultural needs it satisfied. Ultimately, she sees the romances as variants of a single mythic structure. Like Wittig, Brewer (1988) would describe romance as symbolic narrative but would articulate its meaning in terms of family drama and self-definition. Knight (1986) examined the ideological structure of the Middle English romances and identified three major types: (1) the lonely hero, (2) family disruption and reestablishment, (3) interrogation of the basic romance ideology. Reiss (1985) argued that the audiences themselves were aware of the conventions of romance and that there was a constant interplay between the expected and the unexpected, the traditional and the individual expression. Fewster (1987) notes that there is a self-conscious traditionality in romance and sees this traditionality and a corresponding intertextuality as evidence of an essentially closed and self-referential system.[4]

Many of the English Arthurian romances are found in single copies, and many cluster within a fairly small group of manuscripts— the Auchinleck manuscript, the Thornton manuscript, the Vernon manuscript, the Percy Folio *inter alia*—and Doyle (1982), Hudson (1984), and Thompson (1991) have looked at some of these groupings, exploring the significance of various juxtapositions within the manuscripts. One of the great accomplishments of the past two decades has been the appearance of facsimile reproductions of the most important manuscripts, with introductions containing detailed codicological studies. This has led to wider discussions of manuscript context (e.g., the consideration of manuscript compilations as "super romances" as defined by Karl D. Uitti) and new theories concerning patronage and reception. Marginalia also provide clues about early readers, and exciting new work has been emerging in this area, much generated by former graduate students at the University of York under the supervision of Derek Pearsall and Elizabeth Salter. More generally, using the evidence of dedicatees and known readers of Arthurian romances Felicity Riddy (1991), now also at the University of York, has examined literary subcultures and textual communities.

In the area of women readers and patrons, there has been much recent work, of which that of Carol Meale (1986) is representative. In spite of the evidence that women read romances, however, there is a growing consensus that the romance was not a "feminized" genre as such, standing in opposition to the masculine epic, as has been conventionally assumed. As early as 1976, Nanette McNiff Roberts challenged the view that romances were written for a female audience and showed that they concentrated on "threatening" male protagonists and tended to emphasize women's youthful beauty, denigrating the maturer role of mother or wife. Elizabeth Archibald (1990) has analyzed the general passiveness of the idealized heroines of romance,

---

[4] Intertextuality has been the focus of many recent studies of the French romances in particular, of which those by Bruckner (1987–88) and Taylor (1987–88) are representative.

moreover, and has concluded that "most medieval romances are overwhelmingly concerned with male values, male pursuits, and 'what goes on inside the *man's* head.'"

## Scholarly Accomplishments

As there are problems in defining romance as a genre, so too do scholars disagree about how to create a classification system for the actual texts that constitute the Matter of Britain. Most general studies address themselves to a period (fourteenth-century romances, say), a form (the alliterative revival), or thematic issues (the figure of Kay). In terms of an overview, Ackerman (1959) has suggested that the English Arthurian romances, apart from Malory, can be divided roughly into three categories: those whose main concern is with episodes in King Arthur's life, those dealing with the early history of the Grail and taken from the French Vulgate *Estoire del Saint Graal* and *Merlin*, and those treating individual knights. Barron (1987) presented a slightly different breakdown: dynastic romances, chivalric romances and folk romances, and Gawain romances. In the forthcoming collaborative volume under Barron's editorship, *The Arthur of the English: The Arthurian Legend in Medieval English Life and Literature*, the texts will be divided into the chronicle tradition (Geoffrey of Monmouth, Wace, Laʒamon, *Of Arthour and Merlin*, *Prose Merlin*, Henry Lovelich's *Merlin* and *The History of the Holy Grail*, *Arthur*, *The Legend of King Arthur*, *King Arthur's Death*), dynastic romance (Alliterative *Morte Arthure*, Stanzaic *Morte Arthur*, Malory's *Morte Darthur*, which has a chapter to itself), chivalric romance (*Ywain and Gawain*, *The Awntyrs off Arthure*, *Golagros and Gawain*, *Sir Gawain and the Green Knight*, *Libeaus Desconus*, *Arthur of Little Britain*, *Sir Tristrem*, *Lancelot of the Laik*, *Sir Lancelott of du Lake*, and the Launfal group), and folk romance (*The Grene Knight*, *The Turke and Gowin*, *Syre Gawene and the Carle of Carelyle*, *The Carle off Carlile*, *The Avowynge of King Arthure*, *The Weddynge of Sir Gawen and Dame Ragnell*, *The Marriage of Sir Gawaine*, *The Jeaste of Syr Gawayne*, *King Arthur and King Cornwall*, *Joseph of Arimathie*, *Sir Perceval of Galles*). Not surprisingly, whatever the scheme the same romances tend to be grouped together.

Compared with its ultimate source, Geoffrey of Monmouth's *Historia Regum Britanniae*, Laȝamon's *Brut* has perhaps suffered from scholarly neglect until the last few years.[5] There has been a marked revival of interest in the poem, precipitated perhaps by the appearance of the second volume of the EETS edition undertaken by G.L. Brook and R.F. Leslie (1963, 1978). Admirable in its paleographical expertise, this edition still lacks the third and concluding volume (to be prepared by Françoise Le Saux and Ian Kirby), which will provide full introduction, notes, and glossary and which will act as bibliographical focus for future work. Meanwhile, Le Saux's thorough and painstaking study (1989) serves as a companion to the edition, especially since she undertakes a full discussion of earlier scholarship and gives an extensive bibliographical survey of nineteenth- and twentieth-century critical studies.[6] W.R.J. Barron and S.C. Weinberg have published an edition and translation of the Arthurian section of the poem (1989) and have announced a complete edition and translation. Donald Bzdyl has brought out a prose translation (1989) and Rosamund Allen a verse translation (1992).

In a seminal article on the *Brut*, E.G. Stanley (1968) has argued that the dating of the poem can be only roughly approximated: sometime between 1189 and not very early in the second half of the thirteenth century. Le Saux (1989), on the other hand, would date it to pre-1216. The matter is open to interpretation because neither of the two surviving manuscripts, B.L., Cotton Caligula A. ix or B.L., Otho C. xiii, is an autograph copy and both may postdate the original date of composition by an undetermined period of time. There are also significant differences between the text as presented in the two manuscripts, the precise relationship between which remains unclear.

---

[5] Presumably thinking of other literary works, Johnson (1991) calls it a marginalized text, whereas Matheson, comparing it with chronicles and histories (1990), states that it has received considerable scholarly attention, "primarily on account of [La3amon's] undoubted literary power, his handling of and additions to his major source, the putative metrical links between his work and earlier and later English alliterative verse, and his use of language."

[6] Rudolph Willard (1948) has written on seventeenth- and eighteenth-century critical reception.

Stanley (1969) maintains that Caligula is more reliable; in his view, the scribe of Otho, lacking sympathy with the antiquarian modulation of the poem, cleansed and altered the original. By noting the omissions in Otho, in this interpretation, one can determine what aspects of the language were self-consciously old-fashioned to the thirteenth-century ear. Elizabeth Johnson Bryan (1990) has also analyzed the relationship between the two manuscripts, concentrating, however, on the role of scribe as creator of text and evidence concerning readership.

The positing of an archaistic form leads to other stylistic considerations and to questions about the placement of this poem within a native alliterative tradition. Concrete evidence here, as in other issues relating to vernacular texts in Britain in this period, is woefully sparse. Until recently most scholars, of whom Dorothy Everett (1955) may have been the most influential, have suggested that there must have been a post-Conquest tradition of popular, perhaps oral, materials of which no trace remains. Putative lost manuscripts, too, have often been invoked. James Noble (1985) has argued that the larger rhetorical patterns of the *Brut* provide evidence for the continuity of the Old English poetic tradition into the early Middle English period. In his study of the English alliterative tradition (1991), Thomas Cable has examined the role of the *Brut* as a link between Old English and the fourteenth-century "revival." There is a growing trend, moreover, to see parallels with prose texts of late Anglo-Saxon times and afterward, particularly texts associated with Worcester. Laȝamon's interests resembled those of the "tremulous" glossator in significant ways, and it is tempting to interpret their activities as part of a wider movement. Concurrently, scholars have warned against imposing modern dichotomies between poetry and prose, and N.R. Blake (1969), for example, has argued that the term "rhythmical alliteration" should be used to describe a number of these early Middle English texts. This topic has also been taken up by Elizabeth Salter (1988) and Steven Brehe (1990), who has announced a forthcoming study of Laȝamon's prosody. Angus McIntosh (1982) has undertaken an analysis of the "metrical system" used by Laȝamon, observing that the boundary between prose and poetic texts in the period was extremely fluid and noting too that alliteration is not an inevitable characteristic of the *Brut*. Although many lines reproduce Old English metrical types perfectly, thousands of lines show no alliteration.

Even if he avoided the poetic rigidity of the Old English alliterative verse form, Laȝamon restricted his vocabulary to words of English origin, a surprising feature in a work that is in the broadest sense a translation from French. In Stanley's scheme (1969), this relates to Laȝamon's archaizing tendency: he was consciously preserving (and imitating) old-fashioned diction as well as using the alliterative line. In spite of these archaistic linguistic features, however, Elizabeth Salter (1988) has suggested that we should avoid making a sharp distinction between French and English culture in the period and that we should think of a synthetic cultural scene in which diverse influences in Latin, French, Anglo-Norman, and English can be seen as interacting rather than standing in opposition. Le Saux, building on the work of Herbert Pilch (1960) and the unpublished dissertation by A.C. Gibbs (1962), would add Welsh to the cultural field. Ultimately, she sees the *Brut* as a means of kindling a solidarity between the Welsh and the English against the invaders. Johnson (1991) warns, nevertheless, against the impulse to see Laȝamon and Wace as "synecdoches" for an anachronistic French-English binary opposition, a stereotype that, she observes, can be found even in such critically informed work as that produced by Martin Shichtman (1987).

Laȝamon's archaizing tendency extended to matters of theme as well as orthography and diction, and this can be observed in his descriptions of battle scenes. In this area, however, Laȝamon seemed to lack a full understanding of the old heroic ethos; this is apparent in his use of such terms as *beot*. He portrayed a fictionalized view of the past (the heroic tradition is a "faltering" memory) and can thus be seen, according to Daniel Donoghue (1990), as an antiquary and one of the first students of Old English literature. On the other hand, scholars should not assume that he did not understand Wace's use of a "chivalric" ethos and that he was a backwoods cleric, naively overlooking the subtleties that the courtly Wace, writing for Eleanor of Aquitaine, introduced into Geoffrey of Monmouth's clerical history. In this area, as Gibbs (1962) first pointed out, critics have been misled by his linguistic choices (i.e., because French terms for *amour courtois* have passed into our language we can be insensitive to the nuances of Laȝamon's writing). Indeed, Barron and Le Saux (1989) sharply dispute the critical commonplace that Laȝamon is in some sense anti-*courtois*.

Laȝamon's relationship with his stated sources has long troubled critics, since it is clear that he was being somewhat disingenuous in his prologue; that is, what we can reconstruct about his method is quite unlike what he stated he was doing. Stanley (1969) suggested that this was part of the antiquarian exercise. Le Saux (1989), on the other hand, thinks that the prologue authorizes what follows as a work of "scientific pretentions."[7] She argues that we should not construe Laȝamon's statements about the books he consulted in modern terms but should look at them rather in terms of a Latin pedigree to the work. Using Ronald H. Bathgate's "operational model of the translation process," she is thus able to resolve the differences between his articulated stance and his actual methodology. And as Johnson (1991) points out, further comparative analysis of authorizing passages and historiographical models in other, almost inevitably Latin, texts from the period may indicate that multiple options were available and that there was a sophisticated awareness of these options.

The sheer length of the poem (32,200 hemistichs) has proved to be an obstacle to informed critical response and also raises questions about process of composition and intended audience. Barron (1989) maintains that Laȝamon's technique involved the reading of longish passages and subsequent rearrangement of the components to express his own conception of meaning and interest—a kind of early equivalent of William Morris's advice concerning the re-creation of medieval romance: "Read it through . . . then shut the book and write it out again as a new story for yourself." In terms of narrative segments, Barron postulates units of approximately four hundred lines, each sufficient for an evening's reading. The context of the Caligula version in particular would seem to suggest a more lettered milieu than has generally been associated with the poem.

The question of audience leads to questions of genre. Barron (1980), visualizing the *Brut* in epic terms, quoted Tatlock (*pace* Milton) on its role as a kind of national epic: "By reason of Arthur's position as its climax as well as of the long line of other traditional heroes, events and associations, and of its breadth of treatment, simplicity, intensity, enthusiasm, accord with the supernatural, vitality of imagination,

---

[7] Jeff Rider (1989) comes to a different conclusion when he maintains that Laȝamon's use of dialogue indicates a preference for fictional discourse over historical discourse.

elevation and sometimes nobility and religious feeling, the poem is the nearest thing we have to a traditional racial epic." Swanton (1987) uses the term "verse chronicle," which in his opinion helpfully blurs the modern distinction between historical fact and creative fiction.

Perhaps the issue that has troubled modern scholars most relates to the relationship between the "medium" and the "message." Why did Laȝamon, in other words, write a poem glorifying the Britons in the language of their conquerors? In the most broad sense, what were the politics behind his choices and where did he ally himself? One way to resolve the ironies implicit here is to see the poem as representing a national rather than a racial history, and this position has been explicitly articulated by Kirby (1964) and Swanton (1987).[8] Rider (1989) focuses on Merlin as an agent potentially independent of the line of kings who reflects feelings of defiance against the Normans: "What could not be worked out in action [Laȝamon] worked out in literature: a representation of the world, transformed by the power of fiction, where a king depends on Merlin to engender his story."[9] Noble (1992) argues that Laȝamon saw himself and his contemporaries as descendants of the Angles and not the Saxons and that as Angles they were the legitimate heirs to the British glory, for whom a new Arthur's imminent arrival might reasonably be expected. Donoghue (1990) suggests that Laȝamon had an ambivalent attitude to the past, an ambivalence characteristic of writers of the twelfth and thirteenth centuries. Relying heavily on Stanley and on Robert Hanning's analysis of Geoffrey of Monmouth's historiography, he maintains that "Anglen" and "Brutten" are defined by race (*leod*) rather than nation and that the unifying principle is divine providence. There is an analogy between the English conquered by the Normans and the Celts overrun by the Anglo-Saxons; Laȝamon's very language was part of his endeavor to emphasize this analogy. The poem is part of a historiographical

---

[8] Donoghue (1990) queries the relevance of the modern concepts of irony and nationalism within the thirteenth-century context.

[9] Much of the writing on Merlin as substitute for author has been sparked by Howard Bloch's influential "Le rire de Merlin" (1985).

tradition that takes its root in Gildas and that can be traced through Bede to Geoffrey.[10]

In her review article (1991), Johnson gave an overview of scholarship and argued that Le Saux's volume, by its very existence, will act as a deterrent against the perpetration of the old-fashioned platitudes about the *Brut*. Nevertheless, there is much we do not know about the cultural milieu in which Laȝamon was writing and in particular about production of and reception of historical narratives in verse. We still need, therefore, "some sustained self-reflective discussion of the issues involved in providing a context for the *Brut* and hence of the process of making this narrative 'mean' for a modern audience." In August 1992, the first International Conference on Laȝamon's *Brut* was held in Lausanne, and Le Saux is editing revised versions of several of the papers for publication. This, it seems likely, will be the first of a series of similar volumes, dealing with precisely these sorts of issues.

If Laȝamon's *Brut* is to be classified as a verse *chronicle* or at least part of a historical tradition deriving directly from Geoffrey of Monmouth, then the earliest of the surviving English Arthurian romances *per se* is *Of Arthour and Merlin* (1250–1300), a work drawn in part from the Vulgate *Merlin* and representing the first wave of the "Chrétien" influence as defined by Busby. Although *Of Arthour and Merlin* survives uniquely in the Auchinleck manuscript, a much later rendition of the first section is found in several manuscripts as well as in a Wynkyn de Worde print. The Auchinleck manuscript formed the basis for O.D. Macrae-Gibson's edition (1973–79), and he also printed the text of the Hale manuscript (Lincoln's Inn 150), supplemented from the Percy Folio manuscript. William E. Holland (1971) has prepared a critical edition of the text in the Hale manuscript, and Pearsall and Cunningham (1977) have brought out a facsimile edition of the Auchinleck manuscript.

Although there has been a striking difference in critical response to the poem—Newstead (1967) called it a "skilfully abridged translation"

---

[10] It should be remembered, as Johnson (1991) has pointed out, that there is a pressing need for a sustained analysis of the terminology used to describe the "imagined communities" and how it relates, or does not relate, to modern equivalents.

and Dean (1987) a "very monotonous story in which the poet's love of recounting battles with all their traditional attendant details dominates everything else"—issues of dialect, authorship, and relationship between the early and later version have dominated scholarly debate. Like Eugen Kölbing, who first edited the text in 1890, Macrae-Gibson maintains that the poem was written by the author of *Kyng Alisaunder* and *The Seven Sages of Rome*, but he rejects the suggestion that *Richard Coeur de Lion* is by the same individual. His conclusions stand as a strong response to the case put forward by W.H. French (1946) that linguistic features establish that *Of Arthour and Merlin* and *Kyng Alisaunder* could not be by the same author. Sklar, who argued (1975) that the author "englished" his French source for chauvinistic purposes, rejected Smithers's suggestion that *Of Arthour and Merlin* and *Kyng Alisaunder* originated in London despite variations from the pure dialect. Instead she (1977) posited a Sussex place of origin. Macrae-Gibson (1979) has shown, however, that her thesis is untenable.

Although *Of Arthour and Merlin* is the only medieval English verse romance dealing with Arthur's early life, several concern themselves with his death and its "tragic" implications. In an article first published in 1983, Lee Patterson could argue that the Alliterative *Morte Arthure*, perhaps the most important of the versions in verse, had not truly achieved canonical status among medieval English writings. The quantity and excellence of recent studies have gone a long way toward rectifying this situation, and Dean (1987) considers it "one of the more widely acclaimed poems in Middle English." Although the poem has been edited several times, most notably by Valerie Krishna in 1976, the edition by Mary Hamel in 1984 has provided scholars with a definitive text. It includes a full editorial apparatus, analyzes in depth the critical problems, which had been the focus of an important collection of essays assembled by K.H. Göller (1981), and gives a glossary. Linguistic issues make the poem difficult of access to modern audiences, and fortunately it has also been translated in verse by Krishna (1983) and prose by Brian Stone (1988). Larry D. Benson's version (1974) with regularized spelling and marginal glosses has, moreover, been recently reissued (1986).

The Alliterative *Morte Arthure* survives in a unique copy found in Lincoln Cathedral Library 91, fols. 53-98v (the Thornton manuscript;

copied ca. 1440), which has been published in a facsimile edition
(1975; rev. 1977) and which with its London companion has also been
the subject of further studies (Doyle 1982; Hamel 1983; Thompson
1983). Robert Thornton was scribe rather than author, and the date of
the original composition has never been definitively established;
suggestions range from the mid-fourteenth to the early fifteenth
century. Hamel's endorsement of Benson's dating ca. 1399–1402,
however, has now won wide acceptance. Many of the critics who
argued for an earlier date based their conclusions on descriptions of
clothing and armor—and it has been universally noted that this poem is
exceptionally faithful in terms of details of representation—but Hamel
has pointed out that there is also a certain amount of antiquarianism;
references in other words could have been historically accurate rather
than strictly *à la page*. As Patterson (1983/87) has observed, moreover,
the poem seems to have been composed over a long period of time with
many revisions and accretions, embodying a kind of historical layering.
The date of composition in this case becomes fluid: process rather than
specificity.

Most critics have found this poem to be rich in allusions, and there
has been much work on the relationship to contemporary events,
although George Keiser (1973) has argued against making the parallels
with Edward III's campaigns too detailed. R.E. Kaske (1990) has
summarized scholarship on the Nine Worthies episode, noting parallels
between Arthur and David, Alexander, and Godfrey of Bouillon. Like
Ziolkowski (1988), however, he felt that there may well be submerged
analogies still to be discovered. In an important article, Elizabeth Porter
(1983) warned against imposing anachronistic modern readings
concerning attitudes to war and rejected the characterization by Göller
(1981) and others of the poet as a pacifist.

In her introduction, Hamel pointed out that the survival of a unique
copy dictates a conservative position for the modern editor: she also
discussed the relationship between scribal emendation and copy text
(1983). Nevertheless, she makes approximately three hundred and
twenty emendations in her edition, some of which subsequent studies
have shown to be unnecessary, as in the case of line 1382, emended
from "Feltemour" to "Marcel de Mouce," but for which E.D. Kennedy
(1992) has been able to justify the original reading. In many instances
Hamel has used the Winchester Malory as the basis for emendation,

assuming both that Malory "translated" the Alliterative *Morte Arthure* in his Roman War episode and that the Winchester manuscript is closer to Malory's original text than the Caxton print. Accepting this general position, Terence McCarthy (1985) has argued that there is, nevertheless, no need to hypothesize that Malory had access to a lost better version of the Alliterative *Morte Arthure*; what is far more likely is that Malory imitated the characteristic alliteration himself and "emended" when he saw fit. W.G. Cooke (1986) made this same point, giving specific examples such as lines 277–79, where Hamel's emendation from Malory is, Cooke considers, a result of her lack of sensitivity to Malory's tendency to compose afresh in imitation of his source. In a long review article (1986), Turville-Petre challenged the hypothesis that Malory rewrote from the copy of the Alliterative *Morte Arthure* found in the Thornton manuscript itself: "the proposition is absurd, and only attractive to those who want to believe Thornton's copy of the Alliterative *Morte Arthure* to be a good text, which it patently is not."

Certain other issues continue to spark scholarly debate. Whether or not Arthur is to some degree responsible for his fall is a question that has not yet been resolved to the satisfaction of all commentators. Indeed, even those who see Arthur as guilty cannot agree universally on the nature of his sin. In Loomis's *Arthurian Literature in the Middle Ages*, O'Loughlin (1959) formulated most coherently the widely accepted view that Arthur's incest was the cause of his downfall; nevertheless, the author of the Alliterative *Morte Arthure* does not seem to dwell on this aspect of Mordred's paternity, and Regan (1984/85) argues that Mordred is not even presented as Arthur's son in this poem. Part of Regan's argument hinges on the question of genre, and he, like John Finlayson before him, maintains that the Alliterative *Morte Arthure* fits securely into the chanson de geste tradition.

Other scholars, taking their cue from the groundbreaking work of William Matthews (1960), suggest that Arthur is guilty of pride and overreaching. For these scholars, structural issues are particularly important; that is, the precise relationship between Arthur's rise and fall in what for them is a clearly articulated *de casibus* tragedy. Most see a pyramidlike structure, taking the form abcdcba, but in one of the most illuminating studies of the poem (1988) Ziolkowski posited an abcdabcd form, with lines 1–1221 and 3150–4346 closely linked in balanced structure and imagery. In this reading, then, Arthur loses his life because, like the giant, he forsakes his reason. Or, as Hamel would put it (1988), he has become the "tyrant-ogre" himself.

In another, and altogether opposing, study of the poem's formal structure (1982), Eadie maintained that Arthur's conduct is never condemned, that his limitations are simply those imposed on every human being. This is a point that Patterson (1983/87), like Wurster (1981), makes in his new-historicist reading of the poem, when he emphasizes the paradoxical aspect of the *Fürstenspiegel*: princely pride manifested in emulation of even the greatest examples from the past must ultimately give way to the realization that all heroism comes to dust. Yoking together of the Wheel of Fortune and Nine Worthies motifs, the author of the Alliterative *Morte Arthure* has forcefully reminded us of these two contradictory messages that reading the past imparts. Patterson thus touches on the question of reader response and reception theory, since the poem itself is a recreation of the past with lessons to teach the present: in Patterson's view at least, much of the force of the poem lies in the empathetic response it provokes in its readers, medieval and modern.

Like the Alliterative *Morte Arthure*, the Stanzaic *Le Morte Arthur* was probably written in the second half of the fourteenth century, and both poems, of course, deal with Arthur's death. Here the analogy ends, since the poems reflect the contrasting traditions concerning the causes of the downfall of Arthur's kingdom: the Alliterative *Morte Arthure* grows out of the chronicle tradition whereas the Stanzaic *Morte* is an adaptation of the French Vulgate *Mort Artu*.

As is the case with other Middle English Arthurian texts, including the Alliterative *Morte Arthure*, the Stanzaic *Morte* survives in only one manuscript (B.L. Harley 2252), compiled long after the poem was first written. Meale (1983) has studied the format of the manuscript and has charted the stages of its assemblage. The poem has been edited a number of times, and the editions are listed by Jan Simko (1993). Until recently, the standard edition was P.F. Hissiger's (1975), but it has now been replaced by that of S. Noguchi (1991), who reedited because of the significant number of errors in Hissiger's transcription. There are two verse translations (Kahn 1986; Krishna 1990) and one in prose (Stone 1988). The poem has also been translated into Japanese (Shimizu 1985), which is not surprising since there is a strong scholarly interest in Japan.

Recent studies have tended to focus on the poet's adaptations in his "translation" of the Old French *Mort Artu* and to show how these determine the effects he was trying to achieve. Ikegami (1993) concluded that the changes reflect the interests of the audience for whom the poem was composed, one that wished for a simple, straightforward narrative with an emphasis on the role of human weakness in causing the course of events. In his thorough study (1994), Kennedy shows in fuller detail that Arthur is somewhat transformed in order to suit the tastes of an English audience and that he is not nearly as weak as he is in the *Mort Artu*. In this regard, then, Kennedy would contradict the conclusions put forward by Korrel (1984) and Dean (1987), both of whom see Arthur as a foil to Lancelot. Kennedy's analysis of English chronicle sources, moreover, indicates that the poem presents a view of tragedy influenced by the positive portrait of Arthur in the English chronicle tradition and that it is Arthur's relative blamelessness in the Stanzaic *Morte* that attracted Malory. Simko (1993) believes that the structural buildup creates a tragedy that can be seen almost in Shakespearian terms, even though (unlike Malory's adaptation) there is no hope offered at the end. Both Barron (1987) and Alexander (1983) examine the ways in which irony, rather than overt didacticism, is used to show how misfortune interacts with the weaknesses of basically good men and makes the destruction of the Round Table fellowship inevitable.

The final meeting of Lancelot and Guinevere seems to have been the poet's addition, as Beston and Beston (1973) have argued, and Jansen Jaech (1984) concentrates on this scene to show how the poet has used sophisticated patterns of repetition to pull together significant narrative themes. Bennett (1986), who would maintain that Malory uses the second section in his own "Morte Arthur Saunz Guerdon" but who is less certain about the borrowings in the "Tale of Lancelot and Guinevere," notes the particular mastery here. Indeed, he argues that the poem is exemplary throughout, using a difficult verse form with great suppleness, and that it is a worthy precursor of Malory. This admiration for the Stanzaic *Morte*, most forcefully articulated by Bennett, is implicit in most of the studies undertaken in the past decade or so, and Dean stands as a lone voice in his dismissal of the tragedy—Arthur "is not depicted on a large enough scale to be a genuinely tragic figure"—and technical competence of the poet.

Several adaptations from the French Vulgate Cycle deal with the early history of the Grail, a topic that would presumably have a strong resonance in England after the mid-thirteenth century, when Joseph of Arimathea came to be recognized as founding saint of the English church. *Joseph of Arimathie* (ca. 1375) survives only in the Vernon manuscript, where it is presented as continuous prose rather than in the verse form of the surrounding items. When W.W. Skeat first edited the poem in 1871, he treated it as alliterative verse, signaling the formal characteristics by clearly defined conventions. In his introduction and commentary, he traced the poem's source to the Vulgate *Estoire del saint Graal*, of which it appeared to be a much abbreviated "translation," albeit with several odd changes. Universally acknowledged to be mediocre as poetry, the poem received little further critical attention until the 1970s, when Valerie M. Lagorio undertook a series of studies on the English legends of Joseph of Arimathea. Since then, it has been the subject of a new edition by David Lawton (1983), who elsewhere discussed its place in the alliterative revival of the fourteenth century.

For Lawton (1983), "the major interest of Joseph of Arimathea lies in its form not its content," and his most radical conclusion is that it is the first draft of a poem awaiting revision and alliterative embellishment. This thesis, based on the irregularites of the verse and the presentation in the manuscript, of which Lawton gives a detailed analysis, is reflected in Lawton's layout, and he does not reproduce the capitals and paraphs that seemed to mark off the a-verses. Not entirely convinced by Lawton in this matter, reviewers have generally agreed that it would have taken drastic rewriting to have converted the poem into strict and formal alliterative verse.

Even though Lawton was concerned primarily with formal characteristics, he did look at sources and suggested that the poet knew and used the Vulgate *Queste del saint Graal*, as well as the *Estoire*, a proposition for which there does not seem to be a great deal of textual authority. According to Lawton, moreover, the poet was not particularly concerned with the evangelization aspect of the story. In this area, Lawton's conclusions stand in sharp contrast to those of Lagorio, who has examined the borderline between hagiography and romance and has suggested (1975) that the poet's intentions were to transform the *Estoire* into a hagiographical tale focusing on Joseph as evangelist. Expanding on Lagorio's analysis, Noble (1991) has argued that the changes the poet made to his source—the way he treated the Grail material, emphasized Joseph instead of Josephe, and handled the marvelous—indicate that he was quite consciously recreating the French romance as a didactic saint's life extolling the missionary career of the founder of the English church.

Ca. 1450, a London skinner, Henry Lovelich—inspired perhaps, as Barron suggests, by translators employed in commercial scriptoria—undertook the enormous task of translating the Vulgate *Estoire del saint Graal* and *Estoire de Merlin*; the work was intended as a tribute to the Lord Mayor. A somewhat mechanical translator, who wrote (as Barron puts it) in "limping verse," Lovelich has received surprisingly little attention. The chief modern studies have been by Lagorio (esp. 1978), who has examined his contribution to the evolution of the English Joseph of Arimathea legend. As Lagorio has noted, Lovelich tended to emphasize Joseph over his son, Josephe, and—the most significant change from his source—he gave the burialplace of Joseph as Glastonbury Abbey. In the *Merlin*, moreover, Lovelich stressed Merlin's role as prophet of the Holy Grail, and the Grail seems to have a prominent, highly redemptive, role in his vision of the Arthurian legend.

Whereas Lovelich's translation of the Vulgate *Estoire de Merlin* ends with Arthur's victory over Claudas, the *Prose Merlin* carries the work forward to the births of Lancelot, Lionel, and Bors. It follows its original fairly closely, but there are certain assimilations and stylistic innovations, and it seems virtually certain, as the text's first editor, Henry B. Wheatley, pointed out, that the author was working from a source manuscript different from the one used by Lovelich. In recent times, two innovative studies examine marginal annotations and come to important conclusions about contemporary readers and the cultural milieu in which the text was circulating. Analyzing the many marginal notes made by Elyanor Guldeford, Meale (1986) speculates about the readers of English Arthurian romances in the fifteenth century and concludes that the romances were certainly popular among women readers of high status. In her related study, Stern (1986) urges a sympathetic approach to prose works of this sort and considers that the methodology so successfully applied in Malory studies could be usefully brought to bear on this narrative. Elyanor Guldeford's notes show us not only who was reading Arthurian romance but how it was being read: her fascination with the important female characters is particularly revealing. What the work of Meale and Stern makes clear, then, is that criticism of the late-medieval prose material can more profitably direct itself toward contemporary readership and its response to the texts— obtained through close codicological work—than to studies based on anachronistic standards of literary excellence.

When one turns to romances concerning individual knights, it is surprising to see how thoroughly Gawain dominates the field and how little was written about some of the most prominent knights of the Round Table as portrayed in the continental romances; Tristan, in particular, figures in one romance only (apart from Malory). Although *Sir Tristrem* was one of the first medieval English Arthurian romances to be rediscovered in the nineteenth century (edited and "completed" by Sir Walter Scott in 1806), it has received little scholarly attention. The poem is taken from Thomas d'Angleterre's text but is highly condensed and shows signs of oral transmission. As Pearsall, who considers this to be an important "link" poem in the formal developmental chain from epic romance to lyric romance, has suggested (1965), the difficult eleven-line stanza proved unsuited to narrative. Like T.C. Rumble (1959), nonetheless, he sees a number of merits in the poem, which he characterizes as thoughtful and carefully adapted to its relatively sophisticated audience. Dean (1987) would seem to be at odds with this assessment of the putative audience, and he suggests that in spite of the poet's skill with the battle scenes, the chivalric world has been brought down to the level of the fabliau. The most thorough modern study is by Crepin (1982), who observes that the Old French story has been transformed for a nonaristocratic audience and that it falls on the border between ballad and romance. The production of the manuscript indicates that the poem was intended specifically for a wealthy bourgeois client (Shonk 1985). In terms of style, the poem has more similarities with the Norwegian saga version than with Thomas's romance. Barron (1987) comments on the ineptitude of the "translation" but also points out that some of the problems may arise from the unfamiliarity of the scribe with the dialect (perhaps northern) of the original; it is also possible that the scribe was working from a version damaged in transmission. In more general terms, Barron notes that the tendency of English romances to opt for uncomplicated and positive statements leads here to loss of meaning, and the conflict of love and duty becomes reduced to a series of motiveless incidents.

Like Tristan, Perceval fares badly in the English tradition and is represented by only one "translation," *Sir Perceval of Galles*, surviving in the Thornton manuscript and composed probably in the first half of the fourteenth century. In recent years it has been edited at least twice in doctoral dissertations (Baldwin 1972; Rodriguez 1976), but these have not been published. For many years, it was held that *Sir Perceval* was not directly based on Chrétien's *Perceval* but that it represented a form of the story closer to the "original" source and was perhaps related to Irish tales concerning a fairy cup of plenty (see especially Brown 1943). As recently as 1968, Mehl argued that "*Sir Perceval* is certainly not an adaptation of Chrétien's novel and is related to it only through some earlier versions of the story." Primarily through the work of two scholars, David Fowler (1975) and Keith Busby (1978, 1987), this view has been more or less discredited, and we are thus brought back to the position of the earliest commentators such as Halliwell-Phillips (1844).

Fowler characterizes the poem as a parody and as a work of great merit, a view shared by Eckhardt (1973–74) who treats it as a comedy and insists that it has been well designed and crafted for its intended audience. Busby (1978) shows that the poem combines material from the Chrétien's *Perceval* and from the Gawain Continuation and notes, moreover, that these works appear in immediate proximity to each other in the vast majority of surviving manuscripts.

If one accepts the premise that the poet "english'd" Chrétien, then it is possible to look closely at the changes, the motivations for them, and the results. Busby (1987) considers that the radical abridgment leads to a flattening, a reduction in emphasis on love and chivalry. Most dramatically, the Grail is eliminated because of lack of interest in matters spiritual in this type of popular romance. Rather than assume a "clumsy" adapter, unable to understand the subtleties of the French original (a point maintained as recently as 1980 by Finlayson), Busby suggests that we have a poet keenly aware of the demands of his audience. We can assume that the poem is faster moving, concerned with revenge motifs, less devoted to love interest precisely because it was produced for a male-oriented and nonaristocratic community of readers.

Busby's discussions of audience lead to a consideration of genre, and he suggests that Hans Robert Jauss's distinctions between epic and romance could be usefully applied here. It seems that the author has turned romance into something closer to epic while retaining romance affiliations, that is, the "epic romance" described by Pearsall in his important study of Middle English romance (1965). John J. Thompson has examined the context in which *Sir Perceval of Galles* is found in his wider study of the formation of the Thornton manuscript (1983). Like many recent scholars, Thompson takes a codicological approach and shows that it is impossible to discuss texts in isolation: one must inevitably examine manuscript context and the role of scribe as reader/author.

In summary, then, the most recent work on *Sir Perceval of Galles* has moved beyond questions of hypothetical preliterate source (the anthropological school popularized by Jessie Weston and her followers) and, as a development of the structural criticism of the seventies (such as that of Galloway 1973), has concentrated on adaptation, genre, and reception.

As in the case of romance, scholars have found it difficult to come to a definition of the Middle English lay and chart precisely how it relates to the earlier Old French lai. Finlayson (1984–85) has argued that the eight surviving examples in Middle English do not have enough in common to allow for a single generic definition. In his opinion, there are two distinct types, and *Sir Launfal*, representative of one of these, closely resembles the chivalric romance in its defining characteristics. (The other, of which *Le Freine* is typical, involves ordeal and improbable coincidence, but there are no fairy elements or chivalric adventures.) Marie de France's lais are usually considered to be the ultimate source for the English materials, but in the case of *Sir Launfal* it is not entirely clear what the proximate source may have been. It is, however, generally assumed that the three surviving Middle English versions of the story, including *Sir Landeval*, *Sir Lambewell*, and *Sir Lamwell*,[11] all derive from the same Middle English translation of

---

[11] Elizabeth Williams will undertake a study of *Sir Lamwell* in a collection of essays to be edited by Jennifer Fellows, Rosalind Field, Gillian Rogers and Judith Weiss for publication in 1996. In this same volume, there will be a more general study of the Breton lays by Margaret Robson. Gillian Rogers has observed (personal communication)

Marie's *Lanval* (Barron 1987), and Carlson (1988) has established that this lost Middle English version was probably a redaction of a text of *Lanval* similar to that found in Paris, B.N., nouv. acq. fr. 1104.

The contention that *Sir Launval* must be a debased version of *Lanval* is no longer universally accepted; Bennett (1986), for example, argues that Thomas Chestre was a sophisticated refashioner who skillfully incorporated materials from other lays into his poem. Like Barron (1987), Nappholz (1987–88) suggests that Chestre was well aware of his audience and produced a conscious parody in which "largesse" is changed from an ethical to a physical trait. Barron points out that the poem should be seen in the context of folktale tradition rather than in terms of the French lais, and Rosenberg (1985) would argue that like *Graelant* it is related to Type 313 of the *The Types of Folklore*. In addition to its folklore connections, Veldhoen (1990) maintains that archetypal patterns are present.

Although traditionally attributed to Chestre, *Libeaus Desconus* may have been written by a different and less talented author. Having certain resemblances to Malory's later "Tale of Sir Gareth," it derives ultimately from Renaut de Beaujeu's *Bel Inconnu*, and the manuscript distribution—it survives in six manuscripts—suggests that it was a popular tale with contemporary audiences. Nevertheless, it has not found favor with modern scholars and has generally been neglected; Bennett (1986) is representative in his judgment that it is "romance going down hill."

The hero of *Libeaus Desconus* is Gawain's illegitimate son, Ginglain, and this poem could in a sense, therefore, be considered one of the large group of English Gawain poems.[12] From the time of Madden's 1839 edition of *Syr Gawayne: A Collection of Ancient Romance Poems*, which provided superb transcriptions of eleven of the Gawain poems, scholars have noted how intrinsic Gawain is to the

---

that *Sir Lambewell* is nearer to *Sir Landevale* than to *Sir Launfal* but that it is also very close to the sixteenth-century Malone print, closer than to John Kynge's 1557–58 print (Douce fragment), and this shows that the descent cannot be a simple straight line.

[12] Boardman (1988) observes that the quest in *Libeaus Desconus* is "a projection forward onto his son of Gawain's own *enfances*, necessary because Gawain's textual form is completeness, not growth."

English tradition. Boardman (1988) contends that the figure of Gawain constitutes the "vital center" of the English Arthurian romances. Barron (1987) speculates that Gawain appealed to the English imagination because "he could be most readily identified with the archetypal folk-hero seeking self-knowledge through adventure." In the context of the English materials, it seems significant, as Ackerman observed (1959), that the Gawain poems are much more independent of the French romances than are the works devoted to other heroes.[13] In the case of the *Morte Darthur* in particular, Bonnie Wheeler (1993) argues that we end up with an English Gawain whose definition is the incapacity of definition: "Malory's Sir Gawain is from the earliest moment dense with the possibilities of contrary interpretation and he is an exemplary index of Malory's paratactic causality."

Composed in the first half of the fourteenth-century, *Ywain and Gawain* is the closest adaptation from Old French among the English Gawain romances; nevertheless, as Bennett pointed out (1986), "No other romance is so markedly native in its briskness, not to say brusqueness, and its northern idiom." There is a reliable edition (Friedman and Harrington 1964), and modern studies have concerned themselves for the most part with the continuities and discontinuities between this text and Chrétien's *Yvain*. Structural studies of the 1960s and 1970s (such as those undertaken by Finnie 1965 and Fogg 1975) showed the ways in which the author's changes highlighted action and neglected love and courtly conventions. Hunt (1984) observed that in this poem, unlike its source, the coordination of love and chivalry is not problematic; love is quite simply subordinated to the demands of chivalric "trowth." Barron (1987), who also emphasized the importance of "trowth," pointed out that the abbreviation is aimed at eliminating all the "extranarrative" material so intrinsic in Chrétien's version. Mills (1975) noted that the author has tried to accommodate a sophisticated work to a less sophisticated audience, and Busby (1987) analyzed ways in which the text can give us insight into the makeup of this audience.

Although it does not have Gawain's name in the modern title, *The Awntyrs off Arthure at the Terne Wathelyne* (1400–30), which survives

---

[13]Apart from the materials that are listed in this essay, it should be noted that Gillian Rogers will have a piece on *Gawain and Arthur* in the volume to be edited by Fellows, Field, Rogers, and Weiss (see above, n. 11).

in four manuscripts, is nevertheless devoted to his prowess as a hero. It has been edited in four doctoral dissertations and has formed the focus for a master's thesis (by Rosamund Allen at the University of London in 1967–68) as well. Both Gates (1969) and Hanna (1974) have published revised versions of their dissertations, and Hanna (1988) has subsequently reassessed his critical methodology as well as specific emendations. The poem has also appeared in a modern-spelling edition (Phillips 1988).

The major critical issue centers on the unity or disunity of the two parts of the poem. Hanna's edition has enshrined the proposition that the poem is made up of two distinct works, which he has marked off editorially with the headings *The Awntyrs A* and *The Awntyrs B*. As he interpreted it, the second, considerably less learned, poet removed the final stanza from its original position following the ghost episode and made it his own conclusion. Both Allen (1987) and Fichte (1989) endorse Hanna's "bipartite" position, and Allen considers that the second section was written significantly later.[14] Fichte believes that the two episodes contradict each other, and that the poem is controlled by an irreconcilable dualism of purpose: the condemnation and praise of Arthurian ideals. In his reading, some "kind" soul must have added the final stanza.

As definitively as Hanna's edition appears to establish the bipartite reading, dissenting critics contend that the poem has an intricate and unified structure leading to various types of interplay. Phillips (1993) maintains that there are strong unifying factors: "It may be that these unifying factors are not sufficiently worked out . . . to make the work a great one rather than an endlessly intriguing one, but criticism is unlikely to return again to the view that its design is meagre or naive." A.C. Spearing (1985) used numerical analysis to show that the poem is based on a balanced "diptych" structure with stanzas 27 and 28 at the center. In his reading, the meaning is created by juxtaposing the two adventures in a significant way. Takami Matsuda (1984) suggests that the two-part structure defines the Round Table as a "this-worldly" institution but nevertheless allows for an appreciation of its merits. Phillips (1989) has argued that the reference to the ghost's baptism is

---

[14]Allen has announced a fuller study of the poem in the volume edited by Fellows, Field, Rogers, and Weiss.

part of a coherent scheme of ideas, which forms an organizing principle in the first section and which extends through the rest of the poem. More recently (1993), she has used the three-fitt division found in the Ireland-Blackburne manuscript as a basis for a structural reconsideration.[15] Even if this division cannot be shown to have any kind of absolute authority, it does allow us to notice the themes (in particular, the focus on Arthur as a great leader) that unify the central sections of the poem and to link them to those that come before and after. The secular and eschatological aspects, moreover, provide frames for each other. In the final analysis, Phillips believes, much of the unity debate is a result of the difficulty that a modern audience has in accepting a poem whose values are entirely aristocratic.

*The Awntyrs* is generally viewed as having a social function, and several scholars have dealt with Guinevere and the "place" of women. Stiller (1980) has argued that we have here a clear expression of male fear of female sexuality, whereas Maureen Fries (1981) sees Guinevere as an archetype of combined courtly and spiritual significance. Mathewson (1987) has examined the idealization of Gawain in a masculine world from which the feminine is displaced.

In the past, scholars have seen relationships between this poem and *Sir Gawain and the Green Knight*, which it may even echo. Phillips (1993) notes that it also deals with the theme of mutability in a manner similar to the Alliterative *Morte Arthure* and that there may be a connection. Doyle (1982) turns from intertextual relationships to manuscript contexts and possible audiences, concluding that "wherever and whenever a piece of pronouncedly alliterative character originated, it could have a wide dissemination, by no means all amateur or provincial, and lasting beyond the middle of the fifteenth century outside the northern regions." Turville-Petre (1974) observed that *Summer Sunday, De Tribus Regibus Mortuis,* and *The Awntyrs* were linked formally and thematically; in 1977, he also suggested a similarity to certain of the Harley Lyrics. In his discussion (1989), Lawton questioned Turville-Petre's assumption that the thirteen-line stanza could be an offshoot of aa/ax poetry and gave other possibilities. Bennett (1983) has pointed out that northern alliterative poetry

---

[15] The manuscript has also been studied by Phillipa Hardman (1976), who suggests that Part 1 of the manuscript is a literary unit, adapted by a discerning compiler.

developed not so much from the long line as from the rhyming alliterative stanza: *The Awntrys* and *Golagros and Gawain*, in other words, grow out of the same tradition as *Summer Sunday*.

Among surviving Arthurian romances, *The Avowing of King Arthur, Sir Gawain, Sir Kay, and Baldwin of Britain* is most similar to *The Awntyrs of Arthure*, as Bennett (1986) has pointed out, and it is worth noting that both texts occur in the same manuscript. The major work on the poem has been undertaken by Roger Dahood, who published an edition with full glossary of the unique version (it is found in the Ireland-Blackburne manuscript) in 1984. His method was a conservative one, and he rarely emended the manuscript readings. David Johnson (1990) would apply to this poem the same kind of diptych structure postulated by Spearing to explain the divided nature of *The Awntyrs*. In Johnson's reading, there is a contrast between two types of chivalry, one literary and the other more practical; there is also a hint that the audience would identify readily with the more down-to-earth attitudes of the second part of the poem. Work remains to be done. In particular, it is not clear how precisely *The Avowing of King Arthur* relates to other sixteen-line stanza poems, and this in turn leads to the wider issue of whether or not one can really think of a distinct northern school of tail-rhyme romances.

Studied primarily in relation to Chaucer's *Wife of Bath's Tale*—Wurtele (1987), for example, used it (and the related ballad version *The Marriage of Sir Gawaine* from the Percy Folio manuscript) as a basis of comparison in his study of how the Wife of Bath's "distorted" vision requires the surrender of sovereignty—*The Weddinge of Sir Gawen and Dame Ragnell* has received little independent analysis, although critics now rate it more highly than was the case in the past. There is no modern critical edition as such, but Withrington has provided a modern spelling edition (1991), in the introduction to which he gives a survey of Gawain romances and looks specifically at the ways in which this poem fits into the English Gawain tradition. J.J. Griffiths (1982) has discussed Oxford, Bodleian Library, Rawlinson C.86, which contains the only surviving copy of the poem. Dannenbaum (1982) has related individual phrases to contemporary hunting treatises, and Kooper (1990) has examined the poem in the context of contemporary marriage practice and ecclesiatical views on love and marriage. Tigges (1990) touched upon aspects of parody.

Most radically, P.J.C. Field (1982) postulated that the poem was actually written by Malory himself.

The Percy Folio Gawain romances—*The Turke and Gowin*, *The Carle off Carlile*, *The Grene Knight*, and *The Marriage of Sir Gawain*—have received relatively little attention, although this situation will be rectified when the volume to be edited by Felicity Riddy, Gillian Rogers, Diane Speed, and Elizabeth Williams appears.[16] *The Turke and Gowin*, badly damaged and now containing only about half of its original lines, has been more closely studied than the other romances and has been edited in two unpublished doctoral dissertations (Schlobin 1971; Williams 1987). Jost (1988) has examined the relationship between adventure and violence in *The Turke and Gowin* and in *The Ballad of King Arthur and the King of Cornwall* and suggests the need for a closer analysis concerning what motivated such a strong taste for violence in the fifteenth-century English romances. Nicolas Jacobs (1982) argues that episodes in certain English Gawain poems (*Sir Gawain and the Green Knight*, *The Carle off Carlisle*, and *The Turke and Gowin*) indicate the existence of a motif of disenchantment by beheading, and he finds parallels, for example in the Irish tale *The Destruction of Da Derga's Hostel*. Whitaker (1984) notes parallels with Irish materials and discusses the otherworld-journey motif.

Among the Scottish Gawain materials, *Golagros and Gawain* has received most critical attention in recent years. Basing his text on the "Livre du Chastel Orgueilleus" in the *First Continuation* of Chrétien's *Perceval*, the author of *Golagros and Gawain* has made specific sorts of changes, that in turn lead to major shifts in meaning: the love motif is eliminated, and knightly honor and prowess are emphasized. The poem was probably composed late in the fifteenth century, but no manuscript containing it survives: it is found only in a unique copy of the printed edition of 1508. Several "modern" editions are based on the

---

[16] Provisionally entitled *Arthurian Romances of the Percy Folio Manuscript*, it will also include an edition of the other Arthurian romances in the Percy Folio manuscript, described by Rogers (1991). Speed has provided an edition of *The Grene Knight* in *Medieval English Romances* (Sydney: University of Sydney, 1987). There is an edition of *The Carle off Carlile* by Auro Kurvinen, *Sir Gawain and The Carl of Carlisle in Two Versions* (Helsinki, 1951).

1508 print, but these are relatively inaccessible, and it is particularly fortunate therefore that Barron is engaged on a new edition.

Barron has undertaken several studies of *Golagrus and Gawane*: he has compared it with its source (1963) and concludes that it displays a distaste for love themes and that it indicates a distinctly Scottish conception of romance, where the erotic is rejected and chivalry reinterpreted. In two articles (1974, 1982), he has discussed medieval theories of translation and has observed that medieval authors did not distinguish between creation and redaction. In his opinion, *Golagrus and Gawane* is an independent—creatively exciting—text, as distinct from its original in meaning as it is different in form. Unlike Barron, who argues that we get real heroes engaged in human concerns in this poem, Mathewson (1987) has suggested that the characters are extraordinarily abstract, figures in a morality text. The values are exclusively masculine ones, in her reading, and the feminine is incorporated into the males themselves: we see Arthur as witch, and Gawain at the opposite extreme as Virgin Mary or love heroine. Shichtman (1990), who argues that the Scottish writers used the character of Gawain as a means of appropriating a hostile English legend, maintains that Gawain becomes a metaphor for the Scottish writers themselves and the sources are changed in such a way that he is portrayed as the sole voice of reason in the court.

*Lancelot of the Laik,* which survives only in a fragment contained in a single manuscript, is also an adaptation from the French Arthurian tradition, in this case the French Vulgate *Lancelot.* Although the poem is generally faithful to the original, there are two major changes, one of which emphasizes Arthur's weakness and provides him with advice on how to be a just ruler. It is possible, therefore, that the poem was directed to James III, and Dean (1979) would locate it within the "mirror for princes" genre. An important study of the whole Arthurian/ Scottish nexus was undertaken by Flora Alexander (1975), and Shichtman (1990) has elaborated this theme. Contrary to earlier critics, who have seen the emphasis on Gawain in this poem as inconsistent, Shichtman suggests that Gawain has been deliberately glorified, his frailties in the French version carefully suppressed. The poem is not, as has been claimed, a bad paraphrase but a conscious reworking for a specific audience: the French favorite is ousted, in other words, by the "hometown boy," and the Arthurian legend thus appropriated for a Scottish context.

If critics complain that the "minor" Gawain romances have received insufficient analysis, bibliographers might well groan about the prolixity of treatments of *Sir Gawain and the Green Knight*: according to Blanch (1983), there were over eight hundred scholarly appraisals between 1900 and 1977.[17] Fortunately, however, there have also been a number of reference works and bibliographical studies. One of these, by Malcolm Andrew (1979), provides a comprehensive bibliography from 1839 to 1977 for all four poems contained in Cotton Nero A.x. For *Sir Gawain*, Andrew lists over nine hundred items, but the sheer number of citations necessarily causes his annotations to be somewhat telegraphic. Blanch (1983), on the other hand, limited himself to *Sir Gawain* only and to the years 1968–78, taking up where Ackerman's earlier survey (1968) left off. In his introduction, Blanch has given a useful overview of critical trends. Not surprisingly, Blanch's summary indicates that Gawain scholarship has tended to mirror critical fashions in other areas: roughly speaking, it moved during these ten years from discussions of orality through structuralist studies to questions of feminism and the interplay between reader and audience. From his informed perspective, Blanch suggested a number of remaining desiderata—ambiguity, interlacing among all four Cotton Nero poems, the question of narrator, narrative methods—and stated in particular that further subjects would undoubtedly open up as the *Middle English Dictionary* progressed. More recently, there have been two supplements (Foley 1988–89 and Blanch 1991) for the years up to 1985, both based on Andrew's format and covering all four works attributed to the *Gawain*-poet; Although many of the older critical issues continued to be debated, there was a trend in the early eighties to examine

---

[17] Over the years, *Sir Gawain and the Green Knight* has also been edited a number of times, but Norman Davis's revised version of the Tolkien and Gordon edition (1967) continues to be the standard scholarly text. Felicity Riddy is producing an edition of *Pearl* and *Sir Gawain and the Green Knight* for Oxford University Press to replace Tolkien and Gordon.

ambiguity, the rhetoric of romance, social history in general, and the literary achievement of the Northwest Midlands.[18]

In a shortish and somewhat impressionistic study (1990) completed not long before her death, Jeanne T. Mathewson, herself a student of Ackerman, discussed developments from the time of Ackerman's piece up to the end of the eighties. She noted that there has been a great deal of work on comic elements, on the conventions of genre, on game and the play of the hero, on patterning, on folklore and psychoanalytic theory, on audience response, on contemporary thought and practice, and legal matters. Considering that background studies in particular have only a limited value ("the application of background information has the effect of denying the lighthearted, playful, positive dimension of the poem, and emphasizing doom and gloom—imposing a puritanical sobriety that is belied by almost every line of *Sir Gawain*"), Mathewson concluded that the most fertile source for new insights will be the French Vulgate romances. Whatever else, the Christian context—Christmas does not conjure up game alone—must be kept well in mind.

Since 1985, the period for which there has not been until recently any single standard bibliographical source, the stream of articles and books on *Sir Gawain* has continued to pour forth. Translations into Japanese, Spanish, and Italian have been produced, as well as a useful collection of essays on teaching approaches (Miller and Chance 1986). There has been a slightly higher proportion of psychological studies than in the past; a return of interest in folklore material, ancient motifs, and rituals; provocative work on sign theory (Arthur 1987; Shoaf 1988), speech-act theory (Campbell 1990), chivalry (Clein 1987; Anderson 1989–90) and courtesy (Nicholls 1985); hermeneutics of

---

[18]After this study was completed, Robert J. Blanch and Julian N. Wasserman's review article summarizing the present state of *Sir Gawain and the Green Knight* criticism appeared (1993); this refers to a "cloudburst of scholarly activity devoted to *Gawain*." In their assessment, Blanch and Wasserman focused on the problem of poetic closure and on recent approaches—historical and cultural studies; sociohistorical interpretations; feminist readings; semiotic theories; psychological studies and the use of myth and ritual. In terms of future directions, they suggest that the unity and interrelatedness of the four poems in the manuscript could be profitably explored in the light of contemporary theoretical practices. Meg Stainsby has also produced an updated version of Andrew's bibliography (1992).

laughter, game (Goodlad 1987), and rhetoric (esp. Troyan 1990); and a renewed interest in the manuscript context (esp. Horrall 1986). Feminist readings have appeared, such as Fisher (1988) and Kamps (1989), but Heng (1991) argues that the insufficiency in this area is only beginning to be redressed. Both Shoaf (1984) and Mann (1986) have looked at the poem in the context of medieval economic thought, and Mann suggests that the intended audience must have included a merchant class. Cooke (1989) has argued for an earlier date of composition than has generally been assumed, and Cooper and Pearsall (1988) have contributed an important piece concerning the question of common authorship.

More than any other poem in the medieval English Arthurian tradition, *Sir Gawain* seems to provoke commentary, but this can easily draw scholars away from the poem itself, and Hanning's admonition (1982)—that modern exegetes should "recognize in Gawain's fall and failings as a knight, a Christian, and a human being an instructive analogue to our own imperfections as critics"—seems germane.

Apart from whatever personal merits he may have possessed as a writer, Sir Thomas Malory stands at an important juncture in literary history and pulls together, if only temporarily, the strands of the English Arthurian tradition: chronicle and romance, history and fiction, poetry and prose. The two surviving versions of his Arthuriad also provide a metaphor, or even Johnson's dreaded synecdoche, for the movement from manuscript to print culture. For those coming after Tennyson and the Pre-Raphaelites, it is hard to believe that Malory was virtually unknown for almost two hundred years and that there were no editions of Caxton's version between 1634 and 1816. This all changed in the nineteenth century—one thinks of Georgiana Burne-Jones's comment that "sometimes I think that the book never can have been loved as it was by those two men [Burne-Jones and Morris]"—and at least ten editions appeared between 1816 and 1900, culminating with the Dent version illustrated by Aubrey Beardsley, begun in serial in 1893. Barry Gaines (1990) has undertaken a complete bibliography of all editions between 1485 and 1985, which meticulously charts critical reaction to Malory over the past five hundred years, and Carlson (1994) has given a sharp analysis of the politics of the 1634 Blome-Stansby edition in the context of the post–Civil War Arthurian narrative *Brittains Glory* (1684). Marylyn J. Parins (1988) discusses how nineteenth-century editors abridged Malory in order to make the book fit reading for Victorian audiences. As a complement to the editions themselves, Parins (1988) has provided texts of critical responses, beginning with Caxton's 1485 preface and concluding with a 1912 article by George Saintsbury. The illustrations found in editions from 1498 to 1936 have been analyzed by Muriel Whitaker (1985). Elizabeth Archibald and A.S.G. Edwards are editing a *Companion to Malory* (on the model of the highly successful Cambridge series) to be published by Boydell and Brewer in 1995.

In the twentieth century, Malory scholarship has been dominated by the 1934 discovery (Oakeshott 1963) of the Winchester manuscript (now British Library Add. 59678, issued in facsimile, 1976), which resulted in Eugène Vinaver's critical edition under the title of *The Works of Sir Thomas Malory* (1947, 1948, with corrections; 1967, 1973, with additions and corrections); revised and reissued by P.J.C. Field (1990). There has, not surprisingly, been a strong reaction against Vinaver's revisionist stance, which has led to a reaffirmation of the importance of the Caxton version (issued in facsimile, 1976), of which James Spisak has prepared a new critical edition (1983). With the Spisak edition, we now have, as Basil Cottle observed in his review of Spisak, "all the primary Malory material that we need, with ample tabulated comparisons of the variant forms which it takes." In Japan, where Malorian studies are flourishing, T. Kato (1974) compiled a concordance, which has been a major aid to subsequent word studies and other close readings of the text.

In recent times, the canonization of Malory by literary historians— T. Turville-Petre observed (1986) that "Malory, indeed, is the figure to whom all students of English Arthurian literature must constantly return"—has been accompanied by a proliferation of studies devoted to the *Morte Darthur*. Malory is, as Larry Benson noted (1968), "a critical 'discovery' of the twentieth century."[19] For the period up to 1977, complete bibliographical references can be found in P.W. Life's useful study (1980), which can be supplemented by Toshiyuki Takamiya's bibliography (1981). James W. Spisak (1985; "Intro-

---

[19] Nor is interest in Malory limited to the scholarly forum. In 1990, David Freeman directed a dramatized version at the Lyric Theatre Hammersmith, and Kevin Crossley-Holland has prepared a modernized retelling for radio.

duction") has categorized recent scholarly trends, focusing on (1) biographical studies; (2) use of English sources and translation of French materials; (3) language and style; (4) structure; (5) order of composition; (6) relationship of manuscript version and Caxton's edition to Malory's original text. A section (IX) in *A Manual of the Writings in Middle English 1050–1500. III* has been devoted to Malory and Caxton. In his guide, Terence McCarthy (1988) summarizes the scholarly issues. Boydell and Brewer's important Arthurian Studies series was initiated by the volume edited by Toshiyuki Takamiya and Derek Brewer (1981), in which old methodologies were discussed and new directions signaled, Brewer contending that "our modern interest, as revealed in these essays, tends to be historical and, as it were, technical." These same trends can still be observed,[20] along with increased reference to theoretical issues and, in particular, the implications of the positioning of this text on the cusp between manuscript and print culture.

Until the past few years, the scholarly debate has hinged on two questions: identity of the author and degree of unity among the eight distinct sections. The compendious researches of P.J.C. Field (1974, 1977, 1979, 1979-80, 1982, 1993) have convinced most critics that Thomas Malory of Newbold Revel must be our author, although R.R. Griffith (1981, 1990) has made a strong case for Thomas Malory of Papworth St. Agnes; and Spisak (1985) insists that "the authorship question remains open to further research and debate," a point reaffirmed by R.M. Lumiansky (1987) in his summary of the arguments concerning each of the three possible candidates. Richard Barber (1993) has suggested that, like John Paston III, Malory moved in the lower level of court circles and that he acquired much of his information about the Arthurian romances in this milieu—"squires of the household 'talking of chronicles of kings and other policies' after supper."

Few scholars would still accept unreservedly either Vinaver's premise, first articulated in 1935-36, that Malory composed eight separate and virtually unrelated works or Lumiansky's contrary view

---

[20] For example, the volume edited by Takashi Suzuki and Tsuyoshi Mukai in 1993 has eight essays on Malory: four of them deal specifically with bibliographical matters, and most of the others are concerned with materials covered by Brewer's term "historical."

(1955, 1964, 1987) that the *Morte Darthur* must be seen as a single well-integrated unit. In the past decade, various critics have, in fact, sought to reconcile these two opposing interpretations. Taking "A Noble Tale of Sir Launcelot du Lake" as his model, Brewer (1986) has argued that Malory should not be read using the modern principle of singleness; as a traditional narrative, its interest lies in pattern and structure rather than in cause and effect. Mann (1991) discusses the ways in which the narrative we are reading is "somehow distanced from the events it wishes to embrace." She suggests that it is at the very end, when the narrative finally escapes from us altogether, that it realizes a wholeness that can be achieved only as past event; this, she points out, is the significance of the "hoole book" colophon. In a related study, W.B. Piper (1986) envisages the narrative as a collection of separate entities, all subordinate to a greater whole, whose reality lies outside the discourse and is suggested by Malory's paratactic style. Murray J. Evans (1985) argues that the layout of the manuscript indicates five linked narrative units whose links function as dropped analogies that invite the reader to complete the structure and determine its *significatio*. The degree of unity, then, is to some extent a product of each reader's own interpretation. Andrea Clough (1986) suggests that Malory's narrative reflects his concern with the civil wars disrupting his own life. In his desire to create order out of division, Malory transformed the pattern of the traditional plot (from political unification to social chaos) by including a return to unification in the closing chapters. In her contextualizing study, Riddy (1987) maintains that we should compare the "hoole book" with other similar compilations of the period: in some sense, its integrity is codicological rather than authorial.[21] Carol Meale (1985) has argued that there were a variety of manuscripts containing collections of romances to which Malory may have had access; there is no need, therefore, to posit a single patron such as Anthony Wydville, Lord Scales.

The unity debate inevitably leads to other structural considerations, and this topic has been comprehensively dealt with by Stephen Knight (1969). In a somewhat radical approach, Judson B. Allen (1982) argued

---

[21] Following the same general approach, Karen Helen Cherewatuk (1986) has studied the relationship between the *Morte Darthur* and manuals of chivalry (1986). See also Goodman (1987).

that medieval poetic theory can be applied to the *Morte Darthur* to show that its eight parts define the story in terms of the seven days of creation and the eighth of judgment. James D. Pickering (1983), on the other hand, sees an analogy between the pattern of action in Malory and the development of the Renaissance five-act drama; the tragedy arises from the clash between quest for individual success and service to King and Fellowship. John F. Plummer (1985) suggests that the typology of Pentecost and Babel can be used to chart the disintegration of the Round Table. Andrew Lynch (1990) observes that the disclosure of names is a structural component in the *Morte Darthur*: name does not mean subject-character as it does in the modern realist novel; rather, name becomes the primary "way of meaning" for the story. This relates to theories of personality and definitions of self, on which Caroline E.M.E. Fleming has written a dissertation (1987). Ginger Thornton (1991) argues that "The Book of Sir Tristram" is a structural key: in this book, Arthur's personal weakness becomes apparent, and the final disintegration of the Round Table is foreshadowed.

The study of sources continues apace, and no fewer than four of the essays in *Aspects of Malory* addressed themselves to this issue and the related question of translation from the French. Recent scholars have, moreover, been sensitive to the nuances of what medieval authors meant when they used the term "translation"; Catherine Batt (1989), for example, has examined several motifs in the *Morte Darthur* and has come to the conclusion that Malory can be seen as a critical reader of his sources, well aware of the choices he was making as translator.[22] J.M. Walsh (1985) challenges Vinaver's thesis concerning a lost version of "La Cheualer du Charyot" and suggests that all Malory's revisions in this tale have structural origins, relating to the placement of this episode in his complete Arthuriad. Malory's self-conscious references to "La Chaualer du Charyot" are probably designed to mask the extent of his changes. P.J.C. Field (1989) has studied the different versions of the *Prose Tristan* and compared them with Malory's "Tale of Sir Tristram"; he has also argued (1991) that Chrétien's *Yvain* is the

---

[22] Translation issues closely tie in with considerations of Malory's prose style, and, as Turville-Petre has observed (1986), this is an area that awaits detailed research and careful weighing of the relative influence on Malory of French sources and native prose tradition.

source for two distinct episodes, those where Lancelot frees people from the rule of giants and where Sir Ector provokes the appearance of a knight by striking a basin. Michael N. Salda (1990-91) examines the relationship between Malory's "Tale of Sir Tristram" and two closely related fifteenth-century texts of the *Prose Tristan* and maintains that Malory's lost source may have been a composite text, represented in part by the manuscript that was the basis for the 1489 printed edition. Most recently, E.D. Kennedy (1993) has looked at sources for "The Noble Tale of Sir Launcelot du Lake," which has been used as evidence by both sides in the unity debate. In Kennedy's opinion, this tale was written as a short romance to prepare readers for Lancelot's later role in other tales without obscuring Malory's own emphasis on King Arthur.

Few scholars would still accept Vinaver's view that Malory's "The Tale of the Sankgreal" is the least original of his "translations," and this book has been the focus of a number of recent studies, initiated by Sandra Ness Ihle's book (1983), which used architectural terminology as a basis for comparing Malory's tale with the Vulgate *Queste*. Murray J. Evans (1982) takes the rhetorical device of *sermocinatio* as a means for showing how Malory's portrait of Lancelot indicates a shift from the abstract religious perspective of the French original; this in turn reflects on Lancelot's portrayal before and after the Sankgreal adventures. Robert L. Kelly (1985), on the other hand, argues that the portrayal of Lancelot in the Sankgreal episode emphasizes later discontinuities in his characterization. Stephen C.B. Atkinson (1985) sees the treatment of Lancelot as the feature that links the Sankgreal segment to the rest of the *Morte Darthur*; in the course of the quest, the dichotomy between public and private that dominated his earlier career is replaced by the dichotomy between earthly and heavenly chivalry. Dhira B. Mahoney (1985) also suggests that Malory transmits the dichotomy between secular and spiritual chivalry, but, unsympathetic to the typological method, Malory indicates that ghostly chivalry is a solution only after earthly fellowship has gone. John F. Plummer (1989) maintains that Malory was not obtuse in any way in his reading of the Vulgate *Queste*; his adaptations were deliberately chosen to emphasize the gulf between spiritual and literal planes. Paul H. Caron (1990-91) contends that Malory wished to secularize the Grail theme and thus made Lancelot the most important character in the

Sankgreal quest. S.C.B. Atkinson (1988) argues that readers, like the characters, are unprepared for the allegorical world of the Sankgreal section and are forced to formulate new standards that, in turn, will allow them to approach the complexities of the final tales. Likewise, E.S. Sklar (1988) maintains that "The Tale of the Sankgreal" posits the need for a new value system that is created through a redefinition of secular terms. In particular, the concept of adventure takes on a new meaning, involving right-thinking, passivity, abstention from sexuality, penitence, and openness to God's will. Less concerned with internal structural links, Riddy (1987) views Malory's treatment of the Grail in the context of the introspective piety of the fifteenth-century gentry.

To some extent, studies of individual characters hinge on the relationship between Malory's portrayal and that found in his sources, and Merlin proves to be the principal figure for analysis, as he is in Arthurian studies in general. W.T. Greene (1987) suggests that Merlin regresses as the "hoole book" progresses and that at the end the reader must see him as nothing more than a bumbling magician. Donald L. Hoffman (1991), on the other hand, sees his combination of fore-knowledge and powerlessness as tragic, his fate as helpless slave to passion an exemplum of the fall of the whole kingdom.

In terms of English sources, on which E.D. Kennedy undertook groundbreaking work (1981), the Alliterative *Morte Arthure* is a key document. Terence McCarthy (1985) has challenged the long-held theory that Book 2 can be used as evidence that there was once a better, now lost, version of the Alliterative *Morte Arthure* to which Malory had access. Related to the question of source is the consideration of the relationship between the Winchester version of the Roman Wars episode and that found in the printed text; Vinaver employed Book 2 as a principal means of showing just how radical an editor Caxton was. Drawing on the work of William Matthews, Lumiansky (1987) argued, however, that Caxton's edition was the result of Malory's own revisions rather than external editorial measures; indeed, both he and Charles Moorman (1986) consider that in some sense Caxton's *Morte Darthur* bears witness to Malory's second edition, that is, the lost "copye unto me delyvered."[23]

---

[23] This too, in Lumiansky's opinion, would account for the deleted *explicits* in Caxton's version.

Thematic considerations have been taken up by several individuals, who have concentrated primarily on medieval chivalry. Beverly Kennedy (1985) has suggested that the text can be read as a typology of knighthood, with Gawain representing the heroic knight, Arthur the worshipful knight, and Lancelot the true knight. David V. Harrington (1987) examines the conflicting pulls of chivalric standards and personal obligations, which he sees as typical of the struggle to ennoble chivalry in the fifteenth century. These specific studies of knighthood are complemented by the more general study of chivalry edited by Chickering and Seiler (1988).

Apart from considerations of the actual role of the Winchester manuscript in the production of Caxton's print—on which Hilton Kelliher (1981), Lotte Hellinga (1981), and Toshiyuki Takamiya (1993) have done much important work—there have been a number of studies concerned with the ways in which this text fitted into Caxton's overall publishing agenda. Jennifer R. Goodman (1985) points out that the *Morte Darthur* was one of a series of four chivalric works being published by Caxton in the 1480s, and this provides a context for understanding certain important structural and thematic features. Tsuyoshi Mukai (1993) compares the concept of knighthood presented in these works on chivalry. He also notes how the subtle changes in Wynkyn de Worde's 1498 reprint suggest a trend to "normalize" and "medievalize" Malory's idea of chivalry. Elizabeth Kirk (1985) has observed that a comparison of Caxton's prologue with his other prologues displays a system of assumptions about narrative, genre, and the function of literature quite unlike our own. More generally, N.F. Blake has provided a full bibliographical guide to Caxton's publishing activities (1985).

Margaret F. Nims's translation and study of Geoffrey of Vinsauf's *Poetria Nova* in 1967 opened the way for renewed study of medieval literary theory, but this area has not been as much of a focus in Malory criticism as it has in the equivalent French texts. Nevertheless, Ihle (1984), who dealt with rhetorical strategies in *Malory's Grail Quest*, has shown how Books 7 and 8 demonstrate the use of *abbreviatio* in such a way that a tragedy is produced quite unlike that in its source. Allen (1985) would argue that the best way to read the last tales is as a diptych *distinctio*, whose normal end is definition, rather than as a tragic plot, whose end is conclusion.

There have been recent studies of Malory's use of language. Catherine LaFarge (1987), for example, suggests that characters in the *Morte Darthur* speak at cross-purposes and that we thus lose any sense of unified perception. Ultimately, the instability of narratorial viewpoint may be the defining characteristic of a number of medieval English romances. Ann Dobyns (1990) analyzes Malory's use of dialogue by comparing speeches of Guinevere and Isode, and suggests that dialogue in the *Morte Darthur* is not psychologically revealing but metaphoric; the characters are thus emblems for Malory's own vision of the human condition. She also shows (1986) how Lancelot's speeches exemplify the loss of the fellowship of the Round Table.

Recent years have seen an interest in psychological readings of Malory. F.J. Ringel (1987) would see Gareth's exile in the kitchen in light of Georges Dumézil's third function (i.e., feeding); in this interpretation, Gareth is doing penance for his mother's incest with Arthur. The incest theme is also taken up by Elizabeth Archibald (1989), who examines the Mordred story in the context of the vogue for moralizing incest stories in the twelfth and thirteenth centuries. Bonnie Wheeler (1994) gives a Jungian reading of Gareth and sees the tale as exemplifying the process of individuation worked out through the alchemical process.

Finally, we come to feminist perspectives. Lindsay E. Holichek (1982) argues that Guinevere maintains the code of knightly behavior as much as does Lancelot and that she conforms to what Malory defines as "worshypful." Maureen Fries (1994) observes that one of the roads to "worship" in the *Morte Darthur* consists in the single extended quest that culminates in marriage, and she points to Gareth as a prime example. In many cases, though, marriage can be a hindrance to the pursuit of a chivalric career, and a knight is more likely to achieve success by taking a mistress than by taking a wife. Geraldine Heng (1990) provides a study of the feminine subtext in Malory and looks in particular at the feminine background for most of the knightly adventures. Fries (1991) emphasizes Malory's positive approach by analyzing the ways in which Tennyson transformed the female characters; Tennyson "bowdlerized" the tragedy by focusing it almost entirely on female guilt. The female characters are also the subject of a recent dissertation by Marjorie W. Dobbin, "The Women of Malory's *Morte Darthur*" (1987), and Roberta Anne Davidson has written a thesis on "Three Ladies of Arroy: Sign and Gender in Sir Thomas Malory's Arthuriad" (1987).

## *Desiderata*

In 1971, Lillian Herlands Hornstein provided a survey of scholarship and desiderata in the field of Middle English romances, in which she voiced a concern about the definition of the genre. She also observed that "a methodology, and specifications for editing of [neglected] texts" must precede the much-needed textual reediting and critical apparatuses. Since then, the new philology—and there have been a variety of studies of philology new and old, such as Ziolkowski (1990) and Busby (1993)—has brought the editing question into sharp focus and has also led to reexamination of the manuscript context in which texts occur as part of a "postmodern return to the origins of medieval studies" (Nichols 1990). On the most general level, Bloch (1988) has argued that there can be no unmediated access to the text, "which, because of the degraded nature of verbal signs, requires interpretation or gloss." Every editorial act, in other words, must be seen as part of a political agenda. A similar position has been taken by Lee Patterson (1987), who looks carefully at the exemplary work of Kane and Donaldson on the seemingly multiple issues of *Piers Plowman* and contends that their most basic premises, a combination of belief in the author as romantic genius and in the possibility of logical analysis to get us back to the original text, depend on the academic tradition from which they spring. A.S.G. Edwards (1987) also addresses the Kane-Donaldson edition and observes that the methodology in less scrupulous hands could take us back to the kind of "imaginative folly" employed by Percy and his ilk. Modern editors need to combine the accuracy and candor of Kane and Donaldson with greater restraint. Charlotte Brewer (1991) suggests that the recent work on scribes as well as "original" authors has caused a more self-conscious attitude on the part of editors; she espouses Jerome J. McGann's "sociological" position and maintains that there should be less emphasis on author as presiding genius to whose unadulterated words we are trying to return. In a volume comprising many important articles on the question of editing (1992), Nicolas Jacobs has a piece concerning the possible motives that led scribes to edit their copy-texts. Although she renounces excessive "scribolatry," Jennifer Fellows (Mills, Fellows, Meale, 1991) maintains that the traditional editorial task of pursuing archetypes does not fit the romance mode well and that we should not try to reduce them to single correct versions.[24]

Edwards (1991) has pointed out that of ninety-four verse romances listed in the revised Severs Manual, nearly fifty exist in a single manuscript, and it is particularly hard to posit "superior" readings for troublesome patches in these works, especially since we must also consider oral variation as a factor.[25] In the case where multiple copies exist, on the other hand, there is the problem of incoherence in style in "popular" texts, and this makes access to the putative original virtually impossible. Like Brewer (1991)—who states that "irony is our great modern critical device for protecting ourselves from imaginative experience of an unfamiliar kind"—Edwards is suspicious of modern confidence concerning tone and intention as editorial technique: "notions of burlesque and parody rest on a secure sense of the text and of the firm relationship between authorial design and audience." And it is precisely in these areas where our knowledge continues to be least certain. When there is no stable text, then, where does the possiblity of interpretation lie? Edwards concludes that for the majority of the romances there is little middle ground between textual study and literary criticism, especially since the composition process and the transmission history of these works serve to render notions of purposive design and texture indeterminate. Both Speer (1983) and Hult (1988) have come to this same conclusion, and Hult, in particular, observes (grantedly in the context of Old French texts) that "what is crucial about the editor's craft is its direct placement at that spot where modern concerns meet medieval ones in the very conception of the literary object. In this regard, it is important to keep in mind that editing is not simply prior to interpretation, it is consubstantial with it."

---

[24] Rosamund Allen (1987) raises a number of the same questions and signals the dangers of direct method or eclectic editing.

[25] Corley (1990) has also discussed the editorial issues involved when dealing with single-manuscript texts, although she has used Old French material as her reference point.

What is clear then, is that the field of editing is, as Wenzel (1990) puts it, "in great turmoil." Nevertheless, all parties seem agreed that a basic desideratum is access to the texts in one form or another and that new editions, especially of the lesser-studied works, continue to be a major requirement.[26] Thus, in her review (1990) of Barron's *English Medieval Romance*, Judith Weiss concluded that "what is now needed is publication of accessible editions to support the evidently lively study of a mode that still operates, for better or worse, just beneath the surface of our literary and cultural consciousness." And Brewer (1991) observed in his survey of current scholarly trends that "there is still much to be done in the editing of texts, despite some remarkable achievements, both in Britain and on the Continent, in the last few years."[27] Fortunately, new reference guides are leading us to the neglected texts, and one must single out the *Index of Middle English Prose*, under Edwards's general editorship: all manuscripts containing prose in Middle English are being examined collection by collection and all new or variant forms of texts described. Once we discover these new texts, and come to new understandings of the manuscript context of familiar works, however, it will be the detailed indices, dialect atlases, and reference guides that will provide the critical background with which to assess and reassess.[28]

Although Barron (1980) has suggested that "for the modern sensibility, with its historical perspective, its conscious, if sometimes self-deceptive, disassociation of fact and legend, it is probably impossible to appreciate fully what Arthur may have meant to

---

[26] Interestingly, the whole question of editing has been the focus of a recent thread on an e-mail network, and Busby has voiced the concerns of many in the field: "How many of us actually give courses in editing? Will there be anyone left to edit at all in a couple of generations' time? My hope is that the renewed interest in the manuscript context of medieval literature will lead to a renewal in editing and the presentation of medieval texts, probably in electronic form. We do need to get our students, at least in part, back to basics and to de-emphasize some of the more desperate 'critical' stuff."

[27] What Brewer was too modest to add was that Boydell and Brewer, and the Arthurian Studies Series in particular, have been especially helpful in bringing such materials out.

[28] There are still many desiderata, and in this area Brewer (1991) more or less randomly singled out linguistic studies, a historical social anthropology of literature, a motif index, and full iconographical databases.

Englishmen of the late Middle Ages," what the proliferation of recent studies indicates is that scholarly fascination with the *matière de Bretagne* and its central role in the historical and literary consciousness of medieval Britain continues unabated.

# Bibliography

*Bibliographies and General Surveys*

Ackerman, Robert W. "The English Rimed and Prose Romances." In Roger Sherman Loomis, ed., *Arthurian Literature in the Middle Ages*. Oxford: Clarendon, 1959, pp. 480-519.

————. "*Sir Gawain and the Green Knight* and Its Interpreters." In John W. Ehrstine, John R. Elwood, and Robert C. McLean, eds., *On Stage and Off: Eight Essays in English Literature*. Pullman: Washington State University Press, 1968, pp. 66-73.

Andrew, Malcolm. *The Gawain-Poet: An Annotated Bibliography, 1839-1977*. New York: Garland, 1979.

Barron, W.R.J. *English Medieval Romance*. London: Longman, 1987. Rev. by Judith Weiss, *Medium Ævum*, 59 (1990), 302–303.

Bennett, J.A.W. *Middle English Literature*, ed. Douglas Gray. Oxford: Clarendon, 1986.

Blanch, Robert J. *Sir Gawain and the Green Knight: A Reference Guide*. Troy, NY: Whitston, 1983.

————. "Supplement to the *Gawain*-Poet: An Annotated Bibliography, 1978-1985." *Chaucer Review*, 25 (1990-91), 363-386.

————, and Julian N. Wasserman. "The Current State of *Sir Gawain and the Green Knight* Criticism." *Chaucer Review*, 27 (1993), 401–412.

Brewer, Derek. "Some Current Trends in Arthurian Scholarship and Criticism 1987." 2 vols. In Willy van Hoecke, Gilbert Tournoy, and Werner Verbeke, eds., *Arturus Rex, II: Acta Conventus Lovaniensis 1987*. Leuven: Leuven University Press, 1991, II, 3-18.

Busby, Keith. "Medieval French Arthurian Literature: Recent Progress and Critical Trends." In Mette Pors, ed., *The Vitality of the Arthurian Legend: Proceedings of the Twelfth International Symposium Organized by the Centre for the Study of Vernacular Literature in the Middle Ages Held at Odense University on 16-17 November, 1987*. Odense: Odense University Press, 1988, pp. 45-70.

Dean, Christopher. *Arthur of England*. Toronto: University of Toronto Press, 1987.

Foley, Michael. "The *Gawain*-Poet: An Annotated Bibliography, 1978-1985." *Chaucer Review*, 23 (1988-89), 251-282.

Gaines, Barry. *Sir Thomas Malory: An Anecdotal Bibliography of Editions, 1485-1985*. New York: AMS, 1990.

Johnson, Lesley. "Tracking Laȝamon's *Brut*." *Leeds Studies in English*, n.s., 22 (1991), 139-165.

Jost, Jean Effinger. *Ten Middle English Arthurian Romances: A Reference Guide*. Boston: Hall, 1986. Rev. by Robert J. Blanch, *Quondam et Futurus*, 8, No. 1 (1987–88), 8-9.

Kato, Tomomi, ed. *A Concordance to the Works of Sir Thomas Malory*. Tokyo: University of Tokyo Press, 1974.

Kennedy, E.D. *Chronicles and Other Historical Writing*. In Albert Hartung, ed., *A Manual of the Writings in Middle English, 1050-1500*. Vol. 8. New Haven: Connecticut Academy of Arts and Sciences, 1989.

Life, Page West. *Sir Thomas Malory and the "Morte Darthur": A Survey of Scholarship and Annotated Bibliography*. Charlottesville: University Press of Virginia, 1980.

Mathewson, Jeanne T. "*Sir Gawain and the Green Knight*: Twenty More Years of Fascination." In Lagorio and Day, eds., *King Arthur Through the Ages*, 1990, I, 209-233.

Miller, Miriam Youngerman, and Jane Chance, eds. *Approaches to Teaching Sir Gawain and the Green Knight*. New York: Modern Language Association, 1986.

Palmer, Caroline. *The Arthurian Bibliography III: 1978-1992*. Woodbridge: Boydell and Brewer, forthcoming.

Pickford, Cedric E., Rex Last, and Christine R. Barker. *The Arthurian Bibliography*. 2 vols. Woodbridge: Boydell and Brewer, 1981-83.

Reiss, Edmund, Louise Horner Reiss, and Beverly Taylor. *Arthurian Legend and Literature: An Annotated Bibliography. I: The Middle Ages*. New York: Garland, 1984.

Rice, Joanne A. *Middle English Romance: An Annotated Bibliography, 1955-1985*. New York: Garland, 1987.

Salter, Elizabeth. *English and International Studies in the Literature, Art and Patronage of Medieval England*, ed. Derek Pearsall and Nicolette Zeeman. Cambridge: Cambridge University Press, 1988, pp. 29-74.

Sands, D.B., ed. *Middle English Verse Romances*. New York: Holt, Rinehart and Winston, 1966; rpt. Exeter: University of Exeter Press, 1986.

Spearing, A.C. *Medieval to Renaissance in English Poetry*. Cambridge: Cambridge University Press, 1985.

Stainsby, Meg. *Sir Gawain and the Green Knight: An Annotated Bibliography, 1978–1989*. New York: Garland, 1992.

Swanton, Michael. *English Literature Before Chaucer*. London: Longman, 1987.

Takamiya, Toshiyuki. "A Bibliography to Aspects of Malory." In Takamiya and Brewer, eds., *Aspects of Malory*, 1981, pp. 179-186.

Willard, Rudolph. "Laȝamon in the Seventeenth and Eighteenth Centuries." *Texas Studies in English*, 27 (1948), 239-278.

Wilson, Robert H. "Malory and Caxton." In Albert Hartung, ed., *A Manual of the Writings in Middle English 1050-1500*. Vol. 3.IX. Hamden: Connecticut Academy of Arts and Sciences 1972, pp. 757-807, 909-951.

*Editions and Translations*

Aertsen, Henk, and Alasdair A. MacDonald, eds. *Companion to Middle English Romance*. Amsterdam: VU University Press, 1990.

Allen, Rosamund, trans. *Lawman: Brut*. London: Dent, 1992.

Baldwin, Dean Richard, ed. "*Sir Perceval of Galles*: An Edition." Diss. Ohio State University, 1972.

Barron, W.R.J., and S.C. Weinberg, eds. and trans. *Laȝamon's Arthur: The Arthurian Section of Laȝamon's "Brut."* London: Longman, 1989.

Benson, Larry D., ed. *King Arthur's Death: The Middle English "Stanzaic Morte Arthur" and "Alliterative Morte Arthure."* Indianapolis: Bobbs-Merrill, 1974; rpt. Exeter: University of Exeter Press, 1986.

Bliss, A.J., ed. *Sir Launfal*, by Thomas Chestre. London: Nelson, 1960.

Brook, G.L., and R.F. Leslie, eds. *Laȝamon: "Brut." Edited from the British Museum MS. Cotton Caligula A. ix and British Museum MS. Cotton Otho C. xiii.* London: Oxford University Press, 1963, 1978.

Bzdyl, Donald G., trans. *Layamon's Brut: A History of the Britons.* Binghamton: State University of New York Press, 1989.

Christianson, Clayton Paul, ed. *"The Awntyrs off Arthure*: An Edition." Diss. Washington University, 1964.

Clarke, Susan J., ed. *"The Weddynge of Syr Gawen and Dame Ragnell*: An Edition." Thesis Birmingham University, 1975.

Dahood, Roger, ed. *The Avowing of King Arthur.* New York: Garland, 1984.

Dass, Nirmal, trans. *The Avowing of King Arthur: A Modern Verse Translation.* Lanham, MD: University Press of America, 1987.

Field, P.J.C., revised version, *The Works of Sir Thomas Malory*, ed. Eugène Vinaver. 3 vols. Oxford: Clarendon, 1990.

Finlayson, John, ed. *Morte Arthure.* London: Arnold, 1967.

Friedman, Albert B., and Norman T. Harrington, eds. *Ywain and Gawain.* London: Oxford University Press, 1964.

Gates, Robert James, ed. *"The Awntyrs off Arthure at the Terne Wathelyne*: A Critical Edition of the Douce MS Corrected from Other Manuscripts with All Variant Readings." Diss. University of Iowa, 1967.

———, ed. *The Awntyrs off Arthure at the Terne Wathelyne: A Critical Edition.* Philadelphia: University of Pennsylvania Press, 1969.

Hamel, Mary, ed. *Morte Arthure: A Critical Edition.* New York: Garland, 1984.

Hanna, Ralph, III. "*Awntyrs off Arthure at the Terne Wathelyne*: An Edition Based on Bodleian Library MS. Douce 324." Diss. Yale University, 1967.

———, ed. "*The Awntyrs off Arthure at the Terne Wathelyne*": An Edition Based on the Bodleian Library MS. Douce 324. Manchester: Manchester University Press, 1974.

Hissiger, P.F., ed. "*Le Morte Arthur*": A Critical Edition. The Hague: Mouton, 1975.

Holland, William E., ed. "*Merlin*. MS. Lincoln's Inn 150: A Critical Edition." Diss. Stanford University, 1971.

Kahn, Sharon, trans. *The Stanzaic "Morte": A Verse Translation of "Le Morte Arthur."* Lanham, MD: University Press of America, 1986.

Ker, N.R., intro. *The Winchester Malory: A Facsimile Edition.* London: Oxford University Press, 1976.

*The Knightly Tale of Golagros and Gawane.* Edinburgh: Chepman and Myllar, 1508.

Kock, Ernst A., ed. *Merlin...by H. Lovelich.* London: Kegan Paul, Trench, Trübner, 1904, 1913; London: Oxford University Press, 1932.

Krishna, Valerie, ed. *The Alliterative Morte Arthure: A Critical Edition.* New York: Franklin, 1976.

———, trans. *The Alliterative Morte Arthure: A New Verse Translation.* Washington, DC: University Press of America, 1983.

———, trans. *Five Middle English Arthurian Romances.* New York: Garland, 1990.

Lawton, David A., ed. *Joseph of Arimathea: A Critical Edition*. New York: Garland, 1983.

Lupack, Alan, ed. *"Lancelot of the Laik" and "Sir Tristrem."* Kalamazoo, MI: Medieval Institute, 1994.

Macrae-Gibson, O.D., ed. *Of Arthour and of Merlin*. 2 vols. London: Oxford University Press, 1973-79.

Mills, M., ed. *Lybeaus Desconus*. London: Oxford University Press, 1969.

Needham, Paul, intro. *Le Morte D'Arthur Printed by William Caxton 1485*. London: Scolar, 1976.

Noguchi, Shunichi, ed. *Le Morte Arthur*. Tokyo: University of Tokyo, 1991.

Paton, Florence Ann, ed. "A Critical Edition of the *Aunters of Arthur*." Diss. University of Colorado, 1963.

Phillips, Helen, ed. *The Awntyrs of Arthure at the Terne Wathelyne: Arthur's Adventures at Tarn Wadling*. Lancaster: Lancaster University, 1988.

Rodriguez, Marcia, ed. *"Sir Perceval of Gales*: A Critical Edition." Diss. University of Toronto, 1976.

Schlobin, Roger C., ed. *"The Turke and Gowin, The Marriage of Sir Gawaine*, and *The Grene Knight*: Three Editions with Introductions." Diss. Ohio State University, 1971.

Shimizu, Aya, trans. *The Stanzaic Morte Arthur*. Tokyo: Dolphin, 1985.

Simmons, F.J., ed.; Aubrey Beardsley, illus. *The Birth, Life and Acts of King Arthur*, by Sir Thomas Malory. 2 vols. London: Dent, 1893-94.

Spisak, James W., and William Matthews, eds. *Caxton's Malory: A New Edition of Sir Thomas Malory's "Le Morte Darthur" Based on the Pierpont Morgan Copy of William Caxton's Edition of 1485*. 2 vols. Berkeley: University of California Press, 1983; rev. by Basil Cottle, *Journal of English and German Philology*, 84 (1985), 252–253.

Stone, Brian, trans. *King Arthur's Death: Alliterative "Morte Arthure" and Stanzaic "Le Morte Arthur."* Harmondsworth: Penguin, 1988.

Tolkien, J.R.R., and E.V. Gordon, eds. *Sir Gawain and the Green Knight*. 2nd ed. revised Norman Davis. Oxford: Clarendon, 1967.

Vinaver, Eugène, ed. *The Works of Sir Thomas Malory*. 3 vols. Oxford: Clarendon, 1947; rpt. with corrections 1948; 2nd ed., Oxford: Clarendon, 1967; rpt. with corrections and additions 1973.

Williams, Jeanne Myrla Wilson, ed. "A Critical Edition of 'The Turke & Gowin.'" Diss. University of Southern Mississippi, 1987.

Withrington, John, ed. *The Wedding of Sir Gawain and Dame Ragnell*. Lancaster: Lancaster University, 1991.

Wright, Neil, ed. *The "Historia Regum Britannie" of Geoffrey of Monmouth. I: Bern, Burgerbibliothek, MS. 568*. Cambridge: Brewer, 1985.

——, ed. *The "Historia Regum Britannie" of Geoffrey of Monmouth. II: The First Variant Version*. Cambridge: Brewer, 1988.

## Studies

Adams, Alison, Armel H. Diverres, Karen Stern, and Kenneth Varty, eds., *The Changing Face of Arthurian Romance: Essays on Arthurian Prose Romances in Memory of Cedric E. Pickford*. Cambridge: Brewer, 1986.

Aertsen, Henk, and Alasdair A. MacDonald, eds., *Companion to Middle English Romance*. Amsterdam: VU University Press, 1990.

Alexander, Flora M. "Late Medieval Scottish Attitudes to the Figure of King Arthur: A Reassessment." *Anglia*, 93 (1975), 17-34.

————. "'The Treson of Launcelote du Lake': Irony in the Stanzaic *Morte Arthur*." In P.B. Grout et al., eds., *The Legend of Arthur in the Middle Ages: Studies Presented to A.H. Diverres by Colleagues, Pupils, and Friends*. Cambridge: Brewer, 1983, pp. 15-27.

Allen, Judson Boyce. *The Ethical Poetic of the Later Middle Ages: A Decorum of Convenient Distinction*. Toronto: University of Toronto Press, 1982.

————. "Malory's Diptych Distinctio: The Closing Books of His Work." In Spisak, ed., *Studies in Malory*, 1985, pp. 237-255.

Allen, Rosamund. "Some Sceptical Observations on the Editing of *The Awntyrs off Arthure*." In Pearsall, ed., *Manuscripts and Texts*, 1987, pp. 5-25.

Anderson, J.J. "The Three Judgments and the Ethos of Chivalry in *Sir Gawain and the Green Knight*." *Chaucer Review*, 24 (1989-90), 337-55.

Archibald, Elizabeth. "Arthur and Mordred: Variations on an Incest Theme." *Arthurian Literature*, 8 (1989), 1-27.

————. "Women and Romance." In Aertsen and MacDonald, eds., *Companion to Middle English Romance*, 1990, pp. 153-169.

Arthur, Ross G. *Medieval Sign Theory and "Sir Gawain and the Green Knight."* Toronto: University of Toronto Press, 1987.

Atkinson, Stephen C.B. "Malory's Lancelot and the Quest of the Grail." In Spisak, ed., *Studies in Malory*, 1985, pp. 129-152.

————. "'Now I Se and Undirstonde': The Grail Quest and the Education of Malory's Reader." In Mary Flowers Braswell and John Bugge, eds., *The Arthurian Tradition: Essays in Convergence.* Tuscaloosa: University of Alabama Press, 1988, pp. 90-108.

Barber, Richard. "Malory's *Le Morte Darthur* and Court Culture under Edward IV." *Arthurian Literature*, 12 (1993), 131–153.

Barron, W.R.J. "*Golagrus and Gawain*: A Scot's Conception of Love and Honour." *Bibliographical Bulletin of the International Arthurian Society*, 15 (1963), 131-132.

————. "*Golagrus and Gawain*: A Creative Redaction." *Bibliographical Bulletin of the International Arthurian Society*, 26 (1974), 173-185.

————. "Arthurian Romance: Traces of an English Tradition." *English Studies*, 61 (1980), 2-23.

————. "Alliterative Romance and the French Tradition." In Lawton, ed., *Middle English Alliterative Poetry*, 1982, pp. 70-87.

————, and Françoise Le Saux. "Two Aspects of Laȝamon's Narrative Art." *Arthurian Literature*, 10 (1989), 25-56.

Batt, Catherine. "Malory's Questing Beast and the Implications of Author as Translator." In Roger Ellis, ed., *The Medieval Translator: The Theory and Practice of Translation in the Middle Ages*. Cambridge: Brewer, 1989, pp. 143-166.

————. "Gawain's Antifeminist Rant, the Pentangle and Narrative Space." *Yearbook of English Studies*, 22 (1992), 117–139.

Beer, Jeannette, ed. *Medieval Translators and Their Craft*. Kalamazoo, MI: Medieval Institute, 1989.

Bennett, J.A.W. "Survivals and Revivals of Alliterative Modes." *Leeds Studies in English*, n.s., 14 (1983), 26-43.

Benson, Larry D. "Sir Thomas Malory's *Le Morte Darthur*." In R.M. Lumiansky and Herschel Baker, eds., *Critical Approaches to Six Major English Works: Beowulf Through Paradise Lost*. Philadelphia: University of Pennsylvania Press, 1968, pp. 81-131.

————. *Malory's Morte Darthur*. Cambridge, MA: Harvard University Press, 1976.

Beston, J., and R.M. Beston. "The Parting of Lancelot and Guinevere in the Stanzaic *Le Morte Arthur*." *Journal of Australasian Universities, Modern Language and Literature Association*, 40 (1973), 249-259.

Blake, N.F. "Rhythmical Alliteration." *Modern Philology*, 67 (1969-70), 118-124.

————. *William Caxton: A Bibliographical Guide*. New York: Garland, 1985.

Bloch, R. Howard. "Le rire de Merlin." *Cahiers de l'Association Internationale des Etudes Françaises*, 37 (1985), 7-21.

————. "The Medieval Text — 'Guigemar' — as a Provocation to the Discipline of Medieval Studies." *Romanic Review*, 79 (1988), 63-73.

Boardman, Phillip C. "Middle English Arthurian Romance: The Repetition and Reputation of Gawain." In Mette Pors, ed., *The Vitality of the Arthurian Legend: Proceedings of the Twelfth International Symposium Organized by the Centre for the Study of Vernacular Literature in the Middle Ages Held at Odense University on 16-17 November, 1987*. Odense: Odense University Press, 1988, pp. 71-90.

Bradstock, E.M. "'Honoure' in *Sir Launfal*." *Parergon*, 24 (1979), 9–17.

Brehe, Steven Karl. "Laȝamon's *Brut* and the Alliterative Tradition: An Investigation of Metrics and Literary History." Diss. University of Minnesota, 1990.

Brewer, Charlotte. "Authorial vs. Scribal Writing in *Piers Plowman.*" In Machan, ed., *Medieval Literature: Texts and Interpretation*, 1991, pp. 59-89.

Brewer, D.S., and A.E.B. Owen, intro. *The Thornton Manuscript (Lincoln Cathedral MS. 91)*. London: Scolar, 1975; revised 1977.

Brewer, Derek. "Malory's 'Proving' of Sir Lancelot." In Adams et al., eds., *The Changing Face of Arthurian Romance*, 1986, pp. 123-136.

———. "Escape from the Mimetic Fallacy." In Brewer, ed., *Studies in Medieval English Romances*, 1988, pp. 1-10.

———, ed. *Studies in Medieval English Romances: Some New Approaches*. Cambridge: Brewer, 1988.

Brown, Arthur C.L. *The Origin of the Grail Legend*. Cambridge, MA: Harvard University Press, 1943; rpt. New York: Russell and Russell, 1966.

Bruckner, Matilda Tomaryn. "Intertextuality." In Lacy, Kelly, and Busby, eds., *The Legacy of Chrétien de Troyes*, 1987-88, I, 223-265.

Bryan, Elizabeth Johnson. "Layamon's *Brut*: Relationships Between the Two Versions." Diss. University of Pennsylvania, 1990.

Burnley, J.D. "Late Medieval English Translation: Types and Reflections." In Roger Ellis, ed., *The Medieval Translator: The Theory and Practice of Translation in the Middle Ages*. Cambridge: Brewer, 1989, pp. 37-53.

Burrow, J.A. "*The Avowing of King Arthur.*" In Myra Stokes and T.L. Burton, eds., *Medieval Literature and Antiquities: Studies in Honour of Basil Cottle.* Cambridge: Brewer, 1987, pp. 99-109.

Busby, Keith. "*Sir Perceval of Galles, Le Conte du Graal* and *La Continuation-Gauvain*: The Methods of an English Adaptor." *Etudes Anglaises,* 31 (1978), 198-202.

————. *Gauvain in Old French Literature.* Amsterdam: Rodopi, 1980.

————. "Chrétien de Troyes English'd." *Neophilologus,* 71 (1987), 596-613.

————, ed. *Towards a Synthesis: Essays on the New Philology.* Amsterdam: Rodopi, 1993.

Cable, Thomas. *The English Alliterative Tradition.* Philadelphia: University of Pennsylvania Press, 1991.

Campbell, James. "Some Twelfth-Century Views of the Anglo-Saxon Past." *Peritia,* 3 (1984), 131-150.

Campbell, Kim Sydow. "A Lesson in Polite Non-Compliance: Gawain's Conversational Strategies in Fitt 3 of *Sir Gawain and the Green Knight.*" *USF Language Quarterly,* 28 (1990), 53-62.

Cannon, Christopher. "The Style and Authorship of the Otho Revision in Laȝamon's *Brut.*" *Medium Ævum,* 62 (1993), 187-209.

Carlson, David R. "The Middle English *Lanval,* the Corporal Works of Mercy, and Bibliothèque nationale, nouv. acq. fr. 1104." *Neophilologus,* 72 (1988), 97-106.

————. "Arthur Before and After the Revolution: The Blome-Stansby Edition of Malory (1634) and *Brittains Glory* (1684)." In Shichtman and Carley, eds., *Culture and the King: The Social Implications of the Arthurian Legend,* 1994, pp. 234-253.

Caron, Paul H. "Liturgical Feasts in Malory's *Sankgreal* and *La Queste del Saint Graal.*" *English Language Notes*, 28, No. 1 (1990-91), 26-32.

Cherewatuk, Karen Helen. "Malory's Book of Chivalry: *The Morte Darthur* and Manuals of Chivalry." Diss. Cornell University, 1986.

Chesnutt, Michael. "Minstrel Reciters and the Enigma of the Middle English Romance." *Culture and History*, 2 (1987) 48-67.

Chickering, Howell, and Thomas H. Seiler, eds. *The Study of Chivalry: Resources and Approaches*. Kalamazoo, MI: Medieval Institute, 1988.

Clein, W. *Concepts of Chivalry in Sir Gawain and the Green Knight*. Norman, OK: Pilgrim, 1987.

Clough, Andrea. "Malory's *Morte Darthur*: The 'Hoole Book.'" *Medievalia et Humanistica*, n.s., 14 (1986), 139-156.

Cooke, W.G. "Notes on the Alliterative *Morte Arthure.*" *English Studies*, 67 (1986), 304-307.

―――. "*Sir Gawain and the Green Knight*: A Restored Dating." *Medium Ævum*, 58 (1989), 34-48.

Cooper, R.A., and D.A. Pearsall. "The *Gawain* Poems: A Statistical Approach to the Question of Common Authorship." *Review of English Studies*, n.s., 39 (1988), 365-385.

Copeland, Rita. *Rhetoric, Hermeneutics, and Translation in the Middle Ages*. Cambridge: Cambridge University Press, 1991.

Corley, C. "Editing *Le Bel Inconnu* and Other Single-Manuscript Texts." In Philip E. Bennett and Graham A. Runnalls, eds., *The Editor and the Text*. Edinburgh: Edinburgh University Press, 1990, pp. 11-19.

Crane, Susan. *Insular Romance: Politics, Faith, and Culture in Anglo-Norman and Middle English Literature.* Berkeley: University of California Press, 1986, pp. 189–198.

Crepin, André. "De Tristan à Tristrem." In Danielle Buschinger, ed., *La Légende de Tristan au moyen âge.* Göppingen: Kümmerle, 1982, pp. 89-108.

Crick, Julia C. *The "Historia Regum Britannie" of Geoffrey of Monmouth. III: A Summary Catalogue of the Manuscripts.* Cambridge: Brewer, 1989, 1991.

————. *"The Historia Regum Britannie" of Geoffrey of Monmouth. IV: Dissemination and Reception in the Later Middle Ages.* Cambridge: Brewer, 1991.

Dannenbaum, Susan. "*The Wedding of Sir Gawain and Dame Ragnell*, Line 48." *Explicator*, 40 (1982), 3-4.

Davidson, Roberta Anne. "Three Ladies of Arroy: Sign and Gender in Sir Thomas Malory's Arthuriad." Diss. Princeton University, 1987.

Dean, Christopher. "The 'Mirror for Princes' Genre and Two Late Arthurian Romances." *Bibliographical Bulletin of the International Arthurian Society*, 31 (1979), 267-268.

Dobbin, Marjorie W. "The Women of Malory's *Morte Darthur*." Diss. University of Georgia, 1987.

Dobyns, Ann. "The Rhetoric of Character in Malory's *Morte Darthur*." *Texas Studies in Literature and Language*, 28 (1986), 339-352.

————. "'Shamefull noyse': Lancelot and the Language of Deceit." *Style*, 24 (1990), 89-102.

Donahue, Dennis. *Lawman's 'Brut,' an Early Arthurian Poem: a Study of Middle English Formulaic Composition*. Lewiston, NY: Mellen, 1991.

Donoghue, Daniel. "Laʒamon's Ambivalence." *Speculum*, 65 (1990), 537-563.

Doyle, A.I. "The Manuscripts." In Lawton, ed., *Middle English Alliterative Poetry*, 1982, pp. 88-100.

———, intro. *The Vernon Manuscript: A Facsimile of Bodleian Library, Oxford, MS Eng. poet.a.1*. Cambridge: Brewer, 1987.

Eadie, J. "The Alliterative *Morte Arthure*: Structure and Meaning." *English Studies*, 63 (1982), 1-12.

Eckhardt, Caroline D. "Arthurian Comedy: The Simpleton-Hero in *Sir Perceval of Galles*." *Chaucer Review*, 8 (1973-74), 205-220.

Edwards, A.S.G. "Observations on the History of Middle English Editing." In Pearsall, ed., *Manuscripts and Texts*, 1987, pp. 34-48.

———. "Middle English Romance: The Limits of Editing, the Limits of Criticism." In Machan, ed., *Medieval Literature: Texts and Interpretation*, 1991, pp. 91-104.

Evans, Murray J. "Camelot or Corbenic?: Malory's New Blend of Secular and Religious Chivalry in the 'Tale of the Holy Grail.'" *English Studies in Canada*, 8 (1982), 249-261.

———. "*Ordinatio* and Narrative Links: The Impact of Malory's Tales as a 'hoole book.'" In Spisak, ed., *Studies in Malory*, 1985, pp. 29-52.

Everett, Dorothy. "A Characterization of the English Medieval Romances." In *Essays on Middle English Literature*, ed. Patricia Kean. Oxford: Clarendon, 1955, 1-22.

————. "La3amon and the Earliest Middle English Alliterative Verse." In *Essays on Middle English Literature*, ed. Patricia Kean. Oxford: Clarendon, 1955, pp. 23-45.

Fewster, Carol. *Traditionality and Genre in Middle English Romance*. Cambridge: Brewer, 1987.

Fichte, Joerg O. "The Middle English Arthurian Verse Romance: Suggestions for the Development of a Literary Typology." *Deutsche Vierteljahrsschrift für Literaturwissenschaft und Geistesgeschichte*, 55 (1981), 567-590.

————. "The Middle English Arthurian Romance: The Popular Tradition in the Fourteenth Century." In Piero Boitani and Anna Torti, eds., *Literature in Fourteenth Century-England: The J.A.W. Bennett Memorial Lectures, Perugia, 1981-1982*. Cambridge: Brewer, 1983, pp. 137-153.

————. "*The Awntyrs off Arthure*: An Unconscious Change of the Paradigm of Adventure." In U. Böker, M. Markus, and R. Schöwerling, eds., *The Living Middle Ages: Studies in Mediaeval English Literature and Its Tradition: A Festschrift for Karl Heinz Göller*. Stuttgart: Belser, 1989, pp. 129-136.

————. "Arthurische und nicht-arthurische Texte im Gespräch, dargestellt am Beispiel der mittelenglischen Romanze *Sir Perceval of Galles*." In Friedrich Wolfzettel, ed., *Artusroman und Intertextualität*. Giessen: Schmitz, 1990, pp. 19-34.

Field, P.J.C. "Sir Thomas Malory, MP." *Bulletin of the Institute of Historical Research*, 47 (1974), 24-35.

————. "Sir Robert Malory, Prior of the Hospital of St John of Jerusalem in England (1432-1439/40)." *Journal of Ecclesiastical History*, 28 (1977), 249-264.

————. "Thomas Malory: The Hutton Documents." *Medium Ævum*, 48 (1979), 213-239.

———. "Thomas Malory and the Warwick Retinue Roll." *Midland History*, 5 (1979-80), 20-30.

———. "The Last Years of Sir Thomas Malory." *Bulletin of the John Rylands University Library of Manchester*, 64 (1982), 433-456.

———. "Malory and The Wedding of Sir Gawain and Dame Ragnell." *Archiv für Neuere Sprachen*, 219 (1982), 374-381.

———. "The French Prose *Tristan*: A Note on Some Manuscripts, A List of Printed Texts, and Two Correlations with Malory's *Morte Darthur*." *Bibliographical Bulletin of the International Arthurian Society*, 41 (1989), 269-287.

———. "Malory and Chrétien de Troyes." *Reading Medieval Studies*, 17 (1991), 19-30.

———. *The Life and Times of Sir Thomas Malory*. Woodbridge: Boydell and Brewer, 1993.

Field, Rosalind. "Romance as History, History as Romance." In Mills, Fellows, and Meale, eds., *Romance in Medieval England*, 1991, pp. 163-173.

Finlayson, John. "Definitions of Middle English Romance." *Chaucer Review*, 15 (1980-81), 44-62, 168-181.

———. "The Form of the Middle English *Lay*." *Chaucer Review*, 19 (1984-85), 352-368.

Finnie, W. Bruce. "A Structural Study of Six Medieval Arthurian Romances." Diss. Ohio State University, 1965.

Fisher, Sheila. "Leaving Morgan Aside: Women, History, and Revisionism in *Sir Gawain and the Green Knight*." In Christopher Baswell and William Sharpe, eds., *The Passing of Arthur: New Essays in Arthurian Tradition*. New York: Garland, 1988, pp. 129-151.

Fleischman, Suzanne. "On the Representation of History and Fiction in the Middle Ages." *History and Theory*, 22 (1983), 278-310.

Fleming, Caroline Evine Mary Elizabeth. "Ideas of the Self in Medieval English Literature." Diss. University of Liverpool, 1987.

Flint, Valerie. "The *Historia Regum Britanniae* of Geoffrey of Monmouth: Parody and Its Purpose. A Suggestion." *Speculum*, 54 (1979), 447–468.

Fogg, Sarah Lucille. "Structure and Meaning: A Critical Study of Four Medieval Romances." Diss. Indiana University, 1975.

Fowler, David C. "*Le Conte du Graal* and *Sir Perceval of Galles*." *Comparative Literature Studies*, 12 (1975), 5-20.

Franzen, Christine. *The Tremulous Hand of Worcester*. Oxford: Clarendon, 1991.

French, W.H. "Dialects and Forms in Three Romances." *Journal of English and Germanic Philology*, 45 (1946), 125-132.

Fries, Maureen. "The Characterization of Women in the Alliterative Tradition." In Levy and Szarmach, eds., *The Alliterative Tradition in the Fourteenth Century*, 1981, pp. 25-45.

————. "What Tennyson Really Did to Malory's Women." *Quondam et Futurus: A Journal of Arthurian Interpretations*, 1 (1991), 44-55.

————. "How Many Roads to Camelot? The Married Knight in Malory's *Morte Darthur*." In Shichtman and Carley, eds., *Culture and the King: The Social Implications of the Arthurian Legend*, 1994, pp. 196–207.

Galloway, Patricia Kay. "Transaction Units: An Approach to the Structural Study of Narrative Through the Analysis of *Perceval of Galles*, *Li Contes del Graal*, and *Parzival*." Diss. University of North Carolina, 1973.

Gibbs, A.C. "The Literary Relationships of Laȝamon's *Brut*." Diss. University of Cambridge, 1962.

Gillingham, John. "The Context and Purpose of Geoffrey of Monmouth's History of the Kings of Britain." *Anglo-Norman Studies*, 13 (1990), 99–118.

Göller, Karl Heinz, ed. *The Alliterative Morte Arthure: A Reassessment of the Poem*. Cambridge: Brewer, 1981.

Goodlad, Lauren M. "The *Gamnes* of *Sir Gawain and the Green Knight*." *Comitatus*, 18 (1987), 45-58.

Goodman, J.R. "Malory and Caxton's Chivalric Series, 1481-1485." In Spisak, ed., *Studies in Malory*, 1985, pp. 257-274.

———. *William Caxton and Malory's Prose Romances of 1485*. New York: Garland, 1987.

Greene, Wendy Tibbetts. "Malory's Merlin: An Ambiguous Magician?" *Arthurian Interpretations*, 1 (1987), 56-63.

Griffith, Richard R. "The Authorship Question Reconsidered: A Case for Thomas Malory of Papworth St. Agnes, Cambridgeshire." In Takamiya and Brewer, eds., *Aspects of Malory*, 1981, pp. 159-177.

———. "Caxton's Copy-Text for *Le Morte Darthur*: Tracing the Provenance." In David G. Allen and Robert A. White, eds., *Traditions and Innovations: Essays on British Literature of the Middle Ages and the Renaissance*. Newark: University of Delaware Press, 1990, pp. 75-87.

Griffiths, J.J. "A Re-examination of Oxford, Bodleian Library, MS Rawlinson C.86." *Archiv für neuere Sprachen*, 219 (1982), 381-388.

Hamel, Mary. "Scribal Self-Corrections in the Thornton *Morte Arthure.*" *Studies in Bibliography*, 36 (1983), 119-137.

———. "Adventure as Structure in the Alliterative *Morte Arthure.*" *Arthurian Interpretations*, 3, No. 1 (1988), 37-48.

Hanna, Ralph, III. "A la recherche du temps bien perdu: The Text of *The Awntyrs off Arthure.*" *Text*, 4 (1988), 189-205.

Hanning, Robert W. "Sir Gawain and the Red Herring: The Perils of Interpretation." In Mary J. Carruthers and Elizabeth D. Kirk, eds., *Acts of Interpretation: The Text in Its Contexts, 700-1600: Essays on Medieval and Renaissance Literature in Honor of E. Talbot Donaldson.* Norman, OK: Pilgrim, 1982, pp. 5-23.

Hardman, Phillipa. "The Unity of the Ireland Manuscript." *Reading Medieval Studies*, 2 (1976), 45-62.

———. "Fitt Divisions in Middle English Romances: A Consideration of the Evidence." *Yearbook of English Studies*, 22 (1992) 63–80.

Harrington, David V. "The Conflicting Passions of Malory's Sir Gawain and Sir Lancelot." *Arthurian Interpretations*, 1, No. 2 (1987), 64-69.

Hellinga, Lotte. "The Malory Manuscript and Caxton." In Takamiya and Brewer, eds., *Aspects of Malory*, 1981, pp. 127-141.

Heng, Geraldine. "Enchanted Ground: The Feminine Subtext in Malory." In Keith Busby and Erik Kooper, eds., *Courtly Literature: Culture and Context.* Amsterdam: Benjamins, 1990, pp. 283-300.

———. "Feminine Knots and the Other *Sir Gawain and the Green Knight.*" *PMLA*, 106 (1991), 500-514.

Hoffman, Donald L. "Malory's Tragic Merlin." *Quondam et Futurus: A Journal of Arthurian Interpretations*, 1 (1991), 15-31.

Holichek, Lindsay E. "Malory's Gwenevere: After Long Silence." *Annuale Mediaevale*, 22 (1982), 112-126.

Hornstein, Lillian Herlands. "Middle English Romances." In J. Burke Severs, ed., *Recent Middle English Scholarship and Criticism: Survey and Desiderata*. Pittsburgh: Duquesne University Press, 1971, pp. 55-95.

Horrall, Sarah M. "Notes on British Library, MS Cotton Nero A.x." *Manuscripta*, 30 (1986), 191-198.

Hudson, Harriet Elizabeth. "Middle English Popular Romances." Diss. Ohio State University, 1982.

———. "Middle English Popular Romances: The Manuscript Evidence." *Manuscripta*, 28 (1984), 67-78.

Hult, David F. "Reading It Right: The Ideology of Text Editing." *Romanic Review*, 79 (1988), 74-88.

Hunt, Tony. "Beginnings, Middles, and Ends: Some Interpretative Problems in Chrétien's *Yvain* and Its Medieval Adaptations." In Leigh A. Arrathoon, ed., *The Craft of Fiction: Essays in Medieval Poetics*. Rochester, MI: Solaris, 1984, pp. 83-117.

Hynes-Berry, Mary. "A Tale 'breffly Drawyne oute of Freynshe,'" In Takamiya and Brewer, eds., *Aspects of Malory*, 1981, pp. 93-106.

Ihle, Sandra Ness. *Malory's Grail Quest: Invention and Adaptation in Medieval Prose Romance*. Madison: University of Wisconsin Press, 1983.

———. "The Art of Adaptation in Malory's Books Seven and Eight." *Arthurian Interpretations*, 15, No. 2 (1984), 75-85.

Ikegami, Tadahiro. "The Structure and Tone of the Stanzaic Morte Arthur." In Suzuki and Mukai, eds., *Arthurian and Other Studies Presented to Shunichi Noguchi*, 1993, pp. 169-177.

Jacobs, Nicolas. "The Green Knight: An Unexplored Irish Parallel." *Cambridge Medieval Celtic Studies*, 4 (1982), 1-4.

———. "Regression to the Commonplace in Some Vernacular Textual Traditions." In A.J. Minnis and C. Brewer, eds., *Crux and Controversy in Middle English Textual Criticism*. Cambridge: Brewer, 1992, pp. 61-70.

Jansen Jaech, Sharon L. "The Parting of Lancelot and Gaynor: The Effect of Repetition in the Stanzaic *Morte Arthur*." *Arthurian Interpretations*, 15, No. 2 (1984), 59-69.

Johnson, David. "The Real and the Ideal: Attitudes to Love and Chivalry as Seen in *The Avowing of King Arthur*." In Aertsen and MacDonald, eds., *Companion to Middle English Romance*, 1990, pp. 189-208.

Johnson, Lesley. "Robert Mannyng's History of Arthurian Literature." In Ian Wood and G.A. Loud, eds., *Church and Chronicle in the Middle Ages*. London: Hambledon, 1991, pp. 129-147.

Jost, Jean E. "The Role of Violence in Aventure: 'The Ballad of King Arthur and the King of Cornwall' and 'The Turke and Gowin.'" *Arthurian Interpretations*, 2, No. 2 (1988), 47-57.

Kamps, Ivo. "Magic, Women, and Incest: The Real Challenges in *Sir Gawain and the Green Knight*." *Exemplaria*, 1 (1989), 313-336.

Kaske, R.E. "Godfrey's Vengeance for God on Good Friday: Alliterative *Morte Arthure*, 3430-1." *Medium Ævum*, 59 (1990), 128-133.

Keiser, George R. "Edward III and the Alliterative *Morte Arthure*." *Speculum*, 48 (1973), 37-51.

Kelliher, Hilton. "The Early History of the Malory Manuscript." In Takamiya and Brewer, eds., *Aspects of Malory*, 1981, pp. 143-158.

Kelly, Robert L. "Wounds, Healing, and Knighthood in Malory's Tale of Lancelot and Guenevere." In Spisak, ed., *Studies in Malory*, 1985, pp. 173-197.

Kennedy, Beverly. *Knighthood in the "Morte Darthur."* Woodbridge: Boydell and Brewer, 1985.

Kennedy, Edward D. "Malory and his English Sources." In Takamiya and Brewer, eds., *Aspects of Malory*, 1981, pp. 27-55.

———. "John Hardyng and the Holy Grail." *Arthurian Literature*, 8 (1989), 185-205.

———. "The Text of the Alliterative *Morte Arthure*: The Disappearance of Sir Feltemour." *Poetica*, 35 (1992), 41-52.

———. "Malory's 'Noble Tale of Sir Launcelot du Lake,' the Vulgate *Lancelot* and the Post-Vulgate *Roman du Graal*." In Suzuki and Mukai, eds., *Arthurian and Other Studies Presented to Shunichi Noguchi*, 1993, pp. 107-129.

———. "The Stanzaic *Morte Arthur*: The Adaptation of a French Romance for an English Audience." In Shichtman and Carley, eds., *Culture and the King: The Social Implications of the Arthurian Legend*, 1994, pp. 91-112.

Kirby, Ian. "Angles and Saxons in Laʒamon's *Brut*." *Studia Neophilologica*, 36 (1964), 51-62.

Kirk, Elizabeth. "'Clerkes, Poetes and Historiographs': The *Morte Darthur* and Caxton's 'Poetics' of Fiction." In Spisak, ed., *Studies in Malory*, 1985, pp. 275-295.

Knight, Stephen. *The Structure of Sir Thomas Malory's Arthuriad*. Sydney: Sydney University Press, 1969.

————. "The Social Function of the Middle English Romances." In David Aers, ed., *Medieval Literature: Criticism, Ideology and History*. Brighton: Harvester, 1986, pp. 99-122.

Kooper, Erik. "Love and Marriage in the Middle English Romances." In Aertsen and MacDonald, eds., *Companion to Middle English Romance*, 1990, pp. 171-187.

Korrel, Peter. *An Arthurian Triangle: A Study of the Origin, Development and Characterization of Arthur, Guinevere and Modred*. Leiden: Brill, 1984, pp. 225-245.

Lacy, Norris J., Douglas Kelly, and Keith Busby, eds. *The Legacy of Chrétien de Troyes*. 2 vols. Amsterdam: Rodopi, 1987-88.

La Farge, Catherine. "Conversation in Malory's Morte Darthur." *Medium Ævum*, 56 (1987), 225-238.

Lagorio, Valerie M. "The *Joseph of Arimathie*: English Hagiography in Transition." *Medievalia et Humanistica*, 6 (1975), 91-101.

————. "The Glastonbury Legends and the English Arthurian Grail Romances." *Neuphilologische Mitteilungen*, 79 (1978), 359-366.

————, and Mildred Leake Day, eds. *King Arthur Through the Ages*. 2 vols. New York: Garland, 1990.

Lawton, David A. "The Unity of Middle English Alliterative Poetry." *Speculum*, 58 (1983), 72-94.

————. "The Diversity of Middle English Alliterative Poetry." *Leeds Studies in English*, n.s., 20 (1989), 143-172.

————, ed. *Middle English Alliterative Poetry and Its Literary Background*. Cambridge: Brewer, 1982.

Leckie, R. William, Jr. *The Passage of Dominion: Geoffrey of Monmouth and the Periodization of Insular History in the Twelfth Century*. Toronto: Toronto University Press, 1981.

Le Saux, Françoise. *Layamon's "Brut": The Poem and Its Sources*. Woodbridge: Boydell and Brewer, 1989.

Levy, Bernard S., and Paul E. Szarmach, eds. *The Alliterative Tradition in the Fourteenth Century*. Kent, OH: Kent State University Press, 1981.

Lumiansky, R.M. "The Question of Unity in Malory's *Morte Darthur*." *Tulane Studies in English*, 5 (1955), 29-39.

———. "Sir Thomas Malory's *Le Morte Darthur*, 1947-1987: Author, Title, Text." *Speculum*, 62 (1987), 878-897.

———, ed. *Malory's Originality: A Critical Study of Le Morte Darthur*. Baltimore: Johns Hopkins Press, 1964.

Lynch, Andrew. "Good Name and Narrative in Malory." *Nottingham Mediaeval Studies*, 34 (1990), 141-151.

McCarthy, Terence. "Malory and the Alliterative Tradition." In Spisak, ed., *Studies in Malory*, 1985, pp. 53-85.

———. *Reading the "Morte Darthur."* Cambridge: Brewer, 1988.

McGillivray, Murray. "Memorization in the Transmission of the Middle English Romances." Diss. University of Toronto, 1986.

Machan, Tim William, ed. *Medieval Literature: Texts and Interpretation*. Binghamton: State University of New York Press, 1991.

McIntosh, Angus. "Early Middle English Alliterative Verse." In Lawton, ed., *Middle English Alliterative Poetry*, 1982, pp. 20-33.

Macrae-Gibson, O.D. *"Of Arthour and of Merlin* in Sussex?" *English Language Notes*, 17, No. 1 (1979), 7-10.

Mahoney, Dhira B. "The Truest and Holiest Tale: Malory's Transformation of *La Queste del Saint Graal.*" In Spisak, ed., *Studies in Malory*, pp. 109-128.

Mann, Jill. "Price and Value in *Sir Gawain and the Green Knight.*" *Essays in Criticism*, 36 (1986), 294-318.

————. "The Narrative of Distance, the Distance of Narrative in Malory's *Morte Darthur.*" The William Matthews Lectures 1991. Birkbeck College, University of London, 1991.

Matheson, Lister M. "King Arthur and the Medieval English Chronicles." In Lagorio and Day, eds., *King Arthur Through the Ages*, 1990, I, 248-274.

Mathewson, Jeanne T. "Displacement of the Feminine in *Golagros and Gawane* and the *Awntyrs off Arthure.*" *Arthurian Interpretations*, 1, No. 2 (1987), 23-28.

Matsuda, Takami. *"The Awntyrs off Arthure* and the Arthurian History." *Poetica*, 19 (1984), 48-62.

Matthews, William. *The Tragedy of Arthur: A Study of the Alliterative "Morte Arthure."* Berkeley: University of California Press, 1960.

Meale, Carol M. "Manuscripts, Readers and Patrons in Fifteenth-Century England: Sir Thomas Malory and Arthurian Romance." *Arthurian Literature*, 4 (1985), 93-126.

————. "The Manuscripts and Early Audience of the Middle English *Prose Merlin.*" In Adams et al., eds., *The Changing Face of Arthurian Romance*, 1986, pp. 92-111.

―――. "The Compiler at Work: John Colyns and BL MS Harley 2252." In Pearsall, ed., *Manuscripts and Readers*, 1987, pp. 82-103.

Mehl, Dieter. *The Middle English Romances of the Thirteenth and Fourteenth Centuries*. London: Routledge and Kegan Paul, 1968 [1969].

Mills, Maldwyn. "The Englishness of Ywain and Gawain." *Bibliographical Bulletin of the International Arthurian Society*, 27 (1975), 214-215.

―――, Jennifer Fellows, and Carol Meale, eds. *Romance in Medieval England*. Cambridge: Brewer, 1991.

Moorman, Charles. "Caxton's *Morte Darthur*: Malory's Second Edition?" *Fifteenth-Century Studies*, 12 (1987), 99-113.

Mukai, Tsuyoshi. "De Worde's Displacement of Malory's Secularization." In Suzuki and Mukai, eds., *Arthurian and Other Studies Presented to Shunichi Noguchi*, 1993, pp. 179-187.

Nappholz, Carol J. "Launfal's 'Largesse': Word-Play in Thomas Chestre's 'Sir Launfal.'" *English Language Notes*, 25, No. 3 (1987-88), 4-9.

Newstead, Helaine. "Arthurian Legends." In J. Burke Severs, ed., *A Manual of the Writings in Middle English, 1050-1500*. New Haven: Connecticut Academy of Arts and Sciences, 1967, pp. 38-79.

Nicholls, Jonathon. *The Matter of Courtesy: Medieval Courtesy Books and the Gawain-Poet*. Woodbridge: Boydell and Brewer, 1985.

Nichols, Stephen G. "The New Philology. Introduction: Philology in a Manuscript Culture." *Speculum*, 65 (1990), 1-10.

Noble, James. "The Larger Rhetorical Patterns in Laȝamon's *Brut*." *English Studies in Canada*, 11 (1985), 263-272.

————. "The Grail and Its Guardian: Evidence of Authorial Intent in the Middle English *Joseph of Arimathea.*" *Quondam et Futurus: A Journal of Arthurian Interpretations*, 1 (1991), 1-14.

————. "Patronage, Politics, and the Figure of Arthur in Geoffrey of Monmouth, Wace, and Layamon." *The Arthurian Yearbook*, 2 (1992), 159-178.

O'Loughlin, J.L.N. "The English Alliterative Romances." In Roger Sherman Loomis, ed., *Arthurian Literature in the Middle Ages*. Oxford: Clarendon, 1959, pp. 520-527.

Oakeshott, Walter F. "The Finding of the Manuscript." In J.A.W. Bennett, ed., *Essays on Malory*. Oxford: Clarendon, 1963, pp. 1-6.

Parins, Marylyn Jackson. "Malory's Expurgators." In Mary Flowers Braswell and John Bugge, eds., *The Arthurian Tradition: Essays in Convergence*. Tuscaloosa: University of Alabama Press, 1988, pp. 144-162.

————, ed. *Malory: the Critical Heritage*. London: Routledge, 1988.

Patterson, Lee. "The Historiography of Romance and the Alliterative *Morte Arthure.*" *Journal of Medieval and Renaissance Studies*, 13 (1983), 1-32; revised and reprinted in his *Negotiating the Past: The Historical Understanding of Medieval Literature*, 1987, pp. 197-230.

————. *Negotiating the Past: The Historical Understanding of Medieval Literature*. Madison: University of Wisconsin Press, 1987.

Pearsall, Derek. "The Development of Middle English Romance." *Mediaeval Studies*, 27 (1965), 91-116; rpt. in Brewer, ed., *Studies in Medieval English Romances*, 1988, pp. 11-35.

————. "The Origins of the Alliterative Revival." In Levy and Szarmach, eds., *The Alliterative Tradition in the Fourteenth Century*, 1981, pp. 1-24.

————, ed. *Manuscripts and Readers in Fifteenth-Century England*. Cambridge: Brewer, 1983.

————, ed. *Manuscripts and Texts: Editorial Problems in Later Middle English Literature*. Cambridge: Brewer, 1987.

————, and I.C. Cunningham, intro. *The Auchinleck Manuscript. National Library of Scotland Advocates' MS. 19.2.1.* London: Scolar, 1977; rpt. 1979.

Phillips, Helen. "The Ghost's Baptism in *The Awntyrs off Arthure*." *Medium Ævum*, 58 (1989), 49-58.

————. "*The Awntyrs off Arthure*: Structure and Meaning. A Reassessment." *Arthurian Literature*, 12 (1993), 63–89.

Pickering, James D. "Malory's *Morte Darthur*: The Shape of Tragedy." *Fifteenth-Century Studies*, 7 (1983), 307-328.

Pilch, Herbert. *Layamons "Brut": Eine literarische Studie*. Heidelberg: Winter, 1960.

Piper, William Bowman. "The Whole Book of King Arthur and of His Noble Knights." *Modern Language Quarterly*, 47 (1986), 219-234.

Plummer, John F. "*Tunc se Coeperunt non Intelligere*: The Image of Language in Malory's Last Books." In Spisak, ed., *Studies in Malory*, 1985, pp. 153-171.

————. "The Quest for Significance in *La Queste del Saint Graal* and Malory's *Tale of the Sankgreal*." In Norris J. Lacy and Gloria Torrini-Roblin, eds., *Continuations: Essays on Medieval French Literature and Language in Honor of John L. Grigsby*. Birmingham, AL: Summa, 1989, pp. 107-119.

Porter, Elizabeth. "Chaucer's Knight, the Alliterative *Morte Arthure*, and Medieval Laws of War: A Reconsideration." *Nottingham Mediaeval Studies*, 27 (1983), 56-78.

Reeve, Michael D. "The Transmission of the *Historia Regum Britanniae*." *Journal of Medieval Latin*, 1 (1991), 73-117.

Regan, Charles Lionel. "The Paternity of Mordred in the Alliterative *Morte Arthure* Once More." *American Notes and Queries*, 23 (1984-85), 35-36.

Reiss, Edmund. "Romance." *Tennessee Studies in Literature*, 28 (1985), 108-130.

Richley, Florence H. "Attila the Hun and King Arthur: A Question of Affinities." *Idovilegium*, 11 (1992), 101–115.

Riddy, Felicity. *Sir Thomas Malory*. Leiden: Brill, 1987.

————. "Glastonbury, Joseph of Arimathea and the Grail in John Hardyng's Chronicle." In Lesley Abrams and James P. Carley, eds., *The Archaeology and History of Glastonbury Abbey*. Woodbridge: Boydell and Brewer, 1991, pp. 317-331.

————. "Reading for England: Arthurian Literature and National Consciousness." *Bibliographical Bulletin of the International Arthurian Society*, 43 (1991), 314-332.

Rider, Jeff. "The Fictional Margin: The Merlin of the *Brut*." *Modern Philology*, 87 (1989), 1-12.

Ringel, Faye J. "Pluto's Kitchen: The Initiation of Sir Gareth." *Arthurian Interpretations*, 1 (1987), 29-38.

Roberts, Nanette McNiff. "Making the Mold: The Roles of Women in the Middle English Metrical Romances, 1225-1500." Diss. New York University, 1976.

Rogers, Gillian. "Themes and Variations: Studies in Some English Gawain-Romances." Diss. University of Wales, 1978.

———. "The Percy Folio Manuscript Revisited." In Mills, Fellows, and Meale, eds., *Romance in Medieval England*, 1991, pp. 39-64.

Rooney, Anne. *Hunting in Middle English Literature*. Woodbridge: Boydell and Brewer, 1993.

Rosenberg, Bruce A. "Medieval Popular Literature: Folklore Sources." *Tennessee Studies in Literature*, 28 (1985), 61-84.

Rumble, T.C. "The Middle English *Sir Tristrem*: Towards a Reappraisal." *Comparative Literature*, 11 (1959), 221-228.

Salda, Michael N. "Reconsidering Vinaver's Sources for Malory's *Tristram*." *Modern Philology*, 88 (1990-91), 373-381.

Shichtman, Martin B. "Malory's Gawain Reconsidered." *Essays in Literature*, 11 (1984), 159-176.

———. "Gawain in Wace and Laȝamon: A Case of Metahistorical Evolution." In Shichtman and Finke, eds., *Medieval Texts and Contemporary Readers*, 1987, pp. 103-119.

———. "The Gawains of English Arthurian Romance." Diss. University of Iowa, 1981.

———. "Sir Gawain in Scotland: A Hometown Boy Made Good." In Lagorio and Day, eds., *King Arthur Through the Ages*, 1990, I, 234-247.

———, and James P. Carley, eds. *Culture and the King: The Social Implications of the Arthurian Legend*. Albany: State University of New York Press, 1994.

————, and Laurie A. Finke. "Profiting from the Past: History as Symbolic Capital in the *Historia Regum Britanniae.*" *Arthurian Literature*, 12 (1993), 1–35.

————, and ————, eds. *Medieval Texts and Contemporary Readers.* Ithaca: Cornell University Press, 1987.

Shoaf, R.A. *The Poem as Green Girdle: "Commercium" in "Sir Gawain and the Green Knight."* Gainesville: University Presses of Florida, 1984.

————. "The 'Syngne of Surfet' and the Surfeit of Signs in *Sir Gawain and the Green Knight.*" In Christopher Baswell and William Sharpe, eds., *The Passing of Arthur: New Essays in Arthurian Tradition.* New York: Garland, 1988, pp. 152-169.

Shonk, Timothy A. "A Study of the Auchinleck Manuscript: Bookmen and Bookmaking in the Early Fourteenth Century." *Speculum*, 60 (1985), 71-91.

Simko, Jan. "Modernity of the Middle English Stanzaic Romance *Le Morte Arthur.*" In Suzuki and Mukai, eds., *Arthurian and Other Studies Presented to Shunichi Noguchi*, 1993, pp. 153-168.

Sklar, Elizabeth S. "*Arthour and Merlin*: The Englishing of Arthur." *Michigan Academician*, 8 (1975-76), 49-57.

————. "The Dialect of *Arthour and Merlin.*" *English Language Notes*, 15, No. 2 (1977), 88-94.

————. "Adventure and the Spiritual Semantics of Malory's Tale of the Sankgreall." *Arthurian Interpretations*, 2, No. 2 (1988), 34-46.

Smithers, G.V., ed. *Kyng Alisaunder.* 2 vols. London: Oxford University Press, 1952-57.

Spearing, A.C. "Readings in Medieval Poetry." Cambridge: Cambridge University Press, 1987, pp. 195-215.

————. "Marie de France and Her Middle English Adapters." *Studies in the Age of Chaucer*, 12 (1990), 117–156.

Speer, Mary B. "Textual Criticism Redivivus." *Esprit Créateur*, 23 (1983), 38-48.

Spisak, James W. "Introduction: Recent Trends in Malory Studies." In Spisak, ed., *Studies in Malory*, 1985, pp. 1–12.

————, ed. *Studies in Malory*. Kalamazoo, MI: Medieval Institute, 1985.

Stanley, E.G. "The Date of Laȝamon's *Brut*." *Notes and Queries*, 213 (1968), 85-88.

————. "Laȝamon's Antiquarian Sentiments." *Medium Ævum*, 38 (1969), 23-37.

Stern, Karen. "The Middle English *Prose Merlin*." In Adams et al., eds., *The Changing Face of Arthurian Romance*, 1986, pp. 112-122.

Stiller, Nikki. *Eve's Orphans: Mothers and Daughters in Medieval English Literature*. Westport, CT: Greenwood, 1980.

Strohm, Paul. "The Origin and Meaning of Middle English Romance." *Genre*, 10 (1977), 1-28.

————. "Middle English Narrative Genres." *Genre*, 13 (1980), 379-388.

Suzuki, Takashi, and Tsuyoshi Mukai, eds. *Arthurian and Other Studies Presented to Shunichi Noguchi*. Cambridge: Brewer, 1993.

Takamiya, Toshiyuki. "Editor/Compositor at Work: the Case of Caxton's Malory." In Suzuki and Mukai, eds., *Arthurian and Other Studies Presented to Shunichi Noguchi*, 1993, pp. 143-151.

————, and Derek S. Brewer, eds. *Aspects of Malory*. Cambridge: Brewer, 1981.

Tatlock, J.S.P. *The Legendary History of Britain*. Berkeley: University of California Press, 1950.

Taylor, Andrew. "The Myth of the Minstrel Text." *Speculum*, 66 (1991), 43–73.

————. "Fragmentation, Corruption and Minstrel Narration: the Question of the Middle English Romances." *Yearbook of English Studies*, 22 (1992), 38–62.

Taylor, Jane H.M. "The Fourteenth Century: Context, Text and Intertext." In Lacy, Kelly, and Busby, eds., *The Legacy of Chrétien de Troyes*, 1987–88, I, 267-332.

Thompson, John J. "The Compiler in Action: Robert Thornton and the 'Thornton Romances' in Lincoln Cathedral MS 91." In Pearsall, ed., *Manuscripts and Readers*, 1987, pp. 113-124.

————. "Collecting Middle English Romances and Some Related Book-Production Activities in the Later Middle Ages." In Mills, Fellows, and Meale, eds., *Romance in Medieval England*, 1991, pp. 17-38.

Thornton, Ginger. "The Weakening of the King: Arthur's Disintegration in *The Book of Sir Tristram*." *The Arthurian Yearbook*, 1 (1991), 135-148.

Tigges, Wim. "Romance and Parody." In Aertsen and MacDonald, eds., *Companion to Middle English Romance*, 1990, pp. 129-151.

Troyan Scott D. "Rhetoric Without Genre: Orality, Textuality and the Shifting Scene of the Rhetorical Situation in the Middle Ages." *Romanic Review*, 81 (1990), 377-395.

Turville-Petre, Thorlac. "'Summer Sunday,' 'De Tribus Regibus Mortuis,' and 'The Awntyrs off Arthure': Three Poems in the Thirteen-Line Stanza." *Review of English Studies*, n.s., 25 (1974), 1-14.

————. *The Alliterative Revival*. Cambridge: Brewer, 1977.

————. "Arthurian Studies." *Nottingham Mediaeval Studies*, 30 (1986), 106-115.

Veldhoen, Bart. "Psychology and the Middle English Romances: Preliminaries to Readings of *Sir Gawain and the Green Knight, Sir Orfeo*, and *Sir Launfal*." In Aertsen and MacDonald, eds., *Companion to Middle English Romance*, 1990, pp. 101-128.

Walsh, John Michael. "Malory's 'Very Mater of La Cheualer du Charyot': Characterization and Structure." In Spisak, ed., *Studies in Malory*, 1985, pp. 199-226.

Wenzel, Siegfried. "Reflections on (New) Philology." *Speculum*, 65 (1990), 11-18.

Wheeler, Bonnie. "Romance and Parataxis and Malory: the Case of Sir Gawain's Reputation." *Arthurian Literature*, 12 (1993), 109–132.

————. "'The Prowess of Hands': The Psychology of Alchemy in Malory's *Tale of Sir Gareth*." In Shichtman and Carley, eds., *Culture and the King: The Social Implications of the Arthurian Legend*, 1994, pp. 180–195.

Whitaker, Muriel A. "Otherworld Castles in Middle English Arthurian Romance." In Kathryn Reyerson and Faye Powe, eds., *The Medieval Castle: Romance and Reality*. Dubuque, IA: Kendall/Hunt, 1984, pp. 27-45.

————. "Illustrating Caxton's Malory." In Spisak, ed., *Studies in Malory*, 1985, pp. 297-319.

Williams, Elizabeth. *"Lanval* and *Sir Landevale*: A Middle English Translator and His Methods." *Leeds Studies in English*, n.s., 3 (1969), 85–99.

Wittig, Susan. *Stylistic and Narrative Structures in the Middle English Romances*. Austin: University of Texas Press, 1978.

Wurster, Jutta. "The Audience." In Karl Heinz Göller, ed., *The Alliterative Morte Arthure: A Reassessment of the Poem*. Cambridge: Brewer, 1981, pp. 44-56.

Wurtele, Douglas J. "Chaucer's Wife of Bath and Her Distorted Arthurian Motifs." *Arthurian Interpretations*, 2, No. 1 (1987), 47-61.

Ziolkowski, Jan. "A Narrative Structure in the Alliterative *Morte Arthure* 1-1221 and 3150-4346." *Chaucer Review*, 22 (1987-88), 234-245.

———. "'What Is Philology?'" *Comparative Literature Studies*, 27 (1990), 1-12.

# SCANDINAVIA

## Marianne E. Kalinke

Contemporary scholarship on the Scandinavian *matière de Bretagne* is partly indebted to and partly reflects Henry Goddard Leach's pronouncement of 1921 that the Old Norse translations of "the romances and other foreign works were originally a court literature, intended by Hákon as much for profit as for pleasure, to instruct those who surrounded him, in the ideals and customs, accoutrement and ceremonials of chivalry" (153). The reference is to King Hákon IV Hákonarson, who ruled Norway from 1217 until 1263 and who was, according to Leach, responsible for "no less than fifty translations from foreign romance—usually Anglo-Norman poems—which can confidently be assigned to Hákon's reign and the period before 1290" (151).

Nearly four decades later, P.M. Mitchell concurred more or less when he wrote in his essay on Scandinavian literature (1959) that "the early prose translations of Arthurian romance were made in Norway" (470) during Hákon's reign and that the Norwegian king was motivated to undertake his program of translation both for the sake of entertainment and to "establish the general ecclesiastical culture of Europe . . . and to introduce also the secular and courtly culture of France and England" (464). Both Leach and Mitchell endeavored not only to survey the Scandinavian Arthurian matter but also to account for its appeal and transmission to the North. At the time of their writing, not a single Old Norse-Icelandic Arthurian text was available in an edition that meets contemporary standards of editing. Indeed, aside from Leach and Margaret Schlauch, whose now classic monograph *Romance in Iceland* addressed all manner of romances, both medieval and post-medieval and not merely those romances constituting the *matière de Bretagne*, scholars did not evince any remarkable interest in northern Arthurian literature.

The extent to which attitudes toward and acquaintance with this imported literature have changed is reflected in the history of the writing of the chapter on Scandinavian Literature in R.S. Loomis's *Arthurian Literature in the Middle Ages: A Collaborative History* (hereafter *ALMA*). To judge by a series of letters, commencing in May of 1952, written by Loomis to P.M. Mitchell, the editor had difficulty finding someone qualified and willing to write the chapter.[1] John Jay Parry had proposed Mitchell as a reliable contributor. The latter demurred, arguing that he was neither a medievalist nor an Arthurian, and suggested that Loomis turn to Henry Goddard Leach instead. In 1953, Loomis reported to Mitchell, "I have written to Henry Leach, but as I expected he is more interested in writing a novel & in a universal language than in refurbishing the work that he did on the Scandinavian romances forty years or so ago. He had no one else to suggest as a specialist in the field." Mitchell finally agreed, albeit reluctantly, to undertake the task. When, in a letter dated August 3, 1953, Loomis acknowledged having received Mitchell's chapter, he remarked, "Isn't it strange how little seems to have been done with the material in recent years?" Not until after the publication of *ALMA*, albeit not necessarily as a consequence, there was to arise a notable interest in the Old Norse-Icelandic *matière de Bretagne*.[2]

What is this "material" to which Loomis referred? Arthurian literature in Scandinavia is predominantly a medieval phenomenon.[3] It was produced primarily in the Old West Norse language area, that is, in Norway and Iceland, during the thirteenth century and it was chiefly a literature of translation, consisting of four romances—Chrétien de Troyes's *Erec (Erex saga)*, *Yvain (Ívens saga)*, and *Perceval (Parcevals*

---

[1] I am grateful to P.M. Mitchell, who made his correspondence with R.S. Loomis available to me.

[2] I use the term Old Norse-Icelandic because the literature, while mostly translated in Norway, is nonetheless preserved primarily in Icelandic manuscripts.

[3] The literatures subsumed under "Scandinavian" are Danish, Faroese, Icelandic, Norwegian, and Swedish.

*saga* and *Valvens þáttr*),[4] as well as Thomas de Bretagne's *Tristan* (*Tristrams saga ok Ísöndar*)—and three lais, the *Lai du cort mantel* (*Möttuls saga*), *Chievrefoil* (*Geitarlauf*), and *Lanval* (*Januals ljóð*); the last two are part of an anthology of Breton lais entitled *Strengleikar* ("Stringed Instruments"). Noteworthy is the fact that the translators rendered these metrical narratives in prose. Two works transmit pseudo-historical matter from Geoffrey of Monmouth's *Historia regum Britanniae*: *Breta sögur* and *Merlínús spá*.

The Norwegian court provided the primary impetus for the transmission of the Arthurian matter to Scandinavia, but there are two noteworthy exceptions. Gunnlaugr Leifsson (†1218), an Icelandic monk at the Benedictine monastery of Þingeyrar, produced *Merlínús spá*, a translation, mostly into the native metre *fornyrðislag*, of "Merlin's Prophecies" in the *Historia regum Britanniae*. *Ivan Lejonriddaren*, dated 1303, is the sole Arthurian romance known to have been translated into Swedish. The latter stands also alone in that unlike the other translations of French romances, which were prose renditions, *Ivan Lejonriddaren* was written in rhymed couplets, the so-called *Knittelvers*. The translation was commissioned by Queen Eufemia, the German wife of King Hákon Magnússon, who ruled from 1299 to 1319 as Hákon V and who was the grandson of Hákon Hákonarson.

Three works enjoyed a special appeal in the North, to judge by their existence in more than one version: they are *Tristan*, *Yvain*, and the *Lai du cort mantel*. Each of these is transmitted as two quite different texts: *Tristan* is transmitted in an Old Norse prose translation, *Tristrams saga ok Ísöndar*, and an Old Icelandic prose adaptation, *Saga af Tristram ok Ísodd*; *Yvain* in an Old Norse prose translation, *Ívens saga*, and an Old Swedish verse translation, *Ivan Lejonriddaren*; and the *Lai du cort*

---

[4] Chrétien's *Perceval* is transmitted as two works, *Parcevals saga* and *Valvens þáttr*. The division of the romance into two independent narratives presumably obtains from the incompleteness of Chrétien's text and the transition of the plot and change of focus from Perceval to Gawain after the Good Friday episode. Consequently, commencing with v. 6519—the story of Perceval concludes with v. 6513; vv. 6514–18 are transitional (cf. William Roach, ed., *Chrétien de Troyes: Le roman de Perceval ou Le conte du graal* [Geneva: Droz, 1959])—the Old Norse-Icelandic translation is known as *Valvens þáttr*. The translator was presumably dissatisfied with the incomplete source and added a concluding section to the Parceval plot in which the protagonist returns to Blankiflúr and marries her.

*mantel* in the Old Norse prose translation *Möttuls saga* and an Old Icelandic metrical version deriving from this saga, *Skikkju rímur*. While the chief sources for the production of a corpus of Scandinavian Arthurian literature were Old French narratives of the twelfth century, a secondary, less well-known stage of importation occurred in the seventeenth and eighteenth centuries, as part of a trend to translate popular German literature, the so-called *Volksbücher*, into Danish. Two fifteenth-century German prose romances were rendered into Danish: *Her Viegoleis med Guld Hiulet* ("Sir Viegoleis with the Golden Helmet," 1656) derives from an anonymous German prose redaction (1472) of the early thirteenth-century *Wigalois* by Wirnt von Grafenberg; similarly, *En tragoedisk Historie om den ædle og tappre Tistrand* ("A Tragic Story of the Noble and Courageous Tistrand"), published in 1775, presumably is based on a fifteenth-century German prose redaction of Eilhart von Oberge's *Tristan*, which itself was translated from Béroul's French romance. The Danish Tristan version, however, parts of which first appeared in serial form in a Norwegian weekly in 1771 and 1772, is so far removed in spirit from the medieval romance that it must be considered a reinterpretation, indeed a recreation of the Tristan myth (Kalinke 1991). These two Danish prose romances in turn generated Icelandic versions, a translation of the former, *Gabons saga og Vigoleis* ("Saga of Gabon and Vigoleis," late seventeenth century), and two metrical versions, so-called *rímur*, of the latter, *Tistrans rímur og Indíönu* by Níels Jónsson (1782–1857) and *Rímur af Tistrani og Indiönu* (1831) by Sigurður Breiðfjörð (1798–1846). In addition to translations of the two postmedieval prose romances, the Arthurian matter in Scandinavia is represented in early-modern times in short forms, such as ballads and folktales, but it is substantially transformed, primarily the result of oral transmission, it would seem.

Contrary to what occurred, for example, in the German-language realm, the translated Arthurian romances did not generate an indigenous subgenre—that is, Arthurian romance—in Scandinavia. Rather, the primary impact of Arthurian literature in the North may be seen in the introduction of new themes in such short narrative forms as ballads and folktales and in the transmission of certain motifs, chiefly from the Tristan legend, that reappeared in indigenous Icelandic romances and even in some Sagas of Icelanders.

At a colloquium on Franco-Scandinavian relations held in 1975 in Liège, Jónas Kristjánsson noted that the individual best suited to produce a critical edition of a literary work is often also the one best suited to undertake scholarly research on it as well. The remark is well taken, provided that individual combines the necessary editorial and literary-critical skills. Although unfortunately this is usually not the case, the remark addresses an important issue of recent scholarship— for our purposes, the publications of the last three decades—in Scandinavian Arthurian studies. A couple of years later, Peter Foote raised the same problem but specifically addressed the issue of comparative, that is, Franco-Norse studies:

> Self-evident prerequisites for elucidation of a work of literature are meticulously established texts and as perfect a comprehension as possible of what the texts say—demanding knowledge of customs and *realia* as well as of language. In these terms it seems virtually impossible nowadays for any single scholar, except in the rarest of cases and probably only when dealing with limited or solitary texts, to be fully competent in both the Romance and the Norse fields.[5]

To extrapolate from Jónas Kristjánsson's and Peter Foote's concerns: the necessary bases for research on the Scandinavian Arthurian matter are good editions, an understanding of the manuscript transmission, and familiarity with two quite different literary traditions.

Not only the burgeoning of literary studies on the Arthurian *riddarasögur* but also the nature of those studies is directly related to the availability of critical editions that meet contemporary standards. These editions in turn are inevitably dependent on manuscript studies, which have affected not only the type of edition produced but also our knowledge of the medieval texts themselves. The complexities of the textual transmission of the Arthurian *riddarasögur* have played a marked role in determining two directions that research in the Scandinavian Arthurian matter has taken.

Many recent publications have addressed such questions as the intended audience, the function of the translations, and the relationship of the extant texts to those produced by the translators. The respective

---

[5] Peter Foote, "Saman er brœðra bezt at sjá: A Personal View of Recent Scholarship in Fields of Mutual Norse-Romance Interest," *Bibliography of Old Norse-Icelandic Studies*, 1975 (Copenhagen: The Royal Library, 1977), p. 11.

answers to these questions have had a direct impact on the hypotheses advanced concerning translational methodology and the reception of the texts in thirteenth-century Norway. Much recent scholarship is predicated on the willingness, or refusal, to posit the production of all the Arthurian sagas in Norway and to accept postmedieval Icelandic manuscripts as faithful representatives of translations antedating the transmitted texts by several centuries. Scholars, however, disagree in their assessment of the relationship of the transmitted texts to the original translations, the one side claiming that the romances we know today represent the thirteenth-century translations; the other arguing that the translations underwent gradual transformation at the hands of Icelandic scribes and thus that the extant texts may be far removed from their thirteenth-century antecedents. The former group (e.g., Barnes; Kretschmer) interprets the at times major textual differences between the translations and their sources as expressive of thirteenth-century attitudes toward royalty and the church, and maintains that didactic intentions inspired the "program" of translation. Consequently, the extant texts are read as attestations of the philosophy and outlook of the thirteenth-century court of King Hákon. This group ascribes additions, omissions, and changes to an intentionally revising translator. The latter scholars (e.g., Kalinke; Sverrir Tómasson) understand the discrepancies between the extant Icelandic texts and their ultimate French sources as the work of one or more Icelandic redactors. They argue that the divergences tell us more about the reception of the romances and the scribal practices and attitudes in Iceland than about translational methodology and ideology in Norway.

The nature of most contemporary research on the Scandinavian Arthurian matter, which on the whole is limited to medieval literature, is directly related to a striking peculiarity of this body of narratives: with one exception, the Arthurian *riddarasögur* ("sagas of knights"), as these narratives are called, are transmitted solely in Icelandic manuscripts. Furthermore, the oldest more or less complete texts are at best one hundred and fifty years removed from what is generally believed to be the time of their translation (Kalinke 1985). The exception is the codex containing the *Strengleikar*, that is, the collection of lais that includes the Arthurian *Geitarlauf* and *Januals ljóð*, a Norwegian manuscript produced in the period 1260–80. This means that most of the literature that was presumably produced for the

Norwegian court is known to us solely through manuscripts written by Icelanders several centuries later. To be sure, Icelandic redactors were subjects of the crown—as of 1262 the Norwegian and by the end of the fourteenth century the Danish crown—but the Icelandic literary and general culture was quite different from that enjoyed in thirteenth-century Norwegian courtly circles. The situation is further complicated both by the long history of manuscript transmission—in the case of *Erex saga*, *Ívens saga*, *Möttuls saga*, and *Parcevals saga*, this reaches into the nineteenth century (cf. *Bibliography of Old Norse-Icelandic Romances*)—and the indisputable fact that the oldest manuscripts, which one would expect to contain a reasonable facsimile of the translations, do not *ipso facto* transmit the best approximations of the original texts.

Unlike the nineteenth-century editor Eugen Kölbing, whose editions of the Arthurian *riddarasögur* were considered standard until the mid-1960s, scholars today not only have recourse to all manuscripts in preparing their editions but also publish unnormalized texts. Indeed, one noteworthy aspect of the critical editions of the Arthurian matter, published by the Arnamagnæan Institute in Copenhagen commencing in 1965, is that they contain the texts of the primary manuscripts (on split pages) and that a thorough accounting of all manuscripts and their stemmatic interrelations is provided in the extensive introductions (*Erex saga*, [Blaisdell] 1965; *Ívens saga*, [Blaisdell] 1979; *Mottuls saga*, [Kalinke] 1987). In the last three decades, editors have repeatedly demonstrated a remarkable aspect of Icelandic manuscript transmission, what Foster W. Blaisdell dubbed "the value of the valueless" (1967).

In the process of editing *Ívens saga*, Blaisdell increasingly came to realize the negative significance for textual scholarship and literary criticism of certain erroneous notions held by nineteenth-century editors; these affected not only the editions they produced but also the subsequent literary-critical work dependent on them. A case in point was Eugen Kölbing's standard—until 1979—edition of *Ívens saga* in the collected edition *Riddarasögur* (1872). Kölbing had chosen to ignore a late seventeenth-century Icelandic manuscript of *Ívens saga* (Stockholm 46 fol.) because it is a late paper manuscript, more than four centuries removed from the time of translation, and he therefore considered it worthless. As modern scholarship has in the meantime been able to show (Blaisdell 1967, 1979; Kalinke 1981), however, the paper manuscript from 1690, although containing a more condensed text than the older manuscripts, nevertheless transmits readings from the original translation that do not exist in the primary manuscripts antedating it by more than two centuries.

The same situation obtains in other instances. The editions by Paul Schach of two different fragments of *Tristrams saga* (1964, 1969) similarly revealed the deficiencies of Kölbing's edition of that work (1878; rpt. 1978) and attested at the same time that Brother Robert had translated more of Thomas's *Tristan* than the nineteenth-century edition permitted us to suspect. The most recent edition of an Arthurian narrative, *Möttuls saga*, based on all extant manuscripts, confirms the importance of late Icelandic manuscripts for assessing the character of the thirteenth-century Norwegian translations by providing striking evidence of the process of complementary attrition (Kalinke 1981, 1987), that is, the phenomenon of dissimilar corruption and loss of text in the aggregate of manuscripts, which, if considered in conjunction with the extant Old French texts, not only facilitates an estimate of the nature of the original Old Norse translation but also throws light on the character of the French text itself (Kalinke 1987).

A striking example by way of indictment of medieval scribal practices is presented by a postmedieval Icelandic redaction of a text in the only Norwegian manuscript containing Arthurian matter, a manuscript produced in the same century as the translations, the De la Gardie codex of the *Strengleikar*. The Icelandic manuscript Lbs. 840 4to, dated 1737, contains a redaction of the translation of *Guigemar*, which reveals that the thirteenth-century Norwegian manuscript, despite its proximity to the original translation—it was produced at most within a half-century of the translation—is a corrupt copy that had already suffered loss of text. The serendipitous discovery of this eighteenth-century Icelandic sister manuscript of the thirteenth-century Norwegian manuscript (Kalinke 1979) contributed to a more accurate assessment of both the Norwegian redaction and translation and to a better understanding of medieval translation in Norway. The Icelandic manuscript proved the first editors of the *Strengleikar* (1850) wrong.[6] They had

---

[6] R. Keyser and C.R. Unger, *Strengleikar eða Ljóðabok: En Samling af romantiske Fortællinger efter bretoniske Folkesange (lais), oversat fra Fransk paa Norsk ved Midten af trettende Aarhundrede efter Foranstaltning af Kong Haakon Haakonssön* (Christiania: Feilberg and Landmark, 1850).

deemed the Norwegian manuscript the first fair copy of the translator's draft (xix). Furthermore, it became apparent that Rudolf Meissner's magisterial comparative study of the *Strengleikar* (1902)[7] and its sources was flawed, since it was predicated on the assumption that the extant Norwegian manuscript faithfully represents the translator's work, which we now know it does not. The text of *Gvímars saga*, as the Icelandic redaction is called, attests that aspects of Meissner's analysis of the Norwegian *Guiamars ljóð* miss the mark and suggests that most of the differences between the Old Norse and French texts are to be attributed not to the translator but rather to a copyist, thus supporting scholarly suggestions about other lais in the collection (cf. Jakobsen 1978, Skårup 1979).[8] While *Guigemar* is not an Arthurian lai, its transmission in Scandinavia suggests that some of the problems attending this text of the *Strengleikar* may obtain in other cases as well, including the Arthurian lais.

While the eighteenth-century Icelandic manuscript of one of the lais demonstrates on the one hand that post-Reformation Icelandic manuscripts can enable scholars in some instances to project a more accurate estimate of the Norwegian translations, this very same manuscript and other postmedieval Icelandic redactions lay bare the constant process of revision, including corruption, reduction, and augmentation of text, in the course of transmission (cf. Blaisdell 1972). The contemporary emphasis on studying the entire manuscript transmission has resulted on the one hand in a better understanding of medieval translation but on the other hand an awareness of the dissimilar reception of texts at the hands of Icelandic scribes. Thus, contemporary editors of the Arthurian texts, including fragments—*Parcevals saga* (Simek 1982), *Tristrams saga* (Schach 1964, 1969), *Erex saga* (Blaisdell 1964; Benedikt Jakobsson 1951; Slay 1985; cf. Jakobson 1988, 1989), *Ívens saga* (Blaisdell 1979), *Möttuls saga*

---

[7] Rudolf Meissner, *Die Strengleikar: Ein Beitrag zur Geschichte der altnordischen Prosalitteratur* (Halle: Niemeyer, 1902).

[8] Unfortunately, Robert Cook and Mattias Tveitane, the editors of the 1979 edition of the *Strengleikar*, were unable to take into consideration the text of *Gvímars saga*, since their edition was already at an advanced stage of page proof (p. xi). See also Marianne E. Kalinke, "Stalking the Elusive Translator: A Prototype of *Guiamars ljóð*," *Scandinavian Studies*, 52 (1980), 142–162.

(Kalinke 1987)—while having produced reliable editions and conjectures of better readings, have thereby also furthered the cause of literary criticism.

Whereas the nineteenth-century editions of Eugen Kölbing (*Ívens saga*, *Parcevals saga*, *Tristrams saga*) and Gustaf Cederschiöld (*Erex saga*, *Möttuls saga*) were groundbreaking for their time, they no longer meet the demands of contemporary scholarship. Unfortunately, editions of three major Arthurian sagas are still outstanding. While the Arnamagnæan Institute in Copenhagen has been announcing for years in its biennial bulletins forthcoming editions of not only *Tristrams saga ok Ísöndar* and *Parcevals saga* with *Valvens þáttr*, but also of the pseudo-historical *Breta sögur*, the publication of these texts is not imminent.[9] Especially in the case of *Tristrams saga*, an edition based on all the manuscripts is imperative. The saga is the only thirteenth-century translation for which we know the names of both the patron, Hákon Hákonarson, and the translator, a Brother Robert; it is also the only work bearing a date: 1226. This information is found in an introductory passage to the translation, and even though it is transmitted only in seventeenth-century Icelandic manuscripts (the older fragments do not contain the beginning of the saga), an analysis of all the evidence suggests that the passage can be accepted as documenting literary history (Sverrir Tómasson 1977). *Tristrams saga* has pride of place among the Scandinavian Arthurian translations inasmuch as it is the sole complete representative of the Thomas branch of the Tristan legend. Furthermore, as Paul Schach has noted, *Tristrams saga* "had a revolutionary impact upon the literary taste of the Icelanders in the thirteenth century. The native literature was strongly influenced by it, both in content and spirit" (1957–61, 103). Together with the *Strengleikar* anthology, which represents the third major collection of Breton lais in existence, *Tristrams saga* has significance not only for Scandinavian but especially for medieval European romance. As Joseph Bédier, whose reconstruction of Thomas's *Tristan* would have been

---

[9] The most recent Bulletin is no. 18, published by The Arnamagnæan Institute and Dictionary (1992). Copies of the Bulletin may be obtained by writing to Det Arnamagnæanske Institut, Københavns Universitet / Amager, Njalsgade 76, DK-2300 Copenhagen S, Denmark.

impossible without recourse to the saga, put it, *Tristrams saga* is "notre témoin le plus sûr du poème de Thomas."[10]

A new edition of *Tristrams saga* should have the highest priority. Although the two oldest fragments have been edited by Paul Schach, and these provide some sense of the loss of text incurred in the process of transmission, only a critical edition incorporating all the manuscripts will contain the kind of evidence essential for contemporary scholarship. It should be noted that in her monograph of 1978, *Tristán en el Norte*, Álfrún Gunnlaugsdóttir undertook a comparative study of the Old Norse version and the extant fragments of Thomas's romance. Unfortunately, the monograph, written in Spanish by an Icelander and published in Iceland, is largely unknown to Tristan scholarship. Yet one romance philologist has noted that henceforth one will no longer be able to use Bédier's reconstruction without at the same time having recourse to *Tristán en el Norte*, which furthermore contains a translation of *Tristrams saga* into Spanish (Kjær 1978/79). Although Álfrún Gunnlaugsdóttir took into account the major redactions, only when Paul Schach publishes the critical edition—on which he has been working for a number of decades—will a competent assessment of the romance be possible. As Schach argued more than thirty years ago, the seventeenth-century paper manuscripts of the saga complement each other, and readings in secondary manuscripts occasionally retain original readings that the primary manuscripts have lost. Furthermore, despite the saga's shortcomings—when compared with its source, which unfortunately is transmitted only in a few fragments, and Gottfried's incomparable German romance—"some of the blame for the weakness of the saga in its present form must be shared by the scribes through whose hands it went between 1226 and 1688" (1957-61: 115).

Only in three cases—*Tristrams saga*, *Ívens saga*, and *Möttuls saga*—do we learn from the manuscripts that the translations were commissioned by King Hákon Hákonarson. Yet there is an implicit assumption, albeit not shared by all, that the other Arthurian romances, *Parcevals saga* and *Erex saga*, were also translated in the shadow of the Norwegian court. This inference by virtue of the similarity of the material, courtly and Arthurian, while plausible, overlooks the fact that

---

[10] Joseph Bédier, *Le roman de Tristan par Thomas* (1905), II, 64. Cf. Thomas (1983), who questions the validity of Bédier's observation, but Blakeslee (1986) confirms it.

the Arthurian sagas are comparatively speaking not all cut of one cloth. There are differences in the style of the translations as well as varying degrees of consonance between the plot and structure of the sagas and the extant French narratives. Research in this area has depended to some degree on the scholarly positions taken in regard to the place and time of translation.

The genre of the narratives suggests to many that all the Arthurian sagas were produced in the thirteenth century in the environs of Hákon's court. The considerable disparity among the sagas in style and their fidelity to the sources, however, particularly in the case of *Parcevals saga*, which is unique by virtue of recurring rhymed couplets, and *Erex saga*, a laconic and restructured narrative vis-à-vis the French romance, suggests to other scholars that even if these works had been translated in thirteenth-century Norway, of which we cannot be certain, the extant texts are to be considered more the products of Icelandic scribes than Norwegian translators. Even when there is consensus that a saga was translated at the Norwegian court, scholars diverge when it comes to establishing whose text we are dealing with, that of the Norwegian translator or one or more Icelandic redactors. While there is no doubt concerning the origin of *Tristrams saga*, not everyone is willing to claim that the extant redaction represents the translational practices of thirteenth-century Norway, that it transmits a thirteenth-century Norwegian text. The Icelandic manuscripts of the Arthurian *riddarasögur* reveal substantial scribal intervention (Kalinke 1985: 332–336; Jakobsen 1988, 1989), and thus, no matter what their origin, most of the translations, in the versions transmitted to us, are in fact Icelandic literature, or, as Jónas Kristjánsson put it (1988: 312), "If we have a text only in Icelandic copies, it is obviously hard to demonstrate Norwegian origin, and a succession of such copies undoubtedly brought about a gradual Icelandicisation of the attitudes, taste and language of the work in question."

Sverrir Tómasson (1989), points out that even though *Tristrams saga* was translated during the reign of King Hákon Hákonarson, the extant text is a work of the fourteenth century, that is, an Icelandic text. The issue of the transmission of texts and what the extant manuscripts represent is not peculiar to the translations of the *matière de Bretagne*. The very same problem haunts the medieval literary history of Iceland in general, since the indigenous sagas, like the Arthurian *riddarasögur*, are transmitted in manuscripts from rather different periods. Preben Meulengracht Sørensen has justifiably questioned the validity of a literary history based on the assumption that the extant manuscripts of the sagas represent the original compositions and has suggested that scholarship might be better served by studying the reception of the sagas as attested in the extant manuscripts than hypothetical original creations. Especially in a case where the extant redactions are quite dissimilar—and this obtains for the Arthurian *riddarasögur* as well—the preserved texts might be better understood as interpretations of each other.[11]

In recent years, ever more doubt has been cast on the theory of the Norwegian origin of a number of translations, including *Parcevals saga* and *Erex saga*. Already in 1965, Thorkil Damsgaard Olsen noted that not every one of the works that might be considered courtly of necessity had a Norwegian past (*Norrøn fortællekunst*, 1965). More recently, Stefán Karlssson has argued on the basis of lexical analyses that sections of *Karlamagnús saga*—the collective name for a group of translated chansons de geste, including the *Chanson de Roland*—were translated not by Norwegians but rather by Icelanders.[12] He suggests that the translators might have been some Benedictine monks from the monastery of Þingeyrar who had spent time abroad among French-speaking Bendictines (176). Even the manuscript De la Gardie 4–7, in which may be found, in addition to the *Strengleikar*, the *Pamphilus* (a translation of the Latin dialogue by the same name) and *Elis saga ok Rósamundu* (a translation of *Elie de St. Gille*), and which is the oldest manuscript containing translations of foreign literature, including the two Arthurian lais, *Januals ljóð* and *Geitarlauf*, seems to have benefited from the work of Icelanders. Finn Hødnebø has argued for the presence of at least one Icelander in the scriptorium that produced the manuscript (1987).

---

[11] Preben Meulengracht Sørensen, *Fortælling og ære: Studier i islændingesagaerne* (Århus: Aarhus Universitetsforlag, 1993), pp. 118–119.

[12] Stefán Karlsson, "Hverrar þjóðar er Karlamagnús saga," in *Festskrift til Finn Hødnebø 29. desember 1989*, ed. Bjørn Eithun, Eyvind Halvorsen, Magnus Rindal, and Erik Simensen (Oslo: Novus Forlag, 1989), pp. 164–179. Cf. also his older study "Islandsk bogeksport til Norge i middelalderen," *Maal og Minne* (1979), esp. pp. 5–6.

A work like *Erex saga* poses a special problem, since it deviates substantially not only from the content and structure of Chrétien's *Erec et Enide* but also from the style of the other translations known to have been produced at the Norwegian court. While some scholars consider it a Norwegian translation and predicate their literary analyses on that assumption (Kjær 1992), others read the extant text as an extensively revised Icelandic redaction (Kalinke 1981; cf. Skårup 1984)[13] or, most recently, even as an Icelandic translation preserved more or less in its original state (Jakobsen 1989). Jakobsen proposes that *Erex saga* is the product of a concerted effort to produce a translation imitative of Icelandic saga style. The thesis bears consideration. He proposes that King Hákon commissioned an Icelander to translate the romance, which would explain the saga's deviation from the other works known to have originated at Hákon's court. If an Icelander rather than a Norwegian was the translator, an explanation is at hand for the remarkable similarity in style between *Erex saga* and the indigenous Icelandic sagas.

Jakobsen's thesis confirms both statistical analyses and more recent linguistic and paleographic studies. Hallberg's lexical analysis of the "Tristram-group" of *riddarasögur* and a control group confirmed what scholars had long suspected: a group of sagas that includes the Arthurian *Ívens saga*, *Möttuls saga*, *Parcevals saga* with *Valvens þáttr*, *Strengleikar* (with its two Arthurian lais), and *Tristrams saga* share semantic and syntactic similarities that are lacking in *Erex saga* (Hallberg 1971). Indeed, Hallberg even noted that the statistical evidence supports the thesis that one and the same person, Brother Robert, had been the translator of the works in the "Tristram-group." While Hallberg's statistical analyses have been criticized because they are based on texts (that is, ultimately, manuscripts) that vary widely in their proximity to the original translations (Blaisdell 1974), the fact remains that even despite these variables and without the evidence of

---

[13] My perspective on *Erex saga* has changed over the years: originally, I interpreted the deviations from Chrétien's romance as the work of the translator, whom I thought to be Norwegian, but extended research on the manuscript tradition and the Arthurian matter in general has convinced me that the text as we know it represents the work of an Icelandic redactor. It may even be, as Jakobsen has suggested, that the extant text represents an Icelander's translation.

statistics it is readily apparent that *Erex saga* is unlike the other Arthurian translations.

Jan de Vries recognized the problematic nature of both *Parcevals saga* and *Erex saga* in the second edition of his *Altnordische Literaturgeschichte* (1967) when he decided to assign the translation of *Parcevals saga* to the reign of King Hákon Magnússon, in fact, to the patronage of Queen Eufemia, whom we know to be responsible for the Swedish *Ivan Lejonriddaren*. His explanation was that the language of the saga reveals a younger coloring ("jüngere Färbung") that suggests that it was translated later than the other Arthurian works. *Erex saga*, however, which together with *Parcevals saga* he had thought in the first edition of the literary history to be one of the works translated at Hákon Hákonarson's court (1942), he identified in 1967 as the work of an Icelandic cleric, who intercalated religious commentary into the translation. In his recent article, Jakobsen (1989) thus laid out the evidence for the thesis proposed by de Vries in 1967.

When Thorkil Damsgaard Olsen (1965) presented what may be considered the first contemporary survey of Old Norse-Icelandic courtly literature, he dismissed the extant Icelandic manuscripts as worthless sources of the original Norwegian translations. Kalinke's monograph *King Arthur, North-by-Northwest* scrutinized the manuscript evidence of the Arthurian sagas, and the author concluded on the one hand that the aggregate of the extant manuscripts suggests that the original translations were much more faithful to their sources than has in the past been thought but on the other hand that interference in the texts by Icelandic redactors is a given. A close analysis of the extant manuscripts of *Möttuls saga* yielded similar results (Kalinke, ed. 1987). The Icelandic scribal habit of revising and adapting texts in the process of copying is well attested. Copyists' revisions affected style, through rhetorical ornamentation—a case in point is *Möttuls saga* (Kalinke 1979)—or deletion of the same, as well as content, through the addition or deletion of episodes; the latter of necessity involved structure, as happens in *Erex saga* (Kalinke 1970). Given this phenomenon, the extant texts may be understood to be the result of a progressive Icelandicization, which did not, however, affect the Arthurian sagas uniformly. If one adopts this position, then one is forced to interpret many of the changes vis-à-vis the French romances as the work of Icelandic redactors rather than Norwegian translators.

Not all scholars accept the above. Both implicitly and explicitly some scholars maintain that the extant manuscripts of the Arthurian *riddarasögur* are the equivalent of the thirteenth-century texts, that they testify to Norwegian translational practices (Barnes 1977; Almazan 1988), that by and large they "preserve the substance, and probably the essentials of the style, of their exemplars" (Barnes 1987: 58). A number of comparative studies are predicated on the assumption that the extant Arthurian texts are more or less synonymous with the texts of the translations (Blakeslee 1986), that these were all produced at the Norwegian court (Almazan 1988), and that the extant texts are the key to understanding why they were produced and how they were under-stood. As a result, comparisons with the French counterparts are thought to throw light on the thirteenth-century courtly milieu of Norway. Interpreted in this manner, the translated sagas suggest that audiences evinced a preference for Arthur the historical warrior over his courtly fictional counterpart, that they were incapable of appreciating irony, and that the narratives were both intended and received as exemplary literature (Barnes 1987). Accordingly, the Arthurian sagas were edifying instruments meant to instruct the Norwegian courtiers, fictional counterparts of the Norwegian *Konungs skuggsjá*, a "King's Mirror" in dialogue form composed during the reign of Hákon Hákonarson (Barnes 1975; Kretschmer 1982).

Whereas one might take exception to interpreting the entire Old Norse-Icelandic Arthurian corpus as a *miroir de prince*, one work, *Parcevals saga*, is indisputably more pedantic and edifying than entertaining. Geraldine Barnes undertook a detailed analysis and proposed that "the saga author may have steered his work towards the pattern of a handbook of chivalry when opportunity arose" (1984: 58). Álfrún Gunnlaugsdóttir (1984) interpreted the saga more broadly as a conscious revision of Chrétien's romance into a "þroskasaga," a "Bildungsroman" as it were, emphasizing instruction in morality rather than chivalry. The intent of the author, whom Álfrún prefers to think of as the translator rather than a later Icelandic redactor (1984), in omitting, changing, and augmenting the source was to remove all matter that might distract attention from Parceval and his education in ethical behavior. She concludes by observing that the translator understood Chrétien's *Conte du graal* as a work concerned with morality, and undertook to adapt the French source in order to produce an edifying and useful text for all.

The two important interpretations of *Parcevals saga*, by Geraldine Barnes and Álfrún Gunnlaugsdóttir, both implicitly and explicitly are predicated on the assumption that the saga is a text translated for and received by a Norwegian courtly audience. The fact remains, however, that the text on which this interpretation rests is found in an early fifteenth-century Icelandic manuscript. Whereas no evidence exists that the text interpreted by contemporary scholars is the text heard or read by a Norwegian audience or even that this text was translated in Norway rather than Iceland, extant manuscripts do attest that *Parcevals saga* was received in Iceland as late as the nineteenth century (Kalinke-Mitchell 1985). The question thus remains how an Icelandic audience might have understood the work. Unlike most of the other translations, including non-Arthurian works, *Parcevals saga* also contains a number of rhymed couplets, sometimes at the end of a chapter; these have the character of adages and function as commentary on the narrative. Like *Erex saga*, the story of Parceval concludes with what may be considered an epilogue: in both instances this concluding section projects future events. In addition to the epilogue, *Parcevals saga*, unlike the French romance, also has an introduction commencing like a folktale: "There once was a man who married a woman; they had an only son whose name was Parceval." This "prologue" to the tale is at odds with what is subsequently reported both in the saga and in *Perceval,* and for this reason, as well as the unusual and decidedly uncourtly designations *karl* and *kerling* for the father and mother—the terms belong more properly in the realm of folktale—scholars think that the introduction was not part of the original translation (Álfrún Gunnlaugsdóttir 1984). Clearly an Icelandic redactor had tampered with the narrative, but the question nonetheless remains how extensive the process of revision was.

One textual crux in *Parcevals saga* has repeatedly attracted scholarly attention: the description of the Grail. The discussion centers on the meaning of the object the maiden carries in her hands; it is something "því líkast sem textus væri; en þeir í völsku máli kalla braull; en vér megum kalla ganganda greiða" (Kölbing, ed. 1872: 30). A translation as obfuscating and ambiguous as the Icelandic text might read: "She bore in her hands something just as if it were a *textus*, and they call it *graull* in the French language, but we may call it *gangandi greiði*." The word *braull* is presumably a corruption of *graull* = *graal*, but scholars' opinions on the intended meaning of *textus* and especially *gangandi greiði* diverge (Foote 1969; Kratz 1977; Loomis 1964; Mitchell 1958).

The interpretation of *Parcevals saga* as a didactic instrument at the Norwegian court represents the one approach to reading the Arthurian *riddarasögur*; the other is espoused by scholars who consider the extant texts the products of centuries of transmission, and their deviations vis-à-vis the known French romances the work of scribes rather than translators. The values expressed in the texts are those of Icelandic redactors rather than Norwegian translators. According to this view, a work like *Erex saga* does not express a thirteenth-century Norwegian court culture but rather a later Icelandic rural, possibly clerical culture. *Erex saga* is the most blatant example of adaptation, even recreation, vis-à-vis its French source. The most remarkable aspect is the strikingly different attitude toward women expressed in the Icelandic saga when compared with Chrétien's romance. According to *Erex saga*, the woman has a right to choose her own husband, a right, as Jenny Jochens has argued, which "was brought to pagan Iceland and Norway from the south by Christian churchmen" (169). What is puzzling, however, and has yet to be explained is why, if the notion of a woman's right to self-determination was imported, this found literary expression in Scandinavian literary works but not in their sources.

*Erex saga* and *Ívens saga* evince an attitude toward women quite different from that in the French sources, while King Arthur, by virtue of "deleted" matter, appears as a rather inconsequential figure in the Arthurian sagas, *Möttuls saga* excepted. Political and sociological explanations have been advanced for the relative insignificance of King Arthur in Norway (Reichert 1986; Kjær 1992). Reichert seeks an explanation in Norwegian history for the remarkable absence of Arthur's Round Table in Scandinavian literature (1986), while Jonna Kjær interprets the deviating matter—vis-à-vis the sources—in *Erex saga* and *Ívens saga* as a censure of sexuality at Hákon's court, expressive of

> an ideology of ecclesiastical nature that is revealed in the mistrust of the saga-authors, on the one hand of the splendid generosity and excessive entertainments in Arthurian feasts, and, on the other, of the clear use made by

Chrétien of the Church for purposes of decoration and the enhancement of Arthur's power [1992: 125].

Similar observations had been made earlier by Kretschmer in his study of the translations of all three of Chrétien's romances (1982), which he interpreted as expressing the attitudes of clerical translators (cf. Blakeslee 1987). Gerd Wolfgang Weber suggests that the striking moralizing and didactic tenor in the sagas is on the one hand merely a crystallization of tendencies already existing in their sources and on the other the result of a loss of the semiotic force of the courtly culture prevailing in the French romances (1986). Through changes in content, the Arthurian *riddarasögur* were attracted, according to Weber, into the generic orbits of both hagiography and historiography, narrative forms well established in both Norway and Iceland, and this explains their popularity, especially in Iceland.

A recurring issue informing scholarly discourse is the motivation underlying the program of translation, that is, the function of the texts. The question is: were the Arthurian romances translated for edification or amusement or both? Leach proposed that the translations were to be both edifying and entertaining, and Mitchell interjected a variant by interpreting didactic interests as a desire to elevate the literary level of the Norwegian court to that enjoyed by other monarchs. I devoted an entire chapter to the problem and came down hard on the side of entertainment—in opposition to Barnes (1975)—but also subscribed to the notion that didactic interests can be interpreted as emulation of prestigious courts in literary matters (1981). Subsequently, the issue has surfaced repeatedly, especially in the publications of Geraldine Barnes (1984, 1987, 1989; cf. Weber 1986; Jakobsen 1990). The matter was expressed most succinctly and pointedly by Bernd Kretschmer when he proposed the hypothesis that "the translations of works belonging to continental courtly literature had the function of contributing to changes in the social conditions and forms of behavior within a social group, that is, these translations were produced, in order to achieve a specific effect in regard to a specific public."[14] The social group he is

---

[14] "Diese Übersetzungen von Werken kontinentaler höfischer Literatur hatten die Funktion, zu Veränderungen sozialer Verhältnisse und Verhaltensweisen innerhalb einer sozialen Gruppe beizutragen, d.h. diese Übersetzungen wurden angefertigt, um bei einem bestimmten Publikum eine bestimmte Wirkung zu erzielen" (p. 37).

referring to is the Norwegian court. Geraldine Barnes, noting that Chrétien's authorial voice has been silenced in the translations, draws the following conclusion:

> It is this act of auctoricide, whether by default or by design on the part of the translator-adaptors, redactors, and scribes engaged in the transmission process culminating in the extant manuscripts of the "translated" *riddarasögur*, which inclines these narratives away from the fictional mode of their originals and towards the exemplary [Barnes 1990: 13].

She reviewed the scholarly debate of *delectare/prodesse* as motivation for the translations in her article on "Some Current Issues in Riddarasögur Research" (1989). This brings the discussion full circle. In the last analysis, the issue cannot be resolved as long as we do not know whether Hákon's courtiers were acquainted with the same texts as we are or whether these texts underwent changes in the course of transmission. Not unexpectedly, most literary scholarship devoted to the Scandinavian Arthurian matter has been comparative and has endeavored to analyze King Hákon's motivation in establishing what appears to have been a program of translation. In these studies, the various conclusions concerning the function and reception of the Arthurian *riddarasögur* have been based on textual deviations from the sources. As Jürg Glauser has put it, ". . . it is probably not greatly exaggerating to say that research on the *riddarasögur* during the past decade has been largely devoted to the basic question as to whether *riddarasögur* fulfilled didactic purposes as well as functions of entertainment. The strongly comparativistic nature of research largely predetermined the result of these investigations" (1990: 39).

There is ample testimony in the form of manuscript copies that these sagas were popular in Iceland. What may perhaps be an even more important attestation than transmitted manuscripts of the effect of the *matière de Bretagne* in Iceland is the appearance of Arthurian, including Tristanian, themes and motifs in indigenous compositions and even the production of sagas that may be interpreted as respectively implied criticism or approval of the content and form of the Arthurian romances. Although the Arthurian *riddarasögur* enjoyed circulation in the form of manuscript copies, the genre "Arthurian romance" never gained a foothold. Nonetheless, Icelanders let themselves be inspired by several romances to produce their own versions. In a series of articles, Paul Schach not only showed the impact of the Tristan matter in the incorporation of motifs borrowed from the legend in indigenous Icelandic literature (1964, 1969), but he also proposed that the strange fourteenth-century *Saga af Tristram ok Ísodd* should not be read as "a boorish account of Tristram's noble passion" (Leach 1921: 186) but rather as a deliberate reply to the Norwegian translation, as a parody of the legend (1960). Subsequently, inspired by Schach, I went on to analyze the saga as a parody of the genre of Arthurian romance per se (1981). M.F. Thomas pointed out the limitations of an interpretation of the Icelandic saga based solely on comparison with the Norwegian translation and read the Icelandic *Tristram* in light of the Tristan legend in its entirety. She concluded that the Icelandic saga constitutes "an important witness to the comparatively early knowledge in Iceland of the so-called 'vulgar' Tristram-tradition" (1983: 88). Her conclusion is not surprising—although her theses were subsequently challenged (Blakeslee 1986)—if one considers that Icelanders appear to have been acquainted with the *matière de Bretagne* by means other than the translated sagas.

The Icelandic *Saga af Tristram ok Ísodd* may be considered the most striking adaptation of the imported Arthurian matter, but scholars have recurrently noted the impact of the Tristan legend on indigenous romance in fourteenth-century Iceland. Some compositions, such as *Göngu-Hrólfs saga* and *Jarlmanns saga ok Hermanns*, incorporated motifs from the Tristan legend (Schach 1969); while others, like *Hrólfs saga Gautrekssonar*, may have imitated the multitiered bridal-quest structure (Andersson 1985). Some Sagas of Icelanders (*Íslendinga-sögur*) also reveal the influence of the Tristan matter in their incorporation of Tristan motifs (*Grettis saga, Víglundar saga*) and adoption of the love-triangle dilemma (Schach 1969; Bjarni Einarsson 1961, 1971). The authors of a group of sagas of skalds, notably *Kormáks saga*, presumably were acquainted with the legend of Tristan in versions other than the Norwegian translation (Bjarni Einarssson 1961, 1971), although this thesis has not gone unquestioned (Andersson 1969).

Scholars have devoted their attention almost exclusively to the Old Norse-Icelandic Arthurian *riddarasögur*. Noteworthy, however, are Tony Hunt's analysis of *Ivan Lejonriddaren* (1975) and Matthew J. Driscoll's study of the *Skikkju rímur* (1991), the former text being a second translation of *Yvain* into Swedish, the latter a metrical rendering of *Möttuls saga* in Iceland. The eighteenth-century Danish chapbook *En tragoedisk Historie om den ædle og tappre Tistrand* has been interpreted as a fictional commentary on political events in eighteenth-century Denmark (Kalinke 1991). Jürg Glauser has surveyed the transmission of medieval narratives in Danish manuscripts (1986).

Norway and Iceland became acquainted with the *matière de Bretagne* primarily through translations of the romances. Noteworthy is the absence of an Old Norse-Icelandic version of Chrétien's *Lancelot*. Although it has occasionally been suggested that this work too must have been translated, Povl Skårup more or less laid the matter to rest by arguing convincingly that the "Lancelot" matter could have reached Iceland through oral transmission by a number of routes and through works other than Chrétien's romance (1980). Although there is sufficient evidence that motifs from the romance were known—the "knight of the cart" appears in the indigenous Icelandic romance *Rémundar saga keisarasonar* (as do the hall-of-statues motif and the princess-as-healer from *Tristrams saga*)—there is no reason to think that these could not have been transmitted orally. Whereas the influence, suggested by Simek, of *Lancelot* in the indigenous romance *Samsons saga fagra* is doubtful (Simek, trans. 1982), the appearance in this same saga of the motif of the magic mantle from *Möttuls saga* is a given, and the use of this motif as well as the introduction of a character named King Arthur, albeit not the king of legend, have repeatedly led Icelandic scribes to classify this saga with the Arthurian matter.

Icelanders were acquainted with a number of Arthurian motifs, some derived from the translated *riddarasögur*, others presumably transmitted orally or through acquaintance with foreign texts by means other than in translation. Whereas *Ívens saga* presumably contributed the grateful-lion episode to several indigenous Icelandic romances and a postmedieval folktale (Kalinke 1981), the occurrence of some motifs from Chrétien's *Yvain* in Sagas of Icelanders antedates the Old Norse translation, and this attests that Icelanders were acquainted with the romance before Hákon had it translated (Nordland 1956; Bjarni Einarsson 1975). Similarly, although the lai *Januals ljóð* is transmitted only in the Norwegian manuscript, the indigenous Icelandic *Helga þáttr Þórissonar* contains a motif suggesting Icelandic acquaintance with the lai (Power 1985).[15] The attestation of themes and motifs from lais and fabliaux in indigenous Icelandic literature confirms wide acquaintance with continental literature, as Sverrir Tómasson has argued (1989). Further research in this area is a desideratum (Skårup 1980).

One ordinarily thinks of the Middle Ages in connection with the Scandinavian Arthurian matter, while post-Reformation literature has been largely ignored. Whereas scholars have in recent years addressed the transmission of medieval texts in manuscripts of this later period, the same cannot be said about the literature itself that was produced during this time. Hubert Seelow's study of the German chapbooks in Icelandic translation reveals the treasures lying in manuscript, among which is a translation of the German Arthurian romance *Wigalois*. Jürg Glauser's discussion of courtly romance in late-medieval and early-modern Denmark invites further attention (1986).

As noted above, editions of *Breta sögur*, *Parcevals saga*, and *Tristrams saga* have been projected by the Arnamagnæan Institute in Copenhagen, but their date of publication is uncertain. The editions presumably will follow the pattern of previously published Arthurian sagas in that they will contain a thorough survey of the manuscripts, the texts of the primary manuscripts, and a translation into English. It should be noted that the translations are "working" translations rather than literary, the point being to make the Arthurian *riddarasögur* accessible to those with little or no ability in Old Norse–Icelandic. The nature of the translations of *Erex saga* and *Ívens saga* is debatable: they are cumbersome word-for-word translations. Furthermore, the editions tend to be long on details about manuscripts but short on the kind of information a literary scholar would seek. Foster Blaisdell's reticence to delve into the literary aspects of the two Arthurian texts is understandable, however, since he was a linguist.

In the same year that *Ívens saga* was published, Robert Cook and Mattias Tveitane published a collaborative edition of the *Strengleikar*, which includes the two Arthurian lais. Unlike the Arnamagnæan

---

[15] Similarly, Carol Clover has suggested that the author of *Völsunga saga* was acquainted with the lai *Eliduc*, which is not one of the lais translated into Old Norse. ("Volsunga saga and the Missing Lai of Marie de France." In *Sagnaskemmtun: Studies in Honour of Hermann Pálsson on his 65th Birthday, 26th May 1986*, ed. Rudolf Simek et al. [Vienna: Böhlau, 1986], pp. 79–84).

editions, which append a translation to the text, this Nowegian publication placed a literary translation on facing pages. Indeed, the edition is exemplary and should be in the hands of every Romance philologist, since the Old Norse translation is our third major collection of Breton lais and contains four narratives that are otherwise unknown.

Partly as an expresssion of dissatisfaction with the two earlier editions of Arthurian romances and my own literary and comparative inclinations, the edition of *Möttuls saga,* that is, the Mantle Lay, looks rather different from the earlier editions published in Copenhagen. *Möttuls saga* includes a long introduction dealing with the transformations of the *Lai du cort mantel* through the nineteenth century. In addition, Philip Bennett revised his 1975 edition of the French lai[16] and it was published facing the saga. The edition thus serves the needs of scholars of both Old Norse and Old French, and the translation of the text of the three main Icelandic manuscripts makes the saga accessible to anyone who can read English. One hopes that the tradition of publishing the Old Norse–Icelandic texts together with their sources will be continued.

In conclusion, it should be pointed out that despite the lack of critical editions of the entire corpus of Arthurian texts, scholarship seems to be alive and well. The Liège conference on Franco-Scandinavian relations of 1972 was noted above; the Acta were published in 1975 (cf. *Les relations littéraires franco-scandinaves au Moyen Age*). In 1982, an international congress was held in Toulon, France, devoted to the topic of Old Norse–Icelandic romance. Many papers focused on the Arthurian matter and are available in the published Acta (cf. *Les sagas de chevaliers* 1975). More recently, a similar but smaller conference was held in 1989 at the University of Sydney in Australia, the papers of which were published in 1990 in Volume 8 of *Parergon,* the Bulletin of the Australian and New Zealand Association for Medieval and Renaissance Studies. Although international scholarship has until recently not paid the attention to the Scandinavian Arthurian matter that it deserves, it is comforting to know that Iceland has never forgotten it. Already in 1944, Einar Ól. Sveinsson had published an anthology, *Leit eg suður til landa,* that

---

[16] Philip E. Bennett, ed., *Mantel et Cor: Deux lais du douzième siècle,* Textes littéraires, XVI (Exeter: University of Exeter, 1975).

contains the two Arthurian lais of the *Strengleikar* anthology. In recent years, several Arthurian romances have been published in editions intended for eighth- and ninth-graders. *Tristrams saga* appeared in 1987, while in 1988 *Parcevals saga* and *Möttuls saga* were included in an Icelandic textbook entitled *Með kurt og pí*, which means something like "in a chivalric manner." Here each chapter of the romances is followed by questions intended to elicit discussion by pupils.[17] These editions testify that the texts have not lost their appeal to the Icelanders without whose manuscripts the medieval Arthurian tradition in Scandinavia would have perished. In May and June of 1994 Icelandic National Radio broadcast *Parcevals saga* in serialized form during an early evening program and supplemented the readings with discussions by scholars of the text, its origin, function, and reception. The ancient tradition of storytelling and reading aloud in Iceland has been transformed in our own century by modern technology, so that Arthurian romance, which formerly was received in the context of a household, can now reach an entire nation.

---

[17] Vésteinn Ólason, *Saga af Tristram og Ísönd* (Reykjavik: Mál og Menning, 1987). *Með kurt og pí: Riddarasögur handa grunnskólum*, ed. Baldur Hafstað and Kolbrún Bergþórsdóttir (Reykjavik: Mál og Menning, 1988).

# Bibliography

*Bibliographies*

Kalinke, Marianne E., and P.M. Mitchell, compilers. *Bibliography of Old Norse–Icelandic Romances*. Ithaca: Cornell University Press, 1985.

Kennedy, John. "The Riddarasögur in Modern English Translation." *Parergon: Bulletin of the Australian and New Zealand Association for Medieval & Renaissance Studies* 8 (1990), 53–68. [Pp. 65–68 contain bibliography of *riddarasögur* in English translation.]


*Editions*

Bjarni Vilhjálmsson, ed. "Saga af Tristram og Ísönd." In *Riddarasögur*. [Reykjavik:] Íslendingasagnaútgáfan, Haukadalsútgáfan, 1949, I, 1–247.

———, ed. "Tristrams saga og Ísoddar." In *Riddarasögur*. [Reykjavik:] Íslendingasagnaútgáfan, Haukadalsútgáfan, 1954, VI, 85–145.

Blaisdell, Foster W., ed. *Erex saga Artuskappa*. Copenhagen: Munksgaard, 1965.

———, ed. *Ívens saga*. Copenhagen: Reitzel, 1979.

Cook, Robert, and Mattias Tveitane, eds. *Strengleikar: An Old Norse Translation of Twenty-one Old French Lais, Edited from the Manuscript Uppsala De la Gardie 4-7—AM 666b, 4°*. Oslo: Kjeldeskriftfondet, 1979.

Jakob Benediktsson, ed. "Nokkur handritabrot." *Skírnir*, 125 (1951), 198.

Jónsson, Eiríkur, [and Finnur Jónsson], eds. "Breta sögur." In *Hauksbók udgiven efter de Arnamagnæanske Håndskrifter No. 371, 544 og 675, 4° samt forskellige Papirshåndskrifter.* Copenhagen: Det Kongelige Nordiske Oldskrift-Selskab, 1892-96, pp. 231-302.

Kalinke, Marianne E., ed. *Mottuls saga*, with an edition of *Le lai du cort mantel* by Philip E. Bennett. Copenhagen: Reitzel, 1987.

Kölbing, Eugen, ed. "Parcevals saga, Valvers þáttr." In *Riddarasögur: Parcevals saga, Valvers þáttr, Ívents saga, Mírmans saga.* Strassburg: Trübner, 1872, pp. 1-71.

————, ed. *Tristrams saga ok Ísondar.* Heilbronn: Henninger; rpt. Hildesheim: Olms, 1978.

Maclean, Helen, ed. "A Critical Edition, Complete with Introduction, Notes, and Select Glossary of Parcevals saga from the Stockholm Manuscript Codex Holmiensis no. 6, Pergament quarto." Thesis, University of Leeds, 1968.

*Romances: Perg. 4:o nr 6 in The Royal Library, Stockholm*, intro. by Desmond Slay. Early Icelandic Manuscripts in Facsimile, X. Copenhagen: Rosenkilde and Bagger, 1972. [Contains *Ívens saga, Parcevals saga, Valvens þáttr, Möttuls saga.*]

Schach, Paul, ed. "An Unpublished Leaf of Tristrams saga: AM 567 Quarto, XXII, 2." *Research Studies* [Washington State University], 32 (1964), 50-62.

————. "The Reeves Fragment of Tristrams saga ok Ísöndar." In Bjarni Guðnason, Halldór Halldórsson, and Jónas Kristjánsson, eds., *Einarsbók: Afmæliskveðja til Einars Ól. Sveinssonar, 12. desember 1969.* Reykjavik, 1969.

Simek, Rudolf, ed. "Ein Fragment der Parcevals saga." *Codices manuscripti: Zeitschrift für Handschriftenkunde*, 8, No. 2 (1982), 58-64.


*Translations*

Blaisdell, Foster W., and Marianne E. Kalinke, trans. *Erex saga and Ívens saga: The Old Norse Versions of Chrétien de Troyes's "Erec" and "Yvain."* Lincoln: University of Nebraska Press, 1977.

Cook, Robert, and Mattias Tveitane, trans. *Strengleikar: An Old Norse Translation of Twenty-one Old French Lais, Edited from the Manuscript Uppsala De la Gardie 4-7—AM 666b, 4°*. Oslo: Kjeldeskriftfondet, 1979.

Hill, Joyce, trans. "The Icelandic Saga of Tristan and Isolt." In *The Tristan Legend: Texts from Northern and Eastern Europe in Modern English Translation*. Leeds: University of Leeds, Graduate Centre for Medieval Studies, 1977, pp. 6-28.

———, trans. "The Norwegian Prose Lay of the Honeysuckle (Geitarlauf)." In *The Tristan Legend: Texts from Northern and Eastern Europe in Modern English Translation*. Leeds: University of Leeds, Graduate Centre for Medieval Studies, 1977, pp. 39-40.

Kalinke, Marianne E., trans. "The Saga of the Mantle." In James J. Wilhelm, ed., *The Romance of Arthur III: Works from Russia to Spain, Norway to Italy*. New York: Garland, 1988, pp. 55-68; rpt. *The Romance of Arthur: An Anthology of Medieval Texts in Translation*. New York: Garland, 1994, pp. 209-223.

Schach, Paul, trans. *The Saga of Tristram and Ísönd*. Lincoln: University of Nebraska Press, 1973.

Rudolf Simek, trans. *Zwei Rittersagas: Die Saga vom Mantel und die Saga vom schönen Samson; Möttuls saga und Samsons saga fagra*. Vienna: Braumüller, 1982.

*Studies*

Álfrún Gunnlaugsdóttir. *Tristán en el Norte*. Reykjavik: Stofnun Árna Magnússonar, 1978.

―――. "Um Parcevals sögu." *Gripla*, VI. Reykjavik: Stofnun Árna Magnússonar, 1984, pp. 218-240.

Almazan, Vincent. "Translations at the Castilian and Norwegian Courts in the Thirteenth Century: Parallels and Patterns." *Mediaeval Scandinavia*, 12 (1988), 213-232.

Andersson, Theodore M. "Skalds and Troubadours." *Mediaeval Scandinavia*, 2 (1969), 7-41.

―――. "'Helgakviða Hjorvarðssonar' and European Bridal-Quest Narrative." *Journal of English and Germanic Philology*, 84 (1985), 51-75.

Barnes, Geraldine. "The *riddarasögur* and Mediæval European Literature." *Mediaeval Scandinavia*, 8 (1975), 140-158.

―――. "The *riddarasögur*: A Medieval Exercise in Translation." *Saga-Book of the Viking Society for Northern Research*, 19 (1977), 403-441.

―――. "Parcevals saga: Riddara Skuggsjá?" *Arkiv för Nordisk Filologi*, 99 (1984), 49-62.

―――. "Arthurian Chivalry in Old Norse." *Arthurian Literature*, 7 (1987), 50-102.

―――. "Some Current Issues in Riddarasögur Research." *Arkiv för Nordisk Filologi*, 104 (1989), 73-88.

―――. "Authors, Dead and Alive, in Old Norse Fiction." *Parergon: Bulletin of the Australian and New Zealand Association for Medieval & Renaissance Studies*, 8, No. 2 (1990), 5-22.

Bjarni   Einarsson.   *Skáldasögur:   Um   uppruna   og   eðli ástaskáldasagnanna fornu.* Reykjavik: Bókaútgáfa Menningarsjóðs, 1961.

———. "The Lovesick Skald." *Mediaeval Scandinavia,* 4 (1971), 21-41.

———. *Litterære forudsætninger for Egils saga.* Reykjavik: Stofnun Árna Magnússonar, 1975.

Blaisdell, Foster W., Jr. "The Composition of the Interpolated Chapter in the Erex Saga." *Scandinavian Studies,* 36 (1964), 118-126.

———. "The Value of the Valueless: A Problem in Editing Medieval Texts." *Scandinavian Studies,* 39 (1967), 40-46.

———. "A Copyist at Work: AM 588a." In John M. Weinstock, ed., *Saga og språk: Studies in Language and Literature.* [Festschrift Lee M. Hollander.] Austin: Jenkins, 1972, pp. 31-38.

———. "The So-Called 'Tristram-group' of the *riddarasögur.*" *Scandinavian Studies,* 46 (1974), 134-139.

Blakeslee, Merritt R. "Mouvance and Revisionism in the Transmission of Thomas of Britain's Tristan: The Episode of the Intertwining Trees." *Arthurian Literature,* 6 (1986), 127-156.

Boyer, Régis, ed. *Les sagas de chevaliers (riddarasögur): Actes de la Ve Conférence Internationale sur les Sagas, Toulon, Juillet 1982.* Paris, 1985.

Campbell, I. "Medieval *riddarasögur* in Adaptation from the French: *Flóres saga ok Blankiflúr* and *Parcevals saga.*" *Parergon: Bulletin of the Australian and New Zealand Association for Medieval & Renaissance Studies,* 8, No. 2 (1990), 23-35.

Damsgaard Olsen, Thorkil. "Den høviske litteratur." In Hans Bekker-Nielsen, Thorkil Damsgaard Olsen, and Ole Widding, eds.,

*Norrøn fortællekunst: Kapitler af den norsk-islandske middelalderlitteraturs historie*. Copenhagen: Akademisk Forlag, 1965, pp. 92-117.

Driscoll, Matthew James. "The Cloak of Fidelity: *Skikkjurímur*, A Late-Medieval Icelandic Version of *Le mantel mautaillié*." *Arthurian Yearbook*, 1 (1991), 107-133.

Foote, Peter G. "Gangandi greiði." In Bjarni Guðnason, Halldór Halldórsson, and Jónas Kristjánsson, eds., *Einarsbók: Afmæliskveðja til Einars Ól. Sveinssonar, 12. desember 1969*. Reykjavik: Prenthús Hafsteins Guðmundssonar, 1969, pp. 45-58.

Glauser, Jürg. "Höfisch-ritterliche Epik in Dänemark zwischen Spätmittelalter und Frühzeit." In Hans-Peter Naumann et al., eds., *Festschrift für Oskar Bandle. Zum 60. Geburtstag am 11. Januar 1986*. Basel: Helbing and Lichtenhahn, 1986, pp. 191-207.

————. "Romances, *rímur*, Chapbooks: Problems of Popular Literature in Late Medieval and Early Modern Scandinavia." *Parergon: Bulletin of the Australian and New Zealand Association for Medieval & Renaissance Studies*, 8, No. 2 (1990), 37-52.

————. "Spätmittelalterliche Vorleseliteratur und frühneuzeitliche Handschriftentradition: Die Veränderungen der Medialität und Textualität der isländischen Märchensagas zwischen dem 14. und 19. Jahrhundert." In Hildegard L.C. Tristram, *Text und Zeittiefe*. *ScriptOralia*, 58. Tübingen: Gunter Narr Verlag, 1994, pp. 377-438.

Hallberg, Peter. "Norröna riddarsagor: Några språkdrag." *Arkiv för Nordisk Filologi*, 86 (1971), 114-138.

————. "Broder Robert, Tristrams saga och Duggals leizla." *Arkiv för Nordisk Filologi*, 88 (1973), 55-71.

————. "Is There a 'Tristram-Group' of the Riddarasögur?" *Scandinavian Studies*, 47 (1975), 1-17.

Hødnebø, Finn. "De la Gardie 4-7 folio." In Jan Ragnar Hagland, Jan Terje Faarlund, and Jarle Rønhovd, eds., *Festskrift til Alfred Jakobsen*. [Trondheim]: Tapir, 1987, pp. 91-105.

Hunt, Tony. "Herr Ivan Lejonriddaren." *Mediaeval Scandinavia*, 8 (1975), 168-186.

Jakobsen, Alfred. "En avskrivertabbe i Bisclaretz lióð." *Maal og Minne*, (1978), 26-29.

―――. "Et misforstått tekststed i *Erex saga*." *Maal og Minne*, (1988), 185-187.

―――. "Var oversetteren av Erex saga islending?" In Bjørn Eithun, Eyvind Fjeld Halvorsen, Magnus Rindal, and Erik Simensen, eds., *Festskrift til Finn Hødnebø 29. desember 1989*. Oslo: Novus Forlag, 1989, pp. 130-141.

―――. "Kong Arthur i det høje nord." *Arkiv för Nordisk Filologi*, 105 (1990), 106-110.

Jochens, Jenny M. "Consent in Marriage: Old Norse Law, Life, and Literature." *Scandinavian Studies*, 58 (1986), 142-176.

Jónas Kristjánsson. "Text Editions of the Romantic Sagas." In *Les Relations littéraires franco-scandinaves au Moyen Age: Colloque de Liège (avril 1972)*. Paris: Les Belles Lettres, 1975, pp. 275-288.

―――. *Eddas and Sagas: Iceland's Medieval Literature*, trans. Peter Foote. Reykjavik: Hið Íslenska Bókmenntafélag, 1988.

Kalinke, Marianne E. "The Structure of the *Erex saga*." *Scandinavian Studies*, 42 (1970), 343-355.

―――. "Alliteration in *Ívens saga*." *Modern Language Review*, 74 (1979), 871-883.

———. "Amplification in *Möttuls saga*: Its Function and Form." *Acta Philologica Scandinavica*, 32 (1979), 239-255.

———. "*Gvímars saga*." *Opuscula*, 7, Bibliotheca Arnamagnæana, 34 (1979), 106-139.

———. "Stalking the Elusive Translator: A Prototype of *Guiamars ljóð*." *Scandinavian Studies*, 52 (1980), 142-162.

———. *King Arthur, North-by-Northwest: The "matière de Bretagne" in Old Norse-Icelandic Romances*. Copenhagen: Reitzel, 1981.

———. "A Werewolf in Bear's Clothing." *Maal og Minne*, 3-4 (1981), 137-144.

———. "Scribes, Editors, and the *riddarasögur*." *Arkiv för Nordisk Filologi*, 97 (1982), 36-51.

———. "Arthurian Literature in Scandinavia." In Valerie M. Lagorio and Mildred Leake Day, eds., *King Arthur Through the Ages*. New York: Garland, 1990, I, 127-151.

———. *Bridal-Quest Romance in Medieval Iceland*. Ithaca: Cornell University Press, 1990.

———. "En tragœdisk Historie om den ædle og tappre Tistran: An Eighteenth-Century King's Mirror." *Danske Studier* (1991), 57-75.

———. "Translator or Redactor? The Problem of Old Norse-Icelandic 'Translations' of Old French Literature." *New Comparisons: A Journal of Comparative and General Literary Studies*, 12 (1991), 34-53.

Kennedy, John. "The Riddarasögur in Modern English Translation." *Parergon: Bulletin of the Australian and New Zealand Association for Medieval & Renaissance Studies*, 8, No. 2 (1990), 53-68.

Kjær, Jonna. Review of Álfrún Gunnlaugsdóttir, *Tristan en el Norte*. *Mediaeval Scandinavia*, 11 (1978/79), 298-304.

―――. "Tristrams saga ok Ísöndar—une version christianisée de la branche dite courtoise du 'Tristan.'" In Keith Busby and Erik Kooper, eds., *Courtly Literature: Culture and Context: Selected Papers from the 5th Triennial Congress of the International Courtly Literature Society, Dalfsen, The Netherlands, 9–16 August 1986.* Amsterdam: Benjamins, 1990, pp. 367-377.

―――. "Franco-Scandinavian Literary Transmission in the Middle Ages: Two Old Norse Translations of Chrétien de Troyes—Ívens saga and Erex saga." *Arthurian Yearbook*, 2 (1992), 113-134.

Kratz, Henry. "Names in *Parcevals Saga* and *Valvers þáttr*." *Names*, 25 (1977), 63-77.

―――. "The *Parcevals saga* and *Li contes del Graal*." *Scandinavian Studies*, 49 (1977), 13-47.

―――. "*Textus, braull* and *gangandi greiði*." *Saga-Book of the Viking Society for Northern Research*, 19 (1977), 371-382.

Kretschmer, Bernd. *Höfische und altwestnordische Erzähltradition in den Riddarasögur: Studien zur Rezeption der altfranzösischen Artusepik am Beispiel der "Erex saga," "Ívens saga" und "Parcevals saga."* Hattingen: Kretschmer, 1982.

Leach, Henry Goddard. *Angevin Britain and Scandinavia*. Cambridge, MA: Harvard University Press, 1921.

Loomis, R.S. "The Grail in the *Parcevals Saga*." *Germanic Review*, 39 (1964), 97-100.

Mitchell, P.M. "The Grail in the Parcevals Saga." *Modern Language Notes*, 73 (1958), 591-594.

————. "Scandinavian Literature." In Roger Sherman Loomis, ed., *Arthurian Literature in the Middle Ages: A Collaborative History*. Oxford: Clarendon, 1959, pp. 462-471.

Nahl, Astrid van. *Originale Riddarasögur als Teil altnordischer Sagaliteratur*. Frankfurt: Lang, 1981.

Nordland, Odd. *Höfuðlausn i Egils saga: Ein tradisjonskritisk studie*. Oslo: Det Norske Samlaget, 1956, pp. 92-97.

Power, Rosemary. *"Le Lai de Lanval* and *Helga þáttr Þórissonar."* *Opuscula*, 8, Bibliotheca Arnamagnæana, 38. Copenhagen: Reitzel, 1985, pp. 158-161.

Reichert, Hermann. "King Arthur's Round Table: Sociological Implications of Its Literary Reception in Scandinavia." In John Lindow, Lars Lönnroth, and Gerd Wolfgang Weber, eds., *Structure and Meaning in Old Norse Literature: New Approaches to Textual Analysis and Literary Criticism*. Odense: Odense University Press, 1986, pp. 394-414.

*Les Relations littéraires franco-scandinaves au Moyen Age. Colloque de Liège (avril 1972)*. Paris: Les Belles Lettres, 1975.

Schach, Paul. "Some Observations on *Tristrams saga." Saga-Book of the Viking Society for Northern Research*, 15 (1957-61), 102-129.

————. "The Saga af Tristram ok Ísodd: Summary or Satire?" *Modern Language Quarterly*, 21 (1960), 336-352.

————. "Tristan and Isolde in Scandinavian Ballad and Folktale." *Scandinavian Studies*, 36 (1964), 281-297.

————. "Some Observations on the Influence of *Tristrams saga ok Ísöndar* on Old Icelandic Literature." In Edgar C. Polomé, ed., *Old Norse Literature and Mythology: A Symposium*. Austin: University of Texas Press, 1969, pp. 81-129.

————. "Some Observations on the Translation of Brother Robert." In *Les Relations littéraires franco-scandinaves au Moyen Age: Colloque de Liège (avril 1972)*. Paris: Les Belles Lettres, 1975, pp. 117-135.

Schlauch, Margaret. *Romance in Iceland*. London: Allen and Unwin, 1934; rpt. New York: Russell and Russell, 1973.

Skårup, Povl. "Oversætter- og afskriverfejl i Strengleikar." *Maal og Minne*, (1979), 30-33.

————. "Forudsætter Rémundar saga en norrøn Lancelots saga kerrumanns?" *Gripla*, 4. Reykjavik: Stofnun Árna Magnússonar, 1980, pp. 76-80.

————. "Tre marginalnoter om Erex saga," *Gripla*, 6. Reykjavik: Stofnun Árna Magnússonar, 1984, pp. 49-63.

Slay, Desmond. "Lbs 1230 8vo III: A Third Reading." *Opuscula*, 8, Bibliotheca Arnamagnæana, 38. Copenhagen: Reitzel, 1985, pp. 149-152.

Stefán Karlsson. "Islandsk bogeksport til Norge i Middelalderen." *Maal og Minne*, (1979), 1-17.

————. "Hverrar þjóðar er Karlamagnús saga." In Bjørn Eithun, Eyvind Halvorsen, Magnus Rindal, and Erik Simensen, eds., *Festskrift til Finn Hødnebø 29. desember 1989*. Oslo: Novus Forlag, 1989, pp. 164-179.

Sverrir Tómasson. "Hvenær var Tristrams sögu snúið?" *Gripla*, 2. Reykjavik: Stofnun Árna Magnússonar, 1977, pp. 47-78.

————. "Hugleiðingar um horfna bókmenntagrein." *Tímarit Máls og Menningar*, 50 (1989), 211-226.

Thomas, M.F. "The Briar and the Vine: Tristan Goes North." *Arthurian Literature*, 7 [1983], 53-90.

de Vries, Jan. *Altnordische Literaturgeschichte*. 2nd rev. ed. Berlin: de Gruyter, 1967, Vol. 2.

Weber, Gerd Wolfgang. "The Decadence of Feudal Myth: Towards a Theory of Riddarasaga and Romance." In John Lindow, Lars Lönnroth, and Gerd Wolfgang Weber, eds., *Structure and Meaning in Old Norse Literature: New Approaches to Textual Analysis and Literary Criticism*. Odense: Odense University Press, 1986, pp. 415-454.

# FRANCE

## Keith Busby and Karen A. Grossweiner[1]

Although the Celts seem to have provided the wealth of tales and motifs on which Arthurian romance is built, and although Geoffrey of Monmouth provided a chronological framework in which the *aventure* of romance could be located, there is little doubt that Arthurian literature in medieval French from the twelfth and thirteenth centuries lays the foundations for most of the subsequent development in the vernaculars. Indeed, we would argue that it is next to impossible to understand the significance of, say, Hartmann von Aue, or of *Sir Gawain and the Green Knight*, or Malory's *Morte Darthur*, without a basic grasp of prior French tradition. French Arthurian literature has not only a chronological advantage but also a quantitative one: there is simply more of it.

There has been no dearth of editions of, and studies on, medieval French Arthurian literature from the mid-nineteenth century onwards. Indeed, a history of scholarship in Arthurian studies could provide a paradigm of medieval literary studies in general: the editing and publishing of texts in the age of philology, the detailed examination and dissection of the texts in source study, the scrutiny of texts for what they can reveal about such phenomena as chivalry, courtesy and courtly love. Only relatively recently, perhaps, have medievalists begun to ask questions about medieval aesthetics as reflected in Arthurian romance and how medieval textuality conditioned their reception in the Middle Ages (and how it may distort our modern readings of them).

It is not the aim of this chapter to offer a complete history of French Arthurian studies, but rather to assess the present state of the

---

[1] In this chapter, Keith Busby prepared the essay; Karen A. Grossweiner had primary responsibility for the compilation of the bibliography.

field with particular reference to scholarship since 1980. It will sometimes be necessary to discuss earlier work, especially large projects whose publication extends over a number of years, but by and large we will do so only to situate works published in the last fifteen years in a context of some sort. The ground covered in this chapter overlaps somewhat with that in Busby (1988), which discussed progress and trends in the period 1962–87, and to which we refer the reader for our view of scholarship in the 1960s and 1970s; the opening pages of that article also constitute a more elaborate exposition of the first two paragraphs above.[2]

Paradoxically perhaps, one of the results of recent interest in literary theory has been a reexamination of medieval textuality and its consequences for the modern reader. This has been at least partly responsible for a surge in the production of text-editions of various persuasions that provide scholars with the basis for further study. Editions are, of course, an absolute prerequisite for scholars (unless one has permanent and easy access to large repositories of manuscripts). We will therefore begin this chapter by looking at the availability, nature, and quality of recent editions of French Arthurian romance.

*Editions and Research Tools*

One edition of Wace's *Brut* has appeared in recent years, namely Emmanuèle Baumgartner and Ian Short's *La Geste du roi Arthur* (1993), which presents the Arthurian part of the text from the hitherto unedited MS. Durham, Cathedral Library C. iv. 27, an early Anglo-Norman copy written in a French close to that of Wace; the text of 4458 lines is accompanied by a modern French prose translation and followed by a French prose translation of Geoffrey of Monmouth's *Historia Regum Britanniæ* as edited from MS. Bern, Burgerbibliothek

---

[2] Although we have tried to be exhaustive in the matter of editions, we have not listed translations (unless they accompany editions) as these are treated in the final chapter of this volume; see also Lacy (1991). Nor have we aimed at exhaustivity in our discussion of scholarship, where we have considered studies that are in our opinion representative and/or groundbreaking.

568 by Neil Wright (1984). Despite its modest paperback format, this book is a major contribution to the study of Geoffrey and Wace and their role in the development of Arthurian literature. The relation between the versions of Geoffrey and Wace has been studied in a recent series of articles by Laurence Mathey-Maille (e.g., "De l'*Historia* . . . étude," 1993; "De l'*Historia* . . . traduction," 1993; "Traduction," 1993).

For many decades, there was a dearth of good editions of the romances of Chrétien de Troyes. This fact is all the more remarkable in the light of Chrétien's crucial role in the evolution of the genre. In essence, scholars had recourse either to the "critical" but often artificially reconstructed editions of Wendelin Foerster (and Alfons Hilka for *Perceval*) or to the "best manuscript" editions of Mario Roques (Alexandre Micha for *Cligés* and Félix Lecoy for *Perceval*) based on Paris, Bibliothèque Nationale, fonds français 794, the so-called "copie de Guiot"; William Roach's edition of *Perceval* from BN, fr. 12576 was also easily available and widely used. The availability and affordability of the Roques-Micha-Lecoy texts in the Classiques Français du Moyen Age, not to mention their legibility, led to their acceptance as the edition that most scholars had to hand. This easy and often unquestioning acceptance was itself rooted to a large degree in a general unawareness of the nature of the medieval text and its manuscript transmission. As scholars began to realize that slavish adherence to the base manuscript ran the risk of substituting one scribe, and only one, for the poet, efforts were undertaken to remedy the situation. William W. Kibler produced editions of *Lancelot* and *Yvain* (1981 and 1985), Carleton W. Carroll of *Erec et Enide* (1987), and Rupert T. Pickens of *Perceval* (1990) for the Garland Library of Medieval Literature; these were somewhat more interventionist, but still based on Guiot, and accompanied by facing English translations. It is perhaps symptomatic of the lesser attention paid to Chrétien's Byzantine romance, *Cligés*, that it has not been the object of an edition in this series. However, a project initiated by members of the British Branch of the International Arthurian Society under the auspices of the Eugene Vinaver Memorial Trust has to date produced truly critical editions of *Cligés* by Stuart Gregory and Claude Luttrell (1993) and of *Perceval* by Keith Busby (ed., 1993). The Gregory-Luttrell *Cligés* is based on Guiot and Busby's *Perceval* on Paris, BN, fr. 12576, but both editions

have a full, critical apparatus in an attempt not only to restore
Chrétien's own words where possible but also to offer the reading of
all individual manuscripts (within the limitations imposed by the format
of the printed book). Chrétien's other romances are being edited by
other scholars according to similar principles.

Although Foerster's editions were presented as parts of Chrétien's
"Sämtliche Werke" and those of Roques-Micha-Lecoy as "Les romans
de Chrétien de Troyes ...," there existed until 1994 no single-volume
"Œuvres complètes" of France's first and most important author of
Arthurian romance. The series "Lettres Gothiques," directed by Michel
Zink and published by the Livre de Poche, included individual editions
and French translations of all of Chrétien's romances, which were then
published collectively in one volume in the series "Classiques
Modernes" in 1994. The romances were purposely based on manuscripts other than Guiot with a view to presenting a different text to the
reading public: *Erec et Enide* was edited by Jean-Marie Fritz (*Erec*,
1992), *Cligés* by Charles Méla and Olivier Collet (1994), *Yvain* by
David Hult (1994), *Lancelot* and *Perceval* by Charles Méla (1990 and
1992). These editions, with their excellent introductions and limited
apparatus, are valuable additions to our knowledge of the transmission
of Chrétien's romances; it is moreover extremely convenient to have
them collected in one affordable volume. The collective edition also
includes and edition of Chrétien's lyrics by Marie-Claire Gérard-Zai
and a translation by Olivier Collet which accompanies a reprint of C.
de Boer's edition of *Philomena*; *Guillaume d'Angleterre* is not included.

The same year saw the appearance of a second "Œuvres
complètes," this time published under the general editorship of Daniel
Poirion in the prestigious series Éditions de la Pléiade (Poirion et al.,
1994). The publication of this volume was accompanied in France by
more media attention than Chrétien de Troyes had ever hitherto
received. The romances are edited by an international team of scholars,
including Peter F. Dembowski, Sylvie Lefèvre, Daniel Poirion, Karl
D. Uitti, Philippe Walter, and Anne Berthelot. The translations into
modern French seem to be the centerpiece of this volume, with the Old
French text (again based on the Guiot manuscript, but with some
measure of intervention) in smaller print at the foot of the page.
Paradoxically, perhaps, in the light of this, there is a substantial amount
of critical and variant apparatus in the back of the book. The Pléiade

edition contains much information that Chrétien scholars will find useful and more than the enlightened non-specialist reader, for whom the series is presumably intended, will ever want to know. While the desire to include an edition of Chrétien in the Pléiade no doubt stimulated the undertaking, the question remains as to whether medieval literature lends itself to such an enterprise. This volume includes Chrétien's lyrics, *Philomena*, and the disputed *Guillaume d'Angleterre*.

Outside of these projects, other editions of Chrétien have appeared, the most notable of which is doubtless the *Lancelot* prepared by Karl D. Uitti and the late Alfred Foulet published in the Classiques Garnier series (1989). This is once more based on the Guiot manuscript, but with numerous interventions justified by the "editorial grid" elaborated by the two scholars in a series of earlier articles; the text is accompanied by a translation into modern French. Also accompanied by modern French translations are editions in the series Garnier-Flammarion of *Lancelot* by Jean-Claude Aubailly (1991, reprinting Kibler's 1984 text), of *Yvain* by Michel Rousse (1990, reprinting Foerster's 1912 text), and of *Erec et Enide* by the same editor (1994, reprinting Foerster's 1934 text).

This extraordinary editorial activity has been preceded and accompanied by much discussion of the principles of editing Old French texts in general and Chrétien in particular. Although viewpoints have varied within the discussion, it has in essence arisen out of a growing realization that the "best manuscript" method in its extreme formulation by Joseph Bédier, long tacitly accepted as the norm, is incapable of doing justice either to Chrétien or to the rich manuscript transmission of his romances. Particularly noteworthy early contributions to the debate were made by Tony Hunt (1979, reprinted 1993) and T.B.W. Reid (1976), who both criticize the CFMA editions from theoretical and practical points of view. From among many other contributions, we would mention as being each in its own way illustrative of a point of view or methodology articles by Ménard (1979), Pickens (1987), and Woledge (1984). Woledge's two volumes of textual commentary on *Yvain* (1986 and 1988) are also in essence required reading for the editorial problem. Finally, mention ought to be made of a spirited exchange of views between David F. Hult (1986 and 1989) and Karl D. Uitti and Alfred Foulet (1988) and in especial connection with the text of *Lancelot*. We will return to matters relating to the manuscript transmission of Chrétien's romance more than once below.

Chrétien de Troyes has not been the only author of verse romance to have benefited from renewed editorial activity and reflection, although his case is obviously the most prominent. 1983 saw the publication of Manessier's *Continuation* of *Perceval* and with it the completion of William Roach's monumental project to edit all of the sequels to Chrétien's last unfinished romance. The five volumes (1949–83) stand as a tribute to the memory of one of the great Old French scholars of our time. Colette-Anne van Coolput-Storms has reprinted Roach's edition of MS. L of the *First Continuation*, accompanied by a modern French translation, in the Lettres Gothiques. Some of the so-called "epigonal" romances have also been reedited: Guillaume le Clerc's *Fergus* by Wilson L. Frescoln (1983); *Yder* by Alison Adams (1983); *Hunbaut* by Margaret Winters (1984); Renaut de Beaujeu's *Le Bel Inconnu* by Karen Fresco with an English translation by Colleen P. Donagher (1992); and Girard d'Amiens's lengthy *Escanor* has just been reedited by Richard Trachsler (1994). Because of their general overall quality and accessibility, these editions are likely to replace the pioneering work of scholars from the late nineteenth and early twentieth centuries. The nature of its textual transmission means that serious study of *Fergus* will probably require consultation of both Frescoln and the older edition of Ernst Martin (1872).

Despite their fragmentary nature and relative brevity, the *Tristan* romances in verse have been frequently reedited: Thomas by Stewart Gregory (1991, with English translation) and by Félix Lecoy (1992), and Béroul by Norris J. Lacy (1989) and Stewart Gregory (1992), both with English translation, and by Herman Braet and Guy Raynaud de Lage (1989).[3] Jean-Charles Payen's 1974 collective edition and translation of *Tristan* material (Béroul, Thomas, the two *Folies*, Marie

---

[3] The "Arthuricity" of the Tristan romances and the *Lais* of Marie de France may be questioned. We have nevertheless surveyed work on the former here, albeit somewhat more cursorily than other fields; as for Marie, we consider only *Lanval* and possibly *Chèvrefeuille* Arthurian. Studies devoted to these texts individually are rare, but commentary on them can be found in general studies on Marie's *Lais*, such as Burgess (1987).

de France's *Chèvrefeuille*) in the Classiques Garnier was published in a revised version in 1986. Another volume in the Lettres Gothiques by Daniel Lacroix and Philippe Walter (1989) includes the same texts collected by Payen plus the Tristan section of the *Donnei des amants*, with French translations, and a French translation of the Norse *Tristramssaga*. Payen edited the texts anew from the manuscripts, Walter claims only to present a "synthèse provisoire" (p. 19) based on other editions, although he makes no mention of the work of Payen. Tony Hunt and Ian Short will publish a newly discovered fragment of Thomas's romance in a forthcoming issue of *Romania*. It is doubtless the unsatisfactory nature of the textual transmission of the verse *Tristan* romances that is responsible for the proliferation of editions: Béroul's corrupt text is a challenge to scholars desirous of proposing a series of satisfactory emendations (see also Gregory 1981 and 1988, and Sandqvist 1984). The Payen and Lacroix-Walter collections were clearly been produced with classroom use in mind.

There have been no major new critical editions of the *Lais* of Marie de France (*Lanval* and *Chèvrefeuille* belong to the *matière de Bretagne*). Alexandre Micha has reedited the poems from MS. London, British Library, Harley 978 (1994) in the Garnier-Flammarion series, and Laurence Harf-Lancner reprinted Karl Warnke's 1925 text in the Lettres Gothiques (1990); both editions are accompanied by modern French translations. Micha has also reprinted Tobin's 1976 text of the anonymous *Lais* (1992; *Tyolet* and *Melion* have Arthurian settings).[4]

Arguably, however, the greatest progress in editing has been in the area of Old French prose romance, where an increasingly mature understanding of these works has both benefited from and stimulated editorial activity. There are now fine editions of the non-cyclic and cyclical versions of the *Prose Lancelot*, by Elspeth Kennedy (2 vols., 1980) and by Alexandre Micha (9 vols., 1978–83) respectively; Kennedy's text has been reprinted with a modern French translation by François Mosès (1991–93) in the Lettres Gothiques series. Scholars will now be able to judge for themselves with confidence the question of priority of the versions of the *Lancelot*, which has figured so largely in recent decades. Of the other parts of the Vulgate Cycle, the *Queste del*

---

[4] The various versions of the Horn/Mantel test, often designated as *lais*, do not correspond to the usual definition of *lai breton*, although they are certainly Arthurian.

*saint Graal* has been edited from an Udine manuscript unknown to Pauphilet by A. Rosellini et al. (1990), and the prose version of Robert de Boron's *Merlin* (together with the verse fragment) by Alexandre Micha (1980). A lifetime of scholarship has gone into Fanni Bogdanow's edition of the partly reconstructed Post-Vulgate *Roman du Graal* published by the Société des Anciens Textes Français (3 vols., 1994). Bernard Cerquiglini has reedited the *mise en prose* of the whole of Robert's trilogy from the Modena manuscript (*Joseph, Merlin,* and *Perceval*) under the title of *Le Roman du Graal* (1981). In what it likely to be the definitive edition, Richard O'Gorman has published both the verse and prose versions of Robert's *Joseph d'Arimathie* (1995). The anonymous *Propheties de Merlin,* finally, has been reedited from the Bodmer manuscript by Anne Berthelot (1993).

While there had always been Sommer's earlier edition of the Vulgate Cycle, those wishing to read the *Prose Tristan* had been more or less obliged to consult Löseth's long summary (1891). In 1985, Renée Curtis published the third volume of her edition of MS. Carpentras 404 (first two volumes 1963 and 1976, both reprinted 1985 to accompany vol. III). While Curtis was convinced of the "quality" of the text in the Carpentras manuscript, it is unfortunately fragmentary, and so although Curtis's edition is complete, the romance itself is not. The manuscript tradition of the *Prose Tristan* is so complex that it is impossible to produce a critical edition akin to those that are least conceivable for Chrétien's romances, and the second major *Prose Tristan* project is also in essence an edition of a single manuscript. Philippe Ménard has been directing a team of French scholars who have published seven volumes based on MS. Vienna, ÖNB, 2542 (1987–94). No doubt out of a desire to make as much of the romance as possible available to colleagues as quickly as possible, Ménard's vol. I begins where Curtis's vol. III ends. The imminent completion of this project will mark a major landmark in the accessibility of French Arthurian prose romance.

It is remarkable to note that many of these editions constitute what are in essence *editiones principes* (at the end of the twentieth century!). This is also true of the prose version of *Floriant et Florete* edited by Claude M.L. Lévy (1983), and of the monumental publication of the enormously long fourteenth-century prose romance *Perceforest* undertaken by Jane Taylor (1979) and Gilles Roussineau (1987, 1988, 1991), hitherto accessible only in manuscript or incunabula. André Giacchetti has provided an edition of *Ysaÿe le Triste* (1989), a prose romance written at the very end of the fourteenth or beginning of the fifteenth century. Together with the editions of the *Prose Tristan*, these publications signify a notable expansion of the canon beyond the traditional confines of Chrétien and the Vulgate Cycle.

Although it will always remain necessary to consult manuscripts of the prose romances, the number and nature of the critical editions currently available reflects much more reliably the complex set of intertextual relations created by the continuous rewriting of the tales. Indeed, the awareness of the nature of medieval textuality and scribal activity has informed the work of most recent editors and a number of critical studies to be dealt with below.

In addition to the general Arthurian reference works treated elsewhere in this volume, a number of important research tools relating specifically to French romance have appeared. As regards bibliographies, Douglas Kelly's volume on Chrétien de Troyes (1976) will soon be followed by a supplement; David Shirt published a bibliographical guide to the Tristan poems (1980); and Glyn S. Burgess has performed a similar service for Marie de France (1977; first supplement, 1986; second supplement forthcoming). An excellent bibliography on the *Prose Tristan*, updating that in her 1975 thesis, has been provided by Emmanuèle Baumgartner (*La Harpe*, 1990). The only concordance of Chrétien's entire *oeuvre* to date is that by Marie-Louise Ollier's *Lexique et concordance de Chrétien de Troyes* (1986), although this is more properly a concordance of the scribe Guiot, being based on the CFMA editions; Gabriel Andrieu and Jacques Piolle had already produced a concordance of the Lecoy edition of *Perceval* (1976). Pierre Kunstmann and Martin Dube have generated a concordance of the Vulgate *La Mort le roi Artu* (1982), and Gérard Gonfroy of vol. I of Philippe Ménard's edition of the *Prose Tristan* (1990). More such work can be expected as progress is made with computerized databases and various types of "word-crunching." Karl D. Uitti has begun a project, known informally as "the Princeton *Lancelot*," already available in partial form for consultation on the network, and Busby is working on a CD-ROM edition of *Erec et Enide*. Such work will eventually make all transcriptions of all manuscripts available for linguistic and stylistic analysis, and digitized scanned images of the manuscripts will accompany the transcriptions. This is likely to be the area in which most textual progress will be made over the next few decades.[5]

*Scholarly Studies*

A number of major studies of Chrétien de Troyes have appeared in the last fifteen years. Jean Frappier's standard introduction to Chrétien was published in an English translation by Raymond J. Cormier in 1982. Norris J. Lacy's *The Craft of Chrétien de Troyes: An Essay in Narrative Art* (1980) provides a fine analysis of the architectonics of the romances. More traditional in their concern with such themes as chivalry, courtly love, and religion are Leslie Topsfield's *Chrétien de Troyes: A Study of the Arthurian Romances* (1981) and Evelyn Mullally's *The Artist at Work: Narrative Technique in Chrétien de Troyes* (1988); Peter Noble studies *Love and Marriage in Chrétien de Troyes* (1982) and concludes, not surprisingly, that Chrétien was a strong supporter of conjugal love, disapproving of adultery. Katalin Halász acknowledges her debt to Paul Zumthor's *Poétique médiévale* and Erich Köhler's study of customs in her *Structures narratives chez Chrétien de Troyes* (1980), in which she concentrates largely on *Erec et Enide* and *Yvain*, while Donald Maddox proposes a detailed and subtle post-Köhlerian reading of custom in Chrétien's work as a whole in *The Arthurian Romances of Chrétien de Troyes: Once and Future Fictions* (1991). Useful guides to the individual romances have been provided in the Grant and Cutler series "Critical Guides to French Texts": *Erec et Enide* by Glyn S. Burgess (1984), *Cligés* by Lucie Polak (1982), *Yvain* by Tony Hunt (1986), and *Perceval* by Keith Busby (study, 1993); there is as yet no volume devoted to *Lancelot*. Although introductory in nature, these studies nevertheless contain much that is of interest to the specialist reader of Chrétien. Joan Grimbert's *"Yvain" dans le miroir* (1988) is a major study, which shows how the romance is predicated on what she calls an "adversative structure," constantly challenging the audience to respond, creating ambiguity and questions as it proceeds. Mention should further be made

---

[5] The computer also promises much in the field of stemmatics, but the results to date have been somewhat disappointing. Cf. Dees (1988) and van Mulken (*Manuscript Tradition*, 1993; and in Busby, Nixon, Stones, Walters 1993).

of Emmanuèle Baumgartner's perceptive monograph on *Lancelot* and *Yvain* (1992), which examines how these two romances echo each other and deal in different ways to some of the basic concerns of romance, such as love and adventure.

The most important recent general study of French Arthurian verse romance is almost certainly Beate Schmolke-Hasselmann's *Der arthurische Versroman von Chrestien bis Froissart* (1980), which rewrites a part of medieval literary history and invites us to redraw the literary and linguistic map of the late twelfth and thirteenth centuries.[6] Drawing on and refining the work of scholars such as Erich Köhler and Hans Robert Jauß, Schmolke-Hasselmann examines the reception of Chrétien in the "epigonal romances," i.e., the verse romances written in his wake. She concludes that Arthurian romance had a special, often political, significance for the highest social classes in Anglo-Angevin society, and that its audience was formed by a limited number of aficionados who knew Chrétien's works in great detail. This study also has the great merit of freeing post-Chrétien verse romance from the tiresome critical practice of odious comparison with the works of the master and assessing it on its own terms. The epigones react consciously to Chrétien's *oeuvre*, adapting it to meet the needs and tastes of their own audiences. The evolution of verse romance is marked by both continuity and disruption, depending on the precise nature of the epigonal response. Schmolke-Hasselmann has also published a number of important articles (1980–84) on related topics. Similar critical concerns inform Busby's *Gauvain in Old French Literature* (Busby 1980), and the two-volume *The Legacy of Chrétien de Troyes* (Lacy, Kelly, Busby 1987–88). Numerous articles have also examined in detail the *Rezeptionsgeschichte* of Chrétien's work in particular thirteenth-century works. Claude Lachet (1992) has produced a thorough study of *Sone de Nansay*, a romance of 21,000 lines dated 1270–80, and even the "last Arthurian romance," Froissart's *Meliador*, has been the center of some recent attention which seeks to situate it in its own time and as part of Froissart's *oeuvre* as well as within the continuum of Arthurian

---

[6] We feel obliged here to make the statutory lament about scholars' failure to assimilate work in German. Had Schmolke-Hasselmann's book been written in English or French, it would doubtless have been as seminal as it deserves to be. An English translation will soon be published by Cambridge University Press.

romance (Dembowski 1980, 1983, 1986; Schmolke-Hasselmann 1984; Bouchet 1991; Wolfzettel 1991). *Meliador,* along with *Le Chevalier du papegau, Ysaïe le triste,* and *Perceforest,* is also studied in a major contribution to our understanding of Arthurian romance (verse and prose) in the fourteenth century by Jane Taylor (1987); Taylor stresses the need for authors in this final phase of the evolution of the genre to integrate the *matière de Bretagne* into a pseudo-historical corpus and to devise the means of escaping from the straitjacket of tradition while at the same time using stock motifs, themes, and topoi provided by the genre.

With the completion in 1983 of Roach's Grail *Continuations,* the way was open for a minor surge in studies of these extraordinary texts. Corin Corley in particular has carried out detailed textual and philological work on the Second *Continuation,* defining its precise parameters (1982) and confirming its authorship by Wauchier de Denain, author of a prose version of the *Vies des Pères* (1984). A thoroughly detailed exposition of these and other issues, followed by a glossary of the Second *Continuation* is contained in Corley 1987, the published version of the author's dissertation. A major study of the Chrétien's *Perceval* and the First *Continuation* by Guy Vial (1987), unfortunately incomplete, was seen through the press by Jean Rychner after the author's premature death. After having proposed a salvation-based reading of Chrétien's romance, Vial considers the bewildering divergences between the various redactions of the First *Continuation*; unfortunately, no version of a planned third part of Vial's planned book, a comparative study of Chrétien and the first continuator, was found among his papers. Monumental is the only word that can be used to describe Pierre Gallais's four-volume *thèse d'état, L'Imaginaire d'un romancier français de la fin du XII*' *siècle: Description raisonnée, comparée et commentée de la "Continuation-Gauvain"* (1988–89), in which the author presents the results of a lifetime's study of the First *Continuation.* From consideration of the quality of each manuscript copy to stylistic analysis, there is little that is not discussed; all study of the First *Continuation* must henceforth begin here. The late John L. Grigsby also investigated Chrétien's legacy and the reception of his aesthetic in the *Continuations* in two perceptive articles (1987, 1988), and Matilda T. Bruckner distills a poetics of continuation from the same corpus (1993). Filippo Salmeri has published the only book-length study to date of Manessier's *Continuation*, concentrating on the religious symbolism and moral problems (1984).

Study of the verse Tristan romances has gone on unabated, but space permits mention here of only a few major studies. The best introduction to this complex matter is now possibly Emmanuèle Baumgartner's densely written *Tristan et Iseut: de la légende aux récits en vers* (1987). This book was clearly written for the French student audience, and two more volumes in the Grant and Cutler Critical Guides series fulfill a similar function for Anglophones, although their approaches are somewhat more traditional than that of Baumgartner. Peter Noble has studied Béroul and the Berne *Folie* (1982) and Geoffrey Bromiley, Thomas and the Oxford *Folie* (1986); the pairings Béroul-*Folie* Berne and Thomas-*Folie* Oxford have long been a critical commonplace and correspond to the "version commune / version courtoise" contradistinction. Also important is Merritt Blakeslee's *Love's Masks: Identity, Intertextuality and Meaning in the Old French Tristan Poems* (1989), a thorough examination of the central figure of Tristan in his manifold guises; central to Blakeslee's purpose is the elucidation of meaning generated by the process of continual rewriting of the story by a succession of authors. Other studies devoted to the Tristan romances in general are discussed below as examples of mythological and psychoanalytical approaches to medieval romance (Walter 1990; Huchet 1990). The *Tristan menestrel* episode from Gerbert de Montreuil's *Continuation* of Chrétien's *Perceval* has been the object of studies by Busby (1983) and by Jonna Kjær (1990).

Interest in the epigonal verse romances, the *Continuations* of *Perceval*, and the Tristan romances has been matched by the growth of critical studies of the prose romances, and has also been facilitated by the availability of reliable editions. Until quite recently, only *La Queste del saint Graal* and *La Mort le roi Artu* had been the object of much critical attention, thanks no doubt to the editions of Pauphilet and Frappier, to the forbidding length of the *Prose Lancelot* and the *Prose Tristan*, and to the disconcerting complexity of their manuscript transmission. Four scholars have dominated the field: Elspeth Kennedy, Fanni Bogdanow (both students of Eugène Vinaver), Alexandre Micha, and Emmanuèle Baumgartner. It is difficult to overestimate the insights that their scholarship has provided into a complex, misunderstood, and quite crucially important part of French Arthurian tradition. First-hand knowledge of the manuscripts has led to considerable emphasis being placed on the roles of scribes and compilers in the genesis of the prose romances. Kennedy's edition was followed in 1986 by a major study of the *Prose Lancelot, Lancelot and the Grail*, while Micha published *Essais sur le Lancelot-Graal* (1987), and *Etude sur le "Merlin" de Robert de Boron* (1980). Much of Bogdanow's meticulous scholarship leading up to her edition has been devoted to the unraveling of the textual tradition of the Post-Vulgate *Roman du Graal*. Baumgartner's important 1975 thesis on the *Prose Tristan* was followed in 1990 by *La Harpe et l'épée: tradition et renouvellement dans le "Tristan en prose."* Colette-Anne van Coolput-Storms's study of the reception of the Grail romances in the *Prose Tristan* (1986) draws directly and indirectly on the work of these scholars. Although Sommer's edition of the *Livre d'Artus* is the only one to date, a number of studies of the text have appeared, for example, by Marie-José Bayard (1985) and Busby (1991).

Emmanuèle Baumgartner has also demonstrated the importance of the Biblical paradigm in the construction and meaning of the prose romances. *L'Arbre et le pain: essai sur la "Queste del saint Graal"* (1981) shows how romance is predicated on scriptural patterns, and paves the way for Michèle Szkilnik's *L'Archipel du graal: Etude de l'"Estoire del saint Graal"* (1991), an important study of one of the least well-known parts of the Vulgate Cycle. Francesco Zambon has also written on Biblical patterns in the *Queste* (e.g., Zambon 1989). Awareness of these same concerns informs E. Jane Burns's important study of the Vulgate (1985) which also stresses notions of writing, rewriting, and the importance of the narrative voice of "li contes." More specialized studies of narrative technique in the prose romances are by Baumgartner ("Techniques," 1987) and Burns (1990); Carol Chase (1986) and Frank Brandsma (1989, 1990, 1991) have pursued the study of the important device of "entrelacement" in the prose romances. The state of studies in the prose romances is radically different from what it was a quarter of a century ago; vastly improved and more sophisticated, it has finally come of age.

Scholarship of this period on both prose and verse romance generally reflects the influence of notions of *mouvance* as developed by Paul Zumthor, according to which the medieval text is fundamentally unstable, moving in both space and time. The practical consequence of this is that no two versions of the same text are identical and indeed frequently exhibit major differences. The *Continuations* of Chrétien's *Perceval* illustrate this point perfectly, as do the various textual states of most of the prose romances, the *Prose Tristan* being a particularly clear case in point. Related to *mouvance* is the concept of *intertextuality*, which views each individual work as part of a larger whole, the intertext; intertextual relationships can be either general or specific. The well-known links between Chrétien's *Lancelot* and *Yvain*, for example, may be viewed in an intertextual perspective, as can Chrétien's response to the Tristan legend, or the rewriting of Chrétien's *Lancelot* in the Vulgate or of his *oeuvre* in the epigonal romances. The basic advantage of such an approach is that it frees scholars from the somewhat restrictive and vague notion of "influence" of one text on another. Important work has been done in this area by Uitti ("Intertextuality," 1980), Bruckner (1987, 1993), and Wolfzettel (1990).

The writing of romance is also conditioned by a rhetorical process governed by the "rules" and prescriptions of the medieval arts of poetry, part of what could be viewed as the literary theory of the Middle Ages. No one has done more to sensitize us to the crucial role played by rhetoric than Douglas Kelly, much of whose work has been devoted to French Arthurian romance in both verse and prose. Kelly's work also shows that while in some respects Arthurian romance obeys its own rules, in others it is part of the mainsteam of vernacular narrative fiction. From his first major study of Chrétien's *Lancelot* (1966) through a series of major articles (e.g., 1978; "Invention," 1984; "Rhetoric," 1984b; 1990) to his landmark study on *The Art of Medieval French Romance* (1992), Kelly has gone beyond the simple search for examples of, say, the prescriptions of Geoffrey of Vinsauf's *Poetria Nova* in vernacular texts, and demonstrated how the precepts of Latin rhetoric lie at the very basis of romance structure and how they evolve in the twelfth and thirteenth centuries within the corpus of romances.

Although few would deny its importance, the relevance of the wider Latin cultural context for a better understanding of Chrétien de Troyes's work has received far less attention that might have been expected. Eugene Vance (1986, 1987) has explored the contribution of logic through the *trivium* to Chrétien's poetics in the transition from a Latinate culture to a vernacular one. Jeanne A. Nightingale has also concentrated on Chrétien in a number of articles ("Chrétien," 1990; "Mirror," 1990; "Romances,"1990) devoted to situating courtly romance within the broader tradition of mythographical discourse, particularly Macrobius and Ovid. The implications of this type of approach have yet to be fully explored and assimilated by scholars.

An approach that has largely ceased to be practiced in recent times is that developed by D.W. Robertson and others, known as the "patristic-exegetical method," according to which medieval literature had to be read necessarily in the light of Augustinian doctrine to generate a meaning pertaining to the concept of *caritas*. While the 1970s produced Jacques Ribard's reading of Chrétien's *Lancelot* (1972) and Tom Artin's study of *Erec et Enide* and *Yvain* (1974), scholars have not pursued this type of work; only Ribard has continued in this vein ("Pour une interprétation," 1984, and 1989). Instead, the undoubted messianic associations of the Arthurian hero and the possibilities of allegorical readings of Arthurian *aventure* have become integrated into other methods such as that which informs the studies of Baumgartner and Szkilnik mentioned above.

If patristic exegesis searches for a "serious" moral message in literature, scholarship has become much more aware in recent years of the possibilities of ironic, parodic, and burlesque intentions on the part of romance authors and the concomitant awareness on the part of their intended audiences. Suzanne Fleischman published a fine study of "chivalry askew" in the Occitan romance of *Jaufre* (1981), but the major work on parody in romance is no doubt Kathryn Gravdal's *Vilain and Courtois: Transgressive Parody in French Literature of the Twelfth and Thirteenth Centuries* (1989), one chapter of which is devoted to Guillaume le Clerc's *Fergus* and its (parodic) relation to earlier tradition. Although only one chapter is directly concerned with Arthurian romance, the method used and the use of "interpretants" may provide a model for further study. Apart from specific studies of parody, the acceptance on the part of scholars that it is widely present in Arthurian romance has meant that it is equally widely discussed.

Whereas work on the rhetoric of romance and its Latin background has stressed the learned nature of the genre, some scholars have moved in the other direction and underlined the "orality" of the genre. Recognition of orality in medieval narrative is not new, and Paul Zumthor's *La Poésie et la voix dans la civilisation médiévale* (1984) has been seminal. Joseph J. Duggan has considered such matters as improvisation, oral performance, and memory in a pair of related articles ("Oral Performance," 1989; "Performance," 1989), but more provocative and radical has been the work of Evelyn Birge Vitz on the Tristan romances and Chrétien (1986, 1987, 1990). The octosyllabic rhyming couplet, the primary form of French Arthurian verse romance, is seen as a preliterary medium, and while not all verse romances were orally composed, some were, and a reevaluation of the critically commonplace dichotomy "oral–written" is urgently called for. Vitz's most controversial suggestion is that Chrétien de Troyes was a minstrel, not a *clerc*, and that he conceived his work as popular entertainment rather than as written literature. The view has not found wide acceptance.

A number of important studies of specific figures or types in Arthurian romance have appeared. Aileen Ann MacDonald (1990) has provided a useful treatment of the figure of Merlin in thirteenth-century prose romances (Robert de Boron, Vulgate and Post-Vulgate Cycles), considering his role as womanizer, kingmaker, and prophet; the three central Merlin texts are interrelated and seen as products of collaboration between royal ladies, their court poets, and the religious of the Fontevrist order. More all-encompassing is Marie-Luce Chênerie's *Le Chevalier errant dans les romans arthuriens en vers des XIIᵉ et XIIIᵉ siècles* (1986) which examines, in the traditional manner of a *thèse d'état*, all aspects of the presentation and role of the errant knight in the verse romance corpus. The book also constitutes a thorough description of the world of Arthurian romance (inhabitants, geography, spaces, sentiment, etc.) as it pertains to the figure of the knight. The *fée* has been studied in important books by Laurence Harf-Lancner (*Les Fées*, 1984), Pierre Gallais (1992), and Jean-Claude Aubailly (1986). These three works are typical of a kind of Arthurian scholarship currently being produced in France in that they are concerned with mythological and folkloric material that they view from various anthropological and psychoanalytical perspectives. Harf-Lancner's thorough study traces the birth in the Middle Ages of what she considers a new mythological figure, the *fée*, before going on to explore its articulation in figures such as Morgan and Mélusine; a final part of the book considers the rationalization and christianization of this mythological and folkloric material in medieval literature. Although not restricted to Arthurian romance, this study is particularly important for its treatment of the figure of Morgan and of the widespread "fairy mistress" theme. Gallais's study, informed by the works of Jung, Bachelard, and Gilbert Durand, seeks to establish the figure of the *fée* as an archetype of the feminine *anima* and the rise of the *fée* in literature as an exaltation of feminine values. In addition to its basic thesis, this book, like that of Harf-Lancner, is also noteworthy for much incidental discussion of romance themes and motifs. Similar conclusions are reached by Aubailly, whose book is concerned mainly with the Breton *lais*, two of which, Marie's *Lanval* and the anonymous *Tyolet*, are specifically Arthurian: Jung's principle of *anima*, the collective idea of woman hidden in man's subconscious, is rehabilitated, revealing the restoration of a lost cosmological harmony.

Inseparable from the *fée* and related figures is the concept of the *merveilleux*, the subject of studies by Daniel Poirion (1981) and Francis Dubost (1991). Three chapters (IV on the *lais bretons*, V on Arthurian romance, and VI on the thirteenth century) of Poirion's volume, *Le Merveilleux dans la littérature française du moyen âge*, in the "Que sais-je" series, are devoted largely or in part to Arthurian texts. This short monograph is intended as an introductory overview of the subject and provides an excellent starting point. Dubost's *thèse d'état* is a comprehensive study of "aspects fantastiques" in twelfth- and thirteenth-century French literature, mainly romances (many of which are Arthurian) and *chansons de geste*. According to Dubost, the disturbing and inexplicable that define the *fantastique* are generated by "alterity." The spaces from which God is absent are likely to be the *loci* of supernatural manifestations and to be inhabited by all manner of fantastic creatures: *chevaliers faés*, dragons, *bestes glastissants*, etc., the Devil, and Merlin. This book should certainly be read in conjunction with MacDonald's previously mentioned study of Merlin by those wishing to assess the role of the enchanter in Arthurian romance. Jean-Marie Fritz (*Le Discours*, 1992) has published an innovative and interdisciplinary study of madness in twelfth and thirteenth-century French literature, subtitled "Etude comparée des discours littéraire, médical, juridique et théologique de la folie." Among the Arthurian romances discussed are Chrétien's *Yvain*, the *Folies Tristan*, the *Prose Lancelot*, the *Prose Tristan* and *Ysaïe le Triste*.

Clearly, many of the studies mentioned in the two previous paragraphs deal, both directly and indirectly, with matters of folklore. More avowedly "folkloristic" in approach is an important article by Anita Guerreau[-Jalabert] (1983) on Chrétien's romances and their thematic analogues in folktales.[7] While acknowledging the value of the Stith Thompson *Motif Index*, Guerreau reveals its shortcomings for the medievalist and revises Thompson's concept of "motif." This is achieved by the implementation of a new method of internal analysis and comparative study of the romances, taking into account their meaning in relation to their sources and cultural context. Stith Thompson's *Motif Index* nevertheless remains the basic model for Guerreau-Jalabert's *Index des motifs narratifs dans les romans arthuriens français en vers (XII<sup>e</sup>-XIII<sup>e</sup> siècles) [Motif-Index of French Arthurian Verse Romances (XIIth-XIIIth Centuries)]* (1992). In the introduction, Guerreau-Jalabert discusses problems of classification, the inevitability of subjectivity, and the impossibility of categorical definition. The general motif index based on Thompson is followed by a motif analysis of each of the twenty-seven romances in the corpus and an alphabetical motif index. This will henceforth be an indispensable reference work for students of Arthurian narrative. E.H. Ruck's *An Index of Themes and Motifs in Twelfth-Century Arthurian Poetry* (1991) is more restricted in its corpus (Wace's *Brut*, Chrétien's work, the verse *Tristan* texts, five *lais*, *Le Bel Inconnu*, *Le Chevalier à l'épée*, and *La Mule sans frein*), but more wide-ranging in that it does not limit itself to narrative motifs; the categories are in essence similar to those used by Mario Roques and Alexandre Micha in the appendices to their editions of Chrétien's *Erec et Enide*, *Yvain*, and *Cligés* in the Classiques Français du Moyen Age.[8]

Joël Grisward has extended his Dumézil-inspired studies of the Old French *chanson de geste* (1981) into the domain of Arthurian romance (1983, 1985, 1988), showing how the Indo-European trifunctional

---

[7] It is apparently no longer fashionable to "do" Propp. Edina Bozóky (1984) is one of the few scholars to have carried out (modified) Proppian analyses of Arthurian romance, in this case of Renaut de Beaujeu's *Le Bel Inconnu*.

[8] A note by Roques at the end of the CFMA *Lancelot* explains the absence of such an index in that volume; Félix Lecoy did not include one in his *Perceval*.

system has been preserved in the stories of Arthur's conception and accession to the throne, and in various transformations of the Grail legend (Chrétien, the *Continuations*, Robert de Boron). Although not drawing directly on Dumézil's work, Gaël Milin's study of Aarne-Thompson 782, *Le Roi Marc aux oreilles de cheval* (1991) underlines the associations between the horse and royalty in Indo-European society and suggests that the episode formed by ll. 1303-50 of Béroul's *Tristan* is based on a Celtic tale. This hypothesis allows Milin to show how Béroul modified a traditional tale to fit into the context of his romance.

Milin's work is also illustrative of what might be termed a "new Celticism" on the part of some French, and notably, Breton, scholars. Gwénolé Le Menn's *La Femme au sein d'or* (1985) compares Breton folksongs collected recently with the legend of St. Enori and with the Caradoc episode from the First *Continuation* of Chrétien's *Perceval*. Le Menn concludes that while Welsh tradition may have been the closest source of the romance, the tale can be traced back to a Breton source. The unity and interrelation of Celtic cultures is also stressed in Le Menn's work. Another scholar who has made significant contributions to the study of the Celtic elements in Arthurian romance is Jean-Claude Lozac'hmeur. Together with Shigemi Sasaki (1982) Lozac'hmeur returns to R.S. Loomis's earlier hypothesis concerning the relations between Celtic tales of vengeance and sovereignty and Chrétien's *Perceval*, concluding, against Frappier, that Loomis was in essence correct. Lozac'hmeur's article on Gauvain's adventures in Chrétien's *Perceval* (1985) restates these conclusions, before ingeniously examining the Celtic nature of this part of the narrative, finally justifying its position in the romance as a whole. Similar concerns inform a third article (1987) in which Lozac'hmeur also underlines the esoteric, Indo-European, nature of the origins of the Grail legend and its relationship to Indo-European rites of royal initiation.

The theories of Claude Lévi-Strauss are used by Jean-Guy Gouttebroze (1982, 1984) to elucidate lineage ties in Chrétien's work, notably in the *Perceval*. Perceval is seen as an "anti-Œdipus" who, by refusing to ask the question at the Grail castle, avoids the danger of incest; the romance is seen as dealing with issues such as stability and instability of lineage, clan, and ultimately royalty. Another type of psychoanalytical approach is that exemplified in Charles Méla's substantial *La Reine et le Graal: La "conjointure" dans les romans du*

*Graal, de Chrétien de Troyes au "Livre de Lancelot"* (1984). Largely inspired by postmodernist theory and the work of Lacan, Méla eschews a chronological approach to the Grail romances in favor of a method that elucidates the "secret life" of the texts, intertextual and intratextual. By examining themes such as the absent father, castration, and incest, Méla demonstrates that the itinerary of the hero in the Grail texts corresponds to the manner of their writing and of their reception by the reader. Méla's work was enthusiastically received by Jean-Charles Huchet (1985), who further argues that the homologous structures that exist between psychoanalysis and medieval romance render each capable of elucidating the other: Méla uses psychoanalysis to read medieval romance while Henri Rey-Flaud in *La Névrose courtoise* (1983) employs medieval romance to refine the results of psychoanalysis. Huchet's study of the Tristan romances, *Tristan et le sang de l'écriture* (1990) is an ingenious and, some might say, subjective reading of the same persuasion.

The Tristan romances are also studied by Philippe Walter (1990) in one of a number of original recent studies on the mythological substructure of Arthurian romance. For Walter, the relationship between the surviving Tristan texts is less important than their ability to reveal the myths, beliefs, and superstitions proper to Indo-European society. In particular, the Tristan story shares features with the story of Cinderella. Such superstitions include astrological ones, and Walter has ingeniously proposed (1988) that Yvain becomes "le Chevalier au Lion" because he is under the influence of Sirius ("Canicule," the Dog Star), a bright star of the constellation Canis Major visible in the summer sky (22 July–23 August) when the sun rejoins the sign of Leo; Sirius brings torrid heat, plague, and melancholic rage in "the dog days of Summer." Walter's *thèse d'état, La Mémoire du temps: Fêtes et calendriers de Chrétien de Troyes à la "Mort Artu"* (1989) is at the same time an analysis of the feasts that punctuate the narratives of Arthurian romance ("nuptial," "dynastique," "curial"), and an attempt to recover their mythological and archaic foundations. The method chosen necessarily entails comparison of seemingly quite disparate and distant cultures. The relationship of this type of study to those of Grisward, Lozac'hmeur, and Milin will be apparent.

In the USA, Peter Haidu (1983) and Eugene Vance (1986) have both attempted poststructuralist, deconstructionist, analyses of Chrétien de Troyes, which attempt however to restore a historical dimension. Haidu in particular, in an article on *Yvain*, explicitly aims to show, contrary to de Man's contention, that deconstruction and historicity are not mutually exclusive. The episodes of the hero's meeting with the hermit, and the Château de Pesme Aventure are seen as illustrating contemporary economic models of exchange. Similar concerns inform Vance's article, which discusses Yvain's crisis, his relationship with Laudine, and the machinations of Lunete in the context of a new view of love as an economic transaction. One chapter of Judith Kellogg's *Medieval Artistry and Exchange: Economic Institutions, Society, and Literary Form in Old French Narrative* (1989) is also devoted to Chrétien de Troyes, whose romances are said to conceal only skimpily the cracks appearing in the outmoded feudal armor of twelfth-century aristocracy. This type of scholarship clearly pursues another path opened up by the important earlier work of Erich Köhler.

French Arthurian romance has naturally been the object of feminist criticism in the 1980s and 1990s. Particularly active in this field have been E. Jane Burns and Roberta L. Krueger, who co-edited a special issue of *Romance Notes* (1985) on the topic of "Courtly Ideology and Woman's Place in Medieval French Literature." Burns's *Bodytalk: When Women Speak in Old French Literature* (1993) is a polemical examination of gender issues raised by the representation of women in texts inspired by misogynous male imagination and fantasy; foremost among these are Chrétien's *Erec et Enide* and Béroul's *Tristan*. Through the speech attributed to them, female protagonists can subvert and restructure the norms of female identity as they are usually perceived in romance. Krueger focuses on the relation between the romances and their female audiences in her *Women Readers and the Ideology of Gender in Old French Verse Romance* (1993). She suggests that works such as *Yvain, Lancelot, Le Roman de Silence, Le Chevalier à l'épée*, and *La Vengeance Raguidel* invite their readers to criticize and resist gender roles at the same time as they appear to present idealized models of behaviour. Current issues in gender studies also inform articles on "The Construction of Manhood in Arthurian Literature," a special section of vol. III of *The Arthurian Yearbook*; particularly relevant to French romance are the articles by Susan Crane (1993) and Gary Ferguson (1993).

*Manuscript Studies*

One of the more noticeable trends in medieval literary scholarship in recent years has been the renewed attention being paid to manuscripts. This has not only resulted in the new editions discussed at the outset of this chapter, but more especially in consideration of the manuscript context of the romances and what can be learned from it. Such studies begin to proliferate in the mid-1980s and are by and large concerned with two, related, areas: the roles of scribes and compilers, and the relationship between text and image. Lori Walters's article on the insertion of Chrétien's romances into the text of Wace's *Brut* in MS. Paris, BN, fr. 1450 (1985) has already become a classic, comparable to Elspeth Kennedy's earlier piece on the manuscripts of the *Prose Lancelot*, in which she coined the phrase "the scribe as editor" (1972); Walters has also examined BN, fr. 1433 (Chrétien, *L'Atre périlleux*, etc.) as a "super romance" formed by the conjoining of originally independent works (1991). Although Sylvia Huot's book, *From Song to Book: The Poetics of Writing in Old French Lyric and Lyrical Narrative Poetry* (1987) is not directly concerned with Arthurian literature, it does deal with some romance codices and is a landmark in Old French studies generally. It is an excellent example of what close examination of manuscripts can reveal about the literature they contain.

The physical layout of particular manuscripts or groups of manuscripts has been the object of a number of studies: Hans Runte (1989) has studied the structuring of Chrétien's romances through the positioning of decorated capitals (see also Middleton in Busby, Nixon, Stones, Walters 1993), Geneviève Hasenohr (1990) has discussed the various types of *mise en page* of verse romance manuscripts, while Emmanuèle Baumgartner ("La 'Première page,'" 1987) and Véronique Roland (1991) have commented on the opening-page layout of manuscripts of the *Prose Tristan* and *Merlin* respectively and their implication for the perception of the romances.

Sandra Hindman (1991, 1994) has argued that certain of the romances in which Chrétien's romances are preserved were written for the Picard aristocracy in the latter half of the thirteenth century. Basing her argument on the scenes chosen for illustration, Hindman suggests that the manuscripts reflect a particular view of chivalry and its social

function. Keith Busby (1988, rpt. in Busby, Nixon, Stones, Walters
1993) and Angelica Rieger (1989) have looked at the relationship
between word and image in the *Perceval* manuscripts and have shown
that the visual reception of the romance confirms what can be deduced
from more strictly textual sources; Busby pursued the same line of
inquiry for the manuscripts of the *Continuations* ("Text, Miniature and
Rubric," in Busby, Nixon, Stones, Walters 1993). Alison Stones (1991)
has provided a basic iconographical update to the Loomises' basic book
on *The Arthurian Legends in Medieval Art* (1938) bringing to bear her
unrivaled knowledge of vernacular manuscript illumination. Although
manuscripts of Gottfried's *Tristan* are richly illustrated, there are few
representations of the verse tradition in French. Tony Hunt (1987),
however, offers the first analysis of a set of drawings based on
Thomas's version in MS. London, British Library, Add. 11619, which
seem to underscore the moral nature of Thomas's text.

The most important recent event in Chrétien studies is doubtless the
monumental, two-volume *The Manuscripts of Chrétien de Troyes*
(Busby, Nixon, Stones, Walters 1993).[9] An international, collaborative
effort, this work presents a complete catalogue of all Chrétien
manuscripts, a photographic inventory of all miniatures, types of
decoration, and scribal hands, along with numerous studies by literary
scholars, art historians, palaeographers, codicologists, etc. The essays
it contains illustrate all of the directions discerned in the previous three
paragraphs, and more besides. Space does not permit a full description
of its contents here, but in addition to lists, catalogues, and descriptions
of the manuscripts, there are essays on textual issues by Tony Hunt,
Margot van Mulken, and Keith Busby; studies of the manuscript transmission and presentation of *Cligés* by Stewart Gregory and Claude
Luttrell, of *Erec et Enide* by Françoise Gasparri, Geneviève Hasenohr,
and Christine Ruby; of the location and significance of colored capitals
in the *Erec et Enide* manuscripts by Roger Middleton; on pen-
flourishing in some Champenois manuscripts by Patricia Stirnemann;
of the artistic context of the illustrated manuscripts by Alison Stones;
on the Pierre Sala *Yvain* manuscript by Elizabeth Burin; on opening
miniatures by Lori Walters; on the iconography of *Perceval* and the

---

[9] The editor, in the presence of authorial modesty, has provided the specific
characterization of this study as "important" and "monumental." (N.J.L.)

*Continuations* by Keith Busby, Angelica Rieger, Lori Walters, and Emmanuèle Baumgartner; and on fantastic elements of the illustrations by Laurence Harf-Lancner.[10] Important sections by Roger Middleton deal in great detail with the history of all the manuscripts and what is known about their former owners.[11]

## Conclusion

If we have come full-circle and returned to the matter of manuscripts, it is because they are the raw material of Old French studies, Arthurian and non-Arthurian. They have yet much to reveal about the manner in which literature was read in the Middle Ages; and without them none of the extraordinary wealth of scholarship reviewed above would be possible. It will be clear, then, that scholarship in Old French Arthurian literature is in a healthy, vigorous, and robust state. Its very diversity reflects not only the fascination it continues to exercise over scholars but also the passion with which those same scholars debate what they regard as fundamental issues of medieval literary studies. For that alone we should be grateful.

---

[10] All of these items 1993.

[11] Middleton's previous studies on the reception of Chrétien in the eighteenth century ("Le Grand d'Aussy's *Erec*," 1986; "Chrétien's *Erec*," 1987) should also be mentioned here as examples of yet another fruitful direction of Chrétien studies.

# Bibliography

*Bibliographies*

Burgess, Glyn S. *Marie de France: An Analytic Bibliography. Supplement No. 1*. London: Grant and Cutler, 1986.

Kelly, Douglas. *Chrétien de Troyes: An Analytic Bibliography*. London: Grant and Cutler, 1976. [Supplement in progress]

Pickford, C.E., and R.W. Last, eds. *The Arthurian Bibliography*. 2 vols. Ipswich: Brewer, 1981–83.

Reiss, Edmund, Louise Horner Reiss, and Beverly Taylor. *Arthurian Legend and Literature: An Annotated Bibliography. Vol. I: The Middle Ages*. New York: Garland, 1984.

Shirt, David J. *The Old French Tristan Poems: A Bibliographical Guide*. London: Grant and Cutler, 1980.

Vielliard, Françoise, and Jacques Monfrin. *Manuel bibliographique de la littérature française du moyen âge de Robert Bossuat: troisième supplément (1960–1980)*. 2 vols. Paris: Editions du CNRS, 1986–91. [For Matter of Britain, see I, 237–392, and II, 702–706.]


*Editions*

Adams, Alison, ed. *Yder, The Romance of*. Woodbridge: Brewer; Totowa, NJ: Biblio, 1983.

Aubailly, Jean-Claude, ed. and trans. *Lancelot ou le chevalier de la Charrette*, by Chrétien de Troyes. Paris: Garnier-Flammarion, 1991.

Baumgartner, Emmanuèle, and Ian Short, eds.. *La geste du roi Arthur*. Paris: Union Générale d'Editions, 1993.

Berthelot, Anne, ed. *Les Prophesies de Merlin (Cod. Bodmer 116)*. Cologny-Geneva: Bodmer, 1992.

Bogdanow, Fanni, ed. *Le Roman du Graal*. 3 vols. Paris: SATF, 1994.

Braet, Herman, and Guy Raynaud de Lage, eds. *Tristran et Iseut: poème du XIIe siècle*, by Béroul. 2 vols. Louvain: Peeters, 1989.

Busby, Keith, ed. *Le Roman de Perceval ou Le conte du graal: édition critique d'après tous les manuscrits*, by Chrétien de Troyes. Tübingen: Niemeyer, 1993.

Carroll, Carleton W., ed. and trans., with an introduction by William W. Kibler. *Erec et Enide*, by Chrétien de Troyes. New York: Garland, 1987.

Cerquiglini, Bernard, ed. *Le Roman du graal: manuscrit de Modène*, by Robert de Boron. Paris: Union Générale d'Edition, 1981.

Curtis, Renée L., ed. *Le Roman de Tristan en prose*. 3 vols. Woodbridge: Brewer, 1985.

Foulet, Alfred, and Karl D. Uitti, eds. and trans. *Le Chevalier de la charrette (Lancelot)*, by Chrétien de Troyes. Paris: Bordas, 1989.

Fresco, Karen, ed., and Colleen P. Donagher, trans; Margaret P. Hasselman, music ed. *Le Bel Inconnu (Li biaus descouneüs; The Fair Unknown)*, by Renaut de Bâgé. New York: Garland, 1992.

Frescoln, Wilson, ed. *The Romance of Fergus*, by Guillaume le Clerc. Philadelphia: Allen, 1982.

Fritz, Jean-Marie, ed. *Erec et Enide: édition critique d'après le ms. BN, fr. 1376*, by Chrétien de Troyes. Paris: Livre de Poche, 1992.

————, et al., eds. *Romans*, by Chrétien de Troyes. Paris: Livre de Poche, 1994. [Includes Jean-Marie Fritz, ed., *Erec et Enide*; Charles Méla and Olivier Collet, eds., *Cligès*; C. Méla, ed., *Le Chevalier de la Charrette* and *Le Conte du Graal*; David Hult, ed., *Le Chevalier au Lion*; Marie-Claire Zai, ed., *Chansons*; O. Collet, ed., *Philomena*]

Giacchetti, André, ed. *Ysaÿe le triste: roman arthurien du moyen âge tardif.* Rouen-Maromme: Qualigraphie, 1989.

Gregory, Stewart, ed. *The Romance of Tristran*, by Béroul. Amsterdam: Rodopi, 1992.

————, ed. and trans. *Tristran*, by Thomas of Britain. New York: Garland, 1991.

————, and Claude Luttrell, eds. *Cligés*, by Chrétien de Troyes. Cambridge: Brewer, 1993.

Harf-Lancner, Laurence, ed. and trans. *Lais*, by Marie de France. Paris: Livre de Poche, 1990.

Kennedy, Elspeth, ed. *Lancelot do Lac: The Non-Cyclic Old French Prose Romance*. 2 vols. Oxford: Oxford University Press, 1980.

————, ed., and François Mosès, trans. *Lancelot du Lac*. 2 vols. Paris: Livre de Poche, 1991–93.

Kibler, William W., ed. and trans. *Lancelot, or The Knight of the Cart (Le chevalier de la charrete)*, by Chrétien de Troyes. New York: Garland, 1981.

————, ed. and trans. *The Knight with the Lion, or Yvain (Le chevalier au lion)*, by Chrétien de Troyes. New York: Garland, 1985.

Lacroix, Daniel, and Philippe Walter, ed. and trans. *Tristan et Iseult. Les poèmes français, la saga norroise*. Paris: Livre de poche,

1989. [Beroul: *Le Roman de Tristan*, pp. 21–231; *Folie Tristan d'Oxford*, pp. 233–281; *Folie Tristan de Berne*, pp. 283–311; Marie de France, *Lai du Chèvrefeuille*, pp. 313–319; "Tristan rossignol" in *Le Donnei des amants*, pp. 321–333; Thomas, *Le Roman de Tristan*, pp. 335–483; *La Saga de Tristan et Yseut*, pp. 495–664.]

Lacy, Norris J., ed. and trans. *The Romance of Tristran*, by Béroul. New York: Garland, 1989.

Lecoy, Félix, ed. *Le Roman de Tristan*, by Thomas. Paris: Champion, 1992.

Lévy, Claude M.L., ed. *Floriant et Florete ou Le chevalier qui la nef maine, Le roman de*. Ottawa: Editions de l'Université d'Ottawa, 1983.

Méla, Charles, ed. *Le conte du Graal ou le roman de Perceval: édition du ms. 354 de Berne*, by Chrétien de Troyes. Paris: Livre de Poche, 1990.

———, ed. *Le Chevalier de la charrette ou le roman de Lancelot: édition critique d'après tous les manuscrits existants*, by Chrétien de Troyes. Paris: Livre de Poche, 1992.

Ménard, Philippe, ed. *Tristan en prose*. Vol. I, ed. Philippe Ménard; Vol. II, ed. Marie-Luce Chênerie and Thierry Delcourt; Vol. III, ed. Gilles Roussineau; Vol. IV, ed. Jean-Claude Faucon; Vol. V, ed. Denis Lalande and Thierry Delcourt; Vol. VI, ed. Emmanuèle Baumgartner and Michèle Szkilnik; Vol. VII, ed. Danielle Queruel and Monique Santucci. Geneva: Droz, 1987– (publication is proceeding on a regular basis).

Micha, Alexandre, ed. *Lancelot: roman en prose du XIIIe siècle*. 9 vols. Geneva: Droz, 1978–83.

———, ed. *Merlin*, by Robert de Boron. Geneva: Droz, 1980.

————, ed. and trans. *Lais féeriques des XIIe et XIIIe siècles.* Paris: GF-Flammarion, 1992.

————, ed. and trans. *Lais,* by Marie de France. Paris: Garnier-Flammarion, 1994.

Mölk, Ulrich, and Irmgard Fischer, eds. *Lancelot en prose: Bonn, Universitätsbibliothek, Handschrift S526. Farbmicrofiche-Edition.* Literarhistorische Einführung von Ulrich Mölk, kodikologische Beschreibung von Irmgard Fischer. Munich: Lengenfelder, 1992.

O'Gorman, Richard, ed. *Joseph d'Arimathie: A Critical Edition of the Verse and Prose Versions,* by Robert de Boron. Toronto: Pontifical Institute of Medieval Studies, 1995.

Otaka, Yorio, ed. *Œuvres complètes,* by Marie de France. Tokyo: Kazama, 1987.

Payen, Jean-Charles, ed. and trans. *Tristan et Yseut: les "Tristans" en vers.* 2nd ed. Paris: Garnier, 1986.

Pickens, Rupert T., ed., and William W. Kibler, trans. *The Story of the Grail ("Li contes del graal"), or "Perceval,"* by Chrétien de Troyes. New York: Garland, 1990.

Poirion, Daniel, ed., with the collaboration of Anne Berthelot, Peter F. Dembowski, Sylvie Lefèvre, Karl D. Uitti, and Philippe Walter. *Œuvres complètes,* by Chrétien de Troyes. Bibliothèque de la Pléiade. Paris: Gallimard, 1994.

Roach, William, ed. *Continuations of the Old French "Perceval" of Chrétien de Troyes.* 5 vols. Philadelphia: University of Pennsylvania Press/American Philosophical Society, 1949-83.

————, ed., and Colette-Anne Van Coolput-Storms, trans. *Première Continuation de Perceval (Continuation-Gauvain): Texte du ms. L.* Paris: Livre de Poche, 1993.

Rousse, Michel, ed. and trans. *Le Chevalier au Lion*, by Chrétien de Troyes. Paris: Garnier-Flammarion, 1990.

————, ed. and trans. *Erec et Enide*, by Chrétien de Troyes. Paris: Garnier-Flammarion, 1994.

Roussineau, Gilles, ed. *Le Roman de Perceforest* Geneva: Droz; Part IV. 2 vols., 1987; Part III, 2 vols., 1988, 1991.

Taylor, Jane H.M., ed. *Le Roman de Perceforest*, Part I. Geneva: Droz, 1979.

Trachsler, Richard, ed. *Escanor*, by Girard d'Amiens. 2 vols. Geneva: Droz, 1994.

Warnke, Karl, ed., and Laurence Harf-Lancner, trans. *Lais*, by Marie de France. Paris: Livre de poche, 1990.

Winters, Margaret, ed. *Hunbaut*. Leiden: Brill, 1984.

Wright, Neil, ed. *The "Historia Regum Brittanie,"* by Geoffrey of Monmouth. Cambridge: Brewer, 1984.

Zink, Michel, ed., with Jean-Marie Fritz, Charles Méla, Olivier Collet, David F. Hult, and Marie-Claire Zai. *Romans*, by Chrétien de Troyes. Paris: Livre de Poche, 1994.

*Critical Studies*

Accarie, Maurice. "L'Eternel départ de Lancelot: roman clos et roman ouvert chez Chrétien de Troyes." In *Mélanges Alice Planche*, 1984, pp. 1–20.

Adams, Alison, Armel H. Diverres, Karen Stern, and Kenneth Varty, eds. *The Changing Face of Arthurian Romance: Essays on Arthurian Prose Romances Cedric E. Pickford*. Cambridge: Brewer, 1986.

Allen, Peter L., "The Ambiguity of Silence: Gender, Writing, and *Le roman de Silence.*" In Wasserman and Roney, eds., *Sign, Sentence, Discourse*, 1989, pp. 98–112.

Andrieu, Gabriel, and Jacques Piolle. *Perceval ou le conte du Graal de Chrétien de Troyes: concordancier complet des formes graphiques occurrentes d'après l'édition de M. Félix Lecoy.* Aix-en-Provence: CUERMA, 1976.

Armstrong, Grace M. "Rescuing the Lion from *Le chevalier au lion* to *La queste del saint graal.*" *Medium Ævum*, 61 (1992), 17–34.

Aronstein, Susan. "Chevaliers estre deüssiez: Power, Discourse, and the Chivalric in Chrétien's *Conte du graal.*" *Assays*, 6 (1991), 3–28.

Arrathoon, Leigh A., ed. *The Craft of Fiction: Essays in Medieval Poetics.* Rochester, MI: Solaris, 1984.

Arthur, Ross G. "The *Judicium Dei* in the *Yvain* of Chrétien de Troyes." *Romance Notes*, 28 (1987–88), 3–12.

Artin, Tom. *The Allegory of Adventure: Reading Chrétien's "Erec et Enide" and "Yvain".* Lewisburg, PA: Bucknell University Press, 1974.

Atanassov, Stoyan. "Les Modèles narratifs dans le *Tristan* de Thomas." In Foulon et al., eds., *Actes du 14e Congrès International Arthurien*, pp. 1–15.

Aubailly, Jean-Claude. *La Fée et le chevalier.* Paris: Champion, 1986.

———. "Plaidoyer pour une mythanalyse: le cas d'*Yvain*." *PRIS-MA*, 3, No. 1 (1987), 3–13.

Bartoli, Renata Anna. "Trinità celeste e trinità diabolica nella *Queste del saint graal.*" *Medioevo Romanzo*, 12 (1987), 89–102.

———. "Bipartition et tripartition dans la *Queste del saint graal*." *Cultura Neolatina*, 50 (1990), 195–208.

Baswell, Christopher, and William Sharpe, eds. *The Passing of Arthur: New Essays in Arthurian Tradition*. New York: Garland, 1988.

Baumgartner, Emmanuèle. *L'Arbre et le pain: essai sur "La Queste del saint graal."* Paris: CDU et SEDES, 1981.

———. "L'Ecriture romanesque et son modèle scripturaire: écriture et réécriture du graal." In *L'imitation: aliénation ou source de liberté*. Paris: Documentation Française, 1984, pp. 129–143.

———. "Remarques sur la prose du *Lancelot*." *Romania*, 105 (1984), 1–15.

———. "Luce del Gat et Hélie de Boron: le chevalier et l'écriture." *Romania*, 106 (1985), 326–340.

———. "La 'Première Page' dans les manuscrits du *Tristan en prose*." In *La présentation du livre: Actes du Colloque de Paris X-Nanterre (4–6 décembre 1985)*. Paris: Centre de Recherches du Département de Français de Paris X–Nanterre, 1987, pp. 51–62.

———. "Les Techniques narratives dans les romans en prose." In Lacy, Kelly, Busby, eds., *The Legacy of Chrétien de Troyes*, I, 1987, 167–190.

———. *Tristan et Iseut: de la légende aux récits en vers*. Paris: Presses Universitaires de France, 1987.

———. "L'Aventure dans le *Lancelot en prose*." In Dallapiazza and Schulze-Belli, eds., *Liebe und Aventiure im Artusroman des Mittelalters: Beiträge der Triester Tagung 1988*, 1990, pp. 93–108.

———. *La Harpe et l'épée: tradition et renouvellement dans le "Tristan" en prose*. Paris: CDU et SEDES, 1990.

————. "Retour des personnages et mise en prose de la fiction arthurienne au XIIIe siècle." *Bibliographical Bulletin of the International Arthurian Society*, 43 (1991), 297–314.

————. *Chrétien de Troyes: Yvain, Lancelot, la charrette et le lion.* Paris: Presses Universitaires de France, 1992.

————. "La Préparation à la *Queste del Saint Graal* dans le *Tristan* en prose." In Busby and Lacy, eds., *Conjunctures: Medieval Studies in Honor of Douglas Kelly*, 1994, 1-14.

Bauschke, Ricarda. "Auflösung des Artusromans und Defiktionalisierung im *Bel inconnu*: Renauts de Beaujeu Auseinandersetzung mit Chrétien de Troyes." *Zeitschrift für Französische Sprache und Literatur*, 102 (1992), 42–63. Expanded version in Mertens and Wolfzettel, eds., *Fiktionalität im Artusroman*, 1993, pp. 84–116.

Beardsmore, Barry F. "*Ysaie le triste*: A Tale of Two Heroes." *Zeitschrift für Romanische Philologie*, 105 (1989), 254–263.

Bellenger, Yvonne, ed. *Le Temps et la durée dans la littérature au moyen âge et à la Renaissance: Actes du Colloque organisé au Centre de Recherche sur la littérature du moyen âge et de la Renaissance de l'Université de Reims (novembre 1984).* Paris: Nizet, 1986.

Beltrami, Pietro G. "Racconto mitico e linguaggio lirico: per l'interpretazione del *Chevalier de la charrette*." *Studi Mediolatini e Volgari*, 30 (1984), 5–67.

Bender, Karl-Heinz. "Beauté et mariage selon Chrétien de Troyes: un défi lancé à la tradition." In Krauss and Rieger, eds., *Mittelalterstudien Erich Köhler*, 1984, pp. 31–42.

Berthelot, Anne. "La 'Merveille' dans les enfances Lancelot." *Médiévales*, 8 (1985), 87–102.

Bertolucci Pizzorusso, Valeria. "Il discorso narrativo su Tristano e Isotta nel sec. XII." In *Actes du XVIIe Congrès International de Linguistique et de Philologie Romanes, Aix-en-Provence, 29 août–3 septembre 1983*. Vol. 8: *Stylistique, rhétorique et poétique dans les langues romanes*. Aix-en-Provence: Université de Provence, 1986, pp. 383–397.

Blacker-Knight, Jean. "Transformations of a Theme: The Depoliticization of the Arthurian World in the *Roman de Brut*." In Braswell and Bugge, eds. *The Arthurian Tradition: Essays in Convergence*, 1988, pp. 54–74.

Blaess, Madeleine. "The Public and Private Face of King Arthur's Court in the Works of Chrétien de Troyes." In Noble and Paterson, eds., *Chrétien de Troyes and the Troubadours*, 1984, pp. 238–248.

Blakeslee, Merritt R. "The Authorship of Thomas's *Tristan*." *Philological Quarterly*, 64 (1985), 555–572.

———. "*Mal d'Acre, Malpertuis* and the Date of Beroul's *Tristran*." *Romania*, 106 (1985), 145–172.

———. *Love's Masks: Identity, Intertextuality, and Meaning in the Old French Tristan Poems*. Cambridge: Brewer, 1989.

Bloch, R. Howard. "Wasteland and Round Table: The Historical Significance of Myths of Dearth and Plenty in Old French Romance." *New Literary History*, 11 (1980), 255–276.

———. "Merlin and the Modes of Medieval Legal Thinking." In Lucie Brind'amour and Eugene Vance, eds., *Archéologie du signe*. Toronto: Pontifical Institute of Mediaeval Studies, 1983, pp. 127–144.

Blumenfeld-Kosinski, Renate. "Transgressing Boundaries: The Oral and the Written in Robert de Boron." *Stanford French Review*, 14, Nos. 1–2 (1990), 143–160.

Bogdanow, Fanni. "The *double esprit* of the Prose *Lancelot*." In Mermier, ed., *Courtly Romance: A Collection of Essays*, 1984, pp. 1–22.

———. "The Changing Vision of Arthur's Death." In Jane H.M. Taylor, ed., *Dies illa: Death in the Middle Ages*. Liverpool: Cairns, 1984, pp. 107–123.

———. "The Mystical Theology of Bernard of Clairvaux and the Meaning of Chrétien de Troyes' *Conte du graal*." In Noble and Paterson, eds., *Chrétien de Troyes and the Troubadours*, 1984, pp. 249–282.

———. "La Chute du royaume d'Arthur: évolution du thème." *Romania*, 107 (1986), 504–519.

———. "An Interpretation of the Meaning and Purpose of the Vulgate *Queste del saint graal* in the Light of the Mystical Theology of St. Bernard." In Adams et al., eds., *The Changing Face of Arthurian Romance*, 1986, pp. 23–46.

Bossy, Michel-André. "The Elaboration of Female Narrative Functions in *Erec et Enide*." In Busby and Kooper, eds., *Courtly Literature: Culture and Context*, 1990, pp. 23–38.

Bouchard, Constance B. "The Possible Nonexistence of Thomas, Author of *Tristan and Isolde*." *Modern Philology*, 79 (1981), 66–72.

Bouchet, Florence. "Froissart et la matière de Bretagne: une écriture 'déceptive.'" In Van Hoecke, Tournoy, and Verbeke, eds., *Arturus Rex: Vol. II*, 1991, pp. 367–375.

———. "Carrefours idéologiques de la royauté arthurienne." *Cahiers de Civilisation Médiévale*, 28 (1985), 3–17.

Bozóky, Edina. "Les Eléments religieux dans la littérature arthurienne." *Cahiers du Cercle Ernest Renan*, 29 (1981), 1–13.

————. "En attendant le héros… (pour une typologie de l'orientation de l'itinéraire du héros dans le roman arthurien)." In Mermier, ed., *Courtly Romance: A Collection of Essays*, 1984, pp. 23–45.

Braet, Herman. "Le Lai de *Tyolet*: structure et signification." In Heur and Cherubini, eds., *Etudes Jules Horrent*, 1980, pp. 41–46.

————. "Béroul et l'amour tristanien." In Krauss and Rieger, eds., *Mittelalterstudien Erich Köhler*, 1984, pp. 60–67.

Brahney, Kathleen J. "When *Silence* Was Golden: Female Personae in the *Roman de Silence*." In Burgess and Taylor, eds., *The Spirit of the Court*, 1983, pp. 52–61.

Brandsma, Frank. "A Dream Boding Ill: Thematic Interlace in the 'Préparation à la Quête.'" *Arthurian Yearbook*, 2 (1992), 13–26.

Braswell, Mary Flowers, and John Bugge, eds. *The Arthurian Tradition: Essays in Convergence*. Tuscaloosa, AL: University of Alabama Press, 1988.

Brewer, Derek S. "Some Current Trends in Arthurian Scholarship and Criticism 1987." In Van Hoecke, Tournoy, and Verbeke, eds., *Arturus Rex: Vol. II*, 1991, pp. 3–18.

Bromiley, Geoffrey N. *Thomas's Tristan and the Folie Tristan d'Oxford*. London: Grant and Cutler, 1986.

Brownlee, Kevin. "Transformations of the *Charrete*: Godefroi de Leigni Rewrites Chrétien de Troyes." *Stanford French Review*, 14, Nos. 1–2 (1990), 161–178.

————, and Marina Scordilis Brownlee, eds. *Romance: Generic Transformation from Chrétien de Troyes to Cervantes*. Hanover, NH: University Press of New England, 1985.

Bruckner, Matilda Tomaryn. "Essential and Gratuitous Inventions: Thomas' *Tristan* and Chrétien's *Lancelot*." In Foulon et al., eds., *Actes du 14e Congrès International Arthurien*, 1985, pp. 120–141.

———. "An Interpreter's Dilemma: Why Are There So Many Interpretations of Chrétien's *Chevalier de la charrette*?" *Romance Philology*, 40 (1986), 159–180.

———. "Intertextuality." In Lacy, Kelly, Busby, eds., *The Legacy of Chrétien de Troyes*, I, 1987, pp. 223–265.

———. "The Poetics of Continuation in Medieval French Romance: From Chrétien's *Conte du Graal* to the *Perceval* Continuations." *French Forum*, 18, No. 2 (1993), 133–149.

———. *Shaping Romance: Interpretation, Truth, and Closure in Twelfth-Century French Fictions*. Philadelphia: University of Pennsylvania Press, 1993.

Brumlik, Joan. "The Knight, the Lady, and the Dwarf in Chrétien's *Erec*." *Quondam et Futurus*, 2, No. 2 (1992), 54–72.

Buettner, Bonnie. "The Good Friday Scene in Chrétien de Troyes' *Perceval*." *Traditio*, 36 (1980), 415–426.

Bullock-Davies, Constance. "The Visual Image of Arthur." *Reading Medieval Studies*, 9 (1983), 98–116.

Burgess, Glyn S. *Chrétien de Troyes: Erec et Enide*. London: Grant and Cutler, 1984.

———. *The "Lais" of Marie de France: Text and Context*. Athens, GA: University of Georgia Press; Manchester: Manchester University Press, 1987.

———, ed. *Court and Poet: Selected Proceedings of the Third Congress of the International Courtly Literature Society (Liverpool 1980)*. Liverpool: Cairns, 1981.

————, and Robert A. Taylor, eds. *The Spirit of the Court: Selected Proceedings of the Fourth Congress of the International Courtly Literature Society (Toronto 1983)*. Cambridge: Brewer, 1985.

Burgwinkle, William. "'L'Ecriture totalisante' de Robert de Boron." *Constructions* (1986), pp. 87–101.

Burns, E. Jane. "Feigned Allegory: Intertextuality in the *Queste del saint graal.*" *Kentucky Romance Quarterly*, 29 (1982), 347–363.

————. *Arthurian Fictions: Rereading the Vulgate Cycle*. Columbus: Ohio State University Press, 1985.

————. "Quest and Questioning in the *Conte du graal.*" *Romance Philology*, 41 (1988), 251–266.

————. "*La voie de la voix*: The Aesthetics of Indirection in the Vulgate Cycle." In Lacy, Kelly, Busby, eds., *The Legacy of Chrétien de Troyes*, II, 1988, 151–167.

————. *Bodytalk: When Women Speak in Old French Literature*. Philadelphia: University of Pennsylvania Press, 1993.

————, and Roberta L. Krueger, eds. *Courtly Ideology and Woman's Place in Medieval French Literature*. Special Issue, *Romance Notes*, 25, No. 3 (1985).

Burrell, Margaret. "The Participation of Chrétien's Heroines in Love's 'covant.'" *Nottingham French Studies*, 30, No. 2 (1991), 24–33.

Busby, Keith. *Gauvain in Old French Literature*. Amsterdam: Rodopi, 1980.

————. "Der *Tristan Menestrel* des Gerbert de Montreuil und seine Stellung in der altfranzösischen Artustradition." *Vox Romanica*, 42 (1983), 144–156.

————. "The Reception of Chrétien's Calogrenant Episode." In A.M.J. van Buuren et al., eds., *Tussentijds: Bundel Studies W.P. Gerritsen*. Utrecht: HES Publishers, 1985, pp. 25–40.

————. *"Le Roman des eles* as Guide to the *sens* of *Meraugis de Portlesguez."* In Burgess and Taylor, eds., *The Spirit of the Court*, 1985, pp. 79–89.

————. "The Illustrated Manuscripts of Chrétien's *Perceval." Zeitschrift für Französische Sprache und Literatur*, 98 (1988), 41–52.

————. "Medieval French Arthurian Literature: Recent Progress and Critical Trends." In Mette Pors, ed., *The Vitality of the Arthurian Legend: A Symposium: Proceedings of the Twelfth International Symposium Organized by the Centre for the Study of Vernacular Literature in the Middle Ages Held at Odense University on 16–17 November, 1987*. Odense: Odense University Press, 1988, pp. 45–70.

————. "Le *Tristan* de Béroul en tant qu'intertexte." In Lacy and Torrini-Roblin, eds., *Continuations: Essays on Medieval French Literature and Language in Honor of John L. Grigsby*, 1989, pp. 19–37.

————. "L'Intertextualité du *Livre d'Artus."* In Van Hoecke, Tournoy, and Verbeke, eds., *Arturus Rex: Vol. II*, 1991, pp. 306–319.

————. *Chrétien de Troyes: Perceval (Le conte du Graal)*. London: Grant and Cutler, 1993.

————, and Erik Kooper, eds., *Courtly Literature: Culture and Context: Selected Papers from the 5th Triennial Congress of the International Courtly Literature Society, Dalfsen, The Netherlands, 9–16 August, 1986*. Amsterdam: Benjamins, 1990.

————, and Norris J. Lacy, eds., *Conjunctures: Medieval Studies in Honor of Douglas Kelly*. Amsterdam: Rodopi, 1994.

Buschinger, Danielle, ed. *La Légende de Tristan au moyen âge: Actes du Colloque du 16 et 17 janvier 1982, Université de Picardie, Centre d'Etudes Médiévales*. Göppingen: Kümmerle, 1982.

———, ed. *Lancelot: Actes du Colloque des 14 et 15 janvier 1984*. Göppingen: Kümmerle, 1984.

———, ed. *Histoire et littérature au moyen âge: Actes du Colloque du Centre d'Etudes Médiévales de l'Université de Picardie (Amiens 20–24 mars 1985)*. Göppingen: Kümmerle, 1991.

Calin, William. "Vers une nouvelle lecture de *Jaufré*: un dialogue avec Marc-René Jung." *Marche Romane*, 33 (1983), 39–47.

Callay, Brigitte L. "The Concept of Destiny in Chrétien's *Perceval*." In Van Hoecke, Tournoy, and Verbeke, eds., *Arturus Rex: Vol. II*, 1991, pp. 134–144.

Caulkins, Janet Hillier. "The Genealogy of the *Prose Tristan* and the Theme of a Debased Knighthood." In Haymes, ed., *The Medieval Court in Europe*, 1986, pp. 105–122.

———. "Récompense et châtiment dans la structure narrative de la généalogie du *Tristan* en prose." In Davies and Kennedy, eds., *Rewards and Punishments in the Arthurian Romances and Lyric Poetry of Mediaeval France*, 1987, pp. 9–19.

Chandès, Gérard. *Le Serpent, la femme et l'épée: Recherches sur l'imagination symbolique d'un romancier médiéval: Chrétien de Troyes*. Amsterdam: Rodopi, 1986.

Chase, Carol J. "Sur la théorie de l'entrelacement: ordre et désordre dans le *Lancelot en prose*." *Modern Philology*, 80 (1983), 227–241.

———. "Multiple Quests and the Art of Interlacing in the 13th-Century *Lancelot*." *Romance Quarterly*, 33 (1986), 407–420.

————. "'Or dist li contes': Narrative Interventions and the Implied Audience in the *Estoire del Saint Graal.*" In Kibler, ed., *The Lancelot-Grail Cycle*, 1994, pp. 117-138.

Chênerie, Marie-Luce. *Le Chevalier errant dans les romans arthuriens en vers des XIIe et XIIIe siècles.* Geneva: Droz, 1986.

————. "Un Recueil arthurien de contes populaires au XIIIe siècle? *Les Merveilles de Rigomer.*" In Michel Zink and Xavier Ravier, eds., *Réception et identification du conte depuis le moyen âge: Actes du Colloque de Toulouse, janvier 1986.* Toulouse: Université de Toulouse-Le Mirail, Service des Publications, 1987, pp. 39–49.

Chocheyras, Jacques. "Les Symboles de la chasteté volontaire: des contes irlandais au *Tristan* de Béroul et à celui d'Eilhart." In *Lectures du moyen âge: hommage à René Ménage.* Recherches et Travaux: Université de Grenoble, 32 (1987), 21–34.

*Chrétien de Troyes. Europe*, No. 642 (October 1982).

*Chrétien de Troyes et le graal.* Paris: Nizet, 1984.

Clark, Susan L., and Julian N. Wasserman. "Putting the Cart Before the Horse: Excess, Restraint and Choices in Chrétien's *Chevalier de la charrete.*" *Essays in Literature*, 11 (1984), 127–135.

Clifford, Paula. *Marie de France: Lais.* London: Grant and Cutler, 1982.

Colby-Hall, Alice M. "Frustration and Fulfillment: The Double Ending of the *Bel inconnu.*" *Yale French Studies*, 67 (1984), 120–134.

Collins, Frank. "A Semiotic Approach to Chrétien de Troyes's *Erec et Enide.*" *Arthurian Interpretations*, 15, No. 2 (1984), 25–31.

Cooper, Kate. "Merlin Romancier: Paternity, Prophecy and Poetics in the Huth *Merlin.*" *Romanic Review*, 77 (1986), 1–24.

Corley, Corin F.V. "Réflexions sur les deux premières *Continuations* du *Perceval*." *Romania*, 103 (1982), 235–258.

———. "Wauchier de Denain et la *Deuxième Continuation* de *Perceval*." *Romania*, 105 (1984), 351–359.

———. "Manessier's Continuation of *Perceval* and the Prose *Lancelot* Cycle." *Modern Language Review*, 81 (1986), 574–591.

———. *The Second Continuation of the Old French Perceval: A Critical and Lexicographical Study*. London: Modern Humanities Research Association, 1987.

Cormier, Raymond J. "Bédier, Brother Robert and the *Roman de Tristan*." In Heur and Cherubini, eds., *Etudes Jules Horrent*, 1980, pp. 69–75.

Crane, Susan. "Brotherhood and the Construction of Courtship in Arthurian Romance." *The Arthurian Yearbook*, 3 (1993), 193–201.

Curtis, Renée L. "Pour une édition définitive du *Tristan en prose*." *Cahiers de Civilisation Médiévale*, 24 (1981), 91–99.

———. "Who Wrote the *Prose Tristan*? A New Look at an Old Problem." *Neophilologus*, 67 (1983), 35–41.

———. "The Validity of Fénice's Criticism of Tristan and Iseut in Chrétien's *Cligés*." *Bibliographical Bulletin of the International Arthurian Society*, 41 (1989), 293–300.

Dallapiazza, Michael. "Emotionalität und Geschlechterbeziehung bei Chrétien, Hartmann und Wolfram." In Dallapiazza and Schulze-Belli, eds., *Liebe und Aventiure im Artusroman des Mittelalters*, 1990, pp. 167–184.

———, and Paola Schulze-Belli, eds. *Liebe und Aventiure im Artusroman des Mittelalters: Beiträge der Triester Tagung 1988*. Göppingen: Kümmerle, 1990.

Davies, Peter V., and Angus J. Kennedy, eds. *Rewards and Punishments in the Arthurian Romances and Lyric Poetry of Mediaeval France: Essays Presented to Kenneth Varty on the Occasion of his Sixtieth Birthday.* Cambridge: Brewer, 1987.

Dees, Anthonij. "Analyse par ordinateur de la tradition manuscrite du *Cligés* de Chrétien de Troyes." In *Actes du XVIIIe congrès de linguistique et de philologie romanes*, vol. VI. Tübingen: Niemeyer, 1988, pp. 61–75.

Deist, Rosemarie. *Die Nebenfiguren in den Tristanromanen Gottfrieds von Straßburg, Thomas' de Bretagne und im 'Cligès' Chrétiens de Troyes.* Göppingen: Kümmerle, 1986.

De Looze, Laurence N. "A Story of Interpretations: The *Queste del saint graal* as Metaliterature." *Romanic Review*, 76 (1985), 129–147.

———. "Generic Clash, Reader Response, and the Poetics of the Non-Ending in *Le Bel inconnu*." In Busby and Kooper, eds., *Courtly Literature: Culture and Context*, 1990, pp. 113–123.

Dembowski, Peter F. *Jean Froissart and His "Meliador": Context, Craft, and Sense.* Lexington, KY: French Forum, 1983.

———. "Chivalry, Ideal and Real, in the Narrative Poetry of Jean Froissart." *Medievalia et Humanistica*, 14 (1986), 1–15.

———. "De nouveau: *Erec et Enide*, Chrétien et Guiot." In *Et c'est la fin pour quoy sommes ensemble: hommage à Jean Dufournet*, 1993, pp. 409–417.

Deschaux, Robert. "Le Monde arthurien dans le *Meliador* de Froissart." In *Mélanges Charles Foulon*, 1980, II, 63–67.

Dirscherl, Ulrike. *Ritterliche Ideale in Chrétiens "Yvain" und im mittelenglischen "Ywain and Gawain": von "amour courtois" zu "trew luf,"* von *"frans chevaliers deboneire"* zum *"man of mekyl mygh. "* Frankfurt am Main: Peter Lang, 1991.

Ditmas, E.M.R. "Béroul the Minstrel." *Reading Medieval Studies*, 8 (1982), 34–74.

Diverres, Armel H. "Yvain's Quest for Chivalric Perfection." In Varty, ed., *An Arthurian Tapestry: Essays in Memory of Lewis Thorpe*, 1981, pp. 214–228.

———. "The Grail and the Third Crusade: Thoughts on *Le conte del graal* by Chrétien de Troyes." *Arthurian Literature*, 10 (1990), 13–109.

Dragonetti, Roger. "Le Vent de l'aventure dans *Yvain* ou *le Chevalier au lion* de Chrétien de Troyes." *Moyen Age*, 96 (1990), 435–462.

Dubost, Francis. *Aspects fantastiques de la littérature médiévale (XIIème-XIIIème siècles): L'autre, l'ailleurs, l'autrefois.* 2 vols. Paris: Champion, 1991.

———. "Le conflit des lumières: lire *'tot el'* la dramaturgie du graal chez Chrétien de Troyes." *Moyen Age*, 98 (1992), 187–212.

Dubuis, Roger. "La Première Rencontre de Perceval avec le graal, dans le *Conte du graal* de Chrétien de Troyes et le *Parzival* de Wolfram von Eschenbach." *Germanisch-romanische Monatsschrift*, 32 (1982), 129–155.

———. "L'Art de la 'conjointure' dans *Yvain*." *Bien dire et bien aprandre*, 7 (1989), 91–106.

Dufournet, Jean. "Une Nouvelle Edition du *Lancelot*, roman en prose du XIIIe siècle." *Moyen Age*, 87 (1981), 105–112.

———, ed. *Approches du Lancelot en prose.* Paris: Champion, 1984.

————, ed. *Chrétien de Troyes: Le Chevalier au lion. Approches d'un chef-d'œuvre*. Paris: Champion, 1988.

————, ed. *Nouvelles recherches sur "Le Tristan en prose."* Paris: Champion, 1990.

Duggan, Joseph J. "Oral Performance of Romance in Medieval France." In Lacy and Torrini-Roblin, eds., *Continuations: Essays on Medieval French Literature and Language in Honor of John L. Grigsby*, 1989, pp. 51–61.

————. "Performance and Transmission, Aural and Ocular Reception in the Twelfth and Thirteenth-Century Vernacular Literature of France." *Romance Philology*, 43 (1989–90), 49–58.

Dulac, Liliane. "L'Epreuve du siège vide: esquisse d'une lecture croisée d'un épisode du *Joseph* et du *Merlin* de Robert de Boron." In Davies and Kennedy, eds., *Rewards and Punishments in the Arthurian Romances and Lyric Poetry of Mediaeval France*, 1987, pp. 31–43.

Durling, Nancy Vine. "Translation and Innovation in the *Roman de Brut.*" In Jeanette Beer, ed., *Medieval Translators and Their Craft*. Kalamazoo, MI: Medieval Institute Publications, 1989, pp. 9–39.

Enders, Jody. "Memory and the Psychology of the Interior Monologue in Chrétien's *Cligés.*" *Rhetorica*, 10 (1992), 5–23.

*Et c'est la fin pour quoy sommes ensemble: hommage à Jean Dufournet: littérature, histoire et langue du moyen âge*. 3 vols. Paris: Champion, 1993.

*Etudes de langue et de littérature françaises offertes à André Lanly*. Nancy: Publications de l'Université de Nancy II, 1980.

Ferguson, Gary. "Symbolic Sexual Inversion and the Construction of Courtly Manhood in Two Old French Romances." *The Arthurian Yearbook*, 3 (1993), 203–213.

Fichte, Joerg O. "'Fakt' und Fiktion in der Artusgeschichte des 12. Jahrhunderts." In Mertens and Wolfzettel, eds., *Fiktionalität im Artusroman*, pp. 45-62.

Fitz, Brewster E. "Desire and Interpretation: Marie de France's *Chievrefoil*." *Yale French Studies*, 58 (1979), 182-189.

Fleischman, Suzanne. "*Jaufre* or Chivalry Askew: Social Overtones of Parody in Arthurian Romance." *Viator*, 12 (1981), 101-129.

Foulet, Alfred. "On Grid-Editing Chrétien de Troyes." *L'Esprit Créateur*, 27, No. 1 (1987), 15-23.

————, and Karl D. Uitti. "Chrétien's 'Laudine': *Yvain*, vv. 2148-55." *Romance Philology*, 37 (1984), 293-302.

Foulon, Charles, et al., eds. *Actes du 14e Congrès International Arthurien (Rennes, 16-21 août 1984)*. 2 vols. Rennes: Presses Universitaires de Rennes 2, 1985.

Frappier, Jean. *Chrétien de Troyes: The Man and His Work*, trans. Raymond J. Cormier. Athens, OH: Ohio University Press, 1982.

Freeman, Michelle A. "Transpositions structurelles et intertextualité: le *Cligès* de Chrétien." *Littérature*, 41 (1981), 50-61.

————. "*Fergus*: Parody and the Arthurian Tradition." *French Forum*, 8 (1983), 197-215.

Fritz, Jean-Marie. *Le Discours du fou au moyen âge, XIIe-XIIIe siècles*. Paris: PUF, 1992.

Fromm, Hans. "Lancelot und die Einsiedler." In Klaus Grubmüller, Ruth Schmidt-Wiegand, and Klaus Speckenbach, eds., *Geistliche Denkformen in der Literatur des Mittelalters*. Munich: Fink, 1984, pp. 198-209.

Gallais, Pierre. *Dialectique du récit médiéval (Chrétien de Troyes et l'hexagone logique)*. Amsterdam: Rodopi, 1982.

―――. *L'Imaginaire d'un romancier français de la fin du XIIe siècle: Description raisonnée, comparée et commentée de la "Continuation-Gauvain" (première suite du "Conte du graal" de Chrétien de Troyes)*. 4 vols. Amsterdam: Rodopi, 1988–89.

―――. "L'Hexagone logique et la 'logique des images.'" In Helder Godinho, ed., *Em torno da idade média*. Lisbon: Universidade Nova de Lisboa, Faculdade de Ciências Sociais e Humanas, 1989, pp. 129–148.

―――. *La Fée à la fontaine et à l'arbre: un archetype du conte merveilleux et du récit courtois*. Amsterdam: Rodopi, 1992.

Giddey, Jean-Luc. "Effets de philtre, efforts du verbe dans le *Tristan* de Béroul." *Etudes de lettres: revue de la Faculté des Lettres de l'Université de Lausanne*, 2–3 (1987), 105–112.

Glasser, Marc. "Marriage and the Use of Force in *Yvain*." *Romania*, 108 (1987), 484–502.

Göller, Karl Heinz, ed. *Spätmittelalterliche Artusliteratur: Ein Symposion der neusprachlichen Philologien auf der Generalversammlung der Görres-Gesellschaft Bonn, 25–29 September 1982*. Paderborn: Schöningh, 1984.

Gonfroy, Gérard, ed. *Le Roman de Tristan en prose: concordancier des formes graphiques occurrentes établi d'après l'édition de Ph. Ménard (tome I)*. Telmoo: Université de Limoges, 1990.

Gottzmann, Carola L. *Artusdichtung*. Sammlung Metzler, 249. Stuttgart: Metzler, 1989.

Goulden, Oliver. "*Erec et Enide*: The Structure of the Central Section." *Arthurian Literature*, 9 (1989), 1–24.

Gouttebroze, Jean-Guy. *Qui perd gagne: le Perceval de Chrétien de Troyes comme représentation de l'Œdipe inversé.* Nice, 1983.

Gowans, Linda. "New Perspectives on the *Didot-Perceval.*" *Arthurian Literature,* 7 (1987), 1–22.

———. *Cei and the Arthurian Legend.* Cambridge: Brewer, 1988.

Goyens, Michèle. "La survivance de la matière arthurienne dans la littérature française." In Verbeke, Janssens, and Smeyers, eds., *Arturus Rex, Vol. I,* 1987, pp. 310-322.

Gracia, Paloma. "La herencia del pecado en el *Lancelot en prose.*" *Medioevo Romanzo,* 16 (1991), 129–139.

Grant, Marshal S. "The Question of Integrity in the First Continuation of Chrétien de Troyes' *Conte du graal.*" *Proceedings of the Patristic, Mediaeval and Renaissance Conference,* 11 (1986), 101–125.

Gravdal, Kathryn. *Vilain and Courtois: Transgressive Parody in French Litera-ture of the Twelfth and Thirteenth Centuries.* Lincoln: University of Nebraska Press, 1989.

Gregory, Stewart S. "Notes on the Text of Beroul's *Tristan.*" *French Studies,* 35 (1981), 1–18.

———. "Fragment inédit du *Cligès* de Chrétien de Troyes: le manuscrit de l'Institut de France." *Romania,* 106 (1985), 254–269.

———. "Further Notes on the Text of Béroul's *Tristan.*" *French Studies,* 42 (1988), 1–20, 129–149.

Grenier-Braunschweig, Laurette. "L'Enigme de la *Folie Tristan d'Oxford.*" In Foulon et al., eds., *Actes du 14e Congrès International Arthurien,* 1985, pp. 241–256.

Grigsby, John L. "L'Empire des signes chez Béroul et Thomas: 'le sigle est tut neir.'" In *Mélanges Charles Foulon*, 1980, II, 115–125.

———. "The Ontology of the Narrator in Medieval French Romance." In Grunmann-Gaudet and Jones, eds., *The Nature of Medieval Narrative*, 1980. pp. 159–171.

———. "Perceval devant l'herméneutique et la grammatologie." *L'Esprit Créateur*, 23 (1983), 25–37.

———. "Truth and Method in Arthurian Criticism." *Romance Philology*, 38 (1984), 53–64.

———. "Heroes and their Destinies in the *Perceval* Continuations." In Lacy, Kelly, Busby, eds., *The Legacy of Chrétien de Troyes*, II, 1988, pp. 41–53.

———. "Remnants of Chrétien's Aesthetics in the Early *Perceval* Continuations and the Incipient Triumph of Writing." *Romance Philology*, 41 (1988), 379–393.

Grimbert, Joan Tasker. "On the Prologue of Chrétien's *Yvain*: Opening Functions of Keu's Quarrel." *Philological Quarterly*, 64 (1985), 391–398.

———. *"Yvain" dans le miroir: une poétique de la réflexion dans le "Chevalier au lion" de Chrétien de Troyes*. Amsterdam: Benjamins, 1988.

———. "Misrepresentation and Misconception in Chrétien de Troyes: Nonverbal and Verbal Semiotics in *Erec et Enide* and *Perceval*." In Wasserman and Roney, eds., *Sign, Sentence, Discourse*, 1989, pp. 50–79.

———. "Love, Honor, and Alienation in Thomas's *Roman de Tristan*." *Arthurian Yearbook*, 2 (1992), 77–98.

Grimm, Reinhold R., ed. *Le Roman jusqu'à la fin du XIIIe siècle. Tome 1: Partie historique. Tome 2: Partie documentaire.* In vol. 4.2, *Grundriß der romanischen Literaturen des Mittelalters.* Heidelberg: Winter, 1978–84.

Grisward, Joël. *Archéologie de l'épopée médiévale: Structures trifonctionnelles et mythes indo-européens dans le cycle des Narbonnais.* Paris: Payot, 1981.

————. "Uter Pendragon, Artur et l'idéologie royale des Indo-Européens: structure trifonctionnelle et roman arthurien." *Europe*, No. 654 (October 1983), 111–120.

————. "L'Arbre blanc, vert, rouge de la Quête du graal et le symbolisme coloré des Indo-Européens, I." In Foulon et al., eds., *Actes du 14e Congrès International Arthurien*, 1985, pp. 273–287.

————. "Le Lit de Paradis et le seigneur coloré: notes sur l'*Ordene de chevalerie* et la *Queste del saint graal*." In Danielle Buschinger, ed., *Sammlung-Deutung-Wertung: Ergebnisse, Probleme, Tendenzen und Perspektiven philologischer Arbeit. Mélanges Spiewok.* Stuttgart: Sprint, 1988, pp. 147–154.

Groos, Arthur. "Perceval and Parzival Discover Knighthood." In *Magister regis: Studies Robert Earle Kaske.* New York: Fordham University Press, 1986, pp. 117–137.

Grout, P.B, R.A. Lodge, C.E. Pickford, and E.K.C. Varty, eds. *The Legend of Arthur in the Middle Ages: Studies Presented to A.H. Diverres by Colleagues, Pupils, and Friends.* Woodbridge: Brewer; Totowa, NJ: Biblio, 1983, pp. 66–75.

Grunmann-Gaudet, Minnette, and Robin F. Jones, eds. *The Nature of Medieval Narrative.* Lexington, KY: French Forum, 1980.

Guerreau, Alain. "Renaud de Bâgé: *Le bel inconnu*, structure symbolique et signification sociale." *Romania*, 103 (1982), 28–82.

Guerreau-Jalabert, Anita. "Romans de Chrétien de Troyes et contes folkloriques: rapprochements thématiques et observations de méthode." *Romania,* 104 (1983), 1–48.

———. *Index des motifs narratifs dans les romans français en vers (XIIe–XIIIe siècles.* Geneva; Droz, 1992.

Guthrie, Jeri S. "The *Je(u)* in *Le bel inconnu*: Auto-Referentiality and Pseudo-Autobiography." *Romanic Review,* 75 (1984), 147–161.

Hahn, Stacey L. "Genealogy and Adventure in the Cyclic Prose *Lancelot.*" In Busby and Lacy, eds., *Conjunctures: Medieval Studies in Honor of Douglas Kelly,* 1994, 139-151.

Haidu, Peter. "The Hermit's Pottage: Deconstruction and History in *Yvain.*" In Pickens, ed., *The Sower and His Seed,* 1983, pp. 127–145; and *Romanic Review,* 74 (1983), 1–15.

Halász, Katalin. *Structures narratives chez Chrétien de Troyes.* Debrecen: Kossuth Lajos Tudományegyetem, 1980.

———. "The Intermingling of Romance Models in a 13th-Century Prose Romance: *Roman de Laurin.*" *Forum for Modern Language Studies,* 22 (1986), 273–283.

———. "L'Ange, Josephes, Merlin, Robert, Gautiers et les autres: approche narratologique de quelques romans en prose." *Le Forme e la Storia,* n.s., 2 (1990), 303–314.

Halverson, John. "Tristan and Iseult: The Two Traditions." *Zeitschrift für Französische Sprache und Literatur,* 93 (1983), 271–296.

Hanning, Robert W. "Arthurian Evangelists: The Language of Truth in Thirteenth-Century French Prose Romances." *Philological Quarterly,* 64 (1985), 347–365.

———. "Love and Power in the Twelfth Century, with Special Reference to Chrétien de Troyes and Marie de France." In Robert

R. Edwards and Stephen Spector, eds., *The Olde Daunce: Love, Friendship, Sex, and Marriage in the Medieval World*. Albany, NY: State University of New York Press, 1991, pp. 87–103, 267–268.

Harding, Carol E. *Merlin and Legendary Romance*. New York: Garland, 1988.

Harf-Lancner, Laurence. *Les Fées au moyen âge: Morgane et Mélusine. La naissance des fées*. Paris: Champion, 1984.

———. "Lancelot et la Dame du lac." *Romania*, 105 (1984), 16–33.

———. "*Le Chevalier au lion*: un conte morganien." *Bien dire et bien aprandre*, 7 (1989), 107–116.

Harrison, Ann Tukey. "Arthurian Women in *Jaufre*." In Keller et al., eds., *Studia occitanica in memoriam Paul Remy*, 1986, II, 65–73.

Hart, Thomas Elwood. "Chrestien, Macrobius and Chartrean Science: The Allegorical Robe as Symbol of Textual Design in the Old French *Erec*." *Mediaeval Studies*, 43 (1981), 250–296.

———. "The *Quadrivium* and Chrétien's Theory of Composition: Some Conjunctures and Conjectures." *Symposium*, 35 (1981), 57–86.

Herman, Harold J. "Sir Kay, Seneschal of King Arthur's Court." *Arthurian Interpretations*, 4, No. 1 (1989), 1–31.

Heur, Jean-Marie d', and Nicoletta Cherubini, eds. *Etudes de philologie romane et d'histoire littéraire offertes à Jules Horrent*. Liège: GEDIT, 1980.

Hindman, Sandra. "King Arthur, His Knights, and the French Aristocracy in Picardy." *Yale French Studies*, special number, *Contexts: Styles and Values in Medieval Art and Literature*, 1991, pp. 114–133.

————. *Sealed in Parchment: Rereadings of Knighthood in the Illuminated Manuscripts of Chrétien de Troyes*. Chicago: University of Chicago Press, 1994.

Hoecke, Willy van, Gilbert Tournoy, and Werner Verbeke, eds. *Arturus Rex, Volumen II: Acta Conventus Lovaniensis 1987*. Leuven: Leuven University Press, 1991.

Höfner, Eckhard. "Zum Verhältnis von Tristan- und Artusstoff im 12. Jahrhundert." *Zeitschrift für Französische Sprache und Literatur*, 92 (1982), 289–323.

Hogetoorn, Corry. "Onzalige paradijzen: tuinen in het werk van Chrétien de Troyes." In R.E.V. Stuip and C. Vellekoop, eds., *Tuinen in de Middeleeuwen*. Hilversum: Verloren, 1992, pp. 131–141.

Holzermayr, Katharina. "Le 'Mythe' d'Arthur: la royauté et l'idéologie." *Annales: Economies Sociétés Civilisations*, 39 (1984), 480–494.

Houstin, Françoise. "Le Drame de la mère de Perceval: Chrétien de Troyes, *Le conte du graal*." *PRIS-MA*, 1 (1985), 72–78.

Huchet, Jean-Charles. "Les Déserts du roman médiéval: le personnage de l'ermite dans les romans des XIIe et XIIIe siècles." *Littérature*, 60 (1985), 89–108.

————. "Psychanalyse et littérature médiévale: recontre ou méprise? (A propos de deux ouvrages récents)." *Cahiers de Civilisation Médiévale*, 28 (1985), 223–233.

————. *Tristan et le sang de l'écriture*. Paris: Presses Universitaires de France, 1990.

Hult, David F. "Lancelot's Two Steps: A Problem in Textual Criticism." *Speculum*, 61 (1986), 836–858.

————. "La Double Autorité du *Chevalier de la charrete.*" In Emmanuèle Baumgartner and Christiane Marchello-Nizia, eds., *Théories et pratiques de l'écriture au moyen âge: Actes du Colloque Palais du Luxembourg-Sénat, 5 et 6 mars 1987.* Paris: Centre de Recherches du Département de Français de Paris X–Nanterre, Saint-Cloud: Centre Espace-Temps-Histoire de l'E.N.S. Fontenay, 1988, pp. 41–56.

————. "Author/Narrator/Speaker: The Voice of Authority in Chrétien's *Charrete.*" In Kevin Brownlee and Walter Stephens, eds., *Discourses of Authority in Medieval and Renaissance Literature.* Hanover, NH: University Press of New England, 1989, pp. 76–96, 267–269.

————. "Steps Forward and Steps Backward: More on Chrétien's *Lancelot.*" *Speculum*, 64 (1989), 307-316.

Hunt, Tony. "Irony and the Rise of Courtly Romance." *German Life and Letters*, 35 (1981), 98–104.

————. "The Medieval Adaptations of Chrétien's *Yvain*: A Bibliographical Essay." In Varty, ed., *An Arthurian Tapestry: Essays in Memory of Lewis Thorpe*, 1981, pp. 201–213.

————. "The Significance of Thomas's *Tristan.*" *Reading Medieval Studies*, 7 (1981), 41–61.

————. "Beginnings, Middles, and Ends: Some Interpretative Problems in Chrétien's *Yvain* and Its Medieval Adaptations." In Arrathoon, ed., *The Craft of Fiction: Essays in Medieval Poetics*, 1984, pp. 83–117.

————. *Chrétien de Troyes: Yvain (Le chevalier au lion).* London: Grant and Cutler, 1986.

————. "The Tristan Illustrations in MS London, BL Add 11619." In Davies and Kennedy, eds., *Rewards and Punishments in the*

*Arthurian Romance and Lyric Poetry of Medieval France*, 1987, pp. 45–60.

———. "Chrestien de Troyes: The Textual Problem." *French Studies*, 33 (1979), 257–271; rpt. in Busby, Nixon, Stones, Walters, eds., *Les Manuscrits de Chrétien de Troyes*, 1993, pp. 27–40.

———. "Chrétien's Prologues Reconsidered." In Busby and Lacy, eds., *Conjunctures: Medieval Studies in Honor of Douglas Kelly*, 1994, 153–168.

Huot, Sylvia. *From Song to Book: The Poetics of Writing in Old French Lyric and Lyrical Narrative Poetry*. Ithaca: Cornell University Press, 1987.

Hyatte, Reginald. "Tristran's Monologues as a Narrative Model in Thomas's *Roman de Tristan*." *Arthurian Interpretations*, 15, No. 2 (1984), 32–41.

———. "Recoding Ideal Male Friendship as *fine amor* in the *Prose Lancelot*." *Neophilologus*, 75 (1991), 505–518.

Ihle, Sandra N. *Malory's Grail Quest: Invention and Adaptation in Medieval Prose Romance*. Madison: University of Wisconsin Press, 1983.

Iyasere, Marla W. Mudar. "The Tripartite Structure of Chrétien's *Erec et Enide*." *Mediaevalia*, 6 (1980 [c. 1982]), 105–121.

Jacobsen, Berit. "Le Merveilleux Merlin." In *Mélanges Helge Nordahl*. Oslo, 1988, pp. 94–102.

Janssens, Jan. "L'Obstacle dangereux dans le *Chevalier de la charrete*." In Foulon et al., eds., *Actes du 14e Congrès International Arthurien*, 1985, pp. 346–353.

———. "Le Prologue du *Chevalier de la charrete*: une clef pour l'interprétation du roman?" *Bien dire et bien aprandre*, 4 (1986), 29–51.

Jefferson, Lisa. "The Keys to the Enchantments of Dolorous Guard." *Medium Ævum*, 58 (1989), 59–79.

———. "Don – don contraignant – don contraint: A Motif and Its Deployment in the French Prose Lancelot." *Romanische Forschungen*, 104 (1992), 27–51.

Jung, Emma, and M.-L. von Franz. *Die Graalslegende in psychologischer Sicht*. 2nd ed. Olten: Walter, 1983.

Kasprzyk, Krystyna. "La Pitié de Marc." *Marche Romane*, 32 (1982), 15–24.

Kay, Sarah. "The Tristan Story as Chivalric Romance, Feudal Epic and Fabliau." In Burgess and Taylor, eds., *The Spirit of the Court*, 1985, pp. 185–195.

———. "Commemoration, Memory and the Role of the Past in Chrétien de Troyes: Retrospection and Meaning in *Erec et Enide*, *Yvain* and *Perceval*." *Reading Medieval Studies*, 17 (1991), 31–50.

Keller, Hans-Erich. "De l'amour dans le *Roman de Brut*." In Lacy and Torrini-Roblin, eds., *Continuations: Essays on Medieval French Literature and Language in Honor of John L. Grigsby*, 1989, pp. 63–81.

———. "The Intellectual Journey of Wace." *Fifteenth-Century Studies*, 17 (1990), 185–207.

———, J.-M. D'Heur, G.R. Mermier, and M. Vuijlsteke, eds. *Studia occitanica in memoriam Paul Remy*. 2 vols. Kalamazoo, MI: Medieval Institute Publications, 1986.

Kellogg, Judith. *Medieval Artistry and Exchange: Economic Institutions, Society, and Literary Form in Old French Narrative.* New York: Lang, 1989.

Kelly, Douglas. "Topic Invention in Medieval French Literature." In James J. Murphy, ed., *Medieval Eloquence: Studies in the Theory and Practice of Medieval Rhetoric.* Berkeley: University of California Press, 1978, pp. 231–251.

————— "The Logic of the Imagination in Chrétien de Troyes." In Pickens, ed., *The Sower and His Seed*, 1983, pp. 9–30.

—————. "L'Invention dans les romans en prose." In Arrathoon, ed., *The Craft of Fiction: Essays in Medieval Poetics*, 1984, pp. 119–142.

—————. "The Rhetoric of Adventure in Medieval Romance." In Noble and Paterson, eds., *Chrétien de Troyes and the Troubadours*, 1984, pp. 172–185.

—————. "Description and Narrative in Romance: The Contextual Coordinates of *Meraugis de Portlesguez* and the *Bel inconnu.*" In Lacy and Torrini-Roblin, eds., *Continuations: Essays on Medieval French Literature and Language in Honor of John L. Grigsby*, 1989, pp. 83–93.

—————. *The Art of Medieval French Romance.* Madison: University of Wisconsin Press, 1992.

—————. "*Fine amor* in Thomas's *Tristan.*" In Pickens, ed., *Studies in Honor of Hans-Erich Keller*, 1993, pp. 167–180.

—————, ed. *The Romances of Chrétien de Troyes: A Symposium.* Lexington, KY: French Forum, 1985.

—————. *Medieval French Romance.* New York: Twayne; Toronto: Macmillan, 1993.

Kennedy, Angus J. "The Portrayal of the Hermit-Saint in French Arthurian Romance: The Remoulding of a Stock-Character." In Varty, ed., *An Arthurian Tapestry: Essays in Memory of Lewis Thorpe*, 1981, pp. 69–82.

―――. "Punishment in the *Perlesvaus*: The Theme of the Waste Land." In Davies and Kennedy, eds., *Rewards and Punishments in the Arthurian Romances and Lyric Poetry of Mediaeval France*, 1987, pp. 61–75.

Kennedy, Elspeth. "The Scribe as Editor." In *Mélanges . . . Jean Frappier*. Geneva: Droz, 1972, II, 521–531.

―――. "Etudes sur le *Lancelot* en prose." *Romania*, 105 (1984), 34–62.

―――. *Lancelot and the Grail: A Study of the Prose "Lancelot."* Oxford: Clarendon Press, 1986.

―――. "The Re-writing and Re-reading of a Text: The Evolution of the *Prose Lancelot*." In Adams et al., eds., *The Changing Face of Arthurian Romance*, 1986, pp. 1–9.

―――. "'Lancelot li mescheans': Mischance and Individual Responsibility in the *Lancelot-Graal*." In Bart Besamusca and Frank Brandsma, eds., *De ongevalliche Lanceloet: Studies over de "Lancelot-compilatie."* Hilversum: Verloren, 1992, pp. 117–136.

―――. "Variations in the Patterns of Interlace in the Lancelot-Grail." In Kibler, ed., *The Lancelot-Grail Cycle*, 1994, pp. 31–50.

Kibler, William W., ed. *The Lancelot-Grail Cycle: Text and Transformations*. Austin, TX: University of Texas Press, 1994.

Kjær, Jonna. "Théorie du mythe et les romans de *Tristan et Iseult*: présentation d'un projet de recherches." *Revue Romane*, 15 (1980), 221–233.

————. "L'Episode de 'Tristan le ménestrel' dans la 'Continuation de Perceval' par Gerbert de Montreuil (XIIIe siècle): essai d'interprétation." *Revue Romane*, 25, No. 2 (1990), 356–366.

Klenke, Sister M. Amelia. *Chrétien de Troyes and "Le Conte del graal": A Study of Sources and Symbolism.* Madrid: José Porrúa Turanzas; Potomac, MD: Studia Humanitatis, 1981.

Knight, Gillian. "Chrétien de Troyes: His 'Rhetoric of Love.'" *Reading Medieval Studies*, 14 (1988), 77–110.

Knight, Stephen. *Arthurian Literature and Society.* New York: St. Martin's; London: Macmillan, 1983.

Kratins, Ojars. *The Dream of Chivalry: A Study of Chrétien de Troyes's "Yvain" and Hartmann von Aue's "Iwein."* Washington, DC: University Press of America, 1982.

Krauss, Henning, and Dietmar Rieger, eds. *Mittelalterstudien: Erich Köhler zum Gedenken.* Heidelberg: Winter, 1984.

Krueger, Roberta L. "'Tuit li autre': The Narrator and His Public in Chrétien de Troyes' *Le chevalier de la charrete.*" In Mermier, ed., *Courtly Romance: A Collection of Essays*, 1984, pp. 133–150.

————. "Contracts and Constraints: Courtly Performance in *Yvain* and the *Charrete.*" In Haymes, ed., *The Medieval Court in Europe*, 1986, pp. 92–104.

————. "Desire, Meaning, and the Female Reader: The Problem in Chrétien's *Charrete.*" In Baswell and Sharpe, eds., *The Passing of Arthur: New Essays in Arthurian Tradition*, 1988, pp. 31–51.

————. *Women Readers and the Ideology of Gender.* Cambridge: Cambridge University Press, 1993.

Kunstmann, Pierre. "Texte, intertexte et autotexte dans le *Tristan* de Thomas d'Angleterre." In Grunmann-Gaudet and Jones, eds., *The Nature of Medieval Narrative*, 1980, pp. 173–189.

———, and Martin Dubé. *Concordance analytique de La mort le roi Artu*. 2 vols. Ottawa: Editions de l'Université d'Ottawa, 1982.

Lachet, Claude. *"Sone de Nansay" et le roman d'aventures en vers au XIIIe siècle*. Geneva: Slatkine, 1992.

Lacy, Norris J. *The Craft of Chrétien de Troyes: An Essay in Narrative Art*. Leiden: Brill, 1980.

———. "Gauvain and the Crisis of Chivalry in the *Conte del graal*." In Pickens, ed., *The Sower and His Seed*, 1983, pp. 155–164.

———. "*Perlesvaus* and the *Perceval* Palimpsest." *Philological Quarterly*, 69 (1990), 263–271.

———. "French Arthurian Literature in English Translation." *Quondam et Futurus*, 1, No. 3 (1991), 55–74.

———. "The *Mort Artu* and Cyclic Closure." In Kibler, ed., *The Lancelot-Grail Cycle*, 1994, pp. 85–97.

———, Douglas Kelly, and Keith Busby, eds. *The Legacy of Chrétien de Troyes*. 2 vols. Amsterdam: Rodopi, 1987–88.

———, and Jerry C. Nash, eds. *Essays in Early French Literature Presented to Barbara M. Craig*. York, SC: French Literature Publications, 1982.

———, and Gloria Torrini-Roblin, eds. *Continuations: Essays on Medieval French Literature and Language in Honor of John L. Grigsby*. Birmingham, AL: Summa, 1989.

Lagorio, Valerie M., and Mildred Leake Day, eds. *King Arthur Through the Ages*. 2 vols. New York: Garland, 1990.

*Lancelot, Yvain et Gauvain: Colloque Arthurian Belge de Wégimont.* Paris: Nizet, 1984.

Lange, Hanne. "Symbolisme, exégèse, littérature profane: intertextualité et intratextualité dans le *Conte du graal* de Chrétien de Troyes." *Actes du XVIIIe Congrès International de Linguistique et de Philologie Romanes,* VI (1988), 289–307.

Lathuillère, Roger. "L'Evolution de la technique narrative dans le roman arthurien en prose au cours de la deuxième moitié du XIIIe siècle." In *Etudes de langue et de littérature françaises offertes à André Lanly,* 1980, pp. 203–214.

Laurie, Helen C.R. "Chrétien's 'bele conjointure.'" In Foulon et al., eds., *Actes du 14e Congrès International Arthurien,* 1985, pp. 379–396.

———. "Chrétien de Troyes and the Love Religion." *Romanische Forschungen,* 101 (1989), 169–183.

———. *The Making of Romance: Three Studies.* Geneva: Droz, 1991.

———. "The Psychomachia of *Yvain.*" *Nottingham French Studies,* 30, No. 2 (1991), 13–23.

Lebsanft, Franz. "Wer lacht über Lancelot? zur Interpretation des Motivs der *demoiselle tentatrice* bei Chrétien de Troyes und im Prosa-*Lancelot.*" *Romanistisches Jahrbuch,* 33 (1982), 85–96.

Le Menn, Gwennolé. *La Femme au sein d'or.* St. Brieuc: SKOL, 1985.

Le Merrer, Madeleine. "Iseut et le pouvoir: du mythe reçu aux poèmes de Béroul et de Thomas." *Actes du Cent cinquième Congrès National des Société savantes Caen 1980.* Paris: Comité des travaux historiques et scientifiques, 1984, pp. 29–44.

Lepri, Alessandra. "I personaggi minori nei romanzi di Chrétien de Troyes." *Quaderni di filologia romanza della Facoltà de Lettere e Filosofia dell'Università di Bologna*, 8 (1991), 7–94.

Leupin, Alexandre. "La Faille et l'écriture dans les continuations du *Perceval.*" *Moyen Age*, 88 (1982), 237–269.

———. *Le Graal et la littérature: étude sur la Vulgate arthurienne en prose.* Lausanne: Age d'homme, 1982.

Liborio, Mariantonia. "La Logique de la déception dans les romans de Tristan et Yseut." *Annali Istituto Universitario Orientale Napoli: sezione romanza*, 23 (1981), 151–163.

Lie, O.S.H. "Guinevere." In R.E.V. Stuip and C. Vellekoop, eds., *Middeleeuwers over vrouwen.* Utrecht: HES, 1985, I, 27–40.

Lindvall, Lars. "Structures syntaxiques et structures stylistiques dans l'œuvre de Chrestien de Troyes." *Romania*, 102 (1981), 456–500.

Lloyd-Morgan, Ceridwen. "The Relationship Between the *Perlesvaus* and the *Prose Lancelot.*" *Medium Ævum*, 53 (1984), 239–253.

Lods, Jeanne. "Amour de regard et amour de renommée dans le *Méliador* de Froissart." *Bibliographical Bulletin of the International Arthurian Society*, 32 (1980), 231–249.

Lozac'hmeur, Jean-Claude. "Origines celtiques des aventures de Gauvain au pays de Galvoie dans le *Conte du graal* de Chrétien de Troyes." In Foulon et al., eds., *Actes du 14e Congrès International Arthurien*, 1985, pp. 406–422.

———. "Recherches sur les origines indo-européennes et ésotériques de la légende du Graal." *Cahiers de Civilisation Médiévale*, 30 (1987), 44–63.

————, and Shigemi Sasaki. "A propos de deux hypothèses de R.S. Loomis: Eléments pour une solution de l'énigme du Graal." *BBSIA*, 34 (1982), 207–221.

Luttrell, Claude. "Chrestien de Troyes and Alan of Lille." *Bibliographical Bulletin of the International Arthurian Society*, 32 (1980), 250–275.

————. "Folk Legend as Source for Arthurian Romance: The Wild Hunt." In Varty, ed., *An Arthurian Tapestry: Essays in Memory of Lewis Thorpe*, 1981, pp. 83–100.

————. "The Prologue of Crestien's *Li contes del graal*." *Arthurian Literature*, 3 (1983), 1–25.

————. "The Arthurian Hunt with a White Bratchet." *Arthurian Literature*, 9 (1989), 57–80.

McCash, June Hall. "Marie de Champagne's 'cuer d'ome et cors de fame': Aspects of Feminism and Misogyny in the Twelfth Century." In Burgess and Taylor, eds., *The Spirit of the Court*, 1985, pp. 234–245.

MacDonald, Aileen Ann. *The Figure of Merlin in Thirteenth-Century French Romance*. Lewiston, NY: Mellen, 1990.

————. "Merlin in the Vulgate and Post-Vulgate: A Study in Contrasts." In *Comparative Studies in Merlin from the Vedas to C.G. Jung*. Lewiston, NY: Mellen, 1991, pp. 3–19.

MacRae, Donald C. "Appearances and Reality in *La mort le roi Artu*." *Forum for Modern Langauge Studies*, 18 (1982), 266–277.

Maddox, Donald. "Trois sur deux: théories de bipartition et de tripartition des œuvres de Chrétien." *Œuvres et Critiques*, 5, No. 2 (1980–81), 91–102.

———. "The Awakening: A Key Motif in Chrétien's Romances." In Pickens, ed., *The Sower and His Seed*, 1983, pp. 31–51.

———. "Lancelot et le sens de la coutume." *Cahiers de Civilisation Médiévale*, 29 (1986), 339–353.

———. "Vers un modèle de la communauté textuelle au moyen âge: les rapports entre auteur et texte, entre texte et lecteur." In *Actes du XVIIIe Congrès International de Linguistique et de Philologie Romanes*, VI (1988), 480–490.

———. *The Arthurian Romances of Chrétien de Troyes: Once and Future Fictions*. Cambridge: Cambridge University Press, 1991.

———. "Coutumes et 'conjointure' dans le *Lancelot* en prose." In Busby and Lacy, eds., *Conjunctures: Medieval Studies in Honor of Douglas Kelly*, 1994, 293–309.

Marchello-Nizia, Christiane. "Les 'Voix' dans la *Queste del saint graal*: grammaire du surnaturel, ou grammaire de l'intériorité?" In *Histoire et société: mélanges Georges Duby*. 4 vols. Aix-en-Provence: Publications de l'Université de Provence, 1992, vol. 4: *La mémoire, l'écriture et l'histoire*, pp. 77–85.

———. *Merlin l'enchanteur, ou l'éternelle quête magique*. Paris: Retz, 1981.

———. *Le Graal*. Paris: Retz, 1982.

Mathey, Laurence. "Le Roi Arthur chez Geoffroy de Monmouth et Wace: la naissance du héros." In Van Hoecke, Tournoy, and Verbeke, eds., *Arturus Rex, Vol. II*, 1991, pp. 222–229.

———. "De l'*Historia regum Britanniae* de Geoffroy de Monmouth au *Roman de Brut* de Wace: Etude d'un écart à valeur idéologique." In *Et c'est la fin pour quoy sommes ensemble: hommage à Jean Dufournet*, 1993, pp. 941–948.

————. "Traduction et création: De l'*Historia regum Britanniae* de Geoffroy de Monmouth au *Roman de Brut* de Wace." In Dominique Boutet and Laurence Harf-Lancner, eds., *Ecriture et modes de pensée au Moyen Age (VIIIe–XVe siècles)*. Paris: Presses de ENS, 1993, pp. 187–193.

Méla, Charles. "'La lettre tue': cryptographie du graal." *Cahiers de Civilisation Médiévale*, 26 (1983), 209–221.

————. *La Reine et le graal: la "conjointure" dans les romans du graal de Chrétien de Troyes au "Livre de Lancelot."* Paris: Seuil, 1984.

————. "Life in *La mort le roi Artu*." In Baswell and Sharpe, eds., *The Passing of Arthur: New Essays in Arthurian Tradition*, 1988, pp. 5–14.

*Mélanges Alice Planche*. 2 vols. Nice: Belles Lettres, 1984.

*Mélanges de langue et littérature françaises du moyen âge et de la Renaissance, offerts à Monsieur Charles Foulon*. 2 vols. Rennes: Institut de Français, Université de Haute-Bretagne (= vol. I), Liège: *Marche Romane*, 30, Nos. 3–4 (= vol. II), 1980.

Melli, Elio. "Commercio, mercanti, prefigurazione di organizzazione industriale nei romanzi di Chrétien de Troyes." *Quaderni di filologsofia romanza della Facoltà di Lettere e Filosofia dell'Università di Bologna*, 2 (1981), 55–80.

Ménage, René. "*Erec et Enide*: quelques pièces du dossier." In *Mélanges Charles Foulon*, 1980, II, 203–221.

Ménard, Philippe. "Note sur le texte du *Conte du Graal*." In *Mélanges de langue et de littérature française offerts à Pierre Jonin*. Aix-en-Provence: CUERMA, 1979, pp. 449–457.

————. "Problématique de l'aventure dans les romans de la Table Ronde." In Van Hoecke, Tournoy, and Verbeke, eds., *Arturus Rex, Vol. II*, 1991, pp. 89–119.

————. "Chapitres et entrelacement dans le *Tristan en prose*." In *Et c'est la fin pour quoy sommes ensemble: hommage à Jean Dufournet*, 1993, pp. 955–962.

Meneghetti, Maria Luisa. "Duplicazione e specularità nel romanzo arturiano (dal *Bel inconnu* al *Lancelot-Graal*)." In Krauss and Rieger, eds., *Mittelalterstudien Erich Köhler*, 1984, pp. 206–217.

————. "Les Modèles culturels: *ante rem, in re, post rem?*" In Morris Halle et al., eds., *Semiosis: Semiotics and the History of Culture in honorem Georgii Lotman*. Ann Arbor: University of Michigan Press, 1984, pp. 27–91.

————, ed. *Il romanzo*. Bologna: Il Mulino, 1988.

Mermier, Guy, ed. *Courtly Romance: A Collection of Essays*. Detroit: Fifteenth-Century Symposium, 1984.

————, ed. *Contemporary Readings of Medieval Literature*. Ann Arbor: Department of Romance Languages, University of Michigan, 1989.

Mertens, Volker, and Friedrich Wolfzettel, eds., with Matthias Meyer and Hans-Jochen Schwiewer. *Fiktionalität im Artusroman: Dritte Tagung der deutschen Sektion der Internationalen Artusgesellschaft*. Tübingen: Niemeyer, 1993.

Micha, Alexandre. *Etude sur le Merlin de Robert de Boron: roman du XIIIe siècle*. Geneva: Droz, 1980.

————. *Essais sur le cycle du Lancelot-Graal*. Geneva: Droz, 1987.

————. "La Géographie de la *Queste* et de la *Mort Artu*." In *Farai chansoneta novele: hommage à Jean-Charles Payen*. Caen: Centre de Publications de l'Université de Caen, 1989, pp. 267–273.

Mickel, Emanuel J., Jr. "Tristan's Ancestry in the *Tristan en prose*." *Romania*, 109 (1988), 68–89.

Middleton, Roger. "Le Grand d'Aussy's *Erec et Enide*." *Nottingham French Studies*, 25 (1986), 14–41.

————. "Structure and Chronology in *Erec et Enide*." *Nottingham French Studies*, 30, No. 2 (1991), 43–80.

Mikhaïlov, A.D. "Le Héros dans la structure du roman de chevalerie: parallélisme et symétrie du *Roman de Tristan*." In Foulon et al., eds., *Actes du 14e Congrès International Arthurien*, 1985, pp. 442–448.

Milin, Gaël. *Le Roi Marc aux oreilles de cheval*. Geneva: Droz, 1991.

Moi, Toril. "'She Died Because She Came Too Late...': Knowledge, Doubles and Death in Thomas's *Tristan*." *Exemplaria*, 4 (1992), 105–133.

Mok, Q.I.M., I. Spiele, and P.E.R. Verhuyck, eds. *Mélanges de linguistique, de littérature et de philologie médiévales, offerts à J.R. Smeets*. Leiden: Presses Universitaires, 1982.

Monson, Don A. "L'Idéologie du lai de Lanval." *Moyen Age*, 93 (1987), 349–372.

Montoya Martínez, Jesús, Aurora Juárez Blanquer, and Juan Paredes Núñez, eds. *Narrativa breve medieval románica*. Granada: Ediciones TAT, 1988.

Morgan, Gerald. "The Conflict of Love and Chivalry in *Le chevalier de la charrete*." *Romania*, 102 (1981), 172–201.

Morris, Rosemary A. *The Character of King Arthur in Medieval Literature*. Woodbridge: Brewer; Totowa, NJ: Rowman and Littlefield, 1982.

———. "Aspects of Time and Place in the French Arthurian Verse Romances." *French Studies*, 42 (1988), 257–277.

Mullally, Evelyn. "The Order of Composition of *Lancelot* and *Yvain*." *Bibliographical Bulletin of the International Arthurian Society*, 36 (1984), 217–229.

———. *The Artist at Work: Narrative Technique in Chrétien de Troyes*. Philadelphia: American Philosophical Society, 1988.

Nelson, Deborah H. "Enide: *amie* or *femme*?" *Romance Notes*, 21 (1981), 358–363.

———. "The Public and Private Images of *Cligès'* Fénice." *Reading Medieval Studies*, 7 (1981), 81–88.

Nelson, Jan A. "A Jungian Interpretation of Sexually Ambiguous Imagery in Chrétien's *Erec et Enide*." In Braswell and Bugge, eds. *The Arthurian Tradition: Essays in Convergence*, 1988, pp. 75–89.

Nightingale, Jeanne A. "The Romances of Chrétien de Troyes as Adventures in Interpretation." *Cincinnati Romance Review*, 7 (1988), 11–28.

———. "Chrétien de Troyes and the Mythographical Tradition: The Couple's Journey in *Erec et Enide* and Martianus' *De Nuptiis*." In Lagorio and Day, eds., *King Arthur Through the Ages*, 1990, I, 56–79.

———. "From Mirror to Metamorphosis: Echoes of Ovid's Narcissus in Chrétien's *Erec et Enide*." In Jane Chance, ed., *The Mythographic Art: Classical Fable and the Rise of the Vernacular in Early France and England*. Gainesville, FL: University of Florida Press, 1990, pp. 47–82.

Nixon, Terry. "*Amadas et Ydoine* and *Erec et Enide*: Reuniting *membra disjecta* from Early Old French Manuscripts." *Viator*, 18 (1987), 227–251.

Noble, James. "Patronage, Politics, and the Figure of Arthur in Geoffrey of Monmouth, Wace, and Layamon." *Arthurian Yearbook*, 2 (1992), 159–178.

Noble, Peter S. *Béroul's "Tristan" and the "Folie Tristan de Berne."* London: Grant and Cutler, 1982.

———. *Love and Marriage in Chrétien de Troyes*. Cardiff: University of Wales Press, 1982.

———. "Chrétien's Arthur." In Noble and Paterson, eds., *Chrétien de Troyes and the Troubadours*, 1984, pp. 220–237.

———, and Linda M. Paterson, eds. *Chrétien de Troyes and the Troubadours: Essays in Memory of the Late Leslie Topsfield.* Cambridge: St. Catharine's College, 1984.

*Le Nombre du temps en hommage à Paul Zumthor*. Paris: Champion, 1988.

O'Gorman, Richard. "Robert de Boron's *Joseph d'Arimathie* and the Sacrament of Penance." In Busby and Lacy, eds., *Conjunctures: Medieval Studies in Honor of Douglas Kelly*, 1994, 375-385.

Ollier, Marie-Louise. "Modernité de Chrétien de Troyes." *Romanic Review*, 71 (1980), 413–444.

———. "Utopie et roman arthurien." *Cahiers de Civilisation Médiévale*, 27 (1984), 223–232.

———. *Lexique et concordance de Chrétien de Troyes d'après la copie Guiot, avec introduction, index et rimaire.* Traitement informatique par Serge Lusignan, Charles Doutrelepont, and Bernard Dorval.

Montreal: Institut d'Etudes Médiévales, Université de Montréal; Paris: Vrin, 1986.

———. "Le Péché selon Yseut dans le *Tristan* de Béroul." In Busby and Kooper, eds., *Courtly Literature: Culture and Context*, 1990, pp. 465–482.

O'Sharkey, Eithne M. "The Character of Lancelot in *La Queste del saint graal*." In Varty, ed., *An Arthurian Tapestry: Essays in Memory of Lewis Thorpe*, 1981, pp. 328–341.

———. "Punishments and Rewards of the Questing Knights in *La Queste del saint graal*." In Davies and Kennedy, eds., *Rewards and Punishments in the Arthurian Romances and Lyric Poetry of Mediaeval France*, 1987, pp. 101–117.

Ostergaard Kristensen, Vibeke. "L'Amour de Tristan et Iseut dans *Le roman de Tristan en prose*: amour fatal ou amour chevaleresque?" *Revue Romane*, 20 (1985), 243–258.

Owen, D.D.R. "The Craft of Guillaume le Clerc's *Fergus*." In Arrathoon, ed., *The Craft of Fiction: Essays in Medieval Poetics*, 1984, pp. 47–81.

———. "Theme and Variations: Sexual Aggression in Chrétien de Troyes." *Forum for Modern Language Studies*, 21 (1985), 376–386.

———. "Reward and Punishment in Chrétien's *Erec* and Related Texts." In Davies and Kennedy, eds., *Rewards and Punishments in the Arthurian Romances and Lyric Poetry of Mediaeval France*, 1987, pp. 119–132.

Panvini, Bruno. *L'"Erec et Enide" di Chrétien de Troyes: "conte d'aventure" e "conjointure."* Catania: C.U.E.C.M., 1986.

———. *Il "Cligès" di Chrétien de Troyes*. Catania: Facoltà di Lettere e Filosofia, Università di Catania, 1989.

Parisse, Michel. "Tournois et tables rondes dans *Sone de Nansay*." *Etudes de langue et de littérature françaises offertes à André Lanly*, 1980, pp. 275-286.

Pastoureau, Michel. *Armorial des chevaliers de la Table Ronde*. Paris: Léopard d'or, 1983.

Payen, Jean Charles. "Le Palais de verre dans la *Folie d'Oxford*: De la folie métaphorique à la folie vécue, ou le rêve de l'île déserte à l'heure de l'exil: notes sur l'érotique des *Tristan*." *Tristania*, 5, No. 2 (1980), 17-27.

———. "Le Peuple dans les romans français de *Tristan*: La 'povre gent' chez Béroul, sa fonction narrative et son statut idéologique." *Cahiers de Civilisation Médiévale*, 23 (1980), 187-198.

———. "Béroul et l'abélardisme." *Romania*, 103 (1982), 374-375.

———, ed. *La Légende arthurienne et la Normandie (hommage à René Bansard)*. Condé-sur-Noireau: Corlet, 1983.

Pearcy, Roy J. "Fabliau Intervention in Some Mid-Thirteenth-Century Arthurian Verse Romances." *Arthurian Yearbook*, 1 (1991), 63-89.

Pemberton, Lyn. "Authorial Interventions in the *Tristan en prose*." *Neophilologus*, 68 (1984), 481-497.

Pensom, Roger. "Rhetoric and Psychology in Thomas's *Tristan*." *Modern Language Review*, 78 (1983), 285-297.

Perret, Michèle. "'Architecture inscrite' dans un roman arthurien du XIIIe siècle: *Le Bel inconnu*." In *Et c'est la fin pour quoy sommes ensemble: hommage à Jean Dufournet*, 1993, pp. 1073-1087.

———. "Atemporalités et effet de fiction dans *Le bel inconnu*." In *Le nombre du temps en hommage à Paul Zumthor*, 1988, pp. 225-235.

Pfeffer, Wendy. "The Love Potion in Béroul's *Tristan.*" In Mermier, ed., *Courtly Romance: A Collection of Essays*, 1984, pp. 169–176.

Pickens, Rupert T. *"Mais de çou ne parole pas Crestiens de Troies...*: A Re-examination of the Didot-*Perceval.*" *Romania*, 105 (1984), 492–510.

————. "Autobiography and History in the Vulgate *Estoire* and in the *Prose Merlin.*" In Kibler, ed., *The Lancelot-Grail Cycle*, 1994, pp. 98–116.

————, ed. *The Sower and His Seed: Essays on Chrétien de Troyes.* Lexington, KY: French Forum, 1983.

————, ed. *Studies in Honor of Hans-Erich Keller.* Kalamazoo, MI: Medieval Institute Publications, 1993.

Pickford, Cedric E. "The Good Name of Chrétien de Troyes." In Varty, ed., *An Arthurian Tapestry: Essays in Memory of Lewis Thorpe*, 1981, pp. 389–401.

————. "The Maturity of the Arthurian Prose Romances." *Bibliographical Bulletin of the International Arthurian Society*, 34 (1982), 197–206.

Pitts, Brent A. "Commerce, Memory and Composition in the French Poems of Tristan." *Medieval Perspectives*, 4–5 (1989–90), 150–160.

————. "Absence, Memory, and the Ritual of Love in Thomas's *Roman de Tristan.*" *French Review*, 63 (1990), 790–799.

————. "The Path of Memory: Imagination and Repetition in Béroul's *Roman de Tristan.*" *Romance Quarterly*, 37 (1990), 3–17.

————. "In Praise of Tristan: Oral Composition and Epic Technique In Beroul's *Roman de Tristan.*" *Romance Philology*, 36 (1992), 1–12.

Poirion, Daniel. *Le Merveilleux dans la littérature française du moyen âge*. Paris: Que-sais-je?, 1981.

———. "Semblance du graal dans la *Queste*." In Mok, Spiele, and Verhuyck, eds., *Mélanges de linguistique, de littérature et de philologie médiévales, offerts à J.R. Smeets*, 1982, pp. 227–241.

Polak, Lucie. *Chrétien de Troyes: Cligés*. London: Grant and Cutler, 1982.

Pollmann, L. "Tristan und Isolde in Kontext der hochhöfischen Literatur Frankreichs (*folie* und szenische Gestaltung)." *Studia M. de Riquer*. Barcelona: Quaderns Crema, 1988, III, 471–498.

Ponti, Annalisa. "I 'Tristani' di Thomas e Béroul: prospettivismo monologico e prospettivismo dialogico." *Medioevo Romanzo*, 13 (1988), 183–202.

Poublan-Couste, Emmanuelle. "Les nombres et leur symbolique dans le *Lancelot-Graal*." *PRIS-MA*, 8 (1992), 195–210.

Pratt, Karen. "Aristotle, Augustine or Boethius? *La Mort le roi Artu* as Tragedy." *Nottingham French Studies*, 30, No. 2 (1991), 81–109.

Press, A.R. "Chrétien de Troyes's Laudine: A *Belle dame sans mercy*?" *Forum for Modern Language Studies*, 19 (1983), 158–171.

———. "Death and Lamentation in Chrétien de Troyes's Romances: the Dialectic of Rhetoric and Reason." *Forum for Modern Language Studies*, 23 (1987), 11–20.

Raabe, Pamela. "Chrétien's *Lancelot* and the Sublimity of Adultery." *University of Toronto Quarterly*, 57 (1987–88), 259–269.

Reichert, Hermann. "Les Origines du motif de la Table Ronde dans le *Brut* de Wace." In Danielle Buschinger and André Crépin, eds., *La Représentation de l'antiquité au moyen âge: Actes du Colloque des 26, 27 et 28 mars 1981*. Vienna: Halosar, 1982, pp. 243–258.

Reid, T.B.W. "Chrétien de Troyes and the Scribe Guiot." *Medium Ævum*, 45 (1976), 1–19.

Reiss, Louise Horner. "Tristan and Isolt and the Medieval Ideal of Friendship." *Romance Quarterly*, 33 (1986), 131–137.

Rey-Flaud, Henri. *La Névrose courtoise*. Paris: PUF, 1983.

Ribard, Jacques. *Chrétien de Troyes: le "Chevalier de la Charrete," essai d'interprétation symbolique*. Paris: Nizet, 1972.

———. "Ecriture symbolique et visée allégorique dans le *Le conte du graal*." *Œuvres et Critiques*, 5, No. 2 (1980–81), 103–109.

———. "L'*Aventure* dans la *Queste del saint graal*." In *Mélanges Alice Planche*, 1984, pp. 415–423.

———. *Du philtre au graal: pour une interprétation théologique du "Roman de Tristan" et du "Conte du graal."* Paris: Champion, 1989.

———. "Figures du chevalier errant dans le *Tristan en prose*." In *Et c'est la fin pour quoy sommes ensemble: hommage à Jean Dufournet*, 1993, pp. 1205–1216.

———. "Tristan/Renart 'revisité.'" In Pickens, ed., *Studies in Honor of Hans-Erich Keller*, 1993, pp. 181–194.

Rider, Jeff. "Courtly Marriage in Robert Biket's *Lai du cor*." *Romania*, 106 (1985), 173–197.

Rieger, Angelica. "Neues über Chrétiens Illustratoren: Bild und Text in der ältesten Überlieferung von *Perceval-le-vieil* (*T*)." *Bibliographical Bulletin of the International Arthurian Society*, 41 (1989), 301–311.

Rieger, Dietmar. "Le Motif de la jalousie dans le roman arthurien: L'Exemple du roman d'*Yder*." *Romania*, 110 (1989), 364–382.

*Le Rire au moyen âge dans la littérature et dans les arts: Actes du Colloque International des 17-19 novembre 1988.* Bordeaux: Presses Universitaires de Bordeaux, 1990.

Robreau, Yvonne. *L'Honneur et la honte: leur expression dans les romans en prose du Lancelot-Graal (XIIe-XIIIe siècles).* Geneva: Droz, 1981.

Rockwell, Paul V. "Writing the Fountain: The Specificity of Resemblance in Arthurian Romance." *Bibliographical Bulletin of the International Arthurian Society*, 42 (1990), 267–282.

———. "The Falsification of Resemblance: Reading the False Guenièvre." *Arthurian Yearbook*, 1 (1991), 27–42.

Roland, Véronique. "Folio liminaire et réception du texte: les manuscrits parisiens du *Merlin en prose.*" *Bibliographical Bulletin of the International Arthurian Society*, 43 (1991), 257–269.

Roloff, Volker. "Der Märchenwald als Traum: zur Interpretation von Märchenmotiven in der Artusepik (*Tristan* und *Lancelot en prose*)." In Wolfzettel, ed., *Artusrittertum im späten Mittelalter*, 1984, pp. 146–158.

Rossi, Marguerite. "Les Duels de Gauvain dans la *Première Continuation de Perceval* ou les ambiguïtés de la prouesse individuelle." In *Mélanges Jean Larmat.* Paris: Belles Lettres, 1982, pp. 275–289.

Rousse, Michel. "Chrétien de Troyes, les femmes et la politique." In Foulon et al., eds., *Actes du 14e Congrès International Arthurien*, 1985, pp. 739–752.

Roussel, Claude. "Le Jeu des formes et des couleurs: observations sur 'la beste glatissant.'" *Romania*, 104 (1983), 49–82.

———. "L'Art de la suite: Sagremor et l'intertexte." *Annales: Economies Sociétés Civilisations*, 41 (1986), 27–42.

Ruck, E.H. *An Index of Themes and Motifs in Twelfth-Century French Arthurian Poetry.* Cambridge: Brewer, 1991.

Ruh, Kurt. *Lancelot: Wandlungen einer ritterlichen Idealgestalt.* Marburg: Pressestelle der Philipps-Universität, 1982.

Ruhe, Ernstpeter. "Der Chevalier errant auf enzyklopädischer Fahrt." In Wolfzettel, ed., *Artusrittertum im Späten Mittelalter*, pp. 159–176.

Runte, Hans R. "Initial Readers of Chrétien de Troyes." In Lacy and Torrini-Roblin, eds., *Continuations: Essays on Medieval French Literature and Language in Honor of John L. Grigsby*, 1989, pp. 121–132.

Rushing, James A., Jr. "The Adventures of the Lion Knight: Story and Picture in the Princeton *Yvain*." *Princeton University Library Chronicle*, 52 (1991), 31–49.

Saccone, Antonio. "La parola di Dio e la parola di Chrétien nel *Conte del graal*: la vera storia di Perceval." *Annali Istituto Universitario Orientale Napoli: sezione romanza*, 33 (1991), 103–143.

Salmeri, Filippo. "Due studi sul *Perceval*: I. Le tre gocce di sangue sulla neve (valore e funzione dell'episodio nella struttura del romanzo). II. Perchevax li Galois." *Quaderni di Filologia Medievale Catania*, 1, No. 1 (1980), 7–64.

———. *Manessier: modelli, simboli, scrittura.* Catania: C.U.E.C.M, 1984.

Saly, Antoinette. "La récurrence des motifs en symétrie inverse et la structure du *Perceval* de Chrétien de Troyes." *Travaux de Linguistique et de Littérature* (Strasbourg), 21, No. 2 (1983), 21–41.

———. "Dépouillement du *Perlesvaus*." *PRIS-MA*, 1 (1985), 29–31.

————. "Perceval-Perlesvaus: la figure de Perceval dans le *Haut Livre du graal.*" *Travaux de Linguistique et de Littérature* (Strasbourg), 24, No. 2 (1986), 7–18.

————. "L'Arbre illuminé et l'arbre à l'enfant." *PRIS-MA*, 5, No. 1 (1989), 81–93.

————. "Joseph d'Arimathie Roi Pêcheur." *Travaux de Littérature*, 5 (1992), 19–36.

Sandqvist, Sven. *Notes textuelles sur le roman de Tristan de Béroul.* Lund: Gleerup, 1984.

Santucci, Monique. "Propos sur la structure de *La mort Artu.*" *Travaux de Littérature*, 5 (1992), 7–17.

Sargent-Baur, Barbara Nelson. "Erec's Enide: 'sa fame ou s'amie'?" *Romance Philology*, 33 (1980), 373–387.

————. "Between Fabliau and Romance: Love and Rivalry in Béroul's *Tristran.*" *Romania*, 105 (1984), 292–311.

————. "*Dux bellorum / rex militum /* roi fainéant: la transformation d'Arthur au XIIe siècle." *Moyen Age*, 90 (1984), 357–373.

————. "Truth, Half-Truth, Untruth: Béroul's Telling of the Tristan Story." In Arrathoon, ed., *The Craft of Fiction: Essays in Medieval Poetics*, 1984, pp. 393–421.

————. "La Dimension morale dans le *Roman de Tristan* de Béroul." *Cahiers de Civilisation Médiévale*, 31 (1988), 49–56.

————. "Perceval and the Adventure Within." In Van Hoecke, Tournoy, and Verbeke, eds., *Arturus Rex: Vol. II*, 1991, pp. 120–133.

————. "Love in Theory and Practice in the *Conte du graal.*" *Arthurian Yearbook*, 2 (1992), 179–189.

Sasaki, Shigemi. "Le Mystère de la lance et la chapelle à la main noire dans trois *Continuations* de *Perceval.*" In Foulon et al., eds., *Actes du 14e Congrès International Arthurien*, 1985, pp. 536–557.

Schaefer, Jacqueline T. "Towards a Poetics of the Mediaeval Tristanian Universe: A Computer-Assisted Analysis of the *Folie Tristan* Poems." *Tristania*, 6, No. 1 (1980), 3–18; 6, No. 2 (1981), 3–22.

Schenck, David P. "Vues sur le temps et l'espace chez Chrétien de Troyes." *Œuvres et Critiques*, 5, No. 2 (1980–81), 111–117.

Schmid, Elisabeth. "Buchstabenwunder, Leseabenteuer und die Bedürftigkeit des Leibes: das Vorspiel zur 'Estoire del saint graal.'" In Mertens and Wolfzettel, eds., *Fiktionalität im Artusroman*, 1993, pp. 117–134.

Schmolke-Hasselmann, Beate. *Der arthurische Versroman von Chrestien bis Froissart: zur Geschichte einer Gattung.* Tübingen: Niemeyer, 1980.

———. "King Arthur as Villain in the Thirteenth-Century Romance *Yder.*" *Reading Medieval Studies*, 6 (1980), 31–43.

———. "Le Roman de *Fergus*: technique narrative et intention politique." In Varty, ed., *An Arthurian Tapestry: Essays in Memory of Lewis Thorpe*, 1981, pp. 342–353.

———. "Untersuchungen zur Typik des arthurischen Romananfangs." *Germanisch-romanische Monatsschrift*, 31 (1981), 1–13.

———. "The Round Table: Ideal, Fiction, Reality." *Arthurian Literature*, 2 (1982), 41–75.

———. "Der französische Artusroman in Versen nach Chrétien de Troyes." *Deutsche Vierteljahrsschrift für Literaturwissenschaft und Geistesgeschichte*, 57 (1983), 415–430.

————. "Ausklang der altfranzösischen Artusepik: *Escanor* und *Meliador.*" In Göller, ed, *Spätmittelalterliche Artusliteratur*, 1984, pp. 41–52.

Schulze-Busacker, Elisabeth. "Etude typologique de la complainte des morts dans le roman arthurien en vers du 12e au 14e siècle." In Varty, ed., *An Arthurian Tapestry: Essays in Memory of Lewis Thorpe*, 1981, pp. 54–68.

Shirt, David J. "*Le Chevalier de la charrete*: A World Upside Down?" *Modern Language Review*, 76 (1981), 811–822.

————. "Was King Arthur Really 'Mad'? Some Comments on the *Charrete* References in *Yvain.*" In Varty, ed., *An Arthurian Tapestry: Essays in Memory of Lewis Thorpe*, 1981, pp. 187–202.

————. "Cligés: A Twelfth-Century Matrimonial Case-Book?" *Forum for Modern Language Studies*, 18 (1982), 75–89.

Short, Ian, ed. *Medieval French Textual Studies in Memory of T.B.W. Reid*. London: Birkbeck College, 1984.

Simes, G.R. "*La Queste del saint graal* as Chivalric Anti-Romance." *Parergon*, 5 (1987), 54–70.

Solterer, Helen. "*Conter le terme de cest brief*: l'inscription dans *La mort de roi Artu.*" In Foulon et al., eds., *Actes du 14e Congrès International Arthurien*, 1985, pp. 558–568.

Speckenbach, Klaus. "Endzeiterwartung im 'Lancelot-Gral-Zyklus': zur Problematik des joachitischen Einflusses auf den Prosaroman." In Klaus Grubmüller, Ruth Schmidt-Wiegand, and K. Speckenbach, eds., *Geistliche Denkformen in der Literatur des Mittelalters*. Munich: Fink, 1984, pp. 210–225.

Stäblein, Patricia Harris. "The Structure of the Hero: Narrative Dynamics and Heroic Power in Beroul's *Tristan.*" In Mermier, ed., *Courtly Romance: A Collection of Essays*, 1984, pp. 223–250.

Staines, David. "*Cliges*: Chrétien's Paradigmatic Experiment." In Mermier, ed., *Courtly Romance: A Collection of Essays*, 1984, pp. 251–272.

Stanesco, Michel. "Le Chemin le plus long: de la parole intempestive à l'économie du dire dans *Le conte du graal*." In Varty, ed., *An Arthurian Tapestry: Essays in Memory of Lewis Thorpe*, 1981, pp. 287–298.

———. "Le Lion du chevalier: de la stratégie romanesque à l'emblème poétique." *Littératures*, 20 (1989), 7–13.

———, and Michel Zink. *Histoire européenne du roman médiéval: esquisse et perspectives*. Paris: Presses Universitaires de France, 1992.

Stones, M. Alison. "Aspects of Arthur's Death in Medieval Illumination," with "Appendices: An Iconographic Survey of Manuscripts Illustrating Arthur's Death." In Baswell and Sharpe, eds., *The Passing of Arthur: New Essays in Arthurian Tradition*, 1988, pp. 52–101 + 12 plates.

———. "Arthurian Art Since Loomis." In Van Hoecke, Tournoy, and Verbeke, eds., *Arturus Rex: Vol. II*, 1991, pp. 21–78.

Strubel, Armand. *La Rose, Renart et le graal: la littérature allégorique en France au XIIIe siècle*. Paris: Champion, 1989.

*Studies in Medieval French Language and Literature Presented to Brian Woledge*. Geneva: Droz, 1988.

Sturm-Maddox, Sara. "Hortus non conclusus: Critics and the *Joie de la Cort*." *Œuvres et Critiques*, 5, No. 2 (1980–81), 61–71.

———. "The *Joie de la cort*: Thematic Unity in Chrétien's *Erec et Enide*." *Romania*, 103 (1982), 513–528.

————. "*Tout est par senefiance*: Gerbert's *Perceval*." *Arthurian Yearbook*, 2 (1992), 191–207.

————, and Donald Maddox. "Description in Medieval Narrative: Vestimentary Coherence in Chrétien's *Erec et Enide*." *Medioevo Romanzo*, 9 (1984), 51–64.

Suard, François. "La Conception de l'aventure dans le *Lancelot* en prose." *Romania*, 108 (1987), 230–253.

————. "The Narration of Youthful Exploits in the *Prose Lancelot*." In Kibler, ed., *The Lancelot-Grail Cycle*, 1994, pp. 67-84.

Sullivan, Penny. "The Education of the Heroine in Chrétien's *Erec et Enide*." *Neophilologus*, 69 (1985), 321–331.

Sweetser, Franklin P. "L'amour, l'amitié et la jalousie dans le *Lancelot en prose*." *Travaux de Littérature*, 2 (1989), 23–29.

Szabics, Imre. "La Fonction poétique des structures syntaxiques récurrentes dans l'*Yvain* de Chrétien de Troyes." In Foulon et al., eds., *Actes du 14e Congrès International Arthurien*, 1985, pp. 584–599.

Szkilnik, Michelle. "Ecrire en vers, écrire en prose: le choix de Wauchier de Denain." *Romania*, 107 (1986), 208–230.

————. *L'Archipel du graal: Etude de l'"Estoire del saint graal."* Geneva: Droz, 1991.

————. "*L'Estoire del saint graal*: réécrire la *Queste*." In Van Hoecke, Tournoy, and Verbeke, eds., *Arturus Rex: Vol. II*, 1991, pp. 294–305.

Taylor, Jane H.M. "The Fourteenth Century: Context, Text and Intertext." In Lacy, Kelly, and Busby, eds., *The Legacy of Chrétien de Troyes*, 1987-88, I, 267–332.

————. "Arthurian Cyclicity: the Construction of History in the Late French Prose Romances." *Arthurian Yearbook*, 2 (1992), 209–223.

————. "The Parrot, the Knight and the Decline of Chivalry." In Busby and Lacy, eds., *Conjunctures: Medieval Studies in Honor of Douglas Kelly*, 1994, 529-544.

Thorpe, Lewis. *The "Lancelot" in the Arthurian Prose Vulgate.* Cambridge: Heffers, 1980.

Topsfield, Leslie T. *Chrétien de Troyes: A Study of the Arthurian Romances.* Cambridge: Cambridge University Press, 1981.

Torrini-Roblin, Gloria. "Oral or Written Model?: Description, Length, and Unity in the *First Continuation.*" In Lacy and Torrini-Roblin, eds., *Continuations: Essays on Medieval French Literature and Language in Honor of John L. Grigsby*, 1989, pp. 145–161.

Traxler, Janina P. "Observations on the Importance of the Prehistory in the *Tristan en prose.*" *Romania*, 108 (1987), 539–548.

————. "Textual Criticism of the French *Prose Tristan.*" *Arthurian Yearbook*, 2 (1992), 225–245.

Tyson, Diana B. "King Arthur as a Literary Device in French Vernacular History Writing of the Fourteenth Century." *Bibliographical Bulletin of the International Arthurian Society*, 33 (1981), 237–257.

Tyssens, Madeleine. "Comment Béroul écrit l'*Estoire.*" In *Miscellanea di studi Aurelio Roncaglia.* 4 vols. Modena: Mucchi, 1989, pp. 1369–1379.

Uitti, Karl D. "Intertextuality in *Le Chevalier au lion.*" *Dalhousie French Studies*, 2 (1980), 3–13.

————. "Vernacularization and Old French Romance Mythopoesis with Emphasis on Chrétien's *Erec et Enide.*" In Pickens, ed., *The*

*Sower and His Seed: Essays on Chrétien de Troyes*, 1983, pp. 81–115.

————. "Chrétien de Troyes and His Vernacular Forebears: The City of Women (I)." *French Forum*, 11 (1986), 261–288.

————. "Chrétien de Troyes's *Cligés*: Romance *Translatio* and History." In Busby and Lacy, eds., *Conjunctures: Medieval Studies in Honor of Douglas Kelly*, 1994, 545-557.

————, and Alfred Foulet. "On Editing Chrétien de Troyes: Lancelot's Two Steps and Their Context." *Speculum*, 63 (1988), 271–292.

Vance, Eugene. "Chrétien's *Yvain* and the Ideologies of Change and Exchange." *Yale French Studies*, 70 (1986), 42–62.

————. *From Topic to Tale: Logic and Narrativity in the Middle Ages*. University of Minnesota Press, 1987.

Van Coolput, Colette-Anne. "La 'Préhistoire arthurienne': quelques réflexions à propos de la première partie du *Tristan en prose*." *Lettres Romanes*, 38 (1984), 275–282.

————. *Aventures querant et le sens du monde: aspects de la réception productive des premiers romans du Graal cycliques dans le "Tristan en prose."* Leuven: Leuven University Press, 1986.

van Mulken, Margot. *The Manuscript Tradition of the "Perceval" of Chrétien de Troyes: A Stemmatological and Dialectological Approach*. Amsterdam, 1993.

Varty, E.K.C. "On Birds and Beasts, 'Death' and 'Resurrection,' Renewal and Reunion in Chrétien's Romances." In Grout et al., eds., *The Legend of Arthur in the Middle Ages*, 1983, pp. 194–212.

————, ed. *Arthurian Tapestry: Essays in Memory of Lewis Thorpe*. Glasgow: French Department of the University of Glasgow, 1981.

Verbeke, W., J. Janssens, and M. Smeyers, eds. *Arturus Rex, Volumen I: La matière de Bretagne et les anciens Pays-Bas.* Leuven: Leuven University Press, 1987.

Verhuyck, Paul, and Anneli Vermeer-Meyer. "Le temps divin d'Yvain." *Revue Belge de Philologie et d'Histoire*, 60 (1982), 527-539.

Vermette, Rosalie A. "*Terrae incantatae*: The Symbolic Geography of Twelfth-Century Arthurian Romance." In William E. Mallory and Paul Simpson-Housley, eds., *Geography and Literature: A Meeting of the Disciplines.* Syracuse, NY: Syracuse University Press, 1987, pp. 144-160.

Verstraete, Daniel. "La Fonction littéraire du silence de Perceval dans le *Conte du graal*." *Revue des Langues Romanes*, 90 (1986), 99-110.

Vial, Guy. *Le Conte du graal: sens et unité. La première continuation: textes et contenu.* Geneva: Droz, 1987.

Vinaver, Eugène. "The Questing Knight." In Marjorie W. McCune, Tucker Orbison, and Philip M. Withim, eds., *The Binding of Proteus: Perspectives on Myth and the Literary Process.* Lewisburg, PA: Bucknell University Press; London: Associated University Presses, 1980, pp. 126-140.

————. *Intreccio, strutture, narrazione e discorso nel romanzo: il caso di Chrétien de Troyes (analisi dell'"Erec et Enide" e dell'"Yvain").* Cagliari: Istituto di Filologia moderna della Facoltà di Lettere e Filosofia dell'Università degli studi di Cagliari, 1980.

————. *Perceval: per un'e(ste)tica del poetico: Fra immaginario, strutture linguistiche e azioni.* Oristano: S'Alvure, 1988.

Vitz, Evelyn Birge. "Rethinking Old French Literature: The Orality of the Octosyllabic Couplet." *Romanic Review*, 68 (1986), 308-321.

————. "Orality, Literacy and the Early Tristan Material: Béroul, Thomas, Marie de France." *Romanic Review*, 78 (1987), 299–310.

————. "Chrétien de Troyes: clerc ou ménestrel? Problèmes des traditions orales et littéraires dans les cours de France au XIIe siècle." *Poétique*, 81 (1990), 21–42.

Voicu, Mihaela. "Modèle et fiction: *L'Eloge de la nouvelle chevalerie* de saint Bernard de Clairvaux et *La queste del saint graal*." *Verbum* (July–December 1991), pp. 73–84.

————. "'Semblance' et 'senefiance' ou de la lecture des signes dans *Le conte du graal*." *Revue Roumaine de Linguistique*, 37 (1992), 79–87.

Walter, Philippe. "Le Solstice de Tristan." *Travaux de Linguistique et de Littérature* (Strasbourg), 20, No. 2 (1982), 7–20.

————. *Canicule: essai de mythologie sur "Yvain" de Chrétien de Troyes.* Paris: CDU et SEDES, 1988.

————. *La Mémoire du temps: fêtes et calendriers de Chrétien de Troyes à la "Mort Artu."* Paris: Champion, 1989.

————. *Le Gant de verre: le mythe de Tristan et Yseut.* La Gacilly: Artus, 1990.

Walters, Lori. "Le Rôle du scribe dans l'organisation des manuscrits des romans de Chrétien de Troyes." *Romania*, 106 (1985), 303–325.

————. "The Creation of a 'Super Romance': Paris, Bibliothèque Nationale, fonds français, MS 1433." *Arthurian Yearbook*, 1 (1991), 3–25 + 13 plates.

White, Sarah Melhado. "Lancelot's Beds: Styles of Courtly Intimacy." In Pickens, ed., *The Sower and His Seed: Essays on Chrétien de Troyes*, 1983, pp. 116–126.

Wild, Gerhard. "Manuscripts Found in a Bottle? zum Fiktionalitäts-status (post)arthurischer Schwellentexte." In Mertens and Wolfzettel, eds., *Fiktionalität im Artusroman*, 1993, pp. 203–241.

Willaert, Frank. "*Matière* et *sens* chez Chrétien de Troyes et Hadewijch (d'Anvers?)." *Moyen Age*, 88 (1982), 421–434.

Williams, Harry F. "*Le Conte du graal* de Chrétien de Troyes: positions critiques et nouvelles perspectives." *Œuvres et Critiques*, 5, No. 2 (1980–81), 119–123, 127–128.

Woledge, Brian. "Notes on Rhythm in Chrétien's *Yvain*." In Grout et al., eds., *The Legend of Arthur in the Middle Ages*, 1983, pp. 213–226.

———. "The Problem of Editing *Yvain*." In Short, ed., *Medieval French Textual Studies in Memory of T.B.W. Reid*, 1984, pp. 254–267.

———. *Commentaire sur "Yvain" ("Le Chevalier au Lion") de Chrétien de Troyes. Tome I: vv. 1–3411. Tome II: vv. 3412–6808.* Geneva: Droz, 1986–88.

Wolfgang, Lenora D. "Perceval's Father: Problems in Medieval Narrative Art." *Romance Philology*, 34 (1980), 28–47.

———. "Chrétien's *Lancelot*: Love and Philology." *Reading Medieval Studies*, 17 (1991), 3–17.

Wolfzettel, Friedrich. "Arthurian Adventure or Quixotic 'Struggle for Life'? A Reading of Some Gauvain Romances in the First Half of the Thirteenth Century." In Varty, ed., *An Arthurian Tapestry: Essays in Memory of Lewis Thorpe*, 1981, pp. 260–274.

———. "Lancelot et les fées: essai d'une lecture psychanalytique du *Lancelot en prose*." *Marche Romane*, 32 (1982), 25–42.

————. "Idéologie chevaleresque et conception féodale dans *Durmart le Galois*: l'altération du schéma arthurien sous l'impact de la réalité politique du XIIIe siècle." In Foulon et al., eds., *Actes du 14e Congrès International Arthurien*, 1985, pp. 668–686.

————. "Zum Stand und Problem der Intertextualitätsforschung im Mittelalter (aus romanistischer Sicht)." In Wolfzettel, ed., *Artusroman und Intertextualität*, 1990, pp. 1–17.

————, ed. *Artusrittertum im späten Mittelalter: Ethos und Ideologie: Vorträge des Symposiums der deutschen Sektion der Internationalen Artusgesellschaft vom 10.–13. November 1983 im Schloß Rauischholzhausen (Universität Gießen)*. Gießen: Schmitz, 1984.

————, ed. *Artusroman und Intertextualität: Beiträge der deutschen Sektionstagung der Internationalen Artusgesellschaft vom 16. bis 19. November 1989 an der Johann Wolfgang Goethe-Universität Frankfurt a. M.*. Gießen: Schmitz, 1990.

Zaddy, Z.P. "Chrétien misogyne." In *Mélanges Charles Foulon*, 1980, II, 301–307.

————. "Yvain as the Ideal Courtly Lover." In *Studies in Medieval French Language and Literature Presented to Brian Woledge*, 1988, pp. 253–275.

Zambon, Francesco. *Robert de Boron e i segreti del graal*. Florence: Olschki, 1984.

————. "Graal et hérésie: le cas du *Joseph* de Robert de Boron." In Foulon et al., eds., *Actes du 14e Congrès International Arthurien*, 1985, pp. 687–706.

————. "La 'cavalleria celeste' e il luogo del racconto nella *Queste del saint graal*." *L'Immagine Riflessa*, 12 (1989), 217–229.

Zemel, Roel. "Fergus, Ferguut en de Graalheld." In *"In onse scole":
Opstellen Margaretha H. Schenkeveld.* Amsterdam: Stichting
Neerlandistiek, 1989, pp. 75–94.

Zink, Michel. "Le Rêve avéré: la mort de Cahus et la langueur
d'Arthur, du *Perlesvaus* à *Fouke le Fitz Waryn.*" In *Littératures:
Mélanges René Fromilhague.* Toulouse: Université de Toulouse-Le
Mirail, 1984, pp. 31–38.

Zuurdeeg, Atie Dingemans. *Narrative Techniques and Their Effects in
"La mort de roi Artu."* York, SC: French Literature Publications,
1981.

# THE LOW COUNTRIES[*]

## Bart Besamusca

Penninc, one of the two Flemish authors of the *Walewein*, observes in his prologue:

> Vanden coninc Arture
> Es bleven menighe avonture
> Die nemmer mee ne wert bescreven.
> Nu hebbic ene scone up heven.
> Consticse wel in twalsche vinden
> Ic soudse jou in dietsche ontbinden:
> Soe es utermaten scone!

("Many a story about King Arthur has not yet been put in writing. I have just started a beautiful one. If I could find it in French, I would translate it for you into Dutch: it is a fine tale indeed!" *Walewein*, edition Van Es, ll. 1–7)

Netherlandists set great store by these words of Penninc, which imply that in the period the poet was active, ca. 1250, many Arthurian stories were still circulating orally. It would also seem that Penninc is informing us that his story is not a translation but an indigenous romance. (Only occasionally does a scholar, such as J.H. Winkelman [1984], question this interpretation of these verses.) It is beyond dispute, furthermore, that the poet suggests that French literature was greatly respected in the Low Countries.

The word *dietsche* (l. 6) was once used in the Low Countries to designate the Dutch language as it was used between ca. 1150 and 1550. Nowadays, "Middle Dutch" denotes this phase of our language,

---

[*] My research has been made possible by a fellowship of the Royal Netherlands Academy of Arts and Sciences. I would like to thank Frank Brandsma and Orlanda Lie for their comments on the first draft of this article. The Dutch version was translated into English by Josephie Brefeld.

as distinguished from Old Dutch and Modern Dutch. *Dietsch* is not a single language; what we now call Middle Dutch is in fact a series of closely related dialects. Two examples will suffice to illustrate this. In most dialects, *ridder* is the word for "knight" but one dialect has a marked preference for *rudder*. In that same Flemish dialect, *soe* is used for the third person singular female personal pronoun, where the other dialects commonly have *si*. Variants of *dietsch* were spoken in an area that roughly encompasses both the Netherlands as it is today (with the exception of Friesland) and the Flemish-speaking part of Belgium. For the Middle Ages, this involves the counties Holland and Flanders and the duchies Brabant and Limburg. Interest in Arthurian literature was markedly greater in some of these areas than in others.

## The Corpus

The tradition of Arthurian romance in verse as written by Chrétien and his followers is strongly represented in Middle Dutch Arthurian literature. Already at the beginning of the thirteenth century, for example, a translation of Chrétien's *Perceval* was made in the province of Holland, in all probability together with a translation of the *First Perceval Continuation. Wrake van Ragisel* ("Revenge for Ragisel"), a Flemish adaptation of *Vengeance Raguidel*, was presumably translated in the same period, as well as *Tristant*, an adaptation of Thomas's *Tristan* made in the eastern part of the Low Countries. About the middle of the thirteenth century, Guillaume le Clerc's *Fergus* was put into Middle Dutch by a Flemish poet. This translation is known as *Ferguut*.

The tradition of the prose romances was also well established in the Low Countries. The *Prose Lancelot* was put into Middle Dutch at least three times (but, curiously enough, two of the translators did not adopt the prose form of their exemplar). Around 1260, a Flemish poet wrote *Lantsloot vander Haghedochte* ("Lancelot of the Cave"), a free verse adaptation of the Old French text. It is presumed that ca. 1280 this romance was followed by the *Lanceloet* translation, again made by a Fleming. In spite of its form—it is a text in verse—*Lanceloet* is a faithful translation of the *Prose Lancelot*. The third Middle Dutch translator of the Old French romance produced a prose text; when and where he worked is not known.

Other parts of the Vulgate Cycle were put into Middle Dutch, too. *Queeste vanden Grale* ("Quest of the Grail") and *Arturs doet* ("Arthur's Death") are translations of the *Queste del saint Graal* and *Mort le roi Artu*, respectively. Both are rhymed translations that date back to the second half of the thirteenth century. Ca. 1261, the Flemish poet Jacob van Maerlant prepared two romances for Albrecht van Voorne, viscount of Zeeland. The *Historie vanden Grale* ("History of the Grail") and the *Boek van Merline* ("Book of Merlin") which form a unity, are verse adaptations of Old French prose versions of Robert de Boron's *Joseph d'Arimathie* and *Merlin*. In 1326, the Brabantine poet Lodewijk van Velthem followed in Maerlant's footsteps with his *Merlijn-Continuatie* ("Merlin Continuation"). Velthem's romance, which was probably made for Gerard van Voorne, the son of Albrecht, is a translation in verse of the *Suite-Vulgate du Merlin* and was meant to complete Maerlant's texts.

In the years 1283–88, Maerlant worked on his *Spiegel Historiael*. In this adaptation of Vincent of Beauvais's *Speculum Historiale*, commissioned by the count of Holland, Floris V, the Middle Dutch poet also gave an account of British history from the arrival of Brutus to the disappearance of Arthur, completing his source with material from Geoffrey of Monmouth's *Historia Regum Britanniae*.

Middle Dutch Arthurian literature does not consist of translations and adaptations only. From the middle of the thirteenth century onward, the *matière de Bretagne* inspired several poets to write indigenous romances. The classic and probably first example of such a work is Penninc's and Vostaert's Gawain romance, *Walewein*. In the second half of the thirteenth century, three more indigenous romances were written: *Moriaen* (about the black knight Moriaen), *Ridder metter mouwen* ("Knight with the Sleeve"), both of them Flemish, and *Walewein ende Keye* ("Gawain and Kay").

About 1320, many of the Middle Dutch Arthurian romances were combined in the so-called *Lancelot* Compilation, a cycle of ten Arthurian romances that came into being in Brabant. The compiler used existing Middle Dutch texts, radically adapting some of them. *Lanceloet*, *Queeste vanden Grale*, and *Arturs doet* form the core of the cycle. Preceding the translation of the *Queste del saint Graal* are versions of *Perchevael* and *Moriaen*; following it are *Wrake van Ragisel*, *Ridder metter mouwen*, *Walewein ende Keye*, *Lanceloet en het hert met de witte voet* ("Lancelot and the Stag with the White Foot," a "novelette" probably based on the *Lai de Tyolet*), and *Torec*, an adaptation of a Middle Dutch translation, now lost, of an Old French Arthurian romance that is also lost, *Torrez, le Chevalier au Cercle d'Or*. According to a note on the last folium of the codex, Lodewijk van Velthem was the first owner of the *Lancelot* Compilation.

Printed Middle Dutch Arthurian romances were extremely rare. Between 1534 and 1544, the Antwerp printer Symon Cock published the *Historie van Merlijn* ("History of Merlin"), an adaptation of *A Lytel Treatyse of y Birth and Prophecye of Marlyn*, which had been printed in London in 1510. No other printed Arthurian romances from the Low Countries have survived.

## Current State of Scholarship

The Middle Dutch Arthurian romances have come to us in a few codices and a great many fragments, most of which came into being in the fourteenth century. J. Deschamps's catalogue (2nd ed., 1972) of a Brussels exhibition on Middle Dutch manuscripts from European and American libraries offers useful information on complete codices with Arthurian texts. Designed for literary historians, my *Repertorium* (1985) presents brief descriptions of all the sources for Middle Dutch Arthurian literature, as well as a bibliography of Middle Dutch Arthurian studies to 1985. A third reference work, by Hans Kienhorst (1988), does not limit itself to the manuscript tradition of Arthurian romances: it describes the written sources of the entire Middle Dutch chivalric literature, stressing codicological aspects.

In 1974, the unique manuscript of *Ferguut* was published in facsimile by M.J.M. de Haan. One year later, the same scholar made accessible in the form of a facsimile edition the quire of the *Lancelot* Compilation that contains *Ridder metter mouwen*. Although these editions are rather simple, the reproduction is good enough to be useful.

Halfway through the nineteenth century, pioneers in the study of Middle Dutch literature began to publish many editions. These editions, meant chiefly to enable scholars to study the language, are now out of date, though they are still being used. W.J.A. Jonckbloet's monumental edition of the *Lancelot* Compilation (1846–49), published under the title *Roman van Lancelot*, is still indispensable. A number of romances are available in full only in this edition: *Lanceloet*, *Perchevael*, *Queeste vanden Grale*, *Walewein ende Keye*, and *Arturs doet*.

Unlike many of his colleagues, Jonckbloet had a keen eye for the literary value of Middle Dutch texts. He is a kindred spirit to the editors of recent decades who seek to present to their readers a reliable image of the text as it has been preserved but who above all approach the text as a literary work. A fine example is M.J.M. de Haan's edition of the *Ridder metter mouwen* (1983), in which punctuation and ample explanation of words help the reader to interpret the romance. E. Rombauts's fine 1976 edition of *Ferguut* is responsible for the text having been widely read and studied over the past years. An obvious deficiency of the *Ferguut* edition has recently been remedied. The manuscript of *Ferguut* contains about two hundred and fifty corrections made by another contemporary hand which were not indicated in Rombauts's edition. In 1989, however, Willem Kuiper, studying the corrections closely, indicated them in an edition of the romance that was appended to his book.

The flawed 1971 edition of *Moriaen* by H. Paardekooper-van Buuren and M. Gysseling, neither punctuates the text nor regularizes the allographemes *i*, *j*, *u*, and *v*. Many potential readers of this romance will prefer Jongen's Modern Dutch translation of *Moriaen* and of *Walewein ende Keye* published in 1992 as *Walewein, de neef van koning Arthur*.

In his review of W.P. Gerritsen's remarkable *editio princeps* of *Lantsloot vander Haghedochte* (1987) Frank Willaert praised Gerritsen's exemplary editing of this fragmentary romance. With a limited number of editorial interventions, the text is presented in such a way that it is accessible to modern readers yet users with linguistic interests have no trouble reconstructing the text as the manuscript has it. Comments at the bottom of the page offer paleographical notes, explanation and translation of words and other interpretative entries, and notes that deal with literary aspects. Gerritsen summarizes those parts of the text that have been lost on the basis of the Old French original.

Although linguistic research is beyond the scope of this essay, E. van den Berg's work is of major relevance to the study of Middle Dutch chivalric romances. His 1983 dissertation studies the relation between verse-line and sentence in Middle Dutch narrative poetry, distinguishing four types of versification. Some poets write short sentences with few enjambments (analytic-static), others write long sentences with few enjambments (synthetic-static), a third category produces short sentences and many enjambments (analytic-dynamic), and finally there are the poets who combine long sentences with many enjambments (synthetic-dynamic). It is fascinating to see that these four types represent different stages in the development of Middle Dutch versification, a development from analytic-static to synthetic-dynamic verse. It follows that relative dates can be assigned to texts on the basis of these versification types. In a later article, Van den Berg links his chronological results to the geographical distribution of the Middle Dutch chivalric romances. It appears that Arthurian romances, like the Charlemagne romances, came into being chiefly in Flanders and that the Romances of Antiquity received a great deal of attention in Brabant and Holland.

The study of the literary aspects of Middle Dutch Arthurian romances has recently gained momentum. Inspired by international medieval studies and in particular by Germanic studies, Dutch and Belgian Arthurian's approach the Middle Dutch texts from various points of view, with no single one having the monopoly. The following are those that are most important.

Comparative research has focused on the direct relation between a Middle Dutch Arthurian romance and its original. When poets wanted to prepare a translation of a romance, they turned to the south, where France dominated the cultural scene; it is this attitude that Penninc hints at in the quotation that opened this essay. One of these poets adapted the *Vengeance Raguidel*. W.P. Gerritsen's 1963 study of *Wrake van Ragisel*, a milestone in the field, has persuaded scholars that the study of techniques of translation and adaptation is valuable. Dutch translations are not mere imitations of Old French originals. Although faithful translations do exist (e.g., *Perchevael*), they are a minority. Usually, Middle Dutch translators break new ground. The same holds for the poet of *Wrake van Ragisel*, who, according to Gerritsen, quite often managed to surpass the original. The adapter increased suspense in certain situations—for example, by ordering events differently. He amplified descriptions of man-to-man fights, festive meals, and the other topoi of Arthurian literature and rewrote the love scenes in such a way that *Wrake*'s Walewein is much more a courtly lover than Gauvain is in *Vengeance*. Influenced by Edmond Faral and Ernst Robert Curtius,[1] Gerritsen stresses that the poet who wrote *Wrake* followed the guidelines of the twelfth- and thirteenth-century *artes poeticae*, with which he had become familiar at school.

Inspired by Maartje Draak's pioneering 1954 study on the Middle Dutch translations of the *Prose Lancelot*, a study that contained an eloquent plea for a renewed and detailed analysis of these texts, Orlanda Lie provided in her 1979 dissertation (published 1987) a study and edition of the Middle Dutch prose translation. Through a rigorous analysis of the manuscript tradition, focusing on groups of textually affiliated manuscripts, Lie determined the place of the prose translation in the French, German, and Dutch *Lancelot* tradition. She proved that the three extant Middle Dutch versions of the *Prose Lancelot* were written independently and that the German *Prose Lancelot* is not based on the Dutch one. In addition, Lie shows that the Middle Dutch prose translator favored a literal, almost word-for-word translation with an occasional replacement of the French reading by a more condensed paraphrase.

In 1981, F.P. van Oostrom studied the adaptation technique of the poet who composed *Lantsloot vander Haghedochte*. Unlike Gerritsen, van Oostrom interprets the differences between the Middle Dutch romance and its Old French source not as the logical consequence of the teaching of rhetoric (e.g., amplification) in the medieval school but as deliberate interventions. In studying the adaptation technique employed in *Lantsloot*, van Oostrom distinguishes three major tendencies. The poet rationalizes, he blurs the exact references to place and time, and, most important, he idealizes, striving to make the manners, speech, courage, and self-control of his characters meet the standards of perfect courtly behavior. It is especially in this last tendency that van Oostrom sees a correspondence with the adaptation

---

[1] Cf. Edmond Faral, *Les arts poétiques du XIIe et du XIIIe siècle: recherches et documents sur la technique littéraire du Moyen Age* (Paris: Champion, 1924), and Ernst Robert Curtius, *Europäische Literatur und lateinisches Mittelalter* (Bern: Francke, 1948).

technique that French Germanists observed in the work of Middle High German poets, the so-called *adaptation courtoise*.[2] In addition, van Oostrom argues, idealization reveals what the poet intended with his work: *Lantsloot* was meant as a mirror of courtly behavior for a court that was not yet familiar with courtly ideals.

Interest in the translation and adaptation technique of Middle Dutch poets has continued. In 1991, I published an edition of a part of *Lanceloet* and an introductory study of the poet's translation technique. Unlike *Wrake van Ragisel* and *Lantsloot vander Haghedochte*, *Lanceloet* is not an adaptation but a brilliant translation. The translator stayed close to the words of his prose original, though writing verse, by means of stylistic "tricks," such as the replacement of pronouns by phrases containing a noun in order to meet poetic requirements.

In 1992, Roel Zemel dealt with the relation between *Lanceloet en het hert met de witte voet* and the *Lai de Tyolet*. He argued that the Middle Dutch poet exercised his creativity and sought to ridicule Lanceloet (who in the Middle Dutch romance took the place of Tyolet), contrasting him with Walewein, the positive and successful hero. In 1991, Zemel studied *Ferguut*, a romance in which, unusually, both a translated part and an adapted one can be distinguished. Two poets may have been at work, as Willem Kuiper argued (1989), or a single poet set out to translate but had to rely on his memory at a later stage, as no manuscript of *Fergus* was any longer available. It is the translated part that Zemel thoroughly analyzed.

A second line of approach to Middle Dutch Arthurian romances gained acceptance in the 1960s: the immanent interpretation of texts. As in the international field of medieval studies (cf. Jean Frappier's publications on the romances by Chrétien de Troyes[3]), Dutch and Belgian scholars studied Arthurian romances first of all as literary products whose structure and meaning need to be examined. An increasing number of Middle Dutch Arthurian romances have become the object of this type of investigation. The early popularity of *Ferguut*

---

[2] See, for example, Michel Huby, *L'adaptation des romans courtois en Allemagne au XIIe et au XIIIe siècle* (Paris: Klincksieck, 1968).

[3] For example, Jean Frappier, *Etude sur Yvain ou Le Chevalier au Lion de Chrétien de Troyes* (Paris: SEDES, 1969).

among critics led to discussion on the structure of the romance. According to Hanneke Paardekooper-van Buuren, *Ferguut* has a rigid structure in which the adventures form two groups of three encounters; these two groups mirror each other. She also argues that the structural deviations from *Fergus* in the second part of the Middle Dutch text are a successful attempt on the part of the poet to surpass the original. K.R. de Graaf rejected Paardekooper's point of view, arguing that it is the triangular relationship among Ferguut, his lady-love Galiene, and Arthur that determines the structure of the romance.

The structure and meaning of other texts have become subjects of investigation as well. Reacting to P. Minderaa's study on the composition of *Walewein*, Toos Verhage-van den Berg in 1983 drew attention to the secondary episodes of this text, which she interprets as a love story. In these secondary episodes, Walewein is said to develop from a courtly knight into a courtly lover. Some years later, Frank Brandsma and I demonstrated that in *Walewein* the *don contraignant* ("blind promise") motif[4] is used frequently and in a varied and complicated way to structure the story.

The structural analysis Jeannette Koekman made of the *Torec* indicates that the romance may have had a didactic purpose: it is possible, as W.P. Gerritsen suggested, that the text was written to be used in the education of young Floris V, the future count of Holland. Another Arthurian romance that has recently been examined for its composition is *Ridder metter mouwen*. According to Simon Smith (1989), the text does not have a truly bipartite structure: the romance is simply made up of two distinct parts, which partially mirror each other. He also holds that some structural elements indicate that the romance as we have it in the *Lancelot* Compilation differs greatly from the original romance, which has come down to us in fragments.

It is striking that with this structural approach progress has been made especially on those Middle Dutch Arthurian romances that belong to the tradition of Chrétien. Only in recent years has attention been

---

[4] For this motif, see Jean Frappier, "Le motif du 'don contraignant' dans la littérature du Moyen Age," in his *Amour courtois et table ronde* (Geneva: Droz, 1973), pp. 225-264; also Lisa Jefferson, "Don—Don Contraignant—Don Contraint: A Motif and Its Deployment in the French Prose Lancelot," *Romanische Forschungen*, 104 (1992), 27-51.

given to the structure of those texts that are part of the tradition of the prose romances. It is also the influence of Elspeth Kennedy's work[5] that made Frank Brandsma devote the introduction to his edition of a part of *Lanceloet* to the function of interlace in this romance and in the *Lancelot* Compilation.

Two scholars interested in narrative structures have successfully turned to the manuscripts. In 1980, Willem Kuiper studied the use of initials and section marks in manuscripts that contain *Ferguut* and *Walewein*. He shows that such markers were most certainly not inserted at random. In most cases, they function to structure the text; in addition, they sometimes served as an aid for those who recited the text, for instance by drawing attention to a change of intonation. Erwin Mantingh's 1992 analysis of structure markers (section marks, initials, and chapter titles) in the manuscripts of *Lanceloet*, *Perchevael*, and *Moriaen* resulted in a useful inventory.

At the beginning of the 1980s, scholars began to focus on the sociocultural context of literature. One might call this the historical-functional approach, which has successfully been propagated by F.P. van Oostrom. In his study of *Lantsloot vander Haghedochte*, he showed his interest in the initial function of this Middle Dutch Arthurian romance in its cultural-historical context; under the influence of Joachim Bumke and others,[6] he emphatically advocated in 1982 that scholars undertake the study of the patrons of Middle Dutch literature, illustrating his plea with an account of Lodewijk van Velthem's relation with the court at Voorne. Van Oostrom proved the value of this approach with his investigation of the literature at the court of Holland ca. 1400 (*Het woord van eer*; translated as *Court and Culture*).

Scholars interested in a contextual approach to Middle Dutch Arthurian romances labor under the difficulty of having scarcely any details at all on the sociohistorical background of their texts. We have already seen that it was especially in Flanders that people were interested in Middle Dutch Arthurian romances, but, owing partly to a

---

[5] In particular, her *Lancelot and the Grail: A Study of the Prose Lancelot* (Oxford: Clarendon, 1986).

[6] See, for example, Joachim Bumke, *Mäzene im Mittelalter: Die Gönner und Auftraggeber der höfischen Literatur in Deutschland 1150-1300* (Munich: Beck, 1979).

poor manuscript tradition, we hardly ever know who were the patrons of these romances. It is therefore only natural that, within the contextual approach of Middle Dutch Arthurian romances, much less attention is being paid at present to the cultural-historical background of these texts than to the functional aspects: the communication among poet, patron, and audience has become an object of study as well. In this context, it is the literary game that poets play with their audiences that is most studied. Most often, poets involve their audiences by means of intertextuality. With J.D. Janssens playing the part of pioneer, this aspect of Middle Dutch Arthurian romances has over the past few years received considerable attention.

In a series of articles, Janssens studied aspects of intertextuality. In 1988, his research resulted in an inspiring book that shows how Middle Dutch poets use passages from other texts to structure their own romances. Such passages are used for the context of the poets' own stories and are, under the principle of analogy, made into the basis of similar or contrasting passages in a new romance. Janssens discusses in great detail how this was done in *Walewein*.

Other Arthurian scholars followed in Janssens's footsteps. Wilma Kossen studied the allusions in *Moriaen* to the adventures of Perceval in Chrétien's *Conte du graal*, arguing that the Middle Dutch poet tried to write a *Perceval* continuation. The poet of *Ridder metter mouwen* plays with the same Old French text; in 1991, Simon Smith pointed this out when he discussed intertextuality in the first episode of the Middle Dutch text. In the same year, Roel Zemel published his book (mentioned above) on Guillaume's *Fergus* and *Ferguut*, where he showed that the Middle Dutch poet played a literary game much less than his French colleague did. Because of its many borrowings from the *Perceval*, the meaning of *Fergus* is determined by its intertextual links with Chrétien's romance. There is, however, no such link between *Ferguut* and *Perceval*.

In my book on *Walewein*, *Moriaen*, and *Ridder metter mouwen*, I employed the intertextual approach to show the connection among these three Flemish romances, a connection that had so far been obscure. *Walewein* is a romance in the tradition of Chrétien, where poets use intertextual passages to react against the Old French *Prose Lancelot* and Gerbert's *Perceval Continuation*. The poet of *Moriaen* knows *Walewein* and reacts to it, borrowing quite a number of the literary characteristics

of his romance from the *Prose Lancelot*. He furthermore presents his
text as a variation on *Perceval*: it is not Perceval but his son Moriaen
who is the hero of the story, and it is not the Grail Moriaen is trying
to find, it is his father. The poet of *Ridder metter mouwen*, who knew
both *Walewein* and *Moriaen*, breaks ground that again is fresh: in
contrast to his two predecessors, he follows in Chrétien's footsteps, and
he does so ostentatiously. Not only did he borrow all sorts of literary
characteristics from Chrétien's texts; he also constantly refers to the
adventures of Chrétien's heroes (Yvain, Lancelot, Perceval).

*Work in Progress*

Over the last ten years, the study of Middle Dutch literature has
flourished, and there is currently a good deal of work in progress. A
monograph on *Torec* by Jeannette Koekman is under way, as is a series
of articles on *Ridder metter mouwen* by Simon Smith. Soetje Klerk-
Oppenhuis de Jong studies the highly intriguing way *Perchevael* is
embedded in the *Lancelot* Compilation, and Marjolein Hogenbirk is
working on *Walewein ende Keye*, which has so far been neglected. (As
a first result, the latter recently published an article on the indigenous
text.) Roel Zemel is studying the adapted part of *Ferguut* and plans to
publish his results in a monograph, meant as a sequel to his 1991 study
on the translated part of the romance. Tom Hage is at work on the
urgently needed biography of Lodewijk van Velthem. In the near
future, van Oostrom's study of Jacob van Maerlant will undoubtedly
give attention to the Arthurian romances this Flemish poet wrote.

The Lancelot Project, an ambitious undertaking that has been carried
out in Utrecht since 1975, aims at opening up to scholars the three
Middle Dutch translations of the *Prose Lancelot* by means of studies
and editions. The results of this long-term project are published in the
series *Middelnederlandse Lancelotromans* under the auspices of the
Constantijn Huygens Institute of the Royal Netherlands Academy of
Arts and Sciences, which assumed sponsorship of the project in 1977.
The first three books in this series are van Oostrom's study of the
adaptation technique used by the poet of *Lantsloot vander Haghedochte*
(Volume 1), Gerritsen's edition of this romance (Volume 2), and Lie's

study and edition of the two fragments of the Middle Dutch prose translation of the *Prose Lancelot* (Volume 3).

Starting with Volume 4, the series has begun to deal with the Middle Dutch translations of the core of the Vulgate Cycle in the *Lancelot* Compilation: *Lanceloet, Queeste vanden Grale*, and *Arturs doet*. As has already been noted, these texts are available only in W.J.A. Jonckbloet's edition, which dates back to the last century and which urgently needs to be replaced. This edition does not do justice to the work of the "Corrector." As W.P. Gerritsen demonstrated in a valuable article (1976), for the purpose of its recitation the Corrector provided a great part of the *Lancelot* Compilation with corrections and with words and signs, usually in the lefthand margins of the columns. Jan Willem Klein has argued that the Corrector took an active part in the original production of the manuscript. Furthermore, several scholars have suggested that the Corrector is to be identified with none other than Lodewijk van Velthem. So far, some sixteen thousand verses of *Lanceloet* have been edited, in Volumes 4 (by Bart Besamusca and Ada Postma), 5 (by Bart Besamusca), and 6 (by Frank Brandsma). Ada Postma is working on the next ten thousand verses. It will take about twenty years for the series to be finished.[7]

Those who are cooperating in the Lancelot Project have increasingly taken an interest in the *Lancelot* Compilation as a fine example of a narrative cycle, comparable to compilations of Old French Arthurian romances like those that came down in Chantilly 472 and in Paris, B.N. f.fr. 112, which Cedric Pickford studied in 1960.[8] This interest resulted in a colloquium on the development of narrative cycles in the chansons de geste and the Arthurian romances (Amsterdam, 1992), the proceedings of which were published by Bart Besamusca, W.P. Gerritsen, Corry Hogetoorn, and Orlanda Lie. I myself am working on an English monograph on the *Lancelot* Compilation as a narrative cycle.

---

[7] For a discussion of four volumes of the series *Middelnederlandse Lancelotromans*, see Geert H.M. Claassens's very recent review article.

[8] Cf. Cedric E. Pickford, *L'évolution du roman arthurien en prose vers la fin du Moyen Age d'après le manuscrit 112 du fonds français de la Bibliothèque Nationale* (Paris: Nizet, 1960).

As part of the Lancelot Project, editions of *Perchevael* and *Walewein ende Keye*, the other two romances from the *Lancelot* Compilation that are available only in Jonckbloet's edition, are also being prepared. W.P. Gerritsen assumed the edition of *Walewein ende Keye*, which as yet has not received the scholarly attention it deserves, partly because no good edition is available. The eagerly awaited edition of *Perchevael*—a text that occupies a key position in the development of Middle Dutch Arthurian romance—is being prepared by Maartje Draak and Soetje Klerk-Oppenhuis de Jong.

Dutch Literature and Culture in the Middle Ages is a project coordinated by F.P. van Oostrom. A five-year research program (1989–94) established by the Netherlands Organization for Scientific Research and Leyden University, it aims at studying Middle Dutch literature from a cultural-historical point of view. A large number of dissertations are being prepared, and the project provides for research by groups of scholars concentrating on specific themes: during half a year specialists join forces to study a problem area in Middle Dutch literature. These study groups have examined such topics as urban literature, lyric poetry, and religious prose. In the first half of 1994, a study group under the direction of J.D. Janssens concentrated on Middle Dutch narrative literature. Matters of obvious importance to Arthurian scholars were discussed: the relation between textual history and manuscript history, the dating and localizing of romances, the importance of prologues and epilogues, and the intertextual dimension of texts. This teamwork among specialists will result in a collection of articles.

Under the auspices of the P.J. Meertens Institute of the Royal Netherlands Academy of Arts and Sciences, and with Willem Kuiper as the moving spirit, an index is being compiled of Middle Dutch literary proper nouns (names of persons, animals, weapons, towns, countries, etc.). The material will be published in book form according to genre, starting in 1995 with the names from the Middle Dutch chivalric romances. Just as specialists in Old French Arthurian literature have for years now been able to turn to G.D. West's indexes,[9] those who study Middle Dutch Arthurian romances will in a few years also be able to profit from an indispensable reference work.

## Desiderata

Maerlant and Velthem still lack adequate modern editions. Maerlant's *Historie vanden Grale* and *Boek van Merline* and Velthem's *Merlijn-Continuatie* were edited in 1880 by J. van Vloten under the misleading title *Jacob van Maerlant's Merlijn*. These three romances were preserved completely in Middle Low German and in one codex only. Although Van Vloten rewrote this dialect in what he felt was proper Middle Dutch, thereby rendering his version useless, it remains the only edition of Velthem's romance. Maerlant's work is available in the more recent but still inadequate edition by Timothy Sodmann, who made many reading errors and presented the text in a way that leaves much to be desired.

Articles dealing with Maerlant and Velthem's romances are few and slight; W.P. Gerritsen's 1981 essay on Maerlant's *Historie vanden Grale* and Arthur's history in the *Spiegel Historiael* is a notable exception. Other romances also suffer from the disproportionate attention some texts (e.g., *Walewein*, *Ferguut*) receive. One would almost believe, for example, that the *Tristant* does not exist for Arthurian scholars. The recent attention given to the *Historie van Merlijn* is restricted to a single article by P.N.G. Pesch, and it appears that Netherlandists go out of their way to avoid *Queeste vanden Grale*, the only exception being J.C. Prins-s'Jacob. The works that have come down to us in sources from the border region between the Low Countries and Germany are often ignored: the fragment of the *Tristant*, a number of *Perchevael* fragments, the Cologne *Lancelot* codex (on which fortunately Orlanda Lie [1991] has provided information), and

---

[9] G.D. West, *An Index of Proper Names in French Arthurian Verse Romances 1150-1300* (Toronto: University of Toronto Press, 1969), and G.D. West, *An Index of Proper Names in French Arthurian Prose Romances* (Toronto: University of Toronto Press, 1978).

the codex Burgsteinfurt (with Maerlant and Velthem's romances). To remedy this, Netherlandists and Germanists, who are now apparently waiting for each other to begin the study of these texts, must join forces.

Such a collaboration is also essential for providing insight into the place of Middle Dutch Arthurian literature in the European development of Arthurian romance. Two examples from my own research will illustrate the conspicuous parallels between Middle Dutch and other Arthurian romance. Like many thirteenth-century Arthurian romances, the Middle Dutch *Walewein* by Penninc and Vostaert and *Wigalois* by the German poet Wirnt von Grafenberg present a perfect hero. The correspondence between these two romances is not, however, limited to this parallel. Both works demonstrate that even a perfect hero requires the help of God. In Wigalois's case, this is shown in his fight with the giantess Ruel. When she is about to kill the knight, God saves him by having his horse neigh, whereupon Ruel flees, thinking that what she hears is the roaring of a dragon. Then God answers Wigalois's prayer and frees him from his chains. In *Walewein*, the hero is apparently beyond hope, imprisoned in King Assentijn's dungeon. Again, God intervenes: Walewein is liberated by the ghost of a knight whom he, at an earlier stage in the story, had confessed and had given a Christian burial. Walewein's chains drop of their own accord, and the grateful dead man, with God's assent, leads him out of the castle.

My second example of a similar generic development deals with *Walewein* and *Diu Crône* by Heinrich von dem Türlin. Heinrich, like Penninc and Vostaert, idealizes a secular knighthood, which has its best representative in Arthur's nephew Walewein/Gawein. It is Gawein who at the end of Heinrich's romance manages to conclude the quest for the Grail successfully. The poet thus takes a stand against the spiritual romances of chivalry, and *Diu Crône* and the *Walewein* agree strikingly in this respect. A closer investigation, preferably carried out by Netherlandists and Germanists working hand in hand, would surely yield interesting results.

A.T. Bouwman has pointed out that cooperation between Netherlandists and Romanists is equally desirable. If we believe that our research should be directed at the milieu in which literature functioned, experts in Dutch and French must cooperate in studying medieval Flanders. At present, Romanists study the French Arthurian romances written and copied in Flanders, while Netherlandists study the Middle Dutch ones. But as these works functioned in one and the same region, the interaction between Old French and Middle Dutch Arthurian romances merits closer investigation. Is there, for example, a relation between the popularity of the Old French *Prose Lancelot* in Flanders and the two extant Flemish Middle Dutch translations of that text? Such scholarly cooperation could also result in a revised edition of M.D. Stanger's article on literary patronage at the court of Flanders.

Our knowledge of Flemish literature is inadequate. As J.D. Janssens (1992) has shown, Flemish interest in Middle Dutch Arthurian romances (*Walewein, Ridder metter mouwen, Lanceloet,* and *Lantsloot vander Hagedochte*) presents some fascinating problems. In 1991, I raised one of those problems in an article: we know far too little about the patrons of Middle Dutch works in Flanders. As literary patrons often belong to the aristocracy, we should obviously look to the high Flemish nobility, but this was, as far as we know, completely Gallicized. The counts of Flanders promoted French literature: commissions to Chrétien de Troyes and Manessier are well-known examples. Is it likely that Middle Dutch romances also came into being and were in circulation at the Flemish court? Was the court bilingual? Perhaps we should look elsewhere for the patrons of Middle Dutch romances. One might think of the so-called peers of Flanders and of members of the rich and influential town patriciate. Filling this gap in our knowledge is of crucial importance.

A last desideratum bears upon the internationalization of Middle Dutch scholarship. Foreign insights are readily incorporated into the study of the Arthurian romances and the same holds for the development of the study of Dutch language and literature as a whole. Dutch scholars surrendered the diachronic approach to their literature for a synchronic approach accompanied by strong specialization. This specialization was beautifully reflected in the literary history edited by M.A. Schenkeveld-van der Dussen. Following Denis Hollier's *A New History of French Literature*,[10] more than one hundred Netherlandists were invited to write a short essay. Specialization drove scholars studying Middle Dutch Arthurian romances into the arms of their

---

[10] Denis Hollier, ed., *A New History of French Literature* (Cambridge: Harvard University Press, 1989).

international colleagues, as evidenced by their references to the secondary literature in other languages.

Yet there is another side to internationalization. Netherlandists have thus far failed to make Middle Dutch literature accessible to international colleagues and to contribute to international discussions. Scholars who wish to become acquainted with Middle Dutch Arthurian literature, for example, have only limited possibilities. They can turn to the articles in *The New Arthurian Encyclopedia* edited by Norris J. Lacy et al., and to J.D. Janssens's essays in *The Legacy of Chrétien de Troyes* and *Arturus Rex, Volumen II*. They can also turn to the 1959 survey that Hendricus Sparnaay published in Loomis's *Arthurian Literature in the Middle Ages*. Sparnaay's survey is, however, unreliable. According to Sparnaay, for example, Lodewijk van Velthem translated the *Livre d'Artus*. To the Arthurian scholar, this information is most valuable: after all, we know very little about this unique continuation of the *Prose Merlin*, which has come down to us in incomplete form. Unfortunately, the truth is less spectacular: Velthem translated not the *Livre d'Artus* but another continuation of the *Prose Merlin*, the well-known *Suite-Vulgate du Merlin*.

Yet a change has set in: Dutch and Belgian Arthurian scholars more and more realize that they owe it to their subject to provide information on Middle Dutch literature to those colleagues who speak other languages. A recent collection of articles on Middle Dutch literature in its European context, edited by Erik Kooper, effectively illustrates this new understanding of duties. The same awareness is evident in the articles on Middle Dutch Arthurian romances in *Arturus Rex, Volumen II* (edited by Willy van Hoecke, Gilbert Tournoy, and Werner Verbeke) and in the articles that both J.H. Winkelman and I devoted to *Walewein* in 1992.

Scholars without Middle Dutch can now acquaint themselves with *Walewein*. They owe this to David Johnson, who edited and translated this undisputed masterpiece into English. It is to be hoped that others will follow the example Johnson set; many more Middle Dutch Arthurian romances merit translation into English. With Johnson's work, the time is ripe for a study in English on *Walewein*, in which Dutch scholars could present the results of their inquiries to their international colleagues who might then use *Walewein* in their own research.[11]

The absence of a general, reliable introduction to the Arthurian romances of the Low Countries stands in the way of increasing international interest in these texts. The Eugène Vinaver Trust Fund has for some years now supported plans to update Loomis's *Arthurian Literature in the Middle Ages*. As a first concrete result, 1991 saw the publication of *The Arthur of the Welsh*;[12] other volumes are to follow. One of them ought to present an up-to-date survey of Middle Dutch Arthurian literature.

---

[11] Meanwhile, three scholars, a Romanist (Norris Lacy), a Germanist (Walter Haug), and an Anglicist (Felicity Riddy), have accepted my invitation to write comparative articles about the *Walewein*. Their essays will be published in the Dutch journal *Tijdschrift voor Nederlandse taal- en letterkunde*.

[12] Rachel Bromwich, A.O.H. Jarman, and Brynley F. Roberts, eds., *The Arthur of the Welsh: The Arthurian Legend in Medieval Welsh Literature* (Cardiff: University of Wales Press, 1991).

# Bibliography

*Editions and Translations*

Besamusca, Bart, ed. *Lanceloet: De Middelnederlandse vertaling van de Lancelot en prose overgeleverd in de Lancelotcompilatie, pars 2 (vs. 5531–10740).* Assen: Van Gorcum, 1991.

———, and Ada Postma, eds. *Lanceloet: De Middelnederlandse vertaling van de Lancelot en prose overgeleverd in de Lancelotcompilatie, pars 1 (vs. 1–5530, voorafgegaan door de verzen van het Brusselse fragment).* Assen: Van Gorcum, forthcoming.

Brandsma, Frank, ed. *Lanceloet: De Middelnederlandse vertaling van de Lancelot en prose overgeleverd in de Lancelotcompilatie, pars 3 (vs. 10741–16263).* Assen: Van Gorcum, 1992.

Es, G.A. van, ed. *De jeeste van Walewein en het schaakbord*, by Penninc and Pieter Vostaert. 2 vols. Zwolle: Tjeenk Willink, 1957.

Gerritsen, W.P., ed., with the cooperation of A. Berteloot et al. *Lantsloot vander Haghedochte: Fragmenten van een Middelnederlandse bewerking van de Lancelot en prose.* Amsterdam: North-Holland, 1987.

Haan, M.J.M. de, ed. *Ferguut: A Facsimile of the Only Extant Middle Dutch Manuscript (Leiden, University Library, Ms. Letterkunde 191).* Leiden: New Rhine, 1974.

———, ed. *Die riddere metter mouwen: Ms. The Hague, Royal Library 129 A 10 fol. 167–177 verso and the Fragment Brussels,*

*Royal Library IV 818*; intro. C.W. de Kruyter. Leiden: New Rhine, 1975.

————, et al., eds. *Roman van den Riddere metter mouwen*. Utrecht: HES, 1983.

Johnson, David F., ed. and trans. *Penninc and Pieter Vostaert: Roman van Walewein*. New York: Garland, 1992.

Jonckbloet, W.J.A., ed. *Roman van Lancelot (XIIIe eeuw)*. 2 vols. The Hague: Van Stockum, 1846–49.

Jongen, Ludo, trans. *Walewein, de neef van koning Arthur*. Griffioen. Amsterdam: Em. Querido's Uitgeverij, 1992.

Paardekooper-van Buuren, H., and M. Gysseling, eds. *Moriaen*. Zutphen: Thieme, [1971].

Rombauts, E., N. de Paepe, and M.J.M. de Haan, eds. *Ferguut*. Culemborg: Tjeenk Willink, 1976; rpt. Hilversum: Verloren, 1994.

Sodmann, Timothy, ed. *Historie van den Grale und Boek van Merline*, by Jacob van Maerlant. Cologne: Böhlau, 1980.

Vloten, J. van, ed. *Merlijn*, by Jacob van Maerlant. Leiden: Brill, 1880.

## Studies

Berg, E. van den. *Middelnederlandse versbouw en syntaxis: Ontwikkelingen in de versifikatie van verhalende poëzie, ca. 1200–ca. 1400*. Utrecht: HES, 1983.

————. "Genre en gewest: De geografische spreiding van de ridderepiek." *Tijdschrift voor Nederlandse Taal- en Letterkunde*, 103 (1987), 1–36.

Besamusca, Bart. *Repertorium van de Middelnederlandse Arturepiek: Een beknopte beschrijving van de handschriftelijke en gedrukte overlevering.* Utrecht: HES, 1985.

————. "De Vlaamse opdrachtgevers van Middelnederlandse literatuur: een literair-historisch probleem." *De Nieuwe Taalgids*, 84 (1991), 150-162.

————. "Gauvain as Lover in the Middle Dutch Verse Romance *Walewein.*" *The Arthurian Yearbook*, 2 (1992), 3-12.

————. *Walewein, Moriaen en de Ridder metter mouwen: Intertekstualiteit in drie Middelnederlandse Arturromans.* Hilversum: Verloren, 1993.

————, and Frank Brandsma. "De toezegging met onvoorziene gevolgen in de *Walewein.*" *De Nieuwe Taalgids*, 81 (1988), 1-12.

————, and ————, eds. *De ongevalliche Lanceloet: Studies over de Lancelotcompilatie.* Hilversum: Verloren, 1992.

————, et al., eds. *Cyclification: Proceedings of the Colloquium on the Development of Narrative Cycles in the Chansons de geste and the Arthurian Romances, Amsterdam, 17-18 December 1992.* Amsterdam: North-Holland, 1994.

Bouwman, A.T. "'Na den walschen boucken': Neerlandistiek en romanistiek." In F.P. van Oostrom et al., *Misselike tonghe: De Middelnederlandse letterkunde in interdisciplinair verband.* Amsterdam: Prometheus, 1991, pp. 45-56, 193-197.

Claassens, Geert H.M. "Die van Utrecht, die 'Lancelote' maken: Overwegingen bij—en voorbij—de Middelnederlandse Lancelotromans II, III, V en VI." *Millennium*, 8 (1994), 44-65.

Deschamps, J. *Middelnederlandse handschriften uit Europese en Amerikaanse bibliotheken.* 2nd ed. Leiden: Brill, 1972.

Draak, Maartje. *De Middelnederlandse vertalingen van de Proza-Lancelot*. 1954; rpt. Amsterdam: North-Holland, 1977.

Gerritsen, W.P. *Die Wrake van Ragisel: Onderzoekingen over de Middelnederlandse bewerkingen van de Vengeance Raguidel, gevolgd door een uitgave van de Wrake-teksten*. 2 vols. Assen: Van Gorcum, 1963.

———. "Corrections and Indications for Oral Delivery in the Middle Dutch Lancelot Manuscript The Hague K.B. 129 A 10." In J.P. Gumbert and M.J.M. de Haan, eds., *Neerlandica Manuscripta: Essays Presented to G.I. Lieftinck 3*. Amsterdam: Van Gendt, 1976, pp. 39–59.

———. "Jacob van Maerlant and Geoffrey of Monmouth." In Kenneth Varty, ed., *An Arthurian Tapestry: Essays in Memory of Lewis Thorpe*. Glasgow: French Department of the University of Glasgow, 1981, pp. 368–388.

Graaf, K.R. de. "Ferguut, Artur en Galiene." *De Nieuwe Taalgids*, 67 (1974), 379–391; rpt. in Oostrom, van, ed., *Arturistiek in artikelen: Een bundel fotomechanisch herdrukte studies over Middelnederlandse Arturromans*, pp. 115–127.

Hoecke, Willy van, Gilbert Tournoy, and Werner Verbeke, eds. *Arturus Rex: Volumen II, Acta Conventus Lovaniensis 1987*. Leuven: Leuven University Press, 1991.

Hogenbirk, Marjolein. "'Die coenste die ie werd geboren': Over *Walewein ende Keye*." *De Nieuwe Taalgids*, 87 (1994), 57–75.

Janssens, J.D. "Le roman arthurien 'non historique' en moyen néerlandais: traduction ou création originale?" In Van Hoecke, Tournoy, and Verbeke, eds. *Arturus Rex, Volumen II: Acta Conventus Lovaniensis 1987*, 1991, pp. 330–351.

———. *Dichter en publiek in creatief samenspel: Over interpretatie van Middelnederlandse ridderromans*. Leuven: Acco, 1988.

————. "The Influence of Chrétien de Troyes on Middle Dutch
Arthurian Romances: A New Approach." In Norris J. Lacy,
Douglas Kelly, and Keith Busby, eds., *The Legacy of Chrétien de
Troyes*. 2 vols. Amsterdam: Rodopi, 1987–88, II, 285–306.

————. "De 'Vlaamse' achtergronden van de *Lancelotcompilatie*: Wat
onzekerheden op een rijtje: Vlaams, Brabants of Hollands?" In
Besamusca and Brandsma, eds., *De ongevalliche Lanceloet: Studies
over de Lancelotcompilatie*, 1992, pp. 21–43.

Kienhorst, Hans. *De handschriften van de Middelnederlandse
ridderepiek: Een codicologische beschrijving*. 2 vols. Deventer: Sub
Rosa, 1988.

Klein, Jan Willem. "Codicologie en de Lancelotcompilatie: De
invoeging van de *Perchevael* en de *Moriaen*." *De Nieuwe Taalgids*,
83 (1990), 526–539.

Koekman, Jeannette. "*Torec*, een vorstelijk verhaal; zinvolle verbanden
in een complexe tekst." *De Nieuwe Taalgids*, 81 (1988), 111–124.

Kooper, Erik, ed. *Medieval Dutch Literature in its European Context*.
Cambridge: Cambridge University Press, 1994.

Kossen, Wilma. "Moriaen en de Graalheld." In Fred de Bree and Roel
Zemel, eds., *'In onse scole': Opstellen over Middeleeuwse
letterkunde voor Prof. Dr. Margaretha H. Schenkeveld*. Amsterdam:
Stichting Neerlandistiek VU, 1989, pp. 95–108.

Kuiper, Willem. "Lombarden, paragraaf—en semiparagraaftekens in
Middelnederlandse epische teksten." *Spektator*, 10 (1980–81),
50–85.

————. *Die riddere metten witten scilde: Oorsprong, overlevering en
auteurschap van de Middelnederlandse Ferguut, gevolgd door een
diplomatische editie en een diplomatisch glossarium*. Amsterdam:
Schiphouwer and Brinkman, 1989.

Lacy, Norris J., et al., eds. *The New Arthurian Encyclopedia*. New York: Garland, 1991.

Lie, Orlanda S.H. "The Flemish Exemplar of Ms W. f° 46* Blankenheim, a fifteenth-century German Translation of the *Suite de la Charrette*." In Van Hoecke, Tournoy, and Verbeke, eds., *Arturus Rex: Volumen II, Acta Conventus Lovaniensis 1987*, 1991, pp. 404–418.

————. *The Middle Dutch Prose Lancelot: A Study of the Rotterdam Fragments and Their Place in the French, German, and Dutch Lancelot en prose Tradition, with an Edition of the Text*. Amsterdam: North-Holland, 1987.

Mantingh, Erwin. "*Lanceloet, Perchevael, Moriaen*, en de spin Sebastiaan: Luisteren met tussenpozen?" In Besamusca and Brandsma, eds., *De ongevalliche Lanceloet: Studies over de Lancelotcompilatie*, 1992, pp. 45–75.

Minderaa, P. "De compositie van de Walewein." In L. Brummel et al., eds., *Opstellen door vrienden en collega's aangeboden aan Dr. F.K.H. Kossmann*. The Hague: Nijhoff, 1958, pp. 155–166; rpt. Van Oostrom, ed., *Arturistiek in artikelen: Een bundel fotomechanisch herdrukte studies over Middelnederlandse Arturromans*, 1978, pp. 77–88.

Oostrom, F.P. van. *Lantsloot vander Haghedochte: Onderzoekingen over een Middelnederlandse bewerking van de Lancelot en prose*. Amsterdam: North-Holland, 1981.

————. "Maecenaat en Middelnederlandse letterkunde." In J.D. Janssens, ed., *Hoofsheid en devotie in de middeleeuwse maatschappij: De Nederlanden van de 12e tot de 15e eeuw*. Brussels, 1982, pp. 21–40; rpt. Frits van Oostrom, *Aanvaard dit werk: Over Middelnederlandse auteurs en hun publiek*. Amsterdam: Prometheus, 1992, pp. 48–64, 290–291.

————. *Het woord van eer: Literatuur aan het Hollandse hof omstreeks 1400*. Amsterdam: Meulenhoff, 1987; trans. as *Court and Culture: Dutch Literature, 1350–1450*. Berkeley: University of California Press, 1992.

————, ed., *Arturistiek in artikelen: Een bundel fotomechanisch herdrukte studies over Middelnederlandse Arturromans*. Utrecht: HES, 1978.

Paardekooper-van Buuren, Hanneke. "Struktuur en zin van de Ferguut." *De Nieuwe Taalgids*, 57 (1964), 148–156; rpt. Oostrom, van, ed., *Arturistiek in artikelen: Een bundel fotomechanisch herdrukte studies over Middelnederlandse Arturromans*, 1978, pp. 105–113.

Pesch, P.N.G. "Het Nederlandse volksboek van *Merlijn*: bron, drukker en datering." In Francine de Nave, ed., *Liber Amicorum Leon Voet*. Antwerp, 1985, pp. 303–328.

Prins-s'Jacob, J.C. "The Middle-Dutch Version of *La Queste del Saint Graal*." *De Nieuwe Taalgids*, 73 (1980), 120–132.

Schenkeveld-van der Dussen, M.A., et al., eds. *Nederlandse literatuur, een geschiedenis*. Groningen: Nijhoff, 1993.

Smith, Simon. "Van koning tot kroonprins: Over de structuur van de *Roman van den riddere metter mouwen*." In Fred de Bree and Roel Zemel, eds., *'In onse scole': Opstellen over Middeleeuwse letterkunde voor Prof. Dr. Margaretha H. Schenkeveld*. Amsterdam: Stichting Neerlandistiek VU, 1989, pp. 109–141.

————. "Dat begin vanden riddere metter mouwen." *Voortgang, Jaarboek voor de Neerlandistiek*, 12 (1991), 151–179.

Sparnaay, Hendricus. "The Dutch Romances." In Roger Sherman Loomis, ed., *Arthurian Literature in the Middle Ages: A Collaborative History*. Oxford: Clarendon, 1959, pp. 443–461.

Stanger, M.D. "Literary Patronage at the Medieval Court of Flanders." *French Studies*, 11 (1957), 214–229.

Verhage-van den Berg, Toos. "Het onderschatte belang van de nevenepisoden in de *Walewein*." *De Nieuwe Taalgids*, 86 (1983), 225–244.

Willaert, Frank. "Lancelot in Utrecht." *Spiegel der Letteren*, 32 (1990), 51–70.

Winkelman, J.H. "De Middelnederlandse Walewein oorspronkelijk?" *Spiegel der Letteren*, 26 (1984), 73–82.

———. "Der Ritter, das Schachspiel und die Braut: Ein Beitrag zur Interpretation des mittelniederländischen 'Roman van Walewein.'" In Johannes Janota et al., eds., *Festschrift Walter Haug und Burghart Wachinger*. 2 vols. Tübingen: Niemeyer, 1992, II, 549–563.

Zemel, R.M.T. "'Hoe Walewein Lanceloet bescudde ende enen camp vor hem vacht': Over *Lanceloet en het hert met de witte voet*." In Besamusca and Brandsma, eds., *De ongevalliche Lanceloet: Studies over de Lancelotcompilatie*, 1992, pp. 77–97.

———. *Op zoek naar Galiene: Over de Oudfranse Fergus en de Middelnederlandse Ferguut*, Vol. 1. Amsterdam: Schiphouwer en Brinkman, 1991.

# THE CELTIC LANDS

## John T. Koch

Celtic speech survived into the Middle Ages in two major linguistic subfamilies: Goidelic or Gaelic spoken in Ireland, northern and western Scotland, and the Isle of Man, and Brittonic spoken in Brittany, Cornwall, Wales, and (until the eleventh or twelfth century) Strathclyde/Cumbria.[1] Fragmentary and indirect evidence points to the existence of a variety of Celtic more akin to Brittonic than to Goidelic among the Picts of North Britain. This language probably died not long after the political subordination of the Picts to the Scots A.D. 845.[2]

All of these medieval Celtic groups have some bearing on Arthurian studies, but not to equal degrees. The Arthur of earliest preliterary tradition (together with the "Arthur of history" who would stand behind that, if any such person existed) belonged to the Brittonic-speaking Celts. The overwhelming preponderance of extant medieval Celtic literature that is concerned with the figure of Arthur himself, as well as with the figure of Myrddin (corresponding to Merlin) and the story of Tristan and Isold, is in the Welsh language. It is also in Welsh that we find Arthurian texts that are earlier in their absolute dating and that do not stand in an overt derivative relationship to other surviving texts. For these reasons, most of the current scholarship still concentrates on the Welsh Arthuriana, as did scholarship of the preceding generation.

---

[1] I wish to thank the following for their generous assistance in responding to my queries: Rachel Bromwich, David Dumville, Doris Edel, Patrick K. Ford, Pierre-Yves Lambert, Jean Le Dû, Ceridwen Lloyd-Morgan, Catherine Mckenna, Brynley F. Roberts, Patrick Sims-Williams, Edgar Slotkin, Stefan Zimmer. Remaining errors of omission and commission are wholly my own responsibility.

[2] The only Pictish literature that survives is a king list and roughly forty difficult inscriptions.

The present study continues in this vein: most attention given to Welsh materials, but with account taken of Breton, Cornish, and Gaelic sources. In addition to texts in the Celtic vernaculars, this chapter will address recent developments in the study of early Arthurian texts in Latin that took shape within a Celtic milieu and that have been largely the province of Celtic scholars. The milestone figure of Geoffrey of Monmouth, though serving as both a repository of and inspiration for Arthurian traditions in Celtic languages, may be viewed as standing alongside rather than within the Celtic world and is accordingly relegated to another chapter.

Because of the extent of the subject and scope of the present book, this study cannot aim to be exhaustive in any particular category. It was necessary to be selective, so that in the end we have one scholar's view of significant developments, which may inevitably remain open to the charge of subjectivity. The earlier material receives greater attention here owing partly to the interests and expertise of the writer, but also in the belief that those Celtic traditions that were in a position to contribute to the formation of other Arthurian literatures would be of greatest interest to readers outside of Celtic studies. As a generally conservative field, the pace of new ideas is perhaps less swift in Celtology than that in the turbulent mainstream. For this reason, I give attention to studies of the 1970s (and occasionally the 1960s), the impact of which has often not yet been fully assimilated in the standard editions and medievalist handbooks.

*The Earliest and Potentially Historical Arthurian Sources: De Excidio Britanniae, Y Gododdin, Marwnad Cynddylan, Historia Brittonum, Annales Cambriae*

Within this combined category, we shall examine references to Arthur in Archaic Welsh poems presenting themselves as composed on the occasion of specific historical events in the sixth and seventh centuries and in Celtic Latin histories predating Geoffrey of Monmouth. The question of the historical Arthur, already referred to, lies outside the scope of this study. One noteworthy general trend in current scholarship is the moderation of incandescent enthusiasm over Arthur's possible existence. Pre-Galfridian Arthurian literature tends now to be dealt with as a subject in its own right and not merely as one avenue for pursuing the historical problem. Nonetheless, insofar as reinterpretation of the early Celtic and Celtic Latin Arthurian literature inevitably reshapes the historical debate, it should be noted that the earliest sources as canvassed in this section do remain consistent with an actual late fifth- to early sixth-century figure but do not appear capable of proving Arthur's historicity along any line of inquiry yet evident.

Recent progress with the oldest Arthurian texts may be noted in the areas of determining the origins of texts, their dates of composition, their authorial character or lack of it, the history of transmission, dating and localizing of manuscript witnesses, and elucidating the place of texts within their broader intellectual and historical contexts. All of these trends remain dynamic, and the most penetrating current scholarship has more the effect of destabilizing old orthodoxies than yet succeeding in establishing new ones.

Though the *De Excidio Britanniae* of Gildas does not name Arthur, it presents for the first time what were to become several of the leading themes of the legendary "Arthurian" history of Britain: the removal of the Roman garrison by the usurper Maxiumus, the incursions of the Picts and Scots, the appeal to the Roman consul "Agitius," the unnamed *superbus tyrannus* ("arrogant usurper," elsewhere called Vortigern, "the Over-lord") and the *Adventus Saxonum*, the Saxon revolt against the Britons, and the rally led by Ambrosius Aurelianus culminating with the victory at Badonicus mons ("Mount Badon"). (The last is attributed to Arthur in *Historia Brittonum* and later sources.) Recent major Gildasian studies include Winterbottom's edition and translation, François Kerlouégan's study,[3] and the collection of essays *Gildas: New Approaches* (ed. Lapidge and Dumville). Current thinking has tended toward skepticism or agnosticism regarding the possibility that Gildas's narrative implies the unnamed Arthur or some "Arthurlike" figure (other than the named Ambrosius) as the victor of Badon, let alone contains some veiled allusion to Arthur. There remains the earlier consensus that *De Excidio* was written around A.D. 540, but this date can no longer be taken as universally accepted. It depends ultimately on the obit of King Mailcun (Modern Welsh *Maelgwn*,

---

[3] *Le "De Excidio Britanniae": Les Destinées de la culture latine dans l'Ile de Bretagne au 6e siècle* (Paris: Publications de la Sorbonne, 1987).

Gildas's Latin vocative *Maglocune)* in 549 in *Annales Cambriae* and the synchronism of the reign of Mailcun with that of Ida of Northumbria (547–59) in *Historia Brittonum,* and we cannot now be certain that either of these notices is contemporary, well informed, or independent of each other.

Concerning the dating of the battle of Badon as extractable from the long and difficult passage in *De Excidio,* Dumville has reaffirmed the established view that Gildas meant to say that he was writing in the forty-fourth year after Badon and likewise after his own birth, hence dating both events to ca. 500+ and the Gildasian present at ca. 545 (*Gildas,* 51–59, 76–83). On the other hand, Ian Wood (22–23) interprets the passage to mean that there were forty-three years between Ambrosius's early victory against the Saxons and Badon and that Badon was one month before Gildas's writing, leading to a date range of 485–520 for the nearly simultaneous battle of Badon and writing of *De Excidio.*

What may be the earliest reference to Arthur is the well-known passage from the Welsh heroic elegies known collectively as *Y Gododdin.* If these elegies are what the internal evidence of the text claims them to be, they are the work of a sixth-century North British heroic poet named Aneirin. In the allusion, Arthur is presented as the unrivaled paragon of martial valor and is thus used to form a highly unusual comparison by rendering explicitly inferior the honorand of the *awdl* ("stanza"). Therefore, if the relevant *awdl* and lines can be sustained as Aneirin's original, this would tell us that by the later sixth century there existed in North Britain a tradition of a Brittonic superhero Arthur who supposedly flourished at some earlier period. *Y Gododdin* also contains a reference to *gwenwawt Mirðyn,* "the fair" or "blessed inspired verse of Myrddin" (i.e., Merlin). The text might therefore also provide evidence for the genesis of a Merlin tradition within the heroic age itself.

During the 1970s, the doctrine of an authentic sixth-century nucleus within *Y Gododdin* was challenged strongly by Greene and in a more circumspect way by Mac Cana (review of Jackson). The criticism was countered by Jackson himself (1973–74), and a new case for authenticity was made from the standpoint of *Y Gododdin*'s representation of heroic society (Charles-Edwards 1978).

Through the 1980s, Sir Ifor Williams's *Canu Aneirin* has remained the standard edition, but Jarman's bilingual English/Modern Welsh composite text (with extensive notes, full glossary, and up-to-date and cautiously innovative introductory essays) does what Jackson's translation did as well or better (*Gododdin*). Huws's 1989 photographic facsimile edition is essential to all scholarship based closely on the manuscript and text. In the same period, the idea of *Y Gododdin* as an epic or a unified composition of any sort, as opposed to a collection, was passionately challenged by O Hehir.

What is perhaps the most significant and positive recent trend with the text may be characterized as a move away from loosely defined consensus of "essential authenticity" to elements of greater specificity in a theory of text history. Milestones in this process include the following. Charles-Edwards's "Authenticity of the *Gododdin*" suggested a method for approaching the archaic nucleus of the text. The technique hinges upon the remarkable fact that the manuscript's two scribes (A and B) often repeated versions of the same verse. Charles-Edwards proposed that such variants had separated from a common archetype as early as the period 642–829 and that the nature of this original could be partly recovered through comparing A and B.

In *Early Welsh Poetry*, Dumville raised the possibility of a long written transmission (going back nearer to the dates of the events commemorated, as opposed to the earlier assumption of centuries of oral transmission before the elegies were first recorded) and showed that the historical context could be radically reinterpreted, so as to push the date of the events back into the mid-sixth century in their absolute chronology and relatively prior to the emergence of Bernicia (Northern Northumbria) as the leading opponents of the North Britons. In "When Was Welsh Literature First Written Down?" I confirmed the existence of a pre–Old Welsh written text of *Y Gododdin* on the basis of orthographic features. Charles-Edwards's approach and my own were endorsed by Geraint Gruffydd, who drew the conclusion "that the texts we now have of *Y Gododdin* had their genesis in a Strathclyde scriptorium sometime in the latter half of the seventh century" (264). In "*Canu Aneirin Awdl* LI," Isaac continued close analysis of internal text history and demonstrated that the manuscript in effect contained three texts, rather than the two previously recognized, concerning which see below.

As to the specific sense of the relevant lines, these read

1241 Go·chore brein du ar·uur
1242 caer — ceni bei ef Arthur.

Presently, the standard translation remains roughly, "He glutted the black crows on the wall of the stronghold, though he was no Arthur" (Jarman, ed. and trans. 1988, 64). "Feeding crows" or "ravens" is a regular poetic figure in this corpus for slaying enemies. Translating the verb *go·chore* as "glutted" is a reasoned guess based on context. However, I am presently engaged in a book-length study of the language, text, and historical context of *Y Gododdin*, in which I propose that *go·chore* is the same compound verb as Early Irish *fo·cuirethar*, "sends down, draws down, entices." "He used to draw down black crows" would of course imply much the same for Arthur and the honorand as had the earlier translation.

The outstanding issue remains the date of *Y Gododdin*'s Arthurian passage, and the elegies more generally. In Jarman's 1988 edition, he reaffirms with some important and promising refinements the doctrine of the essential authenticity and sixth-century composition date for *Y Gododdin*, but he lists the Arthurian *awdl* as a possible interpolation and the reference to Myrddin as a certain interpolation (*Gododdin*, lxiv). This would leave the date of the lines and the prior emergence of Arthur as a superhero open. Charles-Edwards (1991, 15), building on the theory of textual transmission that he set forth in "Authenticity of the *Gododdin*," concluded that the reference to Arthur need not go back before the ninth or tenth century because the lines occurred only in *Y Gododdin*'s B-text and were not paralleled in A. Therefore, he thinks it cannot with certainty be attributed to the archaic common ancestor of the two extant versions (actually the work of two scribes bound into a single thirteenth-century manuscript). Sims-Williams similarly regards *Y Gododdin*'s reference to Arthur as being of uncertain date (1991, 37).

Newer approaches to the text may allow greater antiquity for the mention of Arthur. As opposed to Charles-Edwards's (1978) historical stemma for *Y Gododdin* based upon an early separation of texts A and B, Isaac has argued that we have to do with three texts: scribe A's work, which is fairly consistently in Early Middle Welsh spelling; the first half of B's work (verses B.1–B.23), which is less consistent but also in Early Middle Welsh orthography; and the latter half of B (verses B.24–B.42), which is largely in Old Welsh orthography.

In my own forthcoming book on *Y Gododdin*, I term these Texts A, B[1], and B[2] and suggest that they reflect third/fourth, second, and first recensions, respectively. Following Dumville's approach in *Early Welsh Poetry* (2), it may be shown that the various texts not only differ orthographically but also show significant differences in the incidental background for the elegies. Only the most innovative Text A shows interest in the popular medieval Welsh literary figures, Taliesin, Llywarch Hen, the Coeling dynasts of the North, and Myrddin, thus consistent with Jarman's view that the last is a relatively late addition. Only A regards the kingdom of Bernicia as an enemy of the Britons of Gododdin. B[1] and B[2] diverge from A in having no interest in any of these popular figures and considering Deira (later the southern province of Northumbria), and not Bernicia, as the enemy. The most archaic B[2] contrasts with both A and B[1] in several important negative details: no mention of Wales, no allusion to the fall of the kingdom of Gododdin (which probably occurred in 638), no reference to Strathclyde's victory at Srath Caruin in 642, no identification of the poet, no Christianity. D.S. Evans (1977) had earlier suggested that Aneirin's original work (i.e., the authentic nucleus) had been pre-Christian. The central event, the battle of Catraeth, is presented as a disaster for the Gododdin Britons in A and B[1], but not a disaster and possibly as a victory in B[2].

My ongoing work on the text suggests that the tradition behind B[2] separated from a common intermediary AB[1] in North Britain before the period ca. 638–43 and that that version subsequently underwent minimal modernization and no certain or likely interpolation. That version remained in the North until the ninth century and had no discernible impact on any other Welsh text. It is Text B[2] to which the Arthurian reference belongs, and it is my position that this proves that Arthur was probably viewed as a peerless military superhero in the Brittonic North as early as about 600. The debate will undoubtedly proceed into the next century.

It is possible that we also have reference to Arthur in another archaic heroic elegy, *Marwnad Cynddylan* ("The Death-song of Cynddylan"). The case is in several respects analogous to *Y Gododdin*. Both are in the *awdl* meter and commemorate warriors who fell in a battle against the Anglo-Saxons. *Marwnad Cynddylan*, likewise, would compare Arthur to the later warriors of the occasion, presenting him as the supreme standard of comparison in the line *canawon Art[u]r wras, dinas degyn* ("the whelps of great Arthur, the mighty citadel"). This interpretation requires an emendation, for the manuscript reads *artir*, which yields poor sense. The emendation was supported in the recent edition of the elegy by Gruffydd ("Marwnad Cynddylan," 23) and since then quite confidently by the editors of *Arthur of the Welsh* (5; also Bromwich 1975-76, 177). However, in *Early Welsh Saga Poetry*, Rowland proposes another emendation that would not involve Arthur (186). According to Rowland's convincing theory of the historical context of *Marwnad Cynddylan* (which would not be affected by the presence or absence of the Arthurian reference), the fatal battle is the disastrous defeat of Penda of Mercia and his British allies by Oswiu of Northumbria at Winwæd/Gai Campus on November 15, 655. Scholarly consensus at present favors the possibility that a seventh-century occasional poem was the starting point for the extant text, though the oldest surviving copy belongs to ca. 1631-34 (1990, 180).

The ninth-century Welsh Latin *Historia Brittonum* contains a list of Arthur's battles (§56) and two Arthurian marvels, one concerning Arthur's hound Cabal ("Horse") and the hunt for the boar Troit, the other Arthur's slaying of his own son Amr, both in §73. In addition, the marvel of Linn Liuan in *Historia Brittonum* §69, though not naming Arthur, concerns an army crossing the tidal Severn and would thus also anticipate an episode in the hunt of the monstrous boar Trwyth as it occurs as the climactic adventure in the vernacular Arthurian prose tale *Culhwch ac Olwen*. Devoid of any claim of historicity, *Historia Brittonum mirabilia* will be touched on again in the next section.

David Dumville of Cambridge is the leading figure today in scholarship on *Historia Brittonum*. He is currently engaged in an ongoing project to publish the eight recensions of the text. Volume 3 in the series, *The "Vatican" Recension*, has now appeared. Dumville's ideas on the nature of *Historia Brittonum*, its value as history, and indirectly on the nature of the early Arthurian tradition therein have appeared in the introduction to *The "Vatican" Recension* and a series of provocative articles (e.g., 1975-76; 1986). His general line of argument includes the following key points. *Historia Brittonum*, though employing diverse sources, is essentially a unified work (of uniform

Latinity) by a Welsh cleric working in A.D. 829/30. There is no early or sound basis for assigning the name "Nennius," or the like, to this writer; for the "Nennian" prologue was not part of the first recension. As to genre, *Historia Brittonum* is an example of "synchronizing history" (which seems close to what has been called by others "pseudo-history" or "synthetic history") and is thus comparable to the Middle Irish *Lebor Gabála Érenn* ("Book of Invasions") ("Historical Value"). Accordingly, *Historia Brittonum* can have little or no value for recovering fifth- and sixth-century historical events but is of first importance for assessing the intellectual climate of Wales in the early ninth century.

In a thoughtful critique of Dumville's approach, Charles-Edwards shows some reservations regarding *Historia Brittonum*'s unitary nature and sees its genre as an *origo gentis* comparable to credible histories, such as Gregory of Tours's *Historia Francorum*, Bede's *Historia Ecclesiastica*, and Fredegar's Chronicle (1991, 16–22). Whereas Dumville's appraisal of *Historia Brittonum*'s "uniform Latinity" would preclude that any earlier text had been incorporated verbatim ("Historical Value"), Wendy Davies has flatly denied this assessment, recognizing complex sentence structure in *Historia Brittonum*'s hagiographical material on Germanus (§§32–35, 39, 47–50) and Patrick (§§50–55) contrasting with the laconic entries of "The Northern History" (§§57–65). She concludes that *Historia Brittonum* "presents us with edited documents of varying dates and provenances whose origins are not yet sufficiently understood." The possible separate and earlier identity of "The Northern History" is thus reaffirmed (Davis, 205–206, 244, n. 35). My forthcoming work on *Y Gododdin* suggests that North British entries in *Historia Brittonum* §§57–65 were drawn together by partisans of Uryen's family, the rulers of the kingdom of Reget about Carlisle, not long after the decisive defeat of the Northumbrians by the Picts in 685. On the other hand, Dumville (1986, 15) denies the existence of any such discreet earlier text as an "Original Northern History" (as envisioned, for example, in Jackson 1963) or Kathleen Hughes's northern memoranda (71). Thus, today the question of the origin(s) and very nature of *Historia Brittonum* as a text remains open.

So long as the possibility of a discrete and separable "Northern History" in *Historia Brittonum* §§57–65 remains, the placement of the

Arthurian battle list immediately before it is potentially significant. Though the list is formally and stylistically different from what follows, the famous list of five vernacular poets in §62 (which includes Neirin, i.e., Aneirin, and Taliessin) and Arthur's battles are the only two sections of *Historia Brittonum* that show an interest in native poetry. Therefore, it is not inconceivable that a single North British writer or school with access to a particular body of tradition might have compiled the list of poets and also transcribed the twelve battles.

As to Arthur's twelve battles in *Historia Brittonum* §56, scholars today generally accept the Chadwicks' idea of an underlying Welsh battle-listing poem of the sort that survives for the sixth-century chieftains Kynan Garwyn of Powys, Uryen of Reget, and Gwallawc, and the seventh-century Cadwallawn of Gwynedd (1932-49, I, 154-155). Dumville has recently noted the consensus on this point (1986, 13). That *Historia Brittonum*'s compiler knew this Welsh poem from a written rather than an oral source is implied by the likely confusion of Old Welsh *scuid* 'shoulder' and *scuit* 'shield'; this would explain the odd detail that Arthur is said in the list to have carried the cross on his shoulders at the battle of Castellum Guinnion (Bromwich, 1975-76; Bedwyr Lewis Jones, 32-33). We shall of course not be able to recover much more of the text of this lost Welsh poem than the misread word *scuit* and the names of the battle sites. However, a highly promising suggestion made by Thomas Jones thirty years ago carries implications not yet pursued (1968; 1963): the names of the battles may preserve the rhyme scheme of the poem—battles 2-5 *Dubglas*, battle 6 *Bassas*, battle 7 *Cat Coit Celidon*, battle 8 *Castell Guinnion*, battle 9 *Cair Legion*, battle 11 *Bregion*, battle 12 *Badon*. (For battle 10, *Historia Brittonum*'s *fluminis Tribruit* might stand for Old Welsh *Tribruit Abon*, "the River Tribruit.")

If Jones was essentially on the right track here, two important conclusions follow. First, the battle of Mount Badon was integral to the Old Welsh poem, which is to say that it was not lifted from Gildas by the clerical *literatus* who wrote *Historia Brittonum* and then falsely attributed *for the first time* by that ninth-century writer to Arthur. That still allows that Badon may have been falsely attributed to Arthur by the earlier vernacular poet, which is not impossible, but that would imply either that the Latin *De Excidio Britanniae* had more and earlier impact on native poets than we have any other reason to suppose it did or that there was a vernacular tradition of Badon that had originally attributed the victory to Ambrosius (or at least not to Arthur) but had already been untraditionally drawn into Arthur's orbit at some unspecified date prior to 829/30.

Second, concerning the extant Early Welsh battle lists, examples occur in two meters: the longer monorhyming stanzas called *awdlau* (used for the battles of Kynan, Uryen, and Gwallawc) and the three-line *englynion* (used for Cadwallawn). On the one hand, the poem on Cadwallawn's battles has the short stanzas, and no one is now suggesting that it, or any other surviving poem in *englynion*, could be as old as Cadwallawn's lifetime (died 634/35). On the other hand, *Celidon, Guinnion, Cair Legion, (?Tribruit Abon), Bregion, Badon* would necessarily imply the *awdl* meter. The extant battle-listing *awdlau* noted above deal with figures who, like Arthur, belong to the sixth century. There is no doubt over the historicity of any of those other chieftains. The poems in question are preserved in the early fourteenth-century manuscript known as the *Book of Taliesin*. Sir Ifor Williams regarded them as authentic sixth-century compositions attributable to the historical bard Taliesin (*Poems of Taliesin*), though this view is today more sharply questioned than it was during Williams's lifetime (Dumville, *Early Welsh Poetry*). Though it is thus uncertain whether the closest *comparanda* to the Arthurian lists are in fact compositions contemporary to the battles and persons named, it is at least plain that the *attitude* of these poems is contemporary, their honorands are considered to be living. The same attitude in the original vernacular battle list could yet explain why the battle of Camlann, in which Arthur fell twenty-one years after Badon according to the Welsh Annals, is not named as the final battle in *Historia Brittonum* §56.

There has been one further important respect in which the consensus of Celticists has shifted since the publication of *Arthurian Literature in the Middle Ages* (henceforth *ALMA*, ed. Roger Sherman Loomis 1959) in a way that affects the interpretation of the battle list. According to Jackson,

> Such a catalogue poem [as that underlying *Historia Brittonum* §56] is most unlikely to have been contemporary with Arthur or nearly contemporary. The Welsh language did not yet exist in Arthur's day, when Late British had not yet lost its final syllables and composition vowels, which means that verse composed

at that time would have lost its metric construction and disintegrated a couple of
generations later [*ALMA*, 7–8].

Jackson based this conclusion on the phonological chronology of his
monumental *Language and History in Early Britain*. Of the several
scholars (myself included) who have resifted broad areas of Brittonic
historical phonology over the past decade or so, most if not all favor
a generally earlier and less sharply defined date for the loss of syllables
and consequent emergence of a Neo-Brittonic language that might be
called Welsh (Koch 1983; Sims-Williams 1990, "Dating the
Transition"). Though we all continue to stand on Jackson's shoulders,
the structuralist approach of his day can now be seen in retrospect to
have two serious blindspots: first, a failure to allow a considerable time
lag between the working out of a particular innovation on the phonetic
and then the phonemic level and, second, a failure to recognize that
most of our sources of historical linguistic evidence belong to an
educated standard language that may have been more conservative than
coaeval popular registers. In short, it is doubtful that any scholar today
would be so certain that a poem composed in the late fifth or early
sixth century would necessarily have retained all its Old Celtic syllables
and therefore could not possibly have survived to be transcribed
sometime before 829 and then translated into Latin about that date.
Furthermore, if one allows a partly or largely accentual rather than
purely syllabic metrical basis for the earliest Neo-Celtic poetry, syllable
loss becomes less of a theoretical obstacle to transmission (cf. D.E.
Evans; Haycock 1988).

A further interesting recent idea concerning the battle list is Charles-
Edwards's that the function envisioned with Arthur's famous title
therein, i.e., *dux bellorum*, is comparable to that of the generalship of
Penda vis-à-vis the *reges Brittonum* in their war on Bernicia described
in *Historia Brittonum* §64 (1991, 24).

Concerning the etymology and possible location of Arthur's battle,
three articles published by Jackson in the 1940s and 50s remain the
standard account.[4] However, unresolved questions remain, and the

---

[4] See the following by Kenneth Hurlstone Jackson: "Once Again Arthur's Battles"
(*Modern Philology*, 43 [1945], 44-57); "Arthur's Battle of Breguoin" (*Antiquity*, 23
[1949], 48-49); "The Site of Mount Badon" (*Journal of Celtic Studies*, 2 [1953-58], 152-
155).

issue could now be fruitfully reopened in the light of more recent scholarship on *Historia Brittonum*.

*Annales Cambriae* (also known as "The Welsh Annals") contains two well-known Arthurian entries. The first, at the year corresponding to 516 (or 518), concerns *Bellum Badonis in quo Arthur portauit crucem Domini Nostri Iesu Christi tribus diebus et tribus noctibus in humeros suos et Brittones uictores fuerunt* ("The battle of Badon, in which Arthur carried the cross of Our Lord Jesus Christ three days and three nights on his shoulders, and the Britons were victors"). The second, at 537 (or 539) tells of *Gueith Cam=lann in qua Arthur et Medraut corruerunt* ("the battle of Camlann, in which Arthur and Medraut fell"). This is the first reference to Medraut or Mordred, and it is well recognized that it is not clear from the wording that Arthur and Medraut fought on opposite sides as in later accounts. The Welsh bardic allusions show Medrawd as a heroic paragon and implicitly on good terms with Arthur until the poetry of Tudur Aled (ca. 1465–ca. 1525) (Bromwich, ed., 1961; Varin).

It has long been known that the text of *Annales Cambriae* assumed the form now known in the mid-tenth century. The recent work with *Annales Cambriae* generally and the Arthurian notices in particular has been concerned chiefly with possible earlier sources of the entries. The archaeologist Leslie Alcock's theory (45–55), according to which the Badon and Camlann notices probably reflect contemporary annals kept in a sixth-century Easter table, has not met general acceptance among historians. Kathleen Hughes identified three principal strata in *Annales Cambriae*: (1) a set of Irish Annals served as the framework for the years 453 to 613; (2) 613 to 777 had a nucleus of entries derived from a North British chronicle; (3) finally, Welsh annals kept at St. David's continued from the late eighth century till the mid-tenth (67–100). Hughes envisioned little or no overlap among these sections, in other words, no material from the Chronicle of Ireland after 613, none from the North British Chronicle before that date or after 777, and so on.

One might account for such a state of affairs on the assumption that a scriptorium in Strathclyde (or elsewhere in North Britain) began its own record around 613 by adding to a set of Irish annals they had obtained from Iona and that a copy of these annals were then transferred to South Wales around 777, though Hughes herself envisioned a somewhat different process (85). On the other hand,

Dumville believes the Irish source was used beyond 613 and the North British beyond 777 (*Chronicles and Annals*, 211-224).[5] For our purposes, the key points are that the Badon and Camlann entries do not occur in any extant Irish annals, so such a source can be excluded. This means that they could be either of North British or South Walian provenance. In either case, it seems more likely that we have to do ultimately with retrospective insertions postdating ca. 613 (perhaps considerably), rather than contemporary entries from Brittonic annals kept in the first half of the sixth century.

At this point in any attempt to assess where such retrospective insertions might have come from, we are brought back to the form of the Arthurian entries themselves. As recently noted by Charles-Edwards (1991, 27), it is Arthur's carrying of the icon that seems most strongly to suggest a relationship between the *Annales Cambriae*'s Badon entry and *Historia Brittonum*'s battle list. As Thomas Jones remarked (1963, 5-6), the Badon annal is more elaborate than any other *Annales Cambriae* entry. He therefore thought it possible that an original more characteristically laconic *Bellum Badonis & Brittones uictores fuerunt* might have undergone subsequent expansion (i.e., 955-1100) under the influence of the *Historia Brittonum* battle list, where Badon was credited to Arthur and we have the similar story of Arthur carrying the image of Mary on his shoulders at the battle of Castell Guinnion. In other words, Arthur would thus not have been mentioned in the original annal at all. It may be noted further that if both involve a confusion of written Old Welsh *scuit* 'shield' and *scuid* 'shoulder,' then that error in transmission is hardly likely to have come about twice. In other words, within the history shared between the two accounts, the icon story has first been written down in Old Welsh and then mistranslated into Latin; the divergence is a subsequent third stage. In all details, the *Annales Cambriae* entry is more easily understood as derived from *Historia Brittonum*'s account: *Annales Cambriae*'s "three days and three nights" sounds like a baroque elaboration, the icon story was more likely transferred to the more famous battle (Badon) than from it,

---

[5] Dumville argued that the Irish entries were derived specifically from the Clonmacnoise group of annals, which continued to be used by *Annales Cambriae* until at least 888.

and the substitution of the more common icon (the cross) for Mary is more understandable than the reverse.

A final point may be made about the name forms in these sources. *Gueith Camlann* in *Annales Cambriae* and most of the battle names in *Historia Brittonum* §56 are in purely Old Welsh spellings. In contrast, *Bellum Badonis* in *Annales Cambriae* and *bellum in monte Badonis* in *Historia Brittonum* are Latinized, Romano-British forms. That there was a Latinate, Romano-British written tradition about this battle is something we already know, for the source is the *De excidio Britanniae* already discussed. However, Gildas's *obsessio Badonici montis* is not quite the same Latinization as we have in *Historia Brittonum* and *Annales Cambriae*. So it is possible that the Latin material on this battle had once been more extensive.

On the other hand, in both *Historia Brittonum* and *Annales Cambriae* the commander's name is Old Welsh *Arthur*, just as it is (proved by rhyme) in *Y Gododdin*. As most recently endorsed by the editors of *Arthur of the Welsh* (5), it is generally agreed that name derives from Latin *Artorius*. In this light, the consistent use of purely Welsh, uninflected *Arthur* in the early accounts of the battles has been remarked upon by Markale (198–200). Gildas or a contemporary of his writing Latin would probably have spelled the name as *Artorius* or *Arturius* (the latter developing from the former by regular phonological change). In Arthurian sources, these two spellings are to my knowledge nonexistent and rare, respectively. *Arturius* does occur in the late seventh-century Hiberno-Latin of Adomnán (*Vita Columbae* 19a) for Prince Artúr of Dál Ríata, who died ca. 580. ARTVRIVS curiously appears also in Camden's famous picture of the lost Glastonbury cross, and Ashe suggests that the cross might be authentic, or at least old, on this basis (1985, 176). At any rate, the consistent use of the spelling *Arthur* implies that if *Historia Brittonum* and *Annales Cambriae* were drawing on contemporary or near-contemporary sixth-century Latin notices of the battle of Badon, these evidently did not name Arthur as the commander. Though Arthur's legendary companion Kei does not yet surface in the potentially historical sources reviewed in this section, Rachel Bromwich has recently suggested that the name's origin (Latin *Caius*) may take us back to the same milieu of late Romano-British onomastics, Latin names prevailing for men born before A.D. 450 (1983, 42).[6]

*Other Pre-Galfridian Sources*: Culhwch ac Olwen, Historia Brittonum §73 (the Arthurian *mirabilia*), *Pa Gur yv y Porthaur?*, *Preiδeu Annwfyn, Gereint fil' Erbin, Englynion y Beddau, Arthur and the Eagle, Gwenhwyfar and Melwas, Vitae Sanctorum*

Like the sources treated in the previous section, this group predates Geoffrey. However, they are neither historical nor, as far as can be determined from their own internal say-so, composed for a specific historical occasion. Because we are not yet able to date on purely linguistic criteria early Welsh texts surviving only in later manuscript copies, the absolute chronology of the nonhistorical, unattributed pre-Galfridian Welsh poetry remains up in the air. Sims-Williams (1991, 35) notes the relative lack of progress in this area since the time of Jackson's assessment in *ALMA* more than thirty years ago. Thus, for example, Sims-Williams treats the metrical feature of *trwm ac ysgafn* (the rhyming of original -*n* with -*nn* or -*nt*) as an archaism, rightly I think, though it has been treated as an innovation in some earlier scholarship.

The tendency now is for scholars to give as possible dates of composition ranges spread over several centuries. So, for example, Sims-Williams dates this body of Welsh Arthurian poems roughly between the ninth and twelfth centuries (1991, 34) and adds that no compelling linguistic and metrical criteria have been found to confirm pre-1100 datings for the poems in the Black Book of Carmarthen (38). Similarly, Bromwich proposes that in absolute terms the Black Book poem *Pa Gur yv y Porthaur* "may be dated before 1100—perhaps more than a century earlier" (1983, 45). In such formulations, it is really the earlier terminus that has the softer edge; that is to say, we presently have no hard-and-fast criteria for distinguishing ninth-century from eleventh-century Old Welsh or even for determining what sort of poetry could not have been composed before the inception of the Old Welsh period about 800. Thus, although it is likely that as a group the works

---

[6] For some recently recognized incidental information on the later whereabouts of *Historia Brittonum* and *Annales Cambriae*, see Brett, "John Leland."

dealt with in this section postdate those of the preceding, a wide overlap is probable. The situation could be and no doubt someday will be remedied through diligent work with textual and linguistic detail. At present, the working out of such dating criteria must be placed among the highest desiderata for the study of all early Welsh literature. The following recent and ongoing works will have an important contribution to make toward that end.

Under the general editorship of R. Geraint Gruffydd, the Centre for Advanced Welsh and Celtic Studies (Canolfan Uwchefrydiau Cymreig a Cheltaidd) is publishing *Cyfres Beirdd y Tywysogion*, a comprehensive set of texts of the poetry of the late eleventh- to thirteenth-century Gogynfeirdd (also known as the "Poets of the Princes"). The editorial language of the *Cyfres* is Welsh, and its general plan is to provide an introduction for each poet dealing with his life, patrons, corpus, and themes, as well as an introduction to each poem giving consideration to its historical context, meter, and manuscript witnesses. Each poem is published as (1) the earliest extant manuscript version with variants, (2) a text in standard modern spelling, (3) a Modern Welsh paraphrase, (4) philological notes. Full glossaries are being provided, citing every occurrence of every form. Thus, we shall soon be able to see variations in poetic usage over the period in question within a sizable closely datable corpus. Exhaustive lists of personal names and place-names are also given. This feature should be of particular value to Arthurians. For example, *"Prydydd y Moch"* (ed. E.M. Jones), the only volume with textual notes, a full glossary, and complete lists published to date, has six citations for *Arthur*. That volume and *Cynddelw I* (ed. N.A. Jones and Owen) were published in 1991. The remaining five volumes are planned for publication between 1993 and 1995.

I am currently preparing *A Grammar of Old Welsh, Historical and Comparative*. Though this work is not primarily aimed at text dating, it does note more conservative and innovative usages within the corpus and evidence for absolute and relative dates. *A Grammar of Old Welsh* utilizes both Old Welsh texts surviving in contemporary media and later copies of compositions of ca. 1100 and earlier. It thus includes *Y Gododdin*, *Marwnad Cynddylan*, the early Arthurian poetry, and *Culhwch ac Olwen* in its corpus.

*Culhwch* is the earliest extant Arthurian tale and probably the
earliest, at least the most linguistically and stylistically archaic, sizable
specimen of Welsh prose.[7] In 1992, an edition with extensive English
introduction and notes by Bromwich and D.S. Evans was published.
This follows their slimmer Welsh edition of 1988, which has a substantially different introduction and does not contain the hundred and
twenty-nine pages of textual notes. The two editions share the same
Medieval Welsh text and the same line numbers and provide a full list
of personal names, place-names, and epithets. The same two scholars
are also the compilers of the *Glossary to Culhwch ac Olwen*.

*Culhwch*'s eclectic character, its catalogues of characters and tasks,
and the numerous onomastic tales and telescoped traditional narratives
brought in tangentially render it a "who's who" of early Welsh
Arthuriana. For this reason, the new notes, indexes, and glossaries
have the value of an important reference work, a contribution to the
prosopography of Welsh tradition comparable to Bromwich's monumental *Trioedd Ynys Prydein*. Other important studies on individual
identifications and the general literary implications of the great lists of
characters include Sims-Williams's "Significance of the Irish Personal
Names" and Edel's "Catalogues in *Culhwch ac Olwen*," the former
downplaying the likelihood of meaningful influence from medieval Irish
literature upon the work of the storyteller and scribes of *Culhwch*.
Jackson suggested that the epithet of the tale's principal antagonist, the
grotesque Yspaðaden Pen-kawr ("Chief of Giants") contained a rare
and archaic inflected genitive plural < Celtic *\*kawarom*. Since
Brittonic had given up case inflection by as early as ca. 500, the
etymology would imply an old basis in oral tradition for the epithet and
perhaps the character of the giant himself (Jackson 1982, 12–15). He
explained the perplexing formula *teir Ynys Prydein* ("the Three Islands
of Britain") as south Britain, Britain beyond the Forth, and Ireland
(15–17) and identified the name of a real place *Messur Pritguenn*

---

[7] According to Mac Cana ("Rhyddiaith Gymraeg"; "Celtic Word-Order"; "Notes on
the 'Abnormal' Sentence"; "Further Notes"), *Culhwch*'s priority would not be a mere
accident of survival, but the text would rather stand at or near the beginning of the Welsh
continuum of literary prose. He proposes that at the transition of the Old to Middle
Welsh periods, the so-called "abnormal" sentence (verb-second, topic-initial order),
which was native to the Southern Brittonic dialects Cornish and Breton, was adopted by
Welsh as literary diction for *Culhwch* and subsequent works of prose.

("Measure of [Arthur's ship] Prydwen") in the twelfth-century charters of the Book of Llandaf with the *Messur y Peir* ("Measure of the Cauldron") onomastic tale in *Culhwch* (22–23). Prior to his sudden death in 1984, the leading authority on *Culhwch* had been Sir Idris Foster, whose contributions to *ALMA* and the Welsh survey article "*Culhwch ac Olwen*" are still worth consulting, the latter drawing a number of parallels to other early Welsh and Irish tales.

In terms of its content and literary qualities, *Culhwch* continues to be appreciated as a native tale with traditional Celtic analogues and antecedents. Interesting lines of inquiry in this direction including Edel's comparison of *Culhwch* and the Irish saga *Tochmarc Emire* (*Helden auf Freiersfüssen*) and the illumination of the recurring porcine theme in the story by means of etymology in articles by Ford (1990) and Hamp (1986).

Roberts advances a detailed case for *Culhwch* as the work of a literate author as opposed to an oral performer, albeit one "close to traditional modes of narration" (1991, 77–80). He sees the author's detachment and sense of humor (drawing on Radner's article) as literary qualities. In "From Traditional Tale to Literary Story," Roberts discusses the polished flowing style that some portions of *Culhwch* achieve by means of the sophisticated varied word order of the "abnormal" sentence (verb-second, topic-initial syntax) and contrasts this with the primitive lurching style of the opening sequence (1984, 215–216). He concludes that *Culhwch* is essentially a literary rather than an oral tale.

One cause of the complexity of *Culhwch* is the recognized conflation of two strands. On the one hand, there is the frame story, which does not belong to the fabric of Welsh tradition. This centers upon the characters of the young hero Culhwch and his family, the beautiful maiden Olwen (the object of the quest), and her father, the giant Ysbyðaden, all characters largely confined to this tale.[8] Their story may seen be as a "wooing," or *tochmarc*, in Celtological terms or as a version of the tale "Six Go Through the World" if dealt with as folktale; cf. the mythological analysis by Lozac'hmeur in "Nouvelle

---

[8] The continued survival and popularity of this frame story in late-medieval Wales is indicated by an allusion to Ysbyddaden Pencawr in the mid-fourteenth-century corpus of Dafydd ap Gwilym (Bromwich, "Cyfeiriadau," 59).

herméneutique" discussed below. On the other hand, there is the pre-
Galfridian Arthur, already supreme overlord of all Britain, i.e., *penn
teyrneð yr ynys honn* ("chief of the chieftains of this island").

As is clear from the introduction of the Bromwich and Evans
edition, *Culhwch* is generally understood to be a rich tale that brings
together a range both of sources and of styles of expression. In this
sense, the oral vs. literate debate remains open as an area to be
explored further with a synthetic overview, allowing a role for each
medium.

As to the date of *Culhwch*'s composition, Bromwich and Evans
suggest the last decades of the eleventh century to ca. 1100 as the most
likely period for the redaction of the extant version (1988,
lxxxi–lxxxii). Approximately the same date has been put forward by
other scholars, including Bedwyr Lewis Jones (42–43) and Roberts
(1991, 73), though the latter author previously had suggested a
somewhat earlier redaction of ca. 1050 (1984, 214). For now, such
estimates can only be tentative hypotheses and fairly open-ended; as
Bromwich and Evans allow, the catalogues of Arthurian characters in
*Culhwch* continued to take in accretions between the period of the
redaction and that of the extant fourteenth-century manuscripts (1988,
lxxxii). Sims-Williams notes as an important parallelism with a datable
text the similar roles of Bedwyr and Kei as Arthur's chief companions
in *Culhwch*, the poem *Pa Gur*, and the Latin *Vita Cadoci* of Lifris of
Llancarfan of ca. 1100 (1991, 39), but at present the precise import of
such details for absolute and relative dating of the unattributed
vernacular texts remains inconclusive.

In terms of relative chronology, anyone who has read both *Culhwch*
and the Four Branches of the Mabinogi in the original Welsh will have
been struck by the major qualitative gap in language as well as literary
style. This impression can be specified and quantified in some major
categories thanks to important studies by Watkins (1977; 1987; 1988;
1990), D.S. Evans (1985), and Mac Cana (1973; 1979; 1991), as well
as the linguistic section of Bromwich and Evans's *Culhwch and Olwen*
(xv–xxv).

The fact that the language of *Culhwch* agrees with Old Welsh usage
in many individual points supports the assessment that the redaction
must belong to the Late Old Welsh Period (Bromwich and Evans, eds.,
1992, xv–xxv), whereas the Four Branches have for modern scholars

the status of defining the Middle Welsh linguistic horizon. This gap is most naturally understood as a chronological one, as D.S. Evans suggests (1985, 113).[9] If so, then one might expect a century or more to separate the redaction of *Culhwch* from that of the Four Branches. However, other nonchronological factors may also be at work, such as genre, dialect, literary school, relative proximity to oral tradition as opposed to authorial conception as written literature. At present, there is no certainty regarding the date of the redaction of the Four Branches either, though consensus favors (albeit with considerable caution and qualification) the former half of a range of possibilities from the later eleventh to the late twelfth century. One influential treatment of this question is Charles-Edwards's "Date of the Four Branches," in which he attributed the composition to one man working between 1050 and 1120. In other words, we presently face the problematical and unsustainable circumstance that essentially the same dates of composition are authoritatively proposed for a Late Old Welsh text (*Culhwch*) and a quartet of quintessentially Middle Welsh texts (the Four Branches).

There are important recent studies by Huws and Gifford Charles-Edwards of the two key manuscripts in which *Culhwch* and other Arthurian and related Welsh tales are preserved, the White Book of Rhydderch and Red Book of Hergest. Huws considers the possibility of Cistercian origin for the White Book at the abbey of Strata Florida, in Ceredigion. The patron of the fourteenth-century manuscript was Rhydderch ab Ieuan Llwyd of the same region. It contains the Four

---

[9] The linguistic features considered in D.S. Evans's article include the use of the virtually unique verb *amkawd* 'said' in the White Book text, Old Welsh *ðy* 'to' once in the White Book (Middle Welsh *y* in the Red), the preverbal particle *ry* in the White Book for innovative *a* in the Red, archaic *kwt* 'whence, where' in the White Book for *pa le* in the Red, unusual word use, such as *gwest* for "spending the night" (104–106), the third singular preterite ending *-awð* used consistently with *llad* (but *-wys* being generally the more common ending (107)), third singular *-awd* with future force, the future impersonal in *-awr*, the preverbal particles *neu-r*, *yt* not otherwise found in prose (108–109), and the Watkins–Mac Cana data on the word order of copula sentences (110).

Branches of the Mabinogi and the Three Romances (see below), as well as *Culhwch*.[10]

As mentioned above, *Culhwch* shows some close points of comparison with the *Historia Brittonum*'s topographical *mirabilia*: Arthur's hunt of the boar Troit, Arthur's hound Cabal, and the army crossing the Severn bore. Jackson identified the home of Ehawc Llyn Llliw ("the Salmon of the Pool of Lliw") with Oper Linn Liuan of the *Mirabilia* (§69), which is the site of a tidal phenomenon near the Severn estuary (1982, 17–18). No one at present is pressing a case for these marvels having had a textual basis predating the redaction of *Historia Brittonum* in 829/30. Roberts makes the following important points in "Culhwch ac Olwen" (1991, 88–92). The strong geographical orientation of the marvels to Southeast Wales and the adjacent border country probably reflects the local knowledge of the redactor of 829 himself. The immediate background of the Welsh marvels is oral and folkloric. Though these Arthurian marvels cannot be conclusive by themselves, they must remain important in any consideration of the transference of Arthur from a Cornish and/or North British setting to Southeast Welsh settings. Roberts believes that the ambiguous place-name *Carn Cabal* has undergone creative reinterpretation ("Cairn of the Horse" > "Horse's Hoof" > "Cairn/Footprint of [Arthur's Dog] Cafall," i.e., horse) and that the associated folktale was originally not Arthurian. Ford (1983) discusses the possible multiple meanings and earlier significance of *Carn Cabal*, along with the names of Arthur's other possessions in *Culhwch*, in a mythological light. The marvel of Licat Amr ("Spring Source of the River Amr/Gamber") contains an allusion to an otherwise unknown tale of Arthur slaying his own son Amr. This epitomized tale might yet be usefully explored as an analogue to the fully attested stories of Arthur and Mordred in the romances or kinslayings of Conlaí by his father Cú Chulainn, Hadubrand by Hildebrand, and Sohrab by Rustum. The Arthurian *comparandum* shows the alliterating names of the first two pairs.

*Culhwch* is more or less closely related to a body of nonhistorical pre-Galfridian poetry of uncertain date. The most closely similar is the dialogue poem *Pa Gur yv y Porthaur?* ("Who Is the Porter?") in the

---

[10] At the time of writing, new French translations of the Mabinogi by Pierre-Yves Lambert were in press (Gallimard).

thirteenth-century Black Book of Carmarthen. Jarman places the composition in the tenth or eleventh century (1984–86, 14). In *Pa Gur*, we meet many of the characters of *Culhwch* (Arthur, Kei, Beduir, Mabon son of Mydron, Mabon son of Melld (perhaps the same as the previous with his patronym), Manawidan son of Llyr, Anguas Edeinauc, and the gatekeeper Gleuluid Gauaeluaur) and several of the same or similar adventures (e.g., fights with witches and the monstrous cat, Cath Paluc).[11] As lately stressed by Jarman, a number of these characters, including Mabon, Mydron, and Melld, were attested pagan divinities (1984–86, 14). The flyting at the gate between the surly gatekeeper Gleuluid and Arthur forms the frame of the series of allusions. A similar confrontation with Glewlwyd occurs near the opening of *Culhwch*, where the wrangle at the gate similarly functions to lead to a catalogue of Arthurian personnel and incidentals.

One striking difference between *Pa Gur* and *Culhwch* is that in the latter it is Culhwch who is attempting to pass Glewlwyd to gain entry to Arthur's court whereas in *Pa Gur* it is Arthur himself who is denied entry. I have recently proposed (1992) that the episode is derived from Celtic mythology in which the original protagonist, as in the confrontation at the gate in the Old Irish *Cath Maige Tuired*, was the god Lug (= Welsh Lleu < Celtic Lugus).

What is interestingly altogether absent in the parallels between *Culhwch* and *Pa Gur* is any trace of the wooing story that forms the frame of the former, including the characters Culhwch, Olwen, and Yspyðaden. It seems at least possible therefore that the relationship of the two texts is essentially that *Pa Gur* reflects the same body of Arthurian tradition as *Culhwch* but at a stage prior to the merging of that tradition with the story of the wooing of the giant's daughter. And if it is that merger that moved Arthur and his heroes from outside the gate to inside the court, then it was a significant literary development indeed. Such a conclusion may point to an originally courtless hero reminiscent of the Gaelic Finn. As Edel has noted (1983, 7), the fusion of what she calls traditional "epic-heroic" Arthurian episodes and the wooing frame remains incomplete, as shown by Culhwch's absence

---

[11] Jarman gives a detailed discussion of the relationship of *Pa Gur* and *Culhwch* ("Arthurian Allusions," 107-110).

from the accomplishment of the tasks set by his prospective father-in-law Yspyðaden.

Given the eclectic nature of the adventures and personnel in both *Culhwch* and *Pa Gur*, it is hardly surprising that some details are not shared between the two but can be paralleled in other texts. For example, Sims-Williams discusses the possibility that *Pa Gur*'s reference to Llacheu is an oblique echo, otherwise reflected in scattered references, to a story of the killing of Arthur's son (Lacheu, Loholt, or Amr) by Kei or by Arthur himself (1991, 44). The nine witches slain by Kei in *Pa Gur* recall the Nine Witches of Gloucester in *Peredur*, the nine witches in the seventh-century Breton Latin *Life of Saint Samson*, and the nine otherworldly maidens of the Arthurian poem *Preiðeu Annwfyn* (Sims-Williams 1991, 45). Sims-Williams also devotes attention to Arthur's fight with *cinbin* ("dog-heads"; Mod. *cynbyn*), in *Pa Gur* (1991, 41–42). An apparently cognate word *conchinn* designates fantastic beings in a number of Irish texts. In the poem, this allusion leads to a reference to Beduir's fight with Garvluid ("Rough-gray"). In the Triads, there is a Gwrgi Garwlwyd ("Man-dog Rough-gray"), which in light of the comparison with *Pa Gur* looks like another cynocephalus. It is increasingly clear that Minit Eidin, the place of Arthur's fight with the dogheads, is Edinburgh's Mount, capital of the old Brittonic kingdom of Gododdin (Koch 1993). Sims-Williams questions how they got there, assuming the Celtic *cinbin/conchinn* to be derived from the classical accounts of the cynocephali of India (e.g., Pliny, *Natural History* 7.2.23). It is possible that the same geographic transference/confusion is behind the Old Welsh gloss *innð ir Guotodinou* ("of the Gododdin people/regions") in a passage relating to the winter winds of India in the late ninth-century Breton manuscript Angers 477 (13ª).

New and accurate translations of *Pa Gur* are provided by Bromwich (1983, 45–46), Bollard (1984, 19–20), Sims-Williams (1991, 40–45), and Bromwich and Evans (1992, xxxv–xxxvi). A Modern Welsh version is published by Gwyn Thomas (1976, 69–71). An annotated edition is included in Roberts "Cerddi Ymddiddan," 296–309. Jarman's exemplary 1982 edition of the entire manuscript contains a discursive introduction, textual notes, and full glossary in Modern Welsh, and complete lists of proper names. A future English (or French or German) version would be useful for non-Welsh Arthurians, especially so if it were to reflect the prosopographical cross-referencing made possible by *Cyfres Beirdd y Tywysogion*, *Culhwch and Olwen*, and other subsequent advances in the field.

The poem *Preiðeu Annwfyn* ("Spoils of the Un-world") concerns a series of otherworldly overseas adventures by Arthur and his followers. It occurs in the famous manuscript of the earlier fourteenth century known (from the later seventeenth century onward) as Llyfr Taliesin, "The Book of Taliesin,"[12] more accurately Aberystwyth, National Library of Wales MS, Peniarth 2.[13] For Loomis, *Preiðeu Annwfyn* and most particularly its cauldron episode represented important earlier stages in the evolution of the Grail legend (1956, 131–178).[14] In that study, Loomis presented a translation with notes for the first four *awdlau* of the poem only. A complete translation is presented by Bollard (1984, 21–23). A full edition and translation, together with valuable analysis of literary sources and metrics, is now published by Haycock (1983–84). This newer study has the further advantage of understanding the poem in light of the balance of the so-called "mythological" poems within the Book of Taliesin itself and thereby reaches the conclusion that the voice of the poem (presenting himself as one of Arthur's fellow adventurers) is the Taliesin persona. This character has developed out of the sixth-century bard of the same name mentioned above. He is the super-poet of Welsh tradition, an immortal shapeshifter, all-knowing concerning events past, present, and future, and the repository of every aspect of arcane knowledge. He is connected in Welsh sources with the similar prophet-bard figure Myrddin and in many properties anticipates the Arthurian Merlin, who has developed from the latter. Identifying this mythological Taliesin as

---

[12] This was the coining of the pioneer Oxford Celticist Edward Lhuyd.

[13] On the manuscript, its date, and its traditional designation, see Haycock, "Llyfr Taliesin."

[14] Among scholarship on the Celtic sources of the continental Grail romances, note Sterckx ("Têtes coupées," discussed below) and Lozac'hmeur ("Bendigeit Vran"), who explains the name of the Grail castle, *Chastel del Cor(b) Benoit* (> Corbenic) as a literal translation of *Dinas Bendigeit Vran*, "Stronghold of the Blessed Crow" = Dinas Bran, near Llangollen, thus contrasting with Loomis's explanation of *cor beneoit*, "blessed horn" (objective case), as a name for the supernatural vessel itself (*Grail*, 242-244).

the voice of *Preiðeu Annwfyn* underscores the desideratum of a new complete edition and translation of the Book of Taliesin. Haycock's dissertation (1982) might serve as the foundation for any such edition, also utilizing her other relevant studies, such as "*Llyfr Taliesin*" and "Some Talk of Alexander." A new edition of the poetry of the Red Book of Hergest would also be of vital use to Arthurians. One hopes also that photographic facsimiles on the model of Huws's *Llyfr Aneirin* might follow.

One important innovative direction in Haycock's scholarship has been to examine possible sources for the Taliesin persona's ostentatious special knowledge in early-medieval book learning, that is, sources including Isidore of Seville, Bede's scientific works, and Orosius's *History* (1983–84, 56). These lead her, in contrast to Loomis and other scholars of his generation, away from the tendency to see *Preiðeu Annwfyn* and the other mythological poems as highly archaic and reflecting the pre-Christian ideas of the Druids. Most recently, Sims-Williams has similarly opined that the poems in the Book of Taliesin "do not reflect a genuine conflict between Christian-Latin knowledge and surviving types of esoteric native knowledge; those conflicts must have been settled long before the period of the extant Welsh poems" (1991, 34). This formulation would be altogether unimpeachable if one were to read "contemporary" for "genuine." But to say that the mythological Taliesin poems do not at all "reflect" Celtic paganism and its struggles with Christianity (in the sense that the Welsh language reflects the Proto-Celtic and Indo-European) goes too far. A synthetic view is attempted in my "Figure of Taliesin."

Concerning dating, Haycock does not believe that the unique occurrence in *Preiðeu Annwfyn* of the inherited third plural mediopassive verbs (*clywanawr* 'they will hear/will be heard'; *gwiðanhor* 'they know'; and *gwiðanhawr* 'they will know') necessarily indicates an early date of composition ("'*Preiddeu Annwn*'"). Nor does Sims-Williams regard the poem as a special case to be taken out of his omnibus ninth- to twelfth-century dating category. However, such plural deponent verbs had otherwise died out altogether in Brittonic and thus require that we look over to Old Irish for explanation and back to the Common Celtic linguistic horizon (Koch 1984). The further fact that *glywanawr* is mistakenly written for *-or* suggests a written exemplar predating (the writing of) the diphthongization of Welsh *q* to *au* in the later eighth century (Koch 1985–86, 57).[15] In light of the foregoing points, an eighth-century composition and writing of *Preiδeu Annwfyn* is defensible.

As most recently canvassed by Sims-Williams (1990, 62), the Welsh word for the otherworld as used in this poem and elsewhere in the tradition (prominently in the Mabinogi of *Pwyll*, for example) is *annwfyn*. The later *annwn* occurs marginally. *Annwfyn* has two possible etymologies. The basic etymon is W *dwfn* < Celtic *\*dumno-* < *\*dubno-*, basically meaning "deep," from which at an early date it acquired the secondary sense "world." The prefix is either Celtic *ande-* 'in' or *an-* 'not, un-.' The former alternative, which goes back to Sir Ifor Williams (*Pedeir Keinc y Mabinogi*, 99–101), is now endorsed by Bromwich and Evans (1992, 135). However, de Bernardo Stempel's treatment of the Gaulish dedicatory dative plural ανδοουννaβo as a probable cognate, though disputed by Lambert ("Gaulois ANΔOOYNNABO"), would more easily suit the "Un-world" etymology. If De Bernardo Stempel's interpretation is correct, the Gallo-Greek spelling should be interpreted as meaning [aNduvnaβo] < earlier *[anduμn-], in which the peculiar sequence οουνν reflects an embarrassed attempt to represent a vocalic followed by a consonantal *u* and a nasalized vowel followed by an *n*.[16]

Though Arthur is not the central figure in the saga *englynion* on *Gereint fil' Erbin*, it contains important references to him. He is called *ameraudur* ("emperor"; < Lat. *imperator*), probably the first such reference, and is connected with the men of Diwneint, i.e.,

---

[15] Late Middle Welsh posttonic *o* unhistorically written as *aw* is far less likely here, as that inverse spelling is not a common orthographic feature in compositions dating from the era of this later change.

[16] Attempts to identify or even meaningfully interpret the various supernatural *caerau* ("strongholds") of *Preiδeu Annwfyn* have thus far met with less success. For example, *Caer Wydyr* ("The Glass Stronghold") in the poem has sometimes been connected with *Ynys Afallach* and *Ynys Wydrin*, the Welsh names for Avalon/Glastonbury. But Lloyd-Morgan sees the latter two as secondary to the chronicles, especially to *Historia Regum Britanniae*, and having little or no grounding in native oral tradition. Accordingly, the possibility of the identity of Ynys Wydrin and Caer Wydyr would be "extremely faint," and the earliest mentions of Ynys Afallach and Ynys Wydrin would depend on Geoffrey and Giraldus Cambrensis ("From Ynys Wydrin").

Dumnnonia, English Devon, thus in the same quarter of Britain as we find him in *Culhwch* (Pearce, 153). Versions occur in the Black Book of Carmarthen and the closely related White Book of Rhydderch and Red Book of Hergest, the first being the earliest. There are recent editions by Roberts based on the Black Book with bracketed *englynion* from the other copies (1978, 286–296), Jarman (1982), and Rowland with a composite text (1990, 457–461, 636–639). Rowland provides an English translation (504–505), as does Bollard (1984, 17–18).

Sims-Williams discussion of *Gereint fil' Erbin* in "Early Welsh Arthurian Poems" (46–49) lays out the chief outstanding problems of interpretation. There are more than one Gerontius/Gereint known to British history between the early fifth and early eighth century. We do not know if any was a contemporary of the "historical" Arthur. Nor do we know if the *englynion* are meant to imply that Arthur and Gereint were together present at the battle. It is not certain whether the poem says that Gereint died in the battle or only that some of his men did. We do not know whether the central event of the stanzas, the battle at a place called *Llogporth* (Mod. *Llongborth*) is to be located at Langport, Somerset, or some miscellaneous *llongborth* 'ship harbor'; cf. Ir. *longphort* used for Viking encampments. The late John Morris's proposal in *The Age of Arthur* (104–106) that Llogporth is Portsmouth/ Portchester has found little subsequent support, nor has it been decisively disproved.

The Black Book also contains the earliest extant version of *Englynion y Beddau* ("The Stanzas of the Graves"), where we find the famous line *anoeth bid bet y Arthur* ("*anoeth* of the world, a grave for Arthur"). This reference is well established as the starting point for discussions of Arthur's immortality and expected messianic return. The key word is *anoeth*, which, though fairly well attested in the early literature, has not survived into Modern Welsh, as is apparent from the citations in *Geiriadur Prifysgol Cymru*. *Anoeth* is also crucial to another Arthurian text, namely *Culhwch*, where it is the word used for the seemingly impossible tasks set by the giant Yspyδaden for his prospective son-in-law Culhwch. As Sims-Williams suggests (1991, 49), the line in the poem may in fact be an early allusion to *Culhwch*. The usual gloss is "wonder, marvel, (thing) difficult to find," as in Bromwich and Evans (1992, 186). According to the *Geiriadur Prifysgol*, the root element of the word is the same as in Welsh *cyf-oeth* 'wealth, power,' on which see further Bromwich (1961, 142–143). In my forthcoming *Grammar of Old Welsh*, a derivation from British *\*anuχtā* 'what is not spoken,' from Indo-European *\*n-uk$^w$-tó-*: √wek$^w$- 'utter,' is proposed (§540 note).

In addition to the reference to Arthur himself, *Englynion y Beddau* notes two of the key heroes. The grave of Gwalchmei (the Welsh hero who corresponds to the continental and English Gawain) is located in Peryton (Jarman 1982, 18.24). Sims-Williams explains that there was probably one place so named in North Wales and another in the South (1991, 50), relying on the earlier detailed discussion of Ifor Williams, who suggests a link to the common noun *peryf* 'lord, chief' (*Armes Prydein*, xxxiv–xl). To these suggestions should be added the possible connection with the Celtic tribal name *Parisī/Parisīī* of the lower Marne and East Yorkshire. This could be the earliest reference to *Gwalchmei*, though the name *Walcmoei* occurs in Old Breton. As to the etymology, Jackson's from British *\*Walcos Magesos* 'Hawk of the Plain' (with a petrified inflected genitive as second element) is now the standard (1982, 12–15; Goetinck 1975, 31). In light of more recent work by Dafydd Jenkins ("*gwalch*") and by me (1990, 12–13), an earlier *\*Wolcos Magesos* 'Wolf' or 'Errant Warrior of the Plain,' may now be considered. Bedwir's grave is placed in Alld Tryvan (Jarman 1982, 18.38), which Sims-Williams identifies with Tryfan in Snowdonia (1991, 51). Camlann is mentioned in the same *englyn*; so, as Sims-Williams suggests, we may be seeing early evidence for relocating originally northern heroes to Wales. We have Jarman's new edition of the poem in *Llyfr Du*. The standard discussion remains Thomas Jones's "'Stanzas of the Graves,'" which includes a critical edition and translation.

Two poems that are evidently independent of Geoffrey but that survive only in late manuscripts and show late earmarks are the dialogue *englynion* of *Arthur and the Eagle* and *Melwas and Gwenhwyfar* (alternatively identified as *Arthur and Gwenhwyfar*). Reliable but old editions of the two are Ifor Williams ("Arthur a'r Eryr") and Mary Williams, who gives variant texts and translates

*Melwas and Gwenhwyfar.*[17] A new edition and translation of the former by Haycock are currently in proof (*Cerddi Crefyddol Cynnar*). *Arthur and the Eagle* presents Arthur as a receptive pagan receiving Christian instruction from the eagle, which turns out to be a transformation of his deceased nephew Eliwlod.

Sims-Wllliams's discussion (1991, 57–58) goes considerably beyond Jackson's (*ALMA*, 19) and brings up such important analogues as Patrick's dialogues with pagan heroes of the Irish Fenian cycle, the precept-giving messenger birds of *Englynion y Clyweit* (Williams and Parry-Williams; Haycock, *Cerddi Crefyddol Cynnar*), Geoffrey's prophetic Eagle of Shaftesbury (*Historia Regum Britanniae*, 2.9, 12.18), and Gwydyon's *englynion* addressed to Lleu when transformed into an eagle in the Mabinogi of *Math*. He also highlights the Cornish setting of *Arthur and the Eagle*, which links the dialogue to the same stratum of tradition as *Culhwch*, suggesting plausibly that the place-name *Glyncoet Kernyw* ("Valley-woods of Cornwall") in the poem may mean the wooded Glynn Valley near Bodmin. He links Arthur's title *penn kadoeð Kernyw* ("chief of the hosts of Cornwall") with the *dux bellorum* of *Historia Brittonum*'s battle list. As Jackson saw (*ALMA*, 18–19; cf. Sims-Williams 1991, 58–61), *Melwas and Gwenhwyfar* is based on a version of a story of the queen's abduction that we know otherwise from Chrétien de Troyes's *Chevalier de la Charrete* and the Welsh *Life of Gildas* of Caradoc of Llancarfan. Caradoc wrote in the twelfth century prior to the publication of *Historia Regum Britanniae*, and his story of Melvas and Guennuvar may go back to oral sources. *Dyfneint* ("Devon") is mentioned in the *englynion*, and Arthur musters the hosts of Cornubia and Dibnenia in Caradoc.

Arthur is mentioned in several Brittonic saints' lives: those of Cadoc, Carantoc, Iltut, Patern, Efflam, Gildas, and Uuohednou. For the first four, the standard edition remains Wade-Evans's 1944 *Vitae Sanctorum Britanniae et Genealogiae*. They are all pre-Galfridian in content, and most probably predate publication of *Historia Regum Britanniae* in absolute terms. Arthur is generally portrayed in these sources as ruler of Britain. With the exception of the *Life of Iltut*,

---

[17] Ifor Williams, ed., "Ymddiddan Arthur a'r Eryr," *Bulletin of the Board of Celtic Studies*, 2 (1923-25), 269-286; Mary Williams, ed. and trans., "An Early Ritual Poem in Welsh," *Speculum*, 13 (1938), 38-51.

Arthur's role in these Lives is that of tyrannical, or at best morally ambivalent, foil to the saint. For Arthurian studies, the two most important *vitae* are Lifris of Llancarfan's *Life of Cadoc* (written 1061–1104 according to Wendy Davies, 208) and Caradoc's *Life of Gildas*, each of which contains two developed Arthurian episodes.

Caradoc's tale of Melvas and Guennuvar was dealt with above. The story of Cau of Pictland and his sons (one of whom was St. Gildas) is reflected also in *Culhwch* and the earlier Breton (Ruys) *Life of Gildas* as well as Caradoc. The account of Hueil son of Kaw's feud with Arthur was traced by Thomas Jones through modern folkloric sources, the sixteenth-century Elis Gruffydd, and twelfth-century Gerald of Wales back to *Culhwch* and the saints' lives ("Huail"). An edition of Caradoc's *Life of Gildas* newer than Hugh Williams's of 1901 is a desideratum. In the first Arthurian episode in the *Life of Cadoc*, Arthur in an inversion of his usual role has to be dissuaded by his comrades Cei and Bedguir from raping the passing maiden Guladus. The second episode concerns Arthur's arrogant demand for cows of a particular color as compensation for the slaying of three of his warriors. Roberts compares the heroic inversion of Arthur's character with similar effects in Irish hagiography ("*Culhwch*," 82–84). A full list of manuscripts, editions, and studies of Celtic Latin hagiography to 1200 is contained in the *Bibliography* of Lapidge and Sharpe.

*Multiperiod Corpora with Arthurian Connections*: The Myrddin/Merlin Tradition, Tristan and Isold, the Triads

Today, as for the preceding four decades, the leading authority on the early Welsh literature relating to the figure Myrddin (corresponding to the Merlin of Geoffrey and the romances) is A.O.H. Jarman of Cardiff. In his extensive series of editions and published discussions, Jarman personally has provided scholars with reliable texts for the bulk of the corpus and a well-argued explanation of its origins.

At the beginning of his "Merlin Legend," Jarman makes the key point that it was Geoffrey of Monmouth in *Historia Regum Britanniae* who first connected "Merlin" with Arthur. In this sense, the pre-Galfridian Myrddin material is only "proto-Arthurian" in the sense of having once existed as an independent tradition, then subsequently being drawn into the high-medieval Arthurian orbit.

There is no Welsh prose account of Myrddin's biography independent of Geoffrey. Rather, we have six poems that are largely prophetic in content and go by the following conventional titles: *Ymddiddan Myrddin a Thaliesin* ("The Dialogue of Myrddin and Taliesin"), *Yr Afallennau* ("The Apple-Trees"), *Yr Oianau* ("The Greetings"), *Cyfoesi Myrddin a Gwenddydd ei Chwaer* ("The Conversation of Myrddin and His Sister Gwenddydd"), *Gwasgargerdd Myrddin yn y Bedd* ("The ?Scattered Song of Myrddin in the Grave"), and *Peirian Faban* ("Commanding Child"). The first three poems occur in the thirteenth-century Black Book of Carmarthen. Standard editions appear as §§1, 16, and 17 of Jarman's *Llyfr Du*. The stanzas of *Y Bedwenni* ("The Birch Trees"; *Llyfr Du*, §15), occur immediately before the *Afallennau* in the manuscript and are stylistically very close, so they were perhaps intended to form a group, but they do not mention Myrddin or any part of his story. *Myrddin a Thaliesin* was earlier published by Jarman as a monograph with more detailed introductory matter. The *Cyfoesi* and the *Gwasgargerdd* occur in the Red Book of Hergest and are hence available in the aging diplomatic edition of J.G. Evans. Versions of the *Cyfoesi*, *Afallennau*, and *Oianau* occur also in Peniarth 3 and were published by Sir Ifor Williams. The *Gwasgargerdd* also occurs in the formerly detached portion of the White Book of Rhydderch and was published by Phillimore in the last century. *Peiryan Vaban* occurs in a fifteenth-century manuscript and has been published by Jarman.

New translations by Bollard of all six poems were published in *The Romance of Merlin*. For the *Ymddiddan*, *Afallennau*, and *Oianau*, there are also translations by Jarman (in Tolstoy 1985, 251–255) and by Pennar. A portion of the *Afallennau* is modernized by Gwyn Thomas (1976, 71–73). That Myrddin was known in the pre-Norman period as a prophet and an inspired poet is shown also by the reference in *Y Gododdin* mentioned above and the verse opening "Myrddin foretells" in the tenth-century political prophecy *Armes Prydein*, which is one variant of a formula that otherwise reads "poetic inspiration (*awen*) foretells" and "druids foretell." (Tolstoy sees in the Myrddin legend the survival of a complex of pre-Christian druidical beliefs, which he believes survived vigorously in the less Romanized Highland Zone of Britain in the Dark Ages [1985, 71–86].)

In addition to the vaticinatory material in the six poems, we find an accumulation of allusions to a frame story concerning Myrddin and his associates, which does not survive in a complete or explicit form. Jarman discusses the complex relationship of the Black Book vaticinations and the broader corpus of Merlin literature in "Arthurian Allusions" (1983, 102-105). The skeletal story recoverable includes the following details. Myrddin once enjoyed a courtly life as the dependent of a chieftain Gwenddolau. Gwenddolau was defeated and slain by Rhydderch (a historical king of late sixth-century Strathclyde) at the battle of Arfderydd (*Annales Cambriae* Armterid A.D. 573), Myrddin went mad and received his prophetic powers and lived many years as a wildman in Coed Celyddon, "the Caledonian Forest." Some details can be filled in from other sources. Thus, Gerald of Wales (ca. 1146-1223) in his *Itinerarium Kambriae* tells that Myrddin was driven mad by a horrendous celestial vision that he saw as the member of a host drawn up in an array for battle.

A fuller reconstruction requires comparison with traditions of the Strathclyde prophet-wildman Laloecen (or Lailoken) and the Irish Suibne Gelt ("S. the Wildman"). Lailoken narratives are found in twelfth-century Latin texts connected with Kentigern, the patron saint of Glasgow. (The editions, by Forbes and Ward, are over a hundred years old.[18]) The Welsh, Irish, and Scottish parallels are of a nature to suggest (to Carney most particularly) that we are not dealing simply with analogous or cognate themes, but rather the transfer of a specific story from one Dark Age Celtic country to the others. Lailoken of Strathclyde would be the starting point. Like Myrddin, the North British wildman is connected with King Rederech (i.e., Rhydderch) of Strathclyde. He lost his sanity during a battle that appears to have been fought in the same place and the same period as Arfderydd (eight miles north of Carlisle) when he beheld a horrendous vision in the sky at the opening of the battle.

In the Welsh *Cyfoesi*, Myrddin is addressed by his sister as *Llallawc* and its diminutive *Llallogan*. These may mean "fellow, companion" and "dear companion" respectively. The latter is in fact most probably the very same word or name as *Lailoken*. On the Irish

---

[18] A.P. Forbes, ed., *The Lives of St. Ninian and St. Kentigern* (Edinburgh, 1874); H.L.D. Ward, "Lailoken (or Merlin Silvester)," *Romania*, 22 (1893), 504-526.

side, Wild Suibne's descriptive epithet is *Gelt*, which is now widely
agreed to derive from a borrowing of the Brittonic word that supplies
Myrddin's descriptive epithet *Gwyllt*. In a forthcoming article
("*Goídil*"), I conclude that *gelt* was borrowed into Gaelic from
Strathclyde Brittonic along with a block of Brittonic loanwords and
literary themes not long after the historical battle that serves as the
occasion of Suibne's madness (Mag Roth, A.D. 637); that would be the
century prior to the date to which Carney assigned the borrowing
(chapter 4). Suibne is connected with the unidentified place Dún
Rodairce, which can be interpreted as "Fort of Rhydderch" (Carney,
151–152). In one episode of the *Buile Suibne* ("Suibne's Frenzy"),
Suibne visits Strathclyde and meets the British wildman Alladhán,
which may very well be Lailoken himself. Following Carney, Carey
has more recently discussed broader early Irish connections for the
Myrddin/Lailoken complex.

Taken together, these narrative elements imply that the common
original belonged geographically to North Britain (nearby to Carlisle,
Strathclyde, and the Caledonian Forest) and included the wildman and
the historical King Rhydderch, and that the wildman was called
Cumbric *Lallöcan* and had the epithet *Guïlt*, "Wild." Accordingly,
the name *Myrddin* might not be original. Jarman argues that the name
was extracted from *Caerfyrddin*, or "Carmarthen" (< British
*Moridûnon* 'Sea-Fort') as an eponym of the town (and the tribal
kingdom of Dyfed more generally) after the etymology was forgotten
(1991, 137–138). "At some time between the sixth century and the
eleventh the [Strathclyde] legend of Lailoken must have migrated to
Wales, where it took root in Dyfed, and the name 'Myrddin' replaced
that of 'Lailoken'" (1991, 138).

Alternative etymologies have been suggested for *Myrddin* as a
personal name (also containing Celtic *Mori-* 'sea' as the first element),
but these alternatives would not rule out the likelihood that any such
personal name came to be popularly understood as an eponym of
*Caerfyrddin*. Tolstoy argues that it is *Lailoken* that is a secondary
intrusion in Strathclyde, a misunderstanding of the appellative use of
*llallogan* preserved in the *Cyfoesi* (1983–84). References in the *Cyfoesi*
to Myrddin's father, Morfryn, and brothers, Morgenau, Morial,
Mordaf, and Morien, imply that, when the tradition was formed, the
name was still understood to contain the element *môr* < *mori-* 'sea'

when the tradition was formed. Fleuriot has interestingly mentioned the Old Breton anthroponymic element *Merthin-* in ninth-century charters of Redon (1987, 155–156). This vast cartulary (available in the unsatisfactory and rare 1863 edition of de Courson) is a treasure trove of early Brittonic onomastics and could enlighten numerous Arthurian names if more accessible for systematic reexamination.

Bromwich (1966) and Tolstoy (1983–84; 1985) have argued for a historical sixth-century poet named Myrddin at the foundations of the tradition. The alternative view, in which Myrddin arose as an eponym of Caerfyrddin, is cogently reargued by Jarman ("Bardd Hanesyddol").

The publication of Geoffrey's *Historia Regum Britanniae* ca. 1136 and *Vita Merlini* (ca. 1150) spurred interest in the truly Arthurian Merlin for a wide audience. This included a set of reflux or hybridized literary developments in the Celtic countries. Roberts (1977) discusses the several Welsh manuscript versions of Geoffrey's *Prophetiae Merlini*, permitting a stemma and the conclusion of an original Welsh adaptation as old as the end of the twelfth or beginning of the thirteenth century. Forms quoted from the text of Peniarth 311 will remind Celticists of the usage in early Welsh poetry and easily support Roberts's dating: e.g., *diguydaut* 'will befall,' *mygedort* 'vapor.' In "Esboniad Cymraeg ar Broffwydoliaeth Myrddin" (1966), Roberts describes Welsh and Latin explanations of the prophecies with an edition of the Peniarth 16 text, which he dates ca. 1216–ca. 1250 on the basis of a reference to the death of King John.

The post-Galfridian *Prophetia Merlini* of John of Cornwall (ca. 1155) has been the subject of recent publications by Fleuriot (1974), Flobert, and Curley (1982; 1984–86); see also Brett (1989, 12–13). Flobert gives a text and French translation of the dedicatory preface and verse, and Curley a complete edition with copious commentary (1982). Curley concludes that the Brittonic glosses, some of them clearly Cornish, point toward a vernacular tradition of Arthur in Cornwall together with a literary awareness of Geoffrey in the twelfth century. Fleuriot's analysis suggests a possible pre-Galfridian literate vernacular tradition based in either Cornwall or Brittany. Analogues to the medieval Merlin legend in later Breton vernacular literature are pursued by Laurent and Philippe (cf. also Sterckx 1992). Fleuriot also proposed that the prophetic wildman of the woods named Guynglaff who converses with Arthur in the versified Middle Breton *Dialog etre*

*Arzur Roe d'an Bretonet ha Guynglaff* is a further avatar of the Brittonic Merlin figure (1987, 157–158; J.-P. Piriou, 477). Jean-Pierre Piriou interprets the name Guynglaff as meaning "blessed sick man" and presents some indirect evidence for the idea of epilepsy as a disease accompanied by supernatural powers (492–493). Piette (190) and Fleuriot (1987, 157–58) suggested a date of composition ca. 1450 for the *Dialog*. But it survives only in poor and late (eighteenth-century) copies at multiple removes from the original (J.-P. Piriou, 474–475). There clearly have been later modifications; for example, some of the prophecies can be related to events in the later sixteenth century (J.-P. Piriou, 478–480).

Ford published a text and discussion of "The Death of Merlin in the Chronicle of Elis Gruffydd." (Gruffydd and his Chronicle are discussed further below.) Gruffydd's sixteenth-century account is eclectic in detail and offers points of comparison with pre-Galfridian and post-Galfridian Welsh texts, the Vulgate and Post-Vulgate cycles, and Malory. For example, the spirit of Gruffydd's Merddin reappears as Taliesin in the time of King Maelgwn and is said to live still in Caer Sidia (which is to be equated with Caer Sidi, one of the supernatural strongholds of *Preiðeu Annwfyn*). Gruffydd's Merddin makes a glass house in *Ynys Wydrin*, "The Glass Island," and is imprisoned there by the Lady of the Lake. The glass house is reminiscent of a mysterious glass tower that appears in the middle of the sea in *Historia Brittonum* §13 and a glass fortress confronting Arthur's band in *Preiðeu Annwfyn*. For Gruffydd, Ynys Wydrin is near Gloucester; for Gerald of Wales, it was the Welsh name of Glastonbury. In the Vulgate version, Merlin is imprisoned in a magic tower. In Malory, he is imprisoned under a stone in Cornwall by one of the Lady of the Lake's maidens.

It is now, as it has been for many years, consensus that the Tristan story is of Celtic origin. An important recent discussion of Tristan's origins and the relevant Welsh texts is Rachel Bromwich's "*Tristan of the Welsh*" (1991) in which she emphasizes that the chief *dramatis personae* (Drystan, Essyllt, and March) bear names of Brittonic origin (209). A generation ago, Pictish *cum* Old Irish origin was widely accepted, as in the influential article by Newstead (in *ALMA*), a position reaffirmed by Pearce in the 1970s.[19] This theory hinges largely upon the recurrence of the names *Drust(an)* and *Talorc(an)* in the Pictish King List (for which see Anderson, *Kings and Kingship*) and the similarity of the Tristan love triangle to certain Irish wooing tales, chiefly *Diarmaid and Gráinne*. The Pictish name *Drust(-)* would be none other than the cognate of Welsh *Drystan* (= Tristan, etc. in the romances). *Talorc(-)* has been taken as similar to *Tallwch*, Drystan's patronym in the Welsh sources.

The difficulties with the latter are that nothing like *Talorc/Tallwch* occurs in the romances (and therefore by no means certainly in their Celtic source) and that *Talorc* and *Tallwch* cannot possibly be cognates. *Talorc* could be etymologized (popularly by speakers of the early Celtic languages, not actually) as "Pig-Brow" and *Tallwch* as Welsh *tal* 'brow' + *hwch* 'swine, sow'[20] so at best a partial loan translation would be involved. Insofar as Drystan son of Tallwch figures in the Welsh Triads as one of the "Three Powerful Swineherds," where he happens to be connected with Arthur (Bromwich 1961, 44–48), an underlying Pictish dynastic tale is not necessary to motivate the unique name *Tal-hwch*. Since the appearance of Nessa Ní Shéaghdha's edition of an Early Modern Irish version of *Diarmaid and Gráinne*, scholars have become aware that the Irish tale is too late to be credibly taken as Tristan's source and even that the reverse relationship is possible, at least in part (Bromwich 1991, 222–223). A second suggested Irish analogue involves a monster-slaying episode in *Tochmarc Emire*, "The Wooing of Emer" (ed. Van Hamel). Though it is not so chronologically problematical as *Diarmaid and Gráinne*, the *Tochmarc Emire* sequence has no echoes in the Welsh Tristan material.

Padel (1981) gives a well-argued case emphasizing the early Cornish connections of the Tristan story and discrediting the Pictish theory. Key points in the case for a Cornish Tristan include the fifth-

---

[19] It should be noted that some of Pearce's reasons for dismissing Cornish origin are questionable: for example, the belief that the name *Cornwall, Cornubia, Kernyw*, etc., cannot be older than the eighth century (148) and her theory that the southwestern localization of Arthurian tradition in general belongs to a secondary development of the eighth to eleventh centuries.

[20] The different treatment of the consonants at the compositional boundary of *Cul-hwch* can be explained as a result of the apparent etymology of the name preserved in the tale.

to seventh-century inscription DRVSTA(N)VS HIC IACIT CVNOMORI FILIVS, "here lies Drystan son of Cynfawr" (located near Béroul's locale of the tale at Castle Dore), and the place-name *Hryt Eselt*, "Isold's Ford," in a tenth- or eleventh-century Anglo-Saxon charter, probably reflecting an older form of one of the two episodes occurring at fords in Béroul. Fleuriot discussed the possible correspondence of King Mark (Welsh March son of Meirchiawn) and the historical sixth-century Breton chief Marc Conomor, whose surname is equivalent to the *Cunomor-* of the inscription (1987, 127–129). Though *Drystan* and *March* are rare Brittonic names, *Con(o)mor* etc. was extremely common in the early Middle Ages; the identification is therefore not completely certain. Padel has decisively shown that despite Béroul's *Tristan* geography, Lantien (now Castle Dore) was a pre-Roman Iron Age site and therefore could not possibly have been the stronghold of a historical Dark Age Marc Conomor (1991, 240–243).[21]

There is no complete and coherent medieval Celtic version of the Tristan story. As recently itemized by Bromwich (1991, 209), the Welsh Tristan fragments comprise: (1) a poem or fragments of two poems in the Black Book of Carmarthen (Jarman, *Llyfr Du*, no. 35); (2) allusions in the Welsh Triads to Drystan (Bromwich 1961, nos. 19, 21, 26, 41, 71, 72, 73, 80), Esyllt (ibid., nos. 26, 71, 80), and March (ibid. nos. 14, 26, 71, 73); (3) allusions by poets to Drystan and Esyllt beginning with the *Gogynfeirdd* of the thirteenth century and more commonly with the *cywyddwyr* of the fourteenth to sixteenth; (4) *Ystorya Trystan*, "The Tale of Tristan," a mixed prose-verse text occurring only in sixteenth- to eighteenth-century manuscripts. The poem from the Black Book, as well as occurring in Jarman's edition of the manuscript, has been published in a full translation and annotated edition by Bromwich (1979–80). Her discussion underscores the uncertainty of the relationship of the poem(s) to the Tristan story, despite containing the names *D(i)ristan* and *March*. As to the date, she draws attention to the retention of the verbal noun ending *-iμ* (proved by internal rhyme). This form was already shortened to *-i* in the Old Welsh Computus fragment of the late ninth to mid-tenth century. Bromwich's *Trioedd* remains the standard edition and discussion of the

---

[21] Pearce (157) dismisses the evidence of the DRVSTANVS inscription.

Triads, to which add "*Tristan* of the Welsh" (1991, 214–216). In the verse references, the recognizable love story was apparently known beginning with Gruffudd ap Maredudd in the mid-fourteenth century. This evidence, which is not extensive, is canvassed by Bromwich (1991, 216).[22]

*Ystorya Trystan* exists in several manuscript copies.[23] There is a translation by Thomson. Newly discovered texts are edited and a basically twofold stemma is established by Rowland and Thomas. An important recent discussion by Rowland focuses on the likelihood of a separate history and authorship for the prose and verse and sharp differences distinguishing the texts from the continental Tristan romances (1990, 252–254).[24]

In addition to the references to the Drystan story, the Welsh Triads are a general repository of Arthurian and other early Welsh narrative tradition. The style is brief and concise, and it is widely assumed that these are not the primary narratives themselves but epitomized allusions to an extant body of oral and/or written tradition. There is a sparer early version of the corpus reflected in the mid-thirteenth-century manuscript Aberystwyth, National Library of Wales, Peniarth 16, the contents of which are generally pre-Galfridian. The later version reflected in the closely related manuscripts known as the Red Book of Hergest (ca. 1400) and White Book of Rhydderch (mid-fourteenth century) shows the influence of Geoffrey at several points, but is not in the main derived from him. The definitive edition, translation, and discussion are today, as they have been for the past three decades, Rachel Bromwich's *Trioedd Ynys Prydein*. An important recent

---

[22] It is possible that the *Cyfres Beirdd y Tywysogion* mentioned above will reveal earlier allusions.

[23] Various versions edited many years ago remain essential: Tom Peete Cross, ed., "A Welsh Tristan Episode," *Studies in Philology*, 17 (1920), 98-110; Ifor Williams, ed., "Trystan ac Esyllt," *Bulletin of the Board of Celtic Studies*, 5 (1930), 115-129; E.D. Jones, ed., "Trystan ac Esyllt," *Bulletin of the Board of Celtic Studies*, 13 (1948), 25-27.

[24] Special importance has been attached to this text because it mixes verse dialogue and prose. According to the influential theory of Sir Ifor Williams, this had been the original oral form of the saga englynion in general. For a recent discussion of the controversial "lost prose matrix" theory, see Rowland, "Prose Setting."

overview of the Arthurian Triads is Roberts (1991, 80–82). A detailed comparison of the great Arthurian court list in *Culhwch* and the Triads is made by Bromwich and Evans, reaching the conclusion that there is a pattern of long-term and complex mutual influence (1988, xl–xlii). In papers presented at Ottawa in 1986 and Swansea in 1987, Maria Tymoczko proposed that a comparison of the shared vs. nonshared elements among *Culhwch*, other Arthurian narratives, and the Triads could form the basis for calculating and reconstructing the totality of the Welsh Arthurian cycle of ca. 1050–1225. These two papers are to be developed as a monograph-length work. Bollard shows that the Triads (as well as *Culhwch* and *Gereint*) were quarried for the names in the lists in *Breuddwyd Rhonabwy* (1980–81, 160–161).

*Texts Postdating the Advent of Anglo-Norman Influence*: Breuddwyd Rhonabwy, *the Three Romances,* Brut y Brenhinedd

Within this category, *Breuddwyd Rhonabwy* is somewhat anomalous. The frame tale is set in the reign of Madawc son of Mareduδ of Powys (1130–60); therefore, it most probably dates in absolute terms later than the publication of Geoffrey's *Historia Regum Britanniae* (ca. 1135–39) and could be considerably later. On the other hand, Galfridian influence is not pervasive. As Sir Ifor Williams noted many years ago, there are roughly twelve words of French origin in *Rhonabwy* (*Pedeir Keinc*, xxxiii–xxxiv). However, Anglo-Norman literary influence is considerably less obvious. A literary tale that is often cited as similar (as a topical satire whose centerpiece is a fantastic dream vision) is the Middle Irish *Aislinge Meic Con Glinne*, "The Dream of Mac Con Glinne" (e.g., Dafydd Glyn Jones, 189–190). There is a new edition of *Aislinge Meic Con Glinne* by Jackson. Similarly, Carson discusses the Celtic affinities of the pivotal episode in which *Rhonabwy* sleeps on an animal skin as a prelude to gaining otherworldly wisdom. On the other hand, Lloyd-Morgan (1991, 190–191; citing an unpublished thesis by Dafydd Glyn Jones) sees parallels to medieval English and French dream poems, particularly the *Roman de la Rose*, though she stops short of positing direct influence from any particular non-Celtic text.

The standard edition is Richards's Welsh version of 1948. A version with English introduction and notes would prove useful to Arthurian scholars. *Rhonabwy* has been repeatedly anthologized as part of the Mabinogi, broadly construed, including the translations of Jones and Jones and of Gantz.

In recent scholarship, the unusual literary qualities of *Rhonabwy* have attracted attention. Dafydd Glyn Jones (194–195) is struck by how *Rhonabwy* fails to take its storytelling seriously. Mac Cana calls the text "a prolonged parody of native genres and styles" (1977, 83). Bollard likewise draws attention to the tale's self-consciously literary qualities and its overt intention of confusing readers with excess of detail and description. He concludes (1980–81)that the author was satirizing in particular the rhetorical devices of *amplificatio* and *digressio*. Slotkin also views Rhonabwy as a satire by a skilled literary man who distrusts his craft. He sees in its untraditional handling of the Arthurian themes a commentary on the ill effects of the heroic ideal upon Powys and Wales. The Arthurian conflict in the dream is taken as comment upon the conflict between the twelfth-century brothers Iorwerth and Madawc in the frame tale. Slotkin also makes the important observation that the traditional Arthurian biography is retrograde in *Rhonabwy*, with Camlann preceding Baðon (cf. Roberts 1976 ["Tales"], 233). According to Roberts,

> There now seems to be general agreement that these faults [its lack of progression, its descriptive passages, and inconsequentiality of its episodes] are intentional and that the story (an ystoria read from a book) is a pastiche of traditional episodes composed as a parody of interlacing and of the episodic style of a *roman d'aventure* [1984, 225].

Similarly, Lloyd-Morgan emphasizes the authorial and innovative qualities of the tale as a parody of a highly developed Arthurian tradition well known to both the author and his intended audience (1991, 190–193). The most sweeping assessment of *Rhonabwy*'s radical literary qualities is Mac Cana's:

> The fact is that *The Dream of Rhonabwy* is not a story in the sense that the other texts in the *Mabinogi* are stories. . . . It does not tell a tale, but rather creates a situation comprising several sustained images. It uses some of the technical and stylistical devices of oral narrative, but it has no "plot" worth mentioning, no real progression of incident and none but the most inconclusive of endings [1977, 86–87].

Possible dates of composition for *Rhonabwy* range from Madawc fab Mareduð's lifetime (fl. 1130–60) to nearly the date of the Red Book of Hergest (ca. 1400), the single manuscript in which the tale occurs. Charles-Edwards (1971, 266) and Hamp (1974, 99) propose a composition during Madawc's reign because the satire of the puny stature of the men of Powys in his day, as opposed to the great physical stature of the Arthurian heroes of the dream, would be pointless otherwise. This point is weakened (though not wholly disproved) by the analogue of the Late Middle Irish *Acallam na Senórach* ("Colloquy of the Old Men") in which St. Patrick and his followers also appear absurdly puny in contrast to the surviving Fenian heroes (Mac Cana 1977, 85). That text dates to the late twelfth century and contrasts the early Christians of the fifth century with pagan heroes of the third.

Roberts believes that *Rhonabwy* may be later than the Romances, which he places near the beginning of the thirteenth century (1984, 214). Carson argues that internal evidence shows that the tale was composed no earlier than the late fourteenth century. She sees a complex tripartite structure of opponents and their messengers as a comment on the political situation in Wales at that time. As well as adducing heraldic evidence for this date (299–300), her chief support rests on equating of the house of Heilyn-Goch son of Kadwgawn son of Iðon in Dilystwn in the frame tale's setting with the historical Heilyn son of Cadifor of Dudleston, who would have flourished ca. 1385. However, Carson's chronology (at 293–294, n. 15) is muddled and involves impossibly long generations. Furthermore, the name *Heilyn* is not rare in medieval Welsh sources. Such an extreme date is at least slightly too late to accommodate the allusion to "Rhonabwy's Dream" by the poet Madog Dwygraig (fl. 1370–80) as noted by Lloyd-Morgan (1991, 191–192).

The three tales *Owein neu Iarlles y Ffynnawn* ("Owein or the Lady of the Fountain"), *Peredur*, and *Gereint uab Erbin*, are usually treated as a distinct subclass, termed *Y Tair Rhamant* ("the Three Romances"), though they are not so plainly a unity in their style, content, and manuscript tradition as, for example, the Four Branches of the Mabinogi (Roberts 1992, 142–144). In defense of the terms "romance" or *rhamant* for this group, Roberts writes,

> The essence of the romance is not knight errantry, chivalry, the setting, but the significance of the quest. . . . If we have to choose a general theme, it is that of self discovery, the discovery of the identity and the balancing of prowess,

refinement and self-realization by trial, adventure and military skill [1992, 139–140].

Each of the Three Romances occurs in part or wholly in the Red Book of Hergest and White Book of Rhydderch and therefore in the old diplomatic editions of J.G. Evans. Thomson's edition of *Owein*, with English introduction, notes, and full glossary, remains standard. Bollard's discussion of the detailed relationships of the four early manuscripts of *Peredur* is also noteworthy in this connection and tends to underscore the established view of an especially close connection between the White Book and the Red ("Peredur"; see also Goetinck 1975, 304–317). There is a full Welsh edition of *Peredur* by Goetinck, an English version of which would prove useful for Arthurian scholarship. A critical edition of *Gereint*, long a serious lacuna, is in preparation by R.L. Thomson and will be published by the Dublin Institute for Advanced Studies. The Three Romances are included in the translations of *The Mabinogion* of Gantz and of Jones and Jones.[25]

As to the date of the Romances, Bromwich places their writing in the second half of the twelfth or beginning of the thirteenth century, citing obvious influence of the *Historia Regum Britanniae* (1974, 154–155). Similarly, Lloyd-Morgan sees the comparison of the Romances and Chrétien as attesting literary contact between Wales and France around the late twelfth or thirteenth century (1985, 397). Diverres favors a narrower and later span of 1250–84. At the other extreme, Goetinck believes that the spelling found in the manuscripts of *Peredur* reflects a twelfth-century copy, which could be pre-Galfridian (1976, xxiii; 1975, 317; 1988, 231).

In keeping with the general trend in Celtic scholarship in the 1980s, which increasingly views medieval written literature as the monopoly of monastic scriptoria, Goetinck proposes that the *Peredur* author may have been a monk. She adduces the negative portrayal of the military classes (similar to the heroic inversion of Arthur's character in some saints' lives) and the hero's sexual abstinence (1988).

---

[25] For an orthographic modernization and regularization of all three Romances based on the Red Book text for nonspecialist Welsh readers, see Bobi [Robert Maynard] Jones, ed., *Y Tair Rhamant*, 1960; Aberystwyth: Cymdeithas Lyfrau Ceredigion, 1979.

What may be termed the central literary fact of the Three Romances is that they correspond more or less closely to *Yvain ou le Chevalier au Lion*, *Perceval ou le conte du graal*, and *Erec et Enide* (respectively) of Chrétien de Troyes. The precise basis of this detailed correspondence has long remained controversial; this is the so-called *Mabinogionfrage*. Goetinck (1975, 2, n. 2) and Patricia Williams usefully review earlier scholarship assigning priority alternately to the Welsh romances, to Chrétien, or to a lost common source.

One approach to the question of priority has been to consider which version has preserved a theme or motif closer to its supposed original form (Roberts 1977). Along these lines, Goetinck and Patricia Williams draw special attention to detailed correspondences between the Three Romances and other Celtic narratives manifesting the theme of a hero wooing a woman personifying the sovereignty of the land.[26] This complex extends to such details as the preliminary hunt of a magical beast (Goetinck 1965, 171). In a similar vein, Goetinck sees pervasive reflections of a Celtic concept of the otherworld in Peredur and sees the prototype of the Grail as a Celtic talisman of sovereignty from the otherworld, comparing the Early Irish allegory of sovereignty *Baile in Scáil* ("The Phantom's Frenzy"; 1975, 275–303). In this, Goetinck perhaps relies excessively on the passé interpretations of Irish mythology of O'Rahilly.

Sterckx, in his far-ranging and seemingly exhaustive study of Celtic head hunting and related rites (1985–86), draws special attention to the well-attested pagan Celtic practice of using severed heads as ritual cups (a fate that befell, for example, the Roman general Lucius Postumius at the hands of Cisalpine Boii, according to Livy [23.24]). Sterckx concludes that the mysterious severed head and vessel (*dyscyl*) that Peredur beholds in the Stronghold of Wonders (*Caer yr Enryfeðodeu*) are ultimately one and the same. These items correspond to the Grail in the continental romances. Otherwise, Goetinck accepts the pagan origins of the severed head but sees in the *dyscyl* (which she translates as "platter") a fusion with the biblical story of John the Baptist (1988, 229).

---

[26] Watson's thus far unique discussion of medieval gender relations as a subversive subtext of *Gereint* could open a worthwhile door for future reexamination of the theme of the Celtic sovereignty goddess.

Lozac'hmeur (1985) assumes two archetypes of Celtic origin shared by the *Didot-Perceval, Perlesvaus,* and *Peredur*: vengeance and the quest for mysterious objects. The obscurities of Chrétien's version are explained as due to the elimination of the vengeance archetype. Lozac'hmeur concludes that *Owein* and *Yvain* descend independently from a common source, because, on the one hand, *Owein* has misunderstood the description of a tree after a storm, which Chrétien has handled correctly, whereas on the other, *Owein* is closer to Celtic sources in its description of the gigantic and grotesque *coydwr* ("wood-man") than is Chrétien; according to this interpretation, the Celtic source is represented by the *Fer Caille* ("Wood-Man") of the tragic and macabre Irish tale *The Destruction of Da Derga's Hostel* ("Mabinogi d'Owein").[27]

In another broadly conceived study (1992), Lozac'hmeur posits the following archetypal myth: a king's death by one of his descendants is prophesied. His only daughter, though confined, nonetheless conceives a son. The suitor is slain by the king. The grandson is hidden and after coming of age learns his identity and avenges his father, fulfilling the prophecy. Among the many Indo-European myths and legends that Lozac'hmeur derives from this pattern are the biographies of the Irish Lug and Finn, the wooing frame tale of *Culhwch,* and the Grail legend (including *Peredur*). The various inherited themes enumerated above are often more apparent in the Welsh romances than in Chrétien and also better attested in extant Irish *comparanda* than in Welsh. However, Bromwich argues that they belonged to a common fund shared by all Celtic groups and thus were not necessarily borrowed by the Welsh from the Irish (1983, 50–51; 1974, 166).

Coming at the *Mabinogionfrage* head on, Thomson judges that *Owein* reflects the original form of the tale upon which Chrétien's was based. The reasoning is based largely on economy of cross-Channel and interlanguage borrowings (1968, lxxxiii–lxxxiv).

On the other hand, the Three Romances also exhibit considerable evidence of non-Celtic high-medieval courtly themes and French linguistic influence. Roberts (1988) envisions the development in medieval Wales of a hybrid style he terms the "literary *cyfarwydd*"

---

[27] See Marie-Thérèse Brouland, *Le Substrat celtique du lai Breton anglais "Sir Orfeo"* (Paris: Diffusion Didier Erudition, 1990).

("i.e., literary [Welsh] storyteller") and thinks it possible that the Romances represent retellings of Chrétien in this native style. Edel gives detailed scrutiny to what she sees as a formulaic style in *Peredur* contrasting with the typical continental literary interlace of *Perceval*, leading to the conclusion that Chrétien's poem was first translated orally into Welsh and that the text of *Peredur* then reemerged from Welsh oral tradition. Consistent with such conclusions, Goetinck describes *Peredur*'s general lack of interest in the thoughts and feelings of characters and its concise and lively technique, thereby contrasting sharply with Chrétien's attitude and style (1964–65). Diverres concludes that a thirteenth-century Welsh writer steeped in Welsh tradition and methods and working for a Welsh patron in the Welsh Marches produced *Owein* as an adaptation of Chrétien's *Yvain*; *Gereint* is likewise seen as a thirteenth-century adaptation of *Erec et Enide*.

A compatible line is taken by Lloyd-Morgan, who believes that the Three Romances are probably based on Chrétien, albeit employing a loose mode of translation and an essentially Welsh style of storytelling. Refreshingly, she regards the whole *Mabinogionfrage* to be of secondary interest and even regards the preoccupation with origins (personified to her by R.S. Loomis) as clouding the study of the literature in its own right. She is concerned instead with the circumstances, patronage, techniques, and procedures of medieval Welsh translation literature. In this, she sees a continuum with no abrupt changes in the pattern of French-Welsh literary contacts and activities from the Three Romances down to such undoubtedly translated later works as *Y Seint Greal* (1985; 1991 ["French Texts"]). She believes that the French Arthurian tales lent themselves especially well to Welsh adaptations because they possessed analogous characters and well-known episodes paralleled in the native tradition (1985, 402–403). It is particularly clear from Lloyd-Morgan's "Narrative Structure of Peredur" (1981) that her approach leads to viewing the Romances as having a more accomplished and coherent synchronic structure than in the view of other writers, such as Goetinck, who are more concerned with mythological origins. Though approving of Lloyd-Morgan's synchronic vantage, Lovecy regards *Peredur* as a poorly assembled muddle of diverse and partially duplicated elements.

Synthetic positions include Patricia Williams's, according to which Arthur personified both chivalry and sovereignty and therefore provided a vehicle for modernizing the archaic Celtic theme in twelfth-century fashion. In her substantial study of *Peredur*, Goetinck offers a detailed argument for positing a lost common original in French. Her view hinges partly on defense of the independent literary merits of the Romances (1–40), though this line of argument is less conclusive than her detailed comparison of the narrative details of *Perceval* and *Peredur*, where she finds that derivation of the latter from the former would involve an implausible degree of truncation and rearrangement (59–79). A similar approach drawing on *Parzival* indicates that Wolfram worked from a source whose contents were closer to the Welsh than to Chrétien (80–102).

R.M. Jones draws the important distinction between the study of the vertical and horizontal (roughly, diachronic and synchronic) structure of the Romances (171). He is struck by the intense local, Southeastern Welsh associations of the Romances and constructs a three-layer theory of the tales' prehistory, which accounts for the tales' strongly Celtic content (171–175): (A) mythological raw material (not necessarily localized); (B) (i) *Chwedl Frutaidd* (roughly, "Tale of Legendary British History") localized in the vicinity of Caerllion from pre-Norman times, ca. 1060–1170; (B) (ii) *Rhamant* ("Romance"), again localized, belonging to the period of Norman/Breton influence in the area of Monmouth, ca. 1100–1200.[28] He goes on to discuss the Breton presence (173–175). It is almost unavoidable to conclude that this proved a catalyzing cultural contact for more than one branch of Arthurian literature.[29] The subject would repay further scrutiny, particularly from the perspective of Breton studies.

Another potentially penetrating approach to the Celtic origins of the Romances is the names of the chief characters. Goetinck discusses one North British hero named *Peredur* in *Y Gododdin* and another falling

---

[28] This discussion is more elaborate than his earlier treatment of the same ground in *Tair Rhamant* xiii, though it continues along basically the same lines.

[29] For example, Bullock-Davies thinks the lais of Marie de France came from a local source in the Caerwent-Caerllion region and presents a case for interaction along Welsh Marches of "*Cyfarwyddiaid*, latimers, and French, Welsh, and English minstrels" (*Professional Interpreters*, 14–18).

in another battle in A.D. 580 in *Annales Cambriae* (*Peredur*, 26).[30]
However, we have no good reason not to suppose that the familiar
name was simply substituted by the Welsh storyteller for the unfamiliar
but vaguely similar *Perceval* in his prototype. On the other hand,
Chrétien's Yvain son of Urien and the Welsh Owein son of Urien
clearly derive from the historical sixth-century North British chieftain
(Bromwich 1983, 47).[31] Sims-Williams discusses the several historical
Gerontii and Gereints apropos the Gereint *englynion* (1991, 46–47).
The contrast of Arthurian names of the noncognate *Perceval/Peredur*
or *Gawain/Gwalchmei* type with those of the directly equivalent
*Owein/Yvain* type implies a complex interrelationship.

Though her discussion of the Arthurian names and themes applies
to the continental romances generally, Bromwich's conclusions are most
relevant to the problem of Chrétien and the Three Romances: (1) the
character names in the French Arthurian romances that are of Celtic
derivation are specifically of Brittonic (i.e., Welsh and/or Cornish
and/or Breton) origin and are frequently identifiable in sources that are
too early to be attributed to Geoffrey or other Anglo-Norman influence;
(2) Arthur became the center of the cycle during the indigenous stage
of development; (3) the character names and Celtic themes penetrated
French independently of one another; (4) Arthur's rise to fame in
western literature is essentially a Welsh literary problem (1983). She
makes the further important point that some of the French forms of the
names have undergone garbling indicative of oral transmission (44). In
the case of the Romances, we must envision a complex reflux and
reacclimation of Brittonic tradition, which had passed through an
intermediate French stage. Despite the amount of attention the subject
has already received, a rigorously philological and historical linguistic
study of the onomastics of the continental Arthurian literature by a

---

[30] The name *Gwalchmei* is prominent in all three Romances. Though the form is
linguistically archaic the character is ahistorical. Recent work on the name was mentioned
above.

[31] In a not recently edited poem in the Book of Taliesin and implicitly in the Welsh
Triads (Bromwich, *Trioedd*, no. 70), Owein is connected with the mythological figure
Mabon. Lozac'hmeur makes the attractive suggestion that the Arthurian name
*Mabonograin* in Chrétien's *Erec* is a contraction of the names *Mabon* and *Owein* (Old
Welsh *Ougein*) ("Mabonograin"; cf. Ovazza).

scholar with expertise in all the requisite languages remains a desideratum.

For the case of *Gereint* at least, Bromwich's studies of the character names *Erec/Gereint* and *Enit* provides a significant breakthrough allowing a series of stages in the tale's prehistory to be traced (1956–58; 1960–61; 1961, 347–348; 1974, 163–164). The key point is that as *Erec* must reflect Old Breton *Uueroc* (the name of the historical sixth-century founder of the Breton kingdom in the Vannetais), and thus the name of his destined consort *Enit* must reflect *Uuenet*, the Old Breton name of Vannes from the Gaulish tribal name *Venetī*. The common germ of Chrétien's *Erec* and *Gereint* had therefore originally been a dynastic sovereignty legend from southeastern Brittany. In the making of the Welsh version, a key event was substituting the known hero Gereint for the unfamiliar Erec or Gueroc. Bromwich suggests that this replacement took place in Cornwall, where one or more Gerents were known as local heroes, before passing on to Southeast Wales (cf. Goetinck 1975, 29). I have shown that the account in *Gereint* of how Enit's father Niwl lost his land corresponds more or less exactly to Gregory of Tours's historical report of how Uueroc's father lost his realm (1987, 42–44). As there is no corresponding incident in Chrétien, *Gereint* clearly cannot derive from Chrétien, but rather must reflect the Breton dynastic tradition independently. This point is more decisive than the relative weakness of the various Celtic sovereignty motifs in Chrétien, because these could conceivably have been strengthened anew once the French romance had returned to a Celtic milieu.

Bromwich also notes how the *Gereint* storyteller evidently quarried *Culhwch* for characters and compares the thematic and narrative structure of the tale to that of the pre-Galfridian Mabinogi *Pwyll* (1974, 155). This pair of references to other medieval Welsh prose tales only serves to underscore the complexity of the issue; for although the influence of *Culhwch* has no analogue in Chrétien and most probably belongs to the final stages of evolution after the French-Breton story had been localized in Wales, the similarities with the underlying sovereignty tale of *Pwyll* is shared with *Erec et Enide* and thus goes deeply into *Gereint*'s vertical structure.

The popularity of the Three Romances in late-medieval Wales is indicated by references to all three in the poems of Dafydd ap Gwilym, who flourished ca. 1340–70 (Bromwich 1982, 61–62).

There is general agreement about the sorts of pre-Norman Welsh sources to which Geoffrey of Monmouth had access when he wrote the *Historia Regum Britanniae*. As covered in the discussion of Roberts (1991), these include Gildas's *De Excidio Britanniae*; *Historia Brittonum*; *Annales Cambriae*; Old Welsh genealogies similar or even identical to those surviving in London, British Library Harley 3859 (eleventh–twelfth century; ed. Bartrum); saints' lives akin to those in the Book of Llandaf (twelfth century; ed. J.G. Evans and Rhŷs).[32] However, owing to Geoffrey's extremely creative handling of his material, it has as yet seldom been possible to determine with certainty whether Geoffrey possessed the texts in more or less precisely the versions known to us or as lost parallel versions. This uncertainty even goes so far as to cast doubt over whether any particular "Welsh" source was known by Geoffrey through a nonsurviving Cornish or Breton analogue. Unresolved questions of orality, Geoffrey's linguistic competence, and ethnolinguistic identity enter here (Crawford). The issue of Geoffrey's Brittonic sources is one in which close textual and philological work (in the area of onomastics, for example) could yet give us some firm answers.

Approximately sixty extant manuscripts contain Welsh-language versions of *Historia Regum Britanniae*. Most of these are listed with brief descriptions in Griscom (585–599; see also Reiss; Roberts 1971, xxiv—xxxix). Three thirteenth-century translations have been identified. Their oldest manuscript witnesses are in the National Library of Wales: Llanstephan 1, Peniarth 44, and the Dingestow Court Manuscript (Roberts 1991, 116, n. 39). A diplomatic edition of the Red Book of Hergest version (the best witness of its subfamily, which conflates the Dingestow and Llanstephan 1 versions) was published by J.G. Evans in 1890 and has not been superseded. A late version embodied in Oxford, Jesus College 61, as translated by R.E. Jones, is contained in Griscom's edition of Geoffrey. In 1937, J.J. Parry produced a

---

[32] Miller suggested that Geoffrey's list of early kings was based on a now lost ninth–/tenth-century manuscript based on Jerome's Chronicle, Bede, and Isidore ("Geoffrey's Early Royal Synchronisms").

diplomatic edition and translation of a version (probably earlier fourteenth century) reflected in British Library Cotton Cleopatra Bv (fifteenth century?). The most important published text is Henry Lewis's 1942 Welsh-language critical edition of the Dingestow version. Roberts's more recent edition of episodes from the Llanstephan 1 contains a valuable introduction and appendix on *"Historia Regum Britanniae* in Wales." As explained by Roberts (1980), the so-called *Brut Tysilio* represents an abridged fourteenth- or fifteenth-century conflation of known earlier translations of *Historia Regum Britanniae*, but was long mistaken by the early-modern Welsh antiquaries and subsequent scholars as Geoffrey's putative Brittonic source.

It is plain from the foregoing that a great deal of basic editorial work remains to be done or redone on *Brut y Brenhinedd*. Important recent studies of the textual relationships include Roberts's "Fersiwn Dingestow" (1977) and "Red Book of Hergest Version" (1977–78). As translation literature whose source is extant, the *Brutiau* are often regarded as being of secondary importance. However, it should be borne in mind that these are not straight translations in the modern sense. Welsh tradition frequently reasserts itself on Geoffrey's text in the areas of names and the alteration or supplementation of narrative content. For example, the Llanstephan 1 version inserts the native mythological tale of *Lluδ and Lleuelys*. Important studies of the onomastics and epithets in *Brutiau* are Roberts's "Treatment of Personal Names" (1973) and "Testunau Hanes" (1974, 290–291), but the subject has not yielded up all its mysteries. In some cases, like the *Brutiau's Beli* for the *Historia Regum Britanniae's Hely*, the Welsh translations recover a traditional form that Geoffrey misread.[33] Though *Historia Regum Britanniae* is now assigned priority over all of the *Brutiau*, the latter, because they have access to the same texts and traditions used by Geoffrey in the first place, may sometimesthrow light on his sources.

Roberts (1991) traces the emergent Welsh sense of nationhood beginning with Gildas, through *Historia Britonnum, Historia Regum Britanniae,* and the *Brutiau,* down to *Drych y Prif Oesoedd* (1716) and beyond. As itemized by Roberts, the medieval Welsh conception of

---

[33] In "Manawydan, Mandubracios," I repeatedly turn to the *Brutiau* as having a value in reflecting elements of Welsh tradition independent of Geoffrey.

their own history as manifested in the *Brutiau* centered upon five elemental themes: the Unity of the Island of Britain, the *Adventus Saxonum*, Prophecy, the Trojan origin of the Britons, and Rome (1974, 277–280).

## Welsh Arthurian Literature of the Fourteenth to Sixteenth Centuries: *Ystoryaeu Seint Greal, Darogan yr Olew Benigaid, Elis Gruffydd*

The Reverend Robert Williams's 1876 edition of the Late Middle Welsh *Y Seint Greal* (*Holy Greal*) is at last being superseded in the 1990s. This text was translated in the fourteenth century for the South Welsh patron Hopcyn ap Thomas from the French, the former part based on the *Queste del saint Graal* and the latter on the *Haut livre du graal* or *Perlesvaus* (Lloyd-Morgan 1985, 399). Thomas Jones's Welsh edition of "Part I: The Quest" appeared more than twenty years after the editor's death. Part II is soon to be brought to publication by Lloyd-Morgan. Lloyd-Morgan (1986) provides a discussion of the interaction of the French texts with Welsh narrative tradition, which led frequently to the insertion or replacement of native characters and episodes. Most of the manuscripts agree closely with the text found in the oldest surviving copy (Aberystwyth, National Library of Wales, Peniarth 11), but the fifteenth-century Peniarth 15 contains a highly atypical version based (possibly independently) on *Perlesvaus*. Lloyd-Morgan (1978) uses this text as a case study to show that written translation literature could reenter a largely oral repertory of surviving Welsh Arthurian legend, which at that time still retained a sense of what constituted foreign elements, that is, elements that were to be excluded from a naturalized Welsh adaptation.

*Darogan yr Olew Bendigaid* ("Prophecy of the Blessed Oil"), also known as *Hystdori yr Olew Bendigaid* ("Story of the Holy Oil"), is a political prophecy in prose that probably dates to the first half of the fifteenth century. The oldest surviving manuscript, which may be the redactor's autograph, is Aberystwyth, National Library of Wales, Peniarth 50, possibly written at Neath Abbey (Lloyd-Morgan 1991 ["From Ynys Wydrin"], 306–307; 1985 ["Welsh Nationhood"], 20). Edited texts are published by R.W. Evans. The redactor has adapted an English Latin prophecy concerning Thomas Becket. The oil in question is heaven-sent for anointing the rightful kings of England. In the Welsh version, England becomes *yr ynys honn* ("this island"), i.e., the whole of Britain, and the story is given an Arthurian frame drawing in established Glastonbury legends. Thus, the oil is brought to Britain by followers of Joseph of Arimathea and is later used by Archbishop Dubricius to consecrate Arthur. The oil, together with divine support, is then credited with enabling Arthur to vanquish giants and to "trample pagan Saxons underfoot" (Lloyd-Morgan, "Welsh Nationhood," 16). Lloyd-Morgan suggests that the immediate political context may reflect the fall and disappearance of the Welsh insurgent leader Owein Glyndŵr (1408–1413) (1985 ["Welsh Nationhood"], 20–22).

Elis Gruffydd, known as "the soldier of Calais," was a native of the Welsh county of Flint and a Tudor courtier, flourishing in the early to mid-sixteenth century. His ponderous "Chronicle of the Six Ages of the World" survives in his autograph between two manuscripts, Aberystwyth, National Library of Wales, 5276D and Mostyn 158. This eclectic Early Modern Welsh text has never been published in its entirety. A list of published excerpts is provided in Ford, *Ystoria Taliesin*, x. Gruffydd's "Death of Merlin" episode was mentioned above. Ford's edition of *Ystoria Taliesin* ("The Legend of Taliesin") is Gruffydd's version of the popular biography of the mythological persona of the arch-poet of Welsh tradition. A translation is available in Ford's *Mabinogi*. Considerable time elapses during the course of the story. In the beginning, the protagonist is the youth Gwion Bach in the days of King Arthur. After receiving supernatural inspiration from the hag Ceridwen's cauldron, he is cast adrift in a covered coracle for forty years, then released in the days of Maelgwn Gwynedd. In his obscure and bombastic verse, Taliesin tells King Maelgwn, *Shihannes ddewin a'm gelwis J Merd[d]in*: "Johannes the magician called me Merlin." At any rate, though *Ystoria Taliesin* is not in the main an Arthurian text, it was plainly well established in Welsh tradition in the Middle Ages and offers numerous parallels and points of contact with Arthurian tradition. Lloyd-Morgan is now preparing an edition of previously unpublished Arthurian material from Gruffydd's Chronicle.

*Medieval Arthurian Literature from the Other Celtic Countries*

At various points above, traces of Arthurian tradition in the other Brittonic countries—Cornwall, Brittany, and Cumbrian North

Britain—have been noted. The former two have no surviving
continuous vernacular prose or verse texts as early as the Welsh though
they do have Arthurian medieval Latin texts. In Cumbrian per se, we
have nothing, though the likelihood that this was the original domain
of *Y Gododdin*, the story of Lailoken, and northern elements in
*Historia Britonnum* and *Annales Cambriae* has already been discussed.

In 1965, Piette published a case for a Breton contribution to
Arthurian literature. He discussed several earlier theories of the sources
of the Matter of Britain in French, noting (183) that Lot, Loth, Marx,
and Jackson believed that the Anglo-Normans acquired the tradition
mainly from the Welsh in Britain. T. Stephens, W.J. Gruffydd,
Zimmer, Brugger, Voretzsch, Joseph Bédier, and Loomis saw the
Bretons as chief intermediaries. Piette viewed the case against early
Breton oral literature as largely an *argumentum ex silencio* compounded
by the ambiguity of the term *Britones* (and the like) employed in the
medieval sources for both Bretons and the Brittonic peoples of Britain
(184–185). Piette concluded that native Arthurian tradition was
transmitted to Brittany as early as it developed, which is to say long
before the Norman Conquest (189). This finding is consistent with
Jean-Pierre Piriou's point that four names corresponding to *Arthur*
occur in the Redon Charters between 868 and 878 (489).

Fleuriot has defended the internal date of 1019 for the introductory
epistle of *The Life of St. Goueznou*. This epistle contains the famous
précis of the legendary history of Britain, including Arthur's victories
against the Saxons and on the Continent (1987, 98; Ashe 1991).
Various parts of the *Vita* were edited in the last century by de la
Borderie and more recently supplemented by le Duc and Sterckx.

Another important pre-Galfridian Breton Latin text was called by
the fifteenth-century historian Le Baud *Le livre des faits d'Arthur*. The
original poem was probably composed between 954 and 1012. It
survives fragmentarily in a hundred and seventy-three hexameters in the
fifteenth-century manuscript Rennes, Archives d'Ille-et-Villaine 1 F
1003, which is probably Le Baud's workbook (Brett 1989, 4). It
concerns the familiar exploits of the Romano-British general Maximus
(so called using the correct form of his name, thus contrasting with the
*Historia Regum Britanniae, Historia Britonnum*, and *Maxen Wledig* [ =
?*Maxentius*]) and the Briton Conan Meriadec on the Continent. That
this is a more primitive version of the story than Geoffrey's is also

evidenced by further details, including Conan's title *dux*, rather than *rex* as in *Historia Regum Britanniae* (Brett 1989, 16–17). Arthur himself is absent from the extant *Livre des faits*. At present, this text remains unpublished. Important studies addressing *St. Goueznou* and the *Livre de faits d'Arthur* and emphasizing that both were among Geoffrey's sources are le Duc; Fleuriot 1980 [*Origines*], 245–246, 277; 1980 ["Trois textes"]; 1981.

Fleuriot also drew attention to a number of other Breton Latin texts of Arthurian interest. The early twelfth-century *Cartulary of Quimperlé* contains in a brief passage the story of Kenan and Beli, sons of Outham the Old, who went to Rome and settled Laeticia. The last detail probably involves the general medieval Celtic confusion of Irish *Letha*, Old Welsh *Litau*, Latinized *Letavia*, meaning both "Brittany" and "Latium." The details here are close to those of the Welsh *Dream of Maxen Wledig* (Brett 1989, 16). Fleuriot argued that the spelling *Outham* (= Welsh *Eudaf*) pointed to an original Early Old Breton written source of the ninth century, which he identifies as the lost *Historia Britannica* (1987, 99; 1980, 123, 264). The *Historia Britannorum Versificata* (otherwise known as *Gesta Regum Britanniae* or *Pseudo-Nennius*) was probably composed 1234–37 by William of Rennes and was dedicated to Bishop Cadioc of Vannes. The text remains untranslated, the 1862 edition of Michel is largely inaccessible, and the text's relationship to *Historia Regum Britanniae* is unclear (1987, 100–101).

The likelihood of Breton sources for the Breton lays was reexamined by Fleuriot, drawing attention to a number of Breton personal names, sometimes in badly garbled form; e.g., *Guigemar* < Late Old Breton *Guiuhomarch* is better preserved than the norm (*Histoire littéraire*, 1–38). Lozac'hmeur provides a valuable reevaluation of the Breton and pan-Celtic component in the Matter of Britain, again drawing attention to the likely derivation from Breton of Arthurian names in the Romances ("Romans bretons").

An unusual case for a non-Brittonic but Celtic mythological source is that of de Pontfarcy, who sees in Marie de France's *Lai des deus amanz* the survival of a local Gaulish sovereignty myth in Normandy comparable to the legend of the foundation of Marseille preserved by Athenaeus (*Deipnosophistae*, 13.576, quoting Aristotle) and Justin/ Trogus Pompeius (*Philippic Histories*, 43.3).

Goidelic literature has two levels of Arthurian interest: (1) tales of the Old and Middle Irish periods (ca. 600–900 and 900–1200) that are not Arthurian per se but, through *comparanda* of shared themes, episodes, and names, throw light on Common Celtic sources and early inter-Celtic borrowings contributing to the formation of Arthuriana; (2) late-medieval and early-modern material from Ireland, Scotland, and Man that is truly Arthurian and derived from texts otherwise known to us (though often via lost intermediaries). Under the first heading, we may note Boutet's paper recognizing that the character of Guenièvre in the continental romances reflects a partial assimilation of Medb as the sovereignty of Ireland (17; cf. Goetinck 1965, 172).

Gillies's two-part "Arthur in Gaelic Tradition" concerns mostly material postdating the Middle Irish period (ca. 900–1200) and extends beyond the limits of the Middle Ages, but all based in medieval Arthurian tradition. The earliest literary reflections of Arthur in Irish belong to the twelfth century. Thus, for example, in the well-known Fenian tale *Acallam na Senórach* ("Colloquy of the Old Men") an Artú(i)r figures as the son of Béinne Brit, king of the Britons. This need only mean that Artúr was a suitable name for a British prince of long ago. Fuller adoption of the traditions came later. *Lorgaireacht an tSoidhigh Naomhtha* ("The Quest for the Holy Grail") is a fifteenth-century rendering into Early Modern Irish of a lost English version of the Vulgate *Queste* and was edited by Sheila Falconer in 1953 (Gillies 1982, 42–43). In some cases, a character is wholly or partly borrowed from foreign Arthurian sources, but not the name. Thus, "The Great Fool," *An tAmadán Mór*, corresponds to Perceval/Peredur (Gillies 1981, 51–53).

The Early Modern Irish *Eachtra an Amadáin Mór* ("Adventure of the Great Fool") is closer to Chrétien's *Perceval* and its setting more explicitly Arthurian than the later oral version in Scottish Gaelic (Gillies 1982, 47–48). The Gaelic names and titles used for Arthurian characters point toward sources: for example, the forms *Cing Artúr* in *An Lorgaireacht* and *Eachtra an Amadáin Mór* (where he is also called *Rí Breatan*, "King of the Britons") and *Ceann Artair, Caoin Artúr* in the later folk material clearly point toward an English source (Gillies 1982, 49; 1981, 49–51). *Sir Ballbuaid* in *An Lorgaireacht* and the folk *Sir Uallabh O' Còrn* go back to a (Scots) English preform < *Walway*. This interestingly resembles the Welsh name Gwalchmei more than it does Gawain. Nonetheless, Gillies sees no certain evidence of direct Welsh influence on the Irish romances (1982, 63). *Caithréim Chonghail Chláiringnigh* ("The Martial Exploits of Conghal Flat-nail") represents an interesting conflation of Arthurian tradition with the native Ulster Cycle, including some direct borrowings from the Middle Irish Tale *Fled Dúin na nGéd*. In it Artúr Mór mac Iubhair ("Arthur the Great son of Uther") is King of the Britons and faces a Saxon threat (Gillies 1982, 46–47). Gillies emphasizes the degree to which the Modern Irish Arthurian romances have assimilated a Gaelic cultural milieu, citing the king's *geasa* ("tabus") and Gawain as Arthur's *dalta* ("foster son") (1982, 55).

Dealing next with the modern Scottish Gaelic and Irish folk material, Gillies has illustrated in detail the extent to which Arthurian literature was grafted onto an existing native stock of narrative tradition. The recurrent theme of Arthur and his knights hunting is apparently patterned after the native Fenian heroic cycle. Gillies interprets such features as reflecting a relatively long period of naturalization in a Gaelic setting, during which Arthurian figures came to float within Gaelic tradition among the stock of minor characters; hence, for example, Artúr and Úr (< Uther) are peripheral figures in versions of tales concerning the heroes Iollann Airmdhearg and Conall Gulban (1981, 57–58).

An interesting insight into the transmission process is afforded by orally collected versions of the Arthurian ballad *Am Bròn Binn* ("The Melodious Sorrow" or "The Dream of the King of the Britons"), the subject of which is the fateful dream of a king in which he sees a beautiful girl, analogous to the Old Irish *Dream of Óengus*, the Welsh *Dream of Macsen Wledig*, and the Breton Latin *Vita Iudicaeli*. Though there are no early manuscript versions, the modern texts collected from performances as a ballad or waulking song show confusion of *f*, *s*, *r*, pointing to a written original with Gaelic letter forms (1981, 59–62). Gillies suggests that *Am Bròn Binn* was possibly of Scottish origin, noting the Scottish localization in one version and the absence of Irish versions (1981, 63–64). The ballad *Laoidh an Bhruit* ("The Lay of the Mantle") is not an Arthurian but a Fenian Tale, but its theme, a chastity test, links it to *Le mantel mautaillié* and the *Lai du cor*, and further Celtic parallels for ordeals tests. It is attested as early as the early sixteenth-century Scottish Book of the Dean of Lismore and the seventeenth-century Irish Duanaire Finn (1981, 64–65).

# Bibliography

*Editions and Translations*

Anderson, Alan Orr, and Marjorie Ogilvie Anderson, eds. and trans. *Adomnán's Life of Columba* [*Vita Columbae*], 1961; rev. ed., Oxford: Clarendon, 1991.

Bartrum, P.C., ed. *Early Welsh Genealogical Tracts*. Cardiff: University of Wales Press, 1966.

Bollard, John K., trans. "Arthur in Early Welsh Tradition." In James J. Wilhelm, ed., *The Romance of Arthur*. New York: Garland, 1984, pp. 13–25; rpt. *The Romance of Arthur: An Anthology of Medieval Texts in Translation*. New York: Garland, 1994, pp. 11–23. [*Gereint fil' Erbin* from the Black Book of Carmarthen, *Pa Gur*, *Preiðeu Annwfyn*.]

———, trans. "Myrddin in Early Welsh Tradition." In Peter Goodrich, ed., *The Romance of Merlin*. New York: Garland, 1990, pp. 13–54. [*Ymddiddan Myrddin a Thaliesin, Y Bedwenni, Yr Afallennau, Yr Oianau, Myrddin a Gwenddydd ei Chwaer, Peirian Faban, Gwasgargerdd Myrddin*]

Bromwich, Rachel, ed. and trans. *Trioedd Ynys Prydein, The Welsh Triads*. Cardiff: University of Wales Press, 1961; 2nd ed., 1978.

———, ed. and trans. "The 'Tristan' Poem in the Black Book of Carmarthen." *Studia Celtica*, 14/15 (1979–80), 54–69.

———, and D. Simon Evans, eds. *Culhwch ac Olwen*. Cardiff: Gwasg Prifysgol Cymru, 1988.

————, and ————, eds. *Culhwch and Olwen: An Edition and Study of the Oldest Arthurian Tale*. Cardiff: University of Wales Press, 1992.

Clarke, Basil, ed. and trans. *The Life of Merlin: Geoffrey of Monmouth, Vita Merlini*. Cardiff: University of Wales Press, 1973. [Trans. Lailoken Fragments.]

Curley, Michael J., ed. "A New Edition of John of Cornwall's *Prophetia Merlini*." *Speculum*, 57 (1982), 217–249.

Dumville, David N., ed. *The Historia Brittonum: 3. The "Vatican" Recension*. Cambridge: Brewer, 1985.

Evans, R. Wallis, ed. "*Darogan yr Olew Bendigaid a Hystdori yr Olew*." *Llên Cymru*, 14 (1981–82), 86–91.

Flobert, P., ed. and trans. "La 'Prophetia Merlini' de Jean de Cornwall." *Etudes Celtiques*, 14, No. 1 (1974), 31–41.

Ford, Patrick K., ed. and trans. "The Death of Merlin in the Chronicle of Elis Gruffydd." *Viator*, 7 (1976), 379–390.

————, trans. *The Mabinogi and Other Medieval Welsh Tales*. Berkeley: University of California Press, 1977.

————, ed. *Ystoria Taliesin*. Cardiff: University of Wales Press, 1992.

Galyon, Aubrey, and Zacharias P. Thundy, trans. "Lailoken." In Peter Goodrich, ed., *The Romance of Merlin*. New York: Garland, 1990, pp. 3–11.

Gantz, Jeffrey, trans. *The Mabinogion*. Harmondsworth: Penguin, 1976.

Goetinck, Glenys Witchard, ed. *Historia Peredur vab Efrawc*. Cardiff: Gwasg Prifysgol Cymru, 1976.

Griscom, Acton, ed. *The Historia Regum Britanniae of Geoffrey of Monmouth*. London: Longmans, Green, 1929.

Gruffydd, R. Gereint, ed. "'Marwnad Cynddylan.'" In R. Gereint Gruffydd, ed., *Bardos: Pennodau ar y Traddodiad Barddol Cymreig a Cheltaidd*. Cardiff: Gwasg Prifysgol Cymru, 1982, pp. 10–28.

Huws, Daniel, ed. *Llyfr Aneirin: A Facsimile*. Aberystwyth: National Library of Wales, 1989.

Jackson, Kenneth Hurlstone, trans. *The Gododdin: The Oldest Scottish Poem*. Edinburgh: Edinburgh University Press, 1969.

——, ed. *Aislinge Meic Con Glinne*. Dublin: Dublin Institute for Advanced Studies, 1990.

Jarman, A.O.H., ed. *Ymddiddan Myrddin a Thaliesin*. 1951; 2nd ed., Cardiff: Gwasg Prifysgol Cymru, 1967.

——, ed. "Peiryan Vaban." *Bulletin of the Board of Celtic Studies*, 14 (1951–52), 104–108.

——, ed. *Llyfr Du Caerfyrddin: Gyda Rhagymadrodd, Nodiadau Testunol a Geirfa*. Cardiff: Gwasg Prifysgol Cymru, 1982.

——, ed. and trans. *Aneirin: Y Gododdin, Britain's Oldest Heroic Poem*. Llandysul: Gomer, 1988.

Jones, Elin M., ed., with the assistance of Nerys Ann Jones. *Gwaith Llywarch ap Llywelyn "Prydydd y Moch."* Cyfres Beirdd y Tywysogion. Cardiff: Gwasg Prifysgol Cymru, 1991.

Jones, Gwyn, and Thomas Jones, trans. *The Mabinogion*. London, 1949; rev. ed., London: Dent, 1974.

Jones, Nerys Ann, and Ann Parry Owen, eds. *Gwaith Cynddelw Brydydd Mawr I. Cyfres Beirdd y Tywysogion.* Cardiff: Gwasg Prifysgol Cymru, 1991.

Jones, Thomas, ed. and trans. "The Black Book of Carmarthen 'Stanzas of the Graves.'" *Proceedings of the British Academy 1967,* 53 (1968), 97–137.

———, ed. *Ystoryaeu Seint Greal. Rhan I. Y Keis.* Cardiff: Gwasg Prifysgol Cymru, 1992. [2 vols. projected.]

Le Duc, Gwenael, and Claude Sterckx, eds. "Les fragments inédits de la vie de S. Goueznou." *Annales de Bretagne,* 78 (1971), 277–285.

Morris, John, ed. and trans. *Nennius: British History and the Welsh Annals.* London: Phillimore, 1980.

Ni Sheaghdha, Nessa, ed. and trans. *Tóraidheacht Dhiarmada agus Ghráinne.* London: Irish Texts Society, 1967.

Pennar, Meirion, trans. *The Black Book of Carmarthen* [with diplomatic text by J. Gwenogvryn Evans]. N.p.: Llanerch, 1989. [Eleven selected poems.]

Philippe, Jef, ed. *War roudoù Merlin e Breizh.* Mouladurioù Hor Yezh: Lesneven, 1986.

Roberts, Brynley F., ed. *Brut y Brenhinedd: Llanstephan MS 1 Version.* Dublin: Dublin Institute for Advanced Studies, 1971.

———, ed. "Rhai o Cerddi Ymddiddan: Llyfr Du Caerfyrddin." In Bromwich and Jones, eds., *Astudiaethau ar yr Hengerdd (Studies in Old Welsh Poetry) cyflwynedig i Syr Idris Foster,* 1978, pp. 281–325. [*Gereint fil' Erbin, Pa Gur.*]

Rowland, Jenny, and Graham Thomas, eds. "Additional Version of the Trystan Englynion and Prose." *Journal of the National Library of Wales,* 22 (1982), 241–253.

Thomson, R.L., ed. *Owein or Chwedyl Iarlles y Ffynnawn*. Dublin: Dublin Institute for Advanced Studies, 1968.

———, trans. "The Welsh Fragment of Tristan (Trystan ac Esyllt)." In Joyce Hill, ed., *The Tristan Legend*. Leeds: University of Leeds Graduate Centre for Medieval Studies, 1977, pp. 1–5.

Wade-Evans, A.W., ed. *Vitae Sanctorum Britanniae et Genealogiae*. Cardiff: University of Wales Press, 1944.

Williams, Ifor, ed. *Pedeir Keinc y Mabinogi*. Cardiff: Gwasg Prifysgol Cymru, 1930.

———, ed. *Canu Aneirin*. Cardiff: Gwasg Prifysgol Cymru, 1938.

———, ed., and J.E. Caerwyn Williams, trans. *The Poems of Taliesin*. Dublin: Dublin Institute for Advanced Studies, 1968.

———, ed., and Rachel Bromwich, trans. *Armes Prydein: The Prophecy of Britain*. Dublin: Dublin Institute for Advanced Studies, 1972.

Winterbottom, Michael, ed. and trans. *Gildas: The Ruin of Britain and Other Works*. Chichester: Phillimore, 1978.

## Studies

Alcock, Leslie. *Arthur's Britain*. Harmondsworth: Penguin, 1971.

Anderson, Marjorie O. *Kings and Kingship in Early Scotland*. 1973; rev. ed., Edinburgh: Scottish Academic Press, 1980.

Ashe, Geoffrey. "'A Certain Very Ancient Book:' Traces of an Arthurian Source in Geoffrey of Monmouth's *Historia*." *Speculum*, 56 (1981), 301–323.

———. *The Discovery of King Arthur*. New York: Doubleday, 1985.

———. "*Goeznovii, Legenda Sancti* ('Goeznovius, Legend of St. Goeznovius')" In Norris J. Lacy et al., eds., *The New Arthurian Encyclopedia*. New York: Garland, 1991, pp. 204–205.

Bammesberger, Alfred, and Alfred Wollmann, eds. *Britain 400–600: Language and History*. Heidelberg: Winter, 1990.

Bollard, John K. "*Peredur*: The Four Early Manuscripts." *Bulletin of the Board of Celtic Studies*, 28 (1979), 365–372.

———. "Traddodiad a Dychan yn *Breuddwyd Rhonabwy*." *Llên Cymru*, 13, Nos. 3–4 (1980–81), 155–163.

Boutet, Dominique. "Carrefours ideologiques de la royauté arthurienne." *Cahiers de Civilisation Médievale*, 28 (1985), 3–17.

Bowen, Geraint, ed. *Y Traddodiad Rhyddiaith yn yr Oesau Canol*. Llandysul: Gomer, 1974.

Brett, Caroline. "Breton Latin Literature as Evidence for Literature in the Vernacular, AD 800–1300." *Cambridge Medieval Celtic Studies*, 18 (1989), 1–25.

———. "John Leland, Wales, and Early British History." *Welsh History Review*, 15 (1990), 169–182.

Bromwich, Rachel. "Enit, Enide." *Bulletin of the Board of Celtic Studies*, 17 (1956–58), 181–182.

———. "*The Welsh Triads*." In Loomis, ed., *Arthurian Literature in the Middle Ages: A Collaborative History*, 1959, pp. 44–51.

———. "Celtic Dynastic Themes and the Breton Lays." *Etudes Celtiques*, 9 (1960–61), 439–474.

———. "Y Cynfeirdd a'r Traddodiad Cymraeg." *Bulletin of the Board of Celtic Studies*, 22 (1966), 30–37.

————. "Dwy Chwedl a Thair Rhamant." In Bowen, ed., *Y Traddodiad Rhyddiaith yn yr Oesau Canol*, 1974, pp. 143–175.

————. "Concepts of Arthur." *Studia Celtica*, 10/11 (1975–76), 163–181.

————. "Cyfeiriadau Dafydd ap Gwilym at Chwedl a Rhamant." *Ysgrifau Beirniadol*, 12 (1982), 57–78.

————. "Celtic Elements in Arthurian Romance: A General Survey." In P.B. Grout et al., eds., *The Legend of Arthur in the Middle Ages: Studies Presented to A.H. Diverres*. Cambridge: Brewer, 1983, pp. 41–55.

————. "'The Mabinogion' and Lady Charlotte Guest." *Transactions of the Honourable Society of Cymmrodorion* (1986), 127–141.

————. "The *Tristan* of the Welsh." In Bromwich, Jarman, and Roberts, eds., *The Arthur of the Welsh: The Arthurian Legend in Medieval Welsh Literature*, 1991, pp. 209–228.

————, A.O.H. Jarman, and Brynley F. Roberts, eds. *The Arthur of the Welsh: The Arthurian Legend in Medieval Welsh Literature*. Cardiff: University of Wales Press, 1991.

————, and R. Brinley Jones, eds. *Astudiaethau ar yr Hengerdd (Studies in Old Welsh Poetry) cyflwynedig i Syr Idris Foster*. Cardiff: Gwasg Prifysgol Cymru, 1978.

————, and D. Simon Evans, comp. *A Glossary to Culhwch ac Olwen*. Lewiston, NY: Mellen, 1992.

Budgey, Andrea. "*Preiddeu Annwn* and the Welsh Tradition of Arthur." In Cyril J. Byrne, Margaret Harry, and Pádraig ó Siadhail, eds., *Celtic Languages and Celtic Peoples: Proceedings of the Second North American Celtic Congress, 1989*. Halifax: McGee, 1992, pp. 391–404.

Bullock-Davies, Constance. *Professional Interpreters and the Matter of Britain*. Cardiff: University of Wales Press, 1966.

———. "'*Exspectare Arturum*': Arthur and the Messianic Hope." *Bulletin of the Board of Celtic Studies*, 29 (1981), 432–440.

Carey, John. "Suibne Geilt and Tuán mac Cairill." *Eigse*, 20 (1984), 93–105.

Carney, James. *Studies in Irish Literature and History*. Dublin: Dublin Institute for Advanced Studies, 1955.

Carson, J. Angela. "The Structure and Meaning of *The Dream of Rhonabwy*." *Philological Quarterly*, 53 (1974), 289–303.

Chadwick, Hector Munro, and Nora Kershaw Chadwick. *The Growth of Literature*. 3 vols. Cambridge: Cambridge University Press, 1932–40.

Chadwick, Nora. *The British Heroic Age: The Welsh and the Men of the North*. Cardiff: University of Wales Press, 1976.

Charles-Edwards, Gifford. "The Scribes of the Red Book of Hergest." *Journal of the National Library of Wales*, 21 (1979–80), 246–256.

Charles-Edwards, Thomas M. "The Date of the Four Branches of the Mabinogi." *The Transactions of the Honourable Society of Cymmrodorion*, Session 1970, Part 2 (1971), 263–298.

———. "The Authenticity of the *Gododdin*: An Historian's View." In Bromwich and Jones, ed., *Astudiaethau ar yr Hengerdd (Studies in Old Welsh Poetry) cyflwynedig i Syr Idris Foster*, 1978, pp. 44–71.

———. "The Arthur of History." In Bromwich, Jarman, and Roberts, eds., *The Arthur of the Welsh: The Arthurian Legend in Medieval Welsh Literature*, 1991, pp. 15–32.

Crawford, T.D. "On the Linguistic Competence of Geoffrey of Monmouth." *Medium Ævum*, 51 (1982), 152–162.

Curley, Michael J. "Gerallt Cymro a Siôn o Gernyw fel Cyfieithwyr - Proffwydoliaethau Myrddin." *Llên Cymru*, 15 (1984–86), 23–33.

Davies, Wendy. *Wales in the Early Middle Ages*. Leicester: Leicester University Press, 1982.

De Bernardo Stempel, Patrizia. "A Welsh Cognate for Gaul: ανδοουννaβo?" *Bulletin of the Board of Celtic Studies*, 36 (1989), 102–105.

de Pontfarcy, Yolande. "Le lai des *Deus amanz* et la survie en Normandie d'un mythe celtique authentique." In Foulon et al., eds., *Actes du 14e Congrès International Arthurien*, 1985, pp. 500–510.

Diverres, A.H. "*Iarlles y Ffynnawn* and *Le Chevalier au Lion*: Adaptation or Common Source?" *Studia Celtica*, 16/17 (1981–82), 144–162.

Dumville, David N. "'Nennius' and the *Historia Brittonum*." *Studia Celtica*, 10/11 (1975–76), 78–95.

———. "The Chronology of *De Excidio Britanniae*, Book I." In Lapidge and Dumville, eds., *Gildas: New Approaches*, 1984, pp. 61–84.

———. "Gildas and Maelgwn: Problems of Dating." In Lapidge and Dumville, eds., *Gildas: New Approaches*, 1984, pp. 51–59.

———. "The Historical Value of the *Historia Brittonum*." *Arthurian Literature*, 6 (1986), 1–26.

———. "Sub-Roman Britain: History and Legend." *History*, n.s., 62 (1977) 173–192.

Edel, Doris. *Helden auf Freiersfüssen: "Tochmarc Emire" und "Mal y kavas Kulhwch Olwen": Studien zur frühen inselkeltischen Erzähltradition.* Amsterdam: North Holland, 1980.

————. "The Catalogues in *Culhwch ac Olwen* and Insular Celtic Learning." *Bulletin of the Board of Celtic Studies,* 30 (1982), 253–267.

————. "Rhai Sylwadau ar Arddull *Peredur* a Pherthynas y Chwedl Gymraeg â Perceval Chrétien." *Llên Cymru,* 14 (1982–84), 52–63.

————. "The Arthur of 'Culhwch and Olwen' as a Figure of Epic-Heroic Tradition." *Reading Medieval Studies,* 9 (1983), 3–15.

Evans, D. Ellis. "Rhagarweiniad i Astudiaeth o Fydryddiaeth Y *Gododdin.*" In Bromwich and Jones, eds., *Astudiaethau ar yr Hengerdd (Studies in Old Welsh Poetry) cyflwynedig i Syr Idris Foster,* 1978, pp. 89–122.

Evans, D. Simon. "Aneirin — Bardd Cristnogol?" *Ysgrifau Beirniadol,* 10 (1977), 25–44.

————. "Culhwch ac Olwen: Tystiolaeth yr Iaith." *Ysgrifau Beirniadol,* 13 (1985) 101–13.

Fleuriot, Léon. "Les fragments du texte brittonique de la 'Prophetia Merlini.'" *Etudes Celtiques,* 14 (1974), 43–56.

————. *Les origines de la Bretagne.* Paris: Payot, 1980.

————. "Sur trois textes bretons en latin du Xe et de début du XIe siècle: leur date, leur contenance et les sources de Geoffroy de Monmouth." *Archéologie en Bretagne,* 27 (1980), 16–27.

————. "Sur quatre textes bretons en latin, le *Liber uetustissimus* de Geoffroy de Monmouth et le séjour de Taliesin en Bretagne." *Etudes Celtiques,* 18 (1981), 197–213.

————. "Histoires et légendes" and "Prophéties, navigations et thèmes divers." In Léon Fleuriot and Auguste-Pierre Ségalen, eds., *Histoire littéraire et culturelle de la Bretagne: 1. Héritage celtique et captation française — Des origines à la fin des Etats.* Paris: Champion, 1987, pp. 97–129, 153–172.

Ford, Patrick K. "On the Significance of Some Arthurian Names in Welsh." *Bulletin of the Board of Celtic Studies*, 30 (1983), 268–273.

————. "Celtic Women: The Opposing Sex." *Viator*, 19 (1988), 417–433.

————. "A Highly Important Pig." In Matonis and Melia, eds., *Celtic Language, Celtic Culture: A Festschrift for Eric P. Hamp*, 1990, pp. 292–304.

Foster, Idris Llewelyn. "*Culhwch and Olwen* and *Rhonabwy's Dream.*" In Loomis, ed., *Arthurian Literature in the Middle Ages: A Collaborative History*, 1959, pp. 31–43.

————. "*Gereint, Owein,* and *Peredur.*" In Loomis, ed., *Arthurian Literature in the Middle Ages: A Collaborative History*, 1959, pp. 192–205.

————. "*Culhwch ac Olwen.*" In Bowen, ed., *Y Traddodiad Rhyddiaith yn yr Oesau Canol*, 1974, pp. 65–82.

Foulon, Charles, et al., eds., *Actes du 14e Congrès International Arthurien (Rennes, 16–21 août 1984).* Rennes: Presses Universitaires de Rennes 2, 1985.

*Geiriadur Prifysgol Cymru.* Cardiff: Gwasg Prifysgol Cymru, 1950–.

Gillies, William. "Arthur in Gaelic Tradition. Part I: Folktales and Ballads." *Cambridge Medieval Celtic Studies*, 2 (1981), 47–72.

————. "Arthur in Gaelic Tradition. Part II: Romances and Learned Lore." *Cambridge Medieval Celtic Studies*, 3 (1982), 41–75.

Goetinck, Glenys Witchard. "Peredur a Perceval." *Llên Cymru*, 8, Nos. 1–2 (1964–65), 58–64.

————. "Sofraniaeth yn y Tair Rhamant." *Llên Cymru*, 8, Nos. 3–4 (1965), 168–182.

————. *Peredur: A Study of Welsh Tradition in the Grail Legends*. Cardiff: University of Wales Press, 1975.

————. "*Peredur* . . . Upon Reflection." *Etudes Celtiques*, 25 (1988), 221–232.

Goodrich, Peter, ed. *The Romance of Merlin*. New York: Garland, 1990.

Grabowski, Kathryn, and David Dumville. *Chronicles and Annals of Mediaeval Ireland and Wales*. Woodbridge: Boydell and Brewer, 1984.

Greene, David. "Linguistic Considerations in the Dating of Early Welsh Verse." *Studia Celtica*, 6 (1971), 1–11.

Gruffydd, R. Geraint. "Where Was *Rhaeadr Derwennydd*?" In Matonis and Melia, eds., *Celtic Language, Celtic Culture: A Festschrift for Eric P. Hamp*, pp. 261–266.

Hamp, Eric P. "On Dating and Archaism in the *Pedeir Keinc*." *Transactions of the Honourable Society of Cymmrodorion*, Session 1972–73 (1974), 95–103.

————. "*Culhwch*, the Swine." *Zeitschrift für Celtische Philologie*, 41 (1986), 257–258.

Haycock, Marged. "*Llyfr Taliesin*: Astudiaethau ar Rai Agweddau." Diss. University of Wales, 1982.

———. "'Preiddeu Annwn' and the Figure of Taliesin." *Studia Celtica*, 18/19 (1983–84), 52–78.

———. "'Some Talk of Alexander and Some of Hercules': Three Early Welsh Poems from the Book of Taliesin." *Cambridge Medieval Celtic Studies*, 13 (1987), 7–38.

———. "Llyfr Taliesin." *The National Library of Wales Journal*, 25 (1988), 357–386.

———. "Metrical Models for the Poems in the Book of Taliesin." In Brynley F. Roberts, ed., *Early Welsh Poetry: Studies in the Book of Aneirin*. Aberystwyth: National Library of Wales, 1988, pp. 155–178.

———. *Blodeugerdd o Gerddi Crefyddol Cynnar*. Swansea: Barddas, forthcoming.

Hughes, Kathleen. *Celtic Britain the Early Middle Ages: Studies in Scottish and Welsh Sources*. Woodbridge: Boydell and Brewer, 1980.

Huws, Daniel. "Llyfr Gwyn Rhydderch." *Cambridge Medieval Celtic Studies*, 21 (1991) 1–37.

Isaac, Graham R. "*Canu Aneirin* Awdl LI." *Journal of Celtic Linguistics*, 2 (1993), 65–91.

Jackson, Kenneth Hurlstone. *Language and History in Early Britain*. Edinburgh: Edinburgh University Press, 1953.

———. "Arthur in Early Welsh Verse." In Loomis, ed., *Arthurian Literature in the Middle Ages: A Collaborative History*, 1959, pp. 12–19.

———. "The Arthur of History." In Loomis, ed., *Arthurian Literature in the Middle Ages: A Collaborative History*, 1959, pp. 1–11.

————. "On the Northern British Section in Nennius." In *Celt and Saxon: Studies in the Early British Border*. Cambridge: Cambridge University Press, 1963, pp. 20–62.

————. "Some Questions in Dispute about Early Welsh Literature and Language." *Studia Celtica*, 8/9 (1973–74), 1–32.

————. "Rhai Sylwadau ar 'Kulhwch ac Olwen.'" *Ysgrifau Beirniadol*, 12 (1982), 12–23.

Jarman, A.O.H. "The Welsh Myrddin Poems." In Loomis, ed., *Arthurian Literature in the Middle Ages: A Collaborative History*, 1959, pp. 20–30.

————. "A Oedd Myrddin yn Fardd Hanesyddol?" *Studia Celtica*, 10/11 (1975–76), 182–197.

————. "Early Stages in the Development of the Myrddin Legend." In Bromwich and Jones, eds., *Astudiaethau ar yr Hengerdd (Studies in Old Welsh Poetry) cyflwynedig i Syr Idris Foster*, 1978, pp. 326–349.

————. "The Arthurian Allusions in the Black Book of Carmarthen." In P.B. Grout et al., eds., *The Legend of Arthur in the Middle Ages*. Cambridge: Brewer, 1983, pp. 99–112, 240–242.

————. "Y Darlun o Arthur." *Llên Cymru*, 15 (1984–86), 3–17.

————. "The Merlin Legend and the Welsh Tradition of Prophecy." In Bromwich, Jarman, and Roberts, eds., *The Arthur of the Welsh: The Arthurian Legend in Medieval Welsh Literature*, 1991, pp. 117–145.

Jenkins, Dafydd. "*gwalch: Welsh*." *Cambridge Medieval Celtic Studies*, 19 (1990), 55–68.

Jones, Bedwyr Lewis. *Arthur y Cymry — The Welsh Arthur*. Cardiff: University of Wales Press, 1975.

Jones, Dafydd Glyn. "Breuddwyd Rhonabwy." In Bowen, ed., *Y Traddodiad Rhyddiaith yn yr Oesau Canol*, 1974, pp. 176–195.

Jones, Robert Maynard. "Narrative Structure in Medieval Welsh Prose Tales." In D. Ellis Evans, John G. Griffith, and E.M. Jope, eds., *Proceedings of the Seventh International Congress of Celtic Studies*. 1983; Oxford: Evans, 1986, pp. 171–198.

Jones, Thomas. "Datblygiadau Cynnar Chwedl Arthur." *Bulletin of the Board of Celtic Studies*, 17 (1958), 237–252.

———. "The Early Evolution of the Legend of Arthur." *Nottingham Mediaeval Studies*, 7 (1963), 3–21. [English version of previous item.]

———. "Chwedl Huail ap Caw ac Arthur." In Thomas Jones, *Astudiaethau Amrywiol a gyflwynir i Sir Thomas Parry-Williams*. Cardiff: Gwasg Prifysgol Cymru, 1968, pp. 48–66.

Kerlouégan, François. "Les destinées de la culture latine dans l'île de Bretagne au VIème siècle: recherches sur le De excidio Britanniae de Gildas." Diss. Paris, 1977.

Koch, John T. "The Loss of Final Syllables and Loss of Declension in Brittonic." *Bulletin of the Board of Celtic Studies*, 30 (1983), 201–233.

———. "*gwyðanhor, gwyðyanhawr, clywanhor.*" *Bulletin of the Board of Celtic Studies*, 31 (1984), 87–92.

———. "When Was Welsh Literature First Written Down?" *Studia - Celtica*, 20/21 (1985–86), 43–66.

———. "A Welsh Window on the Iron Age: Manawydan, Mandubracios." *Cambridge Medieval Celtic Studies*, 14 (1987), 17–52.

———. "Brân, Brennos: An Instance of Early Gallo-Brittonic History and Mythology." *Cambridge Medieval Celtic Studies*, 20 (1990), 1–20.

———. "Further to *tongu do dia toinges mo thuath*, &c." *Etudes Celtiques*, 29 (1992), 249–261.

———. "Thoughts on the *Ur-Godoðin*: Rethinking Aneirin and Mynyðawc Mwynvawr." *Language Sciences*, 25 (1993), 81–89.

———. *A Grammar of Old Welsh, Historical and Comparative*. Dublin Institute for Advanced Studies, forthcoming.

———. "Obscurity and the Figure of Taliesin." *Medievalia*, 20, forthcoming.

Lambert, Pierre-Yves. "Gaulois ANΔOOYNNABO." *Etudes Celtiques*, 27 (1990), 197–199.

Lapidge, Michael, and David Dumville, eds. *Gildas: New Approaches*. Woodbridge: Boydell and Brewer, 1984.

———, and Richard Sharpe. *A Bibliography of Celtic-Latin Literature 400–1200*. Dublin: Royal Irish Academy, 1985.

Laurent, Donatien. "La gwerz de Skolan et la légende de Merlin." *Ethnologie Française*, n.s., 1 (1971), 19–54.

Le Duc, Gwenael. "L'*Historia Britannica* avant Geoffroy de Monmouth." *Annales de Bretagne*, 79 (1972), 819–835.

Lloyd-Morgan, Ceridwen. "The Peniarth 15 Fragment of *Y Seint Greal*: Arthurian Tradition in the Late Fifteenth Century." *Bulletin of the Board of Celtic Studies*, 28 (1978), 73–82.

———. "Narrative Structure in *Peredur*." *Zeitschrift für Celtische Philologie*, 38 (1981), 187–231.

————. "*Darogan yr Olew Bendigaid*: Chwedl o'r Bymthegfed Ganrif." *Llên Cymru*, 14 (1981–82), 64–85.

————. "Continuity and Change in the Transmission of Arthurian Material: Later Medieval Wales and the Continent." In Foulon et al., eds., *Actes du 14e Congrès International Arthurien*, 1985, pp. 397–405.

————. "Prophecy and Welsh Nationhood in the Fifteenth Century." *Transactions of the Honourable Society of Cymmrodorion* (1985), 9–26.

————. "Rhai Agweddau ar Gyfieithu yng Nghymru yn yr Oesoedd Canol." *Ysgrifau Beirniadol*, 13 (1985), 134–145.

————. "Perceval in Wales: Late Medieval Welsh Grail Traditions." In Alison Adams, Armel H. Diverres, Karen Stern, and Kenneth Varty, eds., *The Changing Face of Arthurian Romance: Essays on Arthurian Prose Romances in Memory of Cedric E. Pickford*. Cambridge: Brewer, 1986, pp. 78–91.

————. "*Breuddwyd Rhonabwy* and Later Arthurian Literature." In Bromwich, Jarman, and Roberts, eds., *The Arthur of the Welsh: The Arthurian Legend in Medieval Welsh Literature*, 1991, pp. 183–208.

————. "French Texts, Welsh Translators." In Roger Ellis, ed., *The Medieval Translator II*. London: Centre for Medieval Studies, Queen Mary and Westfield College, 1991, pp. 45–63.

————. "From Ynys Wydrin to Glasynbri: Glastonbury in Welsh Vernacular Tradition." In Lesley Abrams and James P. Carley, eds., *The Archaeology and History of Glastonbury Abbey: Essays in Honour of the Ninetieth Birthday of C.A. Ralegh Radford*. Woodbridge: Boydell and Brewer, 1991, pp. 301–315.

————. "Trystan ac Esyllt: Y Ddau Draddodiad." *Ysgrifau Beirniadol*, 18 (1992), 29–42.

Loomis, Roger Sherman. *Wales and the Arthurian Legend*. Cardiff: University of Wales Press, 1956.

———. "The Legend of Arthur's Survival." In Loomis, ed., *Arthurian Literature in the Middle Ages: A Collaborative History*, 1959, pp. 64–71.

———. "The Oral Diffusion of the Arthurian Legend." In Loomis, ed., *Arthurian Literature in the Middle Ages: A Collaborative History*, 1959, pp. 52–63.

———. "The Origin of the Grail Legends." In Loomis, ed., *Arthurian Literature in the Middle Ages: A Collaborative History*, 1959, pp. 274–294.

———. *The Grail: From Celtic Myth to Christian Symbol*. Cardiff: University of Wales Press; New York: Columbia University Press, 1963.

———, ed. *Arthurian Literature in the Middle Ages: A Collaborative History*. Oxford: Clarendon, 1959.

Lovecy, Ian C. "The Celtic Sovereignty Theme and the Structure of Peredur." *Studia Celtica*, 12–13 (1977–78), 133–146.

———. "*Historia Peredur ab Efrawg*." In Bromwich, Jarman, and Roberts, eds., *The Arthur of the Welsh: The Arthurian Legend in Medieval Welsh Literature*, 1991, pp. 171–182.

Lozac'hmeur, Jean-Claude. "A propos des sources du Mabinogi d'Owein et du roman d'Yvain." *Etudes Celtiques*, 15 (1978), 573–575.

———. "Bendigeit Vran et Corbenic." *Etudes Celtiques*, 16 (1979), 283–285.

———. "Guinglain et Perceval." *Etudes Celtiques*, 16 (1979), 279–281.

————. "A propos de l'origine du nom de Mabonograin." *Etudes Celtiques*, 17 (1980), 257–262.

————. "Origines celtiques de aventures de Gauvain au Pays de Galvoie dans le Conte du Graal de Chrétien de Troyes." In Foulon et al., eds., *Actes du 14e Congrès International Arthurien*, 1985, pp. 406–422.

————. "Les Romans bretons." In Léon Fleuriot and Auguste-Pierre Ségalen, eds., *Histoire littéraire et culturelle de la Bretagne: 1. Héritage celtique et captation française — Des origines à la fin des états*. Paris: Champion, 1987, pp. 139–152.

————. "Pour une nouvelle herméneutique des mythes: essai d'interprétation de quelques thèmes celtiques." In Gwennolé Le Menn, ed., with the collaboration of Jean-Yves Le Moing, *Bretagne et pays celtiques — langues, histoires, civilisation: mélanges offerts à la mémoire de Léon Fleuriot*. Rennes: Presses Universitaires Rennes, 1992, pp. 389–401.

Mac Cana, Proinsias. Rev. of Kenneth H. Jackson, *The Gododdin: The Oldest Scottish Poem. Celtica*, 9 (1971), 316–329.

————. "On Celtic Word-Order and the Welsh 'Abnormal' Sentence." *Ériu*, 24 (1973) 90–120.

————. "hyddiaith Gymraeg." *Ysgrifau Beirniadol*, 10 (1977), 79–90.

————. *The Mabinogi*. Writers of Wales. 1977; 2nd ed., Cardiff: University of Wales Press, 1992.

————. "Notes on the 'Abnormal' Sentence." *Studia Celtica*, 14/15 (1979), 174–87.

————. "Further Notes on Constituent Order in Welsh." In James Fife and Erich Poppe, eds., *Studies in Brittonic Word Order*. Amsterdam: Benjamins, 1991, pp. 45–80.

Markale, Jean. *Le Roi Arthur et la société celtique*. Paris: Payot, 1976.

Matonis, A.T.E., and Daniel F. Melia, eds. *Celtic Language, Celtic Culture: A Festschrift for Eric P. Hamp*. Van Nuys: Ford and Bailie, 1990.

Milin, Gael. *Le Roi Marc aux Oreilles de Cheval*. Geneva: Droz, 1991.

Miller, Molly. "Geoffrey's Early Royal Synchronisms." *Bulletin of the Board of Celtic Studies*, 28 (1979), 373–389.

Morris, John. *The Age of Arthur: A History of the British Isles from 350 to 650*. New York: Scribner, 1973.

Morris, Rosemary. *The Character of King Arthur in Medieval Literature*. Cambridge: Brewer; Totowa, NJ: Rowman and Littlefield, 1982.

Newstead, Helaine. "The Origin and Growth of the Tristan Legend." In Loomis, ed., *Arthurian Literature in the Middle Ages: A Collaborative History*, 1959, pp. 122–133.

Noble, Peter. "The Heroic Tradition of Kei." *Reading Medieval Studies*, 14 (1988), 125–137.

O Hehir, Brendan. "What Is the *Gododdin*?" In Brynley F. Roberts, ed., *Early Welsh Poetry: Studies in the Book of Aneirin*. Aberystwyth: National Library of Wales, 1988, pp. 57–95.

O'Rahilly, Thomas F. *Early Irish History and Mythology*. Dublin: Dublin Institute for Advanced Studies, 1946.

Ovazza, Maud. "D'Apollon-Maponos à Mabonograin: les avatars d'un dieu celtique." In Foulon et al., eds., *Actes du 14e Congrès International Arthurien*, 1985, pp. 465–472.

Padel, Oliver. "The Cornish Background of the Tristan Stories." *Cambridge Medieval Celtic Studies*, 1 (1981), 53–82.

―――. "Les éléments celtiques." In Ulrich Müller, Franz Hundsnurscher, and Cornelius Sommer, eds., *La legende de Tristan au Moyen Age*. N.p.: Kümmerle, 1982, pp. 81–87.

―――. "Some Southwestern Sites with Arthurian Associations." In Bromwich, Jarman, and Roberts, eds., *The Arthur of the Welsh: The Arthurian Legend in Medieval Welsh Literature*, 1991, pp. 229–248.

Pearce, Susan M. "The Cornish Elements in Arthurian Tradition." *Folklore*, 85 (1974), 145–163.

Pennar, Meirion. "Tynghedfen Peredur." *Ysgrifau Beirniadol*, 11 (1979), 52–62.

Piette, J.R.F. "Yr Agwedd Lydewig ar y Chwedlau Arthuraidd." *Llên Cymru*, 8 (1965), 183–190.

Piriou, Yann-Ber [Jean-Pierre]. "Contributions à une histoire de la littérature bretonne perdue." Diss. Université de Rennes 2, 1982.

Piriou, Jean-Pierre. "Un texte arthurien en moyen-breton: le dialogue entre Arthur roi des Bretons et Guynglaff." In Foulon et al., eds., *Actes du 14e Congrès International Arthurien*, 1985, pp. 473–499.

Radner, Joan. "Interpreting Irony in Medieval Celtic Narrative: The Case of Culhwch and Olwen." *Cambridge Medieval Celtic Studies*, 16 (1988), 41–59.

Reiss, Edmund. "The Welsh Versions of Geoffrey's *Historia*." *Welsh History Review*, 4 (1968), 97–127.

Roberts, Brynley F. "Esboniad Cymraeg ar Broffwydoliaeth Myrddin." *Bulletin of the Board of Celtic Studies*, 21 (1966), 277–300.

————. "The Treatment of Personal Names in the Early Welsh Versions of *Historia Regum Britanniae.*" *Bulletin of the Board of Celtic Studies*, 25 (1973), 274–290.

————. "Testunau Hanes Cymraeg Canol." In Bowen, ed., *Y Traddodiad Rhyddiaith yn yr Oesau Canol*, 1974, pp. 274–302.

————. "Geoffrey of Monmouth and Welsh Historical Tradition." *Nottingham Mediaeval Studies*, 20 (1976), 29–40. [Reissued in Roberts, *Studies on Middle Welsh Literature*, 1992, pp. 25–40.]

————. "Tales and Romances." In A.O.H. Jarman and Gwilym Rees Hughes, eds., *A Guide to Welsh Literature I*. Swansea: Christopher Davies, 1976, pp. 203–244. [Reissued in Roberts, *Studies on Middle Welsh Literature*, 1992, pp. 41–80.]

————. "*Ystoria.*" *Bulletin of the Board of Celtic Studies*, 26 (1976), 13–20.

————. "Copïau Cymraeg o *Prophetiae Merlini.*" *Cylchgrawn Llyfrgell Genedlaethol Cymru*, 20 (1977), 14–39.

————. "Fersiwn Dingestow o *Brut y Brenhinedd.*" *Bulletin of the Board of Celtic Studies*, 27 (1977), 331–361.

————. "Owein *neu* Iarlles y Ffynnon." *Ysgrifau Beirniadol*, 10 (1977), 124–143.

————. "The Red Book of Hergest Version of *Brut y Brenhinedd.*" *Studia Celtica*, 12/13 (1977–78), 147–186.

————. *Brut Tysilio*. Swansea: Coleg Prifysgol Abertawe, 1980.

————. "Nodiadau: I. Pen Penwaedd a Phentir Gafran, II. Yr India Fawr a'r India Fechan, III. Gwyn ap Nudd." *Llên Cymru*, 13 (1980–81), 278–289.

————. "The Welsh Romance of the *Lady of the Fountain (Owain)*." In P.B Grout et al., eds., *The Legend of Arthur in the Middle Ages*. Cambridge: Brewer, 1983, pp. 170–182.

————. "From Traditional Tale to Literary Story: Middle Welsh Prose Narratives." In Leigh A. Arrathoon, ed., *The Craft of Fiction: Essays in Medieval Poetics*. Rochester, MI: Solaris, 1984, pp. 211–230. [Reissued in Roberts, *Studies on Middle Welsh Literature*, 1992, pp. 81–94.]

————. "Dosbarthu'r Chwedlau Cymraeg Canol." *Ysgrifau Beirniadol*, 15 (1988), 18–46.

————. "Oral Tradition and Welsh Literature: A Description and Survey." *Oral Tradition*, 3 (1988), 61–87. [Reissued in Roberts, *Studies on Middle Welsh Literature*, 1992, pp. 1–24.]

————. "*Culhwch ac Olwen*, The Triads, Saints' Lives." In Bromwich, Jarman, and Roberts, eds., *The Arthur of the Welsh: The Arthurian Legend in Medieval Welsh Literature*, 1991, pp. 73–95.

————. "Geoffrey of Monmouth, *Historia Regum Britanniae*, and *Brut y Brenhinedd*." In Bromwich, Jarman, and Roberts, eds., *The Arthur of the Welsh: The Arthurian Legend in Medieval Welsh Literature*, 1991, pp. 97–116.

————. "Sieffre o Fynwy a Myth Hanes Cenedl y Cymry." *Cof Cenedl*, 6 (1991), 3–32.

————. *Studies on Middle Welsh Literature*. Welsh Studies, 5. Lewiston, NY: Mellen, 1992.

————. "Sylwadau ar 'Ramant' *Gereint ac Enid*." *Ysgrifau Beirniadol*, 18 (1992), 29–42.

Rowland, Jenny. "The Prose Setting of the Early Welsh *Englynion Chwedlonol*." *Ériu*, 36 (1985), 29–43.

————. *Early Welsh Saga Poetry.* Woodbridge: Brewer, 1990.

Sims-Williams, Patrick. "The Evidence for Vernacular Irish Literary Influence on Early Mediaeval Welsh Literature." In Dorothy Whitelock et al., eds., *Ireland in Early Mediaeval Europe: Studies in Memory of Kathleen Hughes.* Cambridge: Cambridge University Press, 1982, pp. 235–257.

————. "The Significance of the Irish Personal Names in *Culhwch ac Olwen.*" *Bulletin of the Board of Celtic Studies,* 29 (1982), 600–620.

————. "The Irish Geography of *Culhwch and Olwen.*" In Donnchadh Ç Corráin, Liam Breatnach, and Kim McCone, eds., *Sages, Saints and Storytellers: Celtic Studies in Honour of Professor James Carney.* Maynooth: An Sagart, 1989, pp. 412–426.

————. "Dating the Transition to Neo-Brittonic: Phonology and History, 400–600." In Alfred Bammesberger and Alfred Wollmann, eds., *Britain 400–600: Language in History.* Heidelberg: Winter, 1990, pp. 217–261.

————. "Some Celtic Otherworld Terms." In Matonis and Melia, eds., *Celtic Language, Celtic Culture: A Festschrift for Eric P. Hamp,* 1990, pp. 57–81.

————. "The Early Welsh Arthurian Poems." In Bromwich, Jarman, and Roberts, eds., *The Arthur of the Welsh: The Arthurian Legend in Medieval Welsh Literature,* 1991, pp. 33–71.

Slotkin, Edgar. "The Fabula, Story, and Text of *Breuddwyd Rhonabwy.*" *Cambridge Medieval Celtic Studies,* 18 (1989), 89–111.

Sterckx, Claude. "Les Têtes coupées et le graal." *Studia Celtica,* 20/21 (1985–86), 1–42.

————."Débris mythologiques en Basse-Bretagne." In Gwennolé Le Menn, ed., with the collaboration of Jean-Yves Le Moing, *Bretagne et pays celtiques — langues, histoires, civilisation: mélanges offerts à la mémoire de Léon Fleuriot*. Rennes: Presses Universitaires Rennes, 1992, pp. 403–413.

Thomas, Gwyn. *Y Traddodiad Barddol*. Cardiff: Gwasg Prifysgol Cymru, 1976.

————. "Bras Ddosbarthiad ar ein Rhyddiaith Gynnar." *Ysgrifau Beirniadol*, 11 (1979), 28–51.

Tolstoy, Nikolai. "'Merlinus Redivivus.'" *Studia Celtica*, 18/19 (1983–84), 11–28.

————. *The Quest for Merlin*. Boston: Little, Brown, 1985.

Trindade, W. Ann. "Irish Gormlaith as a Sovereignty Figure." *Etudes Celtiques*, 23 (1986), 143–156.

Tymoczko, Maria. "The Lost Welsh Arthurian Cycle." In Glanmor Williams and Robert Owen Jones, eds., *The Celts and the Renaissance, Tradition and Innovation: Proceedings of the Eighth International Congress of Celtic Studies . . . Swansea . . . 1987*. Cardiff: University of Wales Press, 1990, p. 173. [Abstract.]

Varin, Amy. "Mordred, King Arthur's Son." *Folklore*, 90 (1979), 167–177.

Ward, Charlotte. "Arthur in the Welsh Bruts." In Cyril J. Byrne, Margaret Harry, and Pádraig ó Siadhail, eds., *Celtic Languages and Celtic Peoples: Proceedings of the Second North American Celtic Congress, 1989*. Halifax: McGee, 1992, pp. 391–404.

Watkins, T. Arwyn. "Trefn yn y Frawddeg Gymraeg." *Studia Celtica*, 12/13 (1977), 367–395.

———. "Constituent Order in the Old Welsh Verbal Sentence." *Bulletin of the Board of Celtic Studies*, 34 (1987), 51–60.

———. *Constituent Order in the Positive Declarative Sentence in the Medieval Welsh Tale "Kulhwch ac Olwen."* Innsbruck: Institut für Sprachwissenschaft, 1988.

———. "Constituent Order in the Negative Declarative Sentence in the White Book Version of *Kulhwch ac Olwen.*" In Matonis and Melia, eds., *Celtic Language, Celtic Culture: A Festschrift for Eric P. Hamp*, 1990, pp. 247–252.

———, and Proinsias Mac Cana. "Cystrawennau'r Cyplad mewn Hen Gymraeg." *Bulletin of the Board of Celtic Studies*, 18 (1958), 1–25.

Watson, Jeanie. "Enid the Disobedient: The *Mabinogion*'s *Gereint and Enid.*" In Carole Levine and Jeanie Watson, eds., *Ambiguous Realities: Women in the Middle Ages and Renaissance*. Detroit: Wayne State University Press, 1987, pp. 114–132.

Williams, J.E. Caerwyn. "Brittany and the Arthurian Legend." In Bromwich, Jarman, and Roberts, eds., *The Arthur of the Welsh: The Arthurian Legend in Medieval Welsh Literature*, 1991, pp. 249–272.

Williams, Patricia. "Y Gwrthdaro rhwng Serch a Milwriaeth yn y Tair Rhamant." *Ysgrifau Beirniadol*, 12 (1982), 40–56.

Wood, Ian. "The End of Roman Britain: Continental Evidence and Parallels." In Lapidge and Dumville, eds., *Gildas: New Approaches*, 1984, pp. 1–25.

Wood, Juliette. "Maelgwn Gwynedd: A Forgotten Welsh Hero." *Trivium*, 19 (1984), 102–117.

Wright, Neil. "Geoffrey of Monmouth and Gildas." *Arthurian Literature*, 2 (1982), 1–40.

# ITALY

## Christopher Kleinhenz

I n Novella 114 of his *Trecentonovelle*, Franco Sacchetti recounts
how one day in Florence Dante passed through the gate of San
Pietro and heard a blacksmith singing the verses of the *Divine Comedy*,
in the same manner as one sings a *cantare* ("come si canta uno
cantare").[1] The blacksmith "was making a muddle of the verses,
cutting some short and adding to others," so much so that Dante was
greatly offended ("tramestava i versi suoi, smozzicando e appiccando,
che parea a Dante ricever di quello grandissima ingiuria"). At this
point, the great Florentine poet entered the shop and began taking the
blacksmith's various tools—hammer, pincers, scales, etc.—and
throwing them around and out into the street. At this display of *follia*,
the blacksmith asked: "What the devil are you doing? Have you gone
crazy?" ("Che diavol fate voi? Sète voi impazzato?"); to which Dante
replied: "And you? what do you think you're doing?" ("O tu che
fai?"). Noting that he was merely performing his trade, his *arte*, the
blacksmith observed that Dante was ruining his tools by throwing them
into the street ("Fo l'arte mia . . . e voi guastate le mie masserizie,
gittandole per la via"). In the manner and tradition of the *tenzone*, the
poetic exchange that often involves a "risposta per le rime" of the
"botta e risposta" variety, Dante replies: "If you do not want me to
ruin your things, then don't ruin mine" ("Se tu non vuogli che io guasti
le cose tue, non guastare le mie"). And, to the blacksmith's
bewilderment as to what these "things" are that he is ruining, Dante
explains: "You are singing my book, and you are not saying it as I
wrote it; I do not have any other trade, and you are spoiling the one I

---

[1] The text of the novella is found in Franco Sacchetti, *Il Trecentonovelle*, ed. Antonio
Lanza (Florence: Sansoni, 1984), pp. 231–233.

have" ("Tu canti il libro [mio] e non lo di' come io lo feci; io non ho altr'arte, e tu me la guasti"). Sacchetti concludes this episode as follows: "The smith, completely upset and not knowing how to respond, gathered up his things and returned to his work; and whenever he decided to sing in the future, he sang of Tristan and of Lancelot, and left Dante alone . . ." ("Il fabbro, gonfiato, non sapendo rispondere, raccoglie le cose e torna al suo lavorío; e se volle cantare, cantò di Tristano e di Lancelotto e lasciò stare il Dante . . .").

What emerges from this anecdotal tale of everyday life, local personalities, and popular entertainment in early fourteenth-century Florence is the distinction between literature for popular consumption and literature for the intelligentsia. The tale would seem to say that it is acceptable to butcher those versions of the Tristan and Lancelot legends that are presented in the *cantari*, but that one should not mess with, harm, or do injustice to the verses of the *Divine Comedy*, a work that has decidedly more lofty didactic and allegorical intentions. Although he sang these verses badly, the smithy was nevertheless acquainted with the verses of the *Divine Comedy*, and this has been taken as evidence of the early diffusion and knowledge of Dante's poem among people at various levels of society. We assume—and hope at least for his audience's sake—that the smithy was more adept in his renditions of the "Matter of Britain"!

The contrast between what we could call "high" and "low" literature is interesting for what it tells us about the place of chivalric literature in thirteenth- and fourteenth-century Italy and for what it suggests about its diffusion. The large body of extant literature that concerns the fabulous tales and high adventures of King Arthur and the knights of the Round Table, as well as of other figures who come to be associated with that court, attests to their popularity in this period. Their prime purpose lay in their value as "entertainment": the adventures of knights-errant and their ladies, and the marvelous events, magnificent tournaments, and fierce individual combats in which they took part. However, the evocation of this aristocratic world and its values also served in some instances as a sort of mirror for actions and societal behavior. It is precisely this "exemplary" role of literature, functioning both as a model and as a go-between, that induced Dante's famous lovers Paolo and Francesca to fall irrevocably into the sin of lust. Canto 5 of Dante's *Inferno* has always been a favorite of critics, and much recent work has focused on general questions concerning the act of reading and the power and purpose of literature, as well as on more specific points relating to the nature of Paolo and Francesca's sin and to the implications of their misreading or misinterpretation of the passage in the Old French *Prose Lancelot*.[2]

In his treatise on language and poetry, *De Vulgari Eloquentia*, Dante refers to the "most attractive wandering adventures of King Arthur" ("Arturi regis ambages pulcerrime," I, X, 2), and this comment suggests that he was at one point in his life an avid and appreciative reader of Arthurian literature.[3] However, while the term *ambages* was employed in a positive way in this treatise, it has undergone a complete transformation in its unique appearance in the *Divine Comedy*.[4] In *Paradiso*, Dante contrasts Cacciaguida's "plain words" and "clarity of thought" with the enigmatic and ambiguous phrases of pagan prophets—*ambage*—thus placing in opposition the errant beliefs of pagans and the true word of God:[5]

---

[2] On Dante's relationship with Arthurian literature in Italy, see my essay "Dante as Reader and Critic of Courtly Literature" and the important studies (listed in the bibliography) by Carozza, Crescini, Dronke, Farinelli, Hatcher, Noakes, Picone, Poggioli, Popolizio, Quaglio, Rajna, Scott, Toynbee, and Zingarelli.

[3] For Dante, Arthurian literature was essentially synonymous with courtly literature, and his knowledge of this material was limited almost exclusively to the prose romances, and specifically to the *Prose Lancelot* and the *Mort Artu*.

[4] For the debated meaning of this term, see, among others: Aldo Duro, "Ambage," in *Enciclopedia dantesca*, I, 199–200; Aristide Marigo, in his commentary to the second edition of *De Vulgari Eloquentia*, Opere di Dante, 6 (Florence: Le Monnier, 1948), pp. 77–78; Pier Vincenzo Mengaldo, in his commentary to *De Vulgari Eloquentia*, in Dante Alighieri, *Opere minori* (Milan: Ricciardi, 1979), II, 84; and Pio Rajna, "*Arturi regis ambages pulcerrime*," *Studi Danteschi*, 1 (1920), 91–99.

[5] The passage from the *Comedy* follows the text established by Giorgio Petrocchi, *La commedia secondo l'antica vulgata*, Società Dantesca Italiana, Edizione Nazionale (Milan: Mondadori, 1966–67). The translation is that of Allen Mandelbaum: *Purgatorio* (New York: Bantam, 1984).

> Né per *ambage*, in che la gente folle
> già s'inviscava pria che fosse anciso
> l'Agnel di Dio che le peccata tolle,
>     ma per chiare parole e con preciso
> latin rispuose quello amor paterno . . . .

("Not with the *maze of words* that used to snare the fools upon this earth before the Lamb of God who takes away our sins was slain, but with words plain and unambiguous, that loving father replied..." [*Paradiso* 17.31-35; emphasis mine])

By employing the pregnant term *ambage* in the *Comedy*, Dante is able not only to correct his earlier view but also to place the entire courtly tradition into a more universal perspective.[6]

To be sure, much of the critical treatment of Arthurian material in Italy has focused on Dante, and it is perhaps because of this that the other manifestations of this tradition have been undervalued or even ignored. While the flood of criticism on Dante shows no signs of abating, we can take heart in the fact that more recently scholars have turned their attention to other writers and works in this period, and first among these Boccaccio. In several recent studies, Daniela Delcorno Branca has treated both the general reception of Arthurian material in the works of Boccaccio (in particular, his chapter on Arthur in *De Casibus Virorum Illustrium*) and his reworking of Arthurian themes and motifs in the *Decameron, Amorosa Visione, Corbaccio*, and *Elegia di Madonna Fiammetta*.[7]

---

[6] These verses set the stage for Cacciaguida's foretelling of Dante's exile from Florence for political reasons, a prophecy expressed in simple, direct, and unequivocal language. This use of *ambage* in the *Comedy*, coupled with the allusion to the Lady of Malehaut and the first fault of Guinevere in the previous canto (*Paradiso* 16.13-15), suggests that Dante was consciously thinking of and referring to the Arthurian tradition in this episode.

[7] The three essays are "Tradizione arturiana in Boccaccio," *Lettere Italiane*, 37 (1985), 425-452; "Tristano, Lovato e Boccaccio," *Lettere Italiane*, 42 (1990), 51-65; and "*De Arturo Britonum rege*: Boccaccio fra storiografia e romanzo," *Studi sul Boccaccio*, 19 (1990), 151-190. These three essays have been reprinted with different titles as chapters in *Boccaccio e le storie di re Artù*, to which Delcorno Branca has added an appendix ("Geografia britannica nel *De montibus*"), a bibliography, and indexes.

These brief introductory notes on the presence of Arthurian material in the works of two of the "three crowns of Florence" suggest that scholars should perhaps look to the works of the third "crown"—Francesco Petrarca—as a potentially fertile yet virtually unmined source for future investigations. This essay will consider recent scholarship on Italian Arthuriana by dividing it into several sections, proceeding from more general treatments of the subject to genre-based discussions and to more specialized topics concerning individual figures and the artistic tradition. It will conclude with some remarks on possible directions that scholarship may profitably take in the future. The bibliography that concludes this essay contains full references for those authors and works cited in the body of the text and notes, as well as other important contributions not specifically mentioned herein.

*

The classic study of the subject remains Edmund G. Gardner's *The Arthurian Legend in Italian Literature* (1930), which provides an excellent overview of the presence of the Matter of Britain in Italy. Although unsurpassed in its breadth of coverage, Gardner's work has been supplemented by Antonio Viscardi in his essay in the Loomis collection and by several encyclopedia entries on the subject (e.g., Delcorno Branca). In addition, Donald Hoffman has written an admirable and well-documented survey of "The Arthurian Tradition in Italy" from the Middle Ages to the present. Aldo Scaglione's 1992 wide-ranging, monumental study, *Knights at Court: Courtliness, Chivalry, and Courtesy from Ottonian Germany to the Italian Renaissance*, contains some references to Italian Arthurian materials, but these are not central to its focus. Most recently, Daniela Delcorno Branca has completed a magisterial review of the scholarly production (mainly Italian) on Arthurian material in Italy for a seven-year period, 1985–1992, and Fabrizio Cigni has compiled an extensive *Bibliografia degli studi italiani di materia arturiana*, which contains more than 750 entries and covers a half-century of criticism on Arthurian literature written by Italian scholars, but not focused exclusively on the Italian tradition.

Traditionally most of the critical attention on Italian Arthuriana has focused on the two major prose romances, the *Tavola ritonda* and the *Tristano Riccardiano*.[8] Daniela [Delcorno] Branca's ground-breaking study *I romanzi italiani di Tristano e la "Tavola ritonda,"* the most complete and suggestive to date, has had the great virtue of rekindling interest in the *Tavola ritonda*, which had received relatively little critical commentary since its publication more than a century before (cf. Graf 1885; Malavasi 1903; Barini 1904; Sommer-Tolomei 1910). In recent years, several critics have approached the *Tavola ritonda* from a variety of philological and codicological perspectives. Saverio Guida has been concerned primarily with the text of the romance and its relationship to the earlier Old French *Roman de Tristan* and the other Italian versions, for it appears that he is in the process of preparing a new critical text of the work. Mario Eusebi has examined the influence of Thomas's *Tristan* on the *Tavola ritonda* and provided a new edition of pertinent passages. Anne Shaver's fine translation of this romance, *Tristan and the Round Table*, will allow non-Italianists access to its many wonders, thus generating increased interest in it for its own merits, as well as from a comparative critical perspective.

The other major prose romance of this period, the *Tristano Riccardiano*, has also received increased attention in recent years, being the object of several important studies by Marie-José Heijkant. Her book-length study *La tradizione del "Tristan" in prosa in Italia e proposte di studio sul "Tristano Riccardiano"* treats matters both philological and literary, including the thorny question of its relationship to the Old French *Tristan en prose*.[9] Heijkant has also contributed to the current "rediscovery" of the *Tristano Riccardiano* by reissuing E.G. Parodi's 1896 edition in a reduced format and by providing a new introduction and notes. In 1990, Antonio Scolari published a new critical edition of the *Tristano Riccardiano* with the

---

[8] The *Tavola ritonda* is one of the works discussed by Joan M. Ferrante in her fine comparative study, *The Conflict of Love and Honor: The Medieval Tristan Legend in France, Germany and Italy*.

[9] For the discovery and discussion of fragmentary Old French Arthurian texts in Italy in the Middle Ages, see the studies in the Bibliography by Benedetti, Brunel-Lobrichon, Cingolani, Fontanella, Longobardi, and Scalon.

title *Il romanzo di Tristano*. Scolari has also written on the linguistic dimension of this prose romance in anticipation of his edition.

Two other prose romances, the *Tristano Veneto* and *Tristano Corsiniano*, are only now beginning to receive critical attention, many years after their initial discovery and/or publication.[10] In 1993, Marco Infurna published a critical edition of an Italian version of the Old French *Queste del saint Graal*, which adds another valuable text to our store of Arthurian *volgarizzamenti*. In a related vein, Fabrizio Cigni has announced that his current work in progress will result in a critical edition of the complex *Compilazione* of Rustichello da Pisa.[11] It is a curious fact that, unlike the extremely popular legends of Tristan, the Old French *Lancelot* was never "volgarizzato" in Italy, although we know from archival sources and related documents that a number of manuscript copies of the *Lancelot* were circulating in medieval Italy.[12]

The *cantari*, popular narrative poems composed in *ottave* and sung by a jongleur, display a broad range of Arthurian subject matter, for they draw upon both the prose romances and the Breton lais.[13] Indeed, in its listing of the numerous subjects on which he is able to sing, the anonymous poet of the *Cantare dei cantari* allows us a rare glimpse both into his extensive repertoire and into the literary tastes of contemporary society.[14] The poet declares his ability to perform on a

---

[10] Although a complete critical edition of the *Tristano Veneto* does not yet exist—Aulo Donadello is preparing one for publication—several episodes have been made available by Ernesto G. Parodi ("Dal *Tristano Veneto*") and Felice Arese (*Prose*). The *Tristano Corsiniano* has been edited by Michele Galasso, and this edition has been partially reproduced by Luigi di Benedetto (*Leggenda*). Piera Tomasoni of the Università di Pavia is currently preparing a new edition of the *Tristano Corsiniano* and a study of its language.

[11] See his essay, "Pour l'édition de la *Compilation* de Rustichello da Pisa: la version du ms. Paris, B.N., *fr. 1463*."

[12] See Daniela Delcorno Branca, "Tradizione italiana dei testi arturiani: note sul *Lancelot*."

[13] Most of the *cantari* are preserved in late fourteenth- or early fifteenth-century manuscripts. The fundamental studies of these texts remain those by Ezio Levi.

[14] See Pio Rajna, "Il Cantare dei Cantari e il Sirventese del Maestro di tutte le arti."

wide variety of topics and devotes nine full stanzas (out of fifty-nine) to displaying his vast range of expertise in Arthurian material. Of these many subjects, two principal protagonists are Tristan and Lancelot (as the *novella* by Sacchetti noted at the beginning of this essay suggested).[15] One of these *cantari* deals, for example, with the combat between Lancelot and Tristan at the "Merlin stone" ("il petrone di Merlino")[16] and another treats the death of the lovers in Cornwall.[17] This latter *cantare* has recently appeared in English translation by James J. Wilhelm. In three finely tuned essays Daniela Delcorno Branca reviews the textual and literary fortune of Tristan in the Italian *cantari* and the relationship between the *Tavola ritonda* and the *cantare* tradition with regard to common episodes.[18] In addition to Tristan and Lancelot, the *cantari* feature a host of protagonists, and a brief survey of several titles will provide some idea of their diversity: the anonymous *Pulzella gaia*, *Bel Gherardino*, *Liombruno*, *Carduino*, and *Febusso e Breusso*, and Antonio Pucci's *Gismirante* and *Brito di Brettagna*.[19] In 1990, Maria Bendinelli Predelli published a well-documented study of the sources and literary merits of *Bel Gherardino*, which builds in part on her earlier contributions in this area. The *cantari* were the focus of a major international conference held in Montreal in 1981; Michelangelo Picone and Maria Bendinelli Predelli have edited the volume of proceedings.

---

[15] Texts of the Tristan *cantari* may be found in the following works by Pio Rajna (*I cantari di Carduino*), Giulio Bertoni (*Cantari di Tristano*), Malavasi (*Materia poetica*), Polidori (*Tavola ritonda*), Di Benedetto (*Leggenda*), Natalino Sapegno (*Poeti minori del Trecento*), and Delcorno Branca ("I cantari di Tristano").

[16] See Rajna, *Cantari*, pp. 46–64.

[17] The text is found in Di Benedetto (*Leggenda*), Sapegno (*Poeti minori*), and Bertoni (*Cantari di Tristano*). Bertoni has also written an interesting essay on this episode, "La morte di Tristano."

[18] "I cantari di Tristano," "Il cavaliere dalle armi incantate," and "Il cantare di Astore e Morgana."

[19] For editions of these works, see, among others, Balduino (*Cantari del trecento*) and Levi (*Fiore di leggende*).

Some individual figures from Arthurian literature have been the focus of critical studies. Donald Hoffman has investigated the mysterious figure of Merlin and provided an overview of his presence in Italy from the late twelfth century (in Godfrey of Viterbo's *Pantheon*) through the sixteenth century (Ariosto, in particular). The figure of Dinadan, the seeming anticourtly, antilove character, has also received some attention, though not nearly so much as his maverick French counterpart.[20]

The artistic tradition of Italian Arthuriana—frescoes, illuminated manuscripts, sculptural reliefs, etc.—is not as extensive as that in other countries. In addition to the fundamental study by Roger Sherman Loomis and Laura Hibbard Loomis, *Arthurian Legends in Medieval Art*, and the essay by Pio Rajna on some early embroidery work featuring the Tristan legend ("Intorno a due antiche coperte..."), some research has been done on the carved portals of the cathedrals of Modena[21] and Bari and the mosaic pavement of the cathedral of Otranto.[22] In her study *The Gonzaga of Mantua and Pisanello's Arthurian Frescoes*, Joanna Woods-Marsden includes a section on "Arthurian Romance in Italian Art Before Pisanello's Cycle" (pp. 26–31), and Pisanello's frescoes have been the subject of numerous studies over the years. In terms of manuscript illustration, the lavish cycle of pen drawings in manuscript Palatino 556 of the *Tavola Ritonda*, held in the Biblioteca Nazionale Centrale in Florence, has received much critical attention. Alison Stones has investigated and is currently working on a study of these illustrations. Recently, Annajulia Mariani has written on the *Donna del Vergiù* and its artistic representation—the late fourteenth-century fresco cycle in the Palazzo Davanzati in Florence.

---

[20] For the figure of Dinadan in Italian literature, see my "Tristan in Italy: The Death or Rebirth of a Legend." For his presence in Old French literature, see, among others, Alfred Adler ("Dinadan, inquiétant ou rassurant?") and Eugène Vinaver ("Un chevalier errant à la recherche du sens du monde").

[21] See, for example, Jacques Stiennon and Rita Lejeune, "La Légende arthurienne dans la sculpture de la cathédrale de Modène."

[22] See, for example, Chiara Settis Frugoni, "Per una lettura del mosaico pavimentale della cattedrale d'Otranto."

At one time, with the exception of the work done on Dante, much of the modern criticism on Arthurian material in Italy remained either at a broad descriptive and informative level or at a very technical, philological one. This was to be expected, given the lack of general critical awareness of Italian Arthurian literature, even among Italian specialists. In more recent years, however, the scholarly pace in Italian Arthuriana has increased, although it has not, nor will it perhaps ever, come close to approximating that produced in France or England. One promising sign of the increased interest in this area is that several theses and doctoral dissertations have been or are being written on these subjects in Italy and North America.[23]

Given the current state of studies, several potentially rich areas suggest themselves for future scholarly work on Arthurian material in Italy. The first lies in the area of philology and codicology and concerns the discovery, edition, and reedition of basic texts.[24] The texts of the principal prose romances, which were established in the nineteenth century, are now being reedited, and other works, which had never or only partially been edited (e.g., the *Tristano Veneto, La inchiesta del san gradale*) are now appearing in more proper critical

---

[23] In the United States, the following dissertations have been written on these subjects: Lenore Marie Padula, "The *Tristano Riccardiano*: A Study of Its Composition and Its Relations with the French Versions" (Boston College, 1983); Davide-Paul Bénéteau, "The Reader and the Scribe: Translations from French and the Origins of Italian Prose" (University of California, Berkeley, 1991), which deals in part with Arthurian material; and Gloria Allaire, "The Chivalric 'Histories' of Andrea da Barberino: A Re-evaluation" (University of Wisconsin, 1993). In one chapter of her thesis, Dina Maria Consolini ("Parodies of Love in the Middle Ages: The Poetics of Re-Writing," Yale University, 1993) explores the Italian discourse on love and particularly on the *beffa* in the *Tavola Ritonda*. In Italy, Fabrizio Cigni investigated "Il romanzo arturiano di Rustichello da Pisa" for his *tesi di laurea* (University of Pisa, 1986–87); the topic of Aulo Donadello's *Thèse de Doctorat* was the *Tristano Veneto*: "La redazione veneta del *Romanzo di Tristano*" (University of Padua, 1986–87), and Alessandra Stefanin will be completing her *tesi*, "La materia di Francia e la materia di Brettagna nella letteratura italiana delle origini e nell'opera di Dante Alighieri," at the University of Florence in late 1994 or early 1995.

[24] See the article by Giancarlo Savino, "Ignoti frammenti di un 'Tristano' dugentesco."

guise.[25] An exhaustive inventory of Arthurian materials extant in the Italian libraries and archives is a major desideratum; for it is only through this sort of patient and painstaking codicological research that we will eventually know how much material survives from the Middle Ages. In addition to the necessity of providing reliable critical texts of these works, we hope that English translations of representative Italian Arthurian works will be undertaken, in order that this vibrant and dynamic tradition may be made known to a broader audience.

A second major area for future research concerns the complex relationship between communal society in medieval Italy and the Matter of Britain. Günter Holtus has written on the question of the reception of Arthurian material in the bourgeois society of Italy in the thirteenth and fourteenth centuries, and Franco Cardini has discussed the presence of chivalric literature in Tuscan society in this same period and its relationship to the formation of sociopolitical organizations in Pisa and other Tuscan centers. From a different perspective, following to some degree the more "folkloristically" oriented study of Arturo Graf (*Artù nell'Etna*), Antonio Pioletti has investigated the early manifestations of the Arthurian legend in Sicily and has discussed the use of this legend as part of the political and ideological program of Norman Sicily. These studies should encourage other scholarly efforts in this area.

A third potentially profitable area of investigation involves the broad range of visual materials illustrative of the Arthurian tradition in Italy and how these diverse artistic representations relate to the written documentation and to the society that produced them.[26] All in all, the field of Arthurian studies in Italy has made great strides forward in the past two decades and offers many possibilities for future research.

---

[25] For the questions concerning knowledge of the Old French versions of the Grail quest in Italy and the presence of this subject in medieval Italian literature, see, among others, the studies by Pierre Breillat, P.H. Coronedi, and Gardner, as well as two recent editions: the Italian *volgarizzamento* of the *Inchiesta del san gradale* by Marco Infurna, and the recent edition of the Old French version copied and illustrated in Italy in the late thirteenth century, *La grant queste del saint Graal* (and the important review of this work by Daniela Delcorno Branca in *Lettere Italiane*, 43 [1991], 308–318).

[26] See, for example, the recent volume by Muriel Whitaker, *The Legends of King Arthur in Art*, which includes some discussion of Italian artistic representations.

# Bibliography

*Editions*

Arese, Felice, ed. *Prose di romanzi: il romanzo cortese in Italia nei secoli XIII e XIV.* Turin: UTET, 1950. [Contains selected passages from the *Tristano Riccardiano* (pp. 33–260); *Tristano Veneto* (pp. 261–275); *Tavola ritonda* (pp. 277–463); *Storia di Merlino* (pp. 465–501).]

Balduino, Armando, ed. *Cantari del Trecento.* Milan: Marzorati, 1970. [Contains *Cantare di Fiorio e Biancifiore, Il Bel Gherardino, Ultime imprese e morte di Tristano, Cantare di Pirramo e di Tisbe, Storia del calonaco di Siena, La passione* (Niccolò Cicerchia), and *Cantare della guerra degli otto santi.*]

Bertoni, Giulio, ed. *Cantari di Tristano.* Modena: Società Tipografica Modenese, 1937.

De Robertis, Domenico. "Cantari antichi." *Studi di Filologia Italiana,* 28 (1978), 67–175. [Contains, among others, *Il libro di Fiorio e Biancifiore, Cantare del Bel Gherardino,* and *Cantari di Tristano.*]

di Benedetto, Luigi, ed. *La leggenda di Tristano.* Bari: Laterza, 1942. [Contains the complete *Tristano Riccardiano,* selections from the *Tavola Ritonda* (pp. 299–343) and the *Tristano Corsiniano* (pp. 344–359), and *La morte di Tristano* (pp. 360–367).]

Galasso, Michele, ed. *Il Tristano Corsiniano.* Cassino: Casa Editrice "Le Fonti," 1937.

Infurna, Marco, ed., pref. by Francesco Zambon. *La inchiesta del san gradale: volgarizzamento toscano della "Queste del san graal."*

Florence: Olschki, 1993. ["La mistica travatura della *Queste del saint Graal*," pp. 7–22].

Levi, Ezio, ed. *Fiore di leggende: cantari antichi*. Bari: Laterza, 1914. [Contains *Il Bel Gherardino, Pulzella gaia, Liombruno, Istoria di tre giovani disperati e di tre fate, La donna del Vergiù, Gibello, Gismirante, Bruto di Bretagna, Madonna Lionessa, Reina d'Oriente, Madonna Elena*, and *Cerbino*.]

Parodi, E[rnesto] G., ed. "Dal *Tristano Veneto*." In *Nozze Cian-Sappa-Flandinet*. Bergamo: Istituto Italiano Arti Grafiche, 1894, pp. 105–129.

————, ed. *Tristano Riccardiano*. Bologna: Romagnoli-Dall'Acqua, 1896. [Reissued with a new introduction and notes by Marie-José Heijkant. "Biblioteca Medievale," 16. Parma: Pratiche, 1991.]

Polidori, Filippo-Luigi, ed. *La tavola ritonda o l'istoria di Tristano*. 2 vols. Bologna: Romagnoli, 1864–65.

Rajna, Pio, ed. *I cantari di Carduino, giuntovi quello di Tristano e Lancielotto quando combattettero al petrone di Merlino*. Bologna: Romagnoli, 1873.

————. "Il Cantare dei Cantari e il Sirventese del Maestro di tutte le arti." *Zeitschrift für Romanische Philologie*, 2 (1878), 220–254 and 419–437.

Rosellini, A., ed. and trans. *La grant queste del saint Graal. La grande ricerca del santo graal: versione inedita della fine del XIII secolo del ms. Udine, Biblioteca Arcivescovile, 177*. Tricesimo (Udine): Vattori, 1990.

Sapegno, Natalino, ed. *Poeti minori del Trecento*. Milan: Ricciardi, 1952. [Contains the following *cantari: Cantare di Fiorio e Biancifiore, La donna del Vergiù, Storia di Liombruno, Brito di Brettagna, Madonna Lionessa, Spagna* (selections), *Gibello, La morte di Tristano, Istoria di Pirramo e Tisbe,* and *Orlando* (selections).]

Scolari, Antonio, ed., intro. by Alfredo Giuliani. *Il romanzo di Tristano.* Genoa: Costa and Nolan, 1990.

Segre, Cesare, and Mario Marti, eds. *La prosa del Duecento.* Milan: Ricciardi, 1959. [Contains selected passages from the *Tristano Riccardiano* (pp. 555–661) and the *Tavola ritonda* (pp. 663–735).]

*Translations*

Shaver, Anne, trans. with intro. and notes; editorial assistance by Annette Cash, illus. Catherine M. Hiller. *Tristan and the Round Table: A Translation of "La tavola ritonda."* Binghamton: Medieval and Renaissance Texts and Studies, 1983.

Wilhelm, James J., trans. "Cantare on the Death of Tristan." In *The Romance of Arthur III: Works from Russia to Spain, Norway to Italy.* New York: Garland, 1988, pp. 177–184; rpt. *The Romance of Arthur: An Anthology of Medieval Texts in Translation.* New York: Garland, 1994, pp. 295–303.

*Studies*

Adler, Alfred. "Dinadan, inquiétant ou rassurant? (Encore quelques remarques à propos du rôle de ce chevalier arthurien dans la 'Second Version' du *Tristan en prose).*" In *Mélanges offerts à Rita Lejeune.* 2 vols. Gembloux: Duculot, 1969, II, 935–943.

Ambrosini, Riccardo. "Su alcuni dittonghi aberranti del *Tristano Corsiniano.*" *Annali della Scuola Normale Superiore di Pisa,* 24 (1955), 110–114.

———. "Spoglio fonetico, morfologico e lessicale del *Tristano Corsiniano.*" *Italia Dialettale,* 20 (1956), 29–70.

Barini, Giorgio. "Tristano in Italia." *Nuova Antologia*, 39 (1904), 658–674.

Bendinelli Predelli, Maria. "Modelli strutturali del cantare *fiabesco* italiano." *Quaderni d'Italianistica*, 2 (1981), 1–38.

————. "Dal cantare romanzesco al cantare novellistico. Vicissitudini di una forma." In Michelangelo Picone, Giuseppe Di Stefano, and Pamela D. Stewart, eds., *Formation, codification et rayonnement d'un genre médiéval: la nouvelle. Actes du Colloque International de Montréal (McGill University, 14–16 octobre 1982)*. Montreal: Plato, 1983, pp. 174–188.

————. "Fonti e struttura: il caso del *cantare fiabesco* italiano." In Picone and Predelli, eds., *I cantari: struttura e tradizione*. Florence: Olschki, 1984, pp. 127–141.

————. "Storia delle storie di Lanval." *Quaderni d'Italianistica*, 6 (1985), 1–30.

————. "La città incantata: un episodio del *Carduino*." *Yearbook of Italian Studies*, 8 (1989), 98–118.

————. *Alle origini del "Bel Gherardino."* Florence: Olschki, 1990.

————. "Il *Cantare di Madonna Elena* e l'elaborazione del poemetto cavalleresco in Italia." *Yearbook of Italian Studies*, 10 (1991), 53–107.

Benedetti, Roberto. "Appunti su libri francesi di materia bretone in Friuli." In Paola Schulze-Belli and Michael Dallapiazza, eds., *Liebe und Aventure im Artusroman des Mittelalters*. Göppingen: Kümmerle, 1990, pp. 189–190.

Bertolucci Pizzorusso, Valeria. "I cavalieri del Pisanello." *Studi Mediolatini e Volgari*, 20 (1972), 37–48.

Bertoni, Giulio. "La morte di Tristano." In the collection of his essays *Poesie leggende costumanze del medio evo*. 2nd ed. Modena: Orlandini, 1927, pp. 231–268.

Branca, Daniela. *I romanzi italiani di Tristano e la "Tavola ritonda."* Florence: Olschki, 1968.

Branca, Vittore. *Il cantare trecentesco e il Boccaccio del "Filostrato" et del "Teseida."* Florence: Sansoni, 1936.

Bregoli-Russo, Mauda. "La leggenda di Sir Lancillotto del Lago e l'*Innamorato* del Boiardo." *Esperienze Letterarie*, 12 (1987), 47–55.

Breillat, Pierre. "La quête du saint-graal en Italie." *Mélanges d'Archéologie et d'Histoire de l'Ecole Française de Rome*, 54 (1937), 262–300.

———. "Une traduction italienne de la *Mort le Roi Artu*." *Archivum Romanicum*, 21 (1937), 437–469.

———. "Le manuscrit Florence Palatin 556: La *Tavola ritonda* et la liturgie du graal." *Mélanges d'Archéologie et d'Histoire de l'Ecole Française de Rome*, 55 (1938), 341–373.

Brunel-Lobrichon, G. "Un nouveau fragment des *Prophéties de Merlin* à Bologne." In Anna Cornagliotti, ed., *Miscellanea di studi romanzi offerti a Giuliano Gasca Queirazza*. Alessandria: Edizioni dell'Orso, 1988, I, 91–98.

Cabani, Maria Cristina. *Le forme del cantare epico-cavalleresco*. Lucca: Maria Pacini Fazzi, 1988.

Cardini, Franco. "Concetto di cavalleria e mentalità cavalleresca nei romanzi e nei cantari fiorentini." In *I ceti dirigenti nella Toscana tardo comunale*. Comitato di studi sulla storia dei ceti dirigenti in Toscana, Atti del III Convegno: Firenze, 5–7 dicembre 1980. Florence: Francesco Papafava Editore, 1983, pp. 157–192.

Carozza, Davy. "Elements of the *roman courtois* in the Episode of Paolo and Francesca (Inferno V)." *Papers on Language and Literature*, 3 (1967), 291–301.

Cigni, Fabrizio. *Bibliografia degli studi italiani di materia arturiana (1940–1990)*, intro. Valeria Bertolucci Pizzorusso. Fasano: Schena, 1992.

———. "Pour l'édition de la *Compilation* de Rustichello da Pisa: La version du ms. Paris, B.N., fr. 1463." *Neophilologus*, 76 (1992), 519–534.

Cingolani, Stefano M. "Frammenti di codici in volgare dall'Archivio di Stato di Viterbo." *Pluteus*, 4–5 (1986–87), 247–253.

Coronedi, P.H. "La leggenda del san graal nel romanzo in prosa di Tristano." *Archivum Romanicum*, 15 (1931), 83–98.

Crescini, Vincenzo. "Il bacio di Ginevra e il bacio di Paolo." *Studi Danteschi*, 3 (1921), 5–57.

Dardano, Maurizio. "Il *Tristano Riccardiano* e la *Tavola ritonda*." In *Lingua e tecnica narrativa nel Duecento*. Rome: Bulzoni, 1969, pp. 222–248.

Delcorno Branca, Daniela. "I cantari di Tristano." *Lettere Italiane*, 23 (1971), 289–305.

———. "Tavola rotonda: materia arturiana e tristaniana: tradizione e fortuna." In *Dizionario critico della letteratura italiana*. Turin: UTET, 1973, 471–476; 2nd ed., 1986, IV, 270–276.

———. *Il romanzo cavalleresco medievale*. Florence: Sansoni, 1974.

———. "Per la storia del *Roman de Tristan* in Italia." *Cultura Neolatina*, 40 (1980), 211–229.

———. "Il cavaliere dalle armi incantate: circolazione di un modello narrativo arturiano." *Giornale Storico della Letteratura Italiana*, 159 (1982), 353–382. [Also in *I cantari: struttura e tradizione*, pp. 103–126.]

———. "Romanzi arturiani." In *Enciclopedia Dantesca*. 2nd ed. Rome: Istituto della Enciclopedia Italiana, 1984, IV, 1028–1030.

———. *Boccaccio e le storie di re Artù*. Bologna: Il Mulino, 1991.

———. "Il cantare di Astore e Morgana." In Luigi Reina, ed., *Humanitas e poesia: studi in onore di Gioacchino Paparelli*. 2 vols. Salerno: Laveglia, 1991, pp. 5–20.

———. "Sette anni di studi sulla letteratura arturiana in Italia: Rassegna (1985–1992)." *Lettere Italiane*, 44 (1992), 465–497.

———. "Tradizione italiana dei testi arturiani: note sul *Lancelot*." *Medioevo Romanzo*, 17 (1992), 215–250.

Dronke, Peter. "Francesca and Heloise." *Comparative Literature*, 26 (1975), 113–135.

Eusebi, Mario. "Reliquie del *Tristano* di Thomas nella *Tavola Ritonda*." *Cultura Neolatina*, 39 (1979), 39–62.

Farinelli, Arturo. *Dante e la Francia dall'età media al secolo di Voltaire*. 2 vols. Milan: 1908; Geneva: Slatkine, 1971, esp. I, 8–22.

Ferrante, Joan M. *The Conflict of Love and Honor: The Medieval Tristan Legend in France, Germany and Italy*. The Hague: Mouton, 1973.

Fontanella Vitale-Brovarone, Lucia. "Due frammenti francesi all'Accademia delle Scienze di Torino: *L'estoire du graal* e il *Tristano Torinese*." In Anna Cornagliotti, ed., *Miscellanea di studi romanzi offerti a Giuliano Gasca Queirazza*. Alessandria: Edizioni dell'Orso, 1988, I, 291–314.

Gardner, Edmund G. "The Holy Grail in Italian Literature." *Modern Language Review*, 20 (1925), 443–453.

――――. *The Arthurian Legend in Italian Literature*. London: Dent; New York: Dutton, 1930.

Graf, Arturo. "Appunti per la storia del ciclo brettone in Italia." *Giornale Storico della Letteratura Italiana*, 5 (1885), 80–130.

――――. "Artù nell'Etna." In *Miti, leggende e superstizioni del Medio Evo*. Turin: Loescher, 1893, II, 303–335. [Also available in a new single-volume edition with preface, notes, and appendix by Giosue Bonfanti. Milan: Mondadori, 1984, pp. 321–338.]

Guida, Saverio. "Sulle 'fonti' della *Tavola ritonda*." In *Umanità e storia: scritti in onore di Adelchi Attisani. Letteratura e Storia*. Naples: Giannini, 1971, II, 129–155.

――――. "Per il testo della *Tavola ritonda*: una redazione umbra." *Siculorum Gymnasium*, 32 (1979), 637–667.

Hatcher, Anna G., and Mark Musa. "The Kiss: *Inferno* V and the Old French Prose *Lancelot*." *Comparative Literature*, 20 (1968), 97–109.

Heijkant, Marie-José. "Le *Tristano Riccardiano*, une version particulière du *Tristan en prose*." In Charles Foulon et al., eds, *Actes du 14e Congrès International Arthurien (Rennes, 16–21 août 1984)*. Rennes: Presses Universitaires de Rennes 2, 1985, pp. 314–323.

――――. "L'emploi des formules d'introduction e de transition stéréotypées dans le *Tristano Riccardiano*." In Keith Busby and Erik Kooper, eds., *Courtly Literature: Culture and Context: Selected Papers from the 5th Triennial Congress of the International Courtly Literature Society, Dalfsen, The Netherlands, 9–16 August, 1986*. Amsterdam: Benjamins, 1990, pp. 271–282.

———. "L'assedio della città d'Agippi nel *Tristano Riccardiano*." In Giovanna Angeli and Luciano Formisano, eds., *L'imaginaire courtois et son double*. Naples: Edizioni Scientifiche Italiane, 1992, pp. 323–331.

———. *La tradizione del "Tristan" in prosa in Italia e proposte di studio sul "Tristano Riccardiano."* Diss. Katholieke Universiteit, Nijmegen. Nijmegen: Sneldruck Enschede, 1989.

Hoffman, Donald L. "The Arthurian Tradition in Italy." In Valerie M. Lagorio and Mildred Leake Day, eds., *King Arthur Through the Ages*. 2 vols. New York: Garland, 1990, I, 170–188.

———. "Merlin in Italy." *Philological Quarterly*, 70 (1991), 261–275.

Holtus, Gunter. "La 'matière de Bretagne' en Italie: quelques réflexions sur la transposition du vocabulaire et des structures sociales." In Charles Foulon et al., eds., *Actes du 14e Congrès International Arthurien (Rennes, 16–21 août, 1984)*. Rennes: Presses Universitaires de Rennes 2, 1985, pp. 324–345.

Infurna, Marco. "La *Queste del Saint Graal* in Italia e il manoscritto udinese." In A. Rosellini, ed. and trans., *La grant queste del saint graal: la grande ricerca del santo Graal. Versione inedita della fine del XIII secolo del ms. Udine, Biblioteca Arcivescovile, 177*. Tricesimo (Udine): Vattori, 1990, pp. 49–57.

Kleinhenz, Christopher. "Tristan in Italy: The Death or Rebirth of a Legend." *Studies in Medieval Culture*, 5 (1975), 145–158.

———. "Italian Arthurian Literature." In Norris J. Lacy et al., eds., *The Arthurian Encyclopedia*. New York: Garland, 1986, pp. 293–299; rev. ed., *The New Arthurian Encyclopedia*. New York: Garland, 1991, pp. 245–247.

———. "Dante as Reader and Critic of Courtly Literature." In Keith Busby and Erik Kooper, eds., *Courtly Literature: Culture and Context: Selected Papers from the 5th Triennial Congress of the*

*International Courtly Literature Society, Dalfsen, The Netherlands, 9–16 August, 1986).* Amsterdam: Benjamins, 1990, pp. 379–393.

————. "Perspectives on the Quest Motif in Medieval Italian Literature: Comic Elements in Antonio Pucci's *Gismirante.*" Forthcoming in Donald Maddox and Sara Sturm-Maddox, eds., *Literary Aspects of Courtly Culture: Selected Papers from the 7th Triennial Congress of the International Courtly Literature Society.* Woodbridge: Boydell and Brewer, 1994, pp. 249–256.

————. "The Quest Motif in Medieval Italian Literature." In Keith Busby and Norris J. Lacy, eds., *Conjunctures: Medieval Studies in Honor of Douglas Kelly.* Amsterdam: Rodopi, 1994, pp. 235–251.

Krauss, Henning. "Der Artus-Roman in Italien." In H.R. Jauss and E. Köhler, eds., *Grundriß der romanischen Literaturen des Mittelalters*, vol. 4, *Le roman jusqu'à la fin du XIIIe siècle*, tome 1 (partie historique). Heidelberg: Winter, 1978, pp. 667–675.

Lacy, Norris J., and Geoffrey Ashe. "Italian Literature." In *The Arthurian Handbook.* New York: Garland, 1988, pp. 125–130.

Levi, Ezio. *I cantari legendari del popolo italiano nei secoli XIV e XV: Giornale Storico della Letteratura Italiana*, Supplemento 16, 1914.

————. "I lais brettoni e la leggenda di Tristano." *Studj Romanzi*, 14 (1917), 113–246.

Longobardi, Monica. "Un frammento della *Queste* della Post-Vulgata nell'Archivio di Stato di Bologna." *Studi Mediolatini e Volgari*, 33 (1987), 5–24.

————. "Frammenti di codici dall'Emilia-Romagna: primo bilancio." *Cultura Neolatina*, 48 (1988), 143–148.

————. "Nuovi frammenti del *Guiron le Courtois.*" *Studi Mediolatini e Volgari*, 34 (1988), 5–24.

————. "Altri recuperi d'archivio: le *Profécies de Merlin*." *Studi Mediolatini e Volgari*, 35 (1989), 73–140.

————. "Frammenti di codici in antico francese dalla Biblioteca Comunale di Imola." In Roberto Antonelli, Fabrizio Beggiato, Anna Ferrari, and Adriana Solimena, eds., *Miscellanea di studi in onore di Aurelio Roncaglia a cinquant'anni dalla sua laurea*. Modena: Mucchi, 1989, II, 727–759.

Loomis, Roger Sherman, and Laura Hibbard Loomis. *Arthurian Legends in Medieval Art*. New York: Modern Language Association of America, 1938.

Malavasi, Giuseppe. *La materia poetica del ciclo brettone in Italia: in particolare la leggenda di Tristano e quella di Lancillotto*. Bologna: Zanichelli, 1903.

Mariani, Annajulia. "La donna del Vergiù: cantare ed affresco." In Antonio Franceschetti, ed., *Letteratura italiana e arti figurative I: Atti del XII Convegno dell'Associazione Internazionale per gli Studi di Lingua e Letteratura Italiana (Toronto, Hamilton, Montreal, 6–10 maggio 1985)*. Florence: Olschki, 1988, I, 369–373.

Noakes, Susan. "The Double Misreading of Paolo and Francesca." *Philological Quarterly*, 62 (1983), 221–239.

Paccagnini, Giovanni. *Pisanello e il ciclo cavalleresco di Mantova*. Milan: Electa, 1972; English trans. *Pisanello*, trans. Jane Carroll. London: Phaidon, 1973.

Picone, Michelangelo. "Dante e la tradizione arturiana." *Romanische Forschungen*, 94 (1982), 1–18.

————. "La *matière de Bretagne* nei cantari." In Picone and Predelli, eds., *I cantari: struttura e tradizione*, 1984, pp. 87–102.

————, and Maria Bendinelli Predelli, eds. *I cantari: struttura e tradizione: Atti del convegno internazionale di Montréal, 19–20 marzo 1981*. Florence: Olschki, 1984.

Pioletti, Antonio. *Forme del racconto arturiano: Perceval, Peredur, Bel Inconnu, Carduino*. Naples: Liguori, 1984.

————. "Artù, Avallon, l'Etna." *Quaderni Medievali*, 28 (1989), 6–35.

Poggioli, Renato. "Tragedy or Romance? A Reading of the Paolo and Francesca Episode in Dante's *Inferno*." *PMLA*, 72 (1957), 313–358.

Popolizio, Stephen. "Literary Reminiscences and the Act of Reading in *Inferno* V." *Dante Studies*, 98 (1980), 19–33.

Quaglio, Antonio Enzo. "Francesca." In *Enciclopedia Dantesca*. 2nd ed. Rome: Istituto della Enciclopedia Italiana, 1984, III, 1–13.

Ragni, Eugenio. "Cantari." In *Dizionario critico della letteratura italiana*. Turin: UTET, 1973, I, 480–488; 2nd ed., 1986, I, 492–500.

Rajna, Pio. "Intorno a due antiche coperte con figurazioni tratte dalle storie di Tristano." *Romania*, 42 (1913), 517–579.

————. "Dante e i romanzi della Tavola Rotonda." *Nuova Antologia*, 206 (1920), 223–247.

Rasmo, Nicola. "Il codice Palatino 556 e le sue illustrazioni." *Rivista d'Arte*, 21 (1939), 245–281.

Ruggieri, Jole M. "Versioni italiane della *Queste del saint Graal*." *Archivum Romanicum*, 21 (1937), 471–486.

Savino, Giancarlo. "Ignoti frammenti di un 'Tristano' dugentesco." *Studi di Filologia Italiana*, 37 (1979), 5–17.

Scaglione, Aldo. *Knights at Court: Courtliness, Chivalry, and Courtesy from Ottonian Germany to the Italian Renaissance.* Berkeley: University of California Press, 1992.

Scalon, Cesare. *Libri scuole e cultura nel Friuli medioevale.* Padua: Antenore, 1987.

Scolari, Antonio. "Volgarizzamenti e intertestualità: il sogno erotico di Pallamides." In Massimo Bonafin, ed., *Intertestualità.* Genoa: Il Melangolo, 1986, pp. 89–100.

———. "Sulla lingua del *Tristano Riccardiano.*" *Medioevo Romanzo,* 13 (1988), 75–89.

Scott, John A. "Dante's Francesca and the Poet's Attitude Towards Courtly Literature." *Reading Medieval Studies,* 5 (1979), 4–20.

Settis Frugoni, Chiara. "Per una lettura del mosaico pavimentale della cattedrale d'Otranto." *Bullettino dell'Istituto Storico Italiano per il Medio Evo e Archivio Muratoriano,* 80 (1968), 213–256.

Sommer, Elvira. "Per la leggenda di Tristano in Italia." *Atti del Reale Istituto Veneto di Scienze, Lettere ed Arti,* 67 (1907–08), 967–978.

Sommer-Tolomei, Elvira. "La leggenda di Tristano in Italia." *Rivista d'Italia,* 13 (1910), 73–127.

Stiennon, Jacques, and Rita Lejeune. "La légende arthurienne dans la sculpture de la cathédrale de Modène." *Cahiers de Civilisation Médiévale,* 6 (1963), 281–296.

Stones, M. Alison. "Aspects of Arthur's Death in Medieval Illumination." In Christopher Baswell and William Sharpe, eds., *The Passing of Arthur: New Essays in Arthurian Tradition.* New York: Garland, 1988, pp. 52–101.

Toynbee, Paget. "Dante and the Lancelot Romance." In *Dante Studies and Researches*. 1902; rpt. Port Washington: Kennikat, 1971, pp. 1–37.

Vinaver, Eugène. "Un chevalier errant à la recherche du sens du monde: quelques remarques sur le caractère de Dinadan dans le *Tristan en prose*." In Jean Renson, ed., *Mélanges de linguistique romane et de philologie médiévale offerts à M. Maurice Delbouille*, II, *Philologie médiévale*. Gembloux: Duculot, 1964, pp. 677–686.

Viscardi, Antonio. "La quête du saint-Graal dans les romans du Moyen Age italien." In René Nelli, ed., *Lumière du graal: études et textes*. Paris: Cahiers du Sud, 1951, pp. 263–281.

———. "Arthurian Influences on Italian Literature from 1220 to 1500." In Roger Sherman Loomis, ed., *Arthurian Literature in the Middle Ages: A Collaborative History*. Oxford: Clarendon, 1959, pp. 419–429.

———. "Romanzi cortesi." In *Enciclopedia Dantesca*. 2nd ed. Rome: Istituto della Enciclopedia Italiana, 1984, IV, 1030–1032.

Weaver, Elissa. "Tristan Studies in Italy: A Review of Current Scholarship." *Tristania*, 4, No. 1 (November 1978), 3–14.

Whitaker, Muriel. *The Legends of King Arthur in Art*. Cambridge: Brewer, 1990.

Woods-Marsden, Joanna. *The Gonzaga of Mantua and Pisanello's Arthurian Frescoes*. Princeton: Princeton University Press, 1988.

Zingarelli, Nicola. "Le reminiscenze del *Lancelot*." *Studi Danteschi*, 1 (1920), 65–90.

# GERMANY

## William C. McDonald

The German Arthurian romance (*Artusroman* or *Artusepik*) has never been a stepchild of research. It has, however, stimulated exceptional scholarly interest in the past decade, as the perspectives and postulates proposed in earlier investigations are worked out. The "classical" texts, *Erec* and *Iwein* of Hartmann von Aue and *Parzival* of Wolfram von Eschenbach, all of which were composed around 1200, were widely circulated and imitated in the German cultural region. Virtually all scholars are conversant with these works because of recent English translations and an array of literary studies, the range of which is unusual. Both Hartmann and Wolfram are the subject of special bibliographies, the former in 1977 by Elfriede Neubuhr and the latter in 1968 by Ulrich Pretzel and Wolfgang Bachofer. The best general treatment of German Arthurian literature is the comprehensive introduction in *The Arthurian Handbook* by Norris J. Lacy and Geoffrey Ashe, who argue persuasively for the inclusion of the German Tristan tales of Eilhart von Oberge (fl. 1180) and Gottfried von Strassburg (fl. 1210) in the scholarly discussion. Since Eilhart's *Tristrant* casts the protagonist as a knight of the Round Table, his may be, in the words of the translator J.W. Thomas, the "first Arthurian novel in German" (32). Karin R. Gürttler, in her brief but informative review of German Arthurian literature in *The New Arthurian Encyclopedia*, also refers to Eilhart.

There have been periodic attempts to sketch the contours of research. In 1979, Wolfgang Haubrichs outlined the present state of scholarship in five pages, listing two hundred and twenty-two items in his bibliography. Apologizing for the incompleteness of his results, Haubrichs nevertheless isolates the two tendencies dominating research of the 1970s: interdisciplinary scholarship and attention to the social, political, and cultural contexts of literature, this latter embracing literary reception and the relationship of author and public. In 1986 Carola L. Gottzmann observed that one could scarcely command a view of the secondary literature on Wolfram and Hartmann alone (9). Topics of recent scholarship include court customs and such cultural practices as feasts and social gatherings (Marquardt, Haug and Warning);[1] aristocratic ideals, chiefly courtliness (Scaglione); the benefits of interdisciplinary research (Haage); poetic motifs, such as the steed (Ackermann-Arlt), trickery (Semmler), and shame and disgrace (Martin); the narrative function of knightly combat (Sieverding); courtly love (Peters, Jones); sexuality and obscenity (Beutin); the role of feeling and emotion (Dinzelbacher); fantastic elements in courtly fiction (Haug); and the status and function of King Arthur (Brunner, Schirok).

German Arthurian literature of the classical period is grist for reception theory, inasmuch as it was inspired by French source texts, most prominently the verse romances of Chrétien de Troyes. Although Hartmann von Aue and Wolfram von Eschenbach were not dependent solely on Chrétien, Chrétien's romances were, in the words of William Henry Jackson, "of central importance in establishing the theme of knighthood in German literature" (37). Since German authors took many liberties with sources and invented freely, the term "adapters" is perhaps too imprecise to characterize them. Whichever word we choose, Hartmann, generally recognized as the first author of Arthurian romance in Germany, reworked Chrétien's *Erec et Enide* in the 1180s or early 1190s; Hartmann's *Iwein* was adapted from Chrétien's *Yvain* some years after 1190; and Wolfram von Eschenbach refashioned Chrétien's *Perceval*, as *Parzival*, ca. 1200.

German Arthuriana continued through the fifteenth century; examples are the verses by Ulrich Fuetrer (examined by Bastert), the prose romances (Blamires), and the Shrovetide play (Walsh, Moser). The German courtly romance of the fourteenth century is the topic of an article by Thomas Cramer. Commenting on the adoption of French

---

[1] Names given in parentheses indicate authors as found in the bibliography. I would like to thank Professors Albrecht Classen, Klaus M. Schmidt, and Ulrich Müller for suggestions and items for essay and Bibliography. Even the most casual reader of the present essay will notice how significantly Müller's series, Göppinger Arbeiten zur Germanistik, has contributed to scholarship.

aristocratic culture in Germany, Joachim Bumke, in the translation of Thomas Dunlap, speaks of the break (after 1220) from the pattern of adapting foreign sources:

> Most of the later Arthurian romances got by without any French models. Der Stricker seems to have been the first poet (ca. 1230?) who constructed a new Arthurian romance (*Daniel von dem Blühenden Tal*) from existing motifs after the pattern of Hartmann's *Iwein*. The same technique was later employed by Berthold von Holle, Der Pleier, and others. The extensive production of French romances in the thirteenth century had little influence on Germany.[2]

The last French romances to be translated by German poets were the thirteenth-century stories *Meraugis de Portlesguez* by Raoul de Houdenc, and the anonymous *Blancandin et l'Orgueilleuse d'amour*, as *Segremors* and *Blanschandin*, both adaptations surviving only in fragments.

Because the secondary literature on German Arthuriana is so considerable, the research landscape is strewn with bibliographical compilations (e.g., Neubuhr, Pretzel and Bachofer) that have been abandoned because of the sheer number of new studies. How crucial a few years of scholarship are to the record is evident from the 1993 volume on Chrétien de Troyes and the German Middle Ages, edited by Martin H. Jones and Roy Wisbey. Valuable though the book is—primarily in reminding the reader that, in contrast to the canonical triad *Erec–Yvain–Perceval*, Chrétien's *Cligés* and *Lancelot* enjoyed only limited currency and literary reception in German lands—the research essays are already dated. The Jones–Wisbey collection is based on oral papers from 1988, and one is struck by the amount of research that has been accomplished in the few years between conference and publication. So profuse, in fact, is recent scholarship on German Arthuriana that the bibliography in Volker Mertens's 1984 summary essay on King Arthur seems quaint. A recent issue of the bibliographical journal *Germanistik*, taken at random (No. 33, 1992),

---

[2] *Courtly Culture: Literature and Society in the High Middle Ages*, p. 95. The German version of the book is *Höfische Kultur: Literatur und Gesellschaft im hohen Mittelalter* (Munich: Deutscher Taschenbuch Verlag, 1986). Concerning the *Daniel* of Der Stricker, its translator, Michael Resler, more accurately labels the work "the first original, self-conceived German romance centering on the Arthurian legend" (*Daniel of the Blossoming Valley*, p. lii).

helps make the point: some twenty entries concern Wolfram von Eschenbach alone.

Although Hartmann von Aue established the basis for the German Arthurian romance with his work, which comes ultimately from Chrétien, it is only in recent decades that modern criticism has begun to acknowledge his contribution and to place the poet side by side with "classical" narrative authors. "It has been his fate," Francis G. Gentry has observed, "until fairly recently, to be neglected by modern scholars and to stand in the shadow of his illustrious contemporaries, Wolfram von Eschenbach, Gottfried von Strassburg, and the anonymous *Nibelungenlied* poet" (154). Noting that literary critics have attempted to remedy this neglect, Timothy McFarland and Silvia Ranawake summarize the many topics that help account for the recent dominance of Hartmann's poetry in scholarship:

> . . . the relationship between the sources and Hartmann's adaptation of them; his craft of composition and his stylistic and rhetorical skills; the provenance and the function of Hartmann's motifs and their symbolism; the ethical values that find expression in his work; and . . . the unique position occupied by Hartmann in relation to both the rapidly changing social and cultural world of the medieval lay nobility on the one hand, and to the tradition of clerical learning and the intellectual developments of the period on the other [viii].

Of Hartmann's works, *Iwein* traditionally holds pride of place among scholars. The protagonist is insane for a time, and some of the critical interest in the poem is no doubt motivated by this aspect, making the text a fount of medieval psychology. An index of Hartmann's popularity is the range of scholarly projects devoted to his work, concordances and translations appearing regularly (Boggs). A summary of research on *Erec* is sufficient to fill a volume of some 450 pages by Gudrun Haase; equally imposing is Lambertus Okken's exhaustive inventory of commentary on both Arthurian romances.

Hartmann, in adapting Chrétien's techniques of narration, was no mere translator. The German poet recasts his source text into a network of textual glosses, transmitted through a sophisticated array of narrative personae. The masks of storytelling are a defining features of his tales of the Round Table (Kuttner, Arndt, Kramer), as is Hartmann's conception of King Arthur, which became the paradigm for the German Middle Ages. Hilkert Weddige summarizes:

Artus ist der Repräsentant vollendet höfischen Rittertums . . . [Er] verharrt in
tatenloser Idealität. Er setzt nicht sich selbst, sondern andere in Bewegung. Er
gibt den Rittern seiner Tafelrunde Gelegenheit zur *aventiure* und inszeniert nach
glücklicher Rückkehr prächtige Hoffeste. Letztlich verkörpert Artus das Idealbild
einer statischen Ordnung der höfischen Welt.[3]

Of the attempts to treat the work of Hartmann von Aue as a unified
whole, the most successful is by Susan Clark, who examines cognitive
allusions. Her thesis is that Hartmann "takes as his abiding and
overriding concern the workings of the *mind*—and by mind shall be
understood cerebral functions as well as the emotive and perceptual
functions tied to mind—and translates mind into terms individual to
each of his poems" (3).

Despite the notorious difficulties presented by the *Parzival* of
Wolfram von Eschenbach, critical appreciation for the work has
advanced in scope and substance. The poet has remained in the public
consciousness, not least because of Dieter Kühn's bestseller *Parzival
des Wolfram von Eschenbach* (1986), a peculiar amalgam of biography,
autobiography, medieval montage, and translation. Enigmas surround
the poem, as is well known, and among them is the very purpose for
its composition. Henry Kratz postulates in his ambitious monograph
that *Parzival* bears a political message:

Only through a well-ordered system of succession to the Imperial throne could
lasting peace and prosperity be achieved . . . . To avoid the chaos that is caused
when an unfit person or a minor comes to a throne, there should be some kind
of a system to test the prospective monarch's fitness and maturity before he is
allowed to reign and to depose him if he reigns incompetently . . . [448].

---

[3] "Arthur is the representative of perfect courtly knighthood. . . . He persists in
quiescent ideality. He does not rouse himself to action, instead inspiring action in others.
To the knights of the Round Table he offers the chance for adventure; after their
felicitous return [to him] he organizes sumptuous court festivities. Lastly, Arthur
personifies the ideal image of static order in the courtly world" (Weddige, 204). Unless
otherwise indicated, all translations are my own. On King Arthur, see also Schmidt, "Das
Herrscherbild im Artusroman der Stauferzeit," 181-194.

Wolfram's aims, a persistent topic in scholarship, are addressed in the journal *Wolfram-Studien*,[4] as well as in the essays of Werner Schröder and in the Festschrift that honors him, edited by Kurt Gärtner and Joachim Heinzle. Interesting special approaches to *Parzival* include the depiction of love (Schnell), the motif of female suffering (Brackert), treatment of the poetic figures Keie (Classen) and Gawein (Schopf), an interpretation based on analytical psychology (McConnell), evidence of mathematical design techniques (Hart), and an analysis of power and powerlessness from a feminist perspective (Eder). Regina Unger traces the influence of Wolfram's poetry in later periods. Clifton Hall's long-awaited concordance to *Parzival* promises to provide the basis for a variety of textual investigations. Recent scholarship focuses on no special topic, making it easier to speak of two poorly represented research areas: the traditional topics of Wolfram's religiosity and Parzival's intellectual development.

Although critical interest in Wolfram has not kept pace with the Hartmann "boom," the secondary literature by 1970 was so extensive that it merited a summary volume of scholarship from 1945 forward by Bumke. That no similar review has been attempted from the early 1970s to recent times, beyond Bumke's own specimen bibliography up to the year 1991 in his Wolfram monograph, is a direct reflection of the number of studies that have been produced, making it unlikely that any single researcher can complete the necessary task of tabulation and evaluation.[5] It is not only Wolfram scholarship that is too daunting for a single person to command; the latest handbook on Hartmann von Aue is the work of two scholars, Christoph Cormeau and Wilhelm Störmer. Typical, too, is dual or triple authorship for commemorative volumes, Festschriften, and the like.

To deal with the flood of Arthurian studies, which increased exponentially from about 1965, some researchers offer a skeletal,

---

[4] *Wolfram-Studien*, founded in 1970, are published under the auspices of the Wolfram von Eschenbach-Gesellschaft. See the recent issue devoted exclusively to Wolfram, No. 12, *Probleme der Parzival-Philologie. Marburger Kolloquium 1990*, ed. Joachim Heinzle et al. (Berlin: Schmidt, 1992).

[5] Renate Decke-Cornill is attempting a Wolfram bibliography, the latest installment of which, through the year 1990, appears in *Wolfram-Studien*, 12 (1992), 244-276. See the previous note.

representative bibliography (Gottzmann, De Boor). Another response is to leave in print an out-of-date volume, such as Peter Wapnewski's monograph on Hartmann von Aue (7th ed., 1979). Considerable scholarly activity notwithstanding, no dominant direction of criticism has emerged beyond a return to the research concerns of the 1970s. Nor have glib generalizations successfully characterized the essence of the Arthurian stories, as when Harald Haferland claims, "Das Thema der Artusepik ist zugleich die Aufhebung von Gefangenschaft und die Herstellung der Freiheit des Verhaltens."[6] Criticism in the 1970s had a distinctive face, the sociology of literature, as witnessed by a periodical that commenced with the new decade, *Zeitschrift für Literaturwissenschaft und Linguistik*. Early in its existence, under the editorship of Wolfgang Haubrichs, there appeared a special number, "Soziologie mittelalterlicher Literatur" (1973). In treating aspects of the sociology of medieval literature—social characteristics of hagiography, literary reception, sociopsychological structures in literature, communicative discourse between text and reader, and the concept of medieval "classicism"—this volume provides a valuable point of orientation, illustrating as it does the preoccupations of researchers. A subsequent issue on the courtly period, again edited by Haubrichs (1977), has the provocative title "Höfische Dichtung oder Literatur im Feudalismus?" ("Courtly Literature, or Literature in the Time of Feudalism?"). The essays do not resolve this question, but have stimulated discussion on the conditions under which German medieval literature arose.

Our sketch of some trends in recent criticism shows no distinctive, controlling configuration beyond the literary sociology grounded in earlier periods. There is a unifying element, however, derived from scholarly consensus in three important areas. First, the so-called "postclassical" (*nachklassisch*) Arthurian poems of the thirteenth century and beyond deserve attention, unaccompanied by insistent comparisons with the canonical works of Hartmann and Wolfram. This essay employs the term "postclassical" because it is established in scholarship, as attested in the subtitle of the 1992 book by Neil

---

[6] "The theme of the Arthurian romance is the termination of imprisonment and, concurrently, the establishment of the freedom of human conduct" (206).

Thomas: *The Defence of Camelot: Ideology and Intertextuality in the "Post-Classical" German Romances of the Matter of Britain Cycle.*

As recently as 1971, it was possible for a leading researcher, Karl Otto Brogsitter, to label the later Arthurian romances "Epigonenepen" in a standard reference work and to claim:

> Sattsam bekannte Motive und Motivketten werden wahllos wiederholt, neu kombiniert und mitunter in wildem Wirrwarr zu Epen von oft erheblicher Länge zusammengestoppelt . . . Abenteuer folgen auf Abenteuer, ohne daß man gewöhnlich von vernünftiger Durchgestaltung des Stoffes oder gar einem größeren Sinnzusammenhang reden könnte.[7]

Today, this kind of observation is seen as informed by a flawed understanding of late-medieval aesthetics, and no one would venture to doubt the relevance of the postclassical texts.

The situation has in truth reversed itself to the degree that German Arthurian works after 1200 threaten to dominate criticism. Ironically, it was Brogsitter who in 1984 summarized the scholarly consensus over the role of the Arthurian hero: ". . . Der Held [erscheint] nun nicht mehr als der Träger von Konflikten, sondern von vornherein als ideale Musterfigur."[8] The literary analysis of German Arthurian tales in transition to the later period is most clearly in the debt of Walter Haug, who has explored such characteristic motifs as the absence of existential crises involving the protagonist. Haug, outstanding among scholars bringing forth fundamental work on the Arthurian legend, composed a ground-breaking study in 1971 ("Die Symbolstruktur") on the dissolution of the symbolic structure of the courtly narrative and Wolfram's role in this dissolution. The essay, proposing outlines for further study, which Haug himself took up in "Paradigmatische Poesie," was pioneering in its recognition that medieval aesthetics of

---

[7] "Sufficiently known motifs and sequences of motifs are repeated indiscriminately, combined in new ways, and cobbled together—at times in wild confusion—to make narratives of often considerable length. . . . Adventure follows adventure, so that it would be impossible to speak of rational shaping of the material, or of substantial coherence of meaning" (117).

[8] "Now the hero is no longer the locus of conflicts, but is from the start an ideal, exemplary figure" (16).

the classical period inspired narrative mutations and that these emerged already in Wolfram's poetry.

Two studies appearing only a year apart, in 1976 and 1977, are indispensable for appreciating the marked shift in critical perception that, as a departure from the canonical approach, took place among scholars in the 1970s. These books are *Künec Artus der guote* by Karin R. Gürttler and *Wigalois und Diu Crone* by Christoph Cormeau, both of which challenge the dominant critical assumptions that the later authors were second-rate imitators and that their poems, in emphasizing entertainment, document a decline in artistic sensibility. Gürttler's monograph, the most comprehensive treatment of the Round Table in the German cultural area, challenges the canon by ascribing importance to Arthurian poems by Heinrich von dem Türlin, Der Stricker, Der Pleier, Konrad von Stoffeln, Ulrich von Zatzikhoven, Wirnt von Grafenberg, and the anonymous author of *Wigamur*. Her general conclusion, that the German "Artusbild" ("image of King Arthur") was by no means immutable and a formal ideal, but rather was highly subjective and variable, depending on the individual poet, is accepted by scholars to the degree that it now appears commonplace. The figuration of the ruler, all agree, conforms to no generally accepted model or pattern. In sum, the German Arthur is essentially a good man with noble impulses but flawed in his perception, court mores, and choice of members of the Round Table. In German eyes, the Arthurian court milieu is inadequate to the knightly protagonist.

Cormeau, narrowing his focus to Wirnt's *Wigalois* (1204-15) and Heinrich's *Crône* (1220-30), locates in a historical investigation of genre development the means to lay the groundwork for a close, serious consideration of the postclassical German romance (see also the research of Dorothea Müller). In 1977, the same year in which Cormeau's research appeared, J.W. Thomas produced a translation of *Wigalois* into English, subtitled *The Knight of Fortune's Wheel*, appending a detailed introduction of almost one hundred pages to the poem. According to his usual methodology, Thomas offers an introduction, a review of scholarship, a commentary, and a reliable rendering in prose. He observes that Wirnt's romance, which had broad appeal in its day, has suffered from literary criticism "strongly influenced by a sterile and outmoded positivism that has little appreciation of purely aesthetic matters" (1977, 70). Thomas's challenge has been taken up by several essay volumes (Göller, Schulze-Belli and Dallapiazza, Wolfzettel, Haug and Wachinger), all of which seek to open the canon even wider. For example, there is an essay by Walter Haug, "Von *aventiure* und *minne*," on the anonymous *Reinfried von Braunschweig* (after 1291), which he calls a high-courtly novel of adventure.

Peter Kern, writing in 1981, cites Cormeau and Gürttler when interpreting the Arthurian tales of Der Pleier (fl. 1260). Kern's is an early direct assault on epigonism as a category of criticism. A measure of the success of revisionist research is the disappearance from literary histories of the adjective *epigonenhaft* ("epigonous, decadent"), where it had appeared as a descriptive yet pejorative term. Among those contributing to a fresh understanding of the aesthetics of German Arthurian romance are Klaus M. Schmidt, whose conceptual glossary for the *Lanzelet* (ca. 1200) of Ulrich von Zatzikhoven opens the way for literary analysis, and Neil Thomas, who has investigated the revised canon. Thomas's research on the postclassical works is the most sustained and provocative. He argues vigorously—for example, regarding *Wigalois* by Wirnt von Grafenberg and *Gauriel von Muntabel* (which he attributes to Konrad von Stoffeln)—that

> the two authors' close, even proprietorial attitude to the "canonical" works springs from their identification with the values implied in their predecessors' narratives. This gives them a privileged title as critics of the classical romances. . . . Their two romances provide documentary evidence that the canonical romances, although admired, were not received uncritically [*Arthuriad*, 155].

Thanks particularly to Carola L. Gottzmann and James A. Schultz, it is now possible credibly to put forth a second tier of German Arthurian works, the postclassical, which includes theatrical presentations: *Ain hupsches vasnachtsspil*; *Anteloy*; Albrecht's *Jüngerer Titurel*; *Der Luneten Mantel*; Ulrich Fuetrer's *Prosa-Lantzilet* and *Buch der Abenteuer*; Heinrich von dem Türlin's *Diu Crône, Kinig Artus Hauf* (=*Widuwilt*); Konrad von Stoffeln's [?] *Gauriel von Muntabel*; *Mantel*; Der Pleier's *Garel von dem blühenden Tal*, *Meleranz*, and *Tandareis und Flordibel*; *Prosa-Lancelot*; Der Stricker's *Daniel von dem blühenden Tal*; Ulrich von Zatzikhoven's *Lanzelet*; *Vasnachtsspil mit der Kron*; *Wigamur*; Wirnt von Grafenberg's *Wigalois*; Claus Wisse and Philip Colin's *Parzival*. Of these later works, the two stimulating the most research are *Diu Crône* of Heinrich von dem Türlin and *Daniel von dem blühenden Tal* by Der Stricker, both from the first third of the thirteenth century. Also attracting interest are two other poems from the century, Albrecht's *Jüngerer Titurel* (Guggenberger) and the *Prosa-Lancelot*, the latter the subject of a colloquium which resulted in a special issue of *Wolfram-Studien* (vol. 9, 1986). The inclusion of German Tristan tales in the discussion of Arthurian literature is still somewhat controversial, although it is strongly ratified by Walter Haug ("Gottfrieds von Strassburg *Tristan*"), by me (*Arthur and Tristan*), and by Carola L. Gottzmann (*Artusdichtung*).

Since both *Diu Crône* and *Daniel* have been translated into English, the conclusion suggests itself that a direct connection exists between translation and research. An additional aspect—the poet's lofty aims—helps explain the appeal of *Diu Crône*, a work of some 30,000 lines. J.W. Thomas, translator of Heinrich's romance, has this to say about the poet's ambitions: "Determined to outdo all competitors, the author made his narrative poem into a great storehouse of Arthurian lore, utilizing most of the popular themes and motifs of the period in ceaseless endeavors to astound and amuse" (ix; see Schröder 1992). In his 1992 article on *Diu Crône*, Neil Thomas resolves to find a thesis in a poem that he calls "rather prolix, sometimes comic, occasionally coarse" (169). For Thomas, the Arthurian court "is shown to be powerless and imperilled, entirely dependent for its salvation on the good offices of Gawein," who plays a "messianic role" (174). Gawein, the exemplar of chivalry, thus emerges in Arthurian criticism here and elsewhere as a kind of interpretive category, his preeminence serving as a sign both of authorial intention and of the relationship of writers to literary predecessors (see Thomas, 1989 [*Arthuriad*], 152–153, on Gawein in *Wigalois*).

Similarly enlightening are the remarks of Michael Resler, the translator of Der Stricker's *Daniel*. He makes the point that Der Stricker was undertaking an experiment with his poem, the boldness of which has drawn (not always favorable) scholarly interest:

Frequently Der Stricker has been labelled a poor epigone, even a reactionary for his melding of older, outmoded literary strains with the new and fashionable Arthurian romance. Yet once one discards the artificial standards of the century past, a realization emerges that *Daniel*—the first original, self-conceived German romance centering on the Arthurian legend—is fully able to stand alone and be judged on its own merits [lii].

Resler refutes past critical assumptions, largely negative, but the fact that he believes it necessary to do so as recently as 1990 is testimony to their staying power. The current challenge to *Daniel* scholarship is to move beyond sterile questions of taxonomy to fresh critical approaches. An example of the latter is Albrecht Classen's reading (1991), which emphasizes the instruction, the moral suasion, of the text. Classen argues that Der Stricker has created a protagonist of intelligence and cleverness: "Die Vorbildlichkeit des Helden ruht nicht mehr in seiner Tugendhaftigkeit, sondern in seiner Fähigkeit, seine Intelligenz flexibel einzusetzen und sich stets auf neue Situationen einzustellen."[9] Sharp-wittedness and cunning are also categories of criticism in Jürgen Egyptien's treatment of *Daniel*; he extends these, as well, to *Garel von dem blühenden Tal* by Der Pleier. Egyptien's monograph, which concerns *Verstädterung* ("urbanization") in late-medieval Germany, brings into relief the tendencies isolated in the present study: appreciation for postclassical poems, attempts to establish principles of aesthetics, and sociohistory as the refracting lens for literary criticism.

The second area of consensus is unstated but readily apparent from the critical literature. For all the attention paid to postclassical writings, the exploration of which has sharpened appreciation for later medieval aesthetics in general, current research is preoccupied with topics that came to prominence during the 1970s. There are exceptions (for instance, the investigation of rhetorical patterns), but for the most part contemporary debates proceed from the preoccupations and categories of an earlier time, such as the nature of court culture and courtly ideals (Kaiser; J.-D. Müller); the qualities of noble society (Jaeger); the significance of patrons and sponsors of the arts (McDonald, Bumke); literary reception (Unger); the efficacy of the "idea of knighthood" (Arentzen; Ruberg); structuralist poetics (Simon, Schultz); the role of the narrator (Nellmann); genre theory (D. Müller); the relevance of psychological, mythological, and fairy-tale theory for interpretation

---

[9] "The hero is worthy of imitation, not for his rectitude, but for his capacity to enlist his intelligence with flexibility, and for his continual readiness for new situations" (189).

(Giesa, Ebenbauer and Wyss); the subject of political sovereignty (Thum 1979); the contribution of women to the literary scene (Bennewitz, Henderson); the representation of reality in the arts (Classen); and the place of the *ministeriales* in the hierarchical structure of society and in the composition of Arthurian poems.

In important respects, then, scholars are working out the postulates and thematic concerns that were first articulated years ago. An example is the theories of Erich Auerbach in *Mimesis* regarding the place of questing literature. He contends that a "self-portrayal of feudal knighthood with its mores and ideals is the fundamental purpose of courtly romance" (131), and his thesis—that the aristocratic elite found, through literary adventure, a validation of its power and mission—has proved authoritative, as has his stance on narrative fantasy. Modern scholarship, in its emphasis on the social context of German Arthurian literature as recently emblematized in Ursula Liebertz-Grün's volume in the series Deutsche Literatur: Eine Sozialgeschichte (ed. Horst A. Glaser), tends to be backward-looking in its inspiration. Thus it is that James A. Schultz conducts a structural analysis of German Arthurian romance by seeking semantic building blocks. His book, were it not for its recognition of "less familiar romances," might have been written decades ago. Surprisingly, scholars, when analyzing the romances, neglect religious belief; they replace theology with an amorphous social dimension and a kind of structuralist poetics that is almost parodical in its use of jargon: "Individualität ist die Leerstelle dialogisierender Stimmen und Texte."[10] Of all the structuralist studies on German Arthurian literature, the most valuable is one of the earliest: Hugo Kuhn's pioneering investigation of the similarities between *Artusstruktur* ("the tectonics of the Arthurian romance") and the epic architecture of the bridal quest. It was Kuhn who as early as 1959 argued that one must distinguish sharply between *soziale Realität* ("social reality") and *dichterische Fiktion* ("poetic invention"), a play of contrasts that continues to influence critical perspectives on German Arthurian romance.

It is not surprising that the most influential Arthurian study remains the 1973 monograph by Gert Kaiser. His subtitle has become a kind of

---

[10] "Individuality is the blank space between discoursing voices and texts" (Simon, 202).

catchword: *Aspekte einer sozialgeschichtlichen Interpretation* . . . ("Aspects of a Sociohistorical Interpretation"). Since Kaiser's book helped set the context for the critical discussion, it went into a second edition, which is indicative of its status. Following Kaiser's lead on the relevance of social, economic, legal, and constitutional forces for interpreting the romances of King Arthur, researchers, primarily in Germany, adopted a sociohistorical slant on the Arthurian tales.[11] The best example of this approach is the Hartmann volume by Hubertus Fischer. Devoting fully a third of his book to what he calls the *historische Ort der Gattung* ("historical locus of the genre"), concerning courtly society and the mission of the protagonist, Fischer looks to the historical method to provide a poetics of the romance. He is joined in this methodology by Otfrid Ehrismann and Hans Heinrich Kaminsky, who, while admitting the value of the Arthurian stories as entertainment, stress those factors that make the texts both a critique of social reality and a means to validation in knightly society. The social dimension is again prominent in Will Hasty's definition of knightly adventure. His views emerge most clearly from an analysis of Wolfram's *Parzival*:

> . . . The guilt of court society as a whole is overcome by Parzival in knightly combat, in the performance of the adventure. . . . The hero is not merely an individual desperately seeking the proper personal relationship to God, but rather the representative figure of the court as a whole, a scale-model messiah fulfilling functions dictated by the secular interests of a developing court society [41].

If the Arthurian romance is the most significant narrative expression of the knightly-courtly culture and worldview, as Rolf Bräuer has said, then its configurations and concerns are decidedly social and philosophical, widening the net that must be cast to embrace the genre.

Kaiser's willingness to blend the psychological and social aspects of Arthurian romance has been particularly influential, for example, as regards the class, or estate, of the *ministeriales*. This amorphous group of retainers, who in Germany were traditionally servile, were involved

---

[11] The sociohistorical approach has been so dominant that already in 1977 Helmut Brall saw the need for a status report. Even in scholarship in which the social aspect does not overshadow the others (for example, Voss 1983), the author privileges sociocultural norms (*soziokulturelle Normen*), alluding to them in the subheading to his book.

in the composition, performance, and preservation of Arthurian literature (Bumke, 1976; 1986). Hartmann von Aue and Wolfram von Eschenbach are usually cited as the most prominent artists belonging to this social station, which was very concerned with status. Kaiser's thesis is that the standing of the historical poet influenced the narrative statement—as wish-fulfillment. To make his case, Kaiser raises the issue of the strong identification of the poet with his subject matter (*Identifikationsangebot*). The writer's achievement lies, according to Kaiser, in self-interpretation (*Selbstinterpretation*), as he projects onto the stories his own societal encumbrances and expectations for noble existence. The creative act leads to awareness of self (*Selbstverständnis*) within the community of aristocrats. Seen against this backdrop, Hartmann's *Iwein* and *Erec* contribute to social discourse, according to which the Arthurian story affirms the knightly caste to which the poet belongs.

A full articulation of these ideas is found in Thomas Cramer's conclusion to his modern prose translation of Hartmann's *Erec*, commonly called the first German Arthurian tale:

War also die Aufgabe, Ritter zu sein, ursprünglich den Ministerialen zudiktiert, so bedeutet dies: ein niederer, unfreier Stand übt einen wenig geschätzten Beruf aus, der gleichwohl zur Erhaltung der bestehenden Gesellschaftsform von eminenter Wichtigkeit ist. Dieser Befund ist für die Einschätzung der Funktion des Artusromans von ganz fundamentaler Bedeutung; denn es scheint sich zunächst ein ganz eindeutiger Sachverhalt zu ergeben: Die ersten Artusromane (in Deutschland) sind geschrieben von Ministerialen. Der unterprivilegierte Stand der Ministerialenritter stellt sich selbst, also die Ritter, entgegen der Wirklichkeit literarisch so dar, als sei diese Existenzform etwas äußerst Erstrebenswertes. Die ständische Bezeichung Ritter wird beladen mit ideologischen Wertvorstellungen, so daß Rittersein nun nicht mehr als Berufstätigkeit beschrieben wird, die einem bestimmten (niederen) Stand auferlegt ist, sondern als Partizipation an einer stilisierten sozialen Aura. Treten also im Artusroman Könige, Königssöhne und Grafen als Ritter auf, so ist dies nicht Bild der sozialen Wirklichkeit, sondern Ideologie.[12]

---

[12] "The task of being a knight, thrust upon the *ministeriales*, meant that those of a low, unfree social station practiced a little-valued profession, which at the same time was of utmost importance in preserving the existing societal structure. This finding is fundamental for assessing the function of the Arthurian romance, since . . . the first such poems in Germany were written by ministerials. The underprivileged caste of ministerial-knights portrays itself . . . poetically [in Arthurian literature], in stark contrast to reality,

Here are the outlines for a discussion that has continued for two decades and has had its share of controversy. Speaking of the knightly adventure in fiction, Will Hasty identifies as Marxist in orientation the sociological approach, which "in its critical bias . . . has traditionally attempted to challenge hermetic, formalistic interpretations by relating the adventure to the plight of the subservient class of *ministeriales* at the large courts" (7–8). At its worst, the sociohistorical dimension is reflexively invoked to account for internal and external reality, reducing Arthurian poet and poem to category and stereotype. That this method is pervasive is shown when, as recently as 1988, Klaus Grubmüller attacks it in reference to the narrative poetry of Hartmann von Aue. Seeking to cast doubt on the existence of a *Kommunikations-gemeinschaft* ("communication fellowship") made up of the *ministeriales*, Grubmüller (1988) asks to what extent one can reconstruct the interests of this social group (228). "Die Wortgeschichte ist gerade in der Ritterfrage ein Teil der Sozialgeschichte," Kaiser argues in another place (1985, 39).[13] It is precisely this kind of reductionist claim that Grubmüller targets (1988). He impresses upon the reader the doubtful efficacy of purely sociological readings of Hartmann's poetry: "Hartmann, der gebildete Ritter, Ministeriale derer zu Aue . . . , wird nicht auf eine ständische Perspektive festzulegen sein . . ." (228).[14] In this spirit, Rudolf Voss, when treating Hartmann's Arthurian romances, can speak of sociocultural norms, but he clearly is prepared to counterbalance these with the precepts of the Christian faith.

---

as if knighthood were a type of existence well worth striving after. The social position and vocational-designation 'Ritter' is so fraught with ideological expostulation and value judgments that being a knight is no longer described as an occupation which is the lot of a lower social stratum, but rather as participation in a stylized, social milieu. In the Arthurian romance, when kings, princes and counts appear as knights, this reflects not social reality, but ideology" (447–448).

[13] "In the case of knights/knighthood, etymology is a branch of social history" ("Der Ritter in der deutschen Literatur des Mittelalters."

[14] "Hartmann, the educated knight, ministerial at Aue . . . , cannot be circumscribed by a societal perspective."

Returning to Cramer's phrase that addresses knighthood as an ideological concept, "Partizipation an einer stilisierten sozialen Aura" (448), we see that it contains two recurrent terms in scholarship, "stylized" and "social." Mention of stylization underscores the essential fictitiousnᴜss at the core of the genre. Already in 1982, Per Nykrog brought the topic of Arthurian romance as fiction into the critical discussion, where it has since enjoyed extraordinary currency (see, recently, Mertens 1993). The *matière de Bretagne*, as Ehrismann and Kaminsky reason, induced the audience to become sensitive in unprecedented degree to fantasy and to suspend the boundary between reality and fictionality (175). All critics acknowledge the (sometimes tenuous) relation between courtly fiction and social reality in the German Arthurian tales, between what George T. Gillespie calls ideal and real images of knightly endeavor and love. All agree that the romances not only reflect, but also shape reality. Cramer, drawing on the research of Johanna Maria van Winter, speaks of the Arthurian stories as representing a form of social utopia: the conscious removal of the romances from the flow of history allegedly bespeaks an ideological program. A recent exploration of Arthurian fact and fancy is by Harald Haferland, who muses over *soziale Realität* in his examination of the intersecting poetological categories, *die mögliche Wirklichkeit der höfischen Epik* ("the possible truth-value of courtly narrative poetry"), and *die Realität der höfischen Gesellschaft* ("the reality of courtly society," 12). This kind of philosophical and interpretive designation is anticipated by Karl Bertau, who has spoken of *verifizierbare Wirklichkeit* ("verifiable reality") in respect to Wolfram's narrative poetry (1976, 146ff.).

The duality to which Haferland and scores of others refer is a needed reminder that the German stories of King Arthur are neither pure fiction nor the faithful replication of the feudal milieu of the individual poet but are instead a peculiar amalgam that owes to real life a sometimes elusive debt. Scholarly concern with fantasy, history, and story has in turn reinvigorated the time-honored debate over truth and fiction in medieval narrative literature. So popular is the pairing of fictionality and the Arthurian romance that it was the topic of a recent conference, papers of which were collected by Mertens and Wolfzettel. Of those exploring the limits of poetic invention—indeed, fabrication—Walter Haug has made the most lasting contribution. The same can be said of Haug's studies on the later medieval period in general, which are fundamental; his 1971 essay on Wolfram, "Die Symbolstruktur . . . ," is arguably the beginning of the reassessment of the aesthetics of the German Arthurian romance. Haug identifies *programmatische Fiktionalität* ("programmatic fictionality") in the prologue to Hartmann's *Iwein*, for example (1985 [*Literaturtheorie*], 118ff.). Haug has argued in his "Wandlungen des Fiktionalitäts-bewußtseins" that authorial consciousness of fictional discourse as fiction increases from the twelfth century onward, providing a line of demarcation between the high and late Middle Ages. It should be observed that Haug and other researchers, in their conception of fictitiousness, are indebted to the theories of narrative articulated by Wolfgang Iser.

"Social," the second aspect mentioned by Cramer, continues to influence interpretation of the Arthurian stories. For example, the standard monograph on Hartmann von Aue by Cormeau and Störmer devotes an entire section to the German aristocracy of ca. 1200, a discussion intended to promote the thesis that the Arthurian romance is a vehicle for the self-awareness of nobles. Cormeau and Störmer explain key feudal terminology, social stratification, political developments, old versus new noble families, changes in enfeoffment practices, and the link between classical education and the writing of vernacular literature. Attention to the social sphere thus complements the older, philological component of criticism, so-called historical phenomenology, which concerns the manuscript record of the text, the chronology of individual works, and the biography of the historical poet.

Awareness of the social context within which Arthurian literature arose is, to state it again, the dominant critical mode of recent years. Social influences behind the Arthurian romance are unquestionably important, and sometimes fundamental, to interpretation. There are basic difficulties, however, beginning with imprecise definitions of the term "social" itself. It now signifies a variety of topics and elicits a range of responses, not all of which are predictable. One reason for the difficulty is the preponderance of overlapping terms, such as "self," a ubiquitous key word that has valence in the sociological, anthropological, historical, literary, and psychological realms. An index of the current scholarly discussion is the flood of compounds with *selbst* ("self"), as, for example, *Selbstbewußtsein* ("self-awareness, self-assurance"), *Selbstverständnis* ("self-knowledge"), and *Selbstverwirklichung* ("self-realization"), which threatens to make the German Arthurian romance a playground for social psychology and psychohistory. With John F. Benton, we acknowledge that consciousness of self and perceptions of individuality are a mark of twelfth-century culture and literature. It seems another matter, however, to engage in psychological speculation over romance hero/heroine and historical ministerial alike, positing the identity of the two in fiction and creating interpretive categories from such words as *Selbstverständnis*. This is not to state that psychology and its subfields are inappropriate to literary criticism of Arthurian romance. Assuming that the standards that we would apply to other methods of criticism obtain, psychology proves a useful interpretive tool. Undeniably, the ministerials' social climbing and striving for recognition, witnessed in the projection of self onto literary fiction, are legitimate topics of inquiry.

The very blurring of lines of intellectual demarcation, the blending of fields of inquiry (history, sociology, psychology), has resulted in interdisciplinary assays into German Arthurian romance. Of critical perspectives, the psychological holds special appeal, revealing a central concern of scholarship. An early and perhaps extreme example from the formative 1970s is Rolf Endres's treatment of *psychologische Strukturen* ("psychological structures/constructs") in the medieval text. (See also the research of Monica Meinert.) Also from this period are the provocative essays by Wolfgang Beutin on psychoanalytical categories as a means for interpreting Middle High German sources. Beutin's analysis of the *Lebensweg* ("path through life") of the literary hero has complemented his other evaluations of the relationship between literature and psychology. Controversial are such psychological speculations regarding Wolfram's *Parzival* as Karl Bertau's treatment of the allegedly aggressive fantasies of the poet (with reference to ego structure), Walter Blank's theory that Parzival might be a melancholic, and Dieter Welz's employment of psychoanalytical socialization theory. More persuasive is the Jungian reading of Wolfram's Gawein figure by Winder McConnell and Walter Suess, which, appearing in a specialized periodical, attests to the persistence and seriousness of analytical psychology as a means to literary analysis (see also McConnell 1992). The potential of the psychological method is realized in the intelligent and well-received essays collected by Ulrich Müller et al., which are the fruit of an international symposium under the broad title *Psychologie in der Mediaevistik* ("Psychology in Medieval Studies"). As might be expected, two of those articles (Schmitt, Krause) concern Iwein's insanity; but another breaks fresh ground in surveying in a single study the feminine principle and mythical reception of Hartmann's *Iwein* (Steiner). Oral communication, a dimension with psychological resonance, is the topic of a monograph by Herta Zutt concerning speech acts within *Iwein*, which has become the most popular of Hartmann's poems.

Among German Arthurian poets, Hartmann von Aue enjoys almost universal critical favor and has attracted the greatest scholarly interest in recent times. In explaining the former neglect of his work, Susan L. Clark rightly observes that Hartmann did not benefit "from the exposure that good English translations bring" (3). Clark's unspoken assumption is that scholars are increasingly dependent on translators, as knowledge of Middle High German declines in Europe and in the United States. Whereas the standard modern German translations of *Iwein* and *Erec* were made by Thomas Cramer in 1968 and 1972, respectively, it was only in 1979 that J.W. Thomas authoritatively rendered *Iwein* into English and in 1982 that he brought out *Erec*. Not to be underestimated is the access that these translations allow, for a share of the "changing perspectives" on Hartmann von Aue, to use the words of McFarland and Ranawake, is surely attributable to them.

Hartmann's *Erec* and *Iwein* have been viewed from an impressive number of angles in recent times. Among these approaches are the fairy tale, enlisted by Gerhard Giesa as an interpretive key (with a bow to C.G. Jung); psychology, which Burkhardt Krause examines as it relates, in *Iwein*, to communication and interaction; and medicine, which is the basis for Michael Graf's analysis of *Iwein*. Although the insanity of the protagonist occupies most of his book, Graf contends that the affective states of love, anger, and sorrow or grief also play a part under the designation "pathogenesis." Ample documentation now exists on medicine in the Middle Ages, and it is possible to make use of the healing arts for literary interpretation; witness the remarks by Saul N. Brody on leprosy in *Der arme Heinrich* of Hartmann von Aue (148ff.; see also Meister; Haage 1993, 519–554). However, since Brody limited the scope of his inquiry to a single malady, the question remains whether it is possible to extrapolate a general critical perspective from our knowledge of medieval medicine.

The third area of scholarly consensus flows from the sociohistorical perspective that has dominated research for over two decades. It is the belief that the fullest articulation of the social dimension in the German Arthurian romance is courtliness itself, in all its permutations, such as civility, ceremony, manners, manhood, and gracious living. Following the intensive critical scrutiny of recent times, court culture and its semantic field are accepted as a full field of inquiry. One salutary result is clarification of the loosely employed epithet *höfisch* ("courtly"), which requires careful qualifiers as, for example, when one uses "courtly literature" as a genre designation. Fundamental scholarship on the ideals of courtliness dates from the late 1970s, when it was merely one more of those topics falling under the sociology of literature. Peter Ganz then began examining the use and misuse of the designation *höfisch* in scholarship. Instantly clear was the need for research on the social influences and contexts of court ethics, as well as on the etymology of the German vocabulary of gentility. Ganz (1986; 1990) has helped to expand the semantic range of German courtesy terminology to include Latin equivalents: *curialis* now vies for attention with *cortois*.

Gert Kaiser, mentioned above for his landmark sociohistorical work on Hartmann's Arthurian romances, has also made his influence felt here, in a book on courtly literature, court society, and courtly life—*Höfische Literatur*—which he coedited with Jan-Dirk Müller following a 1983 conference. Not published until 1986, the articles in the volume include Kaiser's own on the Arthurian court and love, as well as Ganz's important investigation of the term *höfisch* (see also Kaiser's collection, *An den Grenzen höfischer Kultur*). There followed three books on court culture, the importance of which can scarcely be overstated. The authors are C. Stephen Jaeger (1985), Joachim Bumke (1986; English version 1991), and Aldo Scaglione (1991). Casting a wide net to include medieval Latin and national literatures other than German, all three scholars argue that the study of courtesy, courts, and courtiers has been seriously neglected and that courtliness, as a social phenomenon, is a firm base upon which aesthetics and literary analysis may rest. As Jaeger expresses it, the court ideal became the literary ideal, nourishing the chivalric narrative (e.g., *Parzival*, *Erec*, and

*Iwein*), which espouses a sublime ethical code (242). In *Iwein*, Hartmann von Aue explores the borders and limits of courtliness, which extend from fine clothes to "compassion and a refined and humane sense of respect for the feelings of others."[15] Read as primers on civility, Hartmann's Arthurian romances advance the melding of ceremony, manners, conviviality, polite speech—and humanism—that modern scholarship understands as "courtly."

Finally, it should be mentioned that researchers, prompted by the findings just alluded to, have intensified their efforts to appreciate courtly forms and norms. I am thinking here of the books by Harald Haferland (1988), Hedda Ragotzky and Horst Wenzel (1990), Josef Fleckenstein (1990), and Gert Kaiser (1991), as well as the essay sketching the state of research by Bumke (1992). In this last, Bumke's premise is that the recent flood of scholarship on courtliness makes it time now for taking stock. Although the critical dialogue about court culture ranges over many works and aspects of courtesy, it is arguable that the Arthurian romance has benefited most from the discussion. Female courtliness, for example, is now in our field of vision, thanks especially to Susann Samples. Her thesis, applied to *Diu Crône* of Heinrich von dem Türlin, is that Guinevere is the female representative and embodiment of idealized courtliness. We close with the observation that the concept of courtly love has not elicited great controversy among German scholars. In Fleckenstein's volume, devoted to courtly-chivalric culture, Rüdiger Schnell (1990) offers a status report on the question, thus complementing Joachim Bumke's discussion in his volume *Courtly Culture* (1986; 1991). Bumke summarizes the meaning of courtly love as societal ideal by claiming that "Courtly love was a thing of social value which manifested itself in the practice of courtly virtues and the adherence to courtly etiquette. Courtly love was the love of a person who was striving for courtly perfection" (374).

---

[15] Jaeger, 243. See also William C. McDonald, who examines the language of courtesy in Hartmann's *Iwein* (in "Observations on the Language of Courtesy") and locates a sophisticated system of communication, that is intended to illustrate how a courtly person (*ein hövesch man*) should behave.

## Work in Progress and Desiderata

A major German publisher, Deutscher Klassiker Verlag in Frankfurt am Main, has set up a translation series, Bibliothek des Mittelalters, to be completed about 1995. Begun in 1987 with the *Carmina Burana*, the series has Walter Haug as general editor. The format is bilingual, the Middle High German or Latin original accompanied by a modern German translation; detailed commentaries are planned. Laudable is the intention to translate the *Prosa-Lancelot* (in five volumes, trans. Hans-Hugo Steinhoff), which promises to inspire research on a poem whose overall structural conception is as yet dark. (Professor Steinhoff of Paderborn is engaged in a long-term project on the same work, a *Namenwörterbuch*, a compendium of proper nouns.) Less salutary is the decision of the Deutscher Klassiker Verlag to publish still another rendering of Hartmann's *Erec* and *Iwein*, Gottfried's *Tristan*, as well as Wolfram's *Parzival*. (This last is stranger yet, since the translator, Dieter Kühn, has already published significant sections of the poem in his volume on Wolfram von Eschenbach and *Parzival*.) Since very few of the German postclassical Arthurian romances are available in English or modern German, these should now take priority over further translations of canonical texts.

The canon is also Thomas Elwood Hart's concern in his ongoing project on mathematically oriented design techniques in medieval literature. As sketched in his studies on *Parzival* (1989; 1991), Hart's method is to ascertain the presence of numerical composition (e.g., proportion) and to bring his data to bear on literary interpretation. Besides *Parzival*, Hart intends to treat *Iwein* and the increasingly popular *Daniel* of Der Stricker. Notably, Hart does not confine himself to German works; *Sir Gawain and the Green Knight* also falls within his purview.

As planned and pending, the bibliographical periodical *Germanistik* listed the following editing projects as of spring 1992, without the names of the editors: Ulrich von Zatzikhoven, *Lanzelet*; Wirnt von Grafenberg, *Wigalois*; Heinrich von dem Türlin, *Der Aventiure Crône*; Konrad von Stoffeln, *Gauriel von Muntabel*; and Albrecht, *Der jüngere Titurel*. The extent of the activity seen here is both verification of the need for modern critical editions and testimony to the importance of the postclassical romances.

The most recent of Klaus M. Schmidt's important conceptual glossaries and indices, *Begriffsglossar und Index zu Ulrichs von Zatzikhoven Lanzelet* (1993), uses the COBOL and PASCAL DIGITAL DBMS system to create an index organized according to *lemmata*, as well as to concepts and ideas, such as human beings, man as a social being, knighthood, and weapons. The book fills a gap in postclassical studies and affirms the utility of computer-assisted content analysis and conceptual text analysis. Working in collaboration with the University of Kiel, Schmidt's team at Bowling Green State University plans a series of conceptual glossaries and indices to include Der Stricker's *Daniel* and the works of Hartmann von Aue.

Despite the recent surge in interest in German Arthuriana, lacunae remain, especially in regard to the so-called postclassical romances. For these, we need modern critical editions, translation editions, and bibliographies. To illustrate, for textual passages Roland Rossbacher cites the edition of Ulrich von Zatzikhoven's *Lanzelet* from 1845 (ed. Hahn). Jürgen Egyptien looks back even farther, listing in his bibliography of primary literature Georg F. Benecke's 1819 edition of *Wigalois* by Wirnt von Grafenberg. Not all postclassical poems have been reprinted, and even if they have been, reprints with a "modern" introduction and a current bibliography cannot substitute for a new edition. Commenting on the need for such an edition of *Diu Crône* of Heinrich von dem Türlin, Werner Schröder (1992) expresses the wish that the editors not content themselves with mere "improved" reproductions of manuscripts. He envisions a fundamentally new critical edition, using recent scholarship, particularly on the manuscript fragments.

That the two critical editions just mentioned are from the nineteenth century is not the exception but the rule. Curiously, editions of the postclassical Arthurian romances appeared during the past century, when critical appreciation for them was very slight. The edition of *Diu Crône* (ed. Scholl) dates from 1852, *Gauriel von Muntabel* (ed. Khull) from 1885, Der Pleier's *Garel von dem blühenden Tal* (ed. Walz) from 1892 and his *Meleranz* (ed. Bartsch) from 1861, and *Tandareis* (ed. Khull) from 1885, *Der Mantel* (ed. Warnatsch) from 1883, *Parzival* of Wisse and Colin (ed. Schorbach) from 1888, and Ulrich Fuetrer's *Prosaroman von Lanzelot* (ed. Peter) from 1885. These editions should be redone, one reason being that they are difficult of access. Not all have been reprinted, and even the reissues, dating from 1965 to 1974, are not easy to obtain.[16] The older editions, let it be stressed, are not defective for reasons of age alone; they are unsafe to rely on because they have not benefited from manuscript finds and advances in editorial practices. Even the edition of *Wigalois* from this century, by J.M.N. Kapteyn (1926), fails to meet modern standards. There are three striking exceptions: in 1983, Michael Resler brought out the critical edition of Der Stricker's *Daniel von dem blühenden Tal* (Altdeutsche Textbibliothek, 92); in 1987, Danielle Buschinger edited *Wigamur*, under the general editorial supervision of Ulrich Müller (Göppinger Arbeiten zur Germanistik, 320); in 1989 Karl-Eckhard Lenk edited some 1,100 strophes of Ulrich Fuetrer's *Lannzilet*, which is from the poet's *Buch der Abenteuer* (Altdeutsche Textbibliothek, 102).

The postclassical poems mentioned in this study as requiring new critical editions remain for the most part untranslated and thus are inaccessible to an English-speaking audience. (This is in contrast to the classical romances, for which there is almost a surfeit of translations, most recently Lambertus Okken's *Hartmann von Aue erzählt* of 1992; see also Wehrli.) To have its greatest effect, a critical edition should be followed by a translation. The two, edition and translation, may therefore be viewed in tandem, neither of full value without the other. The best illustration is the work of Resler, who translated into English the text of the critical edition that he had edited, *Daniel von dem blühenden Tal*, as *Daniel of the Blossoming Valley*, for the Garland Library of Medieval Literature. The critical edition therefore provides a solid philological basis for the translation, which in turn has introduced the poem to readers who have no German. As the rendering of Eilhart's *Tristrant* by J.W. Thomas has shown, a reliable translation

---

[16] Even the reprints proceed from differing editorial conceptions. For example, the Karl Bartsch edition of Der Pleier's *Meleranz*, originally published in 1861 in Stuttgart by the Litterarischer Verein, was reprinted in 1974 by Olms Verlag (Hildesheim) with a concluding essay, including bibliography, by Alexander Hildebrand. In contrast, the Gottlob H.F. Scholl edition of *Diu Crône* by Heinrich von dem Türlin, originally published in 1852 in Stuttgart, again by the Litterarischer Verein, was reprinted in 1966 by Rodopi (Amsterdam) exactly as in 1852, that is, without any modern essay or bibliography. Also a "mere" reprint is the edition, Ulrich Fuetrer, *Prosaroman von Lanzelot*, ed. Arthur Peter, 1885; rpt. Hildesheim: Olms, 1972.

can stimulate interest and research, and the same could be expected for the postclassical German Arthurian romances.

Here again, it is Thomas, the pioneer and premier translator, who shows the way, offering with the *Wigalois* of Wirnt von Grafenberg in 1977 the first English translation of a "second-tier" romance since the version of Ulrich von Zatzikhoven's *Lanzelet* in 1951 by Kenneth G.T. Webster, which was revised by Roger Sherman Loomis. Thomas made a further contribution by his 1989 rendering of *Diu Crône*, as *The Crown*, which attracted favorable attention and received wide circulation. He provides the coda to our plea for new editions and translations by noting that Scholl's edition of *Diu Crône* from 1852 occasionally "makes little or no sense" (xxiv).

Other desiderata include bibliographies. Two types are desired, the specialty bibliography of research titles on a single poet (continuing, e.g., Elfriede Neubuhr's bibliography of Hartmann von Aue); and the annotated, descriptive bibliography for a literary genre or poet (updating Joachim Bumke's Wolfram von Eschenbach volume, for instance). We especially need bibliographies for the postclassical authors, beginning with Der Stricker and Heinrich von dem Türlin.

As bibliographical scholarship on Hartmann von Aue and Wolfram von Eschenbach shifts to exhaustive annotations of specialized areas, such as Okken's *Kommentar zur Artusepik Hartmanns von Aue* (1993), research on the postclassical romances is not even in the first bibliographical phase, namely a "rudimentary" compilation of titles of studies, without copious notes or detailed commentary. Such lists concerning poets and poems are necessary, as groundwork, if serious scholarship, bibliographical and other, is to follow. At present, the best summaries of literary criticism accompany the translations of Resler (*Daniel*) and Thomas (*Wigalois*; *Crône*).

# Bibliography

*Editions and Translations*

Benecke, G.F., K. Lachmann, and L. Wolff, eds.; Thomas Cramer, trans. *Iwein*, by Hartmann von Aue. 3rd ed. Berlin: de Gruyter, 1981.

Buschinger, Danielle, ed. *Wigamur*. Göppingen: Kümmerle, 1987.

Cramer, Thomas, trans. *Erec*, by Hartmann von Aue. Frankfurt am Main: Fischer, 1972.

Hatto, A.T., trans. *Parzival*, by Wolfram von Eschenbach. Harmondsworth: Penguin, 1980.

Keller, Thomas L., trans. *Erec*, by Hartmann von Aue. New York: Garland, 1987.

Leitzmann, Albert, ed. *Parzival*, by Wolfram von Eschenbach. 3 vols. 1905–06; 6th ed. Wilhelm Deinert. Tübingen: Niemeyer, 1961–65.

——, and Ludwig Wolff, eds. *Erec*, by Hartmann von Aue. 6th ed. Christoph Cormeau and Kurt Gärtner. Tübingen: Niemeyer, 1985.

Lenk, Karl-Eckhard, ed. *Lannzilet: Aus dem Buch der Abenteuer, Str. 1–1122*, by Ulrich Fuetrer. Tübingen: Niemeyer, 1989.

McConeghy, Patrick M., trans. *Iwein*, by Hartmann von Aue. New York: Garland, 1984.

Okken, Lambertus, trans. *Hartmann von Aue erzählt: Erec, Iwein oder der Löwenritter, Gregorius oder Der gute Sünder, Der arme Heinrich*, by Hartmann von Aue. Frankfurt am Main: Insel, 1992.

Resler, Michael, ed. *Daniel von dem Blühenden Tal*, by Der Stricker. Tübingen: Niemeyer, 1983.

————, trans. *Erec*, by Hartmann von Aue. Philadelphia: University of Pennsylvania Press, 1987.

————, trans. *Daniel of the Blossoming Valley*, by Der Stricker. New York: Garland, 1990.

Thomas, J.W., trans. *Wigalois, The Knight of Fortune's Wheel*, by Wirnt von Grafenberg. Lincoln: University of Nebraska Press, 1977.

————, trans. *Tristrant*, by Eilhart von Oberge. Lincoln: University of Nebraska Press, 1978.

————, trans. *Iwein, the Knight with the Lion*, by Hartmann von Aue. Lincoln: University of Nebraska Press, 1979.

————, trans. *Erec*, by Hartmann von Aue. Lincoln: University of Nebraska Press, 1982.

————, trans. *The Crown: A Tale of Sir Gawein und King Arthur's Court*, by Heinrich von dem Türlin. Lincoln: University of Nebraska Press, 1989.

Webster, Kenneth G.T., trans. *Lanzelet*, by Ulrich von Zatzikhoven. Rev. with additional notes and intro. by Roger Sherman Loomis. New York: Columbia University Press, 1951.

Wehrli, Mas, trans. *Iwein*, by Hartmann von Aue. 2nd ed. Zurich: Manesse, 1992.

*Studies*

Ackermann-Arlt, Beate. *Das Pferd und seine epische Funktion im mittelhochdeutschen Prosa-Lancelot*. Berlin: de Gruyter, 1990.

Andersen, Elizabeth. "Heinrich von dem Türlin's *Diu Crone* and the *Prose Lancelot*: An Intertextual Study." *Arthurian Studies*, 7 (1987), 23–49.

Arentzen, Jörg, and Uwe Ruberg, eds. *Die Ritteridee in der deutschen Literatur des Mittelalters: Eine kommentierte Anthologie*. Darmstadt: Wissenschaftliche Buchgesellschaft, 1987.

Arndt, Paul H. *Der Erzähler bei Hartmann von Aue: Formen und Funktionen seines Hervortretens und seiner Äußerungen*. Göppingen: Kümmerle, 1980.

Ashcroft, Jeffrey, Dietrich Huschenbett, and William Henry Jackson, eds. *Liebe in der deutschen Literatur des Mittelalters: St. Andrews-Colloquium 1985*. Tübingen: Niemeyer, 1987.

Auerbach, Erich. *Mimesis: The Representation of Reality in Western Literature*, trans. Willard R. Trask. Princeton: Princeton University Press, 1953.

Bäuml, Franz H. "Mittelalter." In *Geschichte der deutschen Literatur: Kontinuität und Veränderung. Band I: Vom Mittelalter bis zum Barock*. Tübingen: Francke, 1987, pp. 1–244.

Bastert, Bernd. *Der Münchner Hof und Fuetrers Buch der Abenteuer: Literarische Kontinuität im Spätmittelalter*. Frankfurt am Main: Lang, 1993.

Batts, Michael S. "Author and Public in the Late Middle Ages." In Kathryn Smits et al., eds., *Interpretation und Edition deutscher Texte des Mittelalters: Festschrift für John Asher*. Berlin: Schmidt, 1981, pp. 178–186.

Bayer, Hans. "'guotiu wip, hant die sin' (*Parz.* 827, 25). Wolfram von Eschenbach und der thüringische Landgrafenhof." *Euphorion*, 74 (1980), 55–76.

Behr, Hans-Joachim. *Literatur als Machtlegitimation: Studien zur Funktion der deutschsprachigen Dichtung am böhmischen Königshof im 13. Jahrhundert.* Munich: Fink, 1989.

Bennwitz, Ingrid. ed. *Der frauwen buoch: Versuche zu einer feministischen Mediävistik.* Göppingen: Kümmerle, 1989.

―――. "Feministische Literaturwissenschaft und Mediävistik: Versuche zur Positionsbestimmung." *Mitteilungen des Deutschen Germanistenverbandes*, 39 (1992), 33–36.

Benton, John F. "Consciousness of Self and Perception of Individuality." In Robert L. Benson and Giles Constable, eds., *Renaissance and Renewal in the Twelfth Century.* Cambridge, MA: Harvard University Press, 1982, pp. 263–295.

Berleth, Richard. *The Orphan Stone: The Minnesinger Dream of Reich.* Westport, CT: Greenwood, 1990.

Bertau, Karl. "Versuch über die Struktur einiger Aggressionsphantasien" (originally 1976). In *Wolfram von Eschenbach: Neun Versuche über Subjektivität und Ursprünglichkeit in der Geschichte.* Munich: Beck, 1983, pp. 126–144.

―――. "Versuch über Wolfram" (originally 1976). In *Wolfram von Eschenbach: Neun Versuche über Subjektivität und Ursprünglichkeit in der Geschichte.* Munich: Beck, 1983, pp. 145–165.

Beutin, Wolfgang. "Zum Lebensweg des 'Helden' in der mittelhochdeutschen Dichtung (*Erec, Iwein, Tristan, Parzival*): Bemerkungen aus psychoanalytischer Sicht." *Zeitschrift für Literaturwissenschaft und Linguistik*, 7 (1977), 39–57.

————. *Sexualität und Obszönität: Eine literaturpsychologische Studie über epische Dichtungen des Mittelalters und der Renaissance.* Würzburg: Königshausen and Neumann, 1990.

Bitsch, Irmgard, Trude Ehlert, and Xenja von Ertzdorff, eds. *Essen und Trinken in Mittelalter und Neuzeit.* Sigmaringen: Thorbecke, 1987.

Blamires, David. "The German Arthurian Prose Romances in Their Literary Context." In Alison Adams, Armel H. Diverres, Karen Stern, and Kenneth Varty, eds., *The Changing Face of Arthurian Romance: Essays on Arthurian Prose Romances in Memory of Cedric E. Pickford.* Cambridge: Brewer, 1986, pp. 66–77.

Blank, Walter. "Wolframs Parzival—ein melancholicus?" In Udo Benzenhöfer, ed., *Melancholie in Literatur und Kunst.* Hürtgenwald: Pressler, 1990, pp. 29–47.

Boggs, Roy A. *Hartmann von Aue: Lemmatisierte Konkordanz zum Gesamtwerk.* 2 vols. Nendeln: KTO, 1979.

Brackert, Helmut. "*der lac an riterschefte tot.* Parzival und das Leid der Frauen." In Rüdiger Krüger et al., eds., *Ist zwivel herzen nachgebur: Günther Schweikle zum 60. Geburtstag.* Stuttgart: Helfant, 1989, pp. 143–163.

Brall, Helmut. "Zur sozialgeschichtlichen Interpretation mittelalterlicher Literatur: Anmerkungen zum Stand der Diskussion." *Zeitschrift für Literaturwissenschaft und Linguistik,* 7 (1977), 19–38.

Bräuer, Rolf, ed. *Dichtung des europäischen Mittelalters: Ein Führer durch die erzählende Literatur.* Munich: Beck, 1991.

Brody, Saul Nathaniel. *The Disease of the Soul: Leprosy in Medieval Literature.* Ithaca: Cornell University Press, 1974.

Brogsitter, Karl Otto. *Artusepik.* 2nd ed. Stuttgart: Metzler, 1971.

———. "Der Held im Zwiespalt und der Held als strahlender Musterritter: Anmerkungen zum Verlust der Konfliktträgerfunktion des Helden im deutschen Artusroman." In Friedrich Wolfzettel, ed., *Artusrittertum im späten Mittelalter: Ethos und Ideologie*. Giessen: Schmitz, 1984, pp. 16–27.

Brunner, Horst. "*Artus der wise höfische man*: Zur immanenten Historizität der Ritterwelt im *Parzival* Wolframs von Eschenbach." In *Germanistik in Erlangen*. Erlangen: Universitätsbund Erlangen-Nürnberg, 1983, pp. 61–73.

Bumke, Joachim. *Die Wolfram von Eschenbach-Forschung seit 1945: Bericht und Bibliographie*. Munich: Fink, 1970.

———. *Ministerialität und Ritterdichtung: Umrisse der Forschung*. Munich: Beck, 1976.

———. *Mäzene im Mittelalter: Die Gönner und Auftraggeber der höfischen Literatur in Deutschland, 1150–1300*. Munich: Beck, 1979.

———. *Höfische Kultur: Literatur und Gesellschaft im hohen Mittelalter*. 2 vols. Munich: Deutscher Taschenbuch Verlag, 1986.

———. *Geschichte der deutschen Literatur im hohen Mittelalter*. Munich: Deutscher Taschenbuch Verlag, 1990.

———. *Courtly Culture: Literature and Society in the High Middle Ages*, trans. Thomas Dunlap. Berkeley: University of California Press, 1991.

———. *Wolfram von Eschenbach*. 6th ed. Stuttgart: Metzler, 1991.

———. "Höfische Kultur: Versuch einer kritischen Bestandsaufnahme." *Beiträge zur Geschichte der deutschen Sprache und Literatur*, 114 (1992), 414–492.

Campbell, Karen J. "Some Types of Incoherence in Middle High German Epic." *Beiträge zur Geschichte der deutschen Sprache und Literatur*, 109 (1987), 350–374.

Clark, Susan L. *Hartmann von Aue: Landscapes of Mind.* Houston: Rice University Press, 1989.

Classen, Albrecht. "Keie in Wolframs von Eschenbach *Parzival*: 'Agent provocateur' oder Angeber?" *Journal of English and Germanic Philology*, 87 (1988), 382–405.

————. "Transformation des arthurischen Romans zum frühneuzeitlichen Unterhaltungs- und Belehrungswerk: Der Fall *Daniel vom Blühenden Tal.*" *Amsterdamer Beiträge zur älteren Germanistik*, 33 (1991), 167–192.

————. "Detail-Realismus im deutschen Spätmittelalter: Der Fall von des Strickers *Daniel von dem Blühenden Tal* und Konrads von Würzburg *Turnier von Nantes.*" *Studia Neophilologica*, 64 (1992), 195–220.

Cormeau, Christoph. "Zur Rekonstruktion der Leserdisposition am Beispiel des deutschen Artusromans." *Poetica*, 8 (1976), 120–133.

————. *Wigalois und Diu Crone: Zwei Kapitel zur Gattungsgeschichte des nachklassischen Aventiureromans.* Munich: Artemis, 1977.

————. "Zur Gattungsentwicklung des Artusromans nach Wolframs *Parzival.*" In Göller, ed., *Spätmittelalterliche Artusliteratur*, 1984, pp. 119–131.

————. "*Tandareis* und *Flordibel* von dem Pleier: Eine poetologische Reflexion über Liebe im Artusroman." In Haug and Wachinger, eds., *Positionen des Romans im späten Mittelalter*, 1991, pp. 39–53.

————, and Wilhelm Störmer. *Hartmann von Aue: Epoche-Werk-Wirkung.* Munich: Beck, 1985.

Cramer, Thomas. "Aspekte des höfischen Romans im 14. Jahrhundert." In Walter Haug, Timothy R. Jackson, and Johannes Janota, eds., *Zur deutschen Literatur und Sprache des 14. Jahrhunderts: Dubliner Colloquium 1981*. Heidelberg: Winter, 1983, pp. 208–220.

————. "*brangend unde brogent*: Repräsentation, Feste und Literatur in der höfischen Kultur des späten Mittelalters." In Ragotzky and Wenzel, eds., *Höfische Repräsentation: Das Zeremoniell und die Zeichen*, 1990, pp. 259–278.

De Boor, Helmut. *Die höfische Literatur: Vorbereitung, Blüte, Ausklang, 1170–1250*. 11th ed. by Ursula Hennig. Munich: Beck, 1991.

Decke-Cornill, Renate. "Wolfram-Bibliographie 1989/90 und Nachträge 1984–1988." *Wolfram-Studien*, 12 (1992), 244–276.

Dinzelbacher, Peter. "Gefühl und Gesellschaft im Mittelalter: Vorschläge zu einer emotionsgeschichtlichen Darstellung des hochmittelalterlichen Umbruchs." In Kaiser and Müller, eds., *Höfische Literatur, Hofgesellschaft, höfische Lebensformen um 1200*, pp. 213–241.

Duby, Georges. *Wirklichkeit und höfischer Traum: Zur Kultur des Mittelalters*. Berlin: Wagenbach, 1986.

Ebenbauer, Alfred, and Ulrich Wyss. "Der mythologische Entwurf der höfischen Gesellschaft im Artusroman." In Kaiser and Müller, eds., *Höfische Literatur, Hofgesellschaft, höfische Lebensformen um 1200*, 1986, pp. 513–539.

Eder, Annemarie. "Macht- und Ohnmachtsstrukturen im Beziehungsgefüge von Wolframs *Parzival*. Die Herzeloydentragödie." In Ingrid Bennewitz, ed., *Der frauwen buoch. Versuche zu einer feministischen Mediävistik*. Göppingen: Kümmerle, 1989, pp. 179–212.

Egyptien, Jürgen. *Höfisierter Text und Verstädterung der Sprache. Städtische Wahrnehmung als Palimpsest spätmittelalterlicher Versromane.* Würzburg: Königshausen and Neumann, 1987.

Ehrismann, Otfrid, and Hans Heinrich Kaminsky. *Literatur und Geschichte im Mittelalter.* Kronberg: Athenäum, 1976.

Endres, Rolf. "Über die gesellschaftliche Bedingtheit psychologischer Strukturen in der mittelhochdeutschen Literatur." *Zeitschrift für Literaturwissenschaft und Linguistik*, 3 (1973), 71–79.

Ertzdorff, Xenja von. "König Artus' site: 'nehein riter vor im az / des tages swenn aventiure vergaz / daz si sinen hof vermeit' (*Parz.* 309, 6ff.)." In Rüdiger Krüger et al., eds., *Ist zwivel herzen nachgebur: Günther Schweikle zum 60. Geburtstag.* Stuttgart: Helfant, 1989, pp. 193–201.

Fischer, Hubertus. *Ehre, Hof und Abenteuer in Hartmanns Iwein: Vorarbeiten zu einer historischen Poetik des höfischen Epos.* Munich: Fink, 1983.

Fleckenstein, Josef, ed. *Curialitas: Studien zu Grundfragen der höfisch-ritterlichen Kultur.* Göttingen: Vandenhoeck and Ruprecht, 1990.

Ganz, Peter. "Der Begriff des 'Höfischen' bei den Germanisten." *Wolfram-Studien*, 4 (1977), 16–32.

———. "*curialis/hövesch.*" In Kaiser and Müller, eds., *Höfische Literatur, Hofgesellschaft, höfische Lebensformen um 1200*, 1986, pp. 39–56.

———. "*hövesch/hövescheit* im Mittelhochdeutschen." In Fleckenstein, ed., *Curialitas: Studien zu Grundfragen der höfisch-ritterlichen Kultur*, 1990, pp. 39–54.

Gärtner, Kurt. "Concordances and Indices to Middle High German." *Computers and the Humanities*, 14 (1980), 39–45.

————, and Joachim Heinzle, eds. *Studien zu Wolfram von Eschenbach: Festschrift für Werner Schröder*. Tübingen: Niemeyer, 1989.

Gentry Francis G. "Hartmann von Aue's *Erec*: The Burden of Kingship." In Valerie M. Lagorio and Mildred Leake Day, eds., *King Arthur Through the Ages*. 2 vols. New York: Garland, 1990, I, 152–169.

Gibbs, Marion E. "The Role of Women in Wolfram's *Parzival.*" *German Life and Letters*, 21 (1968), 296–308.

Giesa, Gerhard. *Märchenstrukturen und Archetypen in den Artusepen Hartmanns von Aue*. Göppingen: Kümmerle, 1987.

————. "Der Artusroman als Märchen und exemplarischer Individuationsprozess." In *Tod und Wandel im Märchen: Nachmittagsvorträge und Referate zum Internationlen Märchenkongreß des Europäischen Märchengesellschaft in Salzburg, 14.–17.9. 1989*. Salzburg: Salzburger Landesinstitut für Volkskunde, 1990, pp. 21–35.

Gillespie, George T. "Real and Ideal Images of Knightly Endeavor and Love in the Works of Hartmann von Aue." In Timothy McFarland and Silvia Ranawake, eds., *Hartmann von Aue, Changing Perspectives: London Hartmann Symposium 1985*. Göppingen: Kümmerle, 1988, pp. 253–270.

Gilroy-Hirtz, Petra. "Der imaginierte Hof." In Kaiser and Müller, eds., *Höfische Literatur, Hofgesellschaft, höfische Lebensformen um 1200*, 1986, pp. 253–275.

Göller, Karl Heinz, ed. *Spätmittelalterliche Artusliteratur*. Paderborn: Schöningh, 1984.

Gottzmann, Carola L. *Deutsche Artusdichtung*. Frankfurt am Main: Lang, 1986.

———. *Artusdichtung*. Stuttgart: Metzler, 1989.

Graf, Michael. *Liebe-Zorn-Trauer-Adel: Die Pathologie in Hartmann von Aues Iwein. Eine Interpretation auf medizinhistorischer Basis.* Bern: Lang, 1989.

Grosse, Siegfried. "Die Erzählperspektive der gestaffelten Wiederholung: Calogreants *aventiure* in Hartmanns *Iwein.*" In Schnell, ed., *Gotes und der werlde hulde: Festschrift für Heinz Rupp*, 1989, pp. 82–96.

Grubmüller, Klaus. "Artusroman und Heilsbringerethos: Zum *Wigalois* des Wirnt von Gravenberg." *Beiträge zur Geschichte der deutschen Sprache und Literatur*, 107 (1985), 218–239.

———. "Artus- und Gralromane." In Ursula Liebertz-Grün, ed., *Aus der Mündlichkeit in die Schriftlichkeit. Höfische und andere Literatur, 750–1320.* Reinbek bei Hamburg: Rowohlt, 1988, pp. 216–235.

———. "Der Artusroman und sein König: Beobachtungen zur Artusfigur am Beispiel von Ginovers Entführung." In Haug and Wachinger, eds., *Positionen des Romans im späten Mittelalter*, 1991, pp. 1–20.

Guggenberger, Herbert. *Albrechts Jüngerer Titurel: Studien zur Minnethematik und zur Werkkonzeption.* Göppingen: Kümmerle, 1992.

Gumbrecht, Hans Ulrich. "Wie fiktional war der höfische Roman?" In Henrich and Iser, eds., *Funktionen des Fiktiven*, 1983, pp. 433–440.

Gürttler, Karin R. *Künec artus der guote: Das Artusbild der höfischen Epik des 12. und 13. Jahrhunderts.* Bonn: Bouvier, 1976.

———. "German Arthurian Literature (Medieval)." In Norris J. Lacy et al., eds., *The New Arthurian Encyclopedia.* New York: Garland, 1991, pp. 182–188.

Haage, Bernhard Dietrich. "Vom Nutzen interdisziplinärer Forschung bei der Interpretation mittelalterlicher Literatur: Am Beispiel von Wolframs von Eschenbach *Parzival.*" *Mediävistik*, 1 (1988), 39–59.

―――. "Prolegomena zum Einfluß der 'Schule von Chartres' auf Wolfram von Eschenbach." In Waltraud Fritsch-Rössler and Liselotte Homering, eds., *Uf der maze pfat. Festschrift für Werner Hoffmann.* Göppingen: Kümmerle, 1991, pp. 149–169.

―――. "Die Heilkunde." In Okken, *Kommentar zur Artusepik Hartmanns von Aue*, 1993, pp. 519–554.

Haase, Gudrun. *Die germanistische Forschung zum Erec Hartmanns von Aue.* Frankfurt am Main: Lang, 1988.

Haferland, Harald. *Höfische Interaktion: Interpretationen zur höfischen Epik und Didaktik um 1200.* Munich: Fink, 1988.

Hall, Clifton D. *A Complete Concordance to Wolfram von Eschenbach's Parzival.* New York: Garland, 1990.

Hart, Thomas Elwood. "Crestien, the Quadrivium, Kyot, and Katabasis: New Evidence of Mathematical Design Techniques in Wolfram's *Parzival.*" In Winder McConnell, ed., *In hohem prise: A Festschrift in Honor of Ernst S. Dick.* Göppingen: Kümmerle, 1989, pp. 83–127.

―――. "Proportionale Textgestaltung als Verkörperung literarischer Theorie: Zu Wolframs Selbstverteidigungen im *Parzival* (114.5–116.4 and 337.1–30)." *Euphorion*, 85 (1991), 342–386.

Hasty, Will. *Adventure as Social Performance: A Study of the German Court Epics.* Tübingen: Niemeyer, 1990.

Haubrichs, Wolfgang. "Impulse und Tendenzen der germanistischen Hochmittelalterforschung seit 1970: Eine Übersicht." *Mitteilungen des Deutschen Germanistenverbandes*, 26 (1979), 4–15.

————, ed. "Soziologie mittelalterlicher Literatur." *Zeitschrift für Literaturwissenschaft und Linguistik*, 3 (1973).

————, ed. "Höfische Dichtung oder Literatur im Feudalismus?" *Zeitschrift für Literaturwissenschaft und Linguistik*, 7 (1977).

Haug, Walter. "Das Fantastische in der späteren deutschen Artusliteratur." In Göller, ed., *Spätmittelalterliche Artusliteratur*, 1984, pp. 133–149.

————. *Literaturtheorie im deutschen Mittelalter: Von den Anfängen bis zum Ende des 13. Jahrhunderts. Eine Einführung*. Darmstadt: Wissenschaftliche Buchgesellschaft, 1985.

————. "Paradigmatische Poesie: Der spätere deutsche Artusroman auf dem Weg zu einer 'nachklassischen' Ästhetik." In his *Strukturen als Schlüssel zur Welt: Kleine Schriften zur Erzählliteratur des Mittelalters*, 1990, pp. 651–671.

————. "Programmatische Fiktionalität: Hartmanns von Aue *Iwein*-Prolog." In his *Literaturtheorie im deutschen Mittelalter: Von den Anfängen bis zum Ende des 13. Jahrhunderts: Eine Einführung*, 1985, pp. 118–130.

————. "Die Symbolstruktur des höfischen Epos und ihre Auflösung bei Wolfram von Eschenbach." In his *Strukturen als Schlüssel zur Welt: Kleine Schriften zur Erzählliteratur des Mittelalters*, 1990, pp. 483–512.

————. "Wandlungen des Fiktionalitätsbewußtseins vom hohen zum späten Mittelalter." In James F. Poag and Thomas C. Fox, eds., *Entzauberung der Welt: Deutsche Literatur 1200–1500*. Tübingen: Francke, 1989, pp. 1–17.

————. "Gottfrieds von Strassburg *Tristan*: Sexueller Sündenfall oder erotische Utopie." In his *Strukturen als Schlüssel zur Welt: Kleine Schriften zur Erzählliteratur des Mittelalters*, 1990, pp. 600–611.

————. *Strukturen als Schlüssel zur Welt: Kleine Schriften zur Erzählliteratur des Mittelalters*. Tübingen: Niemeyer, 1990.

————. "Von *aventiure* und *minne* zu Intrige und Treue: Die Subjektivierung des hochhöfischen Aventürenromans im *Reinfried von Braunschweig*." In Schulze-Belli and Dallapiazza, eds., *Liebe und Aventiure im Artusroman des Mittelalters: Beiträge der Triester Tagung 1988*, 1990, pp. 7–22.

————, and Burghart Wachinger, eds. *Positionen des Romans im späten Mittelalter*. Tübingen: Niemeyer, 1991.

————, and Rainer Warning, eds. *Das Fest*. Munich: Fink, 1989.

Heinzle, Joachim. "Die Entdeckung der Fiktionalität: Zu Walter Haugs *Literaturtheorie im deutschen Mittelalter*." *Beiträge zur Geschichte der deutschen Sprache und Literatur*, 112 (1990), 55–80.

————, L. Peter Johnson, and Gisela Vollmann-Profe, eds. "Probleme der Parzival-Philologie: Marburger Kolloquium 1990." *Wolfram-Studien*, 12 (1992).

Henderson, Ingeborg. *Strickers Daniel vom Blühenden Tal: Werkstruktur und Interpretation*. Amsterdam: Benjamins, 1976.

————. "Die Frauendarstellung im nachklassischen Roman des Mittelalters." *Amsterdamer Beiträge zur älteren Germanistik*, 14 (1979), 137–169.

Henrich, Dieter, and Wolfgang Iser, eds., *Funktionen des Fiktiven*. Munich: Fink, 1983.

Iser, Wolfgang. "Akte des Fingierens, Oder: Was ist das Fiktive im fiktionalen Text?" In Henrich and Iser, eds., *Funktionen des Fiktiven*, 1983, pp. 121–151.

Jackson, William Henry. "Aspects of Knighthood in Hartmann's Adaptations of Chrétien's Romances and in the Social Context." In

Jones and Wisbey, eds., *Chrétien de Troyes and the German Middle Ages*, 1993, pp. 37-55.

Jaeger, C. Stephen. *The Origins of Courtliness: Civilizing Trends and the Formation of Courtly Ideals, 939-1210*. Philadelphia: University of Pennsylvania Press, 1985.

Jillings, Lewis. *Diu Crone of Heinrich von dem Türlein: The Attempted Emancipation of Secular Narrative*. Göppingen: Kümmerle, 1980.

Jones, Martin H. "Formen der Liebeserklärung im höfischen Roman bis um 1300." In Jeffrey Aschcroft et al., eds., *Liebe in der deutschen Literatur des Mittelalters*. Tübingen: Niemeyer, 1987, pp. 36-49.

————, and Roy Wisbey, eds. *Chrétien de Troyes and the German Middle Ages: Papers from an International Symposium*. Woodbridge: Brewer, 1993.

Kaiser, Gert. *Textauslegung und gesellschaftliche Selbstdeutung: Aspekte einer sozialgeschichtlichen Interpretation von Hartmanns Artusepen*. 1973; 2nd ed., Wiesbaden: Akademische Verlagsgesellschaft Athenaion, 1978.

————. "Der Ritter in der deutschen Literatur des Mittelalters." In *Das Ritterbild in Mittelalter und Renaissance*. Düsseldorf: Droste, 1985, pp. 37-49.

————. "Artushof und Liebe." In Kaiser and Müller, eds., *Höfische Literatur, Hofgesellschaft, höfische Lebensformen um 1200*, 1986, pp. 243-251.

————, ed. *Gesellschaftliche Sinnangebote mittelalterlicher Literatur: Mediävistisches Symposium an der Universität Düsseldorf*. Munich: Fink, 1980.

————, ed. *An den Grenzen höfischer Kultur: Anfechtungen der Lebensordnung in der deutschen Erzähldichtung des hohen Mittelalters.* Munich: Fink, 1991.

————, and Jan-Dirk Müller, eds. *Höfische Literatur, Hofgesellschaft, höfische Lebensformen um 1200. Kolloquium am Zentrum für Interdisziplinäre Forschung der Universität Bielefeld (3. bis 5. November 1983).* Düsseldorf: Droste, 1986.

Keller, Ulrich. *Fiktionalität als literaturwissenschaftliche Kategorie.* Heidelberg: Winter, 1980.

Kern, Peter. *Die Artusromane des Pleier: Untersuchungen über den Zusammenhang von Dichtung und literarischer Situation.* Berlin: Schmidt, 1981.

Kohlmorgen, Joachim. "Jetzt solltest du wissen, wer ich bin! *Daniel von dem Blühenden Tal*: Ein etwas anderer Artusroman von dem Stricker." *Horen*, 37 (1992), 13–23.

Kornrumpf, Gisela. "König Artus und das Gralsgeschlecht in der Weltchronik Heinrichs von München." *Wolfram-Studien*, 8 (1984), 178–198.

Kramer, Hans-Peter. *Erzählerbemerkungen und Erzählerkommentare in Chrétiens und Hartmanns Erec und Iwein.* Göppingen: Kümmerle, 1971.

Kratz, Henry. *Wolfram von Eschenbach's Parzival: An Attempt at a Total Evaluation.* Bern: Francke, 1973.

Krause, Burkhardt. "Zur Psychologie von Kommunikation und Interaktion: Zu Iweins 'Wahnsinn.'" In Ulrich Müller et al., eds., *Psychologie in der Mediävistik: Gesammelte Beiträge des Steinheimer Symposions*, 1985, pp. 215–242.

Krohn, Rüdiger, Bernd Thum, and Peter Wapnewski, eds. *Stauferzeit: Geschichte, Literatur, Kunst.* Stuttgart: Klett-Cotta, 1979.

Krüger, Rüdiger, Jürgen Kühnel, and Joachim Kuolt, eds. *Ist zwivel herzen nachgebur: Günther Schweikle zum 60. Geburtstag.* Stuttgart: Fay, 1989.

Kühn, Dieter. *Der Parzival des Wolfram von Eschenbach.* Frankfurt am Main: Insel, 1986.

Kuhn, Hugo. "Soziale Realität und dichterische Fiktion am Beispiel der höfischen Ritterdichtung Deutschlands." In his *Dichtung und Welt im Mittelalter.* 2nd ed. Stuttgart: Metzler, 1969, pp. 22–40.

————. "Tristan, Nibelungenlied, Artusstruktur." *Sitzungsberichte der Bayerischen Akademie der Wissenschaften.* Phil.-hist. Klasse (1973), 3–39.

Kuttner, Ursula. *Das Erzählen des Erzählten: Eine Studie zum Stil in Hartmanns Erec und Iwein.* Bonn: Bouvier, 1978.

Lacy, Norris J., and Geoffrey Ashe. *The Arthurian Handbook.* New York: Garland, 1988.

Liebertz-Grün, Ursula, ed. *Aus der Mündlichkeit in die Schriftlichkeit: Höfische und andere Literatur, 750–1320.* Reinbek bei Hamburg: Rowohlt, 1988.

McConnell, Winder. "The Denial of the Anima in Parzival." *Quondam et Futurus: A Journal of Arthurian Interpretations,* 2 (1992), 28–40.

————, and Walter Suess. "The Gawan Figure in *Parzival:* A Jungian Perspective." *Journal of Evolutionary Psychology,* 12 (1991), 222–239.

McDonald, William C. *Arthur and Tristan: On the Intersection of Legends in German Medieval Literature.* Lewiston, NY: Mellen, 1991.

————. "King Arthur and the Round Table in the *Erec* and *Iwein* of Hartmann von Aue." In Edward D. Kennedy, ed., *King Arthur*. New York: Garland, 1995 [forthcoming].

————. "Observations on the Language of Courtesy in the *Iwein* of Hartmann von Aue." In Ulrich Goebel and David Lee, eds., *The Ring of Words in Medieval Literature*. Lewiston, NY: Mellen, 1993, pp. 219–256.

————, with the collaboration of Ulrich Goebel. *German Medieval Literary Patronage from Charlemagne to Maximilian I: A Critical Commentary with Special Emphasis on Imperial Promotion of Literature*. Amsterdam: Rodopi, 1973.

McFarland, Timothy, and Silvia Ranawake, eds. *Hartmann von Aue, Changing Perspectives: London Hartmann Symposium 1985*. Göppingen: Kümmerle, 1988.

Marquard, Odo, and Karlheinz Stierle, eds. *Identität*. Munich: Fink, 1979.

Marquardt, Rosemarie. *Das höfische Fest im Spiegel der mittelhochdeutschen Dichtung, 1140–1240*. Göppingen: Kümmerle, 1985.

Martin, Ann G. *Shame and Disgrace at King Arthur's Court: A Study in the Meaning of Ignominy in German Arthurian Literature to 1300*. Göppingen: Kümmerle, 1984.

Meinert, Monica C. "Der soziale und psychologische Hintergrund zur Entstehung des frühen deutschen Minnesangs." *Acta Germanica*, 4 (1969), 3–15.

Meister, Peter. *The Healing Female in the German Courtly Romance*. Göppingen: Kümmerle, 1990.

Mertens, Volker. "Artus." In Volker Mertens and Ulrich Müller, eds., *Epische Stoffe des Mittelalters*. Stuttgart: Kröner, 1984, pp. 290–340.

———. *Laudine: Soziale Problematik im Iwein Hartmanns von Aue*. Berlin: Schmidt, 1978.

———, and Friedrich Wolfzettel, eds. *Fiktionalität im Artusroman: Dritte Tagung der Deutschen Sektion der Internationalen Artusgesellschaft in Berlin vom 13. –15. February 1992*. Tübingen: Niemeyer, 1993.

Moser, Dietz-Rüdiger, "Brauchbindung und Funktionsverlust. Zum Nachwirken der Artus-Tradition in Fastnachtsbrauch und Fastnachtsspiel." In Göller, ed., *Spätmittelalterliche Artusliteratur*, pp. 23–39.

Müller, Dorothea. *Daniel vom Blühenden Tal und Garel vom Blühenden Tal: Die Artusromane des Stricker und des Pleier unter gattungsgeschichtlichen Aspekten*. Göppingen: Kümmerle, 1981.

Müller, Jan-Dirk. "Funktionswandel ritterlicher Epik am Ausgang des Mittelalters." In Gert Kaiser, ed., *Gesellschaftliche Sinngebote mittelalterlicher Literatur*, 1980, pp. 11–75.

Müller, Ulrich, et al., eds. *Psychologie in der Mediävistik: Gesammelte Beiträge des Steinheimer Symposions*. Göppingen: Kümmerle, 1985.

Nellmann, Eberhard. *Wolframs Erzähltechnik: Untersuchungen zur Funktion des Erzählers*. Stuttgart: Hirzel, 1973.

Neubuhr, Elfriede. *Bibliographie zu Hartmann von Aue*. Berlin: Schmidt, 1977.

Nykrog, Per. "The Rise of Literary Fiction." In Robert L. Benson and Giles Constable, eds., *Renaissance and Renewal in the Twelfth Century*. Cambridge, MA: Harvard University Press, 1982, pp. 593–612.

Okken, Lambertus. *Kommentar zur Artusepik Hartmanns von Aue.* Amsterdam: Rodopi, 1993.

Peters, Ursula, "Artusroman und Fürstenhof: Darstellung und Kritik neuerer sozialgeschichtlicher Untersuchungen zu Hartmanns *Erec.*" *Euphorion,* 69 (1975), 175–196.

————. "Höfische Liebe: Ein Forschungsproblem der Mentalitätsgeschichte." In Ashcroft, Huschenbett, and Jackson, eds., *Liebe in der deutschen Literatur des Mittelalters,* 1987, pp. 1–13.

Pretzel, Ulrich, and Wolfgang Bachofer. *Bibliographie zu Wolfram von Eschenbach.* 2nd ed. Berlin: Schmidt, 1968.

Ragotzky, Hedda, and Horst Wenzel, eds. *Höfische Repräsentation: Das Zeremoniell und die Zeichen.* Tübingen: Niemeyer, 1990.

Reisel, Johanna. *Zeitschichtliche und theologisch-scholastische Aspekte im Daniel vom dem Blühenden Tal des Stricker.* Göppingen: Kümmerle, 1986.

Rossbacher, Roland. "Artusritter, Königssohn und gewählter König: Ulrichs von Zatzikhoven politische Stellungnahme." *Jahrbuch der Oswald von Wolkenstein Gesellschaft,* 3 (1984/85), 187–201.

Samples, Susann. "Guinevere: A Germanic Heroine." *Quondam et Futurus: A Journal of Arthurian Interpretations,* 1 (1991), 9–22.

Scaglione, Aldo. *Knights at Court: Courtliness, Chivalry, and Courtesy from Ottonian Germany to the Italian Renaissance.* Berkeley: University of California Press, 1991.

Schilling, Michael. "Der Stricker am Wiener Hof? Überlegungen zur historischen Situierung des *Daniel von dem Blühenden Tal.*" *Euphorion,* 85 (1991), 273–291.

Schirok, Bernd. "*Artus der meienbaere man*: Zum Stellenwert der 'Artuskritik' im klassischen deutschen Artusroman." In Schnell, ed.,

*Gotes und der werlde hulde: Festschrift für Heinz Rupp*, 1989, pp. 58–81.

Schmidt, Klaus M. "Frauenritter oder Artusritter? Über Struktur und Gehalt von Ulrichs von Zatzikoven *Lanzelet.*" *Zeitschrift für deutsche Philologie*, 98 (1979), 1–18.

———. "Das Herrscherbild im Artusroman der Stauferzeit." In Krohn, Thum, and Wapnewski, eds., *Stauferzeit: Geschichte, Literatur, Kunst*. Stuttgart: Klett-Cotta, 1979, pp. 181–194.

———. "Conceptual Glossaries: A New Tool for Medievalists." *Computers and the Humanities*, 12 (1978), 19–26.

———. *Begriffsglossar und Index zu Ulrichs von Zatzikhoven Lanzelet*. Tübingen: Niemeyer, 1993.

Schmitt, Wolfram. "Der 'Wahnsinn' in der Literatur des Mittelalters am Beispiel des *Iwein* Hartmanns von Aue." In Ulrich Müller et al., eds., *Psychologie in der Mediävistik: Gesammelte Beiträge des Steinheimer Symposions*, 1985, pp. 197–214.

Schnell, Rüdiger. *Causa amoris: Liebeskonzeption und Liebesdarstellung in der mittelalterlichen Literatur*. Bern: Francke, 1985.

———. "Die 'höfische' Liebe als 'höfischer' Diskurs über die Liebe." In Fleckenstein, ed., *Curialitas*, 1990, pp. 231–301.

———, ed., *Gotes und der werlde hulde: Festschrift für Heinz Rupp*. Bern: Francke, 1989.

Schopf, Alfred. "Die Gestalt Gawains bei Chrétien, Wolfram von Eschenbach und in 'Sir Gawain and the Green Knight.'" In Göller, ed., *Spätmittelalterliche Artusliteratur*, 1984, pp. 85–104.

Schröder, Werner. "Der synkretistische Roman des Wirnt von Gravenberg: Unerledigte Fragen an den *Wigalois.*" *Euphorion,* 80 (1986), 235–277.

———. *Wolfram von Eschenbach.* Band I: *Spuren und Werke*; Band II: *Wirkungen im 13. und 14. Jahrhundert.* Stuttgart: Hirzel, 1989.

———. "Zur Literaturverarbeitung durch Heinrich von dem Türlin in seinem Gawein-Roman *Diu Crône.*" *Zeitschrift für deutsches Altertum,* 121 (1992), 131–174.

Schultz, James A. *The Shape of the Round Table: Structures of Middle High German Arthurian Romance.* Toronto: University of Toronto Press, 1983.

Schulze-Belli, Paola, and Michael Dallapiazza, eds. *Liebe und Aventiure im Artusroman des Mittelalters: Beiträge der Triester Tagung 1988.* Göppingen: Kümmerle, 1990.

Schweikle, Günther. "Mittelalterliche Realität in deutscher höfischer Lyrik und Epik um 1200." *Germanisch-Romanische Monatsschrift,* 32 (1982), 265–285.

Semmler, Hartmut. *Listmotive in der mittelhochdeutschen Epik: Zum Wandel ethischer Normen im Spiegel der Literatur.* Berlin: Schmidt, 1991.

Sieverding, Norbert. *Der ritterliche Kampf bei Hartmann und Wolfram: Seine Bewertung im Erec und Iwein und in den Gahmuret-und Gawan-Büchern des Parzival.* Heidelberg: Winter, 1985.

Simon, Ralf. *Einführung in die strukturalistische Poetik des mittelalterlichen Romans: Analysen zu deutschen Romanen der matière de Bretagne.* Würzburg: Königshausen and Neumann, 1990.

Stein, Alexandra. *'wort unde werc': Studien zum narrativen Diskurs im Parzival Wolframs von Eschenbach.* Frankfurt am Main: Lang, 1993.

Steiner, Gertraud. "Unbeschreiblich weiblich: Zur mythischen Rezeption von Hartmanns *Iwein.*" In Ulrich Müller et al., eds., *Psychologie in der Mediävistik: Gesammelte Beiträge des Steinheimer Symposions*, 1985, pp. 243–257.

Thomas, Neil. "Sense and Structure in the Gawan Adventures of Wolfram's *Parzival.*" *The Modern Language Review*, 76 (1981), 848–856.

————. *A German View of Camelot: Wirnt von Gravenberg's Wigalois and Arthurian Tradition*. Bern: Lang, 1987.

————. *The Medieval German Arthuriad: Some Contemporary Revaluations of the Canon*. Bern: Lang, 1989.

————. *The Defence of Camelot: Ideology and Intertextuality in the "Post-Classical" German Romances of the Matter of Britain Cycle.* Bern: Lang, 1992.

————. "Heinrich von dem Türlin's *Diu Crone*: An Arthurian Fantasy?" *Amsterdamer Beiträge zur älteren Germanistik*, 36 (1992), 169–179.

Thum, Bernd. "Politische Probleme der Stauferzeit im Werk Hartmanns von Aue: Landesherrschaft im *Erec* und *Iwein.*" In Krohn, Thum, and Wapnewski, eds., *Stauferzeit: Geschichte, Literatur, Kunst*. Stuttgart: Klett-Cotta, 1979, pp. 47–70.

————. "Öffentlichkeit und Kommunikation im Mittelalter: Zur Herstellung von Öffentlichkeit im Bezugsfeld elementarer Kommunikationsformen im 13. Jahrhundert." In Ragotzky and Wenzel, eds., *Höfische Repräsentation: Das Zeremoniell und die Zeichen*, 1990, pp. 65–87.

Unger, Regina. *Wolfram-Rezeption und Utopie: Studien zum spätmittelalterlichen bayerischen Lohengrin-Epos*. Göppingen: Kümmerle, 1990.

Urban, Bernd. "Psychoanalytische Interpretation mittelalterlicher Literatur: Forschungsüberblick und Forschungsimpulse." In Ulrich Müller et al., eds., *Psychologie in der Mediävistik: Gesammelte Beiträge des Steinheimer Symposions*, 1985, pp. 361–375.

Voss, Rudolf. *Der Prosa-Lancelot: Eine strukturanalytische und strukturvergleichende Studie auf der Grundlage des deutschen Textes.* Meisenheim am Glan: Hain, 1970.

———. *Die Artusepik Hartmanns von Aue: Untersuchungen zum Wirklichkeitsbegriff und zur Ästhetik eines literarischen Genres im Kräftefeld von soziokulturellen Normen und christlicher Anthropologie.* Vienna: Böhlau, 1983.

Walsh, Martin W. "Arthur Cocu: Comic Abuse of the Round Table in Fifteenth-Century Fastnachtspiele." *Fifteenth-Century Studies*, 15 (1989), 305–321.

Wapnewski, Peter. *Hartmann von Aue.* 7th ed. Stuttgart: Metzler, 1979.

Weddige, Hilkert. *Einführung in die germanistische Mediävistik.* Munich: Beck, 1987.

Wehrli, Max. "Zur Identität der Figuren im frühen Artusroman." In Schnell, ed., *Gotes und der werlde hulde: Festschrift für Heinz Rupp*, 1989, pp. 48–57.

Welz, Dieter. "Episoden der Entfremdung in Wolframs *Parzival*: Herzeloyden-Tragödie und Blutstropfenszene im Verständigungsrahmen einer psychoanalytischen Sozialisationstheorie." *Acta Germanica*, 9 (1976), 47–110.

Wenzel, Horst. "Repräsentation und schöner Schein am Hof und in der höfischen Literatur." In Ragotzky and Wenzel, eds., *Höfische Repräsentation: Das Zeremoniell und die Zeichen*, 1990, pp. 171–208.

Winter, Johanna Maria van. *Rittertum, Ideal und Wirklichkeit*. Munich: Deutscher Taschenbuch Verlag, 1969.

Wolfzettel, Friedrich, ed. *Artusrittertum im späten Mittelalter: Ethos und Ideologie*. Giessen: Schmitz, 1984.

Zach, Christine. *Die Erzählmotive der Crône Heinrichs von dem Türlin und ihre altfranzösischen Quellen: Ein kommentiertes Register*. Passau: Wissenschaftsverlag Richard Rothe, 1990.

Zutt, Herta. *König Artus, Iwein, Der Löwe: Die Bedeutung des gesprochenen Worts in Hartmanns Iwein*. Tübingen: Niemeyer, 1979.

# SPAIN AND PORTUGAL

## Harvey L. Sharrer

F or a detailed overview of Arthurian legend in the Iberian peninsula and the general nature of the literary texts involved, readers should consult the principal surveys: Entwistle's outdated but still valuable monograph *The Arthurian Legend in the Literature of the Spanish Peninsula*; Lida de Malkiel's chapter in *Arthurian Literature in the Middle Ages*, the original Spanish version of which was reprinted in 1984; and my general article in *The New Arthurian Encyclopedia* (1991 ["Spanish and Portuguese"]). In the same encyclopedia, Dayle Seidenspinner-Núñez offers a general survey of the Tristan story in Spain and Portugal (1991), and I have a series of entries on individual Hispanic texts, with several additional entries authored by Norris J. Lacy and Louis A. Murillo; a synthesis of information on the Hispanic texts may also be found in Norris J. Lacy's and Geoffrey Ashe's *The Arthurian Handbook*. Carlos Alvar takes some of the Hispanic prose romance texts into account in his reference tool *El rey Arturo y su mundo: diccionario de mitología artúrica*. For a detailed survey of Hispanic manifestations of the Vulgate Cycle, see my forthcoming article "The Acclimatization."

For additional bibliography, readers may consult works listed in the bibliography at the end of this survey and also the annual *Bibliographical Bulletin of the International Arthurian Society*. Unfortunately, since 1990 the Hispanic section of the *Bulletin* (representing literature published in any Spanish- or Portuguese-speaking country) has not appeared. However, the void is filled in part by entries in the *Boletín Bibliográfico de la Asociación Hispánica de Literatura Medieval*. Concerning primary sources for the medieval period in Spain and Portugal (through the year 1500), one may now consult relational bibliographies for Spanish, Portuguese, and Catalan texts, published on a CD-ROM as part of the program called ADMYTE.

Historians and literary scholars commonly use the year 1500 as an arbitrary *terminus ad quem* for the Middle Ages in the Iberian peninsula, but for the study of medieval Arthurian literature we must consider texts composed within an extended time frame, between the twelfth and sixteenth centuries and even beyond. While the origins of the Arthurian legend in Spain and Portugal remain obscure, Arthurian names and literary references first crop up in the twelfth century. Peninsular interest in the Matter of Britain seems to have declined only after the sixteenth century, although not even Miguel de Cervantes's parody of chivalric romances in *Don Quixote* would sound the death knell to all interest in such material. In the twentieth century, such writers as Benjamín Jarnés, Alvaro Cunqueiro, X.L. Méndez Ferrín, and Paloma Díaz-Mas have given the Arthurian legend new attention, and there has also been a "boom" of translations of medieval Arthurian texts into Spanish, and, to a lesser extent, into Catalan and Portuguese.[1]

Notwithstanding its long historical development, medieval Hispanic Arthurian literature is characterized by a limited corpus of extant texts. The surviving works in Galician-Portuguese, Castilian, Aragonese, and Catalan had as their primary sources of inspiration Geoffrey of Monmouth's *Historia Regum Britanniae* and the French prose romance cycles (the Vulgate or Lancelot-Grail cycle, the Post-Vulgate *Roman du Graal*, and the *Prose Tristan*), as well as prophecies of Merlin derived from Geoffrey and from later prophecies of French origin. Translations and adaptations were made from Latin, French, Provençal, and, in the case of the *Prose Tristan*, perhaps Italian; in turn, the new Hispanic Arthurian texts, particularly the cyclical romances, would come to be translated or adapted into yet other Hispano-Romance languages. There are also examples of late Hispanic Arthurian texts rendered into non-Hispanic languages, specifically Italian and, curiously, Tagalog. Most of the Hispanic texts survive in late copies and frequently reveal significant alterations to the original content and tenor of their source, reflecting changes in literary, social and political interests on the part

---

[1] This is not the place to give a full account of the contemporary revival of the Arthurian legend in Spain and Portugal. However, among the many translations of Arthurian works, one can single out the series of medieval texts directed by Jacobo F.J. Stuart for Ediciones Siruela (Madrid), widely distributed in Spain and Portugal.

of the author and the audience. While scholarship continues to focus on philological concerns, sources, and textual relationships, in recent years studies have also given special attention to questions of reception and the cross-influence and hybridization of literary genres.

## Recent Editions

I include here recent editions of only the principal Hispanic Arthurian texts. In the Scholarly Studies section and the bibliography, I cite editions of other texts containing Arthurian passages (*Libro del Caballero Zifar*, Martorell's *Tirant lo Blanc*) and works inspired by Arthurian prose romances (e.g., *Amadís de Gaula*).

I have prepared a machine-readable transcription of the *Lanzarote del Lago*, the mid-sixteenth-century manuscript copy (Madrid, Biblioteca Nacional 9611) of the Spanish *Prose Lancelot* (corresponding to the very end of Book 1 and Books 2–3 of what would appear to have been a long version of the French *Prose Lancelot*, similar to Paris, Bibliothèque Nationale fr. 751) for the Dictionary of the Old Spanish Language project at the Hispanic Seminary of Medieval Studies, University of Wisconsin–Madison. The Seminary has produced a concordance to the transcription. I plan to publish a microfiche edition in the near future with the Seminary and in the longer term a printed edition with readings from the French clarifying the many garbled passages in the manuscript.

In 1955, Martí de Riquer published in article form an edition and study of the surviving fragments of an incunable version of the fifteenth-century Catalan adaptation by Mossèn Gras of the *Mort Artu*, a reworking to which Riquer gave the title *Tragèdia de Lançalot*. In 1984, Riquer published his edition in the form of a more accessible book, containing an updated introduction and notes to the text and, following the text itself, an edition of poetry in Spanish by Gras, a description of the incunable, and a facsimile of the nine surviving leaves.

The *Prose Tristan* has been the object of considerable editing activity. Ivy A. Corfis, with the aid of a group of graduate students at the University of Pennsylvania, published in 1985 a microfiche edition with concordances of the Vatican manuscript of the Castilian-Aragonese

*El cuento de Tristán de Leonís* for the Hispanic Seminary of Medieval
Studies (Madison). The advantage of the transcription over Northup's
1928 edition of the same manuscript is that it contains duplicate
passages copied by different scribes. The edition is accompanied by a
short booklet containing historico-literary information and a short
bibliography.

Ivy A. Corfis, Dayle Seidenspinner-Núñez, and I are currently
involved in a project to produce for the Seminary a three-volume
printed edition with individual introductions for all the Hispanic *Prose
Tristan* texts. Corfis is responsible for the Vatican manuscript;
Seidenspinner-Núñez and I, the 1501 printing; Seidenspinner-Núñez,
the 1534 printing (the interpolation in books 1 and 2); and I, the
Galician-Portuguese fragment, the Catalan fragments, the Spanish
epistolary exchange between Iseut and Tristan, and other miscellaneous
material. As a preliminary step, Seidenspinner-Núñez and I have in
press with the Seminary a microfiche edition of a new transcription
with concordances of the 1501 *Libro de don Tristán de Leonís*, printed
by Juan de Burgos. The accompanying booklet includes a substantial
introduction and lengthy bibliography.

As mentioned below, in the section on scholarly studies and surveys,
Seidenspinner-Núñez and Cristina Gates have an unpublished
transcription of the 1534 edition, Gates included sections of the text in
her doctoral dissertation for the University of Buenos Aires, and
Luzdivina Cuesta Torre prepared a complete transcription for the
Licenciatura degree at the University of León.

The late fifteenth- or early sixteenth-century epistolary exchange in
Spanish between Iseut and Tristan, in a manuscript miscellany now in
the Biblioteca Nacional in Madrid, has been edited partially by myself
(1981–82) and in its entirety by Fernando Gómez Redondo. Both
editions offer accurate readings, offer textual commentary, and
reproduce passages from other versions of the Iseut letter.

The Post-Vulgate *Roman du Graal* continues to attract a great deal
of interest. Two new editions of the Portuguese *Demanda do Santo
Graal* were published in 1988. Heitor Megale's renders into modern
Portuguese the hard-to-find 1944 and 1955 Rio de Janeiro editions by
Augusto Magne (Volume 2 of the 1955 edition is especially difficult to
locate). Megale offers an introduction providing the general reader with
background information on medieval Arthurian literature, including

other Hispanic versions of the Post-Vulgate *Roman du Graal*, and examples of archaisms and Gallicisms to be found in the Vienna manuscript. Megale fills lacunae in the text with passages from Bonilla y San Martín's 1907 edition of the 1535 Spanish printing and Pauphillet's edition of the French *Queste* of the Vulgate Cycle. At the end of the edition, Megale reproduces in facsimile six folio pages of the manuscript, presents a two-page glossary, and a bibliography.

The second edition offers a reliable, conservative transcription of the manuscript by the German-born linguist Joseph M. Piel, with a seventeen-page introduction by Ivo Castro placing the *Demanda* in its historico-literary context in light of recent scholarship and detailing the history of Piel's edition. The printing was interrupted at Coimbra in 1927, four hundred and thirty-two pages of it rediscovered years later in a collection of printed sheets held in storage at the Imprensa Nacional in Lisbon. Unfortunately, the latter part of Piel's original was completely lost. The last forty-five pages of the new edition contain Irene Freire Nunes's transcription of the text following Piel's transcription norms. At the time of the discovery of the printed sheets, and with no knowledge of Megale's project, Nunes had already prepared her own new edition of the *Demanda*, with regularized orthography for a more general reading public, also to be published by the Imprensa Nacional.

Ivo Castro's dissertation, a partial edition of the *Livro de José de Abarimateia*, the first branch of the Portuguese translation of the Post-Vulgate romance, offers a reading that supersedes in accuracy Henry Hare Carter's useful but difficult to read paleographic edition of the romance. Castro includes a detailed study of the manuscript and its history as well as the relationship of the text to other French and Hispanic versions of the romance. Castro has edited the complete manuscript for publication by the Imprensa Nacional in Lisbon.

Scholars generally assumed that all three branches of the Post-Vulgate *Roman du Graal* were translated into Portuguese, but there was no concrete evidence of a *Merlin* branch until 1979, when Amadeu Soberanas published an edition in article form of fourteenth-century fragments he discovered in the binding of two incunable volumes at the Biblioteca de Catalunya in Barcelona. Soberanas's edition includes a description of the fragments, an accurate transcription, and collations with other French and Spanish versions of the passages. At first seldom cited, Soberanas's important discovery is slowly becoming better known to historians and students of medieval Portuguese literature.

In 1988, Miraguano Ediciones (Madrid) published, in one volume, in its series for the general audience Libros de los Malos Tiempos, what is essentially Justo García Morales's 1956–57 two-volume edition of the Spanish *Baladro del sabio Merlín* as reworked in a 1498 incunable printed at Burgos by Juan de Burgos. José Javier Fuente del Pilar's new reading of Morales's transcription (printed in Gothic type) simplifies and regularizes the orthography and follows current paragraph division and punctuation norms. The book contains a separate insert with an eight-page prologue by Luis Alberto de Cuenca and a short bibliography.

In a 1988 article for the Riquer Festschrift, Giuseppe Di Stefano published what should stand for many years as the definitive edition of the Spanish Tristan ballad. Marred only by a few misprints, the edition includes all the known versions and glosses published in the sixteenth and seventeenth centuries, as *pliegos sueltos* (broadsides) or in song and ballad collections. Di Stefano provides a study and stemma of the complex textual relationships and a "critical" edition of the four principal versions of the ballad.

Thanks to Pere Bohigas and Jaume Vidal Alcover, we now have complete, accessible "critical" edition of Guillem de Torroella's *La Faula*. The edition uses as a base Madrid, Biblioteca Nacional, Res. 48 (the *Cançoner dels Comtes d'Urgell*), filling in missing lines with readings from other extant manuscripts and offering critical notes and an apparatus of variants.[2] The introduction includes a literary study, a description of the manuscripts with stemma, commentary on the language of the manuscripts, a section on versification, and a six-page glossary. In his review of the edition, Cabré, in addition to having questions concerning the literary section of the introduction, expresses disappointment that the glossary is not more detailed and complete.

Gonzalo Santonja's 1988 edition of of the *Tablante de Ricamonte* offers a useful introduction to the text for the general public but does

---

[2] Jacques De Caluwé mistakenly refers to Carpentras, Bibliothèque Municipale 321 (an error for 381), as a previously unknown Catalan adaptation of the *Mort Artu* ("Quelques"). It is one of the known manuscripts of *La Faula* included in Bohigas and Vidal Alcover's critical apparatus.

not inform the reader what edition of the work follows. As noted below, the book provides an edition of the 1564 printing at Estella. This is the same printing published by Adolfo Bonilla y San Martín in the first volume of his *Libros de caballerías* (Nueva Bibliioteca de Autores Españoles, 6, Madrid, 1907).

### Scholarly Studies

Until recently, the earliest known reference to Arthurian material in the Peninsula was in a frequently cited poem, an *ensenyament* (Catalan) or *ensenhamen* (Provençal) written ca. 1170 by the Catalan-born viscount Guerau de Cabrera (Giraut de Cabreira), in which the latter shames a jongleur named Cabra for being unfamiliar with a litany of literary themes, characters and places, including stories about Arthur, his residence at Carduel, and his nephew Gawain, the story of Erec, and the love of Tristan and Iseut. Such material had apparently been in circulation among high society in Catalonia. Important scholarship by David Hook now points to a much earlier penetration of Arthurian material in the north of the Peninsula, particularly in Castile and León. In a meticulous sifting of published documents, Hook has found references to Arthurian names—*Artus* (Arthur), *Galvan* (Gawain), and *Merlin*—as early as the 1130s, or perhaps even earlier, in different parts of the north, from the Catalonian Pyrenees in the east to the kingdom of León in the west. Hook's startling discoveries show familiarity with certain Arthurian names in Spain before Geoffrey of Monmouth produced his *Historia Regum Britanniae*. For Portugal, however, Hook's earliest example of an Arthurian name, *Merlim*, used perhaps as a patronymic, is in a much later document dated 1186. Stimulated by Hook's findings, in the course of my research for the *Bibliografia de Textos Antigos Portugueses*, I have begun examining modern editions of twelfth-century documents and have found two examples from the 1170s: *Merlin* as the family name of a witness to a document dated 1173, apparently issued in Lisbon;[3] and *Galvan* as a

---

[3] Maria Teresa Barbosa Acabado, ed., "Inventário de compras do Real Mosteiro de S. Vicente de Fora," *Arquivo de Bibliografia Portuguesa* 14 (1968), 36–108, no. 4 (p. 44).

witness to a will dated 1178 at Guimarães, in northern Portugal.[4] The Tristan legend, too, seems to have arrived in the Peninsula at an early date, perhaps before any of the early Tristan romances known today had been composed. In a significant piece of research, the Spanish art historian Serafín Moralejo has convincingly shown that the image on a column he dates from the early twelfth century in the cathedral at Santiago de Compostela, where it once formed part of the *Porta Francigena*, is that of Tristan lying wounded on an open boat, with a nicked sword held upright in one of his hands, the missing piece of his sword having been left, as the knowledgeable pilgrim to Santiago would doubtless recall, in Morholt of Ireland's skull. Muriel Whitaker considers the image "unmistakably" that of Tristan, and she places it in the context of other secular themes used for didactic purposes in medieval church art. With Hook's documentary findings and Moralejo's iconographic evidence, we must now consider northern Spain, like northern Italy, with its famous Modena archivolt of identifiable Arthurian figures (dated between 1120 and 1140), as an important early recipient of Arthurian and Tristan legends.

Although there is evidence in early Hispanic chronicles to show that the work of Geoffrey of Monmouth and perhaps that of Wace were known in the Peninsula as early as the mid-thirteenth century (Sharrer 1991 [*"Sumario"*]), recent scholarship has turned more to the prose romances and courtly lyrics of the period for evidence of the early influence and acclimatization of Arthurian romance at the courts of Castile and León and Portugal.

At the turn of the twentieth century, Carolina Michaëlis de Vasconcelos surmised that Afonso III and his entourage brought to Portugal chivalric romances then in vogue in northern France when Afonso returned to Portugal to succeed his brother Sancho II as king in 1245 or early 1246. During his twenty years in exile, Afonso resided at the court of Blanche of Castile, and he became count of Boulogne through his marriage to Mahaud II or Mathilde of Boulogne. The Portuguese philologist Ivo Castro, in an article stemming from his as yet unpublished Lisbon dissertation, provides documentary evidence helping to corroborate the idea that the three branches of the Post-

---

[4] Oliveira Guimarães, "Documentos inéditos dos séculos XII–XV—Mosteiro de Souto," *Revista de Guimarães* 6 (1889), 72-92, no. 4 (p. 75).

Vulgate *Roman du Graal* reached Portugal shortly after their original composition in northern France. He discovers that João Bivas, the Portuguese translator of the Post-Vulgate romance, was associated with the Portuguese court of Afonso III. This new information, joined with Fanni Bogdanow's series of publications offering textual evidence to establish the priority of the Portuguese *Demanda do Santo Graal*, the *Queste/Mort Artu* branch of the Post-Vulgate Cycle, over Spanish versions of the same text, moves us closer to believing that the mid-thirteenth-century Portuguese court of Afonso III was keenly interested in recently compiled or reworked Arthurian prose romances and encouraged their early translation into Portuguese. On this and other French cultural influences at the court of Afonso III, one can profit from a recent dictionary article by Vicente Beltrán.

That the *Lancelot* branch of the Vulgate Cycle was also familiar to courtly audiences in the western part of the peninsula seems evident from a *cantiga d'escarnho*, a satirical poem written by Martin Soares, a Portuguese troubadour who flourished between 1230 and 1260 and who left Portugal for Castile after the civil war of 1245–47, as António Resende de Oliveira has elucidated in a ground-breaking doctoral dissertation (518–521). A 1973–74 article by Jean-Marie d'Heur and a recent explication by Valeria Bertolucci Pizzorusso reveal that Martin Soares's song, surviving in two sixteenth-century copies (*Cancioneiro da Biblioteca Nacional*, 1369; *Cancioneiro da Vaticana*, 977) parodies with humorous effect a long episode from the *Prose Lancelot* involving Lancelot's rescue of Gawain, who was held prisoner by Caradoc. An epigraph to one of the copies of the poem helps explain that a certain cleric, evidently the man mockingly named "Don Caralhote" in the poem, had injured the poet's sister while engaging in sexual intercourse with her. In the song, the woman obtains revenge by holding Caralhote prisoner in her *cárcer* ("jail," a euphemism for "vagina"). The name "Caralhote" resembles that of Caradoc in the French romance, and the *-ote* ending echoes that of "Lançarote"; and it also evokes an obscene association with the Galician-Portuguese term *caralho* ("penis"), found in a number of similarly salacious *cantigas d'escarnho*.

Whether Martin Soares's audience would have been familiar with the *Prose Lancelot* in its original French or in translation is not clear, nor do we know whether the poem was written at the Portuguese court or when the poet went to Castile. The Spanish *Prose Lancelot* romance,

surviving in a mid-sixteenth-century copy bearing the title *El segundo
y tercero libro de don Lanzarote de* [sic] *Lago* (Madrid, Biblioteca
Nacional 9611), may indirectly provide a clue, for it reveals linguistic
evidence of having been originally translated from the French at an
early date into a western Hispano-Romance language (Sharrer 1977,
item Aa3; Sharrer 1981). However, a more thorough study of the
language of the manuscript is required. My hypothesis (proffered with
the assistance of Elspeth Kennedy) that the *Lanzarote del Lago*, at least
for the beginning of the romance, follows a long version of the French
romance similar to that preserved in Paris, Bibliothèque Nationale fr.
751, has recently been corroborated in a conference paper by Antonio
M. Contreras Martín, who also finds a closeness between the two
manuscripts in the famous episode of the cart (MS. 9611, fol.
108v–110r). Contreras Martín briefly studies the faithful translation into
Spanish of French vocabulary concerning virtues, ethics, and arms; and
he projects the possibility that a similar study for the whole manuscript
may help determine the date of the translation and also provide
information concerning its reception in Castile. Based on my machine-
readable transcription of 9611, Contreras Martín is currently preparing
his doctoral thesis for the University of Barcelona on the concept of
chivalry as evidenced in the *Lanzarote del Lago*.

In a survey of the Matter of Britain in pre-1350 Galician-Portuguese
lyrics, I give renewed emphasis to the influence of the Arthurian prose
romances, especially the Post-Vulgate *Roman du Graal*, at the courts
of Castile and León and Portugal (1988 ["La materia"]). Building on
Fanni Bogdanow's research concerning the Post-Vulgate *Roman du
Graal*, I contribute new information concerning the latter as a likely
source of inspiration for two of the so-called *Lais de Bretanha*, a set of
five anonymous songs with prose epigraphs, preserved in two sixteenth-
century copies (*Cancioneiro da Biblioteca Nacional*, 1–5, at fol.
10r–11v; Vatican lat. 7182, fol. 276r–278v). Regarding the epigraph
to the second lai, I find an allusion to the episode of the Roche aux
Pucelles, found in the *Prose Tristan* but adapted anew in the *Merlin*
branch of the Post-Vulgate romance. That the episode circulated in a
Galician-Portuguese translation of the *Merlin* is now known thanks to
Amadeu-J. Soberanas's edition and study of four fragments of an early
fourteenth-century copy, which Soberanas discovered in the binding of
two incunables at the Biblioteca de Catalunya, and an anonymous

summary of the study in Galician, "A versión." I have uncovered additional textual affinity between the last of the five lais and Lancelot material preserved in the so-called *Folie Lancelot* section of the Post-Vulgate *Roman du Graal*, including a line of verse, *Voirement est ce ly escus au meilleur chevalier du monde* ("Truly this is the shield of the best knight in the world"), said in the French text to accompany a *carole*, or dance, of maidens around a pine tree where hangs Lancelot's shield. The Galician-Portuguese lai, supposedly sung by maidens, uses an almost literal translation of the French verse as a refrain and glosses it in a series of strophes that take the form of a *bailada*, a dance form that may have developed at the Portuguese court in the time of Pedro of Portugal, count of Barcelos (ca. 1285–1354), to whom some scholars would ascribe the five lais. Anna Ferrari has recently published a useful dictionary article providing detailed information concerning our knowledge of the origin, transmission, structure and originality of the five *Lais de Bretanha*.

In a recent article Carlos Alvar (1993) reexamines the Matter of Britain in Galician-Portuguese lyrics (excluding the five lais) in the context of similar manifestations in Provençal, French, and Italian texts. Alvar includes a discussion of another satirical poem by Martin Soares, one that makes fun of the short cloak worn by Joan Fernandes, a figure referred to by other contemporary poets as a cuckold and an insincere Muslim convert. The poem recalls for Alvar the test that reveals the fidelity of the wife of Caradoc (not, however, the Caradoc who holds Gawain prisoner), in *Le mantel mautaillié* or the *Lai du cort mantel*, raising the possible influence of short Arthurian narratives alongside that of the cyclical romances.

The survival of so much of the Post-Vulgate in Portuguese and Spanish has, in part, enabled Fanni Bogdanow to reconstruct the original French romance. While no manuscript version exists in French of all three branches as a consecutive narrative—hence some skepticism among Arthurian specialists over Bogdanow's insistence that the romance did indeed exist—Ivo Castro's arguments cited above concerning the likely translation of the full romance at the Portuguese court of Afonso III help reinforce Bogdanow's theory, as do the survival in Spanish of narrative fragments of all three branches in two individual fifteenth-century manuscript compilations. Bogdanow, after devoting over thirty years to the reconstruction of the Post-Vulgate, including a set of recent articles concerning relationships with the extant Hispanic texts, has an edition of surviving sections of the French romance in press with the Société des Anciens Textes Français. This edition should assist scholars working with the Hispanic texts in further refining their own analysis of the transmission and reception of the romance in Portugal and Castile across some three centuries. Concerning the first branch of the Post-Vulgate cycle, Sílvio de Almeida Toledo Neto compares the Portuguese *Livre de Josep ab Aramatia* with Robert de Boron's *Joseph* of *Estoire del saint Graal* and the prose *Estoire* of the Lancelot-Grail cycle and speculates whether the Post-Vulgate *remanieur* had a purpose beyond those that have been pointed out by Bogdanow.

The Portuguese *Merlin* fragments in the Biblioteca de Catalunya offer important textual evidence showing that the Portuguese translation of the romance was probably made soon after its composition in northern France and that the translation was closer to the original French romance than surviving manuscripts of the Post-Vulgate text known today as the *Suite du Merlin*. Only recently have more historians of medieval Portuguese literature given recognition to Soberanas's discovery.

Heitor Megale's important doctoral thesis for the University of São Paulo on the *Demanda* branch of the Portuguese Post-Vulgate remains unpublished, but he has two substantive articles on the Portuguese text. The first (1986) offers an explanation of the narrative structure of the romance, finding a series of broad episodes that commonly present one protagonist in opposition to another knight or a group of knights acting in collaboration; the second (1991) compares readings in Augusto Magne's two editions of the Portuguese romance (1944 and 1955–70) and systematizes Magne's reactions to negative reviews of his first edition. Gerhard Wild examines the reduced status of Lancelot in the Grail quest in the *Demanda* in comparison to the Vulgate Cycle, concluding that the Post-Vulgate treatment of the character would have more appeal to the lay reading public (1989).

The text of the Portuguese *Demanda do Santo Graal* has now become more accessible thanks to two new editions by Joseph Piel and Heitor Megale. Ivo Castro has recently published a series of dictionary articles summing up the current state of scholarship concerning the Portuguese texts. Recent scholarship has given only slight attention to the Spanish translation of the *Demanda* as it survives in late manuscript fragments and in 1515 and 1535 imprints. Gerhard Wild places Lope García de Salazar's reworking of the Post-Vulgate account of Arthur's passing, with Morgan the Fay taking Arthur to the island of Brasil, in the context of early voyages to the New World (1992, 413*b*–*c*). J.B. Hall finds that the 1535 printings of the Spanish *Baladro del sabio Merlín* and *Demanda del santo grial* reflect an exaltation of chivalric ideals prevalent in sixteenth-century Castile. Modifications to the French text reduce criticism of sinful and belligerent knights. Albert Gier proposes that sixteenth-century Spanish readers of the *Demanda* would have associated the dissension among the knights of the Round Table with the struggles knights of Spanish military orders were having with a monarchy seeking to centralize its power. In a recent conference paper, Luzdivina Cuesta Torre complements Megale's structural analysis of the Portuguese *Demanda* in an examination of the theme of rivalry among heroes in the 1535 edition of the *Baladro del sabio Merlín* and *Demanda del santo grial* and the 1528 edition of the *Tristán de Leonís* (1993 ["Algunas notas"]).

We have already observed the apparent knowledge of the Tristan story in a sculpted image at Santiago de Compostela in the early twelfth century and ca. 1170 in the eastern part of the Peninsula in Guerau de Cabrera's *ensenyament*. References to the love story of Tristan and Iseut are also found in thirteenth-century *cantigas d'amor* by Alfonso X of Castile and León and his grandson Dom Dinis of Portugal (Sharrer 1988 ["La materia"]). It is conceivable that the *Prose Tristan* was translated at an early date in the western part of the Peninsula. Three or possibly four of the *Lais de Bretanha* are related to material preserved in manuscripts of the French *Prose Tristan* (Sharrer 1988 ["La materia"]). A fragment of the prose romance in Galician-Portuguese dates from the fourteenth century but may represent a copy of an earlier version, and it probably derives from a version of the romance different from the one translated into Catalan, Aragonese, and Spanish. Luciano Rossi, in a recent dictionary article, briefly studies the Galician-Portuguese fragment (edited in 1962 by José L. Pensado Tomé) in light of corresponding passages in the French *Prose Tristan*, as edited by Renée Curtis (vol. 3, Woodbridge: Brewer, 1985), who uses as a base Carpentras 404; and Philippe Ménard (vol. 1, Geneva: Droz, 1987), who uses Vienna, Österreichische Nationalbibliothek,

2542. Rossi's collation of a section of the fragment with the French of these manuscripts reveals (much as my own findings have in preparing a new edition of the fragment for future publication) that the Galician-Portuguese passages offer a more incisive reading yet remain closely faithful to the French. The comparison corrects Pensado Tomé's belief (based on his reading of a French printing of the romance rather than earlier manuscript versions) that the Galician-Portuguese text was more expansive than its French model. Additional information on the fragment's relationship to its French source may be found in an article Rossi has in press.

Recent scholarship has produced new editions of four Hispanic *Prose Tristan* texts: a complete transcription of the Spanish-Aragonese version of the late fourteenth- or early fifteenth-century manuscript Vatican lat. 6428, known as *El cuento de Tristán de Leonís* (Corfis); a new transcription of the 1501 Spanish imprint (Seidenspinner-Núñez and Sharrer); a partial and a complete edition of a late fifteenth- or early sixteenth-century epistolary exchange between Iseut and Tristan, in Madrid, Biblioteca Nacional 22021, fol. 8v–12v (Sharrer 1981–82; Gómez Redondo); and also partial and complete editions of the 1534 printing that bears the long title *Corónica nuevamente emendada y añadida del buen cavallero don Tristán de Leonís y del rey don Tristán de Leonís, el joven su hijo.* In addition to an important article reappraising the textual transmission of the Catalan, Spanish-Aragonese, and later Spanish versions (Cuesta Torre 1993 ["La transmisión"]), there have been a variety of interpretative and historico-literary studies of the surviving *Tristán de Leonís* texts.

J.B. Hall compares the 1501 and 1528 Spanish imprints to the Castilian-Aragonese text of the Vatican manuscript and observes a change in tone in the later Spanish texts ("A Process"). He finds that certain comic scenes, realistic touches, and material that might give an unfavorable impression of the chivalric knight are suppressed (e.g., for Hall the comic character of Dinadan becomes more courtly in the printed texts). Such changes, Hall believes, reflect a certain nostalgia for chivalric values of the past among Spanish aristocracy of the period. Luzdivina Cuesta Torre has recently questioned some of Hall's conclusions by pointing out passages in the Andorra manuscript fragment of the Catalan *Tristany de Leonis* (dated to the second half of the fourteenth century) that coincide in spirit and expression with corresponding material in the 1501 Spanish imprint, whereas the same passages in the Vatican text show more "color" (1993 ["La transmisión"], 88–89). Thomas Montgomery observes parallels between an episode in the text of the Vatican manuscript—the scene of Tristan's bath at the Irish court, which permits the queen to observe the nick in Tristan's sword, thus identifying Tristan as the slayer of the queen's brother—and traditional accounts of the initiation of Cúchulainn of Ulster and Gonzalo González of Castile as young warriors.

Dayle Seidenspinner-Núñez reconstructs what would have been the original conclusion of the romance that became altered in the 1501 printing of the *Tristán de Leonís* (1981–82). Using Löseth's *Analyse* of the French manuscripts and modern editions of the Italian texts, she concludes that the adapter of the 1501 Spanish version of the romance interpreted the story of Tristan and Iseut as a tragedy, similar to that of lovers in the "sentimental romance" genre, popular in Spain in the second half of the fifteenth century and into the sixteenth. Alicia Yllera, in a recently published conference paper, supplements some of Seidenspinner-Núñez's findings in comparing the episode of the deaths of Tristan and Iseut in the *Tristán de Leonís* to analogous versions in other languages, but she ignores the influence of contemporary Hispanic sentimental literature in the deliberate alteration of the ending of the romance.

John R. Rosenberg, on the other hand, emphasizes the clash between Christian orthodoxy of late-medieval Spain and the poetics or aesthetics of love as expounded in the 1501 edition of the *Tristán de Leonís*. He compares and contrasts this aspect of the Spanish romance with Fernando de Rojas's *Celestina* of the same period, Cervantes's *Don Quixote*, and Goethe's *Elective Affinities*. He finds that the laws of love, which Tristan and Calisto (hero of *Celestina*) profess to the exclusion of theology, coexist with the metaphysical in Don Quixote's love for the mythical Dulcinea; in *Elective Affinities* Rosenberg also sees parallels with *Tristán de Leonís* in the profanation of love and the subversive irreverence toward orthodox religious custom. The Tristan legend in Iberian and contemporary texts is also the subject of a 1987 thesis for the Sorbonne by Patricia Michon. More recently, Elena Moltó Hernández uses the 1528 edition of the *Tristán de Leonís* to argue that the Spanish author softened threats to Tristan from his enemies (including Mark) and ignored the decline of Logres in order to highlight the glory and splendor of the Arthurian world. In a recent article Vincent Serverat proposes an "androgynous" reading of Tristan's character in the Spanish Prose *Tristan*. Alongside Tristan's qualities as a young, virile hero, Serverat also observes a "certain féminité latente," in his sexual awakening and in his relationships with Iseut, Lancelot, and Galahad. Serverat finds parallels too with the sad youthful figure of the servant named Tristan in Fernando de Rojas's reworked tragicomedy version of *Celestina*, printed in the early sixteenth century.

A previously unknown late fifteenth- or early sixteenth-century Spanish Tristan text came to light in 1977 when a manuscript miscellany of the late fifteenth or early sixteenth century was sold to the Biblioteca Nacional in Madrid. A section of the miscellany (MS 22021, fol. 8v–12v) contains an epistolary exchange between Iseut and Tristan. Iseut's letter (*Carta enviada por Hiseo la Brunda a Tristán de Leonís . . .*), a complaint to Tristan for having left her to marry Iseut of the White Hands, is a much expanded version of a similar letter in the *Prose Tristan*; Tristan's letter in response (*Respuesta de Tristán*) is the apparent creation of the Spanish author. My study of the exchange, including a partial edition of the two letters (1981–82), discusses the rhetorical expansion of the letter, especially in its Hispanic versions (the Andorra fragment of the Catalan *Prose Tristan*, the Aragonese and Spanish *Cuento de Tristán de Leonís*, and the sixteenth-century printings of the *Tristán de Leonís*). In Iseut's letter I discover borrowings and verbal echoes from Juan de Flores's sentimental romance *Grimalte y Gradissa*, recalling Pamela Waley's earlier discovery of textual borrowings from the same fifteenth-century Spanish romance in the 1501 edition of the *Tristán*. Subsequent to the publication of my article, I also found in Iseut's letter verbal borrowings from the Spanish translation of Boccaccio's *Elegia di Madonna Fiammetta* as printed at Salamanca in 1497 ("Notas," 330–331, item 9). These examples of plagiary (or possibly the reworking of the Spanish *Prose Tristan* by Juan de Flores himself) present yet another example of the fusion of fictional genres in Spain at the end of the Middle Ages. Fernando Gómez Redondo's complete edition of the Iseut and Tristan epistolary exchange with introduction and analysis supplements and expands upon my study to elucidate further our understanding of the text itself in the context of humanistic tendencies in Spain at the close of the Middle Ages. On the question of authorship, Gómez Redondo hesitantly proposes the earlier fifteenth-century writer of sentimental fiction, Juan Rodríguez del Padrón; but this attribution does not take into account my finding of a verbal borrowing of the Spanish translation of the *Fiammetta* as transmitted in a late fifteenth-century Spanish printing.

In the past decade, Hispano-medievalists have shown interest in studying intergeneric borrowings and cross-influences. Concerning Hispanic Arthurian texts, I have published an article on different manifestations of the fusion of Arthurian romance and sentimental fiction in Spain at the end of the fifteenth century (1984). Expanding on earlier research by Lida de Malkiel, Martí de Riquer, Pamela Waley, and other scholars, I discuss sentimental elements in the 1498 printing of the Post-Vulgate *Baladro del sabio Merlín*, as well as the incunable fragment of Mossèn Gras's Catalan adaptation of the *Mort Artu* branch of the Vulgate Cycle, the 1501 edition of the *Tristan*, and the manuscript epistolary exchange between Iseut and Tristan; and, among Spanish sentimental romances, the adaptation of Arthurian material in Juan Rodríguez del Padrón's *Estoria de dos amadores* (intercalated in the same author's *Siervo libre de amor*), Juan de Flores's *Grimalte y Gradissa* and *Grisel y Mirabella*, and Diego de San Pedro's *Cárcel de Amor*. Following upon my study, Alan Deyermond produced additional examples of apparent Arthurian influences in San Pedro's romance (1984 ["Las relaciones"], 79–82); and Bienvenido Morros points out passages in the 1498 edition of the *Baladro del sabio Merlín* that reveal a rhetoric characteristic of sentimental romances; and through a comparative study with the *Suite du Merlin* and other Hispanic versions, Morros discovers apparent authorial manipulation of the *Baladro* in the use of *amplificatio* and the suppression of certain material. I also study changes in the 1498 *Baladro* and the 1501 *Tristán* that I attribute to the printer, Juan de Burgos. For example, I follow Stephen Gilman's lead in showing that the portrait of Iseut that appears at the end of the 1501 text—thought by Entwistle to derive from a *Tristan* book that served as source for Brunetto Latini's portrait of Iseut in his *Trésor*—is the same as the portrait of Helen in Juan de Burgos's 1490 printing of the *Crónica troyana*; the only substantive change in the 1501 version is the woman's name (1988 ["Juan de Burgos"]). Juan Bautista Avalle-Arce believes that the suicide of Iseut at the end of the

1501 narrative was modeled on that of Oriana, wife of Amadís, in the so-called "primitivo" version of *Amadís de Gaula* (1993, 11).

In the sixteenth century, the Spanish *Prose Tristan* also came under the influence of the contemporary audience's taste for sequels to chivalric romances. In 1534, a new version of the *Tristán de Leonís* was printed in two books, the first containing a version of the text as found in the earlier Spanish imprints, with the addition of a long interpolation, the second book forming an original sequel concerning the adventures of Tristan and Iseut's son and daughter. Gillian Eisele drew new attention to the 1534 printing in two articles, the first (*"Don Tristán de Leonís"*) giving a detailed summary of the sequel, the other ("A Comparison") speculating on the first book's relationship to the 1501 and 1528 printings and a lost intermediary. Subsequent to Eisele's second article, I discovered a 1525 edition of the *Libro de don Tristán de Leonís* in the Bibliothèque Mazarine in Paris, and Clive Willis brought to the attention of Hispanists a 1511 edition in the Rosenwald Collection at the Library of Congress (Sharrer 1986–87, 334, item 23). The 1511 imprint reveals important textual differences vis-à-vis the other editions, prompting María Luzdivina Cuesta Torre to propose a new stemma for the Spanish texts (1993 ["La transmisión"], 77–82).

Seidenspinner-Núñez takes up the evolution of Tristan as a hero and then as a father in the Spanish *Tristán de Leonís* romances, comparing him with two other chivalric heroes, Lancelot and Amadís, who beget sons (1987–88). She contrasts Tristan's eternalness at the end of the French *Prose Tristan*—the perfect knight and lover depicted realistically in the form of a statue, alongside a similar monument representing Iseut—with the alteration to the ending in the Spanish edition of 1501. In the latter, the sepulcher of the two lovers is decorated with a painting of a small boat in a sea of green waves. The painting and a poetic inscription, which reads in part *esta barca de amor / y mar de vana esperança* ("this ship of love / and sea of vain hope"), recall the fatality of Tristan and Iseut's love in the taking of the love potion, reversing Jean-Charles Payen's observation of a tendency toward a *conjuration* of subversive elements in the tragic love story. In the 1534 sequel Seidenspinner-Núñez observes continued emphasis on the fatality of Tristan and Iseut's love, with repeated allusions to the love philter serving to present Tristan's heroism in a sympathetic light. Tristan becomes an ideal ruler (perhaps an indirect criticism, as Eisele pointed out, of Charles I's frequent absence from Spain). His son, Tristan the Younger, is not affected by the love potion and is able to separate private and public demands. Like Galahad in the Lancelot romances and Esplandián in Garci Rodríguez de Montalvo's continuation of *Amadís de Gaula*, Tristan the Younger is a version of the *miles christianus*, and his characterization responds "palimpsestically" to the "pre-text" of his father. Seidenspinner-Núñez points out how Tristan the Younger shows generational superiority in his defeat of the knights of the Round Table and ingenuity in staving off love-smitten female admirers; yet, in contrast to the father-son relationship in the *Amadís* cycle, Tristan the Younger shows no ideological antagonism toward his father. However, Seidenspinner-Núñez concludes that Tristan the Younger, when compared with his father, is uninspiring as a chivalric hero, much as Galahad and Esplandián are inferior to their fathers in demonstrating heroic qualities.

María Cristina Gates, after collaborating with Dayle Seidenspinner-Núñez at the University of California–Irvine on an unpublished transcription of the 1534 edition (based on the exemplar in the library of the University of Valencia), submitted a study of the 1534 text as her doctoral thesis for the University of Buenos Aires, including in an appendix a partial transcription of the second book. Coinciding with Seidenspinner-Núñez and Gates's work, María Luzdivina Cuesta Torre presented an edition of the complete 1534 printing (also based on the Valencia exemplar) as a *Memoria* for the Licenciatura degree and then a literary study of the Spanish *Tristan* romances, with emphasis on the 1534 edition, as her doctoral dissertation for the University of León (published on microfiche). In an article on love and marriage in the second book of the 1534 imprint, Cuesta Torre finds that the author of the sequel rejects the earlier Tristan model in favor of contemporary Castilian attitudes that stress chivalric values leading to moral perfection. Among these values is "true love" consecrated in marriage (1990).

Our knowledge of traditional Spanish ballads is based on a few examples in late-medieval manuscripts, later printed collections and broadsides, and texts collected from twentieth-century oral tradition. Only three such ballads are Arthurian properly speaking, two concerning Lancelot and one Tristan. All three seem ultimately to derive from the cyclical prose romances, but they reveal elements of contamination with a variety of other sources. One of the Lancelot ballads has survived in twentieth-century oral tradition and in its several recorded manifestations shows yet further signs of contamination.

Recent scholarship has focused primarily on the Tristan ballad, "Ferido está don Tristán" ("Wounded Is Sir Tristan"), concerning Tristan lying mortally wounded from his uncle's poisoned lance, visited by Iseut, now pregnant. Pedro F. Campa presents a useful survey of research, provides texts of four extant versions of the ballad, and expresses his own views on the ballad, in particular the image of a lily, watered by the lovers' tears. For Campa, the image not only symbolizes the lovers' sexual union but suggests through Iseut's pregnancy future Tristans to come. Robert L. Surles gives a line-by-line commentary on the ballad and includes a parallel English translation ("Herido está don Tristán"; "Wounded Is Don Tristan"). Julia Kurtz finds the source of the lily image in another traditional Spanish ballad, "La mala hierba" ("The Evil Weed") or the related ballad "La fuente fecundante" ("The Fertile Fountain"). However, observing a similar plant motif in Eilhart von Oberge's *Tristrant*, Kurtz concludes that the borrowing is not random or illogical, for the lily stands for innocence and purity, vindicating the two lovers in a memorial similar to the life-size effigies of the two on their tombs at the end of versions of the *Prose Tristan*. On the other hand, the ballad's contamination produces an ambiguous ending concerning Iseut's immediate death or real pregnancy. Giuseppe Di Stefano has published an important "critical" edition of the Tristan ballad with commentary. Concerning the transmission of the text, he offers valuable insights and suggestions concerning cross-influences, including the possibility of contacts between high literary creation at the end of the fifteenth century or early sixteenth (e.g., the Iseut and Tristan epistolary exchange) and certain areas of traditional balladry.

On the two Lancelot ballads, "Nunca fuera caballero" ("Never Was a Gallant Knight") and "Tres hijuelos había el rey" ("Three Tender Striplings Had the King"), I comment on their complex relationship to the *Prose Lancelot* and other texts and offer a synthesis of interpretative opinion about them as an introduction to a reprinting of J.Y. Gibson's English translations of the late nineteenth century (1988 ["Two Lancelot Ballads"]). Roger Wright offers a new translation of "Tres hijuelos" with textual commentary in his bilingual anthology *Spanish*

*Ballads.* In a student guide to Colin Smith's out-of-print but still commonly assigned anthology, also titled *Spanish Ballads* (Oxford: Pergamon, 1964), Wright provides a brief textual analysis of all three Arthurian poems (1991, 73–75).

At some unknown point, the Provençal Arthurian verse romance *Jaufre*, composed in the late twelfth or early thirteenth century, was rendered into Spanish prose, but without the irony and humor so characteristic of the original. The Spanish romance is extant in a 1513 edition, bearing the cumbersome title *La corónica de los nobles caballeros Tablante de Ricamonte y de Jofre hijo del conde Donasón*, and numerous other editions survive down to the early twentieth century. Nieves Baranda has published a brief summary of the number of editions known (190). Gonzalo Santoja has recently published an edition of Adrián de Anvers's printing of *Tablante de Ricamonte* at Estella in 1564. In 1986, in an unpublished conference paper, I provided a provisional stemma of the many known editions and presented an analysis of textual differences between the 1513 Spanish text and *Jaufre* (1986). I observe in the sixteenth-century Spanish text various influences of the cyclical prose romances, in particular the *Prose Tristan* and possibly the *Prose Lancelot*. I suggest that the printed book may have served as a reader for children, instilling interest in sixteenth-century chivalric ideals. Cervantes cites the title with apparent irony in Part 1, chapter 16, of *Don Quixote* (first printed in 1605). In the mid-eighteenth century, one António da Silva, Mestre de Gramática, adapted episodes of *Tablante de Ricamonte* in his creation of three chivalric chapbook romances in Portuguese (Sharrer 1991 ["Silva"]); and from a late eighteenth- or early nineteenth-century Spanish version, the romance was also translated into a Tagalog verse *awit*. Bearing the title *Tablante de Ricamonte sampo nang magasauang si Jofre at ni Bruniesen* ("Tablante de Ricamonte Together with the Couple Jofre and Bruniesen"), the *awit* survives in an edition printed at Manila in 1902, a copy of which, at the Newberry Library in Chicago (Ayer, 68), also includes a manuscript translation of the Tagalog text into Spanish. In the early nineteenth century, the Spanish romance was condensed and remodeled as a chapbook for popular consumption. New material was also intercalated, most notably the heroine Bruniesen in the role of a knight-errant imitating adventures of her future husband, Jofre. In an article published in 1986, Antony van

Beysterveldt attempts to explain why the original Spanish adaptation of *Jaufre* suppressed or greatly reduced the love element in the story of the hero and heroine, concluding that the prose romance—he cites Bonilla y San Martín's 1907 edition of the 1564 printing at Estella—reflects socioreligious concerns in Castile denying women the privileged role they had had in courtly literature of earlier centuries.

Recent scholarship on the Merlin prophetic tradition deals not with the prophecies of Merlin derived from Geoffrey of Monmouth's *Historia Regum Britanniae*, as intercalated in the 1498 printing of the *Baladro del sabio Merlín*, nor the enigmatic set of prophecies concerning Spanish history in the 1535 printing of the *Baladro*. Rather, individual scholars have explored the prophetic tradition as manifested in other genres: a thirteenth-century Galician-Portuguese miracle story, a fourteenth-century Spanish chronicle, and songbook poetry of the fifteenth century.

Mário Martins, in a book chapter called "Merlim numa cantiga de Santa Maria," identifies an analogous source for *cantiga* 108 of Alfonso X el Sabio's *Cantigas de Santa Maria*, a miracle-story set in Scotland bearing the rubric "[C]omo Santa Maria fez que nacesse o fillo do judeu o rostro atras, como llo Merlin rogara" ("How Holy Mary had the son of the Jew born with his head facing backwards, as Merlin had requested"). The permanent deformity of the child results from Merlin's request that the Virgin help punish the father, Cayphas, after Merlin is unable to convince the latter to accept on faith the Christian doctrine of Incarnation. At the outset of the song, the narrator alludes to an oral source, but Martins finds close parallels to a short Merlin prophecy entitled "Du juif que estoit bossu par derrière" (evidently a garbled title) found in Volume 3 of the *Prophécies de Merlin*. As I point out in a bibliographical essay (1986–87, 335–336, item 29) and my review of Arthurian material in Galician-Portuguese lyrics (1988 ["La materia de Bretaña"], 563–564), Martins's incomplete reference is to Antoine Vérard's printing of the *Prophécies* at Paris in 1498, a book preserving Merlin prophecies that, according to Lucy Allen Paton, were probably originally produced in the Venice area between 1272 and 1279 or, according to Giulio Bertoni, before 1250. More recently, Dwayne E. Carpenter has published much of this same information, including the text from Vérard's edition, in an article that is more important for its exploration of the theological and socioreligious implications of the miracle story and the manuscript illuminations that depict it. Carpenter places *cantiga* 108 in the context of the Barcelona Disputation of 1263 and other Jewish-Christian debates and such tactics as forced sermons to convert Jews to Christianity. *Cantiga* 108 forms part of a new three-volume edition of Alfonso X's *Cantigas de Santa Maria* by Walter Mettmann; José Filgueira Valverde has published a Spanish prose translation (based on an Mettmann's earlier edition published at Coimbra) with brief commentary.[5]

The manuscript tradition of the fourteenth-century *Crónica del rey D. Pedro* by Pero López de Ayala, concerning the reign of Pedro the Cruel of Castile, involves two different versions. The longer version, or *versión vulgar*, contains four interpolated fragments that some historians have regarded as apocryphal or highly suspect. Two of these interpolated texts are letters that a Moorish sage, called Benhatín in the manuscripts, is said to have sent to King Pedro in the years 1367 and 1369. The second letter, supposedly found in chests of the king at the Battle of Montiel, was sent in response to the king's query regarding an obscure prophecy of Merlin. Benhatín's letter explicates the prophecy and goes on to predict that Pedro will be killed at Montiel by his stepbrother Don Enrique. In an article concerning the authenticity of the Benhatín letters, José Luis Moure discusses and transcribes a stylistically different version of the two Benhatín letters, found in an early fifteenth-century copy, Paris, Bibliothèque Nationale esp. 216, which he determines are not of Ayala's creation but rather his source. Both letters in the Paris manuscript identify the Moor as "Benalhatib," a name Moure connects with a proposal (published in 1945) by the Hispano-Arabist Emilio García Gómez that the author of the two letters in the Ayala chronicle was Ibn al-Jatib, an important political and literary figure in Granada during the rein of Muhammad V. Pedro entered into an important alliance with Muhammad V, and Moure provides documentary evidence to show that Ibn al-Jatib became an adviser to Don Pedro in Christian-Muslim relations. Moure's detailed study of the language of the two letters in MS esp. 216 reveals that a Jew made the Spanish translation from an Arabic original. Moure believes that Ayala then polished the translation for insertion in his

---

chronicle. Moure strongly suspects that the letters were authored by Ibn al-Jatib, perhaps after Don Pedro's death, or at least the last part of the second letter predicting Pedro's death. As for the relationship of the second letter to the tradition of Merlin prophecies in Spain, in a long footnote (note 20) Moure finds close similarities with a group of earlier prophecies reworked as political propaganda in favor of Pedro's triumphant stepbrother, Enrique II of Trastámara, called *La visión de Alfonso X en la ciudad de Sevilla* and *Profecías de Merlín acerca de la ciudad de Londres*, manuscript versions of which survive in Catalan and, of the second set, in Spanish.

A use of prophecy attributed to Merlin in a discussion of contemporary history and the Castilian monarchy is also present in poems in the fifteenth-century *Cancionero de Baena*. María Cóndor Orduña takes up the subject, present in poems 332 to 340 in the Baena songbook, in the opening section of an article concerning Gonzalo Martínez de Medina's poetic support of Juan II of Castile. Following upon earlier studies by Charles Fraker that show the clear influence on Medina of both the Merlin prophecies as found in the *Baladro del sabio Merlín* and those of the fourteenth-century French Franciscan John of Rupescissa, Condór Orduña reviews Medina's texts with their strong echoes of Galfridian symbolism in the use of animals to represent Juan II of Castile and figures against and in support of his cause. Linked to the prophecies are lines of text that emphasize the dangers of excessive pride and arrogance, the moral condemnation of Juan II's enemies, and belief in the future glory of Castile under the king. As a device serving to justify and give validity to predictions for the future, Cóndor Orduña cites the poet's frequent enumeration of examples from history and mythology, both classical and biblical.

The indigenous neo-Arthurian Spanish romance *Amadís de Gaula* was probably composed at the end of the thirteenth century, when the Arthurian and Tristan legends formed an important part of the literary milieu of the Castilian and Portuguese courts. It was probably the most original of the Hispanic adaptations of the cyclical prose romances, making use of names and character types, themes, narrative techniques and structural devices, but today only short fragments of a manuscript copy from ca. 1420 are extant of that early version (generally referred to in Spanish as the "*Amadís* primitivo") and a heavily reworked late fifteenth-century version of the romance by Garci Rodríguez de

Montalvo, published in 1508 in four parts. Juan Bautista Avalle-Arce, in a major book on the several versions of the romance, *"Amadís de Gaula": el primitivo y el de Montalvo*, argues for ca. 1285–90 as the original date of composition as part of his reconstruction of the archetype, using as a basis for the latter Lord Raglan's *The Hero: A Study in Tradition, Myth and Drama* and Otto Rank's *The Myth of the Birth of the Hero* (9, 101–132). The influence of the *Prose Lancelot* and *Prose Tristan* on the *Amadís*, and to a lesser extent Trojan romances, has long been a given among literary historians. Avalle-Arce's book, the extensive introduction and annotations to his edition of the *Amadís* (1991), and Juan Manuel Cacho Blecua's earlier edition (1987) with its lengthy introduction and detailed notes, emphasize Arthurian background as well as specific Arthurian elements and borrowings in the *Amadís*. Victoria Cirlot and José Enrique Ruiz Doménec's 1991 edition of the *Amadís* has a two-part introduction providing background on the reception of chivalry and the Arthurian world in the romance.

Martí de Riquer makes numerous textual comparisons with the Arthurian prose romances in an important study of all the references to defensive and offensive arms in the *Amadís* (1980; 1987, 55–187). For example, concerning the knight Bruneo de Bonamar's arms, Riquer suggests direct inspiration in the *Prose Lancelot*, in the passage in which Lancelot, on the Ille de Joie, makes a shield for himself (1980, 425–426; 1987, 177–178). Paloma Gracia compares the rite of initiation to knighthood in the *Prose Lancelot* and the *Amadís* and finds that of the French romance to be more complex (1991, 187–195). Cacho Blecua also examines the investiture ceremony of the principal hero in the *Amadís* in a study of anthropological, historical, and literary interpretations of the rite. He concludes that the Spanish author gives much less attention to description than does the author of the *Prose Lancelot* (in versions edited by Alexandre Micha) but does coincide in introducing the presence of women and the wearing of the right spur followed by a symbolic kiss. He notes certain religious elements in the ceremony in the *Amadís* and partial compliance with the rite as prescribed in the thirteenth-century code of laws known as the *Siete Partidas* and described in Ramon Llull's *Libre de l'orde de cavalleria*; certain departures from these norms may reflect mythical paradigms.

Garci Rodríguez de Montalvo's continuation of the *Amadís* in a fifth book, *Las sergas de Esplandián*, concerning the adventures of Amadís's son Esplandián as a Christian knight crusading against the infidel, is not generally considered Arthurian, but Paloma Gracia points to Arthurian analogues in Montalvo's use of the motifs of Esplandián's birthmark and his association with a grateful lion (1991, 142–143). Susan Giráldez also discusses possible Arthurian echoes in *Las sergas*: the tame lion, the use of prophecy, the hero's sword and his adventures in service of Christianity (chapter 3). William Little has recently published an English translation of *Las sergas*.

The earliest extant indigenous Spanish romance of chivalry is the *Libro del Caballero Zifar* (or *Cifar*), composed ca. 1300–05, perhaps by Ferrán Martínez, archdeacon of Madrid in the church of Toledo. The work, surviving in two redactions in fifteenth-century manuscript copies and a 1512 printing at Seville, is essentially a Byzantine romance laden with didactic and moralistic intent but also imbued with oriental, hagiographic, epic, and Arthurian elements in different sections of the work. Specifically Arthurian are a reference to Arthur's fight with the "Gato Paul" (the Cath Palug of the *Merlin* branch of the Vulgate Cycle) and the evocation of a figure named Yván, son of King Orián, recalling Chétien de Troyes's hero Yvain. Scholars in the past (most notably Marcelino Menéndez Pelayo, Charles P. Wagner, María Rosa Lida de Malkiel, and Jole Scudieri Ruggieri) have argued for Arthurian sources in the supernatural adventures of the Caballero Atrevido (Bold Knight), involving a Lady of the Lake, and the travels of Zifar's son Roboán to the Islas Dotadas, the latter recalling the Island of Apples or Fortunate Isle(s) in Geoffrey of Monmouth's *Vita Merlini*. However, the Arthurian source question has not been definitively resolved but continues to be explored. Elisabeth Schreiner, for example, compares the *Zifar* episodes with analogous material in Old French Arthurian lais and concludes that the reception of Arthurian themes in the *Zifar* is colored by religious and ethical concerns. Reinaldo Ayerbe-Chaux studies "courtly love" in the Islas Dotadas episode, evident from the beginning of the episode through allusions to Chrétien de Troyes's *Yvain* and parallels to the hunting episode in *Erec*. Cristina González puts aside the question of sources and direct influences, emphasizing the structure of the episodes and how their fantasy contributes to the "message" of what is otherwise a narrative based on real customs and institutions. Teresa Ann Sears studies Zifar's and his son Roboán's voyages in relationship to Arthurian quests and suggests that that the *Zifar* be interpreted as a "counter-text to the Arthurian corpus," in which the story of triumphant knights seeking to hold a throne contrasts with that of the flawed and doomed king of Camelot. Paloma Gracia reviews earlier criticism of the Caballero Atrevido episode and discovers new Arthurian analogues in the Post-Vulgate *Roman du Graal*, in particular the *Queste* branch, and in the fourteenth-century *Perceforest* (1992). Three important editions of the *Zifar* have been published in recent years, by González Muela, Cristina González, and Marilyn Olsen. Charles L. Nelson has also published an English translation of the romance.

The most original of the eastern Hispanic Arthurian texts is a verse narrative in Catalan (with some dialogue in a corrupt French) called *La Faula*, by the fourteenth-century Mallorcan poet Guillem de Torroella. Based in large measure on the *Mort Artu* branch of the Vulgate Cycle and a Mediterranean-set story of Arthur's passing, the poet narrates in the first person his travels on the back of a whale to an enchanted island (presumably Sicily), where Morgana (Morgan the Fay) is said to have taken Arthur following the battle on Salisbury Plain. The poet meets Arthur, who gives him a moralistic lesson with possible political implications to give to Mallorcans back home. Following the publication of the first complete and accessible edition of the poem by Pere Bohigas and Jaume Vidal Alcover, a substantive review of the edition and several comparativist articles on the work have appeared. Lluís Cabré takes the recent editors to task for not recognizing in their introductory study Torroella's apparent general knowledge not just of the *Mort Artu* branch of the Vulgate Cycle but also other sections of the cycle. Joan Ors places Torroella's use of the whale in the context of the theme of the hunt of the white stag and the motif of the animal as guide in various French lais and romances and *Blandín de Cornualla*, a late thirteenth- or early fourteenth-century narrative poem with Arthurian connections, written perhaps by a Catalan. Ors points out how the whale in *La Faula*, while preserving certain characteristics of the marvelous common to the Matter of Britain, serves a real narrative function in that it is the poet's means of transport to a land where he can observe the preservation of chivalric virtues, in contrast to the situation in his native Mallorca. On the other hand, the whale also functions as the messenger of Arthur's sister, Morgana, a symbol of the otherworld. Cabré also emphasizes the bestiary tradition behind the image of the whale and associations with medieval travel literature, specifically the voyage of St. Brendan, and also the lapidary tradition in Torroella's use of the snake-and-carbuncle motif.

In a collaborative collection of essays on the marvelous, Anton Espadaler rereads the ending of *La Faula* as a political statement (a suggestion earlier scholars had made but not fully developed): Arthur's observations on kingship constitute a veiled lament on the loss of the Mallorcan monarchy. The contemporary Mallorcan audience would make the association with the death in battle of their last king, Jaume el Dissortat, at Llucmajor in 1349. Lola Badia, in a suggestive study that emphasizes *La Faula*, Bernat Metge's *Llibre de Fortuna e Prudència*, and Joanot de Martorell's *Tirant lo Blanc*, points out that *La Faula* was a sort of "bestseller" in medieval Catalan literature: four manuscript versions (one almost complete, the others more fragmentary) survive; the text came to be adapted almost a century later in chapters 189–202 of *Tirant lo Blanc*; a fifteenth-century document gives testimony to the poet's fame among his descendants (as Bohigas and Vidal Alcover point out); and the poem may be referred to in an inventory of 1459 (1989, 17–32). Badia also believes Metge was influenced by *La Faula* in structuring his *Llibre de Fortuna e Prudència*. Concerning the sources of *La Faula*, she, like Isabel de Riquer in another recent study, emphasizes the hybridization of ingredients in combining a courtly narrative, the *Mort Artu*, with the folkloric legend of Arthur's passing in a Mediterranean location. The tale provides great pleasure for the poet and his audience through the literary stimulus of the fabulous voyage, the magic animals, the garden of delight on the Enchanted Isle, Morgan's beauty, the richness of her palace, and so on. As for the poem's moralistic message about worldly power and fortune, Badia believes the didactic ending turns the narrator's experience into something solemn; without its didactic conclusion, it would be a banal story, exalting fantastic elements common to chivalric literature. She remains skeptical but open to a political interpretation of the work.

Around the year 1460, the Valencian Joanot de Martorell began writing his *Tirant lo Blanc*, a hybrid of chivalric narrative genres (see Thomas R. Hart's recent article on the classification issue) that includes an adaptation of *La Faula* (chapters 189–202). The work, which may have been finished by Martí Joan de Galba, is known through two incunable versions (1490 and 1497) and an early sixteenth-century Spanish translation. Numerous publications have appeared surrounding the five hundredth anniversary of the *editio princeps*, including a new edition by Albert G. Hauf and Vicent Josep Escartí based on the copy in the Biblioteca General i Històrica of the University of Valencia. Martorell's adaptation of *La Faula* is a theatrical farce, with the Arthurian characters—four allegorical damsels, Morgan the Fay, and Arthur—entering into a dialogue with personages at the court of Constantinople, including the hero Tirant lo Blanc (44–50). In 1984, David H. Rosenthal published an English translation that received critical and public acclaim.

For Lola Badia, Martorell's reworking of *La Faula* gives the author the opportunity to reaffirm in a didactic manner certain chivalric principles and values of the past and also to exhibit his rhetorical skills (1989, 40–50). On the latter aspect, she cites Carles Miralles's recent article on Martorell's plagiary of words from the contemporary Valencian prose writer Roís de Corella's *Parlament en casa de Berenguer Mercader*, in the speech of the damsel Esperança (Hope), informing the Emperor of Morgan's arrival at Constantinople. In Arthur's speeches in the same episode Albert Hauf discovers another important didactic borrowing: a summary of various chapters from the second part of the *Dotzè del Crestià* ("Twelfth Book of the Christian"), the encyclopedic guide for the faithful by the fourteenth-century Franciscan Francesc Eiximenis. With such wisdom, Arthur becomes, in Lola Badia's words, a "fountain of chivalry," an "oracle capable of answering all the questions asked of him" (1993, 55–56). In an earlier study, Rafael Beltran Llavador, in reviewing Arthurian and chivalric literature as background for his book on *Tirant lo Blanc*, finds originality in Torroella's fusion of autobiographical realism with fantasy (71). Beltran Llavador finds ambiguity in Martorell's adaptation of *La Faula*, the emphasis on courtly festivity and allegory sharply contrasting with the verisimilitude of the surrounding narrative. The episode becomes believable only because of its framework (135–136). More recently, Emilio J. Sales and Juan Noyes explain the ambiguity of Morgan and Arthur's appearance at the court of Constantinople in terms of Martorell's rejection of the phantasmagoric world of giants and dragons in favor of an aesthetic that seeks to move deeply into reality. Gerhard Wild, in an article that examines Torrella's *La Faula* and Martorell's treatment of it, as well as *Blandín de Cornualla* and Muntaner's *Crònica*, concludes that Catalan authors had trouble accepting Arthurian prose narrative, preferring to introduce the fantastic into their texts by using the Arthurian prose-romance devices of dreams and allegory (1990 ["Ausgrenzung"]). In another article, Wild studies how the crisis of the Arthurian world, as found in the cyclical prose romances, serves as a point of departure for new artistic treatments of Arthur's passing in *La Faula* and Martorell's adaptation (1990 ["Die Geburt"]).

Martí de Riquer cites a series of passages in the first thirty-nine chapters of *Tirant lo Blanc* pointing to Martorell's apparent knowledge of the *Prose Lancelot* and Mossèn Gras's adaptation of the *Mort Artu* or perhaps a lost Catalan translation of the *Mort Artu* (1992, 74–79). In a celebrated recent book on *Tirant lo Blanc*, Riquer also studies the chivalric ceremony immediately following the Arthurian farce: chapters 203–206, in which Tirant, the Viscount de Branches, the constable Diafebus, and Hippolytus all swear solemn vows (1990, 156–159). Albert Soler Llopart has found significant verbal borrowings from a didactic section of the *Prose Lancelot* at the end of chapter 32 and the beginning of 33 of *Tirant lo Blanc*, material that was also used by Ramon Llull in his *Llibre de l'orde de cavalleria* at the end of the thirteenth century; and Júlia Butinyà has discovered a short citation in chapter 28 from the *Mort Artu* of the Vulgate Cycle, material also preserved in the incunable fragment of Mossèn Gras's *Tragèdia de Lancelot*. Lola Badia remains skeptical that this information points to the circulation beginning in the thirteenth century of a Catalan translation of the Vulgate romances (1993, 55); and Riquer believes that Gras's adaptation of the *Mort Artu* may have already existed in 1460 when Martorell began writing *Tirant lo Blanc* (1992, 79).

Miscellaneous occurrences of Arthurian material include the use of Geoffrey of Monmouth in a fifteenth-century Spanish sermon, the Spanish translation of Boccaccio's *De Casibus* (chapter 9 on Arthur), and Cervantes's *Don Quixote*.

Based on Ronald E. Surtz's edition of a fifteenth-century Castilian Corpus Christi sermon (96–97), Alan Deyermond comments on a passage in which the author summarizes the story of Arthur's conception as told in Geoffrey of Monmouth's *Historia Regum Britanniae*. Deyermond is surprised that a preacher in the fifteenth century would adopt a story concerning lust, adultery, rape, and magic in order to clarify doubts concerning the doctrine of Transubstantiation. He finds the summary to be generally accurate but notes that, curiously, the preacher does not cite his patristic sources.

Eric Naylor, as part of an article containing his edition of chapter 9 of the Spanish translation of Boccaccio's *Caída de príncipes*, discusses the importance of the chapter for determining the authorship of the translation. In a prologue found only in three printed editions of the work (1495, 1511, and 1522), Juan Alfonso de Zamora declares that the late fourteenth-century Spanish chronicler, poet, and translator Pero López de Ayala was responsible for translating half the chapter and that he, Zamora, and Alfonso de Cartagena finished it in 1422. Naylor, in his study of eight manuscripts of the *Caída*, discovers two versions: one complete one that was probably written in its entirety by Ayala, and the other incomplete at the middle of chapter 9. Naylor concludes that Zamora and Cartagena probably knew this defective version or one similar to it. The part they supposedly translated remains lost.

In his book *The Half-Way House of Fiction*, Edwin Williamson provides a major comparative study relating Cervantes's *Don Quixote* to early French Arthurian literature, a subject he continues in a recent article, emphasizing similarities and differences in the uses of irony and structural technique (1991). Concerning an Arthurian text still circulating in Cervantes's time, Eduardo Urbina suggests that the parody of the knight-errant in *Don Quixote* might have been influenced by the characterization of the Caballero Anciano in the *Tristán de Leonís* romances, or Bravor le Brun, as the old knight is called in Rusticiano da Pisa's *Compilation*. In a similar vein, Mário Martins sees a possible source of humor and irony for Cervantes in the *Prose Tristan* figure of Dinadan (1983 ["O pré-cervantismo"]).

## Desiderata

Several sixteenth-century printings of Hispanic Arthurian texts remain to be published in modern editions, specifically the 1515 printing of the

*Demanda del santo grial* (Toledo: Juan de Villaquirán) and the 1513 *Tablante de Ricamonte* (Toledo: Juan de Varela de Salamanca). It would be useful to have new, more accessible, and rigorously annotated editions of other texts previously edited: the so-called Spanish Grail or Pietsch fragments of the Post-Vulgate *Roman du Graal* (Salamanca, Biblioteca Universitaria 1877); both the 1498 and 1535 printings of the *Baladro del sabio Merlín*; and the Catalan *Queste* branch of the Vulgate Cycle, *La storia del sant grasal* (Milan, Ambrosiana I.79.sup.). Ian Michael's and my transcription of the lengthy sixteenth-century Spanish translation of *Perceforest* (Madrid, Biblioteca de Palacio 266–267) remains unpublished. It would be extremely useful to have transcriptions of all the principal Hispanic Arthurian texts in electronic form. English translations of several of the longer texts, the Portuguese *Demanda do Santo Graal* and Guillem de Torroella's *La Faula*, for example, would help make Hispanic Arthurian literature better known to non-specialists.

Problems of textual relationships remain. For example, linguistic studies need to be cárried out to help resolve the origin question of the Catalan, Castilian-Aragonese, and Spanish texts of the *Prose Tristan*; and the possible relationship of the these texts to Rusticiano da Pisa's *Compilation* should also be reexamined. Regarding Arthurian models for the *Amadís de Gaula*, my transcription of the *Lanzarote del Lago* can now be considered, as well as versions recently edited of the French *Prose Lancelot* by Elspeth Kennedy and Alexandre Micha. Linguistic and lexical studies of the Hispanic texts should also provide a more solid basis for examining questions of reception. Concerning generic cross-influences and intertextuality, especially in the fifteenth century, it might be useful to examine the language of courtly lyrics in relationship to reworkings of Arthurian romances.

In addition to exploring aspects of texts, there is a need for a detailed monograph to replace William J. Entwistle's outdated *The Arthurian Legend in the Literature of the Spanish Peninsula* (1925). Finally, there is need for volume 2 of my *Critical Bibliography of Hispanic Arthurian Material* and for regular updates of it thereafter.

# Bibliography

*Bibliographies*

ADMYTE [*Archivo digital de manuscritos y textos españoles*]. Disco 0. Coordinated by Francisco A. Marcos Marín and Charles B. Faulhaber. Madrid: Micronet, 1993. CD-ROM.

*Bibliografía de Textos Antigos Portugueses*. Compiled by Arthur L.-F. Askins, Harvey L. Sharrer, Martha E. Schaffer, and Aida Fernanda Dias. In ADMYTE, Disco 0.

*Bibliografía de textos catalans antics*. Compiled by Vicenç Beltran, Gemma Avenoza, and Beatrice Concheff. In ADMYTE, Disco 0.

*Bibliografía española de textos antiguos*. Compiled by Charles B. Faulhaber, Angel Gómez Moreno, and Angela Moll Dexeus. In ADMYTE, Disco 0.

*Boletín Bibliográfico de la Asociación Hispánica de Literatura Medieval*, 1 (1987)–.

Sharrer, Harvey L. *A Critical Bibliography of Hispanic Arthurian Material, I: Texts: The Prose Romance Cycles*. London: Grant and Cutler, 1977.

———. "Notas sobre la materia artúrica hispánica, 1979–86." *La Corónica*, 15 (1986–87), 328–340.

*Editions and Translations*

Bohigas, Pere, and Jaume Vidal Alcover, eds. *La Faula*, by Guillem de Torroella. Tarragona: Tàrraco, 1984.

Castro, Ivo, ed. *"Livro de José de Arimateia* (Estudo e Edição do Cód. ANTT 643)." Diss. Universidade Clássica de Lisbon, Faculdade de Letras, 1984.

Corfis, Ivy A., ed., with the collaboration of Rosa C. Almoguera et al. *Text and Concordances of Vaticana MS 6428, "Cuento de Tristán de Leonís."* Madison, WI: Hispanic Seminary of Medieval Studies, 1985. [Microfiche edition.]

Cuesta Torre, María Luzdivina, ed. *"Don Tristán de Leonís*: el texto de la edición sevillana de 1534." Memoria de licenciatura. Universidad de León, 1993.

Di Stefano, Giuseppe, ed. "El *Romance de don Tristán*: edición 'crítica' y comentarios." In *Studia in honorem prof. M. de Riquer.* Barcelona: Quaderns Crema, 1988, III, 271–303.

García Morales, Justo, ed. *El baladro del sabio Merlín*; rev. José Javier Fuente del Pilar with prologue by Luis Alberto de Cuenca. Madrid: Miraguano, 1988.

Gómez Redondo, Fernando, ed. *Carta enviada por Hiseo la Brunda a Tristán de Leonís*; *Respuesta de Tristán* (Madrid, Biblioteca Nacional, MS 22021). *"Carta de Iseo y respuesta de Tristán,"* *Dicenda*, 7 (1987), 327–356. [For a partial edition, see also Sharrer 1981–82, under Studies.]

González, Cristina, ed. *Libro del Caballero Zifar.* Madrid: Cátedra, 1983.

González Muela, J., ed. *Libro del Caballero Zifar.* Madrid: Castalia, 1982.

Hauf, Albert G., and Vicent Josep Escartí, eds. *Tirant lo Blanch*, by Joanot Martorell and Martí Joan de Galba. 2 vols. Valencia: Conselleria de Cultura, Educació i Ciència de la Generalitat Valenciana, 1990.

Little, William Thomas, trans. *The Labors of the Very Brave Knight Esplandián*, by Garci Rodríguez de Montalvo. Binghamton: Center for Medieval and Early Renaissance Studies, State University of New York at Binghamton, 1992.

Megale, Heitor, ed. *A Demanda do Santo Graal (manuscrito do século XIII)*. São Paulo: Queiroz, 1988.

Mettmann, Walter, ed. *Cantigas de Santa María*, by Alfonso X el Sabio. Madrid: Castalia, 1988, II, no. 108, pp. 30–33.

Nelson, Charles L., trans. *The Book of the Knight Zifar: A Translation of "El libro del Cavallero Zifar."* Lexington: University Press of Kentucky, 1983.

Olsen, Marilyn A., ed. *Libro del Cauallero Çifar*. Madison, WI: Hispanic Seminary of Medieval Studies, 1984.

Piel, Joseph-Maria, ed. (concluded by Irene Freire Nunes). *A Demanda do Santo Graal*. Lisbon: Imprensa Nacional-Casa da Moeda, 1988.

Riquer, Martí de, ed. *Tragèdia de Lançalot amb el facsímil de l'incunable*, by Mossèn Gras. Barcelona: Quaderns Crema, 1984.

Rosenthal, David H., trans. *Tirant lo Blanc*, by Joanot Martorell and Martí Joan de Galba. New York: Macmillan, 1984.

Santonja, Gonzalo, ed. *Crónica de los notables caballeros Tablante de Ricamonte y Jofre, hijo del conde don Asón*. Madrid: Visor, 1988.

Seidenspinner-Núñez, Dayle, and Harvey L. Sharrer, eds. *Text and Concordance of the ["Libro de don Tristán de Leonís"], Printed by Juan de Burgos, 1501, British Library C.20.d24*. Madison, WI: Hispanic Seminary of Medieval Studies, 1994, forthcoming.

Sharrer, Harvey L., ed. *Lanzarote del Lago* (Madrid, Biblioteca Nacional, MS. 9611). Machine-readable transcription, DOSL107. Madison, WI: Hispanic Seminary of Medieval Studies, 1990.

Soberanas, Amadeu-J., ed. "La version galaïco-portugaise de la *Suite du Merlin*: Transcription du fragment du XIVe siècle de la Bibliothèque de Catalogne, ms. 2434." *Vox Romanica*, 38 (1979), 174–193.

Surles, Robert L., trans. "Wounded Is don Tristan." In Surles, "'Herido está don Tristán': Distance, Point of View and 'Piggy-Back' Poetics." *Tristania*, 10 (1984–85), pp. 64–65.

Surtz, Ronald E., ed. *Un sermón castellano del siglo XV con motivo de la fiesta del Corpus Christi*. Published with Alonso de Córdoba, *Conmemoraçión breve de los reyes de Portugal*, ed. Pedro M. Cátedra. Barcelona: Humanitas, 1983, pp. 73–101.

Wright, Roger, ed. and trans. *Spanish Ballads*. Warminister: Aris and Phillips, 1987, pp. 24–25, 152–153.


*Studies*

*Actes del Symposion Tirant lo Blanc*. Barcelona: Quaderns Crema, 1993.

Alvar, Carlos. *El rey Arturo y su mundo: diccionario de mitología artúrica*. Madrid: Alianza, 1991.

———. "Poesía gallego-portuguesa y Materia de Bretaña: algunas hipótesis." In *O cantar dos trobadores*. Santiago de Compostela: Xunta de Galicia, 1993, pp. 31–51.

Avalle-Arce, Juan Bautista. *"Amadis de Gaula": el primitivo y el de Montalvo*. Mexico City: Fondo de Cultura Económica, 1990.

———. *"Amadís de Gaula–Tirant lo Blanc: Tirant lo Blanc–Amadís de Gaula."* In *Actes del Symposion Tirant lo Blanc*, 1993, pp. 7–19.

Ayerbe-Chaux, Reinaldo. "Las *Islas Dotadas*: Texto y miniaturas del manuscrito de París, clave para su interpretación." In Miletich, ed.,

*Hispanic Studies in Honor of Alan D. Deyermond: A North American Tribute*, 1986, pp. 31–56.

Badia, Lola. "De la *Faula* al *Tirant*, passant, sobretot, pel *Llibre de Fortuna e Prudència.*" In *Quaderns Crema, deu anys: miscel•lània*. Barcelona: Quaderns Crema, 1989, pp. 17–57.

———. "El *Tirant* en la tardor medieval catalana." In *Actes del Symposion Tirant lo Blanc*, 1993, pp. 35–99.

Baranda, Nieves. "Compendio bibliográfico sobre la narrativa caballeresca breve." In Lacarra, ed., *Evolución narrativa e ideológica de la literatura caballeresca*, 1991, pp. 183–191.

Beltrán, Vicente, ed. *Actas del I Congreso de la Asociación Hispánica de Literatura Medieval*. Barcelona: PPU, 1988.

———. "Afonso III de Portugal." In Lanciani and Tavani, eds., *Dicionário da Literatura Medieval Galega e Portuguesa*, 1993, pp. 14–15.

Beltran Llavador, Rafael. *"Tirant lo Blanc": evolució i revolta en la novel•la de cavalleries*. Valencia: Institució Alfons el Magnànim, 1983.

Bertolucci Pizzorusso, Valeria. "Martin Soarez." In Lanciani and Tavani, eds., *Dicionário da Literatura Medieval Galega e Portuguesa*, 1993, pp. 441–444.

Bogdanow, Fanni. "The Spanish *Demanda del Sancto Grial* and a Variant Version of the Vulgate *Queste del Saint Graal*: The Final Scene at Corbenic." *Boletim de Filologia* [Lisbon], 28 (1983), 45–80.

———. "The Changing Vision of Arthur's Death." In Jane H.M. Taylor, ed., *Dies illa: Death in the Middle Ages*. Liverpool: Cairns, 1984, pp. 107–123.

————. "A Hitherto Unknown Manuscript of the Post-Vulgate." *French Studies Bulletin*, 16 (1985), 4–5.

————. "The Post-Vulgate *Mort Artu* and the Textual Tradition of the Vulgate *Mort Artu*." In Jesús Montoya Martínez and Juan Paredes Núñez, eds., *Estudios románicos dedicados al Prof. Andrés Soria Ortega*. Granada: Departamento de Filología Románica, Universidad de Granada, 1985, I, 273–290.

Butinyà, Júlia. "Una nova font de *Tirant lo Blanch*." *Revista de Filología Románica*, 7 (1990), 191–196.

Cabré, Lluís. Review of Guillem de Torroella, *La Faula*, ed. Pere Bohigas and Jaume Vidal Alcover. *Llengua & Literatura*, 1 (1986), 609–615.

Cacho Blecua, Juan Manuel. "La iniciación caballeresca del *Amadís*." In Lacarra, ed., *Evolución narrativa e ideológica de la literatura caballeresca*, 1991, pp. 59–79.

Campa, Pedro F. "The Spanish Tristán Ballads." *Tristania*, 7 (1981–82), 60–69.

Carpenter, Dwayne E. "A Sorcerer Defends the Virgin: Merlin in the *Cantigas de Santa Maria*." *Bulletin of the Cantigueiros de Santa Maria*, 5 (1993), 5–24.

Castro, Ivo. "Sobre a data da introdução na Península Ibérica do ciclo arturiano da post-Vulgata." *Boletim de Filologia* [Lisbon], 28 (1983), 81–98.

————. "*Livro de José de Arimateia* (Estudo e Edição do Cód. ANTT 643)." Diss. Universidade Clássica de Lisboa, Faculdade de Letras, 1984.

————. "*Demanda do Santo Graal*." In Lanciani and Tavani, eds., *Dicionário da Literatura Medieval Galega e Portuguesa*, 1993, pp. 203–206.

————. "*Livro de José de Arimateia.*" In Lanciani and Tavani, eds., *Dicionário da Literature Medieval Galega e Portuguesa*, 1993, pp. 409–411.

————. "Matéria de Bretanha: ou literatura arturiana." In Lanciani and Tavani, eds., *Dicionário da Literatura Medieval Galega e Portuguesa*, 1993, pp. 445–450.

————. "Merlim." In Lanciani and Tavani, eds., *Dicionário da Literatura Medieval Galega e Portuguesa*, 1993, pp. 456–458.

Cóndor Orduña, María. "La obra de Gonzalo Martínez de Medina en el *Cancionero de Baena.*" *Revista de Literatura*, 48 (1986), 315–349.

Contreras Martín, Antonio M. "El episodio de la carreta en el *Lanzarote del Lago* castellano (Ms. 9611 BN Madrid)." Paper presented to the V Congreso de la Asociación Hispánica de Literatura Medieval, Granada, September 27–October 1, 1993.

Cuesta Torre, María Luzdivina. "El libro segundo del Tristán de 1534: ideas sobre el amor y el matrimonio." *Estudios Humanísticos— Filología*, 12 (1990), 11–24.

————. "Algunas notas acerca de la rivalidad en tres obras de la materia artúrica hispánica." Paper presented to the V Congreso de la Asociación Hispánica de Literatura Medieval, Granada, September 27–October 1, 1993.

————. "Estudio literario de *Tristán de Leonís.*" Tesis doctoral en microficha, 136. León: Secretariado de Publicaciones, Universidad de León, 1993.

————. "La transmisión textual de *Don Tristán de Leonís.*" *Revista de Literatura Medieval*, 5 (1993), 63–93.

De Caluwé, Jacques. "Quelques réflexions sur la pénétration de la matière arthurienne dans les littératures occitane et catalane médiévales." In Kenneth Varty, ed., *An Arthurian Tapestry: Essays in Memory of Lewis Thorpe*. Glasgow: French Department, University of Glasgow, 1981, pp. 354–367.

Deyermond, Alan. "Problems of Language, Audience, and Arthurian Source in a Fifteenth-Century Castilian Sermon." In Victorio Agüera and Nathaniel B. Smith, eds., *Josep Maria Solà-Solé: homage, homenaje, homenatge (miscelánea de estudios de amigos y discípulos)*. Barcelona: Puvill, 1984, pp. 43–54.

――――. "Las relaciones genéricas de la ficción sentimental española." In *Symposium in honorem prof. M. de Riquer*. Barcelona: University of Barcelona–Quaderns Crema, 1984, pp. 75–92.

Eisele, Gillian. "*Don Tristán de Leonís y don Tristán el Joven*: A Reappraisal of the 1534 Sequel to *Don Tristán de Leonís*." *Tristania*, 5 (1979–80), 28–44.

――――. "A Comparison of Early Printed Tristan Texts in Sixteenth-Century Spain." *Zeitschrift für Romanische Philologie*, 97 (1981), 370–382.

Entwistle, William J. *The Arthurian Legend in the Literatures of the Spanish Peninsula*. London: Dent; New York: Dutton, 1925.

Espadaler, Anton. "El meravellós com a luxe i pedagogia." In *El món imaginari el el món meravellós a l'Edat Mitjana*. Barcelona: Fundació Caixa de Pensions, 1986, pp. 137–149.

Ferrari, Anna. "Lai." In Lanciani and Tavani, eds., *Dicionário da Literatura Medieval Galega e Portuguesa*, 1993, pp. 374–378.

Gates, María Cristina. "*Don Tristán el Joven* y el discurso novelístico marginal como síntoma de una época de transición." Diss. Universidad Nacional de Buenos Aires, 1989 [1990].

Giráldez, Susan. *"Las sergas de Esplandián* y la España de los Reyes Católicos: Pensamiento y literatura."* Diss. University of California–Santa Barbara, 1992.

González, Cristina. *"El Cavallero Zifar"* y el reino lejano. Madrid: Gredos, 1984.

Gracia, Paloma. *Las señales del destino heroico.* Barcelona: Montesinos, 1991.

———. "Varios apuntes sobre el 'Cuento del Caballero Atrevido': la tradición del 'Lago Solfáreo' y una propuesta de lectura." *Cuadernos para Investigación de la Literatura Hispánica,* 15 (1992), 23–44.

Hall, J.B. "La matière arthurienne espagnole: The Ethos of the French Post-Vulgate *Roman du Graal* and the Castilian *Baladro del sabio Merlín* and *Demanda del Sancto Grial." Revue de Littérature Comparée,* 56 (1982), 423–436.

———. "A Process of Adaptation: The Spanish Versions of the Romance of Tristan." In P.B. Grout et al., eds., *The Legend of Arthur in the Middle Ages: Studies Presented to A.H. Diverres by Colleagues, Pupils, and Friends.* Cambridge: Boydell and Brewer, 1983, pp. 76–85.

Hart, Thomas R. *"Tirant lo Blanc*: Between Romance and Epic." In Alan Deyermond and Jeremy Lawrance, eds., *Letters and Society in Fifteenth-Century Spain: Studies Presented to P.E. Russell on His Eightieth Birthday.* Llangrannog: Dolphin, 1993, pp. 59–68.

Hook, David. *"Domnus Artus*: Arthurian Nomenclature in 13th-c. Burgos." *Romance Philology,* 44 (1990–91), 162–164.

———. *The Earliest Arthurian Names in Spain and Portugal.* St. Albans: Hook, 1991.

Kurtz, Julia. "The Multiple Endings of *Ferido está don Tristán*: Triumph of the Flesh or the Spirit?" *Tristania*, 12 (1986–87), 25–43.

Lacarra, María Eugenia, ed. *Evolución narrativa e ideológica de la literatura caballeresca.* Bilbao: Servicio Editorial de la Universidad del País Vasco/Argitarapen Zerbitzua Euskal Herriko Unibertsitatea, 1991.

Lacy, Norris J. "*Tablante de Ricamonte sampo nang magasauang si Jofre at ni Bruniesen.*" In Lacy et al., eds., *The New Arthurian Encyclopedia*, p. 441.

———, and Geoffrey Ashe. *The Arthurian Handbook.* New York: Garland, 1988.

———, et al., eds. *The New Arthurian Encyclopedia.* New York: Garland, 1991.

Lanciani, Giulia, and Giuseppe Tavani, eds. *Dicionário da Literatura Medieval Galega e Portuguesa.* Lisbon: Caminho, 1993.

Lida de Malkiel, María Rosa. "Arthurian Literature in Spain and Portugal." In Roger Sherman Loomis, ed., *Arthurian Literature in the Middle Ages: A Collaborative History.* Oxford: Clarendon, 1959, pp. 406–418.

———. "La literatura artúrica en España y Portugal." In *Estudios de literatura española y comparada.* 1966; rpt. Buenos Aires: Losada, 1984, pp. 167–184.

Martins, Mário. "Merlim numa Cantiga de Santa Maria." In *Estudos de Cultura Medieval.* Lisbon: Brotéria, 1983, III, 45–49.

———. "O pré-cervantismo em *Tristan de Leonis.*" *Boletim de Filologia* [Lisbon], 28 (1983), 33–44.

Megale, Heitor. "'Le jeu des remparts.' A *Demanda do Santo Graal*: la structure idéologique et la construction de la narration." Diss. Universidade de São Paulo, 1980. [Abstract published in *Bibliographical Bulletin of the International Arthurian Society*, 33 (1981), item 299.]

———. "In Search of the Narrative Structure of *A Demanda do Santo Graal*." *Arthurian Interpretations*, 1 (1986), 26–34.

———. "Le texte portugais de la *Demanda do Santo Graal*: les éditions de 1944 et de 1955–1970." In Van Hoecke, Tournoy, and Verbecke, eds., *Arturus Rex, II: Acta Conventus Lovaniensis 1987*, 1991, pp. 436–461.

Michon, Patricia. "La légende de Tristan et Yseut dans l'Occident médiéval: Etude comparée des textes ibériques et contemporains." Diss. Université de Paris IV (La Sorbonne), 1987.

Miletich, John S., ed. *Hispanic Studies in Honor of Alan D. Deyermond: A North American Tribute*. Madison, WI: Hispanic Seminary of Medieval Studies, 1986.

Miralles, Carles. "Raons de Mirra en boca d'Esperança (Sobre un altre plagi de Roís de Corella en el *Tirant lo Blanc*." In *Eulàlia: Estudis de literatura catalana*. Barcelona: Edicions del Mall, 1986, pp. 51–62.

Moltó Hernández, Elena. "'Enemigos' y 'traidores' en el *Tristán* castellano." In Nascimento and Almeida Ribeiro, eds., *Literatura Medieval*, 1991–93, II, 315–319.

Montgomery, Thomas. "The *Ferg* of Gonzalo González." *La Corónica*, 20 (1991–92), 1–17.

Moralejo, Serafín. "Artes figurativas y artes literarias en la España medieval: románico, romance y *roman*." *Boletín de la Asociación Europea de Profesores de Español*, 17 (1985), 61–70, figure 6.

Morros, Bienvenido. "Los problemas ecdóticos del *Baladro del sabio Merlín.*" In Beltrán, ed., *Actas*, 1983, pp. 457–471.

Moure, José Luis. "Sobre la autenticidad de las cartas de Benhatin en la *Crónica* de Pero López de Ayala: consideración filológica de un manuscrito inédito." *Incipit*, 3 (1983), 53–93, 185–196 (documents).

Murillo, Louis A. "Cervantes Saavedra, Miguel de." In Lacy et al., eds., *The New Arthurian Encyclopedia*, 1991, p. 79.

———. "Montalvo, Garci Rodríguez de." In Lacy et al., eds., *The New Arthurian Encyclopedia*, 1991, pp. 326–328.

Nascimento, Aires A., and Cristina Almeida Ribeiro, eds. *Literatura Medieval: Actas do IV Congresso da Associação Hispânica de Literatura Medieval (Lisboa, 1–5 Outubro 1991).* 4 vols. Lisbon: Cosmos, 1991–93.

Naylor, Eric W. "Pero López de Ayala's Translation of Boccaccio's *De casibus.*" In Miletich, ed., *Hispanic Studies in Honor of Alan D. Deyermond*, 1986, pp. 205–215.

Neto, Sílvio de Almeida Toledo. "*Liuro de Josep Ab aramatia* and the Works of Robert de Boron." *Quondam et Futurus*, 3 (1993), 36–45.

Oliveira, António Resende de. "Depois do espectáculo trovadoresco: a estrutura dos cancioneiros peninsulares e as recolhas dos sécs. XIII e XIV." Diss. Faculdade de Letras, Universidade de Coimbra, 1992.

Ors, Joan. "De l'encalç del cérvol blanc al creuer de la balena sollerica: la funció narrativa del motiu de l'animal guia." In *Studia in honorem prof. M. de Riquer*. Barcelona: Quaderns Crema, 1986, I, 565–573.

Riquer, Isabel de. "El viaje al otro mundo de un mallorquín." *Revista de Lengua y Literatura Catalana, Gallega y Vasca*, 1 (1991), 25–36.

Riquer, Martí de. "Las armas en el *Amadís de Gaula*." *Boletín de la Real Academia Española*, 60 (1980), 331–427.

——. *Estudios sobre el "Amadís de Gaula."* Barcelona: Sirmio, 1987.

——. *Aproximació al Tirant lo Blanc*. Barcelona: Quaderns Crema, 1990.

——. *"Tirant lo Blanch," novela de historia y de ficción*. Barcelona: Sirmio, 1992.

Rosenberg, John R. "*Tristan de Leonis*: Medieval Poetics in Perspective." *Hispanic Journal*, 7 (1985), 17–28.

Rossi, Luciano. "*Livro de Tristan*." In Lanciani and Tavani, eds., *Dicionário da Literatura Medieval Galega e Portuguesa*, 1993, pp. 414–415.

——. "I modelli francesi del *Livro de Tristán*." In *Studi portoghesi*, Romanica Vulgaria—Quaderni, 13 (forthcoming).

Sales, Emilio J., and Juan Noyes. "Morgana y Artús en Constantinopla (un episodio del *Tirant lo Blanc*)." In José Manuel Lucía Megías, Paloma Gracia Alonso, and Carmen Martín Daza, eds., *Actas II Congreso Internacional de la Asociación Hispánica de Literatura Medieval*. Alcalá de Henares: Universidad de Alcalá de Henares, 1992, II, 815–826.

Schreiner, Elisabeth. "Die 'Matière de Bretagne' im *Libro del Cavallero Cifar*: Zur Rezeption der 'Matière de Bretagne' in zwei Episoden des *Libro del Cavallero Cifar*." In Dieter Messner, Wolfgang Pöckl, and Angela Birner, eds., *Romanisches Mittelalter Festschrift zum 60 Geburstag von Rudolf Baehr*. Göppingen: Kümmerle, 1981, pp. 269–283.

Sears, Teresa Ann. "Further Adventures: *El Caballero Cifar* and Variations on an Arthurian Theme." In Van Hoecke, Tournoy, and

Verbecke, eds. *Arturus Rex, II: Acta Conventus Lovaniensis 1987*, 1991, pp. 204–212.

Seidenspinner-Núñez, Dayle. "The Sense of an Ending: The Tristan Romance in Spain." *Tristania*, 7 (1981–82), 27–46.

———. "Fathers and Sons: Notes on the Evolution of the Romance Hero." *Tristania*, 13 (1987–88), 19–34.

———. "Tristan in Spain and Portugal." In Lacy et al., eds., *The New Arthurian Encyclopedia*, 1991, pp. 471–473.

Serverat, Vincent. "Portrait en femme du courageux chevalier Don Tristán de Leonís." In Danielle Buschinger and Wolfgang Spiewok, eds., *Tristan-Studien die Tristan-Rezeption in den europäischen Literaturen des Mittelalters*. Greifswald: Reineke, 1993, pp. 117–138.

Sharrer, Harvey L. "The Provenance and Date of the Spanish Prose *Lancelot*." Paper presented to the 13th International Congress of the International Arthurian Society, Glasgow, 11–19 August 1981. [Abstract published in *Bibliographical Bulletin of the International Arthurian Society*, 33 (1981), 311.]

———. "Letters in the Hispanic Prose Tristan Texts," *Tristania*, 7 (1981–82), 3–20.

———. "La fusión de las novelas artúrica y sentimental a fines de la Edad Media." *El Crotalón: Anuario de Filología Española*, 1 (1984), 147–157. Rpt. in abridged form as "La fusión de la novela artúrica y la novela sentimental." In the first supplement to Vol. 1 of Alan Deyermond and Francisco Rico, eds., *Historia y crítica de la literatura española*. Barcelona: Crítica, 1991, pp. 307–311.

———. "*El Tablante de Ricamonte*: novela artúrica y pliego de cordel." Paper presented to the IX Congreso de la Asociación Internacional de Hispanistas, Berlin, August 18–23, 1986. [Summary in Armistead, Samuel G., and Harvey L. Sharrer, "IX

Congreso de la Asociación Internacional de Hispanistas," *La Corónica*, 15 (1986–87), p. 276.]

————. "Juan de Burgos: impresor y refundidor de libros caballerescos." In María Luisa López-Vidriero and Pedro M. Cátedra, eds., *El libro antiguo español: actas del Primer Coloquio Internacional (Madrid, 18 al 20 de diciembre de 1986)*. Salamanca: Universidad de Salamanca, Biblioteca Nacional de Madrid, Sociedad Española de Historia del Libro, 1988, pp. 361–369.

————. "La materia de Bretaña en la poesía gallego-portuguesa." In Beltrán, ed. *Actas*, 1988, pp. 561–569.

————. "Two Lancelot Ballads." In James J. Wilhelm, ed., *The Romance of Arthur III: Works from Russia to Spain, Norway to Italy*. New York: Garland, 1988, pp. 259–264.

————. "*Baladro del Sabio Merlín*." In Lacy et al., eds., *The New Arthurian Encyclopedia*, 1991, p. 31.

————. "*Carta enviada por Hiseo la Brunda a Tristán; Respuesta de Tristán*." In Lacy et al., eds., *The New Arthurian Encyclopedia*, 1991, p. 73.

————. "*Demanda do Santo Graal*." In Lacy et al., eds., *The New Arthurian Encyclopedia*, 1991, p. 114.

————. "*Josep Abaramatia, Livro de*." In Lacy et al., eds, *The New Arthurian Encyclopedia*, 1991, p. 254.

————. "Salazar, Lope García de." In Lacy et al., eds., *The New Arthurian Encyclopedia*, 1991, p. 395.

————. "Silva, António da, Mestre de Gramática." In Lacy et al., eds., *The New Arthurian Encyclopedia*, 1991, p. 418.

————. "Spanish and Portuguese Arthurian Literature." In Lacy et al., eds., *The New Arthurian Encyclopedia*, 1991, pp. 425–428.

————. "*Sumario de historia de los reyes de Bretaña.*" In Lacy et al., eds., *The New Arthurian Encyclopedia*, 1991, p. 436.

Soler Llopart, Albert. "'Mas cavaller qui d'açó fa lo contrari': una lectura del tractat lul • lià sobre la cavalleria." *Estudios Lulianos*, 29 (1989), 1–23, 101–124.

Surles, Robert L. "'Herido está don Tristán': Distance, Point of View and 'Piggy-Back' Poetics." *Tristania*, 10 (1984–85), 53–65.

Urbina, Eduardo. "El caballero anciano en *Tristán de Leonís* y don Quijote, caballero cincuentón." *Nueva Revista de Filología Hispánica*, 29 (1980), 164–172.

Van Beysterveldt, Antony. "El *Roman de Jaufré* y la *Crónica de Tablante de Ricamonte.*" In Hans-Erich Keller et al., eds., *Studia Occitanica in Memoriam Paul Remy*. Kalamazoo, MI: Medieval Institute, 1986, II, 203–210.

Van Hoecke, Willy, Gilbert Tournoy, and Werner Verbecke, eds. *Arturus Rex, II: Acta Conventus Lovaniensis 1987*. Leuven: Leuven University Press, 1991.

"A versión galego-portuguesa da *Suite du Merlin.*" *Grial*, 76 (1982), 215–217.

Whitaker, Muriel. *The Legends of King Arthur in Art*. Woodbridge: Brewer, 1990, pp. 90–93.

Wild, Gerhard. "Säkularisierung und Dissoziation: *A Demanda do Santo Graal.*" *Zeitschrift für Romanischen Philologie*, 105 (1989), 322–336.

————. "Ausgrenzung und Integration arthurischer Themen im katalanischen Mittelalter (von Muntaners *Crònica*, *Blandín de Cornualla* und Torroellas *La Faula* zu Martorells *Tirant lo Blanc).*" *Zeitschrift für Katalanistik*, 3 (1990), 67–89.

————. "Die Geburt der neuen Texte aus dem Geiste von Artus' Tod: Das literarische Gespräch über die *Mort Artu* in den *libros de caballerías.*" In Friedrich Wolfzettel, ed., *Artusroman und Intertextualität.* Giessen: Schmitz, 1990, pp. 215–234.

————. "Überlegungen zu einer welthistorischen Dimension des Fiktiven." *WIFO Journal,* 9 (1992), 408–413.

Williamson, Edwin. *The Half-Way House of Fiction: "Don Quixote" and Arthurian Romance.* Oxford: Clarendon, 1984.

————. "Cervantes y Chrétien de Troyes: La destrucción creadora de la narrativa caballeresca." In Lacarra, ed., *Evolución narrativa e ideológica de la literatura caballeresca,* 1991, pp. 145–163.

Wright, Roger. *Spanish Ballads.* London: Grant and Cutler/Tamesis, 1991.

Yllera, Alicia. "La muerte de los amantes en el *Tristán* castellano." In Nascimento and Almeida Ribeiro, eds., *Literatura medieval,* 1991–93, II, 85–89.

# ARTHURIAN TRANSLATION

## Norris J. Lacy

Not many years ago, it would have been surprising if not unthinkable to include a section on translation in an *état présent* of scholarship on medieval literature. Although translation of classical and of postmedieval texts has long been considered a noble enterprise and an art, the situation has been dramatically different for medievalists, who evidently equated translation with vulgarization. Medievalists long remained indifferent if not hostile to the notion of producing or even reading texts translated into modern languages. Acceptance is still far from universal, but the situation has changed significantly during the past two decades; that is, translation has become an acceptable if not a universally admired activity for medievalists. Why the change?

Cynics might very well (and not entirely without justification) attribute this situation to a simultaneous decline in solid philological training, concluding that we now *need* texts in the modern language far more than we once did. It is certain that few current medievalists can both manage Latin competently and also read more than one or two early languages with comparative ease. Many Anglophones, for example, will manage both Middle English and some Old French (or Italian or Spanish)—but how many scholars, other than Germanists, can deal adequately with Middle High German?[1] And medieval Welsh, in particular, is simply beyond the reach of all but a small handful of medievalists.

---

[1] See William C. McDonald's essay in the present volume; even (or, more likely, *especially*) Germanists recognize the serious decline of training in Middle High German, in Europe as well as the United States, and the consequent need for competent translations of Arthurian texts.

We all recognize that any text suffers in translation: *traduttore traditore*. But this truism is answered by another one, even more self-evident: the beauty of the original is lost on anyone who cannot read it. We might object that instead of providing Englished texts, we should respond to this problem by strengthening philological skills; that solution is devoutly to be wished but scarcely likely to be realized. And failing that, we must ask whether it is better to make texts known through translation or simply leave them unread.

Thus, as we legitimately and even vehemently lament the decline of philological rigor, we ought to recognize also that it has made larger numbers of medieval texts accessible to a far wider public. Medievalists should be pleased to have the texts we study be known to as many readers as possible. And perhaps the pleasures of the medieval text will themselves lead some of those readers back to the original language.

If the current state of philology is a negative factor that has favored the presentation of Arthurian and other medieval texts to an anglophone public, there is a more positive reason as well. Introducing a recent bibliographical essay on translations of medieval French Arthurian literature,[2] I suggested that we may finally be rejecting the assumption that only the very greatest literary masterpieces deserve to be known. I added that

> we have long had modern English versions of Dante, the *Chanson de Roland*, and a handful of other works, but . . . for English versions of romances like *Yder* or the *Roman de Silence*, we had to wait until critics recognized them as literary creations deserving of our attention. Thus, the development of literary criticism in medieval studies has done much during the past twenty or so years to confer legitimacy on the translator's craft and to create the "market" for medieval literary texts in English [p. 55].

Thus, although translators justifiably continue to rework the recognized masterpieces, the more gratifying development in recent translation of Arthurian literature is the awakening of interest in texts once taken as minor or unworthy of a translator's (or reader's) attention.

---

[2] "French Arthurian Literature in English Translation," *Quondam et Futurus: A Journal of Arthurian Interpretations*, 1, No. 3 (1991), 55–74.

## Recent Translations

What follows is by no means a full survey, nor is one needed here. The chapters of this volume include some information about, and bibliographical listings of, translations.

In the following pages, I wish merely to give an indication of the extent of recent translation from each vernacular language,[3] list some of the available texts (even though the listing will duplicate portions of most of the chapter bibliographies),[4] and summarize trends, problems, and needs. In most cases, translations before 1975 or 1980, however important and excellent, are omitted from my discussion, as are the majority of translations of excerpts.

Anthologies are crucial materials for making Arthuriana available to a wide public, including students, and the bibliography includes several of them (Wilhelm, Goodrich, Barber,[5] etc.). In a number of instances, they offer complete texts; elsewhere, they give extensive excerpts, sometimes of texts not otherwise available in English. They are particularly important for languages for which comparatively little Arthurian material appears in English translation: a few texts (e.g., from Welsh, Italian, and Spanish) are presented in translation most conveniently, or in some cases *solely*, in anthologies. In this appendix, I list the more recent anthologies themselves, but only a few of the texts published in them.

---

[3] As I indicate in my introduction, I deal here only with translations into English. Clearly, translations into other languages are equally valuable but are simply outside the range of this volume. In addition, although the focus of the present volume is vernacular literature in the Middle Ages, we should call readers' attention, however briefly, to Latin. In addition to several translations, from past decades, of Geoffrey of Monmouth's *Historia regum Britanniae*, we now have English versions of two important Latin Arthurian texts. Both works (*The Rise of Gawain, Nephew of Arthur* and *The Story of Meriadoc, King of Cambria*) are edited and translated by Mildred Leake Day.

[4] I have taken a good deal of the information about translations from the discussions and bibliographies of other contributors to this volume. I am pleased to express my gratitude to them.

[5] Full publication information is offered in the bibliography that follows this essay.

By far the largest number of Arthurian translations into English are, as noted above, from French. My previous bibliographical essay on that subject included ninety-three entries (although a number were older translations and a good many were excerpts), and several new items have been added since I prepared that essay.

Not surprisingly, the French texts most often put into English are the romances of Chrétien de Troyes. During the past dozen or so years, we have seen nearly twenty translations of one or more of the romances; several of them are documented in the following bibliography. All the romances except *Cligés* have been translated in individual volumes, most more than once. In addition, there are now three recent volumes that offer fresh translations of all five of Chrétien's Arthurian romances: by D.D.R. Owen (1987), David Staines (1990), and William W. Kibler and Carleton W. Carroll (1991).

Even after the appearance of these three volumes, translations of Chrétien continue to appear. The most recent is an *Erec*, translated by Dorothy Gilbert in 1992; her text joins earlier ones by Ruth Harwood Cline as the only verse versions of Chrétien romances in English.

We have a number of translations of French Tristan material. The past decade has seen three parallel-text versions (edition and facing line-for-line translations) of Béroul: by Guy Mermier (1987), Stewart Gregory (1992), and myself (1989). The *Tristan* of Thomas of England, which has been available in a variety of translations, some good and some not, has recently been retranslated (facing a critical edition) by Stewart Gregory. The French *Prose Tristan* has not been translated in full, but Renée L. Curtis has published a translation of large portions, with summaries of the untranslated portions.

Marie de France has long been a favorite author of translators. In recent years, there have been two complete and excellent English texts of the *Lais*: by Robert Hanning and Joan Ferrante (1978) and by Glyn Burgess and Keith Busby (1986).

We have translations of several texts inspired by or related to Chrétien's *Perceval*. Substantial excerpts of the *Continuations* of the *Perceval* were published by Nigel Bryant in 1982, in the volume that also contains his version of Chrétien's last romance; and the *Perlesvaus* was translated by Nigel Bryant in 1978. Robert de Boron's verse *Joseph of Arimathea* has been translated by Jean Rogers, and both the verse text and the *Prose Joseph* are being prepared for publication in an English version by George Diller.

The *Queste del saint Graal* and the *Mort Artu*, two of the five romances of the French Vulgate Cycle (also known as the Lancelot-Grail Cycle, the Pseudo-Map Cycle or the *Prose Lancelot*), have been available in English for some time; the rest of the Vulgate has not. Presently, under my editorship, Garland is issuing the full cycle, as well as the Post-Vulgate, in a five-volume set; publication is expected to be complete by the end of 1995. Corin Corley has translated large portions of the "noncyclic" *Prose Lancelot* romance, *Lancelot of the Lake*.

One of the most salutary developments in translation of French romances is the presentation in English of a number of romances, too often considered secondary or minor, that had long been known only to specialists of Old French literature.[6] These texts include Guillaume le Clerc's *The Romance of Fergus* by D.D.R. Owen; *The Knight of the Parrot* and *The Marvels of Rigomer* by Thomas E. Vesce; Heldris de Cornuaille's *Roman de Silence* by Regina Psaki; *Yder* by Alison Adams; and Renaut de Bâgé's *Le Bel Inconnu* by Colleen P. Donagher. Translations of *Atre périlleux* and other works are in progress.

Far less extensively represented than French, Welsh Arthurian texts are nevertheless available in English in reasonable numbers. The *Mabinogi* have been known to anglophone readers since Lady Charlotte Guest presented them in the middle of the last century; in recent years, both Ford and Gantz have provided new and reliable translations of those texts. Independent tales, some of them popularly if erroneously taken as portions of the *Mabinogion*, have been translated separately or sometimes excerpted in anthologies. In *The Romance of Arthur*, for

---

[6] And, truth be told, not to all such specialists. This is an element of the "masterpiece" syndrome, whereby Chrétien's romances and a few others traditionally dominated, and later texts were deemed inferior to his, not only because he is indisputably the finest writer of romance in medieval France but also—and unjustifiably—because many later romances were fundamentally *different* from his. We have only recently begun to provide a proper reassessment of the aesthetic informing later romances. The principle enunciated here applies as well to other literatures, and especially to German, in which the fully merited respect accorded the earliest compositions (Hartmann, Wolfram, Gottfried) complicated the task of assessing later works and consequently prevented their translation until comparatively recent years.

example, Richard M. Loomis translated *Culhwch and Olwen*, and John
Bollard provided texts of some short poems and excerpts of *Geraint*,
the Triads, and other works; Bollard then translated *Peredur* in *The
Romance of Arthur II*. In *The Romance of Merlin*, he presented some
forty pages of Merlin texts from the early Welsh tradition. Richard
Barber's anthology *The Arthurian Legends* offers short fragments of
*The Annals of Wales*, *The History of the Britons*, and *The Life of St.
Carannog*; it also presents excerpts of *Culhwch and Olwen*, though
from the older translation by Gwyn Jones and Thomas Jones. The
*Gododdin* is available in two modern versions (by Jackson and Jarman).
The Welsh Triads have been translated by Rachel Bromwich, the
*Stanzas of the Graves* by Thomas Jones, and the Taliesin poems by Ifor
Williams and J.E. Caerwyn Williams. A translation of *Arthur and the
Eagle*, prepared by Haycock, is awaiting publication. Outside of Welsh,
Celtic Arthurian materials are practically unknown in English, except
for Sheila Falconer's 1953 rendering of *Lorgaireacht an tSoidhigh
Naomhtha*, the Irish version of the French *Queste del saint Graal*.

In regard to German literature, William McDonald (in his essay in
the present volume) emphasizes the comparative oversupply of
"classical" German Arthurian romances in translation and the
traditional paucity of English versions of the "postclassical." Until
recent decades, it is true, non-Germanists had little access to texts other
than Wolfram, Gottfried, and Hartmann. The last of these has since
become by far the most attractive German subject for translators. His
*Erec* has been translated at least five times; his *Iwein*, three times. As
the bibliography will show, however, there has been significant
progress recently in making the postclassical romances available to
readers of English. The principal effort here has been made by J.W.
Thomas, the most active and prolific translator of German Arthurian
material. Besides translating both of Hartmann's romances and Eilhart
von Oberge's *Tristrant* (1978), Thomas has provided English texts of
Heinrich von dem Türlin's *The Crown: A Tale of Sir Gawein and King
Arthur's Court* (1989), Wirnt von Grafenberg's *Wigalois, The Knight
of Fortune's Wheel* (1977), and a volume containing Der Pleier's *Garel
of the Blooming Valley, Tandareis and Flordibel*, and *Meleranz*. In
addition, Michael Resler has translated Der Stricker's *Daniel of the
Blossoming Valley*.

Although English translations of Scandinavian, Italian, Hispanic, and Dutch materials have given us access to excellent and important works, the volume of such work is slim. That is regrettable but hardly surprising, both because the number of Arthurian texts in each of the areas is comparatively small—the points of comparison being French especially, but English and German as well—and doubtless because the potential audience for such translations is presumed to be small enough that few publishers will risk the venture. It is in such cases that anthologies perform a particularly important service. Of the four languages listed just above, all but Dutch have material represented in one or more of the most recent anthologies, and the reader is directed to those volumes for important additions to the small body of Englished material.

Available Scandinavian translations include the Old Norse *Erex saga* and *Yvens saga*, by Blaisdell and Kalinke; versions of *Möttuls saga* and *Samsons saga fagra* by Rudolf Simek; Tristram/Tristan sagas by Schach and by Hill. Cook and Tveitane have translated the *Strengleikar*, and, finally, Marianne Kalinke has offered the Old Norse *The Saga of the Mantle* in Garland's *The Romance of Arthur III* (retained in the revised edition of *The Romance of Arthur*).

Dutch is at present represented by a single but very important text: the romance of *Walewein*, translated by David Johnson. Fortunately, Johnson is planning editions and facing translations of five other romances from the fourteenth-century Dutch *Lancelot-Compilatie*. Once those are available, the anglophone reader will have important access to a body of texts that deserve to be known far better than they presently are.

Italian material is only slightly better represented than Dutch. Anne Shaver's *Tristan and the Round Table: A Translation of "La Tavola Ritonda"* (1983) was a welcome addition to the available body of Arthuriana in English, and more recently Rosellini has published a translation (along with an edition) of the Italian Grail quest, *La grande ricerca del Santo Graal*. James J. Wilhelm presented the *Cantare on the Death of Tristan* in *The Romance of Arthur III* and retained it in the revised single-volume *Romance of Arthur*.

Several important Hispanic Arthurian texts—Hispanic is taken to include Portuguese and Catalan—are available in English. Charles L. Nelson has published *The Book of the Knight Zifar: A Translation of*

*"El libro del Cavallero Zifar,"* and David H. Rosenthal prepared the translation of Joanot Martorell and Martí Joan de Galba's *Tirant lo Blanc*. Other texts available in recent English versions are *Jaufré*, translated by Ross G. Arthur, and *Amadís de Gaula*, by Place and Behn. William Thomas Little has recently translated Montalvo's *The Labors of the Very Brave Knight Esplandián*, a neo-Arthurian text that is the fifth and last book of the *Amadís*. Some ballads have been published either in anthologies (Roger Wright's translations of Lancelot ballads) or with editions or studies (Robert Surles's "Wounded Is don Tristan").

English, for reasons that are obvious, occupies a curious position. With some initiation and reasonable effort, a reader of modern English can usually manage portions of many, though by no means all, Middle English compositions. Thus, although scholarly editions of those texts are hardly accessible to students and general readers, it may sometimes suffice to present a text in normalized or modernized form, and indeed the lines separating these activities from translation are not always distinct and definite.

The two English texts that are best known and most widely available are Malory's *Morte Darthur* and *Sir Gawain and the Green Knight*. Both have been published repeatedly, in the original and in modern English versions, and Malory can also be read in adaptations or retellings, the value and reliability of which vary dramatically. *Sir Gawain and the Green Knight* has recently been retranslated three times as part of parallel-text versions, by James Winny, Richard Osberg, and William Vantuono.

Both the Stanzaic *Morte Arthur* and the Alliterative *Morte Arthure* are available in several modern versions. Brian Stone presented both in a single volume. The Stanzaic *Morte* also had three other recent translations, by Kahn, Shimizu, and Krishna; and the alliterative romance was put into English by Valerie Krishna.

The first Arthurian text composed in English, Laȝamon's *Brut*, was translated three times in a three-year period, by Barron and Weinberg, by Bzdyl, and by Allen. "Miscellaneous" Middle English texts presented in English include *The Avowing of King Arthur*, translated by Dass, and Krishna's rendering in one volume (along with the Stanzaic *Morte Arthur*) of the *Adventures of Arthur at Tarn Wadling; The Vows of King Arthur, Sir Gawain, Sir Kay, and Baldwin of Britain*; *The Wedding of Sir Gawain and Dame Ragnell*; and *Sir Gawain and the Carle of Carlisle*.

## Desiderata

The suggestion that there is but a single desideratum, the translation of all Arthurian texts into English, is tempting but unrealistic. The following discussion of desiderata is more realistic and selective; to a good extent it is also, inevitably, a subjective listing.

What is certain is that in most literatures, the great Arthurian "masterpieces" are available to an English-reading public. Some of them are in translations that should be improved upon, especially as scholars publish more reliable critical editions, but arguably we need versions of "secondary" or "postclassical" texts more than we need new translations of Chrétien de Troyes, Hartmann, or *Sir Gawain and the Green Knight*.[7]

In Scandinavian, we might want and conceivably expect an English version of *Ivan Lejonriddaren*, both as a curiosity—it is the only translation of an Arthurian text into Swedish—and also to allow comparison with Chrétien's *Yvain* and with its counterparts in other literatures. (The latter argument, relating a text to a French source, is not intended as a restatement of a gallocentric principle, but it may be a way to persuade a publisher that the project is feasible.) The same rationale, in fact, might be given also for *Parcevals saga* and *Valvens þáttr*, the two Norse texts that present the Perceval story from Chrétien.

In German, the *Lanzelet* by Ulrich von Zatzikhoven should be translated; it is one of the earliest German Arthurian texts—and the earliest not available in English. We also need, as McDonald notes, more of the "postclassical" texts, such as *Wigamur* and Albrecht von Scharfenberg's *Jüngerer Titurel*.

---

[7] In French, for example, it has long been remarked that we have no genuinely critical editions of Chrétien de Troyes's romances. Now that such an edition is finally in progress, it might be maintained that new translations based on more reliable editions are needed. In principle, most scholars would doubtless concur, but with several very competent translations of Chrétien (and Hartmann and others) in print, the greater need is to make some romances available for the first time.

David F. Johnson's project to translate several romances preserved in the *Lancelot-Compilatie* will go far in presenting Dutch Arthuriana to the English-speaking world, and the complete text of the *Lancelot-Compilatie*, which Johnson plans eventually to produce, would be an invaluable contribution to our understanding of Middle Dutch Arthuriana.

The primary need in Italian is to have all the Italian *cantari* translated together in a volume; and Paolino Pieri's *Storia di Merlino* and the subsequent *Vita di Merlino con le sue profezie* also present interest and merit translation.

In French, the *Brut* of Wace (or at least the long Arthurian section) needs retranslation. Much important material awaits translation for the first time. Additional thirteenth-century romances should be made available. The same could be said for some of the often fascinating romances from the late Middle Ages and the early to mid-sixteenth century. But note below my comments about problems of scope and market, particularly in regard to the extremely long texts from the later period.

In Hispanic literature, much remains to be done, although a number of the major texts have been translated. Desiderata include Hispanic Tristan texts, derived from the French *Prose Tristan*, and the Spanish and Portuguese manuscripts, fragments, and even incunabula that adapt the Vulgate and Post-Vulgate cycles and that, in some cases, are the only remaining witnesses of the Post-Vulgate. Fortunately, some of those texts, edited by Fanni Bogdanow over the years, are now being put into English by Martha Asher as part of the Garland *Lancelot-Grail* project (see above), but a good many other texts of interest remain known only to a handful of Hispanists.

A number of romances from medieval England merit the wider audience that translation would bring. Of these works, the Middle Scots *Lancelot of the Laik* offers the only text, other than a late ballad, that deals primarily with Lancelot, and it would be of interest if available in modern English, as would be *Sir Tristrem* and the works of Herry Lovelich, *The History of the Holy Grail* and *Merlin*. Some of these desiderata may soon be addressed by a new series known as Arthurian Archives, from Garland Publishing. Each volume of the series, of which I am general editor, will present parallel texts (critical edition and modern English translation) of several Arthurian texts.

The problems facing the translators of such materials are several. First, some of the compositions are available in old, unreliable, or partial editions. Moreover, some of them, especially from the late Middle Ages, are of a length likely to frustrate all but the most patient and hardy translators. But perhaps the most serious hindrance to the translation of additional texts is the presumed limited market for them. An Englished Chrétien or Hartmann can be expected to have reasonable sales (or could have, until the market was saturated), but compositions that are less well known and regarded are not easily sold. (The fact that the phenonenon is circular—in many instances these works are unknown *because* they are unavailable, and availability would permit readers to discover that they have much to commend them—cannot be expected to persuade any but the most adventuresome or idealistic publisher.) University presses should in theory undertake such work, and some, such as the University of Nebraska Press, have done so; we must also be grateful to other publishers—in particular, Garland, Boydell and Brewer, and Penguin—who have undertaken aggressive programs to publish texts in translation.

But the fact remains that, with "acknowledged masterpieces" generally available, large portions of the Arthurian corpus are likely to remain untranslated for the foreseeable future. What solutions are available? First, since both scholarly and general interest in the Arthurian legend remains strong, translators should continue their efforts to interest publishers in their work. Second, regrettable as it may be to present limited excerpts of romances, that may be the only way certain texts can be known at all. Finally, forms of "electronic publishing" may be able in some way to make available translations (and editions) for which the market is severely limited or the cost prohibitive.

# Bibliography

As noted above, the following is by no means a complete bibliography of translations into English. Though it is selective, it includes all the translations mentioned in the preceding remarks, as well as a few, especially in French literature, not mentioned. With only a few exceptions, listed items date from 1975 or later. The purpose of this bibliography is to give a partial idea of what texts are available in translation, as well as to identify the translators in question. Thus, although other bibliographies in this volume are alphabetized by scholars' (or editors') names, with a chronological arrangement whenever more than one title per name is given, this one (except for the initial section on anthologies) lists entries by author or title. It is thus possible at a glance to locate all the listed translations of a given text.

*Anthologies*

Barber, Richard, ed. *The Arthurian Legends: an Illustrated Anthology.* N.p.: Littlefield Adams, 1979; n.p.: Dorset, 1979.

Matthews, John, ed. *Arthurian Reader.* Wellingborough: Aquarian, 1988.

Wilhelm, James J., ed. *The Romance of Arthur: An Anthology of Medieval Texts in Translation.* New York: Garland, 1994. [Contains texts selected from three earlier volumes, entitled *The Romance of Arthur, The Romance of Arthur II,* and *The Romance of Arthur III,* by the same editor.]

Goodrich, Peter, ed. *Romance of Merlin.* New York: Garland, 1990.

## French

Béroul. *The Romance of Tristran*. Ed. and trans. Stewart Gregory. Amsterdam: Rodopi, 1992.

———. *The Romance of Tristran*. Ed. and trans. Norris J. Lacy. New York: Garland, 1989.

———. *Tristan and Yseult*. Ed. and trans. Guy R. Mermier. American University Studies: Romance Languages and Literature, 50. New York: Peter Lang, 1987.

Chrétien de Troyes. *Arthurian Romances*. Trans. William W. Kibler [*Cligés, Lancelot, Yvain, Perceval*] and Carleton W. Carroll [*Erec*]. Harmondsworth: Penguin, 1991.

———. *Arthurian Romances*. Trans. D.D.R. Owen. London: Dent, 1987.

———. *Complete Romances*. Trans. David Staines. Bloomington: Indiana University Press, 1990.

———. *Erec and Enide*. Ed. and trans. Carleton W. Carroll. New York: Garland, 1987.

———. *Erec et Enide*. Trans. Dorothy Gilbert. Berkeley: University of California Press, 1992.

———. *Knight with the Lion, or Yvain*. Ed. and trans. William W. Kibler. New York: Garland, 1985.

———. *Lancelot, or The Knight of the Cart*. Trans. Ruth Harwood Cline. Athens: University of Georgia Press, 1990.

———. *Lancelot, or the Knight of the Cart*. Ed. and trans. William W. Kibler. New York: Garland, 1981.

------. *Lancelot, the Knight of the Cart*. Trans. Deborah Webster Rogers. Intro. by W.T.H. Jackson. New York: Columbia University Press, 1984.

------. *Perceval, or The Story of the Grail*. Trans. Ruth Harwood Cline. New York: Pergamon, 1983.

------. *Perceval: The Story of the Grail*. Trans. Nigel Bryant. Cambridge: Brewer, 1982.

------. *Story of the Grail (Li Contes del Graal) or Perceval*. Ed. Rupert T. Pickens; trans. William W. Kibler. New York: Garland, 1990.

------. *Yvain, or The Knight with the Lion*. Trans. Ruth Harwood Cline. Athens: University of Georgia Press, 1975.

------. *Yvain, The Knight of the Lion*. Trans. Burton Raffel. New Haven: Yale University Press, 1987.

[Continuations of *Perceval*.] Trans. Nigel Bryant. In *Perceval: The Story of the Grail*. Cambridge: Brewer, 1982, pp. 98–302.

Guillaume le Clerc. *The Romance of Fergus, Knight of King Arthur*. *Trans. D.D.R. Owen. London: Dent, 1991.*

*Heldris de Cornuaille. Roman de Silence*. Trans. Regina Psaki. New York: Garland, 1991.

*High Book of the Grail: Perlesvaus*. Trans. Nigel Bryant. Ipswich: Brewer, 1978.

*Knight of the Parrot*. Trans. Thomas E. Vesce. New York: Garland, 1986.

*Lancelot of the Lake*. Trans. Corin Corley. Oxford: Oxford University Press, 1989. [Sizable portion of the "Noncyclic" *Lancelot*, translated from Elspeth Kennedy's edition.]

*Lancelot-Grail: The Old French Vulgate and Post-Vulgate Cycles in Translation*. Ed. Norris J. Lacy. 5 vols. New York: Garland, vols. 1-2, 1993; vols. 3-4, 1995. [Vol. 5 forthcoming 1996.]

Marie de France. *Lais*. Trans. Glyn S. Burgess and Keith Busby. Harmondsworth: Penguin, 1986.

———. *Lais*. Trans. Robert Hanning and Joan Ferrante. New York: Dutton, 1978.

*Marvels of Rigomer*. Trans. Thomas E. Vesce. New York: Garland, 1988.

Renaut de Bâgé. *Le Bel Inconnu*. Ed. Karen Fresco; trans. Colleen P. Donagher. New York: Garland, 1992.

Robert de Boron. *The Grail Trilogy: Joseph, Merlin, and Perceval*. Trans. George Diller. New York: Garland, forthcoming.

———. *Joseph of Arimathea: A Romance of the Grail*. Trans. Jean Rogers. London: Steiner, 1990.

*Romance of Tristan*. Trans. Renée L. Curtis. Oxford: Oxford University Press, 1994. [The French *Prose Tristan*; translation of selected portions, with summaries of untranslated passages.]

*Romance of Yder*. Ed. and trans. Alison Adams. Cambridge: Boydell and Brewer, 1983.

Thomas. *Tristan*. Ed. and trans. Stewart Gregory. New York: Garland, 1991.

———. *Tristan*. In Gottfried von Strassburg, *Tristan*, trans. A.T. Hatto. Harmondsworth: Penguin, 1960, pp. 301-348.

*Celtic*

Anderson, Alan Orr, and Marjorie Ogilvie Anderson, eds. and trans. *Adomnán's Life of Columba* [*Vita Columbae*], 1961; rev. ed., Oxford: Clarendon, 1991.

*Blodeugerdd o Cerddi Crefyddol Cynnar* [*Arthur and the Eagle*]. Ed. and trans. Marged Haycock. Abertawe: Barddas, forthcoming.

Bromwich, Rachel, ed. and trans. *Trioedd Ynys Prydein, The Welsh Triads*. Cardiff: University of Wales, 1961; rev. ed., 1978.

————, ed. and trans. "The 'Tristan' Poem in the Black Book of Carmarthen." *Studia Celtica*, 14/15 (1979–80), 54–69.

Falconer, Sheila, ed. and trans. *Lorgaireacht an tSoidhigh Naomhtha*. Dublin: Dublin Institute for Advanced Studies, 1953.

Ford, Patrick K., trans. *The Mabinogi and Other Medieval Welsh Tales*. Berkeley: University of California Press, 1977.

Gantz, Jeffrey, trans. *The Mabinogion*. Harmondsworth: Penguin, 1976.

Jackson, Kenneth Hurlstone, trans. *The Gododdin: The Oldest Scottish Poem*. Edinburgh: Edinburgh University Press, 1969.

Jarman, A.O.H., ed. and trans. *Aneirin: Y Gododdin, Britain's Oldest Heroic Poem*. Llandysul: Gomer, 1988.

Jones, Thomas, ed. and trans. "The Black Book of Carmarthen 'Stanzas of the Graves.'" *Proceedings of the British Academy 1967*, 53 (1968), 97–137.

Ni Sheaghdha, Nessa, ed. and trans. *Tóraidheacht Dhiarmada agus Ghráinne*. Irish Texts Society, 48. London: Irish Texts Society, 1967.

Pennar, Meirion, trans. *The Black Book of Carmarthen* [with diplomatic text by J. Gwenogvryn Evans]. N.p.: Llanerch, 1989. [Eleven selected poems.]

Williams, Ifor, ed., and Rachel Bromwich, trans. *Armes Prydein: The Prophecy of Britain*. Dublin: Dublin Institute for Advanced Studies, 1972.

————, ed., and J.E. Caerwyn Williams, trans. *The Poems of Taliesin*. Dublin: Dublin Institute for Advanced Studies, 1968.

Winterbottom, Michael, ed. and trans. *Gildas: The Ruin of Britain and Other Works*. Arthurian Period Sources, 7. Chichester: Phillimore, 1978.

## German

Eilhart von Oberge. *Tristrant*. Trans. J.W. Thomas. Lincoln: University of Nebraska Press, 1978.

Hartmann von Aue, *Erec*. Trans. Thomas Cramer. Frankfurt am Main: Fischer, 1972.

————. *Erec*. Ed. and trans. Thomas L. Keller. New York: Garland, 1987.

————. *Erec*. Trans. Michael Resler. Philadelphia: University of Pennsylvania Press, 1987.

————. *Erec*. Trans. J.W. Thomas. Lincoln: University of Nebraska Press, 1982.

————. *Hartmann von Aue erzählt: Erec, Iwein oder der Löwenritter, Gregorius oder Der gute Sünder, Der arme Heinrich*. Trans. Lambertus Okken. Frankfurt am Main: Insel, 1992.

————. *Iwein.* Ed. and trans. Patrick M. McConeghy. New York: Garland, 1984.

————. *Iwein, the Knight with the Lion.* Trans. J.W. Thomas. Lincoln: University of Nebraska Press, 1979.

Heinrich von dem Türlin. *The Crown: A Tale of Sir Gawein und King Arthur's Court.* Trans. J.W. Thomas. Lincoln: University of Nebraska Press, 1989.

Der Pleier. *Arthurian Romances.* Trans. J.W. Thomas. New York: Garland, 1992. [*Garel of the Blooming Valley, Tandareis and Flordibel,* and *Meleranz.*]

Der Stricker. *Daniel of the Blossoming Valley.* Trans. Michael Resler. New York: Garland, 1990.

Wirnt von Grafenberg. *Wigalois, The Knight of Fortune's Wheel.* Trans. J.W. Thomas. Lincoln: University of Nebraska Press, 1977.

Wolfram von Eschenbach. *Parzival.* Trans. A.T. Hatto. Harmondsworth: Penguin, 1980.


*Scandinavian*

*Erex saga and Ívens saga: The Old Norse Versions of Chrétien de Troyes's "Erec" and "Yvain."* Trans. Foster W. Blaisdell and Marianne E. Kalinke. Lincoln: University of Nebraska Press, 1977.

"The Icelandic Saga of Tristan and Isolt." Trans. Joyce Hill. In *The Tristan Legend: Texts from Northern and Eastern Europe in Modern English Translation.* Leeds: University of Leeds, Graduate Centre for Medieval Studies, 1977, pp. 6-28.

"The Norwegian Prose Lay of the Honeysuckle (Geitarlauf)." Trans. Joyce Hill. In *The Tristan Legend. Texts from Northern and Eastern Europe in Modern English Translation.* Leeds: University of Leeds, Graduate Centre for Medieval Studies, 1977, pp. 39-40.

*The Saga of Tristram and Ísönd.* Trans. Paul Schach. Lincoln: University of Nebraska Press, 1973.

*Strengleikar: An Old Norse Translation of Twenty-one Old French Lais, Edited from the Manuscript Uppsala De la Gardie 4-7—AM 666b, 4°.* Trans. Robert Cook and Mattias Tveitane. Norsk Historisk Kjeldeskrift-Institutt. Oslo: Kjeldeskriftfondet, 1979.

*Zwei Rittersagas: Die Saga vom Mantel und die Saga vom schönen Samson; Möttuls saga und Samsons saga fagra.* Trans. Rudolf Simek. Vienna: Braumüller, 1982.

## Dutch

Penninc and Pieter Vostaert. *Roman van Walewein.* Ed. and trans. David F. Johnson. New York: Garland Publishing, 1992.

## Italian

*Grant Queste del Saint Graal. La grande ricerca del Santo Graal: Versione inedita della fine del XIII secolo del ms. Udine, Biblioteca Arcivescovile, 177.* Ed. and trans. A. Rosellini. Tricesimo (Udine): Vattori, 1990.

*Tristan and the Round Table: A Translation of "La Tavola Ritonda."* Trans. Anne Shaver; editorial assistance by Annette Cash, illus. Catherine M. Hiller. Binghamton, NY: Medieval and Renaissance Texts and Studies, 1983.

## Hispanic

*Book of the Knight Zifar: A Translation of "El libro del Cavallero Zifar."* Trans. Charles L. Nelson. Lexington: University Press of Kentucky, 1983.

*Jaufre: An Occitan Arthurian Romance.* Trans. Ross G. Arthur. New York: Garland, 1992.

Martorell, Joanot, and Martí Joan de Galba. *Tirant lo Blanc.* Trans. David H. Rosenthal. New York: Macmillan, 1984.

Montalvo, Garci Rodríguez de. *Amadís de Gaula.* Trans. E.B. Place and H.C. Boehm. 2 vols. Lexington: University of Kentucky Press, 1974, 1975.

———. *Labors of the Very Brave Knight Esplandián.* Trans. William Thomas Little. Binghamton, NY: Center for Medieval and Early Renaissance Studies, 1992.

*Spanish Ballads.* Ed and trans. Roger Wright. Warminister: Aris and Phillips, 1987, pp. 24–25, 152–153.

Surles, Robert L. "'Herido está don Tristán': Distance, Point of View and 'Piggy-Back' Poetics." *Tristania,* 10 (1984–85), 53–65.

## English

*Alliterative Morte Arthure: A New Verse Translation.* Trans. Valerie Krishna. Washington, DC: University Press of America, 1983.

*Avowing of King Arthur: A Modern Verse Translation.* Trans. Nirmal Dass. Lanham, MD: University Press of America, 1987.

*Five Middle English Arthurian Romances.* Trans. Valerie Krishna. New York: Garland, 1990. [Translations of The Stanzaic *Morte Arthur*; *The Adventures of Arthur at Tarn Wadling*; *The Vows of King Arthur, Sir Gawain, Sir Kay, and Baldwin of Britain*; *The Wedding of Sir Gawain and Dame Ragnell*; *Sir Gawain and the Carl of Carlisle*.]

*King Arthur's Death: Alliterative "Morte Arthure" and Stanzaic "Le Morte Arthur."* Trans. Brian Stone. Harmondsworth: Penguin, 1988.

Lawman. *Lawman: Brut.* Trans. Rosamund Allen. London: Dent, 1992.

————. *Laȝamon's Arthur: The Arthurian Section of Laȝamon's "Brut."* Ed. and trans. W.R.J. Barron and S.C. Weinberg. London: Longman, 1989.

————. *Layamon's Brut: A History of the Britons.* Trans. Donald G. Bzdyl. Binghamton: State University of New York Press, 1989.

*Sir Gawain and the Green Knight.* Ed. and trans. Richard H. Osberg. New York: Peter Lang, 1990.

*Sir Gawain and the Green Knight.* Ed. and trans. William Vantuono. New York: Garland, 1990.

*Sir Gawain and the Green Knight.* Ed. and trans. James Winny. Lewiston, NY: Broadview Press, 1992.

*Stanzaic "Morte": A Verse Translation of "Le Morte Arthur."* Trans. Sharon Kahn. Lanham, MD: University Press of America, 1986.

*Stanzaic Morte Arthur.* Trans. Aya Shimizu. Tokyo: Dolphin, 1985.

For Product Safety Concerns and Information please contact our EU
representative  GPSR@taylorandfrancis.com
Taylor & Francis Verlag GmbH, Kaufingerstraße 24, 80331 München, Germany